ARTHUR MARWICK

British Society
since 1945

PENGUIN BOOKS

PENGUIN BOOKS

Penguin Books Ltd, 80 Strand, London WC2R ORL, England
Penguin Putnam Inc., 375 Hudson Street, New York, New York 10014, USA
Penguin Books Australia Ltd, 250 Camberwell Road, Camberwell, Victoria 3124, Australia
Penguin Books Canada Ltd, 10 Alcorn Avenue, Toronto, Ontario, Canada M4V 3B2
Penguin Books India (P) Ltd, 11, Community Centre, Panchsheel Park, New Delhi – 110 017, India
Penguin Books (NZ) Ltd, Cnr Rosedale and Airborne Roads, Albany, Auckland, New Zealand
Penguin Books (South Africa) (Pty) Ltd, 24 Sturdee Avenue, Rosebank 2196, South Africa

Penguin Books Ltd, Registered Offices: 80 Strand, London WC2R ORL, England
www.penguin.com

First published in Pelican Books 1982
Published simultaneously in hardback by Allen Lane
Second edition published in Penguin Books 1990
Third edition 1996
Fourth edition 2003

7

Typeset in 9.5/11.5 pt Adobe Minion
Typeset by Rowland Phototypesetting Ltd, Bury St Edmunds, Suffolk
Printed in England by Clays Ltd, St Ives plc

ISBN-13: 978–0–14–100527–0

www.greenpenguin.co.uk

PENGUIN BOOKS

British Society since 1945

Arthur Marwick was Professor of History at the Open University
from 1969 to 2001. Born in Edinburgh, he studied at Edinburgh
University and at Balliol College, Oxford. He has taught at

Maurice Keen: *English Society in the Later Middle Ages 1348–1500*
Joyce Youings: *Sixteenth-Century England*
Roy Porter: *English Society in the Eighteenth Century*
Jose Harris: *Private Lives, Public Spirit: Britain 1870–1914*
John Stevenson: *British Society 1914–45*

Aberdeen and Edinburgh, and held visiting professorships at the State University of New York at Buffalo, Stanford University, l'Ecole des hautes études en sciences sociales, Paris, Rhodes College, Memphis, and the University of Perugia. In 1981 he received a D.Litt. for his work on twentieth-century cultural and social history. His books include: *The Deluge, British Society and the First World War; Beauty in History; Society, Politics and Personal Appearance, c.1500 to the Present; The New Nature of History; Knowledge, Evidence, Language; The Sixties; Cultural Revolution in Britain, France, Italy and the United States, c1958–c1974;* and *The Arts in the West since 1945.* He is an energetic tennis player.

THE PENGUIN SOCIAL HISTORY OF BRITAIN
General Editor: J. H. Plumb

Other titles in this series:

Contents

Preface

Inevitably in a book of this size much gets left out. Where I deal with literature, science, philosophy, and the arts, I have not sought to mention every distinguished name. Broadly, my concern has been with interaction with the rest of society as it developed after 1945; many of those who had made their names in the pre-war years are left out: Bernard Shaw and Somerset Maugham, for instance.

The extent of economic success, and economic failure, of course, sets limits upon social and cultural developments. I believe I have sketched in enough economic history to make my account comprehensible, but I make no apology for the fact that this is positively a social and cultural history, and not an 'economic and social history' of the traditional type. I do consider political values and voting patterns to be an important part of social history.

In recent years I have had the pleasure and privilege of conducting seminars on Contemporary British Society with European Union civil servants at the Civil Service College. Part Six of this book owes much to these seminars. For constructive criticism and helpful guidance on my original text I am most grateful to the General Editor of the series, Professor Jack Plumb, to Professor Christopher Harvie of Tübingen University and to my colleagues Professor Tim Benton and Dr Henry Cowper; for specialist advice on publishing and censorship, my thanks to Professor John Sutherland. I'd like to make a special acknowledgement to Peter Carson, formerly of Penguin Books, who showed a close and most helpful interest in the first three editions of this book since the time of the late seventies when I insisted that I would write a book on the post-1945 period, not the whole twentieth century as originally envisaged. Warm acknowledgements, too, to Simon Winder of Penguin, who invited me to prepare this fourth edition, which contains new material covering late 1995 to early 2002, and a number of other alterations and additions. My thanks to Angi Rutter, who read the proofs of the original edition, to Karen Smith and Mandy Topham, who produced typescripts relating to the first two editions, and to Sally Eaton, who helped with preparing the third edition, and Debbie Williams and Niki Sherlock for invaluable logistic assistance to this computer inadequate in the production of this fourth edition. Finally, I wish to thank Drs Alex Poteliakhoff and Neela Malviya for providing me with a copy of the super Sex Survey published in *Lancet*, 1 December 2001.

For permission to quote 'A Tribute to the Founder', from *A Look Around the Estate*, thanks are due to the estate of Kingsley Amis and to the publishers Jonathan Cape in London and Harcourt Brace Jovanovich in New York.

For permission to quote from *Wish you Were Here* acknowledgements are due to screen-writer David Leland and publishers Faber and Faber.

For permission to quote from *Nice Work* acknowledgements are due to novelist David Lodge and publishers Martin Secker and Warburg Ltd.

For permission to quote from official publications acknowledgements are due to HMSO.

For permission to quote tables from *British Social Attitudes* acknowledgements are due to Dartmouth Publishing Company Ltd.

Introduction

'How It Was', 'What Went Wrong?', or 'From Consensus to Divided Society and Half-way Back?'

Nobody has ever said precisely how many ways there are of skinning a cat. Probably there are about the same number of ways of writing a Social History of Britain since 1945. There are a number of fundamental factors, institutions and concepts relating to the study of societies, such as population, the family, housing, eating habits, and social class: thus social history can be written as a relatively neutral account of the main changes and developments in these areas. Certainly the basic facts and figures are essential if one is to establish 'How It Was', what it was like to live through these years, and to pin down the nature and extent of social change. However, the British experience since 1945 cries out for a brush more loaded than that.

Whether or not we are able to take the claims that in early 2002 the British economy was a shining example to the rest of the European Union (EU) without a large pinch of salt, we can be in no doubt that much of the writing on Britain throughout most of the period under review has been on the question of 'What Went Wrong?' (my second theme), from Jeremy Seabrook's *What Went Wrong?* of 1978, to David Marquand's *The Unprincipled Society* of ten years later, to Corelli Barnett's monstrous tome of savage imprecations, *The Verdict of Peace* (2001). Barnett had a particular concern with Britain's descent as an international power from 'triumph in 1918 over Imperial Germany to humiliation in 1956 at Suez'. Practically everyone expresses concern over the deplorable state of Britain's public services: seemingly a shining example to the rest of Europe in 1945, Britain by the seventies had slunk behind her neighbours on practically every social statistic which connoted being a healthy civilized society, and stuck there for the next couple of decades. None the less, things did happen in the eighties: nothing less than (to quote the title and subtitle of a book published in 1987 by one of Britain's most respected journalists, Peter Jenkins) 'Mrs Thatcher's Revolution', and 'The Ending of the Socialist Era'. Had the long period of decline been replaced by a new Rebirth, a new age of 'enterprise culture'? To secure a sound and thriving economy was it perhaps necessary and proper to suppress notions of equality and the good life for all? An important component of this theme is the conundrum of whether Thatcherism was essential for providing the economic growth without which the good society would be impossible or whether Thatcherism in itself was inimical to decent public services.

But social trends go in several directions at once; while the alleged betrayal of high hopes may be a relentless historical theme, and the alleged virtues of private involvement in all aspects of public service an insistent contemporary one, much else of significance has taken place in British society. For a third theme I intend to concentrate on the great release from older restraints and controls that took place in the very middle of the period under review. I have nothing political in mind here. Mention commercial television, women's liberation, the Abortion Act, the lowering of the voting age, and the Betting and Gaming Act, and you would probably find people divided for and against on political and moral grounds: but all of these were part of the same movement in which paternalistic Victorian controls were lifted from British society. The upheavals of the 1960s were at least as great as those of the Second World War and have had, I believe, an irreversible influence on British society. This, of course, is a controversial view. Mrs Thatcher's comment of March 1982 is well known: 'We are reaping what was sown in the sixties . . . fashionable theories and permissive clap-trap set the scene for a society in which the old virtues of discipline and restraint were denigrated.' On the Left it is contended that no fundamental shifts took place, and that those features of the sixties culture which hit the headlines were predominantly inegalitarian, commercial, and sexist. In fact the much publicized activities of tiny minorities have distracted attention from a very genuine liberation of the mass of the people. What really happened in the sixties may have pleased no one but ordinary folk: that is no reason at all for denying its significance. Shortly before the 1982 election Mrs Thatcher spoke of her desire to restore Victorian values: but the lumber that had been swept away in the sixties would not be so easily brought back.

My fourth theme is of a rather different order again. Much has been written of 'stability', or 'tolerance', or 'consensus' in British society. Such words can be mere clichés, begging questions rather than answering them. Yet historians and sociologists have traced a connection between the broad political consensus of the mid-twentieth century and the religious tolerance of earlier centuries centred upon an established Anglicanism to which various forms of non-conformity were accommodated without too much fuss. When I spoke on 'social change' at the fiftieth anniversary of the admission of Birkbeck College to the University of London in 1970, I introduced the notion of 'secular Anglicanism', noting in England the lack of extremity of feeling to be found between Catholics and anti-Catholics in France and Italy, among Lutherans and Calvinists in northern European countries, and in the Bible belt of the United States, as also in Ireland and parts of Scotland. Perhaps the phrase is not a very good one; be that as it may, the fourth theme of this book involves questions about the nature and reality of tolerance and consensus in British society and political culture, including the question of whether consensus (if it existed) contributed to a beneficial stability, or to an unfortunate stagnation. Did it become necessary to replace consensus with the abrasive policies of the radical right? I shall be arguing that consensus, strong from the war until the early seventies, began to break up in the middle seventies, and, much more decisively, in the eighties, with the advent of both Thatcherism and of a new left-wing extremism. The big question I pose is whether under the 'New Labour' governments of Tony Blair after May 1997 there is a move back towards restoration of consensus.

But surely, I hear many voices muttering, the impact of science and technology on society must be a major theme. It is a commonplace, though also an accurate and significant truth, that economic developments and social conditions in all industrialized countries since 1945 have been mightily affected by scientific and technological change. However, the correlations are not easy to establish; science and technology are best treated as informing, and being informed by, many aspects of social and economic life, rather than as a separate and perhaps quasi-magic entity somehow having a kind of mechanical 'impact' on an inanimate object, society. Furthermore, it is a purpose of this book to concentrate on what is particular to Britain's social history. All that said, it would be a fool who attempted to write contemporary social history without giving full weight to scientific discovery and technological innovation; I trust that I am not that fool. A persistently nagging question is whether the new structures of industry and commerce, governed by the new technology, have rendered unemployment and job insecurity unavoidable.

It is a long time since 1945. Much in the attitudes and life-styles of people during the later forties seems quite remote from the life-styles of people today. It would do no justice at all to the period under review if I were to treat it as one undifferentiated lump of time within which to follow out my four themes, and follow through developments in population, diet, the family, and so on. Thus I have resorted to one of the fundamental technical devices of historical writing, periodization. To stress the way in which change has taken place since the end of the war, I have divided the book into five parts, though, it scarcely need be said, there are no real turning points in history – general elections certainly are not.

The first period I describe as that of 'Social Consensus', which I take as lasting from 1945 to around 1958. Though, as will quickly become apparent, this period (particularly in its first, highly distinctive few years) was very much dominated by the legacies of the war, 1945 – the year in which the war ended and the general election that brought the Labour Government to power took place – is very much as good a starting point as any and probably better than most. The Labour Government's majority was almost destroyed in the general election of 1950, and it fell from office in 1951. However, the point that one should be aware of generalizing about the country, or the electorate, voting this way or that way, or choosing this or that, is strongly brought out by the fact that actually more people voted Labour in this election than voted Conservative, and more people voted Labour than had voted Labour in 1945. Since there followed thirteen years of Conservative rule, this could not unreasonably be described as a turning point in political history; but as far as social history is concerned it would, in my view, be true to say that the main themes of the late forties continued to be worked out in the early fifties.

In 1954 rationing of most major foodstuffs finally ended; in the same year the bill introducing commercial television became law (though independent television broadcasts did not begin till 1955). These, certainly, were signs of change. It was in 1955 that the Conservatives were returned with a larger and most convincing majority, led by Sir Anthony Eden now that Churchill had finally left the front line of politics. Yet, if we are looking at the more profound developments – particularly growing spending power in all sections of society, not least among young people, and in the provinces – which were to bring about a transformation in British social life, then the critical point of change lies some time in the last two years of the decade.

I take my second period, described as 'Roads to Freedom', as beginning around this time. The Conservatives regrouped themselves under Harold Macmillan, and went on to win a third election victory, with a further increased majority, in 1959. The word 'affluence' began to be bandied around freely. Release came, not just from post-war austerity, but from social controls going back to Victorian times; there was, indeed, something of the air of the eighteenth century about the introduction of premium bonds. There were new critiques of society too: Richard Hoggart's *The Uses of Literacy*, of 1957, and the Boulting Brothers' film *I'm All Right Jack*, of 1959; also released in 1959 were the films *Room at the Top* (completed in 1958, daring in its treatment of both sex and class) and *Sapphire* (a first full recognition of the existence of Britain's already substantial black population). True, a Labour Government, by the skin of its teeth as it turned out, got back into office in 1964. Not only did it end thirteen continuous years of Conservative rule, but it went on to win a comfortable majority in the general election of 1966. Again, however, from the perspective of social history the changes seem but surface ones. Despite the serious weakness of sterling, resulting eventually in devaluation, a general spirit of affluence remained, educational and cultural innovation continued, further libertarian measures were enacted, and 'permissiveness' was abroad in the land.

The Labour Government continued till 1970 when, rather narrowly and somewhat unexpectedly, it lost to the Conservatives. Certainly 1968 and 1969 had been troubled by outbreaks of student activism, but in no way can these be compared with the great upheavals that affected France in 1968. Indeed 1968 and its aftermath, including such developments as the lowering of the age of majority to eighteen, marked a continuing progress on the 'roads to freedom'. Whatever the intentions of the new Conservative administration under Edward Heath, it is hard to detect any significant change in life-styles or attitudes before 1973. But then came the first oil crisis, serious industrial disruption, an escalation of violence. The 'Time of Troubles', marked by depression, decline, and cutbacks, had begun; violence in Northern Ireland, which had entered a new crisis phase in 1968, increasingly overshadowed British life. In 1973 Britain joined the European Economic Community, a move confirmed in the referendum held in 1975 by the Labour Government (which had been elected in 1974). Despite the referendum, it is not easy to generalize about British attitudes towards Europe, but without doubt in the middle seventies there were many manifestations of closer contact with the Continent and of a greater cosmopolitanism, allied perhaps with greater insecurity and less insular pride.

In many respects 1979 is a critical year of change: trade union action in the 'Winter of Discontent' seemed to demonstrate that the spirit of consensus was completely dead. Mrs Thatcher won the election and quickly introduced some radical right-wing legislation, while Labour moved towards the extreme left. However, up till the spring of 1982 it did seem quite likely that Thatcherite policies would soon be replaced by ones more in keeping with the traditions of secular Anglicanism. Only with the Falklands War of 1982 did it become clear that Thatcherism was in the ascendant. At the same time the long-threatened Information Technology (IT) revolution began to seem a reality. There were many continuities, but new social configurations featuring private enterprise and explicitly denying the values of national consensus were clearly apparent by the middle eighties: my fourth period, beginning around 1982, is called 'Privatization, Polarization and IT'. The general election victory of 1987 seemed to confirm the hegemony of Thatcherism.

However, by 1989 there were many signs of the Government's growing unpopularity, particularly over the specifically Thatcherite Community Charge or 'Poll Tax'. At the same time it was very apparent that, despite the puritanical aspirations of the Thatcher Government, the libertarian and innovative developments of the sixties had taken deep root among the populace as a whole. A very clear divide was opening up between the Government and the governed. Perceiving Mrs Thatcher as increasingly a liability, her Cabinet colleagues forced her out of office in November 1990. It seemed that the new Government under John Major might jettison some of the harsher aspects of Thatcherism; Major himself spoke of his wish to create 'a society at ease with itself'. In fact, as the libertarian notions associated with the sixties actually became stronger, and there was something of a revival of the communitarian notions of 1945, what emerged was increasingly 'A Society at Odds with Itself', the title of my fifth period running from 1989 to 1997. Evidence of the government's deep unpopularity mounted, leading to suggestions that just as there had been a 'sea change' (the phrase was that of former Prime Minister James Callaghan) in political values in 1979, so there might well be another 'sea change' in 1996 or 1997. Whatever the truth of that, many of the Thatcherite innovations would remain, and there would be no escaping from the implications of the new technology and a global economic situation in which multi-national companies were dominant players.

'New Labour' under Tony Blair did indeed win the election of 1 May 1997, and then the one of 1 June 2001: in Part Six, running from 1997 to early 2002 I discuss the many disappointments endured under the Blair governments, and discuss how far, if at all, consensus was being restored.

Yet, having identified the themes, and the chronology, there remains the problem of what to put in and what to leave out. Apart from tracing out the four themes and establishing a legitimate periodization, my interest is in the nature, extent, and significance of social change. Accordingly, I now define a list of eleven main clusters of interrelated social facts and developments that I take to be most relevant to the history of British society since 1945. These clusters (they overlap, of course) are: Social Geography (including the physical environment, demography, population, urban and suburban developments, location of industry, etc.); Economic and Technological Change (including innovation in theory as well as techniques and also covering the question of the changing nature of work); Social Class and Social Structure; Social Cohesion (how far is the nation unified? How far are racial, nationalist, or sex differences pulling it apart?); Social Welfare and Social Policy; Material Conditions; Customs, Behaviour and Leisure Activities; the Family and the Role and the Status of Women (I do not assume that these are necessarily intertwined – the latter increasingly becomes an issue in its own right); Social Deviance and Questions of Law and Order; Intellectual (including Scientific) and Artistic Developments; and, finally, Social and Political Values, Institutions, and Ideas. As can be seen, technology and science feature principally under, respectively, the second heading and the second last heading; but as will become clear they emerge in other headings as well.

The ebb and flow of society cannot be contained within the limits set by these eleven signposts. In the five separate parts of this book the eleven headings are shuffled and reshuffled, giving different and, I hope, illuminating juxtapositions. But the signposts are there for readers to use if they wish, for social history should not be a random assemblage of facts and quotations from government papers, still less a swamp of titbits and anecdotes culled from the popular press. Part One, indeed, follows the eleven headings through the order given: chapter 1 takes in social geography *and* economic and technological change; chapter 2 concentrates on social class *and* social cohesion; chapter 3 is limited to social welfare and social policy; chapter 4 covers material conditions, customs, the family and social deviance; chapter 5 sticks to intellectual and artistic developments; while chapter 6 uses the topic of 'values' to assess the period as a whole. The pattern is radically altered in Part Two; then, though the allocation to chapters takes different forms, returning to its original shape in Parts Three and Four. There is a further reshuffle in Part Five, then, in Part Six I once more start with social geography, picking up also on social and political values, institutions and ideas; chapter 28 is largely dominated by social welfare and social policy together with economic and techno-logical change; chapter 29 links social cohesion (topic 4) to topics 3, and 6–10.

But enough of structure. This book seeks to inform, but it aims also to appeal to the general reader. Writing it has been both enjoyable and harrowing. I hope readers will share something of these emotions.

Part One

Social Consensus
1945–57

1

British Journey

On 24 August 1945, J. L. Hodson, a prosperous and well-connected journalist, wrote in his diary:

The war is over; the conditions of war in some respects continue. You need only make a long railway journey in England to become aware of it. I travelled last Sunday to Newcastle on Tyne. The journey which in peace-time took four hours now took eight and a quarter. No food on the train. No cup of tea to be got at the stops because the queues for this remarkable beverage masquerading as tea were impossibly long. At Newcastle an army artillery captain and I got hold of a truck and wheeled our bags along a platform almost impassable through luggage and merchandise waiting to be shifted. No taxi to be got. My hotel towel is about the size of a pocket handkerchief, the soap tablet is worn to the thinness of paper, my bed sheets are torn.

Many of the conditions of war were indeed to continue until early 1950, with rationing and controls enduring still longer. Yet the war itself cracked many of the conventions of British society, so that idealists could genuinely welcome the peace as heralding a new dawn. Between 1945 and 1950, then, the country lay in a crepuscular zone with the shadows of night as firm upon the landscape as the heartening hints of the rising sun. None the less I have taken the full dozen years of 1945 to 1957 as one period because it was only in the later years that certain consequences of the war were clarified, certain continuities of British society re-established, and certain assumptions which were to determine the future course of British society fully worked out.

Life in these dozen years was dominated by the consequences of the war, both negative and positive, though at the same time it largely conformed to patterns of behaviour established earlier in the century.

Over 70 per cent of the nation's dwellings dated back to the late nineteenth or early twentieth century, or earlier; most of the remainder belonged to the various types of more or less 'traditional' housing estates built in the inter-war period. Parking spaces abounded; but then that was because so few people had cars. Sound film and sound broadcasting, both creations of the inter-war years, enjoyed their last golden age. Those just reaching adulthood had spent their formative childhood years in a time when, without doubt, living standards were rising, but when, also, much of the country was affected by severe economic depression. Those already reaching middle-age had lived out the best years of their lives in such conditions.

In waging war Britain had acquired debts of £3,000 million, had allowed domestic capital to deteriorate by around the same amount, had used up overseas investments to the extent of £1,000 million, and had had to let exports fall to one third of their pre-war level. Britain had been able to keep going during the war because of the Lend-Lease agreements with the United States; these, however, were brought to a sudden end with the defeat of Japan. North American loans were secured, but on the condition that the pound should be restored to full convertibility as quickly as possible: when convertibility was restored in the autumn of 1947 it created the first of the sterling crises which were to be the economic trademark of the new era.

With re-building going on everywhere in the world, many materials and foodstuffs were even scarcer than they had been during the war. The coal-mining areas had been shamefully mistreated during the Depression, then conjured into flurried, though not usually very productive, activity during the war. In 1945 coal production was again down at the very low level of 175 million tons and output remained low during the post-war years, matching the pre-war level only in 1950. With the war barely over, there came in the winter of 1946–7 the most serious blizzards and the greatest freeze-up for over a century, followed in turn by floods, though there was a fine summer. During the worst of the cold spell power supplies were cut, creating a wave of temporary unemployment which reached a peak of 800,000 in 1947.

If we survey Britain as it was in the late forties and early fifties, the furthest reaches of mountain and valley, of island and fishing village, as well as the towns and cities and the plumper farming lands, we can identify a number of major forces shaping life within the geographical diversities. In the thirties had come the first halting attempts to control depression and unemployment through diversification and the introduction of new industries into the hardest-hit areas; these policies had scarcely got very far by the time of the outbreak of war, but the idea of diversification and the direction of industry was very much in the minds of Government planners after the war. The war itself had had an enormous direct influence in stimulating all kinds of expanded or new industrial development often in areas remote from the attentions of German bombers. For all that, the traditions, and the hard contours of bricks and mortar, products of a century and a half of industrialization, could not suddenly be wished away.

Planning, direction of the economy, and social engineering in general, it was hoped, would be achieved through nationalization of the major industries, the Distribution of Industry Act (1945), and the channelling of new investment to 'development areas' through the building of new towns, and, on another plane, through the establishment of national parks under the provisions of the National Parks and Access to the Countryside Act (1949). 'Green belts' were to be preserved round London and the major conurbations. Demand after the restrictions of the war years was high, while, at the same time, building materials were in short supply, and, anyway, were deliberately controlled by the Government. Furthermore, it was absolutely vital that Britain achieve its salvation in the post-war world by maximizing exports and, therefore, domestic production. Trends, therefore, were favourable to economic expansion; given the shortages, those areas which had had their industrial capacity extended during the war were at a special advantage. Overall, despite the frustration and austerity of the immediate post-war years, there was modest prosperity, and the bulk of wage and salary earners did reasonably well. There was something of a recession in 1952–3, which served to sort out the areas which had genuinely embarked upon prosperity from the ones where post-war Sellotape and plaster had not fully served to conceal deeper industrial wounds.

The war had had a great influence, also, on the exploitation of science and technology. The Second World War is sometimes called 'the physicists' war', and many of the developments inspired by purely military objectives were to have social repercussions, often rather unexpected ones. The adaptation of nuclear power to the generation of energy for civilian purposes was obvious enough, as was the application of radar to commercial air transport; but radio isotopes, a by-product of the nuclear industry, proved to have important applications in medicine, while the infra-red devices developed during the war for detecting the enemy in the hours of darkness proved invaluable in the scanning techniques developed in medical physics. Penicillin was a pre-war discovery, but it was only exploited in wartime. The successful search for new antibiotics (mainly carried out by American scientists) revolutionized medicine in the post-war years. Within chemicals generally there was a whole range of important developments, including plastics, artificial fibres, fertilizers, and pesticides, and a broad shift from 'light' chemicals to 'heavy' chemicals (detergents are an important example). Out of the war experience came two new, or almost new, science-based industries: electronics and optics; while an older industry was expanded and transformed: engineering. For even more traditional industries, new possibilities opened up: the use of oxygen in the continuous stripmill made possible the rapid production of high-quality thin sheets.

The relationship between the war, science and technology, and post-war British society is rather similar to that between the war, economic and social planning, and post-war society. Many of the great scientific and technological developments could scarcely be attributed to conscious decision-making. Thus, though there was great enthusiasm for, and much talk about, the importance of science and technology to Britain's social regeneration, there was a good deal less understanding of how to set about harnessing science and technology in the most effective manner. As there was to be a hit-and-miss quality about post-war social engineering, so there was to be something of the same quality about the nation's exploitation of science and technology.

For such a small island – 750 miles long, and, at its widest point, 375 miles across – Britain is a very diverse country. The war had been a national and, within limits, a universalizing experience, in much greater degree than had the Depression of the inter-war years. The tangible effects of the war, however, were distributed unevenly as if by some ferocious, but casual, wizardry. Tracts of London, Merseyside, the Midlands, Plymouth, and Clydeside, and many historic towns besides, lay desolate; in other areas, new factories, new roads, new bridges, gave an air of bustle and prosperity which had been lacking for a generation.

When J. B. Priestley, at the height of the Depression in 1933, was collecting material for his *English Journey*, he discovered three Englands: the old England of the guidebooks; nineteenth-century industrial England; and twentieth-century England of bypasses and suburbia: much of nineteenth-century England had in fact become a fourth England,

England of the dole. Probably there had been more Englands than that: rural outposts, for example, mostly enduring hard times; and, outside of England, the remote highlands of Wales and Scotland, the specially deprived industrial areas of these two countries, and the 'Scotland and Wales of the guidebooks'. Priestly's taxonomy had certainly already been partially overturned by the war, yet it continued to have meaning for the post-war years. Indeed there is no completely satisfactory categorization which combines physical and human geography. So let us simply start at the top of the country and work our way steadily down to the bottom.

The Highlands and Islands of Scotland, peopled sparsely with crofters and fishermen, had continued to decay in the inter-war years. Though it was actually in the Orkneys that the first loss of life occurred as a result of an enemy air-raid, this region was hardly affected by the bombing war. But it suffered a renewed outflow of population as young women went, or were directed – a major grievance of the Scottish Nationalists, this – to factories in England. However, the wide spaces and sheltered inlets of the Highlands could be exploited for military training grounds, airfields, and port facilities. An attack was made on the long-neglected problem of communications, new roads being built in the Orkneys, the Shetlands, and on the islands of Lewis, Benbecula, and South Uist, the last two being joined together by the completion of the South Ford Viaduct. New piers were constructed at such shipping ports as Wick, Thurso, Tarbert, and Ullapool. Furthermore, a new hospital for 640 patients was built at Raigmore, Inverness. These were not unmixed blessings, but they served to breathe some semblance of life back into areas which much needed it. More important was the Government's campaign to increase home-produced food supplies. Highland farmers benefited, and even prospered moderately, from grants under the marginal agricultural production scheme and from subsidies for hill sheep and hill cattle.

Hydro-electric schemes had been launched in the inter-war years. During the war, thanks in large measure to the energetic policies of Scotland's Socialist Secretary of State in the wartime coalition, Tom Johnston, had come the establishment of the North of Scotland Hydro-electricity Board. The building of new hydro-electric schemes continued at a rapid pace in the post-war years. Again this meant new life and new amenities for the Highlands. New construction sites provided opportunities for unskilled labourers to make high earnings, so long as they were prepared to live in unattractive temporary accommodation. The Highland economy was not saved, and not all of the changes were welcome ones. But a stop had been put to the absolute decline of pre-war years.

Probably the area of Scotland which benefited most from the war and post-war years was that of the Southern Uplands, the Border Country, where both arable and pasture farming prospered in meeting new demands. In between lies the industrial area of Central Scotland stretching from Glasgow and the Clydeside in the west, with its shipbuilding and heavy engineering industries, to Edinburgh in the east, with its more traditional industries, such as printing and brewing, and its high middle-class professional element, but surrounded, none the less, by coalfields, and northwards through the Fife coalfields, the linoleum factories of Kirkcaldy, to the port town of Dundee, whose staple industry had been jute.

Industrial Scotland, though Edinburgh least of all, had been deep in distress throughout the thirties. Something of a revival seemed to be heralded by the locating of a number of Royal Ordnance factories, as well as other industrial developments, in this area. A Ministry of Supply clothing depot at Motherwell became, in the post-war years, a Metropolitan Vickers engineering factory. A wartime Rolls-Royce factory at Hillington, just outside Glasgow, was the precursor of other factories in what, in the post-war years, became a new industrial estate. Garelochhead acquired a Metal Industries Ltd depot, Falkirk an aluminium rolling mill, and Edinburgh an important Ferranti electronics complex. Government policy deliberately aimed to bring industry to Scotland; and until the early fifties, at least, a new level of prosperity was attained, even if, from the point of view of the national economy, Scotland was not always the most sensible place in which to site new industry. The real basis of prosperity, in any case, lay in the recovery of the traditional heavy industries.

Many of the complications and contradictions involved in the heritage of the war, and the Labour Government's determination to engineer prosperity out of it, show up well in the North-East of England. Coal, iron and steel, and ships, were all in great demand during the war, so the North-East, which had been in the deepest depression in the thirties, prospered. Again wartime Royal Ordnance factories provided the bases for the development of post-war industrial estates. A new urban pattern emerged very clearly. Whereas older industries had been located along the rivers with copious provision of railway sidings, the new industrial estates developed on the outskirts of towns and depended upon the roads. The Royal Ordnance filling factory at Aycliffe became the focal point for the new town of Newton Aycliffe. A site chosen for wartime purposes was scarcely the best choice for a post-war new town, particularly since it was so close to the substantial town of Darlington.

In general, the brave new world tended to be built to contours shaped by the war, or even along lines determined by the bad old industrial world. One of the most striking sights in the North-East was the Consett ironworks (now demolished), rising starkly from a hilly moorland landscape. Unfortunately, judged rationally, this remote spot was scarcely the ideal one. However, the aim after 1945 was to pump prosperity into the former depressed areas, not to carry out a complete rationalization of industry. Hence, under the Labour Government, the Consett ironworks were developed and expanded. But the largest post-war developments in the North-East took place on Teesside, major developments being the establishment of a vast new I C I nylon polymer plant at Wilton and the building of the Lackenby steel smelting shop, which came into production in 1953. As part of its policy of diffusing jobs, and of curbing office development in the South-East, the Government located its new Ministry of National Insurance in Newcastle.

Cumbria, on the other side of the Pennines, has a wilder landscape, and a higher proportion of the population working on the land. Again the small industrial area had suffered greatly during the Depression. Better times were signalled with the establishment at the beginning of the war of the special steel-works at Distington. In the post-war years this became an iron foundry and general engineering works, which, in turn, provided a market for the output from the long-established Workington steelworks. Further employment opportunities were created by the war-generated growth of Vickers at Barrow. But Cumbria was also touched by the greatest of all the technological spin-offs from the war. Already in 1946 work was going ahead on a nuclear plant at Windscale; nearby, at Calder Hall, Britain's first nuclear power station, which began producing electricity in May 1956, was built.

Continuing down the west side of the country, we come first to rural Lancashire, then to the holiday resorts and to the cotton towns heavily stricken during the Depression, for which there was to be no long-term recovery; then to the South-East Lancashire conurbation centring on Manchester, and west, past the old chemical towns of Warrington and Widnes to the great port of Liverpool, which prospered with the post-war productivity drive. New industries, based mainly on synthetics, had been fostered during the war, and the county had been given an injection of metropolitan middle-class life-styles by the settlement of certain civil service departments in the resort towns of Lytham St Annes and Blackpool. The big changes in the chemicals industry brought a new prosperity to Warrington, Widnes, and their vicinity.

Back across the Pennines there was no real recovery for the woollen mills. It was in West Yorkshire that the post-war policies of the Labour Government, aimed at the distribution of industry, were at their most unsuccessful. New industries were excluded, and even established textile firms were encouraged to expand in areas whose need was felt to be greater, for example the North-East. Thus, although the West Riding conurbation itself, mainly through the growth of the service trades, continued to develop, with suburbia filling in the gaps between such main towns as Leeds and Bradford, West Yorkshire was on the way to becoming more a museum than a hive of industry. Yorkshire was a very varied county, of course: the rural areas did well, and the coal-mining regions to the south prospered as a consequence of the wartime and post-war demand for coal. There were important coal-burning electrical power stations in such places as Ferry Bridge. Rather out on a limb was the region of Humberside where modest prosperity came to the main town of Hull, and to such fishing ports as Grimsby which re-established themselves after the disruption of war.

The coal seams of South Yorkshire practically merge into those of the East Midlands. Here, around Nottingham and Derby, we are in D. H. Lawrence country. The coal mines had done moderately well in the Depression, and they did even better in the post-war years. There was considerable growth of light industry in both Nottingham and Derby. Nottingham had its famous Raleigh bicycle works, and Derby had its Rolls-Royce, Midland Railway, and British Celanese factories. Again, we must not take counties or regions as homogeneous. Where the Pennines come to an end in Derbyshire is one of the most famous and popular beauty areas in Britain: in 1949 the Peak District was designated Britain's first national park.

The most striking success story of the war and post-war years was that of the West Midlands. The Black Country, to the north and west of Birmingham, original home of the Midland coal mines and ironworks, certainly had a somewhat desolate air at the end of the war. But Coventry, to the south-east of Birmingham, although blitzed in November 1940, already by the end of the war stood out for its prosperity resulting from the boom in engineering, motor manufacturing, and other light industry;

it was to benefit further from the deliberate attempts to stimulate technological innovation after 1945, as also from the pent-up demand for cars. The West Midlands conurbation can be taken as the most successful example of post-war suburban growth. The potteries of North Staffordshire to the north were always of a rather different character. During the war, 37,000 pottery jobs disappeared here; on the other hand two important Royal Ordnance factories were established which continued, though on a reduced scale, after 1945 and wartime shadow factories located in the potteries were taken up by Rists, AEI, and Simplex. Furthermore pent-up demand, and the general terms of trade, did bring something of a revival in both pottery and coal mining and by 1951 both industries were re-established at almost pre-war employment levels. Development policies perhaps benefited the West Midlands more than strict assessment of need might have suggested: one eighth of the area was declared to be 'development land' and was steadily built on and filled in. When the stop–go came in 1952–3, it had only relatively mild effects on this region, and unemployment always remained at around half the national level.

West of the industrial areas, going towards Wales, lies what has often been described as the cradle of the Industrial Revolution, centred on Ironbridge. This is beautiful countryside, more and more so as one moves towards the heights of south-west Shropshire. These, more sung about than made use of in former years, were reclaimed for pasture farming during the war and in the post-war years, through the exploitation of advanced agricultural technology, continued to yield a good profit as a centre of cattle-rearing.

Central and North Wales met with fewer direct incursions from the war than did the Highlands and Islands of Scotland. Again there was a drive to bring marginal land under cultivation, and on the whole the farming communities of North Wales did well. Industrial South Wales, upon which most attention is usually fixed, is little more than a coastal strip with knotted fingers poking up the valleys as far north as the once-mighty town of Merthyr Tydfil. If the West Midlands can be taken as a paradigm of relatively successful industrial Britain in the first decades after 1945, South Wales, in many ways, forms the paradigm of relatively, though by no means totally, unsuccessful industrial Britain. At the end of the war, South Wales still very much fell within J. B. Priestley's 'nineteenth-century' category, for collapse in demand for coal and steel had made South Wales a scrap-heap in the inter-war period. Because of wartime needs, these two industries again dominated in 1945. As Graham Humphrys (*South Wales*, 1972) has so well put it:

> Individual industries still wore their nineteenth-century forms. Steel sheets were still being hand-dipped in molten tin to make tin-plate in small scattered works. Colliers still picked coal by hand from two-foot seams and afterwards went home to wash in a tin bath in front of the fire. Many of the hospitals were condemned, and in many places things like bread, milk and coal were still being delivered by horse and cart.

Working their effects upon this traditional background, as the post-war decade advanced, was the familiar mix of ideas mooted (and to some extent practised) in the thirties, the forced changes of the war, and the good intentions of politicians and planners. Apart from expansion in the coal and steel industries, munition factories were built at Bridgend, Hirwaun, Glascoed, and Pembrey, together with servicing and stores depots, and a new aluminium works was established. The Treforest Industrial Estate, near Pontypridd, was a brave, if tiny, thirties initiative: after war broke out new factories were set up to produce a range of strategic goods from optical lenses to parachutes.

During the war, and immediately after, a number of amalgamations took place within the steel industry, so that by the late forties it was largely dominated by Richard Thomas and Baldwins (formed in 1944), the Steel Company of Wales (formed in 1946) and Guest Keen and Nettlefolds. Guest Keen and Baldwins were responsible for re-building three blast-furnaces during the period 1943–6. In comparison with these private initiatives, the question of the nationalization of the iron and steel industry, which generated so much political fury, was of little real relevance.

The great symbol of the post-war reconstruction of the iron and steel industry was the building, between 1947 and 1951, of the Port Talbot works at a total cost of £73 million. Its importance is encapsulated in the local nickname given to it of Treasure Island. But as with the expansion of the Consett ironworks, the location of this new massive plant was determined more by tradition and the immediate past, than by any careful analysis of future trends. The Port Talbot site was chosen essentially with tin-plate in mind rather than uncoated sheet-steel and, as David W. Heal has written, it 'represents a prime example of a location which was chosen in the context of one trade, but which has been required to serve another'. The governing factor was the internal development already undertaken by Guest Keen and by Baldwins.

Wartime factories were there to hand for eager industrialists. Deliberate Government policy encouraged the building of the new type of one-storey factories located in open fields outside the towns. The Government sponsored 112 of the 179 new factories (or substantial factory extensions) which were built in South Wales between the end of the war and 1949. Unemployment dropped to 2.8 per cent compared with 20 per cent in the thirties. Prosperity continued right through to the later fifties so that, not unnaturally, the development-area policies were relaxed. But, in the longer term, they were perhaps not as satisfactory as they appeared: diversification was the great panacea, while close attention was not always given to the needs either of the world or even of the national market.

The steel industry had performed competently during the war, and its industrialists, vigorously supported by the Conservative Party in Parliament, were able to delay nationalization. The record, long-term as well as short-term, of the coal industry was very different, and nationalization was carried through in 1946. Much needed investment was channelled largely into the bigger collieries, though the smaller ones lasted till the late 1950s. South Wales in this period, then, was a mixture of refurbished nineteenth-century industry, together with enthusiastically developed new industry with all its accoutrements. It, too, had its new town, Cwmbran, designated in 1948.

Across the Bristol Channel lies the West Country, with Cornwall at the extremity rather barren, Devon much less so, and Somerset joining the other lush counties in stretching eastwards into the heartland of pre-industrial England. Bristol itself did well: out of the war experience burst the growth industries of light engineering, aviation, and electronics; nail-biting civilian demand in a time of austerity created a boom in the age-encrusted tobacco trade. The historic port of Plymouth, its town centre blitzed to the ground, had to embark immediately on an intensive re-building programme. However, it was the whole varied region, both to the north and the south of the Thames, which profited most from the expansion in arable land promoted by the war. This was the area which embraced most enthusiastically new farming methods, and which achieved new levels of prosperity whether in dairy farming or in the fast developing industry of market gardening. In the upper Thames valley such major centres as Reading and Oxford were doing nicely, as were the slightly smaller towns of Banbury and Newbury, already developing as substantial industrial centres.

So we come to London and the South-East, which, in the plottings of planners then, as in the plots of playwrights both before and since, commanded the lion's share of attention. And, although the Industrial Revolution began in the provinces, there can be no gainsaying the special place occupied by London in both history and geography. The war had focused attention on the noisome nature of London's slums, while at the same time destroying numbers of them. Overspill, rehousing, and the establishment of the green belt were key notions. At the same time, the Labour Government sought to restrict office building in Central London. The overall picture was of a movement outwards to new suburban estates, and further afield to the new towns of which London's periphery had a disproportionate number: Basildon, Bracknell, Hemel Hempstead, Hatfield, Stevenage, Harlow, and Crawley, together with the older Welwyn Garden City. By 1956 each of these was expanding at a rate of 9,000 houses a year. Overspill could go yet further afield and in 1952 the first Londoners arrived in Bletchley, a town lying on the frontiers of the Home Counties and the South Midlands, which had itself undergone some transformations during the war due largely to the siting there of large numbers of civil servants and the establishment of the Military Intelligence unit in Bletchley Park.

Whatever the planners' intentions, the Greater London conurbation expanded at a rate comparable with that of the West Midlands. That unique wash of brick-built terrace houses, brightened by little high street shopping centres, which spread across such inner London suburbs as Kentish Town, Islington, Leyton, Hackney, Fulham, and Camberwell, asserted a special charm. It was already clear by the early fifties that there was no rush whatsoever to leave these terraces and that, indeed, they were rising in value as London continued to parade its age-old attractions.

Last we come to East Anglia, often treated as least, since it does not fit easily into any broad taxonomy of British social geography. Still in the forties and early fifties East Anglia retained something of its remote quality, though change was fast breaking in. Predominantly a region of arable farming, it had been in steep decline in the period from 1870 to 1939. As with other areas the war brought new prosperity. The amount of land under arable was actually increased while, in addition to this, there were also increments in livestock farming. By the early fifties there were trading estates at Haverhill and Thetford; more crucially, modest prosperity in other parts, particularly London, intensified tourism on the Broads and round the coasts so that villages and towns were being prodded out of the romantic isolation hymned to every middle-class child in the days of Arthur Ransome and Coot Club.

One characteristic of the depressed industrial areas in the inter-war years had been their loss of population. Over the country as a whole, the birth-rate had been declining in the inter-war years, and was down to sixteen births per year per thousand of the population on the eve of war. However, in 1942 there occurred the first rise in the birth-rate since 1880. This developed into the post-war 'baby boom' which culminated in 1947 with a birth-rate of 20.7 per thousand. However, this appeared to be a purely war phenomenon, for the birth-rate fell again thereafter, causing something of the same concern as there had been in the thirties that Britain was moving towards having a declining population: hence the setting-up of the Royal Commission on Population at the end of the forties.

In the development areas population at least seemed to be stabilized, no longer in decline. There was a definite drift towards the West Midlands and towards London and the South-East; and there was a general drift from country to town. The Highlands of Scotland remained a place apart in that this region continued to suffer a serious loss of population, but for Britain as a whole a new stable prosperity seemed to be recognized when the 1951 census revealed for the first time a net gain by migration of half a million: England and Wales gained three quarters of a million from Scotland, Ireland, and overseas, while Scotland lost a quarter of a million. Britain in the late forties and early fifties, then, was a densely populated country (though with areas of very sparse population), exceeded in population density only by Japan, Belgium, and the Netherlands. Four fifths of the population were living in towns, and half of these town dwellers were to be found in Greater London or in the six provincial conurbations of the West Midlands, South-East Lancashire, Merseyside, West Riding, Tyneside, and Clydeside.

Yet there was still a slightly archaic quality to transport and communications. The expanding sector, certainly, was that of road transport – meaning, however, transport by bus and coach, not by private car. Rail passenger transport remained pretty static, whereas in 1950 passenger mileage by bus and coach had risen to 50.2 thousand million passenger miles (as against 19.4 in 1938), accounting for nearly one half of the total market compared with less than one third before the war; road transport as a whole now accounted for about 75 per cent of all mileage travelled.

In the towns, buses were taking over from trolley-bus and tram: by 1952 bus passenger miles within the cities and towns amounted to 14.5 thousand million, as against 2.9 thousand million clocked up by trolley-buses, and 1.8 thousand million taken by trams.

The great expansion in private car ownership began only in the very last years of the period under review. In 1938 there had been just under 2 million private cars and vans on the roads; in 1948 there were just over 2 million, and in 1950 between 2.25 million and 2.5 million. In 1955 the figure rose steeply to over 3.6 million, though that was still a mild foretaste of things yet to come. Roads were poor, and still served local needs rather than those of national travel. Although dual carriageways had been built near large towns, trunk roads on the whole were narrow and winding. It took a whole day to drive from London to Edinburgh; if going further north, you went up-river to the Kincardine Bridge, or queued for a ferry as medieval citizens had done in the days when Queensferry got its name. To get to South Wales it was necessary to go through Gloucester. Only in 1955 was it announced that Britain's first motorway (planned in the forties) would be built; but the word itself was as yet scarcely known to the wider public, certainly not as a term of abuse. For those with eyes to see it was clear that, compared, say, with Germany, France, and Italy, the British motor industry had taken the soft option of catering to home demand, failing to develop a strong orientation towards exports; while the road transport system, likewise, was inadequate for the needs of the modern world.

However, there were many successes. Britain spent far more on research and development than any of the European countries. The heaviest spending was channelled into aircraft manufacture, telecommunications, precision engineering, and chemicals. By the early fifties a considerable reorientation of Britain's exports had taken place, so that two thirds were drawn from the new science-based and technological industries. But scientific discovery and technological innovation, by their very nature, are international in their consequences. Britain derived much from American pioneering; but other countries took much from Britain. Scientific and technological innovation alone would not keep Britain in the position which, precariously, she still occupied in Europe in the later fifties.

2

That Topic All-Absorbing: Class

Nobody would disagree that it makes sense to divide Britain up geograph-
ically into different regions, though there might be a good deal of disagreement as to how these regions should be defined: is there such an entity as
East Anglia? Should Scotland be divided into three? Should one be guided
by political history, or by physical geography, or by basic occupational
activity? Probably there would be about as much agreement that Britain
in the late forties and early fifties could be divided up into a number of
social classes, though there would also be much disagreement about how
and where lines should be drawn.

If we study the popular vocabulary of the time we find widespread and
quite precise use of the phrase 'working class' or 'working classes' – the
phrases are really synonymous, for the latter one was not intended to
indicate several distinct classes but rather the variety of occupations and
income levels within the one class; we find a rather more varied and less
precise use of 'middle class' and 'middle classes' as well as 'lower-middle
class' and 'upper-middle class' (journalists and academic writers might
also speak of a 'middle-middle class' but that phrase had no standing in
ordinary colloquial English). While the broad notion of there being a
working class and a middle class, however divided up, was well established,
there was less agreement over the use of the term 'upper class': many of
those who might be thought, by objective criteria, to have belonged to
such a class preferred to refer to themselves, and were often described by
others, as 'upper-middle class'. This usage postulated the continuing, if
somewhat etiolated, existence of an 'aristocracy', the real upper class.

The essential difficulty in studying class is that while one can directly
recognize the existence of women, of blacks, of the Catholic Church, or
of council housing estates, one cannot directly apprehend the existence

of classes. All one can do then (unless one has some *a priori* theory, such as Marxism) is agree that class exists when people themselves, explicitly or implicitly, recognize its existence and behave in ways which reflect its existence. Three elements make up class as it actually is. First of all, class is shaped by history. It originates with the Industrial Revolution, which steadily replaced an older society of estates and orders by one made up of the more fluid and imprecise social classes. Industrialization proceeded at different speeds in different parts of the country. Political events, traditions, national characteristics, and the more recent upheavals of war all affected the forms of class as they were after 1945.

Second, class has a very strong subjective element. It is by studying what people say and write about class, by studying, that is, 'images' of class, that we are best able to map out a social structure which conforms with life as actually lived in the period under review, as distinct from merely being an abstract tool of analysis. Third, we can quite unequivocally perceive areas of inequality in modern society: in power, authority, wealth, income, job situation, material conditions, and culture and lifestyles. Once the subjective contours of class have been sketched out, it becomes clear that they do tend to coincide with the major social inequalities.

Was there, then, an upper class in post-war Britain? Long before the Industrial Revolution successful men of business, politics, and the professions had become part of the aristocracy and, within a very short space of time, they and their descendants were behaving as to the manor born. No revolution overthrew this aristocracy which continually renewed itself from below. There used to be much loose talk of 'the rise of the middle class' and of the middle class taking over from the aristocracy with the passing of the Great Reform Act of 1832. In fact the great commercial families, like the Peels and Gladstones, did not overthrow the aristocracy, they joined it, leaving the vast mass of middlingly successful business and professional people to continue occupying a middling station in life.

As the nineteenth century advanced, a new composite upper class emerged consisting of the older aristocracy (many of whose members, anyway, were, a generation or two further back, products of commercial wealth) and a greatly increased number of recruits from commerce, industry, government, and the higher professions. It was still possible, of course, to make a fine distinction between 'aristocrats' on one side, and the 'upper-middle class' (by one definition) on the other. Here we come up against one of the many confusing features of class. When it is a question of fine distinctions, as opposed to the broad historically signifi-cant categories, we find that much depends on the class position of the individual observer. If you belong to the upper class yourself you may well be very aware of the distinction between a true landed aristocrat and a successful industrialist; if you belong to the classes below the distinction may not even be apparent, let alone real. Thus, just before the war, Lord Londonderry could refer to Britain's then Prime Minister, Neville Chamberlain, as 'a Birmingham tradesman' while most of Chamberlain's fellow countrymen may well have been more struck by his projection of the upper-class manner and life-style. For, in the nineteenth century, the upper class elaborated on older traditions in evolving a distinctive ethos inculcated through the major public schools and, in lesser degree, Oxford and Cambridge universities. There was created an upper-class 'box' of attitudes and life-styles into which newcomers could be socialized.

We have to recognize, then, that there is ambiguity in the usage of the phrase 'upper-middle class'. For myself, I prefer the simple phrase 'upper class' to describe what Sir Ian Fraser (in a private letter written in the 1930s) shrewdly defined as that 'reservoir of persons economically free and accustomed to responsibility from an early age' who, as a matter of objective fact, turn out to exercise a dominance in the spheres of power, authority, wealth, and income totally disproportionate to their numbers, and who have a distinctive culture and life-style of their own. I would estimate this class as making up about 2 per cent of the population in the years after 1945. The phrase 'upper-middle class' is then better applied to the upper segment of the class below, a class without this disproportionate dominance of wealth and power. Still, the ambiguity does exist and indeed has a real significance. It was part of the very upper-class ethos that one should be reticent in speaking of class: hence many upper-class people preferred the softer camouflage of the description 'upper-middle-class'; but more than this – 'everybody loves a lord', and there was a very deep vein of snobbishness making for the continued elaboration of a distinction between those truly aristocratic and those who, for lack of a better phrase, must be distinguished as 'upper-middle-class'. Finally, there was the prob-lem of that wretched foreign word *bourgeois*, often translated into English as 'middle-class'. Those who believed that the bourgeoisie now ruled the country thus sometimes confusingly termed the upper class the 'middle class' or the 'upper-middle class'. (In fact the bourgeoisie – the urban élite whose wealth was based on commerce and trade – had been invading the aristocracy since the sixteenth century.)

There was little ambiguity about the composition of the working class. Of the total employed population, well over 60 per cent did manual work of one sort or another, ranging from unskilled roadwork to the craftsmanship of the engine driver or mechanic. Manual workers and their families formed the working class, with which would usually be included small shopkeepers and publicans in working-class areas. Foremen and floor managers occupied an ambiguous position on the fringes, as did the technicians in many of the newer industries. If we mark off the upper class and the working class, we are left with the middle class, or middle classes, in between, amounting to well over 30 per cent of the population. Setting aside all the subtle shades of distinction which exist within all social classes there remains quite an important, though far from rigid, line between the lower-middle class of, essentially, clerical and other types of white-collar worker, and the upper-middle class of local businessmen and the more prestigious professionals.

According to classical Marxist sociology, classes in the modern era are becoming polarized, an upper class of the owners of capital on one side, and a proletariat on the other, with the 'transitional' middle class steadily being forced down into the latter. Increasing polarization, inevitably, means increasing likelihood of class conflict. Conservative sociologists, on the other hand, have presented a thesis of the 'disintegration' of classes, producing a long continuous range of status groups, in place of a small number of discrete social classes. The growth of large-scale industrial organization and the so-called 'managerial revolution' has, it was argued, replaced old-style capitalists with salaried managers. This analysis was at least as superficial as the polarization thesis: owners of capital in the forties and fifties were often also managers; successful managers often acquired capital. Thus there was in fact quite a clear class distinction between major businessmen on the one side, who, combining managerial power with capital ownership, formed part of the upper class, and mere managers on the other, who were part of the middle class.

The disruptions of war had not been without effect on class and relationships between classes. The most important single development was the change in status and bargaining power of the working class. Resorting as necessary to strikes, the workers were able to exploit the very high demand for labour engendered by the necessities of war to push their real earnings up by well over 50 per cent. The much vaunted 'mixing' of social classes during the war was more in spirit than substance, but undoubtedly there was a new upper-class and middle-class concern that, having played so crucial a role in the war effort, the workers should not be plunged back into the economic depression of the inter-war years. The egalitarian policies mooted during the war and, in large degree, carried out by the Labour Government after the war did not, as many hoped (or feared), alter the basic social structure, but in general they favoured the working class. High taxation during and after the war hit the upper-middle class hardest, lowering the barriers between it and the lower-middle class. Overall, the war strengthened the solidarity and self-awareness of the working class. Thus there was both disintegration of class boundaries and consolidation within classes.

The advent of a Labour Government in 1945 did not mean that the upper class necessarily relinquished power. Of Labour leaders, Hugh Dalton, Sir Stafford Cripps, and John Strachey could scarcely be described as anything other than upper class; Clement Attlee, the new Prime Minister, undoubtedly thought of himself as middle class and was usually perceived as such by political opponents; but as the product of a prosperous family of solicitors, who had been educated at the fairly prestigious public school, Haileybury, and at Oxford, he could more reasonably be placed as first-generation upper class. The Haileybury school magazine in November 1945 was able to congratulate itself on the election of only one Conservative old boy, but of four Labour old boys and its first ever Prime Minister, to whom it extended congratulations, 'proud that he is a son of Haileybury, and confident that he will not fail his high trust'.

In any case, the Conservatives were back in power after 1951, by which time, however, there had been a slight shift in the balance of forces within the party: there were more small businessmen and fewer big businessmen, and more representatives of such new growth areas as investment trusts, insurance, property development, advertising and public relations, entertainment, and communications. Whatever party was in office, the higher civil service continued to be dominated by the upper class; of the successful candidates for open entry to the administrative class in 1949–52, 74 per cent came from Oxbridge. Nationalization changed little: in many cases the former private owners and managers simply became the managers and directors of the state enterprises; in others the directorate was filled with established figures from the army, politics, and the civil service, social revolution being represented by a handful of trade unionists.

Rationing, controls, and shortages might have been expected to have had a crippling effect on traditional upper-class life-styles. A quick survey of the sources shows that many within the upper-class fold were able to lead a life of considerable amplitude in the age of austerity. Already in 1946 'Chips' Channon was celebrating the fact that life was back to 'normal' and that the fashionable Carcano–Ednam wedding of that year was a suitably lavish affair. Channon was American-born: his career in high society, charted in his diaries, clearly demonstrates the existence of the upper-class 'box' into which a wealthy outsider, prepared to adopt the appropriate life-style and mannerisms, could readily be absorbed. Harold Nicolson, his family, his wife's family (the Sackvilles), and their associates were not noticeably thrown by rationing either. The Nicolson diaries contain many classic presentations of the upper-class self-image: for example, 'I do believe, as I have always believed, that Social Democracy is the only possible antidote to communism. But I do not like the Labour Party. I am a mixture of an aristocrat and a Bohemian. The bedintness ['a Sackville expression, denoting the attitudes and manners of the lower-middle class,' explains Nigel Nicolson] of the Labour people is as repugnant to me as is their gentility.'

But Harold Nicolson could scarcely match the boisterous élitism of Labour's own Chancellor of the Exchequer, Hugh Dalton, recording in his diary the personal triumph of an old King's man back on the familiar ground of the Cambridge Union:

I scored the first Labour victory of the term by 180 to 170 odd, which was very gratifying. Two points which I think turned votes were:
(i) my declaration that we were spending, and would continue to spend, substantial sums on the Universities, and
(ii) a new declaration of Government policy which I made on the Olympics. I said that I had been informed by the President of the C.U.B.C. [Cambridge University Boat Club] who had the good sense to belong to my old college, that in the Olympics the Boat crews would have to row in old British boats with old British oars against foreign crews in new British-built boats with new British-built oars . . . I was, however, very glad to inform them that that very day, before leaving London, I had been in touch with the Admiralty as well as with the Secretary of State for Air who was not only an old King's man and an old President of the Union, but also an old Olympic Captain, and I was able now to say that the Admiralty would give special consideration to providing, as a most exceptional case, suitable boats and oars for the British crews in the Olympics. 'After that declaration of Government policy,' I cried, 'I am confident that no rowing man will vote for this ridiculous resolution.'

If, instead of flicking through the diaries of the rich, we turn to the meticulous social survey conducted by Professor Margaret Stacey between 1948 and 1951 in the Oxfordshire town of Banbury, we encounter the considered verdict that 'it was impossible to ignore the existence of upper-class people'. Furthermore, 'in so far as this class sets the standards and aspirations of traditional social class attitudes . . . it is important out of all proportion to its size'. Finally, 'members of the traditional upper class in the Banbury district were all educated at one of the major public schools'.

High politics was a traditional occupation for the denizens of Sir Ian Fraser's 'reservoir'; otherwise the city, the diplomatic corps, or the higher civil service. But in a new age, upper-class figures were moving into other jobs as well. After Eton and Balliol, the Hon. John Godley (later Lord Kilbracken) joined the *Daily Mirror*, 'in preference to becoming a diplomat'. By the mid-fifties journalism, publishing, films, radio, television and advertising had become classic refuges for the upper class. More: on the eve of coal nationalization J. L. Hodson visited three up-to-date collieries in the North-East: 'The first surprise was to discover that the chairman of directors, managing director and chief engineer are the sort of men one meets as officers in the Guards or Royal Navy: men in their thirties or forties, beautifully turned out, quietly spoken, with accents traditional to the South.'

Perhaps these men were upper-middle class rather than upper class – that much is suggested by their quiet speech, definitely not an upper-class characteristic. Some insecurity over where the borders of the upper class lay might be suggested by Nancy Mitford's infamous article in *Encounter* (September 1955) defining the distinctions between upper-class usage ('U') and non-upper-class usage ('non-U'). In fact a basic point of the article was to assert that the significant barrier lay between aristocracy and upper-middle class on one side, and middle class and the rest on the other.

The middle-class self-image comes through clearly in some unpublished Mass Observation material dating from 1949. A female civil servant clearly envisaged a three-class society, with herself in the middle, or lower-middle:

I definitely think of myself as middle class. It is difficult to say why. I had a typical middle-class education (small private school and secondary school). I have a middle-class job and I live in a middle-class district. But none of these things would make me middle class in themselves. If I had been clever enough to get a higher post or profession, or rebellious enough to choose a more attractive manual job, I should not thereby have changed my class. Nor should I change it by living in a different district. Besides, my education and job and residence (to a certain extent) were determined by the fact that my parents were middle class so it is like the old riddle of the hen and the egg. Income has something to do with it but is not in itself a deciding factor nowadays as many working-class people get higher pay than the lower-middle class, and many upper-class 'new poor' get less.

A prosperous housewife gave her reasons for allocating herself and her husband to 'the Upper-Middle Classes'. These were 'Financial' – her husband earned a good income and they now lived on the interest from investments; 'Genealogical' – their fathers were respectively architect and headmaster; 'Occupation and Educational' – her husband was an MA of Cambridge and had been Director of Agricultural Research in the Sudan; 'Sartorial' – 'We know what is correct wear even though we may have to make do with our old clothes'; 'Cultural' – they enjoyed good music, books, plays, etc.; 'Conventional' – 'We eat in the dining room and use the conventional speech. We speak grammatical English in accepted pronunciation.'

Another woman, the wife of a production manager in an engineering firm, in declaring herself to be 'lower-middle-class', placed the emphasis on contrasting their position with those below:

. . . our education is of a higher standard than most working-class people. This has produced a standard of tastes in music, art and literature different from those of working-class people. (There are exceptions of course.) Our speech is different than most working-class people in this district, having a particular dialect and a larger vocabulary. Our circle of friends is mainly of the same type of person as ourselves as with two or three exceptions they do not coincide with those of working-class acquaintances. Do not think I am a snob. Can mix easily with working-class people, and do so in church and Parents' Association activities. But as friends, I find them unsatisfying and in conversation limited in subject common to both.

A fourth housewife chose to describe herself simply as of 'professional' status because: 'I can hardly say "middle class" now, though I was brought up in it. Our threadbare conditions seem at variance with the comfortable plumpness one associates with the term "middle class".'

Margaret Stacey found that a common educational background was not a specific middle-class characteristic. This makes sense: the middle class recruited from all sections of society. On the other hand, Professor Stacey found, 'the majority of the working class have received only an elementary education while a much higher proportion of the middle class received a secondary education'.

Historians have argued that, for the late nineteenth and early twentieth century, the distinction between 'respectable' working class and 'rough' working class was at least as significant as that between the working class and the lower-middle class. After 1945 this does not appear to be the case; there were still 'roughs', it is true, but on the whole the working class presents a homogeneous appearance, and a self-confident one, with little aspiration after middle-class values. None the less, it is true that Reginald Bevins, a Conservative Minister in the sixties, wrote in his autobiography, *The Greasy Pole* (1965): 'My mother and sisters dominated the family and, like many women who came from working-class families and have seen the effects of insecurity, her main ambition was that her children should be secure'; but he also recorded that 'she had a positive horror of politics (she would not even vote) which she regarded as an exclusive aristocratic pursuit and, for a shopkeeper, an invitation to bankruptcy'. The new sense of security of the post-war generation was boldly articulated by a plumber (interviewed in 1951): 'There is now so much work to be done and so little unemployment so if the boss rattles at you or threatens you with the sack you can just up and leave . . . The working people are better off and the bosses have lost a lot of their grip.' Above 'the bosses', incidentally, he recognized a 'snob class, the high-ups, senior civil servants, directors and such'. In 1949 a leader of the Transport and General Workers had declared: 'Let there be no mistake about it, we have made substantial progress in working-class conditions during the life-time of this government.'

For all that, the basic fact remained: to be working class meant per- forming manual work, most usually under arduous, uncongenial, or just plain boring circumstances. Conditions of work still demanded special working clothes, and still often left definite physical marks – calloused hands, for instance. When it came to 'life chances' members of the working class were still at a disadvantage compared with all of the rest of society. Individual members might move upwards, but conditions within the working class, not excluding working-class attitudes themselves, discouraged educational aspiration.

Class is a difficult and messy subject, but indisputably neither the upheavals of the Second World War nor the programme of the Labour

Government abolished it. Technological change, certainly, brought new obfuscations and subtleties. Margaret Stacey reckoned that alongside the clearly marked traditional three-tier class structure there also existed 'non-traditionalists' whose mobility through the technocratic sectors of society was such that they could scarcely be placed in any definite class. This is a useful concept, though, personally, I prefer to take it with a pinch of salt. When a representative sample of the British public was polled in 1948 there was little hesitation over opting for appropriate class labels, even if there was an evident tendency for some manual workers to put themselves in the middle class: asked, without prompting, to allocate themselves to a social class, 2 per cent said 'upper', 6 per cent said 'upper-middle', 28 per cent said 'middle', 13 per cent said 'lower-middle', 46 per cent said 'working', and only 5 per cent recorded 'no reply'.

If we are to compare the significance of class with that of other sources of distinction and inequality, such as age, sex, nationality, race, or religious community, class stands out as a key factor in such matters as wealth, political power, educational opportunity, and style of life. The social facts of post-war Britain cannot be *explained* solely by reference to class, but they certainly cannot be fully *understood* without reference to class.

3
The Welfare State

The phrase 'welfare state' (actually coined by Professor Alfred Zimmern in the 1930s) came into widespread use during the war to point a sharp contrast with Hitler's 'warfare state'. The phrase has since been used in a variety of rather loose ways, but essentially it means the totality of schemes and services through which the central Government together with the local authorities assumed a major responsibility for dealing with all the different types of social problems which beset individual citizens.

Most fundamental of these problems is that of income or 'social' security: people can fail to have enough to live on through being unemployed, through being unemployable, through being too old, through having too many children, through being injured, through being pregnant, and through being ill. But if people are ill, they do not just need an income while they are out of work, they need treatment: the second problem is that of the provision of medical services. Sickness, in the past, had often been engendered by bad housing; good housing for everyone, in any case, was the mark of a civilized society. Housing, then, was the third problem to be dealt with by the welfare state. If individuals were to participate fully in a civilized society they should also have a decent education – the fourth problem. But what point in having national insurance benefits, free medical care, proper housing, and wise schooling, if there were no jobs? It was a fundamental assumption of the war and post-war period that all of the different pieces of welfare state legislation would be backed up by an economic policy deliberately designed to create jobs and avoid unemployment. Finally, there were other areas of social life which a government, determined to hoover into spotlessness the Britain of the slums and Woolworth's spectacles, could also suck up: the arts, the environment generally, the care of children.

Whatever Government had come into power in 1945, undoubtedly legislation would had been passed to deal with these various issues. The great symbolic statement of British objectives, one which had been quoted round the world, was the Beveridge Report of December 1942. A vain and difficult man, very much, as a top civil servant and head of an Oxford college, a member of the upper class, Beveridge had deployed much Victorian fustian in his report, borrowing indeed from the language of *A Tale of Two Cities* when he pinned down the problems discussed above as five 'giants': 'want', 'sickness', 'squalor', 'ignorance', and 'idleness'. The report which, formally, was on the rather boring topic of 'social insurance and allied services' recommended a universal social security system covering everyone in the country; but it stressed as 'assumptions' that there should be a national health service, an economic policy directed towards avoidance of mass unemployment, and, more tenuously, an attack on the other 'giants'. Despite recent (erroneous) claims by Margaret Thatcher to the contrary, the Beveridge Report was in fact attacked by many Conservatives, and also by many other vested interests. Churchill, in his 1945 election campaign, emphasized (and who would now say he was totally wrong?) the country's serious economic position and the difficulties in the way of quickly establishing all the social provisions which the Labour Party, in its campaign, promised.

Social security provision, of a sort, went back half a century. Workmen's Compensation dated back to 1893, old-age pensions to 1908, with a more elaborate scheme introduced in 1928, unemployment insurance and health insurance to 1911 (implemented in 1913).

The Labour Government's legislation was in part intended to mark a break with the past, but it was also, on the one hand, constrained by the legislative framework evolved in the past, and, on the other hand, coloured by memories of that same past. Broadly, Labour policies were hitched to the star of 'universality'; the Conservatives would probably have aimed lower at 'selectivity'. Every Labour politician knew of the bitterness of the unemployed man thrown off unemployment insurance once his claim on the system was exhausted; the 'means test' which had to be undergone before unemployment assistance was forthcoming sounded in Labour ears as once the phrase 'Spanish inquisition' had sounded in the ears of Protestant zealots; and the humiliation was still deeply felt over the way in which 'panel patients' got one standard of service from their doctors, while the private patients got another. The Labour idea, then, in stressing the principle of universality was twofold: only by making the state services open to all could it be ensured that the highest standards would be available to all; only by having a universal service could the stigma be removed from those who had to make use of state services.

Actually, the first piece of new social security legislation was carried through by the Conservative 'caretaker' Government, which held office briefly in the period between the resignation of the wartime coalition and the assumption of office of the newly elected Labour Government. The most significant point about family allowances, payable in respect of second and later children in all income groups, was that they were payable to the mother, a very rudimentary sign of feminist influence on social legislation, which recognized women's role as childrearers, and was designed to prevent husbands from spending the money on drink or horses.

Family allowances, in a rather small way, embodied a social philosophy adhered to by many members of the Labour Party: not only did they apply to the whole community, but they were financed by general taxation, and they were, furthermore, themselves subject to taxation; in other words, a need in respect of having two or more children was automatically recognized; the rich in general contributed more and got back less, and yet there was no public distinction between the poor (who in practical terms did best) and the rich. But when it came to the central element in the maintenance of income, the National Insurance scheme as promulgated by the National Insurance Act of 1946, other philosophies prevailed. In the past there had been much Labour hostility to the principle of contributory insurance, but an even stronger hatred from the recent past was of anything that could be presented as a 'dole' or unearned hand-out. Thus the new concept of universality was simply grafted on to the older tradition of National Insurance.

In the Beveridge plan it had been intended that benefits, to be paid at one flat rate, should be sufficient for the maintenance of a basic minimum subsistence standard (Beveridge expected individuals to top this up with private insurance schemes); introducing the National Insurance Bill, the Minister, James Griffiths, formerly a Welsh miner, declared that it marked the introduction of 'the principle of a National Minimum Standard'. Actually, at forty-two shillings (£2.10), the benefits were already falling behind the cost of living, and continued to fall ever further behind. The consequence of the National Insurance scheme, therefore, was that 'every person who on or after the appointed day, being over school-leaving age and under pensionable age, is in Great Britain, and fulfils such conditions as may be prescribed as to residence in Great Britain' would have a National Insurance card upon which weekly National Insurance stamps would have to be stuck; but for many of the well-off, whose earnings often continued anyway even if they were off work, the scheme would be of little real relevance, while for those whose incomes did cease with sickness or unemployment, and who had indeed to go through the whole business of securing sickness notes, the benefits were actually quite inadequate. Although the qualification and requalification conditions were elaborately spelled out, the scheme could never come anywhere near to being an authentic piece of self-financing insurance, since old-age pensions, which were soon taking up two thirds of all expenditure on National Insurance, were to be paid immediately at the full rate. At the same time the scheme could be considered neglectful of the interests of the self-employed, who were not provided with any cover against unemployment.

Yet, since the scheme was theoretically an insurance scheme, there would have to be a further means of providing for those who, in one way or another, failed to meet the qualification conditions. Thus, although the 1948 National Assistance Act formally abolished the old Poor Law, it did retain in new form the autonomous body which had begun life as the ill-famed Unemployment Assistance Board of 1934 and had been continued in 1940 as the Assistance Board. In practice this National Assistance Board had to cope also with those who received insurance benefits but found them inadequate to their needs. Save in emergencies, National Assistance would only be paid out after a personal needs test; it later transpired that many in need were in fact deterred by this from applying for it. The failure was one of misunderstanding how ordinary, bemused, ill-educated people react, rather than one of deliberate harshness; it was, indeed, a failure very much in keeping with the consensus which had developed during the war between upper-class politicians, upper-class civil servants, and self-educated working-class representatives of lofty vision. Compared with the ministerial documents and hand-outs of the 1930s, those of this new era were genuinely friendly and unbureaucratic and pervaded with the spirit of social democracy and welfare for all; yet the probability is that they never got through to those who most needed help.

Still, in one sense, income security, through National Insurance and National Assistance, was a relatively simple matter. All it needed was cash, and that could be raised through National Insurance contributions and through general taxation. With a slight expansion in the lower civil service it could be administered through institutions which in essence already existed. Dealing with the nation's medical problems was not so easy. The range of services required for the maintenance of health is large; the services have to be provided by qualified practitioners, often in specially designed and expensive accommodation, such as hospitals; although medical science yields new means of prevention and treatment, these means tend to be ever more costly. Medical provision before the war depended upon a primitively unstable mixture of class prejudice, commercial self-interest, professional altruism, vested interest, and demarcation disputes. For the rich there was a personal service backed up by private nursing homes, with the substantial fees earned by the doctors to some extent dependent on observing the whims of their patients. Hospitals, in origin, had been for the poor only. By the thirties there were two major types of hospital, both now taking, and charging, middle-class patients, while continuing to treat poor patients free, but bitterly divided against each other. The one thousand or so voluntary hospitals ranged from the tiniest cottage hospitals, where operations were carried out by the local general practitioner, to the great teaching hospitals, which had high-quality specialist services; surgeons made their reputations by working for nothing in the most important of these hospitals, and their incomes by ministering to rich patients. The voluntary hospitals preferred to accept only the more interesting and acute cases; the chronically sick tended to be dumped on the other type of hospital, the local authority hospitals, of which there were about 1,750. The emergencies of war brought a more rational organization, with both types being merged into the Emergency Hospital Scheme organized on a regional basis, though the destruction and disruption of war reduced still further the actual amount of reasonable hospital accommodation available over much of Britain.

The National Health Insurance scheme, administered through private companies known as the 'approved societies', permitted the insured worker to have free medical service from his 'panel' doctor and occasionally, depending on the efficiency of the approved society, to have additional benefits, such as help towards purchasing spectacles. But there was no free medical service for the families of the insured workers, and many others were excluded from the scheme. For these groups doctors provided private services, charging what fees they could, sometimes having to employ professional debt collectors, and always being limited in what they could prescribe by the patients' ability to pay.

Dental care and ophthalmic care were luxuries for the middle and upper classes. The worker went to the dentist only in the last agony of toothache, and then only to have teeth pulled out. Glasses, he obtained direct from Woolworth's or other department stores. For the well-to-do, the private midwife and the nursery nurse supplemented the ante-natal, post-natal, and infant care provided by the general practitioner. For the generality of the nation's mothers one blessing at least of the First World War, much neglected by historians, had been the Maternity and Child Welfare Act of 1918: through the provisions of this Act a separate, inferior, but not inefficient service was provided by health visitors, midwives, and doctors working for the local health authority. Finally, the last tattered elements in this rag-bag of medical provision were to be found in the compulsory inspection and treatment of school children at the state schools, imposed by the Education Act of 1918, and in the distribution of milk and welfare foods developed during the war. The one major piece of social legislation actually enacted by Churchill's National Government was the Education Act of 1944 (pressed on with, in part, in order to divert attention from the costlier and more controversial issues of social security and national health): this Act continued the policy of local authority responsibility for the health care of school children while, in keeping with the tenor of the times, it abolished all charges made to parents.

In planning a national health service the responsible Minister (Aneurin Bevan, like James Griffiths a former Welsh coalminer, though of distinctly patrician tastes) had the advantages of the nationalized hospital system which had in all but name been operated during the war and of the strong current of opinion in favour of radical reform. His major problems concerned the shortage of resources and the (real or perceived) conflicts of interest within the medical profession, and between the profession and the local authorities, and the fact that the British local government system, established in the late nineteenth century, was now seriously out of date.

The National Health Service Act passed into law in the autumn of 1946; but the new National Health Service was not to come into being until 'the appointed day', 5 July 1948. In between, many tense battles had still to be fought out. In broad outline the proposed National Health Service was a monumental expression of the principle of universality. Although a proportion of the income from National Insurance stamps was to be devoted to the Health Service, treatment in no way depended upon insurance contributions: it was entirely open to everyone, and, save in the case of certain specified extra services, it was, at the point of service, entirely free; that is to say, there was no question of having to pay first then recovering the payment later, as was to be the case with health provision in certain other countries. Most important, there was now a firm separation between the question of income need (dealt with by National Insurance and National Assistance) and health need, which had no connection with these schemes.

The biggest innovation was the nationalization of the hospitals, opposed by the Conservatives, though in fact the way had been well prepared by the war experience. No one was to be forced to join the service, whether as doctor or patient. Private pay beds would be allowed to exist within the hospitals, and general practitioners would be able to carry on their own private practice if they so wished. The senior consultants knew that they would be able to go on earning large fees, and they also had the satisfaction of knowing that the special position of the big teaching hospitals would be safeguarded; junior hospital doctors were quite happy to settle for a salaried service; but how the general practitioners were to be paid was not defined in the Act. In fact, these doctors resisted the infringement of their traditional professional status which they believed to be involved in the acceptance of a completely salaried service and held out for a scheme resembling that of the old panel system whereby they received a capitation fee for each patient on their list. Thus, though industrious or popular doctors might be particularly well rewarded, there was no real incentive to good practice.

The establishment of the National Health Service has been widely seen, both at the time and since, as the most significant and successful social innovation of the period. Much of any subsequent criticism was directed towards the failure to achieve a unified administration; it became something of a cliché to inveigh against the 'tripartite' structure though, as a commission of inquiry was to note in the fifties, this bore 'the imprint of the historical circumstances from which it sprang'. Many of the better services upon which the poor had been able to draw in the past were those provided by the local authorities. So it was not altogether unreasonable that important community health services should be left firmly in the hands of the larger local authorities (the smaller authorities were deprived of their health functions): these services included midwifery, maternity and child welfare, health visiting, home nursing, domestic help, vaccination and immunization, local mental health services, ambulance transport, and the provision of health centres (though in Scotland the last two were the responsibility of the Secretary of State for Scotland).

The bulk of the medical profession was not, however, prepared to be placed under the authority of local government when, after all, matters of specialized professional judgement would be involved. Thus for administering the family practitioner services a separate structure of, in England and Wales, 138 executive councils (in all but eight cases responsible for areas coterminous with counties or county boroughs), on which twelve out of twenty-five members were to be representatives of local professional interests, was established; while in Scotland, twenty-five executive councils were established on the same broad principles, though they generally covered areas larger than those of any local authority. These executive councils administered family doctor services, pharmaceutical services, dental services, and ophthalmic services.

To administer the new hospital organization, there were, in England and Wales, fourteen regional hospital boards, each centred on the medical faculty of a university, and appointed by the Minister of Health. Management committees for the 388 hospitals within the system were to be appointed by the regional boards, but the thirty-six teaching hospitals were given a special autonomy in that their boards of governors were to be appointed directly by the Minister. In Scotland, five regional hospital boards were established, four based on universities, and the fifth based on Inverness, and eighty-four hospital boards of management.

Under the National Health Service, the sale of practices was abolished. Though there was no direction of labour, doctors would be refused permission to establish themselves in wealthy areas which already had an excess of doctors, and incentives were offered to induce doctors to settle in poorer areas which were short of doctors. No such restrictions were placed on dentists; here, as was to be expected in the light of the woeful dental history of the 1930s, there simply was an absolute shortage of dentists. The scale of fees devised for dentists in order to yield an 'average' income encouraged speed rather than quality.

In the first five years of the new National Health Service economic circumstances precluded the building of any new hospitals; existing hospitals simply had to be patched and adapted. The demand for attention, for dentures, for spectacles, and for medicines of all types proved to be enormous. The more passionate enthusiasts for the new system declared that this demand simply encompassed the terrible backlog which in itself condemned the appalling neglect of the pre-war system. However, by the early 1950s it was clear that there were no finite limits on the amount of health provision that the inhabitants, even of the new Jerusalem, could consume. In 1951 (when, additionally, Labour's Chancellor, Hugh Gaitskell, was looking for money to finance Britain's contribution to the Korean War) charges were introduced in respect of spectacles, and in 1952 a basic charge was imposed for all prescriptions, and charges were made both for the supply of dentures and for dental treatment.

As public opinion polls revealed, housing was the issue on which people felt most strongly in 1945. People had endured crowded, low-standard housing in the 1930s; during the war they had been bombed out, shunted around, doubled up: now, couples looked forward most of all to a home of their own. Housing is also the area of social policy to which it is most difficult to apply a universalist philosophy. While the actual basic cost of a particular piece of medical treatment does not really vary much, land prices, house prices, the standards accepted as normal by different social classes, vary enormously; different geographical districts tend to assume distinctive class characteristics.

Existing housing legislation was quite explicitly selective: housing Acts were housing Acts 'for the working classes' as were the subsidized council housing estates which resulted from them. Formally, the housing legislation of 1946 made no departure from established principles, though both Bevan, in introducing the English Act, and Joseph Westwood, in introducing the Scottish one, explained that the phrase 'working classes' would be interpreted as meaning 'all sections of the working population'. Bevan expressed a wish to re-create the classless villages of the seventeenth and eighteenth centuries. He hoped to achieve this by raising the standard size of subsidized housing and ensuring that all houses were provided with all the conveniences of modern living.

Understandably enough, given the complexities in both cases, the Government nationalized neither the land nor the house-building industry. Thus council housing continued to be financed in the traditional way: local authorities borrowed the money with which to build the houses, then repaid the loans partly out of an annual Government subsidy, partly out of money it was authorized to raise from the rates, and partly from the rents paid by tenants. Yet, while helpful to those in a position to invest in local government bonds, the Act offered no support whatsoever to private house building. The balance between private landlord and tenant was also kept firmly in favour of the latter by the Rent Control Acts of 1946 and 1949.

The Housing Act of 1949 did, at last, drop the phrase 'for the working classes', and at the same time made subsidies available for conversions and renovations. However, although the rents charged in the new council houses were higher than could be afforded by the lowest-paid workers, those members of the middle class who had any opportunity at all of raising a private mortgage showed no wish to live in them either. The building industry was in disarray, materials were in very short supply: in the upshot only 806,000 houses were built between 1945 and 1950; for the less fortunate there were the 157,000 pre-fabricated houses which were erected in the same period. The Conservatives in opposition spoke of 'a property-owning democracy' which, as a concept, was at least as defensible as Labour's rigid yet confused policies. In 1950 and 1951 local authorities were allowed to authorize only one privately built house for every four they built themselves. With the return of the Conservatives, private houses could be built up to the same quantity as local authority houses, and from January 1953 local authorities were empowered to license smaller private houses without question, and larger ones on their merits. In 1954, 28.5 per cent of all houses completed were constructed by private builders.

Educational policy in the post-war era was governed by the major Act passed in 1944, and, at times more important, the *interpretations* placed upon it. The major strength of the Act was that it ensured that all pupils would, around the age of eleven or twelve, move on to a form of secondary education which would, at the least, be continued till the age of fifteen. As implemented by almost all local authorities this entailed an 'eleven-plus' examination whose results would determine whether the pupil went on to a grammar school or to a secondary modern school. The route to better jobs and to higher education was through the grammar schools; the secondary modern school was the route to the traditional working-class occupations. It also became apparent that middle-class children were far more likely to do well in the eleven-plus than working-class ones who came from a background where academic pursuits were not encouraged. Apart from the non-fee-paying state schools, there continued in existence an older and higher class of grammar schools, charging fees but also supported by a direct grant from the Government (as distinct from a subsidy paid through the local authority). And the expensive and exclusive public schools remained untouched. Thus, although the potential for mobility through the educational system was greater than it had been in the 1930s – rather more working-class children did now get through the eleven-plus into grammar schools – the whole system still very much replicated the division of the social structure into working, lower-middle, upper-middle, and upper classes.

Shortages of accommodation, equipment, and teachers made difficult the achievement of anything more than a bare implementation of the provisions of the 1944 Act. In the 1950s modest advances became possible. By January 1955 the number of pupils throughout the kingdom remaining at school till the age of seventeen and beyond was twice what it had been in pre-war years, although, expressed as a percentage of the total age group, the figures were far from impressive: 7.9 per cent in England and Wales and 9.1 per cent in Scotland. While the Conservatives ruled, the Labour-controlled London County Council opened the first three specially designed comprehensive schools which sought to overcome the eleven-plus segregation between grammar and secondary modern education; other areas, including Leicestershire and Anglesey, followed.

Where significant developments did take place, though affecting only small sections of the population, was in university education. The Labour Government adumbrated the new policy by extending the terms of reference of the University Grants Committee in 1946; the Conservatives carried it out by raising the central grants payable to the universities. By 1956–7 almost 70 per cent of university income was coming direct from the state. Owing to the presence of ex-servicemen, the university population reached a peak of 85,421 in 1949; by 1956–7 it was up to 89,833. At this time over three quarters of all students in England were receiving public grants, with the proportion rather higher in Scotland and Wales. Thus the proportion of students drawn from 'the lower occupational categories' was higher than ever before; but the odds were still heavily weighted against a university education for a working-class child.

While it is not always easy to see just what social philosophies, if any, lay behind policy in the four obvious areas of income security, health, housing, and education, there can be no doubt that both Labour and Conservative Governments were fully committed to a philosophy of the avoidance of mass unemployment. How far their policies, as distinct from world circumstances beyond their control, were directly effective is less easy to establish. There were mild recessions in 1953–4 and 1956–7, but Governments were not really pushed to go beyond the broadly Keynesian macro-economic policies which they were pursuing. Questions of employment protection, industrial retraining, and so forth had scarcely yet surfaced in this period.

Perhaps greatest vision was shown in the realm of environmental planning though, as we saw in our tour around Britain, escape from the legacies of the past was never simple. The Town and Country Planning

Act of 1947 placed a firm obligation on the larger local authorities to prepare comprehensive plans for their entire areas, for which purpose they were given extended powers of compulsory purchase and grants from the Government. A development charge was levied on any increase in land values brought about by development or projected development; this innovation, however, though recommended by the wartime Uthwatt Report, was abolished by the Conservatives in 1955. It was the Conservatives, on the other hand, who were mainly responsible for the practical carrying-out of the provisions of the New Towns Act of 1946. In 1949 came the National Parks and Access to the Countryside Act.

The flurry of legislation carried through by the Labour Government was completed by a number of less well-known Acts which can, perhaps, be seen as adding further dimensions to the concept of the Welfare State. The wartime Council for the Encouragement of Music and the Arts was renamed the Arts Council and given a positive role as the Government's official agent for the support of the arts. The Local Government Act of 1948 empowered local authorities to raise a sixpenny rate purely for the support of the arts. The Children Act of 1948 defined the responsibilities of local authorities towards homeless children. The Legal Aid and Advice Act of 1949 provided legal aid for those too poor to pay for it.

There are two further areas which did not figure at all prominently in contemporary debates over the establishment of the Welfare State but which would usually be considered relevant to any discussion of welfare policies today. There areas concern other mechanisms for the redistribution of income apart from the obvious National Insurance and National Assistance schemes; and the question of the role of the social worker. The post-war era was certainly one of high progressive taxation, moderated however by a system of tax allowances going back to an earlier period. Tax relief on contributions to private pension schemes, on mortgages, and on bank loans were perhaps concessions to the better-off, though, of course, allowances in respect of dependants very much had an egalitarian basis. Food subsidies could also be seen as having a redistributive effect.

Many of the ancillary provisions of the major Welfare State legislation created a new need for trained social workers, though the great explosion in that profession was not to come till a later period. Apart from its main provisions, the National Assistance Act compelled local authorities to provide domiciliary and residential care for the physically handicapped, the elderly, and the homeless. Here few trained social workers in fact were available, and most social work continued to be undertaken by voluntary agencies operating side-by-side with the statutory services. Community care of the mentally disordered was a further responsibility placed upon the local authorities, this time by the National Health Service Act. To begin with, most staff came from a voluntary body, the Central Association for Mental Welfare. A further need for social workers was created within the local authority children's departments set up under the 1948 Children Act. In this connection the Home Office had, with the help of social work departments at certain universities, embarked on training courses. The new regional hospital boards, too, required medical and psychiatric social workers. The great burst of post-war legislation pointed the way, though it was some years before the corps of trained social workers were to become an integral part of what was understood by the Welfare State.

Politicians liked to speak of the 'mosaic' of the Welfare State; in reality it was more of a crazy paving. What was done – and it was a lot – was the result of truly noble vision, but inevitably circumscribed by the country's economic situation, by the continuing barriers and preoccupations of class, by the nature of traditional welfare institutions, and by the perceptions planners had at the time of major social issues, perceptions clouded by a knowledge of life as it had been, rather than by an understanding of life as it would be. The foundation was laid for a more professional approach within a more caring society; at the same time a new vested interest, even if determinedly disinterested, was created.

4
Hearth, Home, and Street Corner

We can allocate people to different social classes, we can allocate them to different regions of the country, but fundamentally life was everywhere lived as a member of a family.

The war had, in many instances, disrupted marriages and family life. Divorces reached a peak of 60,000 in 1947, ten times the pre-war figure. The passing of the Legal Aid Act two years later opened the possibility of divorce to many who had previously been deterred by the expense. By the middle fifties there were about 25,000 divorces a year. Yet there could be absolutely no doubt as to the continued popularity of marriage as a social institution. Even of those divorced, three quarters remarried. The more important historical trend can be seen in the figures relating to women in the twenty to thirty-nine age group: in 1911 only 552 out of every thousand women in this age group were married; in 1951 731 of them were married.

There was a brief 'baby boom' in the immediate post-war years, with the birth-rate reaching a peak of 20.5 per thousand in 1947. Thereafter, the birth-rate levelled off again, and it became apparent that in almost all sections of society deliberate policies of family limitation were being followed. Over the whole country in the mid-fifties the average family size (to give the figure in the absurd way in which averages always come out) was 2.3; the lowest unskilled workers and the very poor tended still to have the larger families, but in a reversal of the trend of the previous half-century, most working-class families were having the smallest number of children, whereas middle-class and upper-class parents were beginning to have slightly larger families. Of all children born in 1955, 5 per cent were illegitimate.

It was a commonplace of American sociology at the time that urbanization everywhere was converting the extended family of earlier times into isolated nuclear units. More locally, the Welfare State could be seen to be having effects in the same direction. If the state was tiding people over bouts of illness and unemployment and offering free medical advice and treatment, perhaps there was less need to call in a grandmother or raise a loan from a more fortunate uncle. Post-war housing policies offered homes in new housing estates, often many miles from the older communities in which grandparents and other relatives lived. In fact, detailed social investigation showed that, much as the family was changing, it was far too soon to write off the extended family. It was in certain sections of the middle class that the movement towards the nuclear family had gone furthest. Professional men, more than any other group, had to go where the job took them; thus professional households could become detached from the network of family relationships. At the same time, professional families were quite likely to have the resources to make possible the transport, or at least the telephones, by which contact could in fact be maintained. The maintenance of family connections was a facet of the upper-class ethos in any case; and upper-class people had greatest freedom of choice in place of occupation and greatest freedom of movement.

Change, and its accompanying stress, was most marked in the working class. But if surveys of the new housing estates revealed the difficulty of keeping up the old family relationships, in which grandparents, particularly on the mother's side, would frequently live close at hand, they also revealed a strong will to keep such relationships in being. By the later fifties we are still in a transitional period. Not many working-class families had cars, and only a few had telephones: but at least the prospect was in view of being able to overcome some of the problems of geographical separation. In 1956, too, though re-housing and slum clearance programmes were well under way, many of the old working-class communities still existed virtually intact.

Even if the social services had diminished the role of the extended family, there were many traditional functions which were scarcely likely to disappear. Social assumptions, moral attitudes, and everyday behaviour are first learned at home. While various sorts of welfare and various kinds of schooling might be on offer, the choices actually made could depend heavily on parental attitudes: working-class children, as we have noted, most often had their educational progress brought to a premature halt. Margaret Stacey's inquiries indicated that on political and religious issues families presented a pretty united front: in 83 per cent of cases husbands and wives had the same politics and 80 per cent of couples shared the same religious affiliation. Religion, even if not actively practised, continued to be very much a family affair. Politics, too, was often a matter of family loyalty: working-class Conservative voters often had Conservative parents and middle-class Labour supporters often had Labour parents. A good case in point is the later Conservative Minister, Peter Walker, whose father, at the end of the war, was a factory worker in the HMV factory in South Harrow and had regularly done voluntary work for the Conservative Party during election campaigns.

In a time of serious housing shortage (there was a shortfall of about a million and a half dwellings in 1951) many couples had to begin married life in the home of one or other parent, more usually the wife's parents. The wife's mother, in fact, continued to have a key role. Often it was the mother who checked out the possibility of any houses becoming vacant in the locality. Two remarks recorded by Michael Young and Peter Willmott say it all: 'We got it through my mother's agent. We had to agree to do it up though and we had to give him a bit of a dropsy,' and 'Her Mum lived in Bethnal Green and she spoke to the landlord for us. She told him we'd pay ten quid if we could get in there.' As families moved, often unwillingly, from private accommodation condemned as slums to council housing, the opportunities for such quiet, personal corruption diminished drastically. Here, indeed, was a clear token of the Welfare State taking over from the extended family: councils awarded houses on the basis of need, those from the worst slums or with the largest families being given priority. But the welfare authorities did not have it all their own way, especially when it came to the ancient mysteries of childbirth and child-rearing: 'I take more notice of my Mum than I do of the welfare. She's had eight and we're all right. Experience speaks for itself, more or less, doesn't it? If you're living near your mother, you don't really need that advice. You've got more confidence in your mother than you would have in the advice they'd give you.' Maternal influence shows itself, too, in the continuance of the old custom of churching, even among the irreligious majority, after the birth of a child. When one young woman explained the custom to Young and Willmott, saying, 'It's after you've had the baby. You go and give thanks to God that you're safe and all that. It's just a matter of form, really,' her husband broke in to remark, 'Because your mother done it, you mean.' Nevertheless, out of the forty-five wives in the Bethnal Green marriage sample, all except four were churched after the birth of their most recent child.

It is perhaps slightly less easy to single out quite such a distinctive role for mothers in middle-class families, though no doubt it existed there as well. Certainly, Margaret Stacey in her survey of Banbury found that middle-class parents together played a critical role in determining what schools their children should be sent to. The special functions of the upper-class family scarcely need stressing: the putting-down at birth of the son's name for the father's public school; the ensuring of the son's succession to the appropriate Oxford or Cambridge college; and, of course, the whole apparatus of debutante balls designed to ensure that a daughter's marriage was to a properly eligible young man.

Once the family had been important as an economic unit. More and more, especially in the freer economy of the 1950s, it was becoming important as a centre of consumption. Advertisements would be directed at wives and at children as much as, or more than, at principal wage-earners. Grandparents, too, sometimes assumed a new role: buying insurance or creating trusts for children's education, devices which were also useful for tax deduction.

The position of women in society, and therefore to some degree within the family, had been changing since the beginning of the century, and the changes had been greatly accelerated by the Second World War. However, the basic principle of a differentiation of roles as between husband and wife prevailed, with a wife's tasks clustering round her function as homemaker and child-rearer, just as a husband's clustered around his function as principal breadwinner. The most rigid segregation of roles was perhaps to be found in the more isolated industrial areas, mining communities in particular. One investigation in a Yorkshire mining village described the family there as 'a system of relationships torn by a major contradiction at its heart; husband and wife live separate, and in a sense, secret lives'; wives, said the report, were placed 'in a position which although they accept it, is more demanding and smacks of inferiority'. This was a situation of tension and potential conflict, which frequently broke out into domestic rows. Middle-class folklore had it that everywhere working-class husbands lorded it over their wives, treating them with brutality and violence.

In our own age of very proper concern for the plight of the battered wife it is important to remember that violence had always featured in a proportion of marriages in all stations of life, and that it had been very prevalent in poorer working-class areas before the First World War, where poverty, bad housing, frustration, and drink produced a vicious combination. Social surveys conducted in the early 1950s found that, while, of course, traditional male attitudes persisted, there were examples in working-class homes of husbands sharing in duties formerly thought of as the wife's alone, and, above all, an acceptance that questions of family size were a matter for joint decision, not a matter of the husband's will alone. Women were having fewer children, earlier, and then often going out to work: some husbands, at least, accepted that if their wives did go out to work then they had a responsibility to help in the home.

One leading authority (Elizabeth Bott) argued that the question of whether husbands' and wives' duties were rigidly segregated or not had nothing to do with social class, but that it was in families where the family network itself, and the network of relationships with friends and neighbours, were most extensive that segregation of roles was most marked; where the family came closest to the isolated, nuclear model, there was greatest likelihood of sharing of jobs between wife and husband. This makes sense; but it should be taken in conjunction with the fact that it was in older working-class communities that networks through the extended family and beyond were most extensive, and among middle-class professional families that they were of least significance. Thus there is much truth in the stereotype that it is in middle-class professional families that husbands would be most likely to share domestic chores with their wives. One must tread carefully, though, in this era long before the advent of women's liberation. Clearly, middle-class professional husbands, dedicated to success in their careers, depended very heavily upon their wives providing them with the comforts and security of domesticity. If we move into the upper class, we can at once see a very clear sense of role separation. The young man, hoping to become a Conservative MP, would find his wife inspected as well as himself; she would have a defined supportive and subordinate role: the constituency party, as has been said, would be counting on getting 'two for the price of one'. In the upper class, more than in any other social milieu in Britain, women were expected to be ornaments and foils to their menfolk, with the further task of maintaining the status of the family.

The most thorough study of British attitudes to marriage, courtship, and sex in this era was contained in the survey conducted by Geoffrey Gorer in January 1951 through the *People* newspaper (and published in book form as *Exploring English Character*). Asked 'Do you think English people fall in love the way you see Americans doing it on the films?' more than three quarters of his respondents said 'no', with a mere 7 per cent saying 'yes'. Two thirds of the married men and half the married women claimed they had never seriously considered marrying anyone else; 27 per cent of the men and 44 per cent of the women had – but the majority of these women belonged to the prosperous middle class of the South of England. Gorer summed up English courtship patterns as follows:

A young man meets a young woman, becomes attracted to her, courts her for between one and two years, and then may have an engagement lasting less than a further year. If the young man is a working lad from the Northern regions his future wife is likely to be the first girl by whom he was seriously attracted; if the girl is of the middle classes and from the big cities or the Southern regions she is more likely to have considered other young men before allowing herself to become seriously attached. There is little here of whirlwind romance, or of playing around before finding Miss or Mr Right; there is also little of the in-group marriage of old acquaintances which characterizes some settled communities.

Gorer further offered the generalization that 'what English men most value in their wives is the possession of the appropriate feminine skills, whereas what English women most value in their husbands is an agreeable character'; 'beauty or strength, good looks or good figure,' he concluded, 'are very seldom mentioned, and then chiefly by the single'.

Expressed attitudes towards sex are notoriously hard to disentangle from actual sexual behaviour. Loudmouths may be the shortest in actual performance; the discreet may be quietly living it up. Just over half the men and nearly two thirds of the women interviewed by Gorer expressed disapproval of sex before marriage; 43 per cent of his total sample admitted to having had a sexual relationship before or outside of marriage, while 47 per cent gave an emphatic denial. Differences both in attitudes and in actual experience (or enjoyment) of sex were apparent as between men and women. It was mainly men who declared sex to be 'very important' in marriage, and mainly women who disagreed with the statement that 'women really enjoy the physical side of sex just as much as men'; 65 per cent of men *agreed* with this statement, and 51 per cent of women. Yet the 'double standard' in sexual morality appeared to be approved more by women than by men. In support of this contention Gorer quoted a sixteen- or seventeen-year-old Liverpool girl, asked first if a man should have sexual experience before marriage: 'I think yes because until a man has such an experience he really cannot define LOVE as anything particular, because men fall victims to their emotions much more easily than women'; but women should not have such experience, 'because although I am a woman and believe in Equality of the sexes, I am still old-fashioned enough to believe a woman should be perfectly pure before she enters into matrimony'.

Lest one such example should deceive, let us balance that emancipated, yet consciously 'old-fashioned' girl against the case history of 'Miss T.' presented by Rowntree and Lavers also in 1951:

Miss T. is aged 24 and is a shop girl. She lives alone in lodgings, but frequently spends her weekends with her parents who 'have been married thirty years and are still in love'.

Miss T. is popular with men as she is very attractive (without being particularly good-looking) and she leads an active sexual life. She is quite open on the subject and says 'I don't see any harm in it. I always have one steady lover and it doesn't hurt him if I have an occasional fellow besides.'

Miss T. bets on horses if she gets a good tip, but 'cannot be bothered' with pools or greyhounds. She smokes heavily and drinks a good deal for a girl – mostly gin and lime. She was in the Land Army during the war and liked the life, except that it was too lonely. She is not happy as a shop girl and her superior is always rebuking her for laziness.

She is not interested in religion, and her sole knowledge of the Christian doctrine is that 'at school we used to read aloud from the Bible – one verse each in turn round the class. I once went to church with my friend, but it was all bobbing up and down, and I couldn't find the place in the book.'

She says her hobbies are dancing and 'going round the shops'.

Rowntree and Lavers clearly disapproved of 'Miss T.' The 'double standard' lived. In fact, there were many evident inequalities between men and women. It is not always easy, however, to distinguish inequalities imposed by social custom (such as unequal pay for perfectly equal work) from those more deeply rooted in biology. Child-bearing and child-rearing, menstruation, lesser physical strength (balanced though by greater dexterity and, often, greater endurance) are facts. Differential ageing is probably a fact too: girls mature more quickly than boys, women last better into old age than do men, but also pass more rapidly into middle age. Where, though, do we place the custom whereby (despite Gorer's verdict on what people value in marital partners) women tended much more universally to be judged on the basis of looks alone than did men? A later generation of women were to fight against all of these facts, fictions, and customs. For the moment we are still in an age when many old traditions governed the rôles and rewards of men and women.

If the fundamental relationship of man and wife had not really changed since the beginning of the century, the relationship of children to parents had changed considerably. Two comments from the Bethnal Green survey placed the difference in the context of the changing generations. First a young mother: 'Dad used to be very strict with us, we are different with our boy. We make more of a mate of him. When I was a kid Dad always had the best of everything. Now it's the children who get the best of it. If there's one pork chop left, the kiddie gets it'; and a young father: 'There's certainly been a change. I whack mine now, but not the beatings like we used to have. When I was a boy most of us feared our fathers more than we liked them. I know I feared mine and I had plenty of reason to.' Geoffrey Gorer found a general belief among parents that toilet training should begin early: within six months of birth, or at most within a year. There was little belief in the innocence or innate goodness of children; 68 per cent of his sample considered that children needed more discipline. 'At least some English parents', Gorer concluded, 'find pleasure without conscious guilt in inflicting severe pain on children as punishment. The majority disapprove of such behaviour, but the emphasis with which such disapproval is voiced suggests the possibility that there is an unconscious temptation against which such defences have to be erected.'

In general, probably, changing attitudes within the working class were a little behind those in the middle and upper classes. The change is related to the limitation of family size, so that instead of being a depressing succession of squalling mouths to be fed, children could be enjoyed, and this was reinforced by the better living standards and job security of the post-war years. Finally, the war, with the evacuation of children and the separation of families, and the destruction of young lives in the bomber raids, seems to have put a new premium on the importance of children and the need to provide them with loving care. Female children were treated differently from male children, of course. The basic assumption in all classes was that girls would become wives and mothers, and should therefore be treated accordingly. Middle-class families might often be willing to send a daughter to a private school, while sending sons to the state schools; but while a son would be encouraged to fight his way on up through the system to university, the daughter's education would usually be terminated much sooner.

Where, in traditional working-class communities, extended family relationships were closest, so too, generally, were relationships with neighbours. Typically, the more isolated middle-class family would have closer associations with 'friends' rather than with 'neighbours'. Much depended on actual geographical and living conditions. To a monied squire in rural Oxfordshire, a neighbour could mean the nearest landowner, several miles away.

In the realm of working-class housing this was a time of rapid transition. The worst conditions of all were in the decaying tenements of industrial Scotland, in the workers' flats that had often been the creation of English philanthropic impulses of an earlier era, and in those larger houses in what had formerly been inner suburbs in London and the big towns, now divided into a multiplicity of, often, one-room flats: in this kind of accommodation primitive facilities were shared by several families – one lavatory on a landing, with, near it, one gas cooker on which several harried housewives had to prepare their meals. The notorious back-to-back was perhaps, by a degree, not quite so appalling: external, shared, lavatories, a rear wall which was also the rear wall of the house on the other side, and so a great shortage of light. The standard working-class house (though with infinite local variations), left intact by the slum clearance drives of the thirties, was the 'two-up two-down'; two bedrooms on the first floor, two rooms on the ground floor, with a tiny scullery at the back, opening on to the yard containing the lavatory. The variable incidence of damp, dilapidation, and vermin could render the intolerable beyond description, and the tolerable degrading. None of these types of houses had baths, a condition shared by one third of all houses in Britain in 1951.

Rents were kept low by legislation, so there was no incentive for private landlords to carry out improvements. In general, local authorities cleared out the multiple-occupancy buildings first. Some families had had a taste of uncongested life outside the cities through the wartime evacuation experience and were glad to go; others were very reluctant to go: all found the local authority rents in the new estates three times as high as what they had been paying before. Husbands, therefore, having less to spend in the pubs, had to spend more time with their families. It was not always easy for middle-class couples to secure housing, at least until the acceleration of private building in the fifties; but they were used to the ethos in which money was saved in order to acquire a mortgage.

Whether life was lived in an overcrowded slum, in a new council house, on a private estate, in a Victorian semi-detached, or in a luxury flat, material conditions for everyone were somewhat different from what they had been in the 1930s. For all the harassment of rationing, shortages, and austerity, the nation as a whole was healthier and fitter in 1951 than it had ever been before. From 1948 onwards around 98 per cent of the country's school children were each drinking one third of a pint of free milk daily. Children in all sections of the community were taller and heavier than in 1936. In 1950, for the first time, infant mortality fell below thirty per thousand.

In the first post-war years almost everything was rationed, with basic foodstuffs on 'coupons', clothing on 'clothing coupons', tinned foods and dried fruits on one kind of 'points', and chocolate and sweets on another, more popularly known as 'sweetie coupons'. Rations fluctuated, but in 1948 they worked out at a weekly allowance per person of 13 oz. of meat, 1½ oz. of cheese, 6 oz. of butter and margarine, 1 oz. of cooking fat, 8 oz. of sugar, 2 pts of milk, and one egg. Between July 1946 and July 1948 even bread was rationed. Officially meals in restaurants were restricted to three courses not costing more than five shillings (the majority of British people did not, in any case, at this time eat meals on that scale in restaurants; the minority who did, though irritated by the restrictions, often were able to find ways round them). Clothes rationing, which did not end till March 1949, was a special bane. J. L. Hodson remarked that the rich were distinguished by their ability to bring a bit of colour into their clothing. A special feature of the autumn of 1946, before the icy winter set in, was that of the 'squatters', homeless families who moved in on army camps (not all of them unoccupied) and empty private mansions. Controls were greatly reduced in 1948 and again in 1950. After the abolition of clothes rationing, milk rationing followed in January 1950, points and the restrictions on restaurant meals in May 1950; in the autumn controls were removed from flour, eggs, and soap. In one of their interview sessions in Bethnal Green, Young and Willmott encountered the father of the family eating his tea: a chop with boiled potatoes and peas. This was a far cry from the late forties, when the weekly meat ration was down as low as half a pound. For the housewife there were indeed specially serious problems in the first five post-war years in coping with shortages and juggling with points and coupons.

As the war ended, there was a great and immediate resurgence of the leisure activities characteristic of the inter-war years. Blackpool, Scarborough, the Isle of Man boomed. Cinema attendances reached a peak in 1946 (when one third of the population were going once a week, 13 per cent twice a week) and remained high; football enjoyed a golden age of large crowds. Slowly, from being a lower-middle-class preserve, the holiday camps were taken over by working-class holidaymakers. These activities drew the family in different directions. Football, and football pools, which embarked on a new lease of life after the war, were largely a male preserve. Cinema attendances divided the family by generation – young people going with other young people most frequently, parents slightly less frequently. Holidays, on the other hand, were a family matter. The more aristocratic sporting venues, Ascot and Henley for instance, provided the perfect opportunity for upper-class women, elegantly attired, to act as foils to their husbands.

The war had given children certain freedoms; economic conditions after the war fostered their independence. Gangs of adolescent, and even younger children, were nothing new; but the post-war years provided a jagged, brittle world, with the sanctions of war removed. In the forties the grown-up generation provided the semi-outcast figure who shocked the respectable and outwitted the sluggish Government: the spiv. With the early 1950s there came the first nationally recognized figure representative of youth's detachment from the rest of society and representative also of the fact that for the first time working-class youth could take the initiative: the Teddy boy.

The name derived from the Edwardian form of dress which, actually, had briefly been assumed by some bright young men of the upper class in the late forties. The family, and all its activities, still rooted in tradition, was being more and more affected by national influences; changing circumstances seemed to be pushing working-class families into middle-class attitudes, but working-class youth was preparing to take initiatives of its own. National influences were reflected in the names with which children were christened. It had been a working-class tradition to name son like father, daughter like mother. Now, in the post-war years, there was a special fashion for names like Len, Garry, Steven, Nicholas, Christopher, Graham, Adrian, Kevin, and for Maureen, Marilyn, Carol, Jacqueline, Janet, June, Susan, Gloria, Lana, and Linda.

One particular national institution served as a fundamental influence on the lives of all young males: National Service. Under the terms of the National Service Act of 1948 something around 160,000 young men were each year called up to undergo basic military training and military service for a period of two years, sometimes in such hot spots as Malaya or Korea. For most men National Service implied boredom and waste, though few denied to it any personal benefit at all. A young factory worker whose personal experience is given in the collection *Called Up* (1955), edited by

Peter Chambers and Amy Landreth, noted: 'When I was back in Civvy Street and looked back on all the good times I'd had with my friends, my National Service didn't seem so bad after all. But I do think that a lot of time is wasted in the Army just hanging around.' While it is probably true that once a Teddy boy had been called up he probably ceased for ever to be a Teddy boy, it is hard to say whether National Service really served as a force for social control (as latter-day right-wing advocates of its restoration have maintained) or whether, by breaking family links, disrupting apprenticeships, opening new horizons, imposing new, and sometimes brutal, stresses it was a potential agent of social disruption. The editors of *Called Up* found it

difficult to estimate to what extent National Servicemen take advantage of the freedom from parental control to gain sexual experience. Certainly a young man unversed in the 'facts of life' will very soon learn the repertoire of sexual possibilities from the conversation of his comrades. If he is posted abroad, he may visit a brothel for the first time in his life, but that does not mean he will avail himself of the opportunities provided by the establishment . . . On the other hand, the moral climate of Service life tends to impel the soldier towards sexual adventures, and if he leaves the Army unexperienced in this field, then it is likely to be for moral or psychological reasons, not for lack of opportunity.

Probably National Service did help to preserve that slightly archaic quality which one finds in British life in the post-war era. Its abolition in 1960 very much fitted into the exuberance and libertarianism of the new age described in Part Two of this book.

5
The Culture of Austerity

'Culture' is a word with many meanings. This chapter is about the intellectual and imaginative life of Britain in the late forties and early fifties. It will include films and radio and television. It might have included football and holidays. Arguably the knowledgeable football fan exercises greater powers of intellect and imagination while at a football match than he does stretched supinely in front of some television parlour game. However, basic leisure activities were included in the previous chapter; this chapter is oriented towards what the quality newspapers of the time would have called 'the arts and entertainment'; it also deals with all forms of reading, as well as all forms of listening and viewing.

It is important to keep in mind the distinction between traditional 'high art', of concern only to a small (and usually wealthy) minority, and the leisure pursuits of the many, sometimes described as 'mass culture' or, more precariously, 'popular culture'. Another distinction was later popularized by C. P. Snow: when he spoke (in the late fifties) of 'the two cultures', he meant 'the sciences' on one side, 'the humanities' on the other. Applied science and technology were touched on in Chapter 1 as elements in the general economic and geographical context; here scientific discovery will feature as one of the important pursuits of the academic minority. Questions of religious belief concern both the minority and also the wider society, though the community of believers was itself steadily shrinking.

This chapter addresses itself to various questions which are more than usually difficult to answer. I take it for granted that just as it is important to ask about the effectiveness of the country's social services, or about the genuineness of its concept of political democracy, so also is it important to ask both about the quality of the highest art produced by that society, and about the accessibility of that art to the majority of the people. One is, in other words, asking questions about what is now often termed 'the quality of life'. Further, in what ways, if any, was artistic and cultural change related to the other social changes already discussed? What light, if any, do the arts throw on the nature of British society in this period? Theories have been put forward accounting for both high art and popular culture as products of the hegemony established over society by the upper class; simpler souls have often talked of art as 'reflecting' society. I adhere to neither position, but hope simply to suggest most tentatively one or two connections between the matters discussed in this chapter and the matters discussed elsewhere in this book. Necessarily, I shall be pronouncing qualitative judgements on particular artists and writers, and on particular works of art; but the purpose is not to award plaudits here, and deduct penalty points there – it is, rather, to establish broadly whether we are talking about high art and minority culture, or about general leisure and popular culture, or about a sort of 'middle-brow' culture in between, or, on occasion, about a mixture of all of these.

Two developments which have already been mentioned expressed the Labour Government's own commitment to the idea that the Welfare State was scarcely complete if provision was not also made for the imaginative and intellectual side of life. The wartime Council for the Encouragement of Music and the Arts, which had done an immense amount to bring forms of high culture to places where they had hitherto been unknown, was in 1946 converted into the Arts Council, with a modest Government grant of £235,000 to dispense. The 1948 Local Government Act made it possible for local authorities to levy up to sixpence on the rates for the support of the arts. Not many did, but the Government commitment was there clearly enough.

For a hundred years the most accessible cultural form had been the novel, consistently priced at about one tenth of the average weekly wage. In the late forties, the audience for the novel was still basically a middle-class one. Most novels made no great profits for their publishers, but publishers expected every now and again to cash in on a bestseller. Chain stores and even quite small shops had circulating libraries from which books were lent out for a penny or two a week. Publishers would hope particularly to do well from the larger circulating libraries: Smith's, the Times Library, Harrods, Mudie's, and Boots. The 'paperback revolution' had not yet materially affected the fiction trade, even though Penguins had been in existence since the 1930s publishing, apart from their serious non-fiction works, a number of contemporary British authors as well as such international giants as Ernest Hemingway.

It is, no doubt, something of a commonplace that the novel had reached its last great apogee in the 1920s, and that there were few, if any, writers after 1945 who could compare with D. H. Lawrence or James Joyce or Virginia Woolf. Though it would be unwise to press the point too far, it could reasonably be said that in the forties and early fifties British political and social thought was inward-looking, concentrating, for instance, on the Welfare State, on the British vision of the brave new world. So the novels of the time, too, perhaps have a national, even parochial, quality.

Evelyn Waugh's war trilogy *Sword of Honour* (*Men at Arms*, 1952; *Officers and Gentlemen*, 1955; and *Unconditional Surrender*, 1961) has been unfavourably compared with the great First World War 'Tietjens' sequence by Ford Madox Ford. Waugh certainly got some important points about the war right:

'Take cover,' said the voice.

A crescent scream immediately, it seemed, over their heads, a thud which raised the paving-stones under their feet; a tremendous incandescence just north of Piccadilly; a pentecostal wind; the remaining panes of glass above them scattered in lethal splinters about the street.

'You know, I think he's right. We had better leave this to the civilians.'

But Waugh was very much a man of the inter-war years, a brilliant satirist of upper-class manners and morals. There is social significance in the fact that he could continue well through the post-war years still focusing on this particular social class (as did a lesser-known writer from the thirties, Anthony Powell, who in 1951 launched a long sequence, *The Music of Time*, which essentially dealt with the life-styles of the upper-class world, beginning with *A Question of Upbringing*, 1951; *A Buyer's Market*, 1952; *The Acceptance World*, 1955; and *At Lady Molly's*, 1957). With special testiness Waugh recorded the problems some members of this class encountered in a changing world: the irascible Gilbert Pinfold in *The Ordeal of Gilbert Pinfold* (1957) abhorred everything 'that happened in his own lifetime'.

The two most consistently lauded writers, also before the public in the 1930s, were Joyce Cary and Graham Greene. Both wrote within a distinctive variation of the traditional English novel. In his wartime trilogy, *Herself Surprised* (1941), *To Be a Pilgrim* (1942), and *The Horse's Mouth* (1944), Joyce Cary, around the splendid characters of the outrageous painter, Gully Jimson, and the shrewd, immoral Sara, deliberately wrote a panorama of certain aspects of English history over the previous sixty years. His post-war trilogy *A Prisoner of Grace* (1952), *Except the Lord* (1953), and *Not Honour More* (1955) dealt more explicitly with political life in the era before, during, and after the First World War. In turn, we see the main characters from the inside. According to the famous Cambridge literary critic F. R. Leavis, the great English novels are 'moral fables'; Cary's books definitely fall into this category.

The agenda for Graham Greene was not the recent past, but the immediate present; sometimes, indeed, he seemed, with the insight of the crack journalist, to anticipate public events. Greene had been a Marxist in the early thirties, then became a Catholic convert: he thus, as we shall see later in this chapter, represented an important social and intellectual phenomenon. Apart from the tortured wrestling over the relationships between God and Man, Greene's novels are probably most celebrated for their power, based on all the devices of style and metaphor at the novelist's disposal, to evoke a particular period and a particular place. Thus for the social historian *The Heart of the Matter* (1948) tells much about a West African colony as British colonialism, mortally wounded by the war, is coming to an end, *The End of the Affair* (1951) evokes the blitz and war-time London in a far more direct way than Waugh's books, and *The Quiet American* (1955) adds its special dimension to the unfolding of the Indo-China tragedy in the Cold War era.

Corporate violence, very much the background to everyone's experience in this period, is ever-present in the novels of Graham Greene. Personal violence and menace, characteristic at this time only of the less well-known and less well-received talents, featured in the highly individualistic novels of Ivy Compton-Burnett. Her mannered, deliberately non-naturalistic novels such as *Parents and Children* (1941) or *Darkness and Day* (1951), set amidst the Edwardian upper class, attracted a cult following. To say that this was in keeping with the rather insular character of much of British minority culture at this time is in no way to deny the high literary repute she enjoyed. The most famous of all commentaries upon the grimness of the times, in which the nightmare of fascist dictatorship had scarcely faded and that of Stalinist oppression was ever-present, was George Orwell's vision of a not-too-distant totalitarian future, *Nineteen Eighty-four* (1948).

With C. P. Snow we return to the mainstream of the British novel. Snow himself described the purpose of his 'Strangers and Brothers' sequence which began in 1940 with the book of that title, and continued with *The Light and the Dark* (1947), *Time of Hope* (1949), *The Masters* (1951), *The New Men* (1954), *Homecomings* (1956), and *The Conscience of the Rich* (1958), as to give insights into British society over the period 1920–50 and to follow the *moral* (my italics) growth of Lewis Eliot, the narrator of the series. Snow, it would be widely agreed, could neither present all of his main characters in the round and from the inside, as could Joyce Cary, nor could he evoke the richness and subtlety of atmosphere of a Graham Greene. The novels, too often, seem much too consciously social and political documents; in many ways, since Snow himself moved in the scientific and governmental circles he describes, this makes them of greater interest to the historian. Here we light on a banal fact: it is often the lesser novels which more consciously and directly tell us about social attitudes and social change. Post-war society, muses Lewis Eliot in *Homecomings*, 'had become more rigid, not less, since our youths'.

A minor novel which hilariously satirized the implications of political consensus was Edward Hyams's *Gentian Violet* (1953). James Blundell was a working-class lad who, like many real-life figures (Edward Heath for instance), had ascended the social scale by means of a distinguished war career. Though as James Blundell he retained his contacts with his humble origins, in upper-class circles he became known as James Stewart-Blundell. Thus he contrived to be elected to Parliament both as a Conservative MP for a rural constituency and as a Labour MP for an industrial one. Any fears he might have of exposure in the House of Commons proved to be groundless:

> Nobody noticed anybody else . . . A member might be on his feet talking away yet boring nobody, as nobody was obliged to listen . . . it reduced the most ambitious and domineering public men to the status of mere prefects, with certain privileges, like putting their feet on the table . . . If democracy was to be found anywhere, Jim felt, it was here in the House of Commons.
>
> And Jim soon began to be very proud of being two members of it.

Among middle-brow readers the most popular genre was that of the detective story. Agatha Christie, the leading practitioner, even had the endorsement of Labour's middle-brow Prime Minister, Clement Attlee. And Agatha Christie largely set the tone: her stories were cunning crossword puzzles filled out to book length, without sex and without gratuitous violence.

Poetry had lost the central position it held in the days of Tennyson or

Kipling: it was not now usually expected to make money and appeared mainly in non-commercial 'little magazines'. Among those who (apart from the long-established T. S. Eliot) enjoyed modest commercial sales were Dylan Thomas, John Betjeman, Laurence Durrell, and Roy Fuller. Thomas, a rumbustious Welshman with a gift for magical incantation, formed the centre of a somewhat self-indulgent romantic bohemia; he died in 1953 at the age of thirty-nine. Betjeman wrote appealing satires on the Welfare State and conjured up nostalgia for an older England. On the whole, literary historians have seen the post-war years as a leaden age for British poetry: Fuller and Durrell, it is said, did better work earlier, and their best work later. Any parallels with international events must be utterly suspect; however, it may be noted that just as America was assuming a primacy in the world of art, so American poetry at this time was eclipsing British. In the middle fifties a number of younger poets, somewhat vaguely described as 'the Movement', joined in attacking the cult, as they saw it, of post-war neo-romantic poetry and its exclusive bohemian trimmings. One of them, Kingsley Amis, declared: 'Nobody wants any more poems about philosophers or paintings or novelists or art galleries or mythology or foreign cities or other poems. At least I hope nobody wants them.' The Movement included almost all of the best-known of recent British poets: Donald Davie, Philip Larkin, Tom Gunn, and Ted Hughes. Many of those who came to dominate poetry (and literary criticism), Raymond Las Vergnas has pointed out, were (or, more accurately perhaps, became) university teachers: 'The result is a kind of enlightened literary class dealing with average beings; of a poetical *élite* preoccupied with the trivialities of daily life.'

War conditions, and especially long nights in the air-raid shelter, encouraged the reading of novels; bombs destroyed theatres, or at least placed them under threat. The same novels could be read all over the country, but drama, before the Second World War, was very much centred on London. Plays aimed at commercial success were put on in the West End theatres, where audiences were predominantly middle class and upper class; a few theatres consciously aimed to put on avant-garde plays for a minority within that same audience. The main theatres in the provincial centres were essentially touring theatres receiving repertory companies, usually London-based, doing standard works, and also West End productions before or after their London run. The war destroyed or badly damaged one fifth of London theatres, and fostered the growth of monopoly in theatrical ownership; yet it also helped to stimulate the beginnings of a theatrical revival in the provinces. In 1942 Prince Littler began to buy up derelict London theatres; by the end of the forties the Prince Littler Consolidated Trust owned eighteen out of forty-two West End theatres and nearly three quarters of the main provincial touring theatres. But in 1943 a group of citizens joined together to save the historic Bristol Old Vic Theatre, and in 1946 it became a part of the London Old Vic Theatre; the establishment of the Coventry Municipal Theatre at the end of the war was essentially a response to the destruction of war and to the desire to build a richer life in the post-war world. Regional repertory companies began to flourish as never before, and in 1948 Basil Dean staged a season of provincial productions at the St James's Theatre calling forth a certain measure of praise from the London critics. At the same time, theatre folk, like everyone else, suffered the restraints and burdens of austerity: 10 per cent of gross receipts was whipped away in entertainments tax.

Anyway, older traditions persisted. The dominance of the consortium, known as 'the Group', in which Prince Littler was a key figure, meant that on the whole commercial considerations were paramount. The actor–manager principle was still very much alive: Sir Donald Wolfit gave a season at the Bedford, Camden Town, in 1949; Sir Laurence Olivier gave two seasons at the St James's in 1950 and 1951; and Sir John Gielgud gave a season at the Haymarket in 1954–5. For serious theatre-goer and serious producer alike, most opportunities were confined to the classics, and 'the classics' almost always meant Shakespeare. It was in *Measure For Measure* that one of what was to prove a new breed of theatrical producers, Peter Brook, established himself. Above all, perhaps, the rather limited theatrical world of the late forties and the early fifties provided a particular kind of golden age for actors working within a strict convention. Kenneth Tynan, the dynamic critic who burst on the public scene in 1951, looking back from the sixties put it this way: 'I claim no intrinsic superiority for the actors of the immediate post-war period over those of today. What is undeniable, however, is that the equivalent actor of today spends far less of his time on the stage than his predecessors did. We may see their like again, but we shall not see the like of their theatrical careers.'

Three names, perhaps, encapsulate the main theatrical fare of the first post-war decade: T. S. Eliot (with, however, only two plays in this period: *The Cocktail Party*, 1949, and *The Confidential Clerk*, 1954), Christopher Fry, and Terence Rattigan. Like Eliot, Fry wrote rich stuff for a time of austerity – *A Phoenix Too Frequent* (1946), *The Lady's Not for Burning* (1949), *A Sleep of Prisoners* (1951) – which sounded like theatre (though it did not always look like it), and struck a fine poetic note (though C. S. Lewis commented that 'Eliot's stage verse imitates prose, with remarkable success'). Terence Rattigan offered 'well-made plays', comfortably upper-class or upper-middle-class British in content: *The Winslow Boy* (1946) centred on a successful barrister's defence of the naval cadet son of a prosperous family, and *The Browning Version* (1948) centred on a public school and its classics master.

In 1954 one of the poets of the Movement, stooping to what he saw as a less important art form, published a novel. *Lucky Jim*, by Kingsley Amis, was a bestseller. A few months earlier John Wain had published *Hurry On Down*, which was also very successful. In 1956 the English Stage Company, with George Devine as artistic director, was established at the Royal Court Theatre in London. In that same year it presented *Look Back in Anger* by John Osborne: only the enormous success of this production kept the company from going bankrupt. In 1957 came John Braine's novel *Room at the Top*, set in the post-war era but cynical about the professed ideals of the then Labour Government: 'the top' was to be achieved not through socialism, but by ruthless individual self-advancement. In one way or another, these works had provincial settings, but they were certainly not working class. The press lumped their authors together as 'angry young men'. All cocked a snook at the comfortable and flowery conventions of the post-war literary scene and also at the comfortable platitudes of consensus politics; they provided an interesting commentary on aspects of social change, on educational opportunity which yet brought no real opportunity, for example. In the wider perspective they can be seen as forerunners of the 'cultural revolution' which erupted in the sixties.

There was no cocking of snooks in the world of music, where the point of change, in so far as there was one, was definitely the Second World War. During the war the Sadler's Wells Opera and the Sadler's Wells Ballet were forced out on tour through the benighted provinces. At the end of the war the Sadler's Wells Theatre was reopened as the home exclusively of English-language opera, while the Sadler's Wells Ballet transferred to the Royal Opera House, Covent Garden. Covent Garden had been the home of opera on the international scale, and in January 1947 a newly assembled Covent Garden Opera gave its first performance: the opera was *Carmen*, by the Frenchman Bizet, just as the gala opening performance of ballet had been of *The Sleeping Beauty*, by the Russian Tchaikovsky. Music at least was not parochial, though it might be argued that a neglect of British composers was a parochial British characteristic.

Opera, self-evidently, commanded a smaller audience than drama; on the whole, it was an audience drawn from higher up the social scale. Covent Garden, at least in its more expensive seats, was a social focus for the upper class and upper-middle class. Sadler's Wells, with its opera in translation, was much more a resort for the middle class and lower-middle class. Since 1934 there had existed what was almost a paradigmatic upper-class institution, the Glyndebourne Opera House in the Sussex Downs.

In the realm of music, as in other spheres, the war had brought destruction and affirmation. The Queen's Hall in London was destroyed for ever; the Free Trade Hall, home of Manchester's famous Hallé Orchestra, was not fit for reoccupation until 1951. The Royal Liverpool Philharmonic and the Hallé became full-time permanent orchestras for the first time in 1942 and 1943 respectively. In 1944 the City of Birmingham Orchestra was re-formed; and at the end of the war the four major London orchestras: the Royal Philharmonic (brought together again in 1946 under the direction of Sir Thomas Beecham), the London Symphony, the London Philharmonic, and the Philharmonia were re-established as self-governing institutions. Developments in the post-war years were the reorganization of the Scottish Orchestra into the permanent Scottish National Orchestra in 1950, and the expansion under Charles Groves of the Bournemouth Symphony Orchestra in 1954. But without doubt the major force in British music was the BBC – through its own Symphony Orchestra, through its regional orchestras, through its broadcasts on its new post-war Third Programme, through its sponsorship each summer of the Royal Albert Hall Promenade Concerts (the Proms), and through the valuable subventions it offered each time it broadcast a concert or music festival.

That creative individuals genuinely aspired to make the new dawn of 1945 a rich and life-enhancing one is best evidenced by the festivals established in the first post-war years. That such aspirations were not confined to individuals alone is evidenced by the success of these festivals. The grandest venture of all was the Edinburgh International Festival of Music and Drama, instituted in 1947 to plans conceived by Rudolph Byng, General Manager of the Glyndebourne Opera, Harvey Wood, Director of the British Council in Scotland, and Sir John Falconer, Lord Provost of Edinburgh. In 1948, under the inspiration of Benjamin Britten, the Aldeburgh Festival on the Suffolk coast was founded.

While the theatres played Shakespeare, Fry and Rattigan, the big orchestras played Mozart, Beethoven, and the nineteenth-century classics.

However, the omens for native British music were probably more auspicious than ever they had been (since the seventeenth century at any rate). Vaughan Williams still bestrode the musical scene like a colossus: he had, as Percy Young has written, 'demonstrated how a new mode of expression could be discovered by bypassing the Romantics, though by no means missing out on Romanticism'. But the composer who was universally recognized at home and abroad as being the one to carry on the torch rekindled by Elgar was Benjamin Britten, whose entire achievements are bound in with the whole deliberate attempt to sponsor a renaissance of the imagination in the post-war years. It was his opera *Peter Grimes* which reopened the Sadler's Wells Theatre on 7 June 1945.

Next only to Britten in critical acclaim was Michael Tippett. Through these composers, and their younger successors, a genuinely English tradition of music-making was maintained and developed, while the composers, at the same time, sought to come to terms with the modes and preoccupations of the mid twentieth century. Thus the more private works tended to be inaccessible to the vast majority of potential listeners. But there could be a real involvement with the wider society as well. One outstanding instance of the serious composer's involvement in the writing of film music was Vaughan Williams's score for *Scott of the Antarctic* which then formed the basis of his *Sinfonia Antartica*.

New works in the visual and plastic arts (in plain English, painting and sculpture) normally reached their rather limited upper-class and upper-middle-class public through the private commercial galleries. For the wider middle-class public, prepared to view but not to purchase, there were municipal galleries in most towns and cities, and the major galleries in London. These, naturally, mainly exhibited works from the great European tradition, showing in greater or lesser degree examples of recent and contemporary British art. Many private art galleries, of course, derived their main income from the buying and selling of 'old masters'. Thus while the indisputable quantitative evidence that art sales boomed during the war certainly supports the thesis that amid the catastrophe of war there is a turning of minds towards the precious elements of civilization, it does not necessarily suggest that native British artists were doing particularly well. Still, I think it would be a valid conclusion that the sponsorship of war artists, the concentration on the specific British heritage, and the general disruption of normal modes of looking at things in the war did serve as a stimulus to British art.

Most firmly within the idiom of the artist pushed by the war into a deeper celebration of Britishness was John Piper, war artist to the Ministries of Information and of War, with a special commission to record bomb damage, and also a member of the Recording Britain Project financed by the Pilgrim Trust. Piper's expressive and romantic renderings of British buildings gained, through the medium of reproductions, quite a wide currency. He provided his own definition of romanticism as pertaining to 'a vision that can see in things something significant beyond ordinary significance: something that for a moment seems to contain the whole world; and, when the moment is past, carries over some comment on life or experience besides the comment on appearances'. Human beings do not intrude upon Piper's buildings, yet, as Robert Melville put it in introducing Piper's 1964 retrospective exhibition, Piper has 'salvaged the Humanist scale and undepicted man remains in his work the measure of all things'. An older British painter who continued to operate within a very restricted British, indeed provincial, perspective was L. S. Lowry. If one mark of the true artist is that his work has an utterly distinctive personal quality, then this distinction certainly attaches to Lowry's Lancashire factory scenes.

For the majority of the better-known British artists, however, though the war might be a minor influence – 'liberating', says Sir John Rothenstein, in the case of Graham Sutherland, 'ambivalent', he says in regard to Ceri Richards – the major influences came from the great European painters of the early twentieth century. Post-war exhibitions of the work of Picasso and Matisse, and of Van Gogh, both showed the great appetite for art among the middle class (20,000 a day attended the 1948 Van Gogh exhibition) and also provided a great stimulus to British painters. Victor Pasmore confessed to being 'very much moved' by the work of Picasso, 'even though I didn't like it'; but by 1947 he had reached the position that 'abstraction is the logical culmination of painting since the Renaissance' – or, as he later put it, 'the solid and spacial world of traditional naturalism . . . could no longer serve as an objective foundation. Having reached this point the painter was confronted with an abyss from which he had either to retreat or leap over and start on a new plane. The new plane is "abstract art".' Yet for some artists, patronage, rather than theory, could still be a critical influence. For Graham Sutherland there came traditional commissions both ecclesiastical and lay. For St Matthew's Church, Northampton, he painted a crucifixion, and for the new Coventry Cathedral, between 1954 and 1957 he designed the tapestry, 'Christ in Glory in the Tetramorph'; for Somerset Maugham, Lord Beaverbrook, and the

Honourable Edward Sackville-West he painted what were to become well-known portraits.

In these scattered fragments there can be no thesis about the artist and society; but let us for a moment look at the social origins, and ultimate careers, of three important figures. Henry Moore was born in 1898, the son of a former miner who had established himself as a mining engineer; Francis Bacon was born in 1909, the son of a well-connected family of the Anglo-Irish ascendancy (he was a collateral descendant of his illustrious Elizabethan namesake); Robert Colquhoun was born in 1914, the son of an engineering worker in the west of Scotland. Moore had already arrived at his distinctive style as a sculptor by the 1930s, though his reputation was still a limited one. During the war he produced a famous series of drawings of people sheltering in the London Tube, drawings which, apart from anything else, showed a somewhat detached and distanced attitude towards suffering humanity around him. In the postwar years Moore emerged as one of the recognized international figures on the British art scene.

Completely untrained, Francis Bacon had made sporadic attempts to set himself up as a painter. An exhibition at the Lefevre Gallery in April 1945, which contained works by such better-known British artists as Matthew Smith and Henry Moore himself, also included a large triptych by Bacon entitled 'Three Figures at the Base of a Crucifixion': this contained those ingredients by which Bacon was eventually to become well known, malignant, ominous, twisted figures, part-human, part-animal. From most critics the response was one of outrage and ridicule. But the sheer power of his work – Bacon spoke of making 'the paint speak louder than the story' – quickly brought paintings first attacked as being obsessive, ferocious distortions into the front line of critical acclaim. Robert Colquhoun, whose work was more obviously in the tradition of Picasso and Braque, had already found acceptance in the bohemian cultural world of Second World War London. Reaching a peak of success in 1945–6, Colquhoun thereafter steadily drank himself to death. Somehow, even in the world of the arts, workers' sons (and Celts) seemed to be more vulnerable than sons of the middle or upper classes.

The personal vision of individual artists, the whims of the coteries within which they worked, may appear quite detached from the social context. Architecture, on the other hand, as is often remarked, is the most socially determined of the plastic arts. Yet, in a way, architecture is the most élitist of all art forms. The public could ignore Moore or Colquhoun;

what the major architects decided was often forced upon it. Wartime planning and socialist vision offered architects a key rôle in rebuilding the post-war Britain, and the young modernists of the thirties (Frederick Gibberd, Denys Lasdun, Maxwell Fry, and others) were given opportunities denied their counterparts in Italy and France where the Old Guard remained in control. The main emphasis till the early 1950s was on building houses and schools. The first generation new towns, started in the 1940s, catered to the traditional taste for low-rise housing set in reasonable space, while at the same time adopting some of the tenets of the international functionalist style. Harlow (planned by Gibberd) has been widely praised, though it also encountered early on a problem which became endemic in post-war architecture: the smart white terraces in the international style by Maxwell Fry and Jane Drew simply wore much less well than some of the more traditional brick-built neighbourhoods. In the big cities local authorities made a start on building massive high-rise housing estates. Denys Lasdun, for example, was involved in the Wholefield Estate, Paddington, in West London; while the LCC Architects Department's realization of Le Corbusier's vision of a high-rise city set in parkland at Roehampton in south-west London was in its day (1952–9) lauded as one of the great achievements of British architecture. Industrial techniques for building schools were pioneered in Hertfordshire, then, in 1948, taken up by the Ministry of Education. Many of these schools, for instance the Henry Hartland Grammar School at Worksop, a secondary modern school at Wokingham, a primary school at Amersham, and a village school at Finmere in Oxfordshire, all light and airy, not specially impressive from the outside, but extremely well designed in their use of space inside, won international reputations.

The first great break from the needs of home, family, and children towards the needs of public spectacle came with the preparation of the bombed-out South Bank site for the 1951 Festival of Britain. Here was a remarkable opportunity to present the British public with a concentrated dose of modern architecture. The entire exhibition area, designed by Sir Hugh Casson, presented the contemporary idea of architecture as a single concept linking together spaces and buildings. The most impressive building was Robert Matthew's Royal Festival Hall, though two temporary constructions, the Skylon and the Dome of Discovery, conveyed even more strongly the feel of a new age.

Many of the new housing estates of the post-war years – and most of the occupants were probably very glad of it – were very traditional in style. How the houses were furnished depended on a number of factors. Wartime necessity had led to the creation of 'utility' furniture; one nationwide economical style. Wartime aspiration had led to the creation of the Council for Industrial Design. Both of those upper-class socialists, Hugh Dalton, President of the Board of Trade during the war, and Sir Stafford Cripps, his successor in the Labour Government after 1945, were enthusiastic supporters of good design. Cripps played an important part in the presentation of the 1946 Design Exhibition at the Victoria and Albert Museum, 'Britain Can Make It'. A million and a half people visited this exhibition of simple, unfussy, rational products, each a tribute to the best in modern functionalism. Unfortunately, few were available for general sale, so that the exhibition was quickly nicknamed 'Britain Can't Have It'.

In 1948 reform was carried through at the Royal College of Art: the theories were those of the great German centre of rational design of the 1920s, the Bauhaus, but the practice was very much that of the progressive element in the British upper class, as in so many of the other experiments of the post-1945 period. The Council for Industrial Design worked hard to cash in on the popularization of good contemporary design achieved by the Festival of Britain. In 1956 the Design Centre was opened in Haymarket, London, and a year later the Design Centre awards began. Gradually manufacturers were persuaded that it was worth trying to attain the label 'Design Centre approved'. Yet, as Fiona MacCarthy has remarked – and how typical this is of the entire British cultural scene: 'Design was still in many ways an amiable clique. Identical professors seemed forever giving prizes to their own RCA students, identical designers were forever smiling thanks to the Duke of Edinburgh.' Much British design was in fact highly derivative, with Scandinavian influences heavily in evidence in the 1950s. Speaking of the Council of Industrial Design, Fiona MacCarthy adds that: 'Through the fifties, its activities were altogether cosy and low-key, with lunch meetings at Overseas House (sample topic: *Design Starvation in the Public Schools*); with musical evenings at the Geffrye Museum; with little exhibitions in Charing Cross Station, "Register Your Choice" and later "Make or Mar". '

Creative work in the realms of the intellect and imagination was carried on in a number of different interlinked groups, each of them a tiny minority within society as a whole, but each of them rooted, however feebly, in the social compost. The least utilitarian items (like philosophy and literary criticism) and the most capital-intensive (science) tend to find their home in the universities. Despite the fact that they form the tiniest of minorities within the minority, British philosophers betrayed an isolationism at least as marked as that of British literature. Leading British philosophers, such as Gilbert Ryle or John Austin, eschewed big metaphysical issues and, under the influence of the great mathematical logician (and, incidentally, publicist of libertarian causes), Bertrand Russell, and of the Austrian-born Cambridge philosopher Wittgenstein, concentrated instead on what many continentals saw as the tedious triviality of 'linguistic philosophy'. Neither in history, which was replacing philosophy and classics as the staple academic subject, nor in sociology, still regarded as a slightly suspect subject in many British universities, was the British achievement marked by any great innovation in content, though history did achieve a new popular appeal, first in the forties through the work of G. M. Trevelyan, then in the fifties through the Pelican History of England series. By 1954 Arnold Toynbee had completed the tenth and final volume of his massive universal history *A Study of History*, begun in the 1930s. Yet, though based on immense knowledge both in classical civilizations and the contemporary world, this was a work of poetic inspiration – particularly as a kind of religious transcendentalism more and more coloured the post-war volumes – rather than a work of methodological innovation or analytical rigour. It won readers round the world but created no great new British school of scholarship.

It was in the most international, and most rapidly changing intellectual universe that British academics did best, science. The physicist Professor G. H. A. Cole (in *The Twentieth Century Mind*, vol. 3) has written: 'Pre-war physics was fun for those lucky enough to be involved with it, but it scarcely affected anyone else; postwar physics was still fun for those lucky enough to be involved in it, but the general world community now could not stand back uncaring.' Much of the pioneering pre-war British work in nuclear physics was now locked up in the United States, but such new sciences as geophysics, medical physics, and molecular biology advanced. In great secret, the British Government proceeded with the development of a British nuclear weapon, principally at the research establishment at Harwell and at the nuclear pile at Windscale. On 3 October 1952 Britain exploded her own test atomic bomb, thus becoming, after America and Russia, the third nuclear power. British physicists, and British finance, played an important role in the setting-up of CERN, the European Centre of Nuclear Research, at Geneva in 1952. For nuclear fission, enormous amounts of energy were required. The major work by J. D. Cockcroft and Ernest Walton in developing a 'voltage multiplier' had been done in Rutherford's Cambridge laboratory before the war; but it was in 1951 that they received the Nobel Prize. Throughout the entire period covered by this book British scientists were to notch up a total of Nobel Prizes second only to that achieved by American scientists.

Developments in radio-astronomy, in which at this time Britain was very much in the lead, again owed much to the war, when it was discovered that signals sent out by the sun in the microwave region were interfering with radar. It soon became clear that the stars also transmitted radio signals. The world's first large-scale radio telescope was built at Jodrell Bank under the supervision of Sir Bernard Lovell. British astronomers played a leading role in debates over the nature and origins of the universe: was it expanding, contracting, oscillating, or remaining in a steady state of continuous creation? W. B. Bonnor was a proponent of the oscillating universe, while Hermann Bondi and Thomas Gold put forward the theory in 1948 of steady state or continuous creation, a theory which was to be greatly developed in the 1960s by Fred Hoyle.

An enormous range of discoveries made by scientists of many nationalities greatly influenced medical science. From the original discovery by Alexander Fleming in 1929, penicillin was developed in the United States by the Australian-born scientist Howard Florey and his German-born associate Ernst Chain; in 1945 Fleming, Florey, and Chain were jointly awarded the Nobel Prize in medicine and physiology. The search for other antibiotics (the word was coined in 1942 by the American bacteriologist Waksman) was on. Thanks to Waksman's discovery of streptomycin, tuberculosis in post-war Britain was no longer the scourge it had been in the inter-war years. The next great advance in pharmaceuticals was the development, based on earlier work carried out at the Harvard Medical School, of the Salk vaccine; it did not, however, come into general use in Britain in the attack on polio till the 1960s. The widespread use in medicine of radioactive tracers also depended heavily upon work carried out in the United States. However, it was the British chemist R. G. Westall who, in 1952, marked an important stage in the attack upon deficiencies of the metabolism by isolating the compound 'porphobilinogen'. In connection with the treatment of pernicious anaemia, the isolation of a pure sample of Vitamin B12 by Ernest Lester Smith in Britain in 1948 was important. The complex molecular structure of Vitamin B12 was eventually determined by the British chemist Dorothy Hodgkin; in carrying through the enormous calculations involved she had to make use of an

American advanced electronic computer. She gained her Nobel Prize for Chemistry in 1964. Another great sphere for international medical research concerned the development of various defences against the viruses which attack the human body. It was a group of British bacteriologists, led by Alick Isaacs who, in 1957, isolated the protein 'interferon' which was to prove in many respects more effective than the older antibiotics.

In April 1953 it was announced that Francis Crick and James D. Watson at Cambridge had discovered that the molecule of deoxyribonucleic acid (DNA), the carrier of genetic inheritance, was in the shape of a double helix. The final discovery was only possible because of the mass of work by scientists in different countries deploying a range of expensive specialist equipment, yet the achievement of the donnish Cambridge biophysicist Crick and the bouncy American viro-chemist Watson, then only twenty-five years old, has much of the romance of a piece of individualistic freebooting in which personal ambition seemed at least as strong a motive as disinterested pursuit of scientific knowledge. The charming human frailties of science, the moods of triumph, the worries over the rival activities of the famous American structural chemist Linus Pauling, the visits to the pub, come through grippingly in Watson's own description of the days after the final breakthrough had been made.

Francis's preoccupation with DNA quickly became full time . . . Constantly he would pop up from his chair, worriedly look at the cardboard models, fiddle with other combinations, and then, the period of momentary uncertainty over, look satisfied and tell me how important our work was. I enjoyed Francis's words, even though they lacked the casual sense of understatement known to be the correct way to behave in Cambridge. It seemed almost unbelievable that the DNA structure was solved, that the answer was incredibly exciting, and that our names would be associated with the double helix as Pauling's was with the alpha helix.

When the Eagle opened at six, I went over with Francis to talk about what must be done in the next few days. Francis wanted no time lost in seeing whether a satisfactory three-dimensional model could be built . . . Though I was equally anxious to build the complete model, I thought more about Linus and the possibility that he might stumble upon the base pairs before we told him the answer.

That night, however, we could not finally establish the double helix. Until the metal bases were on hand, any model building would be too sloppy to be convincing. I went back to Pop's to tell Elizabeth and Bertrand that Francis and I had probably beaten Pauling to the gate and that the answer would revolutionise biology. Both were genuinely pleased, Elizabeth with sisterly pride, Bertrand with the idea that he could report back to International Society that he had a friend who would win a Nobel Prize . . .

The following morning I felt marvellously alive when I awoke. On my way to the Whim I slowly walked towards Clare Bridge, staring up at the gothic pinnacles of King's College Chapel that stood out sharply against the spring sky. I briefly stopped and looked over at the perfect Georgian features of the recently cleaned Gibbs Building, thinking that much of our success was due to the long uneventful periods when we walked among the colleges or unobtrusively read the new books that came into Heffers book store. After contentedly pouring over *The Times*, I wandered into the lab to see Francis, uncharacteristically early, flipping the cardboard base pairs about an imaginary line. As far as a compass and ruler could tell him, both sets of base pairs neatly fitted into the backbone configuration. As the morning wore on, Max and John successively came by to see if we still thought we had it. Each got a quick, concise lecture from Francis, during the second of which I wandered down to see if the shop could be speeded up to produce the purines and pyrimidines later that afternoon.

Actually, the discovery was ignored by the popular press. Acclaim came only in the sixties when, something the popular press *could* understand, Crick and Watson won their Nobel Prize.

The divide between scientists and the rest of society, or rather between scientists and other academics and intellectuals, was the subject of C. P. Snow's first analysis of 'The Two Cultures', published in the *New Statesman* on 6 October 1956. In theory politicians had recognized the immense significance of science in a wartime and post-war world. In the Cabinet, the Lord President of the Council was supposed to act as a kind of Science Minister, and in January 1947 the Advisory Council on Scientific Policy was set up. According to the official statement the appointment of the Council 'marked a further step in the development of close relations between science and the central government'. The reality, echoing, as has already been suggested, the differences between the theory and practice of social planning after the war, was slightly different: as Professor J. G. Crowther has put it (in *Science in Modern Society*) the Advisory Council served more as 'a commentator on' rather than 'a leader of' scientific policy. At the top, British scientific achievements were considerable; there was an impressive reorientation of industry and of medicine towards the new technologies: but there was little effective communication of the significance of science to the wider society, whether by Government agencies or through the press.

Times, indeed, were hard yet cosy for the British press in the post-war years. With papers little more than flimsy fly-sheets there was more than enough advertising to go round, especially since, relative to population, the British were greater newspaper readers than any other nation in the world. In 1950 the total circulation of all the national daily papers reached just under seventeen million; thereafter there was a slight drop, but circulation none the less remained over sixteen million throughout the 1950s. At this point, three press barons dominated the newspaper world: Beaverbrook, Rothermere, and Kemsley. Daily Mirror Newspapers Ltd, with Cecil King as Chairman, emerged in 1951, and in 1953 Roy Thomson, a Canadian millionaire, bought up Scotsman Publications in Edinburgh; but the great upheavals in ownership did not come till the very end of the fifties. As restrictions lifted in the fifties it became clearer that the sharp division in the British press was between the 'quality' papers, *The Times, Manchester Guardian, Daily Telegraph, Observer*, and *Sunday Times* on the one side, and the popular press on the other. The quality press took about two million of the total daily circulation, and was actually expanding in size. It was the in-between papers, in particular the *News Chronicle*, which found conditions hardest, while what remained of the independent provincial press steadily withered away.

Because of a certain repute and authenticity in their presentation of the news the quality papers appealed to upper-middle-class and upper-class readers; they thus could attract advertising at expensive rates. The popular press sought to retain large readerships through presenting sensational, entertaining, and often trivial material rather than hard news and serious comment; in this way they too could attract the advertising necessary for survival.

The one form of communication totally unstained by commercial considerations was the BBC. At the end of the war the radio services were reorganized into three: the Light Programme, the Home Service Programme, and the Third Programme. The audience research which the BBC had pioneered shortly before the war treated the audiences for these three services as synonymous with working-class, middle-class, and upper-middle and upper-class, respectively. Few challenged the validity of the BBC's position or the power of what Lord Reith, first Director General of the BBC, had described as 'the brute force of monopoly' to act for the preservation of certain social and cultural standards.

In reality the BBC was a very upper-class institution. The most successful radio soap opera of all time was 'Mrs Dale's Diary', set in a distinctly
upper-middle-class milieu. There was a strong feeling within the BBC,
dating back to the early years of the war, that an outlet ought to be
provided for genuinely working-class aspirations and that something
equivalent to a working-class Mrs Dale's Diary ought to be put on the air.
Little success attended these efforts and the working-class Mrs Dale's
Diary was never discovered. The Third Programme played an important
part in the musical renaissance after 1945; but many of its serious talks
were characterized by a mannered pedantry and a distinctive academic
parochialism. The war had brought an end to television broadcasting
only in its swaddling clothes at the end of the thirties; it grew again only
slowly in the post-war years though by the early fifties there were five
million television viewers. In order that television might not become an
addiction nor distract children from their studies nor adults from their
duties, television broadcasting was confined to a limited number of hours
per day – also very much in keeping with the BBC ethic. The first serious
debate over the BBC's position took place in 1954 when, in fact, the Act
was passed which made possible the setting-up of a separate commercial
television channel.

The means of communication which were fully developed and ready
to hand got a great boost from the war: paperback books, radio, and also
films. There had been individual British films of considerable merit in
the 1930s, but on the whole it could be said that the war provided
the necessary stimulus, and also opportunity to the more progressive
film-makers, to establish a consistent output of high-level films of a
distinctive British character. It was in the war that Ealing Studios came
to the fore, making films on definite, but low-key, patriotic themes. Ealing
went from strength to strength in the post-war years with a series of
instantly recognizable British genre films both serious and comic. Undoubtedly Hollywood imports continued to be most popular with British
audiences, but Government import restrictions gave a helpful encouragement to British film-makers. Few British films attempted grand themes
but within their limited aims they were, thanks to workmanlike direction,
competent scripts, usually derived from theatrical or literary sources, and
an extremely high level of character acting, artistic successes; usually
aiming at gently satirical comment on British ways they often succeeded
unintentionally in revealing a great deal more about fundamental British
social assumptions. The golden age of Ealing petered out around 1951

when *His Excellency* was generally treated as but a poor successor to *Passport to Pimlico* (1949), *Kind Hearts and Coronets* (1949), and *The Man in the White Suit* (1951). The Government-sponsored Group Three had one great achievement in *The Brave Don't Cry* (1952) which, most unusually, treated, with great sensitivity, an industrial working-class community, a Scottish mining village; but after that, just as a second television channel was on the way, British films relapsed into mediocrity.

In absolute terms there was expansion at all levels of society in opportunities for entertainment, for intellectual stimulus, and for refreshment of the spirit. All of that could not but continue to hasten the decline of traditional religious observance. At the beginning of the fifties under 10 per cent of the population were regular churchgoers. Within the small circle of those who were active and concerned believers there were as yet no very exciting developments. The Catholic Church continued to gain adherents; the non-conformist persuasions continued to do worst. On the whole old positions were held to and sectarian rivalries continued.

In the arts and entertainment, in concern for the environment, in the accessibility of the best to the most, Britain was in a healthier state than it had ever been: if drama was stereotyped, the novel fading, poetry flagging, art was imaginative, architecture positive, music inspiring, and opera and ballet on a more secure basis than they had ever been. Yet in all spheres there was a sense of dominance by established in-groups, a feeling of following the current cult. In all spheres British thought and artistic endeavour were inward-looking, seemingly unconcerned with the great issues which racked continental intellectuals: existentialism and social commitment, the challenge to Marxist faith presented by Stalinist tyranny, the possibilities of a Catholicism attuned to the needs of the modern world. The many British literary works which bring in the Second World War seem somehow to treat it as a little local affair, without epochal significance, when compared, say, with American novels dealing with the same war, or with British literary reactions to the First World War.

6
Consensus Re-examined

Before 1945 Labour had twice formed shaky minority Governments, the second of which collapsed ignominiously in 1931. Never before had Labour had a secure majority. In 1945 the majority in Parliament was a crushing one: Labour had 393 seats to 210 for the Conservatives and their various 'National' allies, with the Liberals having twelve, the Communists two, and various others twenty-three. For those who took the trouble to look, the portents of a Labour victory had been clear enough (the Gallup poll in the *News Chronicle* had forecast a Labour victory, though by a much narrower majority): yet conventional wisdom had firmly predicted a victory for Churchill, 'the man who won the war'.

Shortly after the results were known, a middle-class lady wrote in a private letter: 'We were certainly staggered by the election result especially as I live and work in a very Conservative atmosphere – the end of the world would have occasioned only a little more alarm.' An upper-class one declared: 'But this is terrible – *they've* elected a Labour Government, and the *country* will never stand for that.' An alarmed and disgusted Conservative Member of Parliament described the Labour members flooding over the Government benches as 'just like a crowd of damned constituents'. All the worst fears seemed confirmed when these crowded benches rose to sing 'The Red Flag'. However, it was clear that many Labour men did not actually know the words, and traditional urbanity was restored when the newly re-elected speaker, the Conservative Colonel Clifton-Brown, remarked that he hoped he had been elected Speaker of the House of Commons and not director of some musical chorus.

It was 'a good sign', noted 'Chips' Channon, who was in an excellent position to assess the possibilities of continuing upper-class political dominance, 'that the Labour Party have decided to elect a Conservative

Speaker unanimously'. On the Labour M Ps themselves he was firmly dismissive: 'Never have I seen such a dreary lot of people.' Channon probably had a clearer perception of what was really going on than Sir Hartley Shawcross, one of Labour's recent upper-middle-class recruits, who on 2 April 1946, as the Government was pushing through its Trades Disputes Bill, designed to restore to the trade unions the legal powers they had enjoyed before the 1926 General Strike, declared: 'We are the masters at the moment – and not only for the moment, but for a very long time to come.'

Of votes actually cast, the Conservatives and their allies had received 39.6 per cent, Labour 48 per cent: the country was actually more evenly divided than the House of Commons figures suggested. However, Labour continued to do well in the country, increasing its majorities in the first few by-elections, all in Labour-held seats, and doing very well in the first round of local government elections. In the 1950 election Labour still secured 46.1 per cent of all votes cast, to 43.5 per cent for the Conservatives; and in the 1951 election Labour's share actually went to the highest ever at 48.8 per cent, which was 0.8 per cent ahead of the Conservatives, though, thanks to the single-member-constituency system, the Conservatives actually won a parliamentary majority.

If we concentrate upon the charmed circle of parliamentary politics it is perfectly reasonable to speak of a quick restoration of political consensus. Churchillian thunder pealed more and more distantly as he, and the entrenched right-wingers, became increasingly isolated from the main body of the Conservative Party, whose younger leadership, notably Eden and Butler, deliberately set out to adapt Conservative policy to meet the assumptions of the Welfare State and the full-employment society. But conventional notions of a general consensus receive a jolt if one studies the popular right-wing press, particularly Beaverbrook's *Express* and Rothermere's *Mail*. These kept up an abusive campaign against the Government and all its works, coining a loaded language of their own, such as 'grab' for nationalization, and, of course, always referring to Labour as 'the socialists'. They also coined some witty slogans such as, at the time of the fuel and bread crises, 'Shiver with Shinwell and Starve with Strachey'. Ribbing of the Government, both sharply pointed and more gentle, was to be found in other forms of mass media: the film *The Blue Lamp* (1950), the first to feature a new folk hero, PC George Dixon (he was actually killed in the film, but that did not stop him being revived for innumerable future television series), managed to bring in a bitter criticism of the Government's rationing policies; *Passport to Pimlico* more gently mocked Government bureaucracy.

Parliamentary consensus should not be overstated either. The Conservatives did divide the House on the third reading of the National Health Service Bill. While early nationalization measures went through fairly easily, the Conservatives mounted a powerful and sustained campaign against the nationalization of iron and steel, and indeed used their permanent majority in the House of Lords to frustrate the Government's intentions. Nationalization was very much a major issue between the two parties in the general election campaigns of 1950 and 1951.

Parliamentary consensus was most evident after the return of the Conservatives to power in 1951. Steel, which had not really been nationalized anyway, was denationalized; the practical effects of this political game, as suggested in Chapter 1, were not particularly significant either way in any case. Parts of the road haulage industry were also returned to private ownership. Despite Conservative mutterings over Labour's Trades Disputes Act, trade-union law was not altered, and the Conservative Minister of Labour, Walter Monckton, was noted for his conciliatory policies. 'Butskellism' was the word coined in the early fifties to represent the continuity of economic policy as between the outgoing Labour Chancellor of the Exchequer, Hugh Gaitskell, and the new Conservative one, R. A. Butler. A much publicized political divide did exist between the majority of the parliamentary Labour Party and the left-wing group led by Aneurin Bevan, who had resigned from the Labour administration over the rearmament policy (which, among other things, involved the imposition of health service prescription charges) adopted because of the outbreak of the Korean War. Though a minority in Parliament, the Bevanites had the support of many party activists at constituency level.

Political consensus appeared to be shattered by the Suez Crisis of 1956. But the really significant point with regard to British political attitudes and values is the speed with which passions cooled: Suez was scarcely mentioned in the general election campaign of 1959, despite the fact that the then Conservative leader, Harold Macmillan, had been closely associated with the disastrous policies of Sir Anthony Eden. In collusion with the French and the Israelis, Britain waged war for one week against Egypt in pursuit of Eden's delusion that Colonel Nasser was another Hitler, and vain hope that the Egyptian President could thus be removed from power. Eden's 'armed conflict' lasted just long enough to demonstrate that Britain no longer had the logistic power to mount an efficient sea-borne operation in the Middle East, and for Britain to be branded by the United Nations as an aggressor, before American opposition, Russian threats, and the inevitable run on the pound brought an ignoble venture to a humiliating conclusion. In the early stages of the episode it appeared that Government and Opposition and much of the public were united in xenophobic hostility to Nasser. But once the Labour opposition had decided on outright denunciation of Government policy, public opinion divided very much along party lines. Opinion polls did not support the widely held contention that many Labour supporters found their patriotism agreeably stirred by Eden's venture in gunboat diplomacy. Only one Labour MP, Stanley Evans, supported the Government, and he was shortly forced to resign by his constituency party. On the other side Conservative dissidents were treated with similar roughness by their local organizations. That most Labour voters opposed the Suez venture does not necessarily imply, however, that the entire working class, many of whom voted Conservative in any case, did so.

Public attitudes towards defence policy generally can also be studied through the opinion polls. In January 1949 50 per cent of those interviewed agreed that conscription should be continued in peacetime, while 33 per cent wished it to be discontinued; in November of the same year the percentages were 53 and 38 respectively. In September 1950, before the official announcement that in response to the Korean situation length of service would be increased from eighteen months to two years, 55 per cent gave advance endorsement of this move, while 33 per cent disapproved. Two and a half years later 45 per cent of those polled favoured continuing the two-year term, 45 per cent favoured a reduction to eighteen months. A year later (May 1954), when Churchill's name was introduced into the pollsters' question as a believer in the necessity of Britain's retaining two-year conscription, 49 per cent agreed with Churchill, 35 per cent disagreed. But after the Government had announced in October 1955 that it proposed to cut National Service the majority of those polled echoed the change in policy: 47 per cent favoured cutting the two-year period, 34 per cent thought such a cut would be unwise. In September 1956 44 per cent were in favour of abolishing National Service, 38 per cent were against such abolition.

Reactions over defence expenditure were very similar: majority support (58 per cent in February 1952) for the steady increase in defence expenditure to 1953; a slightly less decisive majority support for cutting defence expenditure after 1956. After the testing of the first British hydrogen bomb in 1955 a more crucial issue stole the scene. Throughout the second half of the fifties opinion polls indicated that between one quarter and one third of the British public favoured Britain's unilaterally renouncing nuclear weapons.

How far, and at what point, a majority of the British people had digested the fact that Britain was no longer a major world power is difficult to determine: probably not till the 1960s, though, objectively, Suez is the watershed. In the imagery of newsreel, press, radio, and television, Britain continued to be presented, along with France, as a 'big' country; the Netherlands, Belgium, Switzerland, and Denmark, though already beginning to demonstrate considerable economic power, were 'small' countries. Undoubtedly a pervasive sentiment was 'we won the war'. While the frequent attribution of low productivity in the pits to the desire of the miners to enjoy the fruits of peace ignored the much more debilitating effects of a long history of appalling industrial relations, it is true that at no level in British society was there a deep commitment to the notion that the continued survival of the nation would depend on a prolongation of the heroic efforts of wartime. In the austerity conditions of the post-war years there were constant exhortations to support the 'export drive', and, indeed, by 1950 immediate export targets had been achieved. But in the fifties, as terms of trade improved, and the economic gloom lightened, very much there was a sense that the British people now had entered into their just inheritance. The consumer market expanded and the pressure to fight for export markets lessened.

Newsreels in the later forties had made something of a fuss over the granting of independence to India, quite possibly because Churchill took a belligerent stand on this issue (not that Britain really had any choice anyway). There has been much theorizing about the impact 'the loss of empire' ought to have had on the British psyche; the empirical evidence is that it really had very little. The most notable consequences were felt by members of the upper and upper-middle classes who no longer had the Raj as a territory in which to exploit their natural gifts of leadership. Apart from a few Victorian regrets over India the official line was one of self-congratulation that Britain once more was leading the way in granting independence to former colonial peoples.

In the formal sense, Britain in the post-war years approached more closely to being a full democracy. Until 1948, businessmen could vote twice, once in their home constituency, and once in the constituency in which their business was situated; at the same time the separate university constituencies, which had provided university graduates with a second vote, were abolished. The non-elective, hereditary House of Lords had been able to frustrate the nationalization of iron and steel, though from 1948 its power to delay legislation was reduced to one year. Yet many aspects of British political culture remained profoundly undemocratic. At parliamentary level individual MPs had few powers to initiate legislation or even to bring Cabinet and senior civil servants under serious scrutiny: there was little in the way of participatory democracy. Politics was left very much to the politicians, apart from the purely temporary excitements of general elections – the turn-out in 1950 and 1951, 83.9 per cent and 82.6 per cent respectively, was impressively high, comparing with 72.7 per cent in 1945, 76.8 per cent in 1955, and 78.7 per cent in 1959.

In one sense industrial relations had been totally transformed by the war; in another sense they had scarcely been changed at all. After 1945 the bargaining power of labour was far stronger than it had ever been in the inter-war years, and this power was maintained by high demand and consequent full employment. Yet, although some attention was given both during and after the war by the TUC to the question of 'industrial democracy' and worker participation in management, traditional attitudes remained very strong here on both sides. It became clear that the TUC was only interested in worker participation in management in respect of the nationalized industries; in private industry management should remain in the hands of the bosses while trade unions continued to uphold their members' interests in the old ways. Sir Stafford Cripps was speaking both as a member of the upper class and of the Labour Government when he stated that workers simply did not have the necessary skills to participate in management. In general, managements went as far as they thought necessary to appease and conciliate their workforce; but in essence the line between was as firmly defined as it had ever been.

By the late fifties it was clear that one central feature of British values was a strong loyalty to the institution of monarchy. The evidence suggested that monarchism was least strong in the immediate post-war period of severe austerity, but that it strengthened as social and economic circumstances improved in the fifties. In the abstract, luke-warm and even hostile sentiments towards the monarchy could be found; but as the great monarchical events, funerals and coronations, focused attention, royalist sentiment strengthened. Overall, monarchist views were expressed most strongly in London, where the great pageants took place, least strongly in the remoter provinces.

In May 1947 George VI and Queen Elizabeth set out on what could well appear a lavish tour of Southern Africa. A majority of those having any defined opinion on the tour at all, 32 per cent of those polled, disapproved of the tour because of the contrast it presented with austere conditions at home; 29 per cent approved of the tour, usually on the grounds that it would strengthen the bonds of Empire. However, the announcement later that year of the engagement between Princess Elizabeth and Prince Philip revealed enormous warmth towards the monarchy, even if there was a widespread view, as Philip Ziegler puts it, 'that the Prince was amiable but dim' – 'a nice enough man even if not over-bright', said one housewife. Yet, in July, 40 per cent of those polled were unenthusiastic about the expenditure involved in the wedding preparations, though 40 per cent also actively approved. But by October those actively approving had risen to 60 per cent, and in November, a fortnight before the wedding, only 29 per cent felt that the arrangements were too costly. The wedding itself, when it came, undoubtedly monopolized attention, with newspapers quickly sold out as the public sought pictures of the royal couple. People interviewed offered various explanations for their enthusiasm: the need for colour and spectacle, the emphasis on the institution of the family, but, above all, a pride in having something in which the British stood out from other countries: 'I expect that some of the royal visitors would feel jealous and wonder whether they would get the same kind of greeting in their own countries,' one man from south-east London commented.

During the night of 5–6 February 1952, George VI died. Again, there was quite evidently a widespread sense of loss and shock, quite different from anything experienced over a civilian leader, even, as it was later to transpire, one as eminent as Churchill himself. Still, the death of one monarch meant the coronation of another one. The nearer the coronation of Queen Elizabeth II came, the more public opinion polls showed enthusiasm for, and interest in, that event. At least two million people turned out in the streets to watch the coronation procession; but the new twist was that almost twenty-and-a-half million people, 56 per cent of the adult population, could watch, and did watch, the entire proceedings on television; a further 32 per cent, 11.7 million, listened on radio. From survey material, it does seem that the coronation was associated in many people's minds, however vaguely, with the idea of a new Elizabethan age in which, through the Commonwealth, if not through the Empire, Britain would still retain a glorious place in the world. The coronation established not so much a peak, but much more a plateau of popular sentiment favourable towards the monarchy: though there were fluctuations in individual polls, it could be said that outright republicans seldom numbered more than about 11 per cent of the population.

Civic loyalty to the established order of things was perhaps even more powerfully demonstrated by attitudes towards the police. Geoffrey Gorer found that 73 per cent of the men and 74 per cent of the women in his sample thought highly of the police. Though 18 per cent were prepared to voice critical opinions, this was over individual police activities, not of the police as an institution. On the other hand, religious observance was undoubtedly in decline – though even here vestiges of traditional loyalties remained strong. At the beginning of the fifties 26 per cent of men and 18 per cent of women admitted to no religious affiliation at all. The figures for regular churchgoing were even lower: 11 per cent of women and 7 per cent of men; 45 per cent of the population could be described as intermittent churchgoers, that is to say they went to church once or twice a year, 40 per cent of the population did not attend church at all, but, and it is an interesting but, all except 7 per cent did expect to attend church for weddings or funerals, furthermore 50 per cent of all parents still sent their children to Sunday school.

In the late fifties commentators of both major political persuasions were ready to argue that the British had done marvellously in the war, had with sense and restraint accepted difficult post-war circumstances, and were now in the fifties reaping the fruits of compromise between collectivist welfare, sponsored by Labour and accepted by Conservatives, and the element of free enterprise and respect for the consumer fostered by the Conservatives. Britain still evoked the admiration of European commentators: 'A progressive social revolution is being sketched out, peaceful and silent,' wrote a French sociologist, Pierre Laroque, in 1955, 'which is apparent to those who after an interval of several months or several years return to England, and take note of the profound transformation taking place there'. An indigenous commentator, writing in the early sixties, was to be much less respectful: 'Far from introducing a "social revolution" the overwhelming Labour victory of 1945 brought about the greatest restoration of traditional social values since 1660.' The words were those of the left-wing, public-school and Oxford-educated journalist, Anthony Howard.

Complacency, parochialism. lack of serious structural change, these are sustainable charges. Did the fault lie with an absence of political leadership? The first two post-war Prime Ministers, Attlee and Churchill, were certainly not weak men, though Churchill was way past his best by the time he returned to office. Political leaders, really, were prisoners of the consensus. If faults have to be looked for, they probably have to be sought at a rather deeper level than that of the actions and thoughts of individual politicians. Consensus was laudable in respect of maintaining social harmony and providing the opportunity for post-war reforms to be worked out. But in some respects, at least, the mixed economy presented the wrong mix. Conservative leaders, mostly upper class, could join with Labour leaders, mostly a mixture of upper class and working class, in supporting the large unit: Labour preferred the State, the Conservatives in certain circumstances preferred large-scale private industry. Both showed little interest in the small businessman, offering little encouragement to true private enterprise.

Part Two

Roads to Freedom
1958–73

7

Affluence, Appliances, and Work

Technology had been a growing force in the shaping of society since the end of the eighteenth century; nevertheless in the sixties there evolved a technological civilization of a sort not previously seen in twentieth-century Britain, characterized by a new ugliness and a new species of modern conveniences, affecting the urban landscape and rural environment, the working day, domestic chores and the pursuit of leisure, the role of women, and the nature of education. Hitherto individual technologies had impinged separately on society, now the concept of one unified technology, based on what its apostles termed 'the systems approach', was beginning to influence every aspect of social organization. New production techniques brought down the price of consumer goods while making it possible to pay higher wages.

Despite recurrent economic crises, the reality for the vast majority of British people was that at last the country seemed to have entered into the kind of high-spending consumer society long familiar from American films. Most of these developments owed little to the deliberate actions of politicians, though the general drift is quite well encapsulated in certain political utterances. The keynote had been sounded in June 1954 by the then Conservative Chancellor of the Exchequer, R. A. Butler, when he asked, rhetorically, 'Why should we not aim to double our standard of living in the next twenty-five years, and still have our money as valuable then as now?' A remark made by the Conservative Prime Minister, Harold Macmillan in 1957, always slightly misquoted, entered popular lore in a vulgar joke which tore round the country during the 1959 election campaign (I heard it first in London and then, within days, in Edinburgh). A woman complains to the police that she has been raped by one of the candidates, who, she insists, was the Conservative; she knows this, 'because she's never had it so good'. (The person who first told me the story was a twenty-two-year-old woman.) What Macmillan actually said was: 'Most of our people have never had it so good'. In the 1964 election campaign, Harold Wilson, as leader of the Labour Party, moved two steps forward by speaking of 'the white heat of technological revolution'.

White heat was perhaps not quite the right image; much of the new technology was concerned with suds, shine, and phoney flavours. Still there could be no doubt about the benefits brought by technology: disinfectants and detergents enormously improved health and hygiene; food was generally purer and fresher than before the war. The British end of the giant multinational conglomerate, Unilever, had set up its first research establishments in the aftermath of the Second World War. By 1963 there were three, when a fourth was established at Welwyn, the team investigating problems of texture and flavour in oils and fats and problems relating to ice-cream moving there from Port Sunlight; the capacity released at Port Sunlight was used for expanded research on detergents. The research was needed, for detergents were already choking up the country's sewers with foam; however, by 1965 a method was found of breaking down detergents biologically. Canning was a traditional method of preserving food (the upper classes in the thirties believed that the feckless working class lived off tinned food); now came freezing and drying as efficient methods of producing convenience foods. The electrical industry directed itself towards producing smaller and more efficient refrigerators, as well as washing machines, spin-driers, dishwashing machines, and bigger and better television sets. Certainly there appeared to be, as disciples of American capitalism had always maintained, a cunning inter-relationship between technology, the market, and the forces of communication. Advertising on commercial television did much to build up and sustain the demand for the new appliances. The chemicals industry produced new plastics. To put the appropriate sheen on the new laminated surfaces new polishes were produced. All of these developments fitted into a social scene where a greater proportion of women than at any time since the war were going out to work and where domestic labour was in short supply. They were also crucial in the movement in the British economy away from the traditional heavy industrial base to the new technological industries.

The systems approach, appropriately dressed up in its own awful jargon, seemed vindicated. Computers were essential to the process known at Unilever as 'Programme Evaluation and Review Technique', translated by

Professor Charles Wilson (in his history of the company) as 'the planning not only of research projects but of research, development and marketing projects so that operations were carried out in the most logical and economical fashion'. The 'scientists' were entering upon their heritage, and in the sixties for the first time they began to appear in numbers on the boards of directors of the major companies dealing in consumer products. (ICI, the larger of the two British chemicals giants, had been the pioneers of placing scientists in important executive positions.) At the receiving end, as it were, of the sophisticated new trading mechanism, supermarkets and self-service stores began to appear. As wages rose, working-class people bought less fish and more meat. Mac Fisheries began to turn their chain of fish shops into small supermarkets selling vegetables and groceries as well as fish. Greater and greater emphasis came to be placed on packaging and advertising. Advertising in itself became a major new growth industry. In 1965 the Chairman of Unilever explained to the shareholders why advertising and packaging had become so important: 'If your goods are to be sold by self-service your package is fighting for you against every other package directly or indirectly competing. You cannot expect it to get much help – at least in self-service stores and supermarkets – from the people running the shop.'

The full version of C. P. Snow's 'The Two Cultures' was delivered as the Rede Lecture at the University of Cambridge in 1959, and published the same year. It quickly aroused a great deal of attention. The incoming Wilson Labour Government of 1964 established a Ministry of Technology with the powerful trade-union leader, Frank Cousins, at its head, and with Snow as Parliamentary Under-Secretary; at the same time Dr B. V. Bowden, Principal of the University of Manchester Institute of Science and Technology, was appointed Minister of State in the Department of Education and Science, being, like Snow, given a peerage. Once again the changes were more paper than reality; within two years Cousins, Snow, and Bowden had all resigned their posts.

On the world's stage momentous events took place at a medical conference held in Tokyo in 1955. The intra-uterine device for contraceptive purposes had been experimented with in the 1920s and 1930s, but had produced such disastrous side-effects that it had been abandoned. At Tokyo, the Japanese reported the successful re-introduction of the intra-uterine contraceptive device. At the same conference the American biologist Gregory Pincus reported his successes with hormonal oral contraceptives. The process by which ovulation is initiated, controlled, and regulated had been understood for fifty years. In the mid-1930s synthetic oestrogens were developed which could prevent the release of pituitary gonadotrophins, so that ovulation would be inhibited and conception controlled. Still lacking, however, was a cheap source of synthetic progesterone-like steroids. Then in the 1940s another American biologist, C. L. Markert, demonstrated that certain plants, particularly the Mexican yam, were rich sources of steroids from which orally effective gestagens could be synthesized cheaply. It was during the year prior to the Tokyo conference that Pincus and his colleagues successfully tried out the combined oestrogen-gestagen product in Puerto Rico. 'The era of the Pill,' a leading medical historian (Dr N. E. Himes) has written, 'had begun.' Always, though, there is a time-lag between scientific discovery and general usage. We shall be discussing later the social consequences of new contraceptive methods, but it may be noted here that the pill only began to be at all widely used in Britain in the late 1960s. And even then, as a 1970 survey reported, only 19 per cent of married couples under forty-five were using the pill, while 29 per cent were using the condom and 37 per cent were using no contraceptive method at all.

New appliances flowing down from the commanding heights of technology formed one of the streams entering the millpond of 1960s Britain; rising income levels formed the other. Even if the phrase had not been invented by Professor J. K. Galbraith for his classic denunciation of American society of the fifties for allowing public squalor to exist side-by-side with private wealth, a distinctive condition, well described as 'the affluent society', undoubtedly existed in the Britain of the 1960s. Back in 1951 the average weekly earnings of men over twenty-one had stood at £8.30 per week. A decade later the figure had almost doubled to £15.35; in 1966 it was £20.30, in 1968 £23.00, in 1969 £24.80, in 1970 £28.05, and in 1971 £30.93. Of course, there was a touch of inflation around as well. Between 1955 and 1960 retail prices rose by 15 per cent; by 1969 they were 63 per cent higher than in 1955. But against that, weekly wage *rates* rose 25 per cent between 1955 and 1960, and had risen by 88 per cent in 1969. When overtime is taken into account, we find that average weekly *earnings* rose 34 per cent between 1955 and 1960, and 130 per cent between 1955 and 1969. This last figure was almost exactly matched by the average earnings of middle-class salaried employees, which rose 127 per cent between 1955 and 1969. While prices of food and other necessities were steadily rising, the prices of small cars, in relation to earnings power, were falling, and the many products of new technology, such as television sets and washing machines, were, despite inflation, actually costing less.

New appliances altered the home more than they altered the work place. Most of the new technological wonders of the consumer age were in fact put together by routine, repetitive work on the assembly line. Where systems approaches prevailed, where research and development really was important, there was employment for the growing breed of 'white-coated workers' who required special training and skills and whose working environment was of a salubrious nature unknown on the assembly line or in the old heavy industries. Many technocrats did indeed come from working-class backgrounds and were well on the way to establishing themselves securely within the middle class. But it was not so much that old work places changed; rather that new work places were created for the fortunate and the upwardly mobile.

Work was much studied by academic researchers towards the end of the sixties. Investigations by Fraser, Warr, Wall, and many others brought out its fundamental dualistic character. On the one hand it is the curse by which almost all human beings are afflicted; on the other it is the activity through which most people establish their identity, feel pride, and, perhaps, find fruition: or, at least, it is the activity which fills the largest slice of any person's time between birth and death. On the whole upper-class (top professional and business) and middle-class (other business and professional) occupations offered most scope for personal satisfaction; lower-middle-class and working-class occupations least. Yet, obviously, the critical significance of work at all levels cannot be ignored. A factory apprentice spoke to Fraser of 'the unforgettable claustrophobic comradeship' of the factory:

It is a friendship generated of common experience, common income and common worktasks. Out of this shared pattern of experience grows a common culture of the workplace. And like other cultures it can never be fully understood by the outsider . . . On that first morning at work I began to learn all the expected patterns of response, all the rewards and sanctions, just as an infant learns its native tongue. I quickly learned the harsh language of aggressive friendship; the need to identify myself with the workgroup in opposition to all forms of authority from the chargehand up. Nothing must be allowed to threaten the cohesion of the workers, for only through this 'sticking together' could we solve the problems facing us.

But another of Fraser's interviews, also recorded in his *Work: Twenty Personal Accounts* (1968), this time with a machine-minder in a knitwear factory, well caught the agony of repetitive, yet highly stressful, work:

Watching the cones, checking the fabric, attending the machines which constantly break down, you're on the go all the time. If a machine stops, it must be started, and when it is going the cones are running out and have to be replaced. Hour after hour without break, from one machine to another and back, putting up ends, changing cones, starting the machines and trying to watch the fabric. The machines aren't designed for the operator. You bend low to see the fabric, and climb up on the machine to reach the arms holding the thread. To see all the cones you have to walk twenty-five feet round. Usually an operative has three machines with a total of 150 cones – many of which you can't see immediately because they're on the other side of the machines; you have to memorize which cones are going to run out. With bad yarn the machines snag constantly; it's gruelling keeping everything running . . .

Hey, the machine's stopped. A top red light? Find a stick, disentangle the thread – break off the balled-up yarn, put the end up, check the thread is not caught, press the button, throw the handle. Peer at the fabric – needles? lines from tight yarn? Feel the yarn as it runs, alter the tension; we're not supposed to, it's the supervisor's job but he's too busy. Change a tight cone. A red light above droppers – cone run out? Press-off? A yellow light – the stop motion has come up, maybe something is out of position on the needles, a build-up of thread or a broken needle. Clear the build-up, change the needle, start the machine again. And the other machines, are they all right? One of them stops every other minute on average. Can't spend more than thirty seconds looking at one, leave it for the two others, make sure they're all right, come back to the first. May take five or ten minutes to clear. By the time the trouble's clear, another one's stopped. Break off the bad yarn, disentangle the cone, restart the machine – a few seconds later do the same again.

Working on his thesis 'The perceived determinants of job satisfaction and job dissatisfaction in a chemical firm', Toby Wall received this account from an employee:

If I thought there was hope of ever having more variety than continuously running out batches and cleaning jobs, but to stand under a blender in one position, day after day, just opening and shutting the valve, it's not my idea of satisfactory. Though, as they say, somebody has to do it, but I don't see why it should be me.

Many schemes were mooted in the middle fifties for improving productivity, in particular incentive production bonus schemes and the increased use of automation. The Secretary of the National Motor Joint

Shop Stewards' Committee, in June 1956, produced a neat reaction to automation proposals at the British Motor Corporation.

> Don't let anyone kid you, Brothers, that we don't welcome automation – we do, but the workers must be in a position to have a say in how automation should be used and to have a fair share of the profits. I don't grumble when I get home from work because my wife has been able to sit down in the afternoons because I have bought her a washing machine, a vacuum cleaner and an electric sewing machine. That is the beginning of automation – making the workers' lives easier. Has it made your life easier? I doubt it. We don't welcome mass introduction of machinery just to help the Government get half-a-million on the dole.

Perhaps the very visible growth in the acquisition of durable consumer goods was necessary to help workers forget the conditions of the work place. In 1956 only about 8 per cent of households had had refrigerators; this rose to 33 per cent in 1962 and 69 per cent by 1971. Television sets had been a rarity in the early 1950s; but by 1961 75 per cent of families had one, and by 1971 91 per cent. By 1971, also, 64 per cent of families had a washing machine. Although technological developments elsewhere were matched in the realm of telecommunications, there was not quite the same expansion in households having a telephone. Subscriber trunk dialling was introduced in Bristol in 1958, in London in 1961, and thereafter was slowly extended to other parts of the United Kingdom. In 1951 1.5 million households had had a private telephone; by 1966 this figure had risen to 4.2 million; nevertheless at the end of the decade more than a half of all households, as yet, had no telephone.

The British in general have not been distinguished for their interest in the culinary skills nor for the quality and variety of the food they eat. Affluence brought important changes, though not always absolutely for the better. After meat rationing ended on 1954, average consumption of all meat, meat products, and poultry ran at something above 2 lb. per week. By 1967 consumption had risen only slightly, but fish was re-assuming a more important role in the diet, mainly, however, in the form of pre-packed frozen 'steaks' or 'fingers'. (Fish and chips from that traditional institution, the fish-and-chip shop, of course, retained a constant popularity.) All in all, convenience foods accounted for about a fifth of expenditure on food in 1960; by 1970 this had risen to a quarter.

As world oil supplies dry up and pollution takes its toll of the environment, it is easy to mock the concept of the private automobile as an instrument of personal freedom and power. Yet, if it is not unapt to speak of 'roads to freedom', it is not, perhaps, inept to stress the importance of the cars which ran along them. The expansion in car ownership began in the fifties, but accelerated rapidly in the early sixties: 2,307,000 cars and vans in 1950; 3,609,000 in 1955; 5,650,000 in 1960; 9,131,000 in 1965; 11,802,000 in 1970. In November 1959 the first modest stretch of the M1 motorway was opened. A new era of cultural spoliation and environmental vandalism, but also of undreamt-of mobility, was opening. If the expansion of private transport threatened chaos on the roads and the possibility of bankruptcy for the nationalized railways, who better fitted to assess the problem than one of the new scientist-industrialists? In 1961 Dr Richard Beeching was appointed Chairman of the British Transport Commission. A couple of years later, the Beeching Report on the railways recommended the axing of all branch lines, reducing the railway network from 13,000 to 8,000 miles with a concentration on freight and inter-city services. In the upshot, the system was stabilized at 11,000 miles, but many small towns lost their railway connections none the less. Mobility, perhaps, was fine for those with cars; for many without, in the country areas, there was almost a return to pre-industrial conditions. At the other end of the scale, domestic air travel doubled between 1961 and 1971 from 1,000 million to 2,000 million passenger kilometres.

Thus there were great changes in industrial organization, social geography, and, in lesser degree, in conditions of work. Technology showed itself in one of its most pernicious forms in the beer industry. Here, small breweries were closed down, and large ones built to produce chemicalized beer. While some of the traditional industrial concentrations remained, as, for instance, in sections of the much shrunk coal-mining industry, on the whole the 1960s was the decade in which the new industry superseded the old. Conditions in light engineering works and motor factories were often as tedious as heavy industrial work had always been; but they were generally less dirty and less arduous.

Hopes were not yet gone that the growth of the fifties and sixties, channelled and shaped by the planning ideals of the forties, could yet create a genuinely better environment, though perceptive commentators noted that such great environmental planners of the war years as Barlow and Abercrombie had scarcely bargained for the new technological civilization of the sixties. As one geographer wrote, neatly encapsulating the complacent optimism and pleasantly fearful exuberance of the time:

The achievements of the post-war years have been great and London's expansion has been braked, if not halted; new development has taken place in a controlled, not in a haphazard, fashion; re-development has created and is creating inner areas of which Londoners need no longer be ashamed; the new towns are built. Yet the circumstances of 1960 are very different from those envisaged by Sir Montague Barlow or Sir Patrick Abercrombie, and new forces have risen to promote further growth.

In 1963 the Buchanan Report recommended urban motorways as the remedy for traffic congestion in towns. Planners and developers came together in a clouded vision of brave new architectural concepts, a wish to set up concrete symbols of progress, a need to accommodate to the motor car, and a desire to make affluence yield a decent profit. So the guts were torn out of such cities as Newcastle, Glasgow, and Birmingham and replaced with an ugly jungle of urban motorways and high-rise buildings.

8

Critiques, Boutiques, and Pop

Never is there an era in which no writers or artists are expressing criticism of the society in which they live. It would be wrong to overstate the case for the late fifties and the sixties as a time of special social criticism; indeed, much that was newest and most characteristic rather formed a self-regarding part of the new culture than a forceful criticism set apart from it. Still, a number of influences, often inter-related, often quite different in strength or in kind, can be detected which together produced that transformation in British ideas and modes of behaviour which can, without quite slipping into bathos, be described as forming a 'cultural revolution'.

First, after the parochial post-war years, there was a new openness to ideas and attitudes from both the Continent and the United States. At the most rarefied level philosophers seemed at last to be peering out from the tunnel of linguistic philosophy, and three works of 1959 can be taken as marking a re-kindling of interest in the wider metaphysical issues which had continued to preoccupy the continentals: *Individuals* by Peter Strawson, *Thought and Action* by Stuart Hampshire, and *Words and Things* by the expatriate Parisian Jew Ernest Gellner. The most powerful (and influential – the book went through six impressions by 1970) demonstration of a new mood in philosophy and of the gathering strength of the social sciences was Peter Winch's *The Idea of a Social Science and Its Relation to Philosophy* (1958): 'Any worthwhile study of society,' he declared, 'must be philosophical in character and any worthwhile philosophy must be concerned with the nature of human society.' Historical writing, too, seemed to be shaking off the dead-hand of relativism which had lain across it for so long, and historians began to take an interest both in the non-European world and in the methodology of social science.

Above all, structuralism – put simply, the attempt to find the underlying structures in apparently the most impressionistic and diverse of human activities – in part through the diffusion of the ideas of the French anthropologist Claude Lévi-Strauss, greatly influenced the humanities and the social sciences, most strikingly, perhaps, in the realm of English literature, so long the softest of all the arts subjects. Structural linguistics, and pursuit of the universals in all human language, were advanced by the disciples of the American Noam Chomsky, particularly at Edinburgh University under the influence of the leading Chomskyite, Professor John Lyons.

Certain other American influences were of such a specific character that they must be separated out into a second category of their own. The point was that America had for years had the style of advanced economic and technological society into which Britain was now edging. Earlier American responses now struck a chord in Britain. Herbert Marcuse's *One-Dimensional Man* (1964) and Marshall McLuhan's *Global Village* (1968) became clichés, along with Galbraith's *Affluent Society*. There was no one political trend: broadly the critiques were of the soullessness and standardization involved in mass technological society; yet from Daniel Bell's *The End of Ideology* (1960) came the view that the old political divisions were redundant.

A more positively political trend, thirdly, was the revivification of the intellectual left. A greater opening to continental influences, and an emphasis, above all, on the lesser-known early writings of Karl Marx, helped to create the more humane 'New Left' which turned away from economic determinism towards the concept of the alienation inherent in contemporary industrial society. The *Universities' and Left Review*, founded in 1957, merged in 1960 into the *New Left Review*.

But, fourthly, there was another purely indigenous school of commentators concerned with the twin problems of Britain's rather poor economic showing (despite affluence) compared with her, by now, flourishing competitors, and her decline in world influence. On the former there was general agreement among those who were to the right of the Labour Party or the left of the Conservative Party that in some way or another Britain had gone 'soft', on the latter there was disagreement between those who accused Britain of maintaining delusions of world grandeur, and those who attacked her for, in the brilliant phrase of John Mander (*Great Britain or Little England?*, 1963), taking a 'holiday from history'. Among those Mander had in mind were members of the Campaign for Nuclear

Disarmament (CND) founded in 1958. Like Richard Hoggart's *The Uses of Literacy* (see below, page 98), CND very much marked a period of transition in British society. Its leaders were largely upper class and upper-middle class; it was very much in the tradition of British radical dissent. Yet it pointed the way towards the participatory sixties: it involved housewives (though usually middle-class ones), and, as opinion polls showed, it had the support of between one quarter and one third of the British public. The campaign reached a peak in 1960 when the annual Labour Party Conference adopted a resolution in favour of Britain's unilateral nuclear disarmament. Thereafter, however, the campaign seemed to lose impetus; a similar resolution was rejected by the following year's Conference, in itself a rather arbitrary matter, given Labour's block-vote system of 'democracy', but, more significantly, the polls suggested a decline in public support.

Typical studies of the economy were Michael Shanks's *The Stagnant Society* (1961), Eric Wigham's *What's Wrong with the Unions?* (1961), and Rex Malik's *What's Wrong with British Industry?* (1964) – all published in paperback by Penguin Books. A wider front was covered by Anthony Sampson's *Anatomy of Britain* (1962), Brian Magee's *The New Radicalism* (1962), and the collection of essays edited by Arthur Koestler, *Suicide of a Nation* (1963). In February 1963 Koestler wrote in the *Observer*:

> In no other country has the national output been crippled on such frivolous and irresponsible grounds. In this oldest of all democracies class relations have become more bitter, trade union politics more undemocratic than in De Gaulle's France and Adenauer's Germany. The motivation behind it is neither communism, socialism, nor enlightened self-interest, but a mood of disenchantment and cussedness.

Much of the economic and political analysis was rather shallow. Far more profound was the shift, in the world of intellect and imagination, away from the literalism and representationalism which had dogged British literature and drama, and to some extent also the visual arts, since the war. At last technology was allowed to influence artistic form. At last intellectuals began to overcome their contempt for the film as a form of expression. New aesthetic concepts influenced art and architecture. There is so much in all this that detailed exemplification must await the closing sections of this chapter. For the moment my concern is to pin down the whole gamut of influences and changes.

Fifthly, then, there were the reactions of those within the little world of art, entertainment, thought, and religion towards the new consumer society in which hitherto underprivileged and silent groups now had, if not a voice, certainly purchasing power. These reactions involved both a general populism, and a special veneer of appealing to and being influenced by youth. Perhaps the best single example is the attempt of the Anglican John Robinson to popularize the more libertarian *avant garde* theology in his book with the catchpenny title *Honest to God* (1963). At its most appealing the reaction within the world of entertainment burst out in the 'satire boom' of the early sixties, which was itself very much grounded in exuberant undergraduate irreverence for authority. Its two major products were the weekly magazine *Private Eye* and the television show *That Was the Week That Was* broadcast, wonder of wonders, by the BBC.

A sixth force is that of youth. At root this was an economic phenomenon related to the new spending power created by the new technological high-wage society. Youth, of course, can mean many different things depending upon the standpoint. The 'angry young men' were certainly not youths. But their writings, and the publicity which surrounded them, helped none the less to create the notion of a culture led by individuals of a rather younger age than had hitherto been usual: there was a kind of 'shunting' effect – intellectuals were now fifteen or twenty years younger than they used to be, so the age of popular entertainers and fashion-setters, too, was shunted back by fifteen or twenty years. Technological developments, allied with the particular turn taken by popular music, were, as we shall see, to give youth a particular hegemony over that aspect of popular culture.

When we speak of youth we begin to move away from influences mediated through the upper and middle classes, or rather through minorities belonging to these classes. And so we make a quantum leap to consider something rather different and of great significance in its own right: the emergence of a new conception of the nature of the working class and its role in society. It became fashionable to speak of the cultural ambience of the sixties as 'classless': a number of individuals from working-class backgrounds did indeed achieve personal eminence, and this is a fact of some considerable significance. But the crucial development was the beginnings of a perception of the working class not as stereotype, not as banner-bearer of the future, but as itself, on its own terms. The seminal work was written by a product of the Leeds working class, a graduate of Leeds University who occupied a faintly low-status appointment on the fringes of academic life at a not very celebrated provincial university: Richard Hoggart was Senior Staff Tutor in Literature at the Department of Adult Education, Hull University, when his *The Uses of Literacy* was published in hardcover in 1957: it was reprinted as a Penguin thirteen times between then and 1977.

Hoggart cautioned against two romantic idealizations of the working class: as the earnest Jude the Obscure seeking after knowledge, or as the class-conscious political activist. Of the seekers after knowledge Hoggart commented: 'They are exceptional, in their nature untypical of working-class people; their very presence at summer schools, at meetings of learned societies and courses of lectures, is the result of a moving-away from the landscape which the majority of their fellows inhabit without much apparent strain.' Those who idealized the political activists, he said, 'overrate the place of political activity in working-class life' and 'do not always have an adequate sense of the grass-roots of that life'. He then went on:

A middle-class Marxist's view of the working classes often includes something of each of the foregoing errors. He pities the betrayed and debased worker, whose faults he sees as almost entirely the result of the grinding system which controls him. He admires the remnants of the noble savage, and has a nostalgia for those 'best of all' kinds of art, rural folk art or genuinely popular urban art, and a special enthusiasm for such scraps of them as he thinks he can detect today. He pities and admires the Jude-the-Obscure aspect of working people. Usually, he succeeds in part pitying and part patronizing working-class people beyond any semblance of reality.

I have spoken of openings towards populism, towards youth, towards the working class. But that certainly did not mean a new culture, more inclusive, more unified than ever before. The very pace of technological change, the very multiplicity of new inputs, meant the opening of a gulf between the proponents of the new culture and the older generation. It was perhaps this, above all, that led the new culture to present itself in an overemphatic, and sometimes even shrill, manner. Always, of course, there has been an *avant garde* cut off from the mass of respectable society. But the new culture was much more widely diffused than any *avant garde* culture had ever been; and it was not necessarily, anyway, in any sense 'progressive'. But the tension between old and new was undoubtedly there, and I would rank that tension eighth of the forces we are now discussing. Ninth is the point that out of all the flux and upheaval new groups were formed protesting against established society on behalf of various minorities. In general there was a current of opinion in favour of what came to be termed 'permissiveness'. This actually had two distinct origins. There were those who argued vociferously for freedom as a part of a human need for self-expression and went to lengths which to others seemed to transgress the frontiers of civilized behaviour. The other source lay with the highly civilized, who saw themselves at the head of a long tradition favouring toleration, dating back to John Stuart Mill and earlier. But there was no one-way trend. In 1964 Mrs Mary Whitehouse set up her 'Clean-up TV' campaign. A running battle between the advocates of permissiveness and tolerance and those of purity and censorship was joined: that battle in itself served to publicize the fact that change indeed was taking place.

Many of these forces came together in what was a kind of overarching characteristic: an attack upon the cosiness, the clichés, the stereotyped assumptions, and the parochialism of British society. But this attack itself became a trend, itself almost became a part of the cosiness of British society. However, that is to debunk too much. In the end, for all the tinsel and for all the posturing, there was an almost un-British vibrance in popular culture, in verbal expression, and in the arts and entertainment, which adds up, as far as anything ever can, to a cultural revolution. Some of the detail will be studied later in the chapter.

Two non-fiction works, published in 1957, both illustrate many of the forces just described and helped to accelerate them. In introducing the collection of essays entitled *Declaration*, which he had edited, Tom Maschler explained that 'a number of young and widely opposed writers have burst upon the scene and are striving to change many of the values which have held good in recent years'. These writers, who had recently achieved fame as 'the angry young men', were, Maschler reminded his readers, 'in their twenties and thirties'. Notably missing from the line-up was Kingsley Amis, whose reply on being invited to contribute had been: 'I hate all this pharisaical twittering about the "state of our civilization" and I suspect anyone who wants to buttonhole me about my "rôle in society". This book is likely to prove a valuable addition to the cult of the Solemn Young Men; I predict a great success for it.'

First among those who did contribute was the socialist novelist Doris Lessing, then in her late thirties. 'British life,' she wrote, 'is at the moment petty and frustrating. The people of these islands are kindly, pleasant, tolerant; apparently content to sink into ever-greater depths of genteel poverty' – the poverty, in her view, was caused by the heavy expenditure on armaments. 'The working people,' she continued, 'get their view of life through a screen of high-pressure advertising; sex-sodden newspapers and debased films and television; the middle classes, from a press which from *The Times* to the *New Statesman* is debilitated by a habit of languid conformity which is attacking Britain like dry rot.'

Colin Wilson, twenty-six at the time *Declaration* was published, stuck to a personal exploration of his own philosophical position, essentially a pseudo-Nietzschean glorification of certain 'outsider' figures, including Nietzsche, T. E. Lawrence, and himself. John Osborne (twenty-eight), while also self-centred, was very pungent. The phrase 'There aren't any good, brave causes left' to which critics of *Look Back in Anger* had attributed a central explanatory role, he explained as merely an expression of 'ordinary despair'. 'At every performance of any of my plays, there are always some of these deluded pedants, sitting there impatiently, waiting for the plugs to come singing in during natural breaks in the action . . . There they sit, these fashionable turnips, the death's heads of imagination and feeling, longing for the interval and its over-projected drones of ignorance. Like the BBC critics, they either have no ear at all, or they can never listen to themselves.'

The fullest and most subtle historical analysis was provided by John Wain (thirty-two). He suggested that great social changes had been initiated at the beginning of the century but had then never been consummated. In the forties writers and intellectuals could still impress by simply being portentous and solemn, but in the fifties a more critical appraisal of society had become imperative: 'How *can* anyone say that he accepts, or rejects, the twentieth century *en bloc*? It is too full of unresolved muddles for that.' Kenneth Tynan and Bill Hopkins, the drama critic and the novelist, both just thirty, confined themselves to the brief of talking about their own special fields. Lindsay Anderson (thirty-four, and second in age only to Doris Lessing) also wrote on his special concern as a film director but managed to make a number of points of considerable general significance. His essay began:

Let's face it; coming back to Britain is always something of an ordeal. It ought not to be, but it is. And you don't have to be a snob to feel it. It isn't just the food, the sauce bottles on the café tables, and the chips with everything. It isn't just saying goodbye to wine, goodbye to sunshine. After all, there are things that matter even more than these; and returning from the Continent, today in 1957, we feel these strongly too. A certain, civilised (as opposed to cultured) quality in everyday life: a certain humour: an atmosphere of tolerance, decency and relaxation. A solidity, even a warmth. We have come home. But the price we pay is high.

For coming back to Britain is also, in many respects, like going back to the nursery. The outside world, the dangerous world, is shut away: its sounds are muffled . . . Nanny lights the fire, and sits herself down with a nice cup of tea and yesterday's *Daily Express*; but she keeps half an eye on us too . . .

After the shock of encountering nanny, one might reflect that at that time not too many British people did go to the Continent, though no doubt many of those who did belonged to that class which employed nannies. In the familiar way, Anderson actually describes himself as 'upper-middle-class', his father having been an army officer, his mother the daughter of a wool merchant; he had been educated at a preparatory and at a public school. However, the open attempt to place himself socially was significant. He then went on to point out that the British cinema had produced practically no proper working-class films. Indeed, he found working in the cinema a great cause for despondency: the British simply did not take film as a serious and creative medium in the way in which foreigners did.

Finally, there was a statement both more personal and more sweeping than any of the others, by Stuart Holroyd, at twenty-four the youngest of the contributors, who, on leaving school, had worked as an author and critic before going to university and becoming a professional philosopher. His declaration was that 'A sense of crisis is one of the first things needful in the writer today. He must see the crisis of our time as a threat to human freedom, and must seek to restore freedom in the only way possible: by deepening inwardness and, by means of his psychological vision, extending the limits of consciousness.'

Against *Declaration* I want to place Hoggart's *The Uses of Literacy*. I have already stressed Hoggart's perception of the working class as it really was, rather than as a figment of upper-class intellectual imagination. Perhaps more graphically than it had ever been done before, Hoggart brought home the physical reality, the geography, of class. Working-class houses, he said,

are fitted into the dark and lowering canyons between the giant factories and the services which attend them; 'the barracks of an industry' the Hammonds called them. The goods-lines pass on embankments in and around, level with many of the bedroom windows, carrying the products of the men's work to South Africa,

Nigeria, Australia. The viaducts interweave with the railway lines and with the canals below; the gas-works fit into a space somewhere between them all, and the pubs and graceless Methodist chapels stick up at intervals throughout. The green stuff of the region forces its way where it can – and that is almost everywhere – in stunted patches. Rough sooty grass pushes through the cobbles; dock and nettle insist on a defiant life in the rough and trampled earth-heaps at the corners of the waste-pieces, undeterred by 'dog-muck', cigarette packets, old ashes; rank elder, dirty privet, and rosebay willow-herb take hold in some of the 'backs' or in the walled-off space behind the Corporation Baths. All day and all night the noises and smells of the district – factory hooters, trains shunting, the stink of the gas-works – remind you life is a matter of shifts and clockings-in-and-out. The children look improperly fed, inappropriately clothed, and as though they could do with more sunlight and green fields.

That Hoggart was writing very much at a time of transition in British social history is brought out by the stress he places on the geographical immobility of the working man:

The car has not reduced distance for him; the trains are no faster than they were three-quarters of a century ago. True, he will usually travel by bus if he has to travel, but the point is that he normally has to undertake very little travel except within a mile or two. The local quality of the day-to-day life of a working-class man is well-illustrated by the way he will still trudge half-way across town with a handcart or old pram, transporting a sixth-hand kitchen table he has picked up cheap from someone who knew someone. It will take the better part of an evening, but seems normal procedure. One is reminded of Tess of the d'Urbervilles moving from one valley to another and seeming, to herself, to move from one country to another. The contrast is not so acute, but the working-man in this instance is nearer Tess than he is to the city solicitor who runs out seven miles for a round of golf. For plenty of working-class people a bus journey to relatives half-way across the county is still a matter for considerable thought and upheaval.

While stressing the cultural homogeneity of the working class, Hoggart also put a special emphasis on what was to appear as one of the characteristic figures of the time, the working-class scholarship child 'emotionally uprooted from their class, often under the stimulus of a stronger critical intelligence or imagination' and who can never escape from 'an underlying sense of some unease'.

However, the dynamic concern of Hoggart's book was with the way in which, while material conditions improved, many of the accompanying cultural changes, particularly the debased popular reading matter referred to also by Doris Lessing, were destroying some of the best things in the working-class heritage.

... it would be a mistake to regard the cultural struggle now going on as a straight fight between, say, what *The Times* and the picture-dailies respectively represent. To wish that a majority of the population will ever read *The Times* is to wish that human beings were constitutionally different, and is to fall into an intellectual snobbery. The ability to read the decent weeklies is not a *sine qua non* of the good life. It seems unlikely at any time, and is certainly not likely in any period which those of us now alive are likely to know that a majority in any class will have strongly intellectual pursuits. There are other ways of being in the truth. The strongest objection to the more trivial popular entertainments is not that they prevent their readers from becoming highbrow, but that they make it harder for people without an intellectual bent to become wise in their own way.

... The new-style popular publications fail not because they are poor substitutes for *The Times* but because they are only bloodless imitations of what they purport to be, because they are pallid but slicked-up extensions even of nineteenth-century sensationalism, and a considerable decline from the sinewy sensationalism of Elizabethan vernacular writers.

Hoggart was no Jeremiah. He noted as encouraging the fact that although the working class might be exploited through the pushing of trivialized entertainment, at least they had now 'to be approached for their consent'. He could see that some of the worst developments that he feared might be a temporary facet of a particular development in technological society. The challenge was to maintain the freedom of an 'open' society while the process of centralization and technological development continued.

The upper-class end of the new social critique of the late fifties was kept up by the publication in 1959 of *The Establishment*, edited by a young diplomat who was to turn historian, Hugh Thomas. As Thomas later explained it, this collection of essays was 'dedicated to the theme that the most sensitive institutions in England were dominated by the same anachronistic master class'; the phrase 'the establishment', meaning this 'master class', had gained a certain currency earlier in the fifties. Nine years later, Thomas published another collection, *Crisis in the Civil Service*, which serves as quite a good measure of the progress of this particular social debate over the 1960s. The assumption in 1959 'was that once class was swept away, proud old England would reassert herself as a society both humane and industrially efficient and capable of exercising by her example a moral force for good in the world'. But by 1968 British weaknesses were rather seen as due to 'well-established and broad national attitudes rather than those of an élite'.

Throughout this book I have stressed the importance of class; I have also stressed the significance of the geographical variety of British society. If we are to talk of new critiques and new social trends we have to try to distinguish between what had a relatively limited impact within London itself, and what spread across the outlying provinces. Boutiques figure in the title of this chapter because they symbolize so many of the points laid out in my opening paragraphs. They represented a reaction against the mass presentation of department stores and big advertising. They had absorbed a *soupçon* of continental dash. Their appeal was to the youthful. They became a self-regarding and self-serving trend. It was actually in 1955 that Mary Quant and Alexander Plunkett-Greene opened their first Bazaar in the King's Road, Chelsea; within a year or two John Stephen had arrived from Glasgow and was opening his first shop in Carnaby Street, near Oxford Circus in London. It took a dozen years or more before boutiques were to be found in every provincial urban centre.

Accompanying the rise of the boutiquier went the rise of the photographer. Cameras were to art and advertising what washing machines were to domestic life: they fitted well into the international (the Germans were the great innovators) and, fairly, classless world of gadgetry. Where an upper-class figure, Anthony Armstrong-Jones, led the way, he was quickly followed by two upwardly mobile products of the London working class, David Bailey and Terence Donovan.

But the central feature, undoubtedly, of the cultural revolution was the transformation of the popular music scene. The pop revolution had all the ambivalence of the other developments characteristic of the sixties. It sprang out of the separate culture of youth, yet it depended upon the spending power of the affluent teenager. It expressed protest against established society and the organized music industry, yet it became a massive commercial enterprise. It was genuinely innovative musically, yet it spawned a mass of repetitive trivia. It had a true do-it-yourself participatory element, yet it became closely bound-up with the wonders of electronics.

American rock and roll music first hit Britain in the middle fifties. The film *Rock Around the Clock* crossed the Atlantic in 1956; Bill Haley went on his epochal tour in 1957. The local, do-it-yourself, response came in the form of skiffle groups. In 1956 lower-middle-class John Lennon and working-class Paul McCartney were playing in the Liverpool group, The Quarrymen. By 1960 the beat group the Silver Beatles had been formed to play in the Liverpool clubs, such as the Cavern and the Jacaranda. Visits to Hamburg equipped the group with new hairstyles and a new cosmopolitan image and exuberance. Decca, Pye, Columbia, HMV, and EMI all refused to record them but in May 1962 they were taken on by George Martin of Parlophone. With a new drummer, Ringo Starr, especially brought in, they recorded and released their first record, 'Love Me Do': it reached the top twenty. Thereafter a series of number-one hits followed. The phenomenon was in origins a local and Liverpool one, though a number of other groups also enjoyed a wider national success through the sale of their records, Gerry and the Pacemakers being the best known.

The Beatles' publicity success reached its peak, and was sustained for several years thereafter, with their American tours of 1964. At the same time, they received the attention of serious music critics. Richard Middleton (in *Pop Music and the Blues*, 1972) has summed up the principal characteristics of their work as including:

first, rhythms, concepts of structure and function and of theme and texture derived, *via* Rock 'n' Roll, from blues, second, a melodic combination of pentatonic and tonal elements, the latter being mostly simply diatonic and folk-like but sometimes having a touch of chromaticism; third, a complex use of harmony, which combines and juxtaposes in different ways tonal progressions of varying complexity, modal progressions, parallel triads and harmonic ostinato, relationship of tonal and non-tonal elements often resulting in an ambivalence of scale and 'key'; fourth, a blues-like but typically 'innocent' vocal style; fifth, a use of vocal response and backing [of a special type]; and sixth, the frequent use, alongside blues-like structures, of verse-and-refrain form, probably derived from folk song and previous popular music traditions. It is the perpetual tempering of one element by another in such a cultural mixture as this (as well as what is retained of the traditional blues techniques of objectification) which is responsible for the sense of irony and control characteristic of the music.

For national and international fame the only possible rivals to the Beatles were the London-based rhythm and blues group the Rolling Stones, who had a stronger pro-youth, anti-establishment, and altogether wilder image than the Beatles. They also came from a social class above the Beatles: when the group was founded, Mick Jagger, lead singer, was a student at the London School of Economics and two other members were at the Sidcup Art School.

Despite the commercial success and hullabaloo attending upon the famous names, this music very definitely had its roots in the hundreds of groups performing in pubs and clubs up and down the country: any collection of young people with a modicum of musical talent could put together the equipment necessary to set themselves up as a pop group. The commercial companies did not initiate the trends; they followed shakily behind. The old song-writer practically disappeared as groups developed their own music and songs. The printed music sheet was passing away, too. A proper record of any number, with all its electronic effects, had to be just that, a *record*. In the fifties, the hit-parade had been judged on sales of sheet music: now it was compiled from the sales of individual records.

It could scarcely be said that the newspapers moulded opinion. More and more, they were themselves a part of mass consumer society. Tighter consolidation of ownership and sharper polarization between quality press on the one side, and popular press on the other, took place. After 1960 a further five national newspapers disappeared; and in 1964 the attempt to run a Labour daily newspaper with some serious political content was finally given up when the *Daily Herald* was transformed into the *Sun*. Between 1959 and 1961 the former Daily Mirror Newspapers Ltd emerged as the massive combine, the International Press Corporation. Roy Thomson took over Kemsley Newspapers, including the *Sunday Times*, in 1959; and in 1966 he bought *The Times* from the Astors. Unlike the Lord Beaverbrook of an earlier era, the great press magnates were not interested in pressing their own personal opinions through their columns: they let the market decide the character of their papers. The deeply entrenched unions in the newspaper industry made sure that however much new technologies might dominate other aspects of British society, they would be kept at bay in the world of newspapers. Yet, in many respects, as money appeared still to be splashing around, such quality papers as the *Sunday Times*, the *Observer*, and *The Times* rose to a level of journalism probably above that seen before in the twentieth century.

Newspapers now had the full competition of television, and the BBC had the full competition of commercial television, which by 1961 was reaching into the homes of 75 per cent of the population. For technical standards, competition proved beneficial; overall the standard of current affairs programmes was high. However, social comedies and dramas showed a ham-handedness which revealed that television was not yet ready to grasp the serious realities of British social structure; broadcasters, and some investigative programmes touching on questions of class, both betrayed the dated upper-class style. The greatest breakthrough was achieved by commercial television when, in late 1960, it presented the first edition of 'Coronation Street', whose characters really did breathe the essence of working-class existence.

But after pop, the most potent evidence of intellectual and artistic renewal in Britain was to be found in the cinema. Three tendencies, relating to what was said at the beginning of this chapter, can be detected: a perceptive social criticism and social satire; an authentic presentation of working-class life-styles; and genuine innovation both in technique and in breaking away from the purely naturalistic film. The classic satire was the Boulting Brothers' film of 1959, *I'm All Right Jack*, which with ruthless gusto exposed the unwitting collusion between the pigheaded, work-shy working class, and the snobbish, arrogant, and corrupt upper class. (Yet within the year, the same production team, without any comment whatsoever, had used a public school setting as the natural background for a vacuous comedy entitled *The French Mistress*.) Clive Donner's *Nothing But the Best* (1966) was a brilliant satire of the enduring upper class: Denholm Elliott, as the black sheep of an upper-class family, coaches Alan Bates, a lower-middle-class clerical worker in a large financial institution, into becoming an accepted member of the upper class: he does not actually have to be able to do anything, but he has to have the right accent and manners, and the proper arrogance. *The* film that ushered in the new explicitness towards not just class, but also sex, was *Room at the Top* (1959), whose social criticism had a sharper cutting-edge than that provided by John Braine's original novel.

The classic portrayal of the working-class environment seen from within was Karel Reisz's interpretation of Alan Sillitoe's *Saturday Night and Sunday Morning* (1960). The disaffection (it is too diffused to be called anger) of the young factory worker is directed against organized society and its bureaucrats, and against the more docile members of the working class, rather than against any identifiable class enemy. Lindsay Anderson had his commercial opportunity with *This Sporting Life* (1963), which, with great subtlety, brought David Storey's inarticulate rugby league footballer to the screen. After the initial failure of his play *The Birthday Party* (1960), Harold Pinter, with his menace-laden plots concentrating on the sudden shifts of dominance in human relationships, emerged as the major playwright of the decade (*The Caretaker*, 1960; *The Homecoming*, 1965); when he teamed up with American-born film director Joseph Losey, British cinema at last abandoned its slavish adherence to the naturalistic conventions (*The Servant*, 1963; *Accident*, 1967). Towards the end of the decade, Lindsay Anderson was responsible for *If* (1968) which after a realistic public school beginning explodes into a futuristic rebellion against this microcosm of British imperial and class rule.

Along the way I have mentioned some of the novels which illustrate the main trends of the times, or were converted into films. As a social commentator, Kingsley Amis became a literary institution: between *Take a Girl Like You* (1960) and *I Want It Now* (1968) a whole sexual revolution had indeed been consummated. John Burgess Wilson, having in 1958 produced *English Literature: A Survey for Students*, emerged briefly in 1963 as Joseph Kell, author of *Inside Mr Enderby*, but was already on the permanent way to literary esteem when, as Anthony Burgess, he published (1962) *A Clockwork Orange* (a futuristic study of excessive mindless violence perpetrated by youth). An imaginative range going outside the traditional novel of social custom was also shown by John Fowles in *The Collector* (1963), *The Magus* (1966), and *The French Lieutenant's Woman* (1969) (which, for example, broke with the naturalistic tradition in offering the reader a choice of conclusions to the story). At middle-brow level – sign indeed of these scientific times – science-fiction was building up a following greater than that ever commanded by thrillers or detective fiction.

Changes were taking place in the means whereby books reached their public. Both the great London commercial circulating libraries and the local twopenny libraries withdrew from business in the early sixties. Two institutions filled the gap. First of all, the public libraries, which up till the Second World War had seen their duties as being basically concerned with the lending of non-fiction works, by the 1964 Libraries and Museums Act had their position confirmed as the officially recognized centre for making books available; libraries were now, as a number of commentators have remarked, the national health service for books. Secondly, the small shops switched over to selling paperbacks. It has been argued that neither development fostered creativity and originality in the production of fiction.

The British were the greatest library users in the world, with about one third of the population registered with a public library; but as buyers of books the British ranked well below the Americans and most West

Europeans. The absolute number of books produced shot up in the sixties as publishers endeavoured to cash in on affluence by publishing works of history, popular sociology, and so on; the number of novels dropped slightly as compared with the fifties. In 1963 2,375 new novels were published which does not compare very impressively with the 2,153 published in 1937. Sales, in general, were poorer than they had been in the thirties. To break even, a first novel had to sell about a thousand copies. An average sale of 1,200–1,400 might be expected, but of this 90 per cent went to libraries. British novels, at 60,000 words, tended to be short compared with American. This, according to John Sutherland, author of *Fiction and the Fiction Industry* (1978), was so that dedicated readers could read six novels a fortnight in the half an hour allocated each evening in bed. Despite innovations elsewhere in Britain, and despite the major experiments taking place on the Continent, the British novel remained fundamentally naturalistic. It now brought in new areas of experience, particularly that of the working class and of women, but in form it was not much changed. Margaret Drabble, successful author of a number of novels, including *A Summer Bird-Cage* (1963), *The Millstone* (1965), and *The Waterfall* (1969), essentially related to the role of women in contemporary society, declared in 1967: 'I'd rather be at the end of a dying tradition, which I admire, than at the beginning of a tradition which I deplore.'

For literary innovation, it was necessary to go to the theatre. A whole clutch of new playwrights, John Mortimer (*What Shall We Tell Caroline?*, 1958), Peter Shaffer (*Five-Finger Exercise*, 1958), Arnold Wesker (*Roots*, 1959), Shelagh Delaney (*A Taste of Honey*, 1959), as well as Harold Pinter, appeared at the end of the fifties. Mortimer declared himself to be particularly concerned with the decline of the upper-middle class; Wesker, unusually for a British playwright, had a very overt, idealist-socialist 'message'. In 1965 Edward Bond exploded violently on to the scene with *Saved*, which explored the condition of society's rejects and their predisposition to senseless violence. The mighty, imaginative, new school of directors went from strength to strength: Peter Hall took over at Stratford in 1960, Peter Brook put on his incredible *Marat/Sade* in 1964. Perhaps partly inspired by transatlantic example, a number of new, often experimental, smaller theatres were opened. In 1959 the Mermaid Theatre opened in the City of London; in 1962 came the Chichester Festival Theatre; in 1963 the Traverse Theatre in Edinburgh; and in 1964 Charles Marowitz began his Theatre of Cruelty (he, like the founder of the

Traverse, Jim Haines, was an American). London, in the 1960s, really could claim to be the drama centre of the world; and the provinces were not doing badly either.

The international artistic style most in vogue in the post-war years had been abstract expressionism. Also from America, there now emanated pop art – the realistic presentation of subjects drawn from advertising, comics, popular idols, and the banal apparatus of everyday life – and optical art. Three British artists, in particular, demonstrated the special vitality of British art in the 1960s, and were in themselves symbols of their times. Two were women and one, when he achieved overnight success, a mere youth. In many ways the sculptor Elisabeth Frink was the most original and most appealing: toughly and uncompromisingly female (rather than feminine) in her powerfully realized, though far from exactly representational, male nudes and horses. Bridget Riley became one of the international leaders of the op-art movement; the critic David Thompson has spoken of 'a kind of optical situation which constantly recurs in her later work – that of a dominant formal pattern under pressure of disintegration'. David Hockney, a lower-middle-class boy from Bradford, vegetarian and conscientious objector, took to etching at college because he could not afford the materials for painting, visited New York on £100 he had managed to save, and produced the series of etchings, The Rake's Progress, which made him £5,000 while still a student. He showed an eclecticism and inventiveness worthy, at times, of Picasso; he drew upon pop art, and showed a healthy disrespect for the canons of wisdom handed down in the colleges: 'I have stopped bothering about modern art, in that at one time you would be frightened of doing things in painting because you would consider them almost reactionary. I have stopped believing that it's possible for art to progress only in a stylistic way.'

Architectural developments, which so closely mirrored the rise and fall of hopes in respect of social policy and social planning, I leave to the last chapter of 'Roads to Freedom'. The achievements of domestic and industrial design, however, were considerable and fit in well with the more optimistic trends discussed in this chapter. First of all, the careful, rational work of the Council of Industrial Design went steadily ahead, its endeavours enjoying added prestige when the former Anthony Armstrong-Jones, now (as Lord Snowdon) Princess Margaret's husband, joined the Council in 1961. Secondly, design shared in the new populism, the new reaction against supermarket and mass-produced shoddy. As with so much in this era, there was a certain ambivalence about the key event, the establishment by Terence Conran of his shop Habitat in South Kensington in 1964. Instead of individuals (middle class, of course, rather than working class) having to search around for their own individual items of style and charm, Habitat and its imitators would do the work for them. As Conran said: 'We hope we have taken the foot-slogging out of shopping by assembling a wide selection of unusual and top quality goods under our roof. It has taken us a year to complete this pre-digested shopping programme and we are confident that many women will take to this new style of buying with enthusiasm.' Still, many of the shops put on sale items made at home by amateur designers. Nowhere was the reaction against supermarket mass production stronger than in the field of children's toys: Galt, Play and Learn, and several others brought a new standard to British toys.

A third influence was that of pop, introducing the jokey and self-indulgent, the use of new plastics and of psychedelic colours. It might seem that the sober-sides of the Council of Industrial Design were being left behind. In the Society of Industrial Arts journal, Michael Wolff stated:

Basically it is true that the sort of designers in Britain who have really given people a bang in the last two years are Ken Adams, Art Director of the James Bond films; Frederick Starke, with his clothes for Cathy Gale [a popular TV character]; and Ray Cusick, with his daleks [the robots in the children's TV series *Doctor Who*]. People like Mary Quant and John Stephen have had the same sort of impact on a more limited age range. It is their zing, and their zest, and their vigorous understanding of what design is all about which should be one of the main contributions of industrial designers to modern society. It'll be a great day when cutlery and furniture designs (to name but two) swing like the Supremes.

True, there was a tension between pop culture and established culture. But the best of serious design, and pop design, were not necessarily totally antithetical. Paul Reilly of the Council of Industrial Design suggested that:

We are shifting, perhaps, from attachment to permanent universal values to acceptance that a design may be valid at a given time for a given purpose to a given group of people in a given set of circumstances, but that outside those limits it may not be valid at all; and conversely there may be contemporaneous but quite dissimilar solutions that can still be equally defensible for different groups – mini-skirt for the teenager, something less divulging for the matron; painted paper furniture for the young, teak or rosewood for the ageing – and all equally of their times and all equally susceptible to evaluation by a selection committee. All this means is that a product must be good of its kind for the set of circumstances for which it has been designed.

Above all, the Council of Industrial Design was at its most successful in its efforts to persuade British industrialists of the importance of contemporary design. 'It had,' wrote Fiona MacCarthy, 'won a famous victory, with questions in the House, over the design of the new Cunard liner, demolishing forever the tendency in industry to leave design decisions to the Chairman's wife.' Council of Industrial Design policies for industry overlapped with a fourth influence discussed in Chapter 7: that of the systems approach dependent on computerization.

The ideas, the images, the literature, the life-styles all showed much of the old cosiness simply transformed into trendiness. But there was a liveliness and a spirit of innovation not seen in British society for generations and which, as never before, had penetrated through so many layers of this still stratified society. In very truth, things would never be quite the same again.

9

The End of Victorianism

The changes in what, in the nineteenth century, the great lawyer-historian A. V. Dicey had called 'law and opinion' – that which was acceptable both in duly constituted courts of law and to prevailing social convention – had little to do with the tenets of socialism or of capitalism. Nor, however, did they just happen. There were pressures from the market place, pressures from youth and popular culture, but also reasoned arguments in favour of a civilized and tolerant society put forward by politicians. The leftist and liberal proponents of a civilized society no doubt had no desire to create a gamblers' paradise; many of those who argued for the individual's rights to waste his money as he willed wanted neither free abortions nor tolerance of homosexuals: but whatever the little local disagreements, all of the 'reforms' of the late fifties and sixties marked a retreat from the social controls imposed in the Victorian era by evangelicalism and non-conformity.

The introduction of commercial television has already been mentioned several times. Next came the introduction in 1956 of the first public lottery since the eighteenth century, the Premium Savings Bonds scheme. Up till 1960 the very strict and somewhat arbitrary legislation governing betting and gaming, itself largely a product of Victorian evangelicalism and snobbery, had resulted in widespread evasion of the law, especially in the form of the passing of betting slips on street corners and in pubs. The main purpose of the 1960 Betting and Gaming Act was the sound conservative one of restoring respect and credibility to the law by openly legalizing certain forms of gambling: street betting shops, gambling clubs, and bingo followed. As the racketeers moved in on the new clubs, it became clear that perhaps there was something to be said for Victorian controls after all.

In the mid nineteenth century drugs had been widely accessible, and controls were established only in the late Victorian period. In the 1950s, drug control was administered in accordance with the best and most liberal paternalistic principles. Drug users, very largely the middle-aged and elderly, were registered, and could receive their particular poison on the National Health Service. British officialdom prided itself on this open system, which seemed to have preserved the country from the horrors of the illicit drug trade which went on in the United States. As the wonders of science marched forward, hand in hand with the wonders of the National Health Service, more and more people, mostly older women, became dependent on the new psychotropic drugs, that is to say, sleeping pills, appetite suppressants, tranquillizers, and anti-depressants. By the early sixties it was clear that the official complacency over the workings of British drug control was quite unjustified: doctors were consistently, though innocently and ignorantly, over-prescribing, and the surplus was finding its way into a new black market.

The new element on the scene was that prosperous and aggressive youth which has been referred to already on several occasions (though it was still far from true that young people were the main drug addicts). In understanding the growth and influence of drug consumption in the 1960s it is important to distinguish between four major areas. First of all, the amphetamines and other pills and capsules operating upon the central nervous system; second, heroin and the other 'needle drugs': together these had been the main sources of narcotic indulgence by adults in the fifties; third, cannabis, a source throughout the ages for a minority, but in the sixties the characteristic drug of youth and the older figures who identified with youth culture; finally, the new invention, LSD, and the other psychedelic drugs.

In 1951 the major pharmaceutical company Smith, Klein, and French came up with the new amphetamine Drinamyl: served up as a blue triangular-shaped pill, it was eventually to become notorious as the 'purple heart'. By the early 1960s it was clear that there was a racket in purveying purple hearts and other amphetamines to certain adolescents, many from a working-class background. The spread of amphetamines coincided with the rise of the particular conservatively dressed youth groups known as the 'mods'. Officialdom was stirred out of complacency and, in what may well seem a contradiction of the general trend against social controls described here, the 1964 Drugs (Prevention of Misuse) Act was passed, making the possession of amphetamines without a prescription an offence.

The central development of the sixties was the spectacular growth in the availability and use of cannabis. *Cannabis sativa* is the name of the hemp plant which grows throughout the world: the flowering leaves and tops provide marijuana, popularly known as pot, and the form most usually taken in the United States; cannabis resin provides hashish, the form usually found in Britain, though here too it is sometimes referred to as pot. Cannabis did become very much the basic drug of a widespread youth culture; and by the later sixties it was also being taken by many of those, no longer young, who were in occupations related to the burgeoning popular culture, or who were in the universities, or who were even in the more traditional professions. The Wootton Committee, reporting in 1968, reckoned that there might be anything from 30,000 to 300,000 cannabis users; other estimates suggested that in 1970 there might have been anything from one million to two million.

LSD (lysergic acid diethylamide) is a synthetic drug which was discovered in 1938 by the Swiss scientist Hofmann; it is derived from ergot, a substance produced, rather easily, by fermenting rye. LSD was used therapeutically, though perhaps dubiously, in Britain from 1954 onwards. Above all, in the middle sixties, it was the drug of the San Francisco underground culture. Its spread to Britain was probably on a very limited scale. However, hashish and LSD were, together, thought of as 'mind-expanding' drugs: they were associated with the San Francisco scene, with resistance to the Vietnam War, with support for peace in general, with transcendentalism, and with 'flower power'. In the summer of 1967 the American hit, Scott MacKenzie's 'San Francisco', also reached the top of the hit-parade in Britain. The influence of the psychedelic drug culture on British popular music after 1967 could be seen, for instance, in such titles as the Beatles' 'Lucy in the Sky with Diamonds' (the initials, of course, spelling out LSD) and Procul Harum's 'A Whiter Shade of Pale'.

The flower-power, psychedelic, dream quickly went sour in America. The wide use of cannabis undoubtedly continued in Britain, but there was also a new, tragic swing in the use of amphetamines: from 1967 onwards certain groups of adolescents were taking amphetamines intravenously in the style of American 'speed freaks'.

For the most part, though, it must be stressed, the use of cannabis proceeded unobtrusively and harmlessly. Illicit drug taking was only a small part of a new sense that, suddenly, the forces of law and order, so painstakingly established in Victorian times, were now suddenly breaking down.

The acceleration in the crime rate was apparent from the mid-fifties onwards. From the mid-thirties to the mid-fifties offences of violence against the person had risen by about 6 per cent a year. From then onwards they went up by about 11 per cent a year. The total figures for crimes of violence went like this: 5,869 in 1955, 11,592 in 1960, 15,976 in 1964, and 21,046 in 1968. The increase in criminality was a feature of the population as a whole, but it was most significant in the seventeen to twenty-one, the fourteen to seventeen, and even the eight to fourteen age groups. The seriousness of the general situation seemed to be highlighted by such spectacular events as the great train robbery of 1963, with its brutal attack on the engine driver, the Moors murders of 1965, which involved particularly sadistic and grisly murders of children, the Shepherds Bush police murders of 1966, and the arrest and trial of the notorious East End criminals, the Kray brothers, in 1969 which brought out just what a vicious, and again sadistic, pair they were. The 1966 general election campaign was the first one in which 'law and order' featured as a major campaign issue.

Some careful researches by Michael Zander have suggested that even a massive increase in the police forces would have very little effect on the actual number of crimes committed; similarly, increasing the severity of penalties seems to have little effect. The roots of the rise in crime must be sought in the economic and cultural changes which we have been discussing. The Committee on Children and Young Persons, reporting in October 1960, offered some wise words on the rise in juvenile crime:

During the past fifty years there has been a tremendous material, social and moral revolution in addition to the upheaval of two wars. While life has in many ways become easier and more secure, the whole future of mankind may seem frighteningly uncertain. Everyday life may be less of a struggle, boredom and lack of challenge more of a danger, but the fundamental insecurity remains with little that the individual can do about it. The material revolution is plain to see. At one and the same time it has provided more desirable objects, greater opportunity for acquiring them illegally, and considerable chances of immunity from the undesirable consequences of so doing. It is not always so clearly recognized what a complete change there has been in social and personal relationships (between classes, between the sexes and between individuals) and also in the basic assumptions which regulate behaviour. These major changes in the cultural background may well have replaced the disturbances of war as factors which contribute in themselves to instability within the family.

With regard to youthful offenders, one might stress the new aggressiveness and hostility to authority of youth in general; one might stress the temptations of the affluent society, going often with frustrations for those who found that in fact nothing opened before them but dead-end jobs. For the crime rate in general, one might stress the acquisitive aspect of the ethos of 'having it good' and the destabilizing influence of a situation in which, although living standards were generally rising, often the contrasts between those who were prospering and those who weren't were becoming sharper; but that would perhaps seem to make too many excuses – much of the villainy of the time was cold and calculated, and carried through with the ruthlessness of a business operation. Perhaps the standards of civic loyalty and respect for law and order had never been as high as conservative romantics affected to believe. There is no easy way of rooting out deviants in society; but certainly the special conditions of the late fifties onwards gave deviants full rein.

Perhaps the increase in crime should be seen more as a return to Victorianism rather than a move away from it, but there can be no doubts about the most significant of all the pieces of civilizing legislation, the abolition of capital punishment. In October 1965 an Act got through Parliament abolishing hanging as a five-year experiment. But before the five years were up, late in 1969, James Callaghan, the Home Secretary, decided to make abolition permanent. The first three years of the experiment had demonstrated convincingly, as was well known in any case to all authorities on the subject, and had been demonstrated from foreign experience, that there was no clear connection between the number of murders committed and the existence of the death penalty.

The solid, respectful, friendly British 'bobby', in so far as he ever fully existed in reality, was the product of the police reorganization of the late Victorian period (and makes some of his most solid appearances in the Sherlock Holmes stories). In the post-war years, the image (strongly presented in the original Dixon of Dock Green film *The Blue Lamp*) was remarkably unchanged, though the TV series *Z Cars* brought a more realistic image in the sixties. Two particular features distinguished the British police from their continental counterparts. First was the manner in which the separate forces (157 of them in the early sixties) were administered locally not nationally; only the Metropolitan Police was directly under the authority, through the Metropolitan Police Commissioner, of the Home Secretary. Second was the fact that, save, very occasionally, for a very few officers under very special circumstances, the

British police were not armed. The Police Act of 1964 did strengthen the supervisory powers of the Home Secretary over all police forces, and at the same time a movement began towards amalgamating the smaller police forces. The spectacularly violent crimes of the sixties produced a situation in which the police themselves were having greater resort to firearms than the traditional image warranted. In 1965 the Special Patrol Group (SPG) of the Metropolitan Police was established on the analogy of the various riot control groups to be found on the Continent. In general the appearance was of a tougher, more professional, police force. In 1964 there were about 80,000 (policewomen as well as policemen) in the various forces; by 1973 there were over 111,000 though this was still below the paper 'establishment'. The legal system and the administration of justice remained little affected by social change in the sixties. Only in the early seventies did standing committees and commissions begin to wrestle with the Herculean task of dragging the law and its procedures out of the nineteenth century.

One of the first public signs of a significant relaxation in the Victorian moral code was the result of the trial for obscenity in 1960 of the publishers of *Lady Chatterley's Lover*. Since its completion by D. H. Lawrence in the 1920s, *Lady Chatterley's Lover* had not been available in this country: Penguin Books took a calculated decision to republish it. With many expert literary witnesses speaking for the defence, and with the prosecution counsel making an ass of himself in a peculiarly significant way by asking the jury whether the book was one they would wish their servants to read, Penguin Books were acquitted, and it was clear that books containing the same sort of explicit sexual material as Lady Chatterley would now be widely available.

The year 1967 was something of an *annus mirabilis* as far as liberal legislation in the sphere of sexual mores was concerned. First, the Abortion Act, put forward by the Liberal MP, David Steel, but supported by the Government, and also by several Conservatives. It had been possible in recent years for the well-off to secure abortions through private clinics, where doctors and psychiatrists were able to steer through the uncertainties of the existing law dating back to the Victorian era. However, penalties for well-intentioned medical men could still be extremely severe. More critically, for the less well-off woman suffering from an unwanted pregnancy the choices were two: to go through with the birth, or to seek a back-street abortion, with all its attendant horror and danger. That classic film of the affluent working-class swinger, *Alfie* (1966), brought the situation out well enough. Under the new Abortion Act, it was merely necessary that two doctors should be satisfied that an abortion was necessary on medical or psychological grounds: the number of private nursing homes providing this service now greatly expanded, but at least their fees were greatly reduced; it was now possible, though often with the prospect of having to go on a waiting-list, to get an abortion on the National Health Service. The National Health Service (Family Planning) Act of the same year made it possible, for the first time, for local authorities to provide contraceptives and contraceptive advice.

Secondly, thanks to the efforts of a private Labour MP, Leo Abse, the Sexual Offences Act ended (in England and Wales) the long and barbaric tradition whereby male homosexuals had been subject to persecution and blackmail: a homosexual act between two consenting adults in private would no longer be a criminal offence. The effects of these three Acts were cumulative: gradually, 'gays' began to 'come out'; advertisements began to appear in public places providing information on contraception and abortion. Matters which the Victorians had buried under shame and evasion by the barrow-load were now entering fully into the public domain.

For any but the very rich, divorce was practically unobtainable in the Victorian era; and even then it was much easier for a husband to divorce his wife than for the wife to divorce the husband. Right on into the sixties the pejorative concept of 'matrimonial offence' remained; without such an offence being committed by one or other party no divorce could be obtained. Representing a special feminist aspect of the Victorian tradition, Dr Shirley Summerskill claimed that the Divorce Reform Act of 1969 was a 'Casanova's charter'. To most people, feminist and non-feminist, it offered freedom to both sexes from an irksome and unjust social control. Clause One of the Act tore apart the shrouds of centuries: 'After the commencement of this Act the sole ground on which a petition for divorce may be presented to the court by either party to a marriage shall be that the marriage has broken down irretrievably.' Henceforth, if a couple had lived apart for two years, and both consented, they had a right to divorce. If separation had lasted five years then either partner was entitled to a divorce, even if the other partner did not agree. Broadly, the trend in this and other legislation was towards recognizing women as independent individuals. The Matrimonial Property Act of 1970 established that a wife's work, whether as a housewife within the home or as a money-earner outside it, should be considered as an equal contribution towards creating the family home, if, as a result of a divorce, that had to be divided. In the same year was passed the Equal Pay Act. There were exceptions and loopholes, and the Act was not to come fully into law for another five years; but at least the principle of equal pay for equal work had been adumbrated even if not universally established.

Theatrical censorship was abolished in 1968. Theatre-going (like divorce) is a minority activity. But if the crudity and the nudity, the frankness and the four-letter words were to be met at their meatiest in the experimental theatre, openness and explicitness spread more widely both in respectable newspapers and in what could be accepted as polite conversation. The censorship system remained for the cinema but there was a noticeable relaxation here too in what was regarded as acceptable.

In part, the new legislation was due to the exertions of active feminists, though it owed more to deeper social and economic forces favourable to a general liberalization of statutes and attitudes. In the middle and later sixties, the feminist movement in Britain was still only in its springtime; the full summer was yet to come. Springtime is an apt metaphor as liberation, in a very non-political sense, showed itself in the fashion, first, for mini-skirts, and then for hotpants. This sort of liberation, as many steelier feminists grumbled, might well mainly mean a picnic for men. Quite simply, as, of course, the Victorians had always known, a girl scantily dressed was a good deal easier to seduce than one more voluminously clad. Under certain circumstances a girl might feel it better to strengthen her defences by opting to wear a pair of jeans. The attitudes and behaviour quickly summed up at the time as 'permissiveness' resulted from a conjunction of circumstances which helped to remove old restraints and fears and positively encouraged the active sexual life as 'normal'. The pill was not the sole factor – many of the sexually active never touched it – but its advent contributed to a general sense of security for women and girls and to a situation in which contraception (something no respectable girl would have dreamt of mentioning ten years before) could be spoken of openly. Much is sometimes made of the influence of the mass media; it is often forgotten that the most potent means of communication is by word of mouth – that is how girls learned what to do to avoid trouble, and what to do when they found themselves in trouble.

Much in arrears of America and many continental countries, women's liberation in its full political sense was scarcely in evidence in Britain at the end of the 1960s. Perhaps this was another facet of that 'secular Anglicanism' which I have mentioned once or twice: there was still something of a tolerance and genuine courtesy as between men and women which softened the potential antagonisms which in America were already producing such violent and hysterical manifestations as SCUM (Society for Cutting Up Men). The critical event, in so far as there was one, in the development of the contemporary feminist movement in Britain was the publication in 1970 of Germaine Greer's *The Female Eunuch*. This work was to influence the seventies rather as *The Uses of Literacy* had influenced the sixties; it will be discussed in the third part of this book.

On the broader question of citizen's rights, and local participation in decision-making, the British were not just far behind the Americans, they were scarcely in the race at all. But in the sixties middle-class groups did begin to stir into action, offering resistance to urban spoliation in the interests of the easy penetration of the motor car. The turning point came in 1965 when a local group in the newly fashionable Barnsbury enclave in Islington in North London successfully resisted a general LCC development order; there were similar movements in Bath, Oxford, and elsewhere.

A crucial aspect of the liberalization of the 1960s was the major development in the realm of higher education. Many colleges, particularly in the spheres of art and design, were upgraded, as were teacher training colleges; quasi-university status was given to leading colleges of technology – rechristened polytechnics, their degrees were awarded by one *national* body (a sharp break with tradition, this), the Council for National Academic Awards (CNAA), founded in 1964; certain colleges of higher technology became full universities, and totally new universities were created: at the top of the prestige scale was Sussex, followed by York and Kent; with Warwick, Lancaster, and East Anglia in the middle; while Essex and Stirling came lowest in the scale. The student movement of 1968 was relatively mild, and in many ways imitative, compared with the French example – secular Anglicanism at work again perhaps. It took its sharpest forms in the austere environment of Essex, or the cramped urban quarters of the London School of Economics. Youth was certainly not made an enemy of by established society; the Family Law Reform and the Representation of the People Acts (both 1968), respectively, lowered the age of legal majority and the voting age to eighteen.

There were profound changes in other sectors of education as well. By 1964 the arguments against the eleven-plus by sociologists, psychologists, and committed social egalitarians were becoming almost deafening. The new Labour Government in July 1965 issued Circular 10/65 calling upon all local authorities to submit proposals for establishing comprehensive schools. Great impetus was certainly given to the replacement of education divided between secondary modern and grammar schools by comprehensive schooling but within a context of great confusion and inconsistency. Government intentions in regard to direct grant schools were far from clear, local authorities anyway had plenty of licence to go their own ways. Confusion was confounded, inconsistency compounded when the new Conservative Government, in June 1970, issued Circular 10/70 which stressed that the reorganization of secondary education was entirely a matter for the local authorities. Thus there was no unified comprehensive system; but at least deep inroads had been made into a system which, with more than a whiff of Victorianism about it, had essentially selected those from deprived backgrounds to go to secondary modern schools, and those from relatively privileged backgrounds to go to grammar schools.

Where innovation took place that was most in accord with the other changes that have been discussed was in the primary schools. For long enough children had been reared under the shadow of the Victorian faith in the three Rs. One of the first major initiatives towards bringing imaginative new approaches to curriculum design came from a private source, the Nuffield Foundation. In 1964 the Schools Council for the Curriculum and Examinations was set up, with finance coming from the local education authorities. From the Schools Council came many initiatives towards making the primary school curriculum more flexible, more imaginative, and more enjoyable. Of course, just as many respectable and far from wrong-headed citizens deplored what was happening in the universities, old and new, and argued that the spread of comprehensive education was destroying the high academic standards once the pride of the grammar schools, so there were many who thought that primary school children were being given far too much latitude while failing to learn the necessary basic skills.

In so many ways, then, British society seemed to have broken out of the straitjacket of dullness and conformity which had pinioned it since Victorian times. It would be wrong to exaggerate changes in everyday life. The growth in wine drinking, the proliferation of foreign restaurants: these things still affected only a minority. But it would be fair to say that there was a new hedonism abroad in the land; that life was lived with greater gusto than ever it had been since the evangelicals set their stamp upon the mores of the middle class. A symbolic case study was provided by Association Football. The abolition in 1961 of the maximum wage, an achievement of the Professional Footballers' Association under the leadership of Jimmy Hill, and in 1963 of the Victorian master–servant transfer system, enabled the best players to escape into a world of high earnings which, though most players remained working-class in background and manner, had something of that veneer of classlessness to be found in other branches of the entertainments industry. Football became fashionable. As well, participatory sports which had once been the preserve of the prosperous or the eccentric became available to people in most sections of the community: new provision was made for sailing and mountaineering, and new leisure and sports centres were built.

One must be careful over the placing in time of the different changes. The absurd Lady Chatterley trial and the sad fuss over the Profumo episode of 1963 show how persistent were the old morality and the old hypocrisy at the beginning of the decade. (John Profumo, Conservative War Secretary, had consorted with Christine Keller, member of an expensive call-girl circle with which Captain Ivanov, formerly of the Russian Embassy, and Stephen Ward, a society osteopath, were also associated; charged with living on immoral earnings, Ward confirmed the allegations which Profumo had at first publicly denied. During his own trial Ward committed suicide.) Many of the changes, such as the new feminist movement and the citizen's rights movement, just apparent at the end of the decade, only really moved on to their full strengths in the 1970s.

10

Social Structure and Social Strains

When the cultural innovations of the sixties were spoken of as being 'classless', the word was being used in a very limited and rather inaccurate way: certain leading cultural phenomena had sprung out of genuinely working-class antecedents; some working-class individuals had achieved great success; regional accents (middle class as well as working class) were no longer smoothed into a sort of standard southern English pronunciation but were boldly projected, red in tooth and claw.

Certainly, the British people were under no illusion as to the disappearance of class boundaries. Regularly throughout the sixties interviews and opinion polls showed that well over 90 per cent of the population recognized the existence of social classes. When, on one typical occasion, a representative sample were asked, without prompting, to allocate themselves to a social class, 67 per cent said they were 'working-class' and 29 per cent said they were 'middle-class'. Of the remainder, 1 per cent said 'upper-working-class', 1 per cent said 'lower-middle-class', and 1 per cent said 'upper-class'; this left only 1 per cent unable to allocate themselves to any of the traditional classes, including 'one twenty-five stone eccentric' who said he belonged to the 'sporting class'. When pressed to allocate themselves to the 'upper' or 'lower' parts of their class, most were reluctant to do so: only 3 per cent of the middle class moved themselves up into the 'upper-middle class', with 4 per cent moving themselves down into the 'lower-middle class'; 10 per cent of the working class moved themselves up into the 'upper-working class', with only 4 per cent allocating themselves to the 'lower-working class'. This suggests a very strong awareness of the broad divisions between the traditional social classes rather than a sensitivity to the subtle distinctions between different occupations, so often insisted upon by social scientists.

A second survey of Banbury conducted between 1966 and 1968, though not published till 1975, it is true, was unable to confirm the clear-cut class distinctions discovered in the first survey; but as the authors say in their introduction 'much had changed in sociology between the two studies'; perhaps that was more important than what had actually changed in Banbury. Reserving the word 'class' to a somewhat pernickety usage, the authors were still prepared to admit the existence in Banbury of 'three social levels', and to hint that something of an upper class was still to be found in the surrounding areas. Actually, there were still plenty of examples of the upper class's image of itself to be found. A leading local lady, interviewed by Ronald Blythe for his study of *Akenfield* (1969), said: 'I suppose we would be called upper class – in fact, we could hardly be called anything else.' Simon Raven, who ought to have known since his father had had independent means and he was himself brought up in 'Surrey stockbrokers' country', educated at an expensive prep school, at Charterhouse, and at King's College, Cambridge, defined the upper class as controlling or consuming 'the cream of the country's resources, its cash, its offices, its perquisites, its youth – and only have to open their mouths in a yawn to be assured of an attentive and nationwide hearing'. In a little piece of heart-searching, Richard Crossman stumbled on a marvellous phrase about the 'facility of freedom and an amplitude of life' which can well be taken as an upper-class hallmark of the 1960s:

I am sitting here in comfort and am therefore bound to wonder whether that fierce old Tory, my brother Geoffrey, is reasonable when he says that I can't be a socialist and have a farm which makes good profits. I tell him the two are compatible provided that as a member of the government I'm ready to vote for socialist policy to take those profits away and even, in the last resort, to confiscate the property. Nevertheless that isn't a complete answer. Having Prescote deeply affects my life. It's not merely that I am more detached than my colleagues, able to judge things more dispassionately and to look forward to retirement, it's also more crudely that I am comfortably off now and have no worries about money. I can eat, drink and buy what I like as well as adding seventy acres to Prescote Manor Farm. Ann and I have a facility of freedom and an amplitude of life here which cuts us off from the vast mass of people . . .

In his study *Middle Class Families* (1968), based on Swansea, Colin Bell neatly summarized a distinction between those who had made it into the upper class, and those who remained in the middle class: Swansea, he wrote, 'may appear in the first chapters of the autobiographies of the famous; it rarely appears in the last'. Awareness of the distinction between middle class and working class is also brought out in two contrasting career autobiographies presented by Colin Bell. A thirty-eight-year-old chemist remarked that there had been a time 'when I used to think that I was a cliché – the working-class boy who made good, a member of the new middle class, the meritocratic technocrat'. The 'whole question of identity' had been 'very difficult for me and my kind'. But this was no longer a problem 'because I now think I know where I am going'. If, he concluded, 'I can get another couple of notches up I will be able to send the boys to a boarding school . . .' The family of a thirty-nine-year-old wholesaler, on the other hand, had 'always been comfortably off'. As he was the eldest, it had always been assumed that he, at least, 'would go into Dad's business'. Describing those now working for him in his warehouses, he remarked that 'about twenty-two men' were 'what you would call working class'.

Older working-class communities, of the type described by Hoggart, continued to exist in the sixties. In writing of Huddersfield, Brian Jackson stressed the continuing importance of the working men's clubs, noting that there were very few businessmen or small tradesmen in the clubs and that those few preferred to keep a very low profile. The view in Huddersfield was:

> They've got their own clubs and political clubs. It's all working men here. Unlike even the pub, the club has the atmosphere of the working man's home: 'I never go into a pub at all now. Clubs are much more sociable like. Look at this. I couldn't rest my legs across a chair in t'pub. Here it is like being at home. As long I don't put me feet on t'seat, I'm all right.'

There was a clear boundary to the community of mill workers; floor managers, clerical workers, and minor officials were excluded. While they collected a general dislike and mistrust, there was, Dennis Marsden found, 'a grudging respect' for the mill owners. You could, said Jackson, 'trace a line through Huddersfield marking the point where the gap showed between middle-class and working-class life'.

The famous Goldthorpe, Lockwood, Bechofer, and Platt survey of 'the affluent worker' in Luton, covering assembly-line workers at Vauxhall Motors, machine operators and craftsmen servicing machines at the Skefco's Ball Bearing Company, and process workers and craftsmen engaged on process maintenance at Laporte Chemicals, did suggest some fragmentation of traditional working-class images and some blurring of class lines. Fourteen per cent claimed for themselves definite 'middle-class' status, while 8 per cent took the view that they could be described equally well as 'working'-class or 'middle'-class. Yet, 67 per cent had no difficulty in allocating themselves to the 'working class'.

Actually, these 'affluent' workers were still a million miles away from middle-class job satisfactions or from middle-class aspiration after social mobility. The Luton workers stressed the unpleasantness of their work, giving the high pay as its only advantage (70 per cent of white-collar workers, by contrast, did not mention pay, and two-fifths – the highest single group – gave the nature of their work as their greatest source of satisfaction). The Luton workers expressed no very strong feelings against separate canteens: 'I don't like the idea of the boss breathing down my neck at meal times,' said one; 'We wouldn't want *them* listening into my conversation,' said another. All three of the Luton firms encouraged promotion from the shop floor to supervisory, technical, and managerial grades. But in fact, the mass of the labour force did not 'think of themselves as one day likely to become something more than merely wage workers'. In brief, Goldthorpe, Lockwood, Bechofer, and Platt concluded, 'for the large majority of men in our sample the possibility of promotion was of no real significance'.

To be working class in the sixties, then, despite the occasional instance of rapid upward mobility, meant a 'life sentence' of hard manual work where, by an implicit irony, the attainment of middle-class living standards was only possible through expending, on overtime, even more excessive amounts of energy in a traditionally working-class way. At the top, to belong to the upper class still offered disproportionate access to positions of power. More than one third of the Labour Cabinet of 1964 were traditional upper-class figures ('patricians' Dr Timothy May calls them), and six Cabinet members were products of the most exclusive public schools, the 'Clarendon Schools'. Only two Ministers had graduated from universities other than Oxford. It is in that context that one has to see the emergence as Prime Minister of the lower-middle-class, but Oxford-educated, meritocrat, Harold Wilson.

The fruits of social mobility over several generations, and the upper-class socialization process, are well brought out in the career of Edward Heath. His great-grandfather had been a merchant seaman, his paternal grandfather, after running a small dairy business which failed, became a porter at Broadstairs Station on the Southern Railway. His son, Will, Heath's father, became a carpenter. His maternal grandmother was the wife of an illiterate farmworker. On leaving school at fourteen, her very good-looking daughter had gone into domestic service with a middle-class family from Hampstead who spent their summers in Broadstairs. Her mother was proud of this position, with its opportunity for learning middle-class ways, but she was not at all pleased with her daughter's association with Will Heath. She lamented that 'with her looks she could do a lot better'.

The First World War, that great engine of social mobility, provided Will Heath with the opportunity to take a job building air frames at the Vickers Aircraft factory in Crayford in North Kent. After the war, he was employed at a good wage by a local builder, while at home his wife worked hard to introduce the middle-class standards she had learned in service. Around 1930 Will Heath took over a small firm which became 'W. G. Heath Builder and Decorator' and the family, as Andrew Roth puts it, 'crossed the line' between the skilled working class and the lower-middle class.

At the age of ten Edward Heath won a scholarship to a grammar school in Ramsgate, which not only set high academic standards but imitated the forms of the public schools. He failed his open scholarship to Balliol but his parents, assisted by a loan, were prepared to fund him; then, after a year, he won the Balliol Organ Scholarship. Heath was well on the way; and the Second World War, in which he ended up a lieutenant colonel in the prestigious Honourable Artillery Company, consolidated his position. He entered the House of Commons in 1950: 'That intake in the Commons,' writes Andrew Roth, 'was exceptional in the large proportion of its new Tory entrants who were ex-officers – and who were professionally competent and had made their way without benefit of family wealth and connections.'

Significantly, however, Heath himself remarked that 'for the new member who has been a member of the Oxford or Cambridge Union, coming to those benches is like coming home'. And Heath quickly showed a knack for associating with the traditional upper-class members of the Conservative Party, though curiously, particularly for a man of his musical talents, he never managed to get the accent right. David Wood of *The Times* noted perceptively that for all his image of 'Wilsonian classlessness', Heath was well in with the Tory 'magic circle', and that 'his is the kind of classlessness that takes on the protective colouring of the company he keeps'. Heath became the first-ever elected leader of the Conservative Party in 1965.

Class showed itself in inequalities in the distribution of power and wealth, and in life-styles and life-chances; above all, it showed itself in the gathering cold war which affected British industrial relations, with a snobbish, and often uninformed, management entrenched on one side, with an immobile, unambitious, workforce, deeply attached to its long traditions, on the other. Class, too, was the biggest single determinant of voting preferences. Yet there was no open evidence in Britain of class conflict: though class distinctions were undoubtedly affecting economic performance, they could still well be held, socially, to be an integrating factor.

The special strength and the special homogeneity of the British working class are represented in two distinctive institutions, the British Labour Party and British trade unions. To be employed as a manual worker in any major British industry was almost certainly to be a member of a trade union. In 1951 male trade-union membership was 7,745,000, 56 per cent of all male employees; in 1961, 1966, and 1971 respectively, the figures were 7,911,000 (53 per cent), 8,003,000 (53 per cent), and 8,382,000 (58 per cent). Trade-union membership figures for women were: 1951, 1,790,000 (25 per cent of female employees); 1961, 2,005,000 (24 per cent); 1966, 2,256,000 (23 per cent); and 1971, 2,753,000 (32 per cent). Since the term 'employees' covers most of those in middle-class as well as working-class occupations it can be seen that union membership among working-class males must have been a good 80 per cent throughout the period since the war.

From the period before the First World War trade unions had enjoyed a special position under the law: even if through strike action unions inflicted considerable financial damage on employers they could not be sued, an entirely reasonable provision in that the strike was the basic weapon wielded by unions in protection of their members' standards of living. Despite their special legal status, unions had not been particularly noteworthy in the inter-war years for asserting economic power. What really was crucial in gauging the relative strengths of unions, employers, and government was the actual state of the economy. In a time of general economic growth and relatively high demand for labour, as was the period after the Second World War, trade-union power was greatly enhanced.

As union membership seemed to bring results, so there was more and more pressure on all employees to join a union, while the truly active membership, those doing the work and making the decisions, tended (in keeping with the non-participatory tradition of British political culture) to be quite a small minority. As we have seen, gross membership figures rose steadily in the fifties and sixties, though at the end of the fifties and in the first half of the sixties trade-union membership actually fell behind the overall growth in employment. In the later sixties trade unions began to grow again, so that in 1971 58 per cent of all male employees and 32 per cent of all female employees belonged to a union. Some of the expansion was due to the way in which white-collar, lower-middle-class unions were beginning to expand (an expansion which really exploded in the 1970s).

In the period with which we are concerned here (that is, essentially, the late fifties and the sixties) the number of strikes, the number of strikers, and the number of days lost due to strikes remained remarkably constant and only a little above those for the period of 'consensus'; only at the very end of the sixties was there a sharp upward turn. For the period 1945–54 the annual averages were, for strikes, 1,791, for workers involved, 545,000 and for days lost, 2,073,000. For the period 1955–64 the annual averages, respectively, were 2,521, 1,116,000, and 3,889,000; and for the period 1965–9 they were 2,380, 1,208,000, and 3,951,000. However, in 1970 the number of strikes had gone up to 3,906, and the number of days lost was up by two and a half times to 10,980,000. The actual number of strikes fell to 2,228 in 1971, but days lost were up again to 13,551,000.

Up till the end of the sixties strikes fitted well into the description I gave above of 'industrial cold war'. Most were not officially sanctioned by the appropriate union, but arose spontaneously from the tensions of the work place. As H. A. Turner put it in 1969, most stoppages 'are over before the unions which might have members involved have even heard of them'. When the Royal Commission on 'Trade Unions and Employers' Associations', chaired by Lord Donovan, reported in 1968 its main criticism of the unions was the failure of union leaders to exercise control over their members; neither the Commission, nor any other informed commentators, held that union leaders were heedlessly or villainously forcing their men into unwanted strikes.

After 1968 circumstances altered: not only was there an increase in strike activity, but an increasing proportion of strikes were now 'official' and led by large unions. The origins of this change of emphasis lay in growing resistance to Government policies aimed at wage restraint and, after 1970, in a wider hostility to the political philosophy of the Heath Conservative Government. It did give some credence to arguments that leaders of major unions could now too readily wield power seriously damaging to the economy. Yet careful study of the actions of union leaders shows them continuing to act with great responsibility and restraint. The surface evidence, as we move on into the early seventies, is of increasing conflict (in so far as strikes represent conflict) between employers and employees, and even between Government and employees; and while Britain's strike record compared with other countries had hitherto been rather good, it now became slightly worse, as Table 1 shows.

Table 1: International trends since Donovan

	Stoppages per 100,000 employees		Strike-days per 1,000 employees	
	1965–9	1970–74	1965–9	1970–74
United Kingdom	9.5	12.0	156	585
Australia	31.4	45.2	217	581
Belgium	1.9	5.1	73	242
Canada	7.6	8.8	659	773
Denmark	1.2	4.1	30	360
Finland	4.2	44.7*	84	600*
France	9.6†	17.7	126†	166
German Fed. Rep.	(not available)		6	49
Ireland	10.2	15.4	543	434
Italy	16.3	25.6	817	1,070
Japan	3.0	6.2	68	115
Netherlands	0.6	0.7	5	48
New Zealand	12.8	30.4	103	187
Norway	0.4	0.8	8	52
Sweden	0.5	1.9	25	56
United States	6.4	6.7	492	531

* Official criteria for recording strikes changed during this period
† 1968 excluded from average
Source: International Labour Office, *Yearbook of Labour Statistics*

The basic point to be stressed is that if up till the late sixties, at any rate, trade-union activity undoubtedly demonstrated the deep sense of cultural identity and class *awareness* of the British working class, it did not provide evidence of the existence of sharp class conflict in British society. At the same time, if we are following up the 'What Went Wrong?' theme it can be seen that industrial relations in Britain were worsening and that there was a case to be made out that in certain spheres trade unions could exercise powers menacing to the community as a whole.

A new source of open social conflict was race. In this book I have already suggested a number of different landmarks indicating the point of change between the post-war age of consensus and the new age of cultural change. Another such landmark occurred in August 1958 when violent race rioting broke out between the heavy concentration of West Indian immigrants in Notting Hill, in west London, and local whites. West Indians had started coming in soon after the war, and the matter had first attracted attention in the early fifties.

One may perhaps detect something of a class division in the way in which the British reacted towards the question of immigration. Those in governing circles were still very much influenced by the notion of Britain's great imperial heritage which, as a concrete legacy, had left a situation in which West Indians, Indians, Pakistanis, and Africans were all full British subjects and entitled, without let or hindrance, to settle in Britain itself. Those in governing circles were also aware of the shortage of labour in post-war and early fifties Britain. Those in the working class and lower-middle class, living in the poorer areas in which, perforce, the new immigrants congregated, were more aware of the disruptions and strains brought to their own everyday lives. Almost a third of all immigrants were concentrated in certain parts of London; there were also heavy concentrations in the West Midlands, in Bradford, and in other impoverished urban areas. Among working-class activists, as well as liberal-minded middle-class and upper-class politicians, there was also a genuine sense of outrage at any discrimination based on race, creed, or colour. While upper-class politicians might become increasingly aware of the mythical quality of Britain's imperial or Commonwealth role, they were also aware of the growing need to maintain tactful relationships with India, Pakistan, and the West Indies. Politicians, of course, were not totally unaware of the potential problems of overcrowding and racial friction. While on the one hand there was some talk in Conservative circles in 1955 and 1957 of bringing in controls on immigration, on the other hand the Institute of Race Relations was set up in 1958.

The cause-and-effect relationship between actual legislation, or the announced intention to legislate, and the increase in immigration has been much argued over. It seems that there was something of an upturn in 1960, then came the Government's announcement of its intention to legislate, followed in turn by a much greater influx than ever before: in the first ten months of 1961, 113,000 immigrants arrived from India, Pakistan, and the West Indies. The Immigration Bill proposed a quota system for ordinary immigrants, with vouchers for those who actually had jobs or who were possessed of special skills; it was hotly attacked by the Labour opposition, but eventually became law on 27 February 1962. An opinion poll at the end of the previous year had indicated that 90 per cent of the population at large supported the new legislation. However, it undoubtedly gave a further stimulus to immigration and perhaps encouraged permanent settlement by those who would otherwise have simply sought temporary employment.

Many Labour members actually abstained in the February vote, and steadily, as complaints arose from working-class areas, Labour moved towards a belief in the need for controls. Once immigrants were in, a complete *laissez-faire* policy was observed: no education, no special training, no attempt at geographical dispersion. Again polls indicated that at least 80 per cent of the population felt that there were too many immigrants in the country already. The immigrants were, indeed, making a valuable contribution to the British economy, usually in the lowest-paid, most unskilled jobs, though a significant contribution to the National Health Service was also being made by Commonwealth doctors. But there were also special social strains, in the schools and in the community generally; many immigrants had little or no English. The British, at the best of times, are a xenophobic people. For their part, the immigrants had long-standing and deeply felt cultural and religious traditions of their own.

To hope for integration, let alone assimilation, was perhaps to hope for too much. Roy Jenkins, Labour Home Secretary and protagonist of the civilized society of the sixties, offered a definition of integration 'not as a flattening process of assimilation but as equal opportunity, accompanied by cultural diversity, in an atmosphere of mutual tolerance'. But Jenkins also recognized that there was a 'social factor' putting limits upon the numbers that could be absorbed. Already, in February 1965, the Wilson Government had introduced stricter restrictions on the number of unskilled workers entering the country. But it also set out positively to legislate against discrimination. Britain's first-ever Race Relations Act set up, in 1966, a Race Relations Board aiming at conciliation in cases of proven discrimination on grounds of race or colour. The two-pronged policy was continued in 1968 when a rather more substantial Bill against discrimination was coupled with new legislation to control entry, the latter being in part a reaction to events in Kenya which seemed likely to provoke a large-scale immigration of Kenya Asians holding British passports. The new Act endeavoured to combat discrimination in employment and housing.

British sentiments, quite simply, were confused. There had been a marked absence of a constructive lead from policy-makers. Deep grass-roots hostility to immigrants, and, above all, to further immigration went along with popular support for some kind of legislation against racial discrimination. Respectable parliamentarians, Labour, Conservative, and Liberal, were agreed in trying to prevent race from becoming a national political issue, agreed on a policy of both maintaining and strengthening controls while at the same time endeavouring to outlaw discrimination against those already settled in the country. Yet race as a political issue led to the establishment, through a fusion of existing groups, of the National Front, as a minority right-wing party, in 1966. Then on 20 April 1968, while Parliament was discussing the new stronger Race Relations Bill, the Conservative front-bench spokesman for Defence, Enoch Powell, delivered a speech in Birmingham in which he envisaged a staggering growth of the non-white population: 'like the Romans, I seem to see "the River Tiber flowing with much blood"'. Apart from a Gallup poll showing 75 per cent of the population broadly sympathetic to the sentiments expressed by Enoch Powell, there were also a number of working-class demonstrations in his support. But Powell was instantly dismissed by Edward Heath from his position in the Conservative Shadow Cabinet.

There were also some home-born stresses upon national cohesion. A new active phase of Scottish Nationalist revival began around 1962. In one of its statements the Scottish Nationalist Party hit off exactly the radical technocratic image of the hour: 'The Scottish Nationalist Party stands for an independent and up-to-date Scotland, and believes this country cannot become up-to-date until it is independent.' The symbol of the 1962 revival was the West Lothian by-election in which the SNP candidate, William Wolfe, a chartered accountant, came a creditable second to Labour, and the Conservative lost his deposit. Thereafter progress was by no means consistent, but the party felt sufficiently confident to put up fifteen candidates in 1964, compared with five in 1959. There were no further significant developments until post-1966 disillusionment with Labour rule began to take effect. In the spring of 1967 the SNP vote in the Pollok (Glasgow) by-election was sufficient to ensure a Conservative victory, and in October Mrs Ewing carried through the greatest Nationalist triumph thus far by winning the by-election at Hamilton. This victory did not necessarily mean that henceforth Nationalist candidates could count on success in similar seats throughout Scotland, but it did provide a tremendous stimulus to party recruitment, with membership reaching 80,000 at the beginning of 1968.

The collapse, in the late seventies, of the movement for a separate Scottish assembly inevitably casts a long shadow backwards over the question of how truly significant the nationalist revival of the sixties really was. Much of it must be seen purely as a protest movement, protest on behalf of Scotland's declining industry, protest against neglect by Westminster, and also against geriatric local Labour politicians and complacent (to put it at its most innocuous) local Labour councils, all mixed up with the cultural upheavals of the time. But there was also a core of very genuine nationalism, a deep and real fear that Scotland as a separate nation, with a distinct and valuable cultural tradition, was doomed to extinction through emigration and the invasion of alien values, unless she resumed complete control of her own affairs. No doubt this sentiment was consistently held only by a small minority, though, as other concerns pressed in, it was capable, from time to time, of firing the enthusiasm of others.

The successes of Plaid Cymru, the Welsh Nationalist Party, were not quite so striking, though their President, Gwynfor Evans, won the Carmarthen seat in July 1966. But Welsh nationalism was perhaps even more closely intertwined than Scottish with the cultural movements of the sixties, and the revived interest in roots and origins. Probably the most significant single event was the Act of 1967 which placed the Welsh language on a par with English in Wales. For some, this was a powerful triumph; for others, it was an unmitigated nuisance as proceedings on committees, at universities, and elsewhere now took twice as long as they were conducted first in one language then in the other.

To many Labour MPs of the more solid sort, those who had never comprehended the romantic appeal of nationalism, the issue was one of regionalism rather than of nationalism. As it became clear in the sixties that the relocation of industry policies of the post-war years were not necessarily solving the problems of the old depressed areas, and as expanding affluence sharpened the distinctions between those who were doing pretty well and those who were doing only moderately well, a certain geographical sectionalism began to appear. Strong competition developed in the late 1960s for allocation of the regional funds made available by the Labour Government in order to try to stimulate flagging industrial areas. While class remained the classic division in British society and while it would be wrong to speak of a 'revolt of the provinces', none the less, taking into account the growth of race, of nationalism, and of regionalism, it could be argued that in this period of change Britain was beginning to be touched by some of the characteristics formerly more closely associated with the United States (though now, perhaps, to be considered common features of all Western industrialized, or post-industrial, countries).

But what of that essential glue of the social fabric, the family? For once in a while the statistics speak volumes (Table 2). No evidence, certainly, of any decline in the popularity of marriage; the proportion of married to single people in the total population remains remarkably constant as between 1951, 1961, and 1971. One specially sad burden borne by women, caused by the greater vulnerability of the male of the species (apart from other factors, the Second World War was still showing its savage effects), can be seen in the tragically high figures for widowed women compared with widowed men. The greatly increased number of divorcees as between 1961 and 1971 is also clearly brought out. If we seek the true seed-pods of social change we must scrutinize the figures for the fifteen to nineteen year olds and the twenty to twenty-four year olds. Here we can see how marriage at an early age became more and more fashionable for both males and females (though at all times, many more young women were getting married than young men) into the late fifties and all through the sixties. Certainly the divorce rate goes up sharply at the end of the sixties (though this was only the dawning of the real age of ready divorce of the seventies): the numbers of divorces were – 1968, 45,794 (3.7 per thousand of the married population); 1969, 51,310 (4.1 per thousand): 1970, 58,239 (4.7 per thousand); 1971, 74,437 (6.0 per thousand).

Generalizing about family size, or indeed about long-term birth-rates, is not as easy as might be thought (indeed much Government planning went badly awry on the latter score). The huge families of the late nineteenth century had certainly gone for good; but whereas in the inter-war years there had been almost universal pressure to limit family size to, say two children, many couples in the sixties were showing a happy predisposition to ignore such old-fashioned prudence. The actual rate of births per thousand of the total population, standing at 16.0 at the beginning of the fifties, rose to 17.9 in 1961, 18.3 in 1962, 18.5 in 1963, 18.8 in 1964 – the peak year, since in 1965 the rate was 18.4, in 1966 it was 18.0, in 1967, 17.6, in 1968, 17.2, in 1969, 16.7, in 1970, 16.3, and in 1971 back to its fifties level of 16.2.

Much of the more engaging detail, which the official statistics leave

Table 2: Marriage in the United Kingdom 1951–71 (figures in thousands)

	Males			Females		
	1951	1961	1971	1951	1961	1971
All ages:						
Single	10,811	11,340	12,014	10,846	10,829	11,055
Married	12,358	13,279	13,976	12,488	13,355	14,050
Widowed	} 944	760	762	} 2,769	2,860	3,139
Divorced		102	200		185	318
Age groups:						
0–14:						
Single	5,781	6,321	6,873	5,544	6,015	6,515
15–19:						
Single	1,556	1,850	1,921	1,542	1,709	1,713
Married	8	20	40	68	116	159
Widowed	—	—	—	—	—	—
Divorced	—	—	—	—	—	—
20–24:						
Single	1,267	1,139	1,350	929	719	848
Married	379	501	779	811	941	1,244
Widowed	} 1	—	—	} 4	2	2
Divorced		1	3		2	10

Source: CSO *Annual Abstract of Statistics* (1980), table 2.8

out, was revealed in the survey which Geoffrey Gorer carried out in April and May 1969, published in 1971 as *Sex and Marriage in England Today*. The results of this survey can be compared with the earlier one of the 1950s, presented in *Exploring English Character*. On courtship, the broad situation had not changed much. Twenty-four per cent of married couples had first met at a dance, 15 per cent at work, 12 per cent at social gatherings, parties (a particularly middle-class phenomenon, this), and outings; 12 per cent had also first met through mutual friends, and again this was a particularly middle-class phenomenon. Eighty-six per cent of women and 74 per cent of men considered that they had really been in love at the time of marriage; 23 per cent of men and 11 per cent of women said that they had not. Twenty-six per cent of men and 63 per cent of women were virgins at the time of marriage; a further 20 per cent of men and 26 per cent of women had married the person with whom they had first had sexual relations.

A clear sign of the emancipation of women achieved in the sixties was to be found in the much higher proportion now declaring sexual love to be very important in marriage: 67 per cent of women made this point, as against 65 per cent of men. Averages and medians almost certainly mean very little in this sphere, but, for what it is worth, Gorer found that the median rate of sexual intercourse per married couple was twice a week. Twenty-four per cent of married couples had what he called 'a high rate of intercourse', three times a week or more; 36 per cent had a medium rate, one to three times a week, and 37 per cent had a low rate, once a week or less.

Despite the developments of the sixties two fifths of all couples were not using any form of birth control: of the 19 per cent of married women on the pill, there was a marked concentration in the younger and also in the wealthier groups. Gorer quoted the views on the pill of a twenty-four-year-old wife of a school teacher, a pious non-conformist: 'Good. I was very biased against it medically when I first heard about it – but nothing based on real scientific knowledge. In all other respects it makes the love side of marriage so much freer, it can only be a good thing.' Gorer's findings did not suggest that the pill was leading to infidelity among the married. To the question, 'Now that the pill provides absolute safety, do you think faithfulness is or is not as important as ever in marriage?', 92 per cent replied in the affirmative.

Of the unmarried interviewed by Gorer, 44 per cent said that they had a special girlfriend or boyfriend. Gorer's general findings supported the view that sexual permissiveness was very far from rampant in the late sixties. What he really found was nothing too surprising: the immense variousness of human behaviour. However, the signs clearly are of a definite trend away from older social controls. Half of those with a regular boyfriend or girlfriend spoke of being on terms of 'real physical intimacy', but for a quarter of these, apparently, this did not include full sexual intercourse. On the one hand there was the twenty-one-year-old daughter of a railway worker who said: 'I have been brought up to believe that you should wait until you are married; and I think if you love someone enough you can be prepared to wait until marriage.' On the other hand was the nineteen-year-old lorry driver, who had been sexually active from the age of fifteen and who remarked: 'If it comes along you don't turn it down';

and the eighteen-year-old daughter of a skilled worker, hoping to go to university, who had been sexually active at sixteen and replied: 'Twice a week if I like the boy. It depends on exams!'

Gorer's findings can be amplified by the more detailed study of 1,873 young people aged fifteen to nineteen carried out by Schofield. Of these, only 12 per cent of the girls had had sexual intercourse, but of the engaged ones, 37 per cent were sleeping with their boyfriends. Another study, this time of third-year university students at Durham carried out in 1970, revealed that 93 per cent of the girls had been virgins when they came to university, but that by the third year only 49 per cent were still virgins.

Use of contraceptives, or perhaps one should say effective use of them, had not kept pace with sixties changes in moral attitudes. Gorer found that the majority of the sexually active unmarried were not regularly using any form of birth control. To turn back to hard official statistics, the number of illegitimate births had been 5 per cent of the total at the beginning of the fifties, was 5.8 per cent at the beginning of the sixties, and had risen to 8.2 per cent at the beginning of the seventies; this was an indication, of course, not merely of promiscuity but of the way in which illegitimacy was losing its Victorian stigma.

The family is usually, and very properly, seen as a force holding society together. However, the family had always also been a source of potential violence: most murders took place within a family context, and by the late sixties attention was coming to be given to the plight of battered wives. As women demanded equal rights, and attempts, though rather faltering ones, were made to try to enforce these, some commentators began to ask whether, just as white was being set against black, and Welsh nationalist against English chauvinist, a new social stress was not also opening between men and women. Again one must not anticipate developments which only reached significance in the seventies but one pregnant statistic, not usually sufficiently stressed, deserves mention. In 1971, in the total population of the United Kingdom, there were still many more women than men: 28,562,000 as against 26,952,000. But already the balance, which for centuries had favoured surviving males, had altered: if we look at the crucial fifteen to twenty-nine age group, we find that in 1951 there were 5,255,000 women and girls to only 5,073,000 men and boys; but already in 1961 there were 5,159,000 men and boys as against 5,100,000 women and girls, and the balance had tipped further in 1971 to 5,915,000 men and boys to only 5,764,000 women and girls. For many men, the advent of permissiveness in the sixties was to prove to be a last golden age; never again would they have it so easy.

What of the stresses and strains between youth and age? In the middle sixties much critical attention was directed at the violent and destructive encounters taking place on Bank Holidays at popular holiday resorts between rival teenage groups of 'mods' and 'rockers'. Yet perhaps one of the most revealing indicators of the condition of British society in the 1960s was the muted and derivative character of the student protests of 1968 and 1969. The older universities were stuffy and authoritarian in their style and government; some of the new universities were bleak and short of cultural amenities. There were good pragmatic reasons for revolt. But much of the student movement was frankly imitative of the much more impressive events taking place in California, Paris, and elsewhere on the Continent. There was no link-up between the students, mostly upwardly mobile members of the middle class, and other dissenting groups. All passed off remarkably uneventfully, with universities making timely concessions in regard to student representation and quietly dropping the more irritating conventions and regulations. As there was not that stridency in male–female relations already to be found in contemporary America, so there was a mildness about the student protest movements. Yet all was not bland in British society. A new activism was afoot among middle-class residents' groups which broke through the standard apathy of British political culture. Motorway schemes, urban and rural, the siting of new airports, the invasion of suburban streets by heavy goods vehicles, all of these brought militant, and often highly successful, protest groups of (relatively) ordinary citizens into being, giving some real substance to the word 'participation' which now, with 'permissiveness', began to be bandied around as part of the signature tune of the late sixties.

Belatedly, for better and for worse, Britain was showing the variety of characteristics familiar for a decade or more in the United States. But still social cohesion held up remarkably well; still, there was that comfortable blanket of secular Anglicanism.

11

False Optimism

Generalizing about 'the mood of the country' is the stock-in-trade of journalists; historians should know better. Of criticism and dissent there was plenty in the Britain of the sixties. Although income levels in fact kept ahead of inflation, there was much frustration among those who were more conscious of rising prices than of periodic wage increases; some sections of the community, anyway, got left far behind. Yet when all the qualifications and exceptions have been totted up, it is not unfair to speak of there being an optimism abroad in British society during the sixties. The austere and slightly prissy good intentions, and the shrill *Daily Express* conservatism which was its reverse, of the forties and early fifties had largely gone; the joyful irreverence that never really stretched social cohesion added to, rather than subtracted from, complacency and good feeling. One of the many choice remarks which one could quote occurs in the autobiography (published in 1967) of Walter Greenwood, author of the great working-class novel of the 1930s, *Love on the Dole*. He speaks of the former slum area in Lancashire where he was brought up:

> Bulldozers are at their work of destruction here ... Over three decades have passed since I stood on the threshold of what proved to be for me a wonderful year, decades that have witnessed another world war, the voluntary liquidation of the Empire and the establishment of a social revolution of which this demolition is but a local aspect.

Bulldozers we shall return to shortly. As for the 'social revolution', even if that phrase must seem exaggerated and inapposite, there actually were very significant developments in the principles and practice of the Welfare State in this decade. Although radical Conservatives were declaring that the notion of a permanent Welfare State was 'not ennobling but degrading', the Welfare State, despite the usual windy posturing of politicians, was scarcely now a matter of political debate. Medical advances, innovations in social theory, greater professionalization and professionalism: these were the forces behind the developing Welfare State of the sixties.

By the late fifties it was clear that while flat-rate contributions to National Insurance were quite burdensome for the lowest-paid, the flat-rate benefits themselves were falling far behind the sort of income expected within an affluent society. Thus, in 1959 there came a new scheme whereby better-off employees paid an additional graduated contribution which in return qualified for an additional earnings-related pension. Employers, provided they paid a higher flat-rate contribution, were permitted to contract out of the scheme if they offered their own employees an adequate pension scheme, protected on change of employment. The new principle was actually extended by the Labour Government in 1966 when it introduced earnings-related contributions and benefits to cover the first six months of loss of earnings from other causes than retirement. The major positive contribution to income security was the Redundancy Payments Act of 1965, which laid down that lump-sum payments, financed partly by the employer and partly by compulsory contributions from all insured employees, must be paid to employees with over two years' service dismissed simply because of a change in the employer's requirements or circumstances.

The most important piece of welfare legislation of 1966 was the Ministry of Social Security Act which, among other things, sought to remove some of the stigmas still attaching to National Assistance by replacing it with Supplementary Benefits. The growing view in official Labour, as well as Conservative, circles was that the universalist principle of 1945 was in reality wasteful of resources in that it spread inadequate benefits too thinly across the entire nation, giving a little to those who had no need, and too little to those who were in deep need. Thus Supplementary Benefits both depended upon a means test, and were administered in a flexible way, with much depending upon the discretion of local officials. Payable to those not in full-time employment, Supplementary Benefits were intended to bring income up to a scale calculated according to the number and age of dependent children together with a rent allowance. Humane and sensitive in many respects (great efforts were made to bring to the attention of the deprived the benefits to which they were entitled), the scheme as it worked in practice had two particularly obnoxious features. First there was the bureaucratic device of the 'wage-stop' designed to ensure that Supplementary Benefits did not act as an encouragement to the work-shy. Those who, when in employment, earned less than the income normally provided by Supplementary Benefits were deliberately, when out of work, paid a level of benefits slightly below their potential earnings when in work. Thus such people were placed in a poverty trap from which, short of a miraculous change in their employment prospects, there was no prospect of escape. Second, there was the 'cohabitation rule': single, separated, or divorced women claiming benefits, often for the support of their children, could have their benefits stopped if the snoopers of the Department of Health and Social Security discovered that they were in fact cohabiting with a man who could then be held to be providing them with financial support.

But the main story is of the deliberate seeking-out of sources of deprivation ignored in the grand strategy of 1945–8: the Rating Act of 1966 allowed for rate rebates for those in need and the National Insurance (Old Persons and Widows Pensions and Attendance Allowance) Act of 1970 directed new benefits towards the disabled and the very old.

The experience of the National Health Service suggested that some commercialism and freedom from the universalist control of the State could co-exist with the maintenance of the ideal of a high-level national service. Medical insurance schemes, offering both care in private nursing homes and access to pay beds in National Health Service hospitals, greatly expanded: they had about a million members at the beginning of the seventies, compared with only fifty thousand at the end of the forties. Supporters of such schemes argued that they actually brought more resources within the national system; opponents argued, probably with greater cogency, that they enabled the wealthy to jump the queue for treatment of non-acute conditions.

A major problem of the Health Service in its first dozen years was the desperate shortage of hospitals. To this, because of Government miscalculation, was added by the late fifties a shortage of doctors. In the sixties genuine attempts were made to deal with both problems. A ten-year hospital building programme was announced by the Conservatives in 1962; the shortage of general practitioners reached a peak in the middle sixties when many doctors actually had more than the maximum permitted number of 3,500 patients on their lists. But after 1966 special additional allowances were earmarked for practice in certain designated areas and by 1971 the average number of patients per doctor was down to

2,421. Attempts to expand private practice, it may be noted, were not greatly successful at this time. A new private scheme launched by the British Medical Association in 1965 came to an unlamented demise within three years. Doctors within the National Health Service had meantime gained a more generous system of remuneration which, in particular, now tended to reward the better and more progressive doctors.

One sphere in which British society had always shown itself to be particularly uncaring was that of mental health. The epoch-making Mental Health Act of 1959, which brought a new flexibility and informality to the treatment of mental disorder, could not of itself carry through a revolution. In the sixties there were disclosures of ill-treatment of mental patients in some of the large, badly managed, and under-staffed institutions. These were followed by the setting-up of the Hospital Advisory Service and a general move towards attending more closely to the plight of mental patients. In 1970 came one of the most civilized pieces of legislation, the Chronic Sick and Disabled Persons Act, which symbolized and ratified a new openness towards, and a new concern for, the problems of the disabled.

On the whole the sixties saw a massive retreat from the original principle of a free health service. Having resisted the imposition of charges in the early fifties, the Labour Party, in office in 1968, reintroduced medical prescription charges and dental charges amounting to half the cost of the treatment. It became a commonplace that Britain was putting less into its health service than other more prosperous Western nations (4.9 per cent of the gross national product was being spent on the National Health Service in 1972 compared with 3.8 per cent in 1962) and there were plenty of commentators to point out that, whatever the achievements of the sixties, crisis was never far away. Still, the majority of the population would probably have echoed Sir George Godber, Chief Medical Officer of the Department of Health and Social Security, when in his Annual Report for 1972 he remarked that 'in time of need for myself or my family I would now rather take my chance at random in the British National Health Service than in any other service I know'.

The arena of most conspicuous boom was that of education, and higher education in particular. If we are to seek 'mood' documents for this period, among the best examples are the Robbins Report on Higher Education and the Newsome Report on Secondary Education (both 1963, and both postulating expansion and envisaging greater social mobility and a society appreciative of the values of education), but also the Plowden

Report (1967, directing attention to the needs of primary education, particularly among the socially deprived) and the James Report (1972, calling for a more systematic training of the country's teachers, with the aspiration, eventually, of an all-graduate profession). Universities were built, colleges of education expanded, there were new jobs at all levels. The publishing trade moved in; academics really had never had it so good; more and worse 'academic' books were published than ever before. Still, it is too easy to let eighties sourness cloud the vision of the sixties. Some of the new developments brought British universities up to the standard of the best American ones and at the end of the sixties the university system, judged as a whole, was in most respects better than any to be found abroad, though in engineering and technology there was still nothing to compare with MIT and Cal. Tech. in the USA. Already at the end of the decade, too, the most ambitious plan of all had come to fruition in that it was in 1969 that the first academics were appointed to the new distance-learning institution for mature students, the Open University.

If educational developments speak volumes for the optimism of the sixties, and some of the false assumptions which underlay it, it is in architecture and redevelopment that we see false promises made concrete. Some magnificent buildings were erected. On the one side was the monumental terraced style of Sir Denys Lasdun, as seen in the University of East Anglia and the National Theatre, as also in Patrick Hodgkinson's Brunswick Centre in Bloomsbury. On the other hand was the gentler more flexible style of, say, Sir Basil Spence with his Sussex University, strongly influenced by Le Corbusier's Jaoul houses in Paris and discreetly blending echoes of a Roman colosseum into a magnificent landscape, or of Sir Robert Matthew in his Edinburgh Airport, with its appropriate Scandinavian styling. It was a very laudable part of the orthodoxy of the time that client and architect should work very closely together. Unfortunately, when the client was a public authority and the actual users ordinary people with no say at all, things began to go sadly wrong.

Yet in the early sixties the spoliation carried out in central Newcastle by T. Dan Smith and his colleagues received the praises of the left-wing intellectual journal the *New Statesman*. When the Kirby housing estate near Liverpool – later to become a paradigm of dereliction and vandalism – was opened, Barbara Castle, left-wing member of the Labour Government, told the local Labour Party: 'This is your chance to build a new Jerusalem.' Those bulldozers lauded by Walter Greenwood appeared to be on a destructive foray against close-knit older communities for the poor trade-off of disruptive urban motorways and ugly, unloved high-rise housing.

In 1968 a gas explosion brought the collapse of Ronan Point, a system-built tower block in East London. Much else collapsed as well; and architects and planners must be given credit for the fact that by the time the seventies had begun they were obviously aware that they had an architecture and planning crisis on their hands. Involved in this was the whole principle of planning ('the architect knows best') and revelations about the commercial exploitation of systems building, and inadequate and often fraudulent support services and amenities. A new emphasis on conservation and a halt to the building of high-rise public housing were announced, though low-cost housing estates of dubious popularity would go on being built, and thousands of people would continue for many years to be marooned in flats hundreds of feet above the ground. (The well-off, however, liked being marooned in such prestige high-rise developments as the Barbican in the City of London.)

The overwhelming majority of people in any country at any time have very little understanding of economics, and do not talk much about such issues as the balance of payments, devaluation, and the money supply. They thus differ from economists and politicians, who talk a lot about the balance of payments, devaluation, and the money supply, and, no doubt, are complete masters of the particular economic theory to which they adhere. In 1964, when the Conservatives left office, there was an enormous balance-of-payments deficit. Left-wing Labour politicians argued for a siege economy, with barriers against imports; right-wing Labour MPs argued for a speedy devaluation; Conservatives, and others, called for curbs on the unions. All thought that if their remedy were adopted, the essential soundness of the nation would reassert itself. The Wilson Government, in the event, did what its Treasury advisers told it to do. It was unable, in face of the opposition of its own supporters, to carry through any changes in trade-union law. There was a great sterling crisis in 1966, a devaluation in November 1967, and further rumblings of crisis in 1968. For those who cared about such things, the country, it seemed, was in a mess. Yet after measures of wage freeze and austerity, which did not, in practice, halt the general upward movement in real living standards, the balance of payments was again in respectable surplus by 1970. Many of the authors of the earlier critiques had focused on the inadequacies of central administration and of local government, as well as on poor industrial relations. The sixties, in fact, was a time of considerable reorganization in central Government; old ministries bit the dust, new departments rose in their place. By the turn of the decade, plans were well advanced for local government reform. As they were, too, for the decimalization of the currency, finally carried through in 1971.

Winning the election of 1970, the Conservatives went hard for a policy of expansion. Edward Heath spoke enthusiastically on television of how export companies had full order books. The year 1972 was one of apparent buoyancy: a good year certainly for finance companies and property speculators. Undoubtedly, trade-union activism, as we saw, was getting more threatening. Even so, Britain's record for days lost because of strikes still wasn't noticeably worse than that of her competitors.

To return, then, to 'moods'. Critics might argue that the British had lost their appetite for work, were no longer interested in the creation of wealth, that the key problems were low productivity and low investment. Yet life was good and all seemed far from lost. Still there was joy in the present, and hope for the future.

Part Three
The Time of Troubles
1973–82

12

Gloom on the Man-Made Island 1973–80

If, in broad outline, the period of 'consensus' with which this book began could be seen as containing the story of the determination to escape for ever from the Depression conditions of the 1930s, the story of the middle and late seventies might well be seen as one of a return to the gloom of that 'devil's decade'. Apart from a general sense of a worsening economy and declining living standards, the special doom-laden features which contemporary commentators singled out were the outbursts of militancy, violence, and terrorism, the revelations of corruption in high places, and the break-up of the optimistic consensus which had, according to one point of view, successfully carried Britain through the difficult post-war years into the affluence of the sixties, or, according to another, had mischievously concealed the desperate realities of Britain's true predicament.

There is no sharp line of divide. The 'roads to freedom' ran on through the seventies, often wider and smoother. Small 'wild-cat' strikes, the characteristic phenomenon of the industrial scene since the early days of the war, ceased to be so around 1968, when observers began to be much more worried by the rise of the large, official strike. The Conservatives, it is true, ousted Labour in 1970; yet a political historian might well prefer to treat 1964–79 as one 'period' of, in general, Labour hegemony. Heath and his Chancellor of the Exchequer Anthony Barber at first propagated a philosophy of expansionism. It was only at the end of 1973 that the spurious boom in share-dealing and property collapsed. The most bitter year since the war of confrontation between Government and unions was certainly 1972; it was the year of the IRA bomb outrage at Aldershot in which five civilians died; and it was also the first year since before the First World War in which a union picket lost his life (albeit in an unfortunate accident). Yet the full-blooded IRA campaign of violence on the British mainland did not materialize till 1974, which was also the year in which Kevin Gately lost his life in the anti-National Front demonstration at Red Lion Square, London. Overall economic trends, no doubt, were downward – as perhaps they had been for a long time; but there were fluctuations. Only in 1976 was it absolutely clear that unemployment was on the up and up. The percentage unemployed out of the total number of employees stood at 2.6 per cent in 1970, rising to 3.5 per cent and 3.8 per cent in 1971 and 1972 respectively, with a fall back to 2.7 per cent in 1973 and 2.6 per cent in 1974; in 1975 it rose to 4.1 per cent, in 1976 to 5.7 per cent, in 1977 to 6.2 per cent, with a slight remission in 1978 to 6.1 per cent, and a further slight decline in 1979 to 5.7 per cent. Inflation, which had been running at an annual average of 5.2 per cent in the later sixties and at 9.3 per cent between 1971 and 1974, reached the frightening height of 27.0 per cent in 1975. However, it came down fairly rapidly thereafter, and after averaging 17.3 per cent over the period 1974–8, was down at 9.3 per cent in 1978–9.

In 1978, the total population of the United Kingdom was 55,835,000 (that is, including the 1,539,000 who lived in Northern Ireland), divided between 27,170,000 males and 28,666,000 females. There had been something under a 10 per cent increase in the total population since 1951 when for the United Kingdom it had been 50,290,000 (1,373,000 in Northern Ireland), divided between 24,152,000 males and 26,138,000 females. It is within these overall totals that we can best assess the significance of regional and local fluctuations in population. The striking national fact which gave pause to the thoughtful and provoked pessimism in the excitable was that in 1975, 1976, and 1977, for the first years since population records began, the population fell slightly. The cause was a sharp fall in the birth-rate. Births in 1977 just outnumbered deaths, but were not sufficient to make up for a net migration out of the country. Figures at the end of the decade suggested a slight rallying, so that statisticians were predicting that on through the rest of the century there would be a steady but very slow increase in population; no bad thing for a crowded island, perhaps. However, it was also noted that a steadily increasing proportion of the population fell into the dependent category, either old people, or the young, together supported by a declining proportion of actual earners. While all that was being digested, it turned out that personal incomes, which had enjoyed an average annual rise of 4.4 per cent from 1950 onwards, actually fell by 0.2 per cent in 1976, and by a further 1 per cent in 1977.

The over-riding economic fact was the shrinkage in Britain's industrial base; there was also, as had been the case in America for many years, a growing mismatch between the characteristics of those seeking work and the kinds of jobs which were available. The total numbers in manufacturing employment declined by 2.2 per cent between 1971 and 1974, and by a further 6.1 per cent between 1974 and 1977. After 1974 the number of males in employment fell, whereas between 1971 and 1976 a further one million married women moved into employment.

Whatever different policies Governments followed, they did little to alter the fundamental facts. In January 1974 the Conservative Government of Edward Heath found itself in confrontation with the miners and involved in an international energy crisis, so that major industries were closed for two days out of five in every week. In the 1940s, Government intervention in industry had been directed towards building, on the basis of the war experience, a post-war Britain in which the mass unemployment of the inter-war years would be abolished. The interventionist policies of the incoming Labour Government after 1974 had more the character of a desperate attempt to shore up failing industries. Certainly considerable sums of money were dispensed, and Britain's only indigenous car firm, British Leyland, was taken into state ownership. Between 1970–71 and 1975–6, Government expenditure on 'trade, industry, and employment' increased (at constant, 1975, prices) from £1,800,400,000 to £2,586,600,000, an increase of 44 per cent. Government, it might be said, was doing its best to preserve or create jobs. Yet, with very minor fluctuations, unemployment figures steadily rose. For Great Britain, they went over the million mark for the first time since the Second World War in August 1975. In 1978 (under Labour) and considerably more drastically in 1979 (under the Conservatives) there were massive expenditure cutbacks, and unemployment continued to soar up towards two million.

Before we go again on our British journey, something old and something new. The something old is that, although Britain remained one of the world's most densely populated countries (593 persons per square mile in Britain, 920 per square mile in England, and 11,432 per square mile in London), considerable parts of the country are quite sparsely populated and the nation was still far from being one continuous urban sprawl; in fact, almost 80 per cent of the land surface was still taken up for agricultural uses, 7 per cent being covered by forest, and only 8 per cent being taken up by towns and cities. The new point is that in the early seventies a complete re-drawing of the local government map had taken place. Obviously the essentials of social geography do not change – the new political lines were intended to recognize such of the social realities as had changed – but on our tour we will find that some historic names had disappeared, and some strange ones had appeared. The new Local Government Acts were passed into law in 1972 (Scotland, 1973), with the new boundaries taking effect in the spring of 1974 (Scotland, 1975). In England and Wales smaller counties were grouped together and the conurbations were formally recognized as metropolitan counties: Tyne and Wear, South Yorkshire, West Yorkshire, West Midlands, Greater Manchester, Merseyside, and Humberside and Cleveland. Scotland was divided into regions (with the bulk of the population going into Strathclyde), and the major cities, for example the City and Royal Burgh of Edinburgh, were now given the undignified title of 'local government district'.

If we start our tour once again in Scotland, we find that whatever optimism there had been in the late 1940s had by now almost completely evaporated, but that a new harbinger of possible wealth was over the horizon. The two most significant features of Scotland's economy were, from the late fifties right through, a deepening depression in the old heavy industries, and from the early seventies onwards the advent of North Sea oil and all its accoutrements. Unemployment ran well above the national average in Scotland: 4.5 per cent in 1973, 4 per cent in 1974, 5.2 per cent in 1975; it rose to 6.9 per cent in 1976, 8.1 per cent in 1977, and 8.2 per cent in 1978. Yet by 1976 around sixty thousand people were in employment directly or indirectly related to oil.

The growth area was the North-East (the new Grampian region). In the post-war years Aberdeen had led a life to match the texture and colouring of its granite buildings. Now it became the capital of the Scottish oil industry. In the process it lost its gentility without gaining many of the attributes of prosperity. Pubs, under new Scottish licensing regulations which in the last years of the decade permitted all-day opening (leaving England far astern), took on a slight transatlantic character. Where once the city's finest restaurant had stood a massive bar brought together oilmen, citizens of various avocations, and ladies of the town. Some historical documents have a special evanescence. The list of drinks on offer in this bar at Easter 1980, rough-hewn into poetic abbreviation, forms a statement of social custom which ought to be recorded:

Whisky	45p	Export	50p
Rum		Lager	50p
Vodka		Pt Bot	
Gin		Cider	48p
De Lux	48p	Bots	
Bacardi		Export	33p
Brandy	58p	Lager	33p
Liqueurs	58p	Carls	35p
S'Comfort	58p	Carls Spec	47p
Port	44p	Guins	35p
Sherry		Stout	33p
Aperitifs		Macks	
Juices	25p	St Ale	35p
Coke	25p	Brown Ale	
Babies	20p	Whits	50p
Cham	35p	Pils	47p
S'Ball		Cordial	4p
Lemonade	24p	Crabbies	7p
		Dashes	4p

The scribblings on the shops at Pompeii are scarcely more evocative.

The black fingers spread further afield than the Grampian coastal towns of Aberdeen and Peterhead. Docking facilities for tankers and construction yards for oil platforms were in demand. Of course, the Highlands had long had hydro-electric schemes, aluminium works, a missile base, a missile-testing range, and an atomic energy station. Now they were well on the way to becoming a type of region specially associated with late twentieth-century civilization: wild, remote, beautiful, neglected, with dotted here and there the advanced industrial-technological complexes which the inhabitants of more developed, more populated, areas preferred not to have sited in their midst. However, one man's environmental poison is another man's daily bread.

But, also, one man's fish is another man's environmental disaster. International agreements on the conservation of fish stocks badly hit Scottish fishermen (who formed nearly half of all fishermen in Great Britain). The tragic story of the Scottish fishing industry highlights the point that the Highlands were still basically in decline, despite the new technological marvels. However, a further point is as relevant to consumer society in general as it is to social life in this particular part of Scotland.

As well as new sources of energy, society, or rather a few more affluent members of it, demanded certain luxuries: thus there was modest prosperity to be found in the Harris tweed industry and in the malt whisky distilleries dotted round the perimeter, from Islay in the south-west, through Talisker in Skye, to Highland Park and Scapa in the Orkneys, and right round to the classic Speyside area in Grampian.

Here and there in the towns and cities of the Lowlands (the new regions of Strathclyde, Central, and Lothian) industry, as heavy engineering declined and electronics expanded rapidly, had moved into the age of automation and the white-coated worker. But for the majority it was a case of working in the old way, or, more and more, of not working at all. One industry (located throughout the Lowlands and Southern Uplands and in Grampian and the North-East) that was doing well was agriculture. There was some prosperity, too, for the quality tweed and knitwear industries in the small towns of the Southern Uplands. And, of course, there were the nuclear power stations, at Hunterston and at Chapelcross.

In many respects the new local government map of England still failed to meet the realities of economic geography as perceived by the central Government. For the purposes of central planning, there was one 'standard region' of the North, which included the historic counties of the North-East, Northumberland and Durham, the new county of Cleveland, the new metropolitan county of Tyne and Wear (old Newcastle-upon-Tyne writ large), and the old North-West, now corresponding with most of, but not the whole of, the new county of Cumbria. This North region was the most depressed of all in Great Britain, for it remained most dependent on traditional industries and most constrained by the worthy but inadequately thought-out policies of the late forties. In 1972 the unemployment rate in the North was, at 6.3 per cent, marginally better than that in Scotland. Although 1973 and 1974 were better years for the country as a whole, it was during them that the North slipped firmly behind Scotland. In the bad year of 1976 the unemployment rate in the North was up to 7.4 per cent, and in 1977 and 1978 it reached 8.3 per cent and 8.8 per cent respectively. The derelict coal-mining villages of Northumberland and Durham set a new bench-mark for dilapidation and deprivation in contemporary Britain. Gloom was least in the farming areas, still vitally important in both Cumbria and Northumberland, and among the new technological complexes on the Teesside area of the metropolitan county of Cleveland.

In preparing their standard textbook *Geography of the British Isles* N. J.

Graves and J. T. White visited the Northumbrian market town of Hexham, one of those towns with a population of around ten thousand which so often get neglected in studies of contemporary Britain. Livestock sales took place there at the auction market four days a week, with cattle being brought from as far away as Ireland, coming via Liverpool docks. In the late seventies as many as 2,000 head of cattle would be auctioned daily. 'In one day,' one of the authors reported, 'I saw lorries from Wooler in the North, Carlisle and Penrith in the West, Northallerton and Knaresborough in Yorkshire.' Many specialized firms had grown up close by the markets, supplying farm machinery, fertilizers, seeds, feed stuffs, and advice and services to farmers. As in so many similar market towns the pubs had special licensing hours to cater for those attending the market. The biggest change during the seventies was the building of a vast car park. Bus services were not good; though the authors might have mentioned, but did not, the frequent train service to Newcastle.

Tesside had the largest concentration of chemical plant in the whole British Isles. It had modern port facilities, and a massive modern steel complex, which was, however, already having its production cut back as the eighties began. The people of Teesside were relatively prosperous, but at the expense of living in an atmosphere often made foul by the chemical works in their midst.

Lancashire still survived as a county and the standard region based on it was recognizably the same distinctive region it had been in the late forties. The North-West, comprising the metropolitan counties of Greater Manchester and Merseyside and the counties of Lancashire and Cheshire, had not seemed to be doing too desperately badly at the beginning of the seventies. However, by the end of the decade unemployment rates here, too, were up above 7.5 per cent. Cotton was no longer king, and the old textile towns of Bolton, Stockport, Oldham, Blackburn, Preston, Rochdale, Burnley, and Bury had, with considerable success, diversified into both man-made fibres and carpets and engineering. Manchester no longer drew prosperity from textiles, but remained Britain's second most important commercial and financial centre and was still, by grace of the Manchester ship canal, an important port. It was a centre, now, of electrical and heavy engineering, electronics, petrochemicals, clothing, dye stuffs, and pharmaceuticals. Among the old chemical towns, Warrington achieved a new fame for its production of vodka. Leyland, home of the original Leyland motor company, now maintained the only really successful division of British Leyland, the one manufacturing commercial vehicles. Blackpool, not quite the holiday centre it once had been as holiday patterns changed, had reasonably successful chemical and other light industries, as had Lancaster itself, never a heavily industrialized town in the nineteenth century, but now, among other things, home of one of the new universities. The farm land of Lancashire is very fertile, and on the whole the agricultural industry did well. There was a nuclear power station at Heysham.

Manchester's great rival, Liverpool, now enveloped in the new metropolitan county of Merseyside, could still boast of being, after London, the largest centre for processing and converting imported foodstuffs and raw materials, such as grain, oils, fats, tobacco, sugar, and rubber. But Liverpool provided the classic case of the city whose heart – in this case the old dockland areas – was dying, and whose prosperity, such as it was, was to be found around the periphery. The geographer Peter Hall had cities like Liverpool in mind when he described the dilemma of the inner city and the predicament of its inhabitants: 'A significant minority of these residents are poorly educated, are unskilled, have incomes too low to travel far, and perceptions too limited to know the possibilities. They could perform the heavy, simple jobs needing much strength but little skill, that were once plentiful. But in the new age of the automated machine and the computer, there is no place for their modest talents.'

Yorkshire we spoke of, when making our earlier tour, as 'an industrial museum'. Compared with other old industrial areas Yorkshire was in fact doing slightly less badly in the later seventies. Standing at 2.8 per cent in 1973, unemployment had risen to 6 per cent in 1978. The 'standard region' is termed Yorkshire and Humberside, and in the new functional (more or less) local government scheme the romance of the Ridings, as divisions of Yorkshire, have gone; instead there are the metropolitan counties of West Yorkshire (Leeds, Bradford, and their surroundings) and South Yorkshire (Sheffield and its surroundings). Again it is just worth remembering that though this area is in parts very heavily industrialized, more than four fifths of Yorkshire and Humberside is open country. The development of new man-made fibres had given the Yorkshire textile trade a slight lift; there had also, as we noted in regard to Harris and the Scottish borders, been a revival in the demand for good woollen products. At the end of the seventies about 70 per cent of Britain's worsted and woollen industry was located in West Yorkshire, with Bradford still having a little of the *cachet* of being the commercial centre of the wool trade. Doncaster and Barnsley continued to be basically coalfield towns, but were profiting from some diversification. York had always stood apart from industrial Yorkshire: it was not doing too badly on two very contemporary trades, tourism and chocolate. Hull and Grimsby, on Humberside, were surviving reasonably well at the beginning of the seventies, their dependence upon fishing balanced out by the establishment of port facilities for European trade together with food processing and cold storage plants. But they were hit hard by the general slump in fishing, and in 1980 the entire Hull trawler trade went bankrupt. Mighty symbol of Humberside's fluctuating fortunes, and Britain's industrial problems in general, was the Humber Bridge, still, after massive expenditure, and one serious accident, uncompleted in 1980, by which time it was being argued that most of the commercial need for it had already vanished.

It was in the Yorkshire coalfield, and in its continuation into the East Midlands, that automation had gone furthest. The geographer (David M. Smith) who wrote that 'the miner in the white coat is the symbol of the 1970s' was exaggerating, but without any doubt automation, based on the inexhaustible possibilities for computerization presented by the silicon chip, for better or for worse, was now beginning to bite deeply into conditions of and opportunities for work. There were huge new power stations around Castleford. Coal made up about one fifth of the industrial output of the East Midlands; major industries were hosiery, knitwear and footwear, trades which, short of a total general depression, tended to do reasonably well as vital parts of contemporary consumer society. Unemployment did not reach 5 per cent in the East Midlands till 1977 and it remained steady at that figure in 1978.

The West Midlands had been the great success area of the war and post-war years. Under the local government reorganization this whole region formed one metropolitan county, with many historic towns now being defined as mere 'districts': Birmingham, Coventry, Dudley, Solihull, Walsall, and Wolverhampton. The area, however, was very dependent upon the vicissitudes of the motor industry, and after having very low unemployment rates in the early seventies, the West Midlands had a 7.5 per cent unemployment rate by 1978. Yet, for seeing what was going on in Britain in this time of troubles, the region was a good one to visit. The Midlands cities, Newcastle-under-Lyme as well as Birmingham and Coventry, had early gone into the business of tearing down their town centres in order to make a land fit for motor cars to live in. In the later seventies, unsteadily because of lack of funds, the attempt was made to restore the conservationist balance. The area's aspiration towards a North

American future was best represented in the building and opening of the National Exhibition Centre on the outskirts of Birmingham which sought to destroy the monopoly which London had so long held on national and international congresses. The region had two quite successful new towns, both based on the metal industries, Telford and Redditch.

On the outermost fringes of the 'Home Counties' (the counties clustered round London), where they begin to merge into the South Midlands, the most famous of all new towns, the new city of Milton Keynes, began to shake itself into some sort of life in the later seventies, and to become as famous a topic for popular journalism as the Loch Ness Monster. Built very much like a large piece of American suburbia, Milton Keynes was much criticized for its 'rabbit-hutch' housing, and for the obvious segregation of its different classes of housing estates. Still, when, according to *New Society*, the community television station, as an April Fool's joke for 1979, broadcast a message saying that the entire city (100,000 inhabitants, half the planned total, at the end of the decade) was to be ploughed back into the ground, a viewer declared that he was not going to go back to London: 'Milton Keynes had given him a garden, something he'd never had before, and he was damned if he was going to give it up now.'

In *Wales: A New Study* (1977), edited by David Thomas, there is, in the chapter by Graham Humphrys, a map of industrial South Wales, showing the collieries still open as black dots, and the collieries closed since 1950 as white dots; the white quite overwhelms the black. The fundamental fact about Wales since the early 1950s has been the concentration of coal production in the deeper central parts of the coal basin, with a drying-up of production around the edges. Small mines closed down leaving only large collieries employing at least five hundred workers. The old life of the village perched on top of the pit was breaking up; the new collieries were often quite some distance from the old villages. If the men did not all work in white coats, though Humphrys speaks of 'a new breed of mining technocrats' replacing 'the men skilled in the arts of manual labour', they were certainly at one with 'post-industrial' twentieth-century civilization in that they had considerable distances to travel to work. For most of the seventies closures did not mean a high level of redundancy; instead there was simply a steady population drift away from South Wales. Hardest hit of all was the anthracite region to the west.

Hopes were still high in the early seventies over the potential of the South Wales steel industry: they had all come crashing down by the end of the decade. First there had been the closure of the small inland works, and a concentration on the vast coastal complexes; but even those were under threat in 1980. Attempts were made to continue and extend the policies of the forties. Substantial growth took place in the electrical goods industry, but the jobs created mainly went to female labour. Historic Merthyr Tydfil was now best known for its Hoover washing-machine factory, whose demand for labour fluctuated with the consumer economy as a whole. Various motor component plants established in the sixties suffered with the problems of the British motor trade in the seventies. In 1971 Wilkinson Sword had established a garden tool manufacturing plant at Waterton Industrial Estate. L'Oreal opened a cosmetics factory at Llantrisant in 1972. There were oil refineries at Milford Haven and Llandarcy and a giant petrochemicals complex at Bagland Bay. There was one nuclear power station at Wilfa on Anglesey and, as a final earnest of the determination of the man-made world to dominate the world of nature, there was another at Trawsfynydd in the middle of the wild and beautiful national park of Snowdonia.

In the West Country (the standard region of the South-West), where, save for the creation of the county of Avon as an expanded version of the former county borough of Bristol, the historic counties had been left intact, the main change since the early fifties was the growth of light engineering and of the various branches of the electronics industry. In addition the West Country had three nuclear power stations, at Berkeley, Aldbury, and Hinkley Point. The South-West had been troubled by unemployment at the end of the sixties (2.8 per cent in 1970), and in 1977 unemployment was running at 6.8 per cent, with a slight drop to 6.5 per cent in 1978.

In the later sixties London and the whole South-East region had been the most prosperous in Britain, with unemployment standing at 1.6 per cent in 1970. This region continued to suffer less than any other, and in 1977 and 1978 was the only region to have unemployment below 5 per cent (4.5 per cent and 4.2 per cent respectively). Yet London itself was steadily losing both employment and population. There was a developing outer ring of light industry, but many of the most characteristic technological developments of the age were being located somewhat outside of Greater London itself: for example the computer industry had important bases at Hemel Hempstead and Letchworth, and the electronics industry was developing at Chelmsford. A special factor in the decline of London's East End was the opening of new deep-sea port facilities down the Thames at Tilbury. There were major oil refineries on both the Thames and the

Medway. Finally, another characteristic of the contemporary age, the major London airports at Heathrow and Gatwick were in themselves now major employers. Outside of London the South-East continued to enjoy a modest prosperity, probably on a rather higher level than was to be found anywhere else in the country. There were nuclear power stations on the south coast at Dungeness. The population of the South-East began to decline after 1972 (when it was 17,600,000); in 1978 it was down to 16,832,000.

In simple cash terms London, though by no means London alone, benefited greatly from the manner in which Britain was becoming a major tourist country, with a record 11.5 million visitors in 1977, spending £2,179 million. But there were those who complained that parts of London, particularly the West End, where tourists took the form of shoppers rather than sightseers, and such towns as Stratford-upon-Avon and Edinburgh, were, in high season, unbearably overcrowded. Many were the new hazards of life in contemporary Britain.

One of the few regions (though, in regard to population, a very tiny one) to show steady growth was East Anglia, which grew from 1,683,000 inhabitants in 1971 to 1,843,000 in 1978. Many East Anglian towns were still steadily absorbing 'over-spill' from London, and the old port towns of Great Yarmouth and Lowestoft had expanded their trade with the Continent as well as becoming North Sea oil bases. The most significant development was the building of the massive continental container port at Felixstowe. There was a nuclear power station at Sizewell.

Yet, again, we must not forget rural England. While the 'revolution in farming' did bring some prosperity to rural areas, the exodus from tiny villages to the towns where the electronics and other technological industries were located, and the drastic changes in British transport policy were leaving less happy consequences. When the petrol crisis of late 1973 first struck, and rationing seemed imminent, the strongest arguments for special consideration came from car owners in East Anglia and other country areas. But for the older and less affluent there were other limitations upon mobility than those threatened by restrictions in the private petrol supply. This and other points were developed in a fine piece of journalism by Philip Norman in the *Sunday Times* of 29 January 1978, when he described a visit to the East Anglian village of Sudbourne in Suffolk.

There was a different village here. It exists now only in clues . . . School Road, Hospital Road, lead one blandly, each to a cul-de-sac of distance and forest edge.

The school has become a private house, its gothic classroom windows shortened, its teachers' quarters severed and lately sold to a barrister from London. Hospital Road divulges only four fir trees in a clump, the scene of fire. There was once a shop, they say, at the Red House. Its vanished window haunts it still in a shape of paler bricks. Inside the telephone kiosk a plaque informs the user he is speaking from 'Sudbourne Post Office and Stores'. Looking out, he sees a white house front, a new double garage, a pale blue, exclusive-looking door.

The Post Office shut down three years ago . . .

The bus time-table, fixed to a wall outside the Chequers, is like a gauge of isolation. It tries to be cheerful, with its promise of money-saving excursions, yet wherever the name Sudbourne occurs on its columns, one might deduce an almost malign wish to keep the village out of step with everywhere. The time-table ordains Woodbridge, eleven miles away, as the nearest town; Saxmundham, Leiston and Aldeburgh, all nearer, are inaccessible from Sudbourne by bus. The morning Ipswich service, calling at Sudbourne just before eight, reaches Woodbridge too late to catch a train. If you take the early evening bus, there is no getting back the same night. The full journey of an hour-and-three-quarters . . . costs £1 each way . . .

For all practical purposes Sudbourne depends on local authority transport, that modern form of charity. School buses take its children to Orford, Butley or Woodbridge. A mobile library calls on alternate Fridays, staying half-an-hour. Once a fortnight, a county council minibus takes the elderly to Orford, to collect their pensions and enjoy a half hour's shopping in the metropolitan atmosphere of a post office, a sweet shop and Elliott's General Store.

The invasion of the rich into the rural territory of the poor, taking over their homes, and everywhere pushing up rates and house prices, was in many places mightily resented. That resentment, allied with nationalism, resulted, early in 1980, in an arson campaign in Wales against the owners of second homes. Still, contemporary discontents should not obscure long-term gains. In Sudbourne, as in villages in Wales and elsewhere, the universal installation of electricity and sewerage was very much an achievement of the period since 1945.

Increasingly, observers were declaring that the crucial divide in British society was one of social geography: between a prospering innovative South (the Midlands, and everything to the south, but excluding Wales), and a backward, depressed North (everything beyond the Midlands). In the general election of 1979, the South, thus defined, overwhelmingly voted Conservative; it was in the North that Labour kept its hopes alive.

Throughout the North wages were lower while more was collected in social security benefits. Scotland had fewest cars per head, but the highest rate of prosecutions for drunken driving. *The Times* summed up Central Statistical Office tables for 1979, in the headline: 'Dirtier, less healthy North; a wealthier South'.

Yet, beneath the geographical and regional variations, there was developing a grimmer social and demographic pattern. All over the country it was becoming difficult for school leavers to find jobs, and older men, unable to acquire newer skills, formed a high proportion of those unemployed. While much unemployment was still relatively short-term, over the country the proportions of those unemployed for over six months and unemployed for over twelve months were remarkably consistent. These dismal points are brought out graphically in Table 3, prepared from Department of Unemployment figures by Kevin Hawkins for his study *Unemployment* (1979).

Work had not lost its double-edged quality; but by the beginning of the eighties a job was becoming again, as it had been in the 1930s, something that you began to thank your lucky stars you had. The paradox

Table 3: Regional analysis of male unemployment by duration and age, January 1978

Region	Male unemployment rate %	Long-term male unemployed as a proportion of all male unemployed		Proportion of all male unemployed	
		Over 6 months	Over 12 months	Under 20	Over 40
South-East	5.8	39.2	21.1	11.2	40.3
East Midlands	6.3	41.6	25.1	11.6	44.1
West Midlands	6.5	47.3	29.0	13.4	40.3
East Anglia	6.6	39.2	24.0	11.5	44.7
Yorks/Humberside	7.3	42.2	25.7	12.4	41.2
South-West	8.9	42.2	24.8	13.4	40.3
North-West	9.2	49.2	29.9	14.7	35.6
Wales	9.9	44.2	26.6	13.6	36.3
North	10.4	46.0	28.5	13.3	39.2
Scotland	10.6	42.1	24.6	11.5	34.6
Great Britain	8.1	43.3	25.4	13.2	39.3

of the late seventies was that although a crucial aspect of industrial relations was dominated by the Employment Protection legislation enacted in 1974 which seemed to affirm the responsibility of society to provide everyone with a job, the economy was so depressed, the provision of new industrial skills so lacking, and the workforce itself so immobile, that, while redundancy payments could be claimed, redundancies themselves were a threat as they never had been since the Second World War. A tentative move towards establishing work as a social right had foundered on adverse economic circumstances and perhaps, indeed, was incompatible with favourable ones. The industrial worker was still at the greatest risk, though his 'rights' had been strengthened; the privileged security of the middle class lay under threat.

In 1955 the first motorways were only promises on the planner's pen. In 1980 there was a widely held predisposition against the building of any new ones. At one level communications, apart from the occasional bottleneck, such as that on the old two-lane stretch of the M1 just north of London, were probably better than they had ever been in the country's history. Much of the rail network was electrified and the Inter-city 125 services on major routes offered journey times as good as any in the world; Cardiff, for instance, was brought within two hours of London and against the tale of South Wales decline can be placed the siting of Companies' House there. It was at the more local level, and in the remoter areas, as we have noted, that transport facilities were declining, though probably almost all individuals, through the irrepressible institution of the extended family, had, in time of need, access to transport by private car. A totally new communications phenomenon was to be found in the pipe lines established to transport gases, natural and otherwise, and petroleum.

It would be wrong to see the environment at the beginning of the 1980s as dominated totally by money-making technologies and their accompanying spoliation and pollution, by the demands of commuter and industrial transport, and by rural decline and the whims of the owners of second homes; and still more wrong to forget that industrial pollution was as old as industry itself. On the side of the angels were three major government bodies: the Standing Royal Commission on Environmental Pollution, the Clean Air Council, and the Advisory Council on Noise; and a whole host of voluntary societies: the National Society for Clean Air, the Noise Abatement Society, the Keep Britain Tidy Group, the Friends of the Earth, and the Council for Nature.

13
Class, Race, and Nationalism

The previous chapter indicated various possible divisions in British society, suggesting, on one plane, the emergence of a division between a deprived North and a relatively prosperous South, and, on another plane, a nationwide divide between young people unable to secure jobs and the rest of society. Clearly both local deprivation and such major structural changes as were brought about by North Sea oil could be expected to have considerable relevance to the progress of nationalism. Already Britain was a society marked by race discrimination and racial tension; often, in the economic gloom, it was the members of racial minorities, particularly the young ones, who could not get jobs. New economic circumstances, then, could be expected also to intensify race divisions.

But for all that, class was very far from losing its traditional significance in British society. In that judgement sociologists, journalists, and commentators of all descriptions seemed to concur, for the seventies ended in an unprecedented flurry of studies of class. From the middle seventies onwards discussions of the all-absorbing topic rumbled through the letter and feature columns of various newspapers. Storm-centres were created by: a Labour Party television broadcast late in 1976 which boldly portrayed a selfish and ineffectual upper class; an acrimonious controversy over the relationship between education and class centring particularly on the relative merits of comprehensive and grammar schools and on the Labour Party's announced intention, at last, to attack the entrenched position of the public schools; and the case, presented most bluntly in the sections of a Milton Friedman American television broadcast shown in this country, that Britain was handicapped compared with her foreign competitors by her rigid class system.

In December 1976, the novelist Lynne Reid Banks in a letter to the

Observer summed up a widely expressed opinion: 'Class is so deeply embedded in our national sub-conscious it is poisoning every aspect of our lives. Not just industrial relations and politics, but our choice of districts to live in, jobs, schools, friends – even which bar to drink in at our local. It's a kind of civil war we are perpetually fighting, wearing out our energy and emotions, wasting our time and money. It holds back progress, destroys prosperity, impedes social and working relations on every side.' Three years and two months later (late January 1980) the same writer, this time in a feature article, had moved from a general critique of British society to a more embattled class position: 'Why should I feel ashamed of the indisputable fact that we, the middle classes, fill the better schools with our children and the theatres with ourselves?' Middle-class idealists, she continued, had given up on the comprehensive educational system: 'What drives them to it is the awful realization that the working people of this country, on the whole, are not interested in educational or cultural self-improvement. They have no ambition for their children apart from material ambition.'

Earlier, a left-wing Labour MP (Robert Kilroy-Silk, writing in *The Times*, December 1976) had welcomed the return to 'a fearless and radical examination and critique of class in Britain today'; the Labour Party, he said, did not seek to divide society, it was divided already. Nowhere was this more clear 'than in the factories where manual workers enter by one gate, eat in segregated canteens and work longer hours in worse conditions than their "betters"'. Also in *The Times*, a right-of-centre Labour MP (John P. Mackintosh) wrote on 'Them and Us: What we can do to heal our divided land': many managements, he noted, would not dream of sitting down to lunch with their shop stewards. The Conservative reply was that 'some form of class structure is inevitable'. The thesis of *Class on the Brain: The Cost of a British Obsession*, written for the right-wing Centre for Policy Studies by Professor Peter Bauer, was that, if class-conscious and variegated, British society was also open and mobile, with the very evident badges of class enhancing mobility by providing additional incentives to hard work and enterprise. This, significantly, is a defence, not a denial, of class distinctions; what characterized all the debates was an open recognition of the existence of classes. The old decade ended with the publication of the lighthearted, but shrewd, study of class by the highly successful journalist Jilly Cooper; and the new one opened with the heavy-footed, but sound, studies of class and social mobility, and class and education, written, respectively, by John Goldthorpe and A. H. Halsey.

There was still no consensus among those who commented so profusely, and indeed promiscuously, over what constituted the upper class, if indeed there was one, or over where the divide came between such an upper class and the upper-middle class. There is no consistency of popular usage, and therefore no rule, over who are included in the upper class and over where the divide comes between the upper class and the upper-middle class. Back in the sixties, in introducing his book *The English Gentleman*, Simon Raven had, as we have seen, revealed that his father had independent means, and that he himself was brought up in 'Surrey stockbrokers' country', educated at an expensive preparatory school, and at Charterhouse and King's College, Cambridge; yet he denied being himself a member of the upper class. In 1979, Jilly Cooper presented a somewhat similar disclaimer:

My paternal grandfather was a wool-merchant, but my paternal grandmother's family were a bit grander. They owned newspapers, and were distinguished Whig MPs for Leeds during the nineteenth century. My mother's side were mostly in the church, her father being Canon of Heaton, near Bradford. Her mother was a beauty. Both sides had lived in the West Riding of Yorkshire for generations. They were very, very strait-laced. To this day there has never been a divorce in the family.

My father went to Rugby, then to Cambridge, where he got a first in two years, and then into the army. After getting married, he found he wasn't making enough money and joined Fords, and he and my mother moved, somewhat reluctantly, to Hornchurch, where I was born. At the beginning of the Second World War he was called up and became one of the army's youngest brigadiers. After the war we moved back to Yorkshire, living first in a large Victorian house. I was eight and, I think for the first time, became aware of class distinction. Our next-door neighbour was a newly rich and very ostentatious wool-merchant, of whose sybaritic existence my parents disapproved . . .

Soon after that we moved into the Hall at Ilkley, a splendid Georgian house with a long drive, seven acres of fields for my ponies, a swimming pool, and tennis and squash courts. From then on we lived an elitist existence: tennis parties with cucumber sandwiches, large dances, and fêtes in the garden.

Jilly Cooper, in effect, defines herself as 'upper-middle class', though she admits that to upwardly mobile, hardworking middle-class professional people, she might well seem 'upper class'.

For myself, I have to say that I would regard both Simon Raven and Jilly Cooper as falling within that 2 per cent or so of the population that I would describe as 'upper class'. By that definition, just to clarify things, an ordinary professor such as myself, well paid, but without influence and totally dependent upon my own earnings, belongs to the upper-middle class. Another usage, just as reputable, though, I think, less exact, would agree with the valuations given by Simon Raven and Jilly Cooper and put them in an upper-middle class which, by all practical indicators, has much the same power, influence, and wealth as the small upper class, restricted in this case to the 'true' aristocracy and gentry, while putting me and my like solidly in the middle class.

In what follows I shall continue to speak of an 'upper class', but readers who do not accept my analysis must then take this category of 'upper class' as including both the upper class and what they would refer to as the 'upper-middle class'. That such a social grouping, whether taken as one integrated entity, or split into two parts, continues to exist is not within the realm of dispute.

Again I must refer to two metaphors employed earlier. First, there is still the upper-class 'box' of ethos, attitudes, and education which perpetuates the tradition and absorbs those not born to the manner. Secondly, this upper class is a 'reservoir'. Not all members of it wield power through being on the boards of multi-national companies or finance corporations; not all members of it stand in the limelight through being Cabinet Ministers or influential backbenchers; not all members of it manipulate the substance of power through the civil service or diplomatic corps. Many other jobs, now, are taken on by sprigs of the upper class, particularly in publishing, journalism, and television. But the point is that all jobs, if wanted, are more accessible to this privileged 2 per cent or so of the population (750,000 individuals; man, woman, and child, or, perhaps, 150,000 family units).

Arguments about the disappearance of a unified upper class are based, we have noted, on the thesis of the 'managerial revolution', on the thesis that influential owners of capital have been displaced by professional managers. Much good work published in the seventies has effectively challenged this gauche thesis. One unique and specially valuable publication, itself a product of one of the more positive and hopeful developments of the 1970s, was the pamphlet *The Making of a Ruling Class* published in 1979 by the Benwell Community Project of Newcastle-upon-Tyne. The careful, detailed research on which this publication was based brought out very clearly how the descendants of Newcastle's old coal-owning, industrial, and banking families of the eighteenth and nineteenth centuries were now powerful components of a nationwide upper class.

Inter-marriage had created great dynasties, such as those of the Joicey, Barnett, and Dickinson families, of the Buddle, Browne, and Brackenbury families, and of the Priestman, Pumphrey, Peile, Bosanquet, and Hodgkin families, as well as families able to go it alone, such as Noble, Pease, and Stephenson. As matters stood in 1980, biographical studies revealed recurrent characteristics: members of these dynasties tended to sit on local authorities (such as the Northumberland County Council), on local planning bodies, on the boards of finance corporations and multi-national companies (where they were also substantial shareholders), had usually been educated at Eton, Harrow, Winchester, or Rugby, held substantial family seats in rural Northumberland, belonged to the Northern Counties Club in Newcastle's Hood Street, and (in the case of eighteen families) to the following exclusive London clubs, Brooks's, the Turf, Pratt's, and the Carlton. 'It is not uncommon,' the authors remark:

to hear the argument that the boards of directors of the banks and insurance companies are purely window dressing; that they are full of titled members of no particular importance, and that effective power lies with the cadre of highly skilled and trained professionals who have worked their way up to the top through the ranks. Thus Anthony Sampson quotes the cartoon in an old Insurance Guild journal showing a decrepit old man staggering through the office: 'No, that's not an accident claim, Clogg,' said one clerk to another, 'that's a director.' While this view seriously underestimates the importance and significance of the interlocking directorships between the finance capital and industrial capital sectors, it is also fundamentally misleading about the class background of the key executives in banking and insurance. The men from the west Newcastle dynasties who have held or now hold some of these key positions are 'professionals' in that they are career accountants, bankers or insurance managers, but there is no doubt about their social and class origins.

Evidence from another earlier study of twenty-seven large financial institutions, the largest clearing banks, merchant banks, discount houses, insurance companies, and the Bank of England, found that out of a total of 341 directors for whom educational data were available 269 (79 per cent) were educated at public schools and 115 (34 per cent) went to Eton alone. Though much of the detailed work remains to be done, the weight of the evidence is that in 1980 there still was a consolidated, coherent, upper class, enjoying quite disproportionate wealth, power, and life chances, in Britain. The evidence also, though, is of greater mobility than ever previously into this upper class; and of members of this class taking jobs which formerly would not have been regarded as appropriate to their social status.

The upper-class self-image was still very much alive, presented facetiously by Jilly Cooper and by Douglas Sutherland in his works on *The English Gentleman*, less facetiously by Michael Nelson, described by his publishers as 'born in England of a good family . . . educated at Bryanston and had a gentlemanly upbringing,' in *Nobs and Snobs*. According to Nelson, 'Britain has continued since the Second World War to be a country made up of many classes, and, though a gentleman is not class-conscious, he is automatically a member of the upper class of British society.' The upper class, Nelson continues, may be subdivided into three:

First, the recognised aristocracy, accepted as such because of their possession of land, wealth, titles and status; second, the lesser landowners, the 'squires', who sometimes marry into the aristocracy, and, third, the lower-upper class, made up of people who . . . have hoisted themselves into the ranks of the upper classes through the right education, service to their country, or marriage.

While the upper-class self-image may be said to have endured, the middle-class self-image had actually become more assertive, as the second quotation from Lynne Reid Banks above might suggest. An even harsher expression of middle-class consciousness emerged from an interview with a woman living in one of London's more expensive suburbs (published by Jane Deverson and Katharine Lindsay in *Voices from the Middle Class*, 1975).

I can't understand people who feel guilty about the working classes. People will always be different, even if everyone has the same houses and the same money. We would always be richer in our minds than the working classes, just by reading books. Labourers can earn a lot of money these days; God, they must have money, the prices they charge! But all they are concerned with is revenge, in the petty ways of their minds. Jealousy and bitching is their main occupation. Look, if everyone had the same amount of money, some people would manage their money better and then things would still be unequal. A person with a different background will live in a different way regardless of money.

Anyway, the Capitalist system helps the poor. If the Stock Market is doing well and the country is richer, that helps the poor. The rich give jobs to the poor. There is always going to be envy, there's always going to be people who are better off than others. It annoys me when people vote Labour out of emotionalism. My best friend voted Labour once, just out of emotion, because she felt it was the right thing to do. Edgar said: 'Are you mad? They are going to nationalise everything and you'll lose all your shares!' She was horrified. 'Oh God, what have I done?' she said. She's mad, completely mad!

There was much talk in the press of the appeal of Thatcherite Conservatism to the middle class. As early as October 1975 David Wood was writing in *The Times* of 'Mrs Thatcher's middle-class uprising'. Subjective comment, as well as the 1979 general election results, suggested that middle-class persons who formerly prided themselves on their progressive sympathies were now swinging away from Labour and back to a more obvious 'class' support of the Conservatives. The best that one middle-class professional who hailed from a working-class background could say was that although he still voted Labour, he no longer cared if the Conservatives won.

The middle class was still the most heterogeneous in educational background. The massive Goldthorpe survey conducted at the beginning of the decade demonstrated that there was indeed mobility out of the working class into the middle class and this trend certainly continued. For those born into the middle class there were opportunities to move up through professional or business success into positions of real influence or power. For the essence of being middle class in 1980 was that, although life was still easier than it was in the working class, there was no ready access to positions of power; jointly, members of the middle class acting together had influence; singly they had little power. Reports of the Royal Commission on the Distribution of Income and Wealth indicated that it was indeed true, as middle-class people felt in their bones, that differentials between them and members of the working class were steadily being eroded both through taxation, and through the strong bargaining power which certain unions possessed.

As always, clear expressions of working-class self-images are hard to find. However, a survey conducted by Richard Scase in 1972 indicated that 93 per cent of all British manual workers believed that classes still existed in Britain; 29 per cent had an overall image of a two-class society, 60 per cent of a three-class society; 74.8 per cent identified both 'upper, top or higher classes' and the 'working class', and 75.6 per cent identified a 'middle class'; 69.8 per cent allocated themselves to the 'working class', 19.3 per cent to the 'middle class', 5 per cent to the 'lower class', 3.4 per cent to 'the poor', and 1.7 per cent declared themselves 'average people'. If any generalization can be made comparing working-class attitudes in the late forties with those of the seventies, it might be said that a certain optimism and sense of confidence in the former period had now been replaced by a sense of bloody-minded resignation and a feeling of 'once a worker always a worker' and why, anyway, aspire to anything better? Huw Beynon collected some characteristic remarks from Ford workers for his book *Working for Ford* (1973): 'It's the most boring job in the world,' said one:

It's the same thing over and over again. There's no change in it, it wears you out. It makes you awful tired. It slows your thinking right down. There's no need to think. It's just a formality. You just carry on. You just endure it for the money. That's what we're paid for – to endure the boredom of it.

If I had a chance to move I'd leave right away. It's the conditions here. Ford class you more as machines than men.

'It's strange this place,' said another:

It's got no really good points. It's just convenient. It's got no interest. You couldn't take the job home. There's nothing to take. You just forget it. I don't want promotion at all, I've not got that approach to the job. I'm like a lot of people here. They're all working here but they're just really hanging around, waiting for something to turn up . . . It's different for them in the office. They're *part* of Fords. We're not, we're just working here, we're numbers.

As the recession bit more and more deeply, it became as clear as ever it was that the working class is the most vulnerable in modern society. Individuals could escape out of the working class, and had increasingly been doing so over twenty years; but the success of isolated individuals does not affect the status and power of a whole class. However, it would be wrong to deny that the organized working class in Britain had greater power and influence than that in any other country in the world. Governments, whether they liked it or not, had to take into account the views of trade-union leaders. In ordinary industrial disputes, the bargaining power of unions was strong. Very largely, the Edward Heath Conservative ministry at the end of 1973 and the beginning of 1974 was destroyed because he foolishly involved himself in a confrontation with the miners. The Callaghan policies in trying to control inflation were only successful as long as he had the co-operation of the trade unions.

The summing-up, then, must be that class divisions had certainly proved remarkably enduring in Britain but that the lines, both between middle class, upper-middle class, and upper class, and between working class and middle class, were now less firm than ever they had been. Within the working class, the expansion of such occupations as that of lorry driver involved a real physical mobility and freedom uncharacteristic of traditional working-class jobs; the growth of white-coated occupations in the former heavy industries also produced a blurring of the line between working and middle class. In industrial confrontations the self-employed lorry driver, most certainly, allied himself against the organized working class. Yet at the same time unionization was expanding; unions themselves were ceasing to be an exclusive indicator of working-classness.

What, then, is the significance of class in contemporary British society? The study by Butler and Kavanagh of the general election of October 1974 indicated that Labour obtained 49 per cent of the skilled working-class vote, compared with 26 per cent for the Conservatives; and Labour got 57 per cent of the unskilled vote, compared with 22 per cent for the Conservatives. Class, then, remained an important factor in political allegiance.

It was also an important factor in the distribution of political power, as an analysis of the social composition of the first Thatcher Cabinet demonstrates. Margaret Thatcher herself is a symbol of the educational opportunity and upward mobility offered by the British system. From a lower-middle-class background (her father was a shopkeeper in Grantham), she went to a local grammar school and then on to Somerville College, Oxford. It might seem a pleasing portent of the times that hers was a science degree, and that she worked as a research chemist from 1947 to 1951. More significant really was the fact that in 1953 she became a barrister. And one cannot leave utterly out of account the fact that when she married her choice was a very wealthy second-generation businessman (by my definition, a member of the upper class). She herself remained ambivalently both subject to the allure of the upper class, and belligerently a representative of the hard-working middle class.

Nothing ambivalent about the next person in the political hierarchy, however. William Whitelaw (Home Secretary), described in *Who's Who* as a 'farmer and landowner', was educated at Winchester and Trinity College, Cambridge, becoming a regular officer in the Scots Guards; his eldest daughter married the second Earl of Swinton. Nor about the Lord Chancellor. Lord Hailsham had inherited a peerage, disclaimed it, then became a life peer. Educated at Eton, he took a double First (it is an absurd error to think of the upper class as stupid or indolent) at Christ Church, Oxford, and became a Fellow of All Souls, and a barrister. He was MP for Oxford at the age of thirty-one. Most secure of all in his position in the upper class was the Foreign Secretary, Lord Carrington, sixth in succession to a barony created in 1796 (in the Irish peerage) and 1797 (in the British peerage). His mother was the daughter of the second Viscount Colville and he himself married the daughter of Sir Francis McClean. Educated at Eton and Sandhurst, he achieved junior Government office at the age of thirty-two. His many directorships included Barclays, Rio Tinto Zinc, and Cadbury Schweppes. His country house is near Aylesbury, his town house in Chelsea.

The Chancellor of the Exchequer, Sir Geoffrey Howe, embodied the possibility of social mobility over three generations. His grandfather was working class, a metal worker and union leader in South Wales. His father, a solicitor in Port Talbot, was comfortably middle class. Howe won scholarships to Winchester and Trinity Hall, Cambridge, where he studied law. He became an extremely prosperous barrister, and received his knighthood in 1970.

Sir Keith Joseph, Secretary of State for Industry, confirmed the position his father, by founding the building firm of Bovis and becoming Lord Mayor of London, and, in 1943, a baronet, had won in the upper class. Joseph was educated at Harrow and Magdalen, Oxford, and, after distinguished war service, was elected a Fellow of All Souls. He became a barrister, and held directorships on Bovis and other companies. Francis Pym, Defence Secretary, is a prize example of the landed gentleman doing rather more than dabble in trade (as a manager with the department-store chain of Lewis's). Pym's father was a Conservative MP; he himself was educated at Eton and Magdalene, Cambridge; his clubs – Buck's, Cavalry, and Guards. The former Sir Christopher Soames (Lord President of the Council), created a life peer in 1978, was educated at Eton and Sandhurst, and married a daughter of Winston Churchill; his main directorships were in finance and banking.

In *Who's Who* James Prior (Employment Secretary) is described as a 'farmer and land agent', though he also held various directorships. After Charterhouse he took a First Class in Estate Management at Pembroke College, Cambridge. Sir Ian Gilmour (Lord Privy Seal) is the third holder of the baronetcy created in 1926. His mother was the daughter of Viscount Chelsea, eldest son of the fifth Earl of Cadogan, and he himself married lady Caroline Margaret Montagu-Douglas-Scott, daughter of the eighth Duke of Buccleuch and Queensberry. It is almost supererogatory to add that Gilmour was educated at Eton and Balliol. The working-class origins of Agriculture Secretary, Peter Walker, have already been mentioned. Walker won his way to a lesser public school, but did not go on to university. Doing well as a successful manager of broker and security companies he set himself up in landed property in Worcester, worth £80,000 in 1970.

Michael Heseltine, Environment Secretary, whose father was a Swansea colonel, was educated at Shrewsbury and Pembroke College, Oxford; his home outside Banbury visibly established him in that upper class whose existence Margaret Stacey had recognized in the first Banbury survey. Educated at Winchester and New College, Oxford, George Younger came from the Scottish brewing family of that name (less well known for its beer than the rival William Younger's, but famous for its close association with the Conservative Party). His father was the third Viscount Younger of Leckie and he himself held directorships in major brewing and whisky concerns. Nicholas Edwards, Secretary for Wales, a merchant banker, was educated at Westminster and Trinity College, Cambridge, and, in 1980, owned three houses, including a town house in Westminster. The Northern Ireland Secretary, Humphrey Atkins, was the son of a captain in 'Kenya Colony' (as *Who's Who* puts it) and was married to the daughter of Sir Robert Spencer-Nairn. Director of a firm of advertising agents, he was educated at Wellington whence he entered the Royal Navy; *Who's Who* lists his club as Brooks's.

Patrick Jenkin, Social Services Secretary, a barrister holding various directorships, was educated at Clifton and Jesus College, Cambridge. Norman St John-Stevas, Leader of the House, was a new arrival in the upper class, his father having been a civil engineer and company director by the name of Stevas, who was able to send his son to Ratcliffe, whence he went to Fitzwilliam College, Cambridge, and then, after taking a First in law, to Christ Church, Oxford. St John-Stevas was for a time a university lecturer in law. John Nott, Trade Secretary, after Bradfield and Trinity College, Cambridge, went on to enjoy the gentlemanly occupations of barrister, merchant banker, and director of various manufacturing companies. David Howell (Energy Secretary), son of a colonel, and educated at Eton and King's College, Cambridge (where he took a First), had entered Parliament at the age of thirty; his club was Buck's.

Neither the Secretary for Education and Science (Mark Carlisle) nor the Chief Secretary to the Treasury (John Biffen) quite had the complete upper-class education of all of their other colleagues apart from Walker and the Prime Minister herself. Carlisle went from Radley College to

Manchester University; Biffen started from Dr Morgan's Grammar School, Bridgwater, but arrived at Jesus College, Cambridge. However, the overwhelmingly upper-class composition of this Cabinet was reasserted by the last figure on the list, Angus Maude (Paymaster General), a gentlemanly journalist, son of a colonel, educated at Rugby and Oriel College, Oxford, and owner of another of those country houses in the vicinity of Banbury.

The purpose of that quick series of potted biographies was not to pillory the Conservative Party but to indicate the continuing hold of the upper class on political power. True, there was considerably less evidence of upper-class political power in the previous Labour Cabinet; yet what is most significant is that in the avowedly *labour* party such upper-class figures as Michael Foot and Anthony Wedgwood Benn continued to be so important. Of the 1977 Cabinet a quarter had been educated at public schools and Oxford (or, in one case, Cambridge). Otherwise Labour at the top proved to be 'meritocratic' (to use the language of Dr Timothy May) middle class, rather than working class.

Was Britain approaching a condition of open class conflict? In the seventies the everyday cold war of the work place many times erupted into large-scale strikes. In January 1979 there were more workers out on strike than at any time since the General Strike of 1926. But there *was* no general strike (as, for single days at a time, there was in France). The British working class was, no more than before, committed to the theory of class conflict; but, for practical economic gains, it was, occupational group by occupational group, prepared to demonstrate both its strength and its sense of apartness from employers, Government, and middle-class society generally. (The point was driven home by the relative failure of the 'day of protest' against Thatcherite economic policies in May 1980.)

It has become a commonplace to attribute Britain's poor economic record to its being a 'class-ridden' society. The epithet is an ambiguous one. In France, to take one instance, the social gulf between management and workers is often at least as great as in Britain; there is more formality and more stress on the dignity of titles and status. There is less educational mobility than in Britain – fewer working-class children at university, for instance. Formality, to the extent of pomposity, is also a feature of American society. Yet it is true that the forms of class are, historically, more deeply entrenched in British society; they were not seriously challenged in the forties, when they might have been, and were only slightly modified in the sixties. In the end, formality and authority in other industrialized societies are related to function: a boss behaves like a boss because he is a boss. In Britain a boss behaves as he does because he belongs to, or has been socialized into, a particular social background.

In all the recent British industrial confrontations, the accents stick out: when an employer's representative opens his mouth he immediately associates himself, not so much with employers as such, but with the upper class; if he happens to have a working-class, or regional middle-class accent, we register that immediately. The pride, traditions, and class awareness of the British worker have, over a period extending back into the nineteenth century, brought him to a position where he wages a constant, but usually very mild, cold war against his employer on the factory floor itself. He expresses little ideological hostility to the employer, and no desire to expropriate him. Feeling no sense of inferiority, his instinct is to stick among his own kind. He feels little involvement in the success of the enterprise in which he works. The French worker is either much more ideologically committed than his British counterpart, or, committed solely to his family and private interests, he goes in for the occasional ritual protest, typically the one-day strike, but otherwise co-operates efficiently with his employer, either because the day of revolution has not yet come, or because he sees it as in his own private interest to do so. The difference here is not between class and absence of class, but between the different ways in which the historical conditioning of the exact nature of class and perceptions of two classes has taken place. In Britain, the persistence of upper-class power, and the advent of organized working-class power, means that there is a constant refrain of hostility towards the middle-class small businessman who only in the 1980 budget at last received the protection of special legislation.

The differences in social habits and culture are greatest in Britain. The British working man eats one kind of rubbish; many middle-class workers eat a similar, more expensively presented, form of rubbish; the upper class does retain some claim to good taste. Managers in Britain are often distinguished most by their clothes, accents, and manners; since these are their main qualifications, they go out of their way to stress them.

Class is a product of history. The particular nature of class relationships in Britain during the Second World War was probably to her advantage; in the 1970s they were very much to her disadvantage. But other factors come in. The British working class has never joined in the 'American' ethos of expansionism, preferring rather to stand on pride in itself and its older traditions. The quirks and trimmings of class are a British preoccupation, and, in the upper reaches, playing the right part has too often been more important than getting things done. The upper class continued to hold too much political power for too long in Britain because there was no effective challenge to it.

The model of class structure presented on contemporary British television is one which recognizes the existence of class differences, but which sees them as largely related to culture rather than power. Most programmes tend to be set within a self-contained cultural milieu, whether upper class, middle class, or working class, with very little direct evidence of friction between different classes. Programmes presenting class conflict tend to be set in an earlier era.

The Butler and Kavanagh study of the October 1974 election brought out the continuing importance of class in voting preferences; but it also brought out that the single most significant factor now was race: 72 per cent of the 'coloured' vote went to Labour, with only 17 per cent going to the Conservatives. Was race now the single most significant divide in British society, eclipsing even the potency of class? One great irony, and perhaps a revealing one about British society, may be that while class was now being openly spoken about when it was no longer the supreme factor in social inequality that it had been in the 1930s, the well-bred reticence that once enveloped discussion of class had now switched itself to discussion of race, just when race was becoming an especially potent cause of inequality. In introducing a series of interviews made in the late seventies with West Indians living in London and published as *Black Testimony* (1978), an American sociologist, Thomas J. Cottle, remarked that:

In Great Britain there is too little discussion of racial matters; too much avoiding the matter in everyday discourse. To listen to some people is to believe there are no racial problems in the United Kingdom. To listen to others, is to hear the problem called minor, easily resolved, barely perplexing, or exaggerated, or subtle. It is none of these. No one who speaks with West Indian, Pakistani, Indian and Mauritian families living in England would call their circumstances minor, exaggerated, or subtle.

About the least combative attitude Cottle found was that of a labourer who admitted that his friends sometimes regarded him as 'being the good Nigger':

You think a white man's going to lose his job before a black one? Not in a life-time. Immigrants come last and go first, man. Everybody knows that. They start their layoffs and I'll be sitting home with my mother all day and talking with all these guys out of work. Then you'll see me talking politics. But what do I do to protect myself? I stay low and work until I drop. I don't let them think they can break me. They got to see how I'm a bull of a worker. And they'll tell you that too. In their minds, see, I'm just the smallest step up from being a slave. But in *my* mind, I know I'm earning what the next guy earns, the white guy, so I am no slave to *nobody*. To nobody, my friend. They can think *their* thoughts, and I'll think mine. I got the laugh so far because I am working, you see what I mean. They want to arrest me for thinking they're all a bunch of racists? hell, they might just as well go arrest every black man and woman in Britain, child too, believe me. These kids know where it's at.

A thirteen-year-old was rather more cynical:

Where's anything going to change for us? Where am I going to get money to help my mother and grandmother? What do you think my brothers can do about anything? Even if they can, it's a lot of years before any of us will be old enough to do anything. We ain't moving at all, man. The country seems to be slowing down too, these days, but families like mine, we haven't moved anywhere for a long, long time already. And see now what happens. My father can't find work over here, work he's fitted for, something he can do well. Are they keeping him from the good jobs because he's black? I'd say yes, sure they are. But how you going to prove it? How can you prove to these boards they have that this person or that person didn't get a job because they were black? Board people are just going to say, look around at all the white men out of work; who didn't give *them* jobs because of the colour of their skin? Or they'll say, look around where you live and you'll find men like your father working. Maybe it's your father. You can't prove these things to anybody. Board people work for the government. They don't make their own rules. The law says everybody has an equal chance, but anybody can see that's a lie.

A school-leaver unable to find employment remonstrated with his father:

If you don't even read the newspaper to find out what kids like me are going through now I pity you. What the hell you think this is all about, man? You think this is a game I am playing, running all over this city begging people to make up work for me to do? Deliver little parcels for them or wipe up floors? You think it's going to get better, that suddenly the government's going to hand down a million new jobs for people? You know what they got planned? They got this thing so worked out it makes me sick. They got a plan that all the little coloured kids, we're told to leave school and think about jobs and making money. Then you know what happens? A few of us get our little rotten work so we're helping them, right? But the most of us, we don't get anything.

Shortly this youth took to organized car stealing and was later sent to borstal.

Many West Indians had a clear picture of how they believed individual whites saw them:

You are unwanted. You are here because some higher order official let you stay, not because I want you. Yet it is my position and not the official's position that is threatened by your presence, your very being. You should have been stopped before you arrived, you should be sent back even if you have been here for a while. You only create problems. You want my job, you want my food, you want to live in my home, you want to use my school, my hospital, my stores. But don't take it personally; I have no quarrel with you as a person. It's immigration I cannot tolerate.

Cottle also recorded the views of a fifty-year-old white dairy worker from the Midlands:

It is a crime, all of it. First they come here where they don't belong, and they know it. Then they want their relatives and their relatives' relatives. And would you believe, the government lets them have anything they wish, at any time they wish. But help those of us already here? no, they haven't an ear for that. I suppose the next step will be the government telling us *we* don't belong here anymore because we're sixth generation, or tenth generation. All you have to do is look at a map and you can see how small the country is. There isn't any room for these people. The laws on immigration are so confused the MPs themselves haven't a clue to what they mean. But they turn their back on it. They just turn their back on it. But help the people who've been here these hundreds of years? oh no. We're the new immigrants. I see what happens in countries where all of this has taken place. This isn't new to the world, you know. But can we learn from it, do you suppose? I should have thought so, but I am pessimistic about it now. I don't see but that they've let it go on too long. They should never have let in those people, people who make all these demands, and complain about their circumstances. There are no jobs for them, no money, the schools are crowded where their children go. It's no good at all.

Then, more emphatically, this white testimony continued:

They're going to bring down this country if they're not careful. They'll topple it. The rich will leave and the rest of us will go it alone with them. It will come down. You remember what I tell you. But there will be blood before it happens because people here won't take it. We've asked for nothing special, but we'll start asking now. That's the only way to stand up to this. You know, I talk about this and I feel my body reacting to those people. It's not just my mind. It's my whole person. Oh, you'll see changes now. They've already started.

West Indians quite clearly felt that racist attitudes in white society spread far beyond the small minority who through the National Front openly advocated violent confrontation with immigrant communities. Much of the National Front support came in decaying urban areas where there were large immigrant populations. Among Jeremy Seabrook's interviewees was one who readily explained why he fought for the National Front:

I don't want parts of my country to become no-go areas, where I feel I can't walk without the risk of being knifed or mugged. I don't want to be with black people, I don't want a multi-racial country. Why should I? I've got nothing in common with them, they don't want to mix with me anymore than I do with them. Why should I be forced to live with them? I want to be able to go into a pub, I want to be able to go to work without seeing a black face. The National Front is saying the sort of things I want to hear. I wouldn't be cruel. If I ran over a black in my car, I wouldn't just leave him lying in the road; I'd kick him into the gutter. I don't want them here. I want them to leave. I understand that this might be a bit disruptive. If the barricades do go up, it won't be the middle class on one side and the working class on the other; it'll be white on one side and black on the other, with just a few race traitors on their side. I want to be just with our own. I don't want to live in a system that falls over itself to favour blacks. If there's anything going in this country, I want it for myself. We've suffered enough in the past, and now it's our turn. We've had one flabby government after another saying, 'We've got to learn to live together.' Well, why? They don't have to live with them, killing goats, wailing at dusk and fasting and being a nuisance.

Predictions about the likelihood of serious racial violence went back some time. The report of the Hunt Committee on Immigrants in the Youth Service back in 1967 had declared that 'If England is not to be the scene of race riots' then 'the time for action is now'. 'Tomorrow', it concluded, would be 'too late'. In 1976, Mark Bonham-Carter, Chairman of the Community Relations Commission, warned that Britain's black population, 40 per cent of whom were born in Britain, would not settle for second-class citizenship 'in exchange for a higher standard of living and the prospect of some employment. They are British, and they take the phrase "equality of opportunity" for what it means. I have no doubt we have not kept pace with the expectations of British-born blacks.' At this very time, the Callaghan Labour Government did introduce a new Race Relations Act which declared all forms of discrimination illegal, and set up a Commission for Racial Equality with powers of enforcement. Some commentators took the view that it is not possible to legislate for people's attitudes. However, legislation is important for establishing what is held to be the norm of correct behaviour in any society.

The basic problems were appalling housing, lack of job opportunities, particularly for the young, the mistrust felt between immigrant communities and the police, and, more simply, the ineluctable vagaries of human behaviour. On the last point one can again quote Cottle's 'good Nigger':

There are four pubs around here where some of the men go for lunch or after work. All I have to do is put my head through the door of all those places and I know I'm not wanted in there. So I don't go. You think I don't know I should, that I have to go in there if I want things to open up in Britain? A good-looking black girl, she can go in there, they'll be happy to have her maybe. But a dirty worker, man from the local construction site, black man, they don't want him, so I am glad to sit in the car and talk, because lunchtime is when the segregation of staff starts up all over again.

There is abundant evidence on the penultimate, and more critical, point: almost every black felt himself to be a potential 'sus' (suspect) and to be subject to constant police harassment. The police, indeed, had problems of their own and the National Police Federation Conference in 1971, devoted to community relations, spoke feelingly of the police being placed on top of a pressure cooker.

The complicated and ambivalent nature of relationships between the police and immigrant communities was brought out at successive Bank Holiday West Indian festivals at Notting Hill. There was evidence there, as elsewhere, of genuine police attempts at fraternization. But there was also appalling violence, thieving, and destruction of property. Community leaders claimed that by their very presence in force the police provoked violence. The police claimed that their very presence was essential to restrain criminality. On the late afternoon of Wednesday, 2 April 1980, and on into the night, a police raid on a club in the poverty-stricken St Paul's district of Bristol led to rioting in which nineteen policemen and six other people were taken to hospital, and in which a bank, other buildings, and police cars were burnt out, with at the same time much looting and vandalism. At one stage the police had been forced to withdraw totally from the area, before coming back with heavy reinforcements. The riot was said not to be a race riot, but one against the police: many of those arrested were white.

It must always be remembered that the immigrant communities themselves are not homogeneous. Ironically, the most energetic and aggressive group, the West Indians, were probably in many ways the most assimilable; it was the Indians and the Pakistanis, generally industrious, often prosperous, and frequently high achievers at school, who more obviously presented the alien ways which stuck in the craw of xenophobic Britons. On 23 April 1979 the National Front deliberately held a meeting in the Town Hall of Southall, a predominantly Asian community in West London. Four thousand policemen were drafted in to confront 3,000 anti-National Front demonstrators. A large number of these were Asians, but there were also many whites; and it was a white teacher, Blair Peach, who was killed that day, quite possibly at the hands of a member of the Metropolitan Special Patrol Group.

Race might well be seen, then, as a more significant, and certainly more dangerous, divide in British society than class. By contrast, the fury of nationalism was much abated. The Scottish National Party did stunningly well in the October 1974 election: gaining eleven seats, it also put at risk a further thirty-five Labour-held seats and seven Conservative seats. While the issue was far less clear-cut in Wales, it certainly seemed throughout most of the seventies that devolution must be granted to Scotland if total separation was to be avoided. Yet when the referendum came in March 1979, only 32 per cent of the Scots (a clear majority of those voting, though, it should be stressed) and 12 per cent of the Welsh actually voted for devolution. Such issues, it was clear, were still minor compared with older class, newer race, and universal economic questions.

At the end of 1973 and the beginning of 1974 press, television, and political platforms were dominated by the question 'Is Britain ungovernable?'. The year 1974 was indeed unprecedented for violent death on the British mainland; that fact, taken along with the miners' strike of 1973–4, the gathering race problem, and the apparent strength of Scottish and Welsh separatism, did suggest that perhaps traditional British social cohesion was breaking down at last. In July 1974 an IRA bomb attack at the Tower of London killed one woman and badly injured forty-one children. In October and November there were IRA pub bombings near army barracks in Guildford and Woolwich: seven were killed. Then at Birmingham in November, in a horrific pub holocaust, twenty-one were killed and 162 injured. The forty-fifth fatality occurred in June 1974, in Red Lion Square, London, Kevin Gateley being killed when a Trotskyist counter-demonstration met a National Front demonstration. Actually, the worst violence associated with a mining strike had taken place in February 1972 at the Saltley Coke Depot, Birmingham: in 1973–4 the mine workers' leaders deliberately enforced restraint upon their pickets. The other violent industrial event of the early seventies was associated with the building workers' strike in the summer of 1972, and arose out of the primitive sub-contracting conditions in that industry, known as 'the lump': the menacing intimidation carried through by pickets at Shrewsbury resulted in three prison sentences. What really made 1974 such a bloody year was the activity of the IRA; hence the enactment of the 1974 Prevention of Terrorism Act.

British attitudes towards the Irish had always been, to say the least, ambivalent. Throughout the period studied by this book Irish jokes based on the premiss of the utter stupidity of the Irish were rampant (for example, an Irishman is asked to explain why he signs his name with three crosses: the first two are for 'Patrick Murphy'; the third, it transpires, is 'for my degree from University College, Dublin'). Most Britons did not discriminate very closely between citizens of the Irish Republic and citizens of Northern Ireland. As violence escalated, the attitude revealed in public opinion polls was very much that of 'a plague on both your houses'. A clear majority believed that British troops should be withdrawn from Northern Ireland allowing both factions, increasingly perceived in Britain as illiterate bigots, to fight things out for themselves.

In Britain violence broke out again in June and July of 1977, during a strike at the Grunwick film-processing factory in West London. Grunwick was run by a tough self-made small businessman, himself of Asian origins; his factory largely employed Asian labour. The attempt at Grunwick to secure basic trade-union conditions for the employees became a *cause célèbre* of the left, bringing in not just Trotskyites, but also respectable leaders of the Labour Party. 'This is the Ascot of the left,' one demonstrator declared. 'It is essential to be seen here, best of all to get arrested.' During the most violent phases, ninety-seven policemen were injured, one very seriously by a milk bottle.

The factors, then, which contributed to the 'ungovernability' thesis, or at least to the view that traditional British tolerance and non-violence were breaking down, were: Edward Heath's failed confrontation with the miners in 1973–4; IRA terror attacks (involving in 1977 the death of a distinguished surgeon, and in 1979 of a leading Conservative politician, Airey Neave); the abandonment by public workers of older civic restraints upon their right to strike (putting patients' lives in danger, for instance); the activities of the National Front; the counter-activities, and involvement in strikes, of Trotskyist groups; the development of the tactic of the flying picket; and the increasing use at demonstrations of the Metropolitan Police Special Patrol Group. There were ugly new scars on the face of British society, to be sure. But against these can be placed trade-union restraint and the social contract observed between 1976 and 1978. And even in the gloomy year of 1980, talk of ungovernability and insurrection had rather less plausibility than it had had in 1974.

14
Living Standards

Year by year throughout the 1970s the Central Statistical Office publication *Social Trends* contained special articles on aspects of recent social history. In 1975, in keeping with what was said in the previous chapter of the way in which class now dared to speak its name, the article was 'Social Class'. The 1980 edition, the tenth issue, featured an article, 'Changes in Living Standards Since the 1950s', which covered both 'material living standards' and 'the rôle of publicly provided services'; in, therefore, borrowing for the title of this chapter the rather colourless phrase 'living standards' I shall be putting together topics 5 and 6 of my original list of major areas of social change: social welfare and material conditions. The article itself is very far from gloomy, the tone being set by a cover drawing in which a family of six, perched on a ration book dated 1951, give place to a family of four wheeling a supermarket trolley full of provisions. 'Consumerism' – the growth of supermarkets, the availability of credit for the purchase of durable consumer goods, and, latterly, the use of credit cards for the whole gamut of purchases from alcohol to dining-room suites – was indeed a central phenomenon of the age.

Tory radicals in the 1960s had argued that as society became more affluent the need for the Welfare State would wither away. In actual fact, as the majority grew more affluent the needs of the individuals and groups left behind were more sharply revealed. Conservative and Labour spokesmen voiced differences over the respective weighting to be given to collectivist initiatives or market forces in the provision of welfare facilities; but as far as welfare policies affected individual members of society there was striking continuity between the policies of the Labour Government which fell in 1970, the Heath Conservative Government which fell in 1974, and the Wilson and Callaghan Labour administrations which lasted till

1979. Over the major part of the decade social policy was determined by six main factors. First, there was the developing awareness of the new types of personal deprivation constantly being revealed in a high-spending consumer society. Secondly, there was a new and far more sophisticated approach to the problem of job protection, deriving partly from a recognition that too often in the recent past working-class jobs had remained rather less secure than any others. Thirdly, in a time of mounting inflation, more elaborate attention was given to the question of income protection. Fourthly, basically on grounds of administrative and financial efficiency, there were alterations in administrative structures (in part related to local government reform) and attempts to avoid making superfluous benefit payments. Fifthly, a factor running against the first three, and in some respects the fourth as well, a worsening economic situation enforced greater attention to questions of economy. Sixthly, demographic changes, and above all the slowing-down in population growth in the middle of the decade, forced changes in broad planning targets and priorities.

Within the realm of income maintenance and social security, the major piece of legislation, the Social Security Act passed by the Heath Conservative Government in 1973, was essentially a consolidating Act. As far as recipients were concerned, not a great deal changed when the provisions of the new Act came into force in January 1976. Income loss due to unemployment continued to be covered through Unemployment Benefit, dependent upon the payment of National Insurance contributions, and Supplementary Benefits. To qualify for Unemployment Benefit the unemployed person had to have paid, or been credited with, fifty weekly contributions in the previous calendar year. Payment did not begin till after three days of unemployment and ceased after one year, though eligibility for benefit could be reviewed after the payment of thirteen contributions. The Earnings Related Supplement did not become payable till after two weeks of unemployment and ended after twenty-six weeks. Where there was no entitlement to Unemployment Benefit, or where such entitlement had become exhausted, Supplementary Benefits came into play, as they did also if a man's National Insurance benefit was below the Supplementary Benefit scale, though, where relevant, the wage stop was applied. Penalties applied where unemployment was voluntary or due to misconduct or where, in the case of a single man, other employment in the area was available. In the former two cases a disqualification for six weeks could apply; in the latter the single man could be refused benefit after four weeks. Though persons on strike could not themselves receive Unemployment Benefit or Supplementary Benefit they could, and this was a matter on which some Conservatives became increasingly outspoken, receive such benefits on behalf of their dependants.

The rather unsatisfactory Redundancy Payment Scheme of 1965 remained in force; but with, after 1974, a new range of devices designed to protect employment, or at least income. The major innovation was the Employment Protection Act of 1975 whose provisions covered the right not to be unfairly dismissed, entitlements to a written statement of terms and conditions of employment, guaranteed pay, time off work for trade-union duties, and also redundancy pay, minimum periods of notice, and maternity rights. It also covered suspension from work on medical grounds and an employee's rights when the employer became insolvent. The Act, as we have seen from Chapter 12, could not act as a bulwark against industrial recession. Nor could various job creation schemes, including the Employment Subsidies Act of 1978, whereby payments were made to employers to enable them to retain or recruit employees, reverse the tide. The Labour Government sought to achieve the aim of income maintenance in old age through linking social security pensions to the cost of living index, and through pressing for the adoption of private schemes whose basic feature was the provision of a pension related to the level of earnings on retirement (such as, for instance, the Universities Superannuation Scheme – USS – in replacement of the older FSSU scheme).

Sickness benefits, for which the self-employed as well as the employed made contributions and therefore were covered, were paid on a rate related to earnings for twenty-six weeks, after which there was an inexhaustible invalidity benefit paid at the basic sickness benefit rate. In practice there were considerable inequalities in the way different social classes were treated, it being quite customary in professional middle-class employments for sick employees to go on being paid their salary, whereas manual workers became immediately dependent upon social security benefits. Employed women who paid the full rate of National Insurance contributions were entitled to maternity benefit enabling them to stay off work for some time before and after confinement. On the birth of a child a maternity grant could be paid provided either the father or the mother had an adequate record of National Insurance payments.

Those disabled at work received Industrial Injuries Benefits. Otherwise, the disabled had to depend upon Supplementary Benefits subject to a needs test. From October 1972 Attendance Allowances were payable to those forced to give special attention to the disabled. A unique product of the Heath Conservative Government's desire to bring back some voluntary element into the Welfare State was the provision in 1973 of £3 million to set up the Family Fund, administered by the Joseph Rowntree Memorial Trust on behalf of the Government, to provide grants to the parents of children under sixteen suffering from severe congenital handicaps. For the first six months after widowhood the Earnings Related Widows' Allowance was paid at a rate higher than the basic Unemployment and Sickness benefits. What happened after six months depended on the age and responsibilities of the widow. The needs of widows and orphans might also be covered by occupational pension schemes. As a general rule these various benefits came to an end if the widow re-married, or, more unsatisfactorily, if she was deemed to be cohabiting with a man. Though stuffiness, and even harshness, continued in regard to the vexed question of cohabitation, there was a general humanizing of attitude towards single-parent families. Where a woman was entitled to maintenance, but was finding difficulty in actually getting it, the Department of Health and Social Security would pay Supplementary Benefits at the full rate and then endeavour to recover the maintenance payments itself. In the administration of Family Income Supplement, a non-contributory scheme introduced by the Heath administration to provide benefits for low-income families with dependent children, single-parent families were treated on a level with two-parent ones.

Though social security was undoubtedly patchy and inadequate in certain areas, Government commitment in this area did not in any way contract in the 1970s. Even making allowances for inflation, the actual increase in Government expenditure is made very clear from Table 4.

Changes in the National Health Service very much follow the same pattern. The major Act, again passed by the Heath Conservative Government, was the National Service Reorganization Act of 1973: however, services for the consumer, as a leading authority put it, had 'not changed. Patients see the same family doctors and attend the same hospitals to see the same specialists.' The essence of the reorganization was the replacement of the much criticized tripartite structure set up by the Act of 1946 by what was intended to be a more unified system, but which, in the upshot, proved more complex and bureaucratic than the old structure. At the top, there was still the Secretary of State, advised by the Central Health Services Council and served by the officers of the Department of

Table 4: Government expenditure on social-security benefits

Central Government current expenditure	Year ended 31 March										£million
	1968/9	1969/70	1970/71	1971/2	1972/3	1973/4	1974/5	1975/6	1976/7	1977/8	1978/9
National insurance:											
Retirement pensions*	1,578	1,663	1,818	2,092	2,422	2,894	3,751	4,898	5,777	6,739	7,719
Widows' benefits and guardians' allowances	159	168	174	203	228	254	323	409	451	485	525
Unemployment benefit	132	135	158	250	219	182	227	473	582	655	660
Sickness benefit	362	401	394	338	306	325	372	460	538	636	688
Invalidity benefit	—	—	—	96	208	255	339	475	596	740	887
Maternity benefit	39	39	42	44	44	44	48	57	84	96	126
Death grant	11	12	11	13	13	14	14	15	15	16	16
Injury benefit	35	34	33	32	33	35	36	40	47	51	52
Disablement benefit	63	64	69	75	83	92	116	152	175	200	226
Industrial death benefit	8	9	9	10	12	14	18	23	26	30	31
War pensions	124	124	127	136	150	164	204	258	283	310	340
Family allowances	310	354	354	359	354	359	359	554	567	906	1,858
Supplementary benefits:											
Old persons	215	233	253	286	285	284	318	419	491	644	757
Unemployed persons	79	80	95	155	191	150	200	381	575	679	706
Sick persons	72	76	81	84	85	96	118	129	134	152	159
Other persons in need	80	100	115	140	154	185	237	306	387	452	484
Other non-contributory benefits:											
Old persons' pensions	—	—	8	24	28	29	32	36	38	38	37
Family income supplement	—	—	—	5	11	14	14	14	20	28	30
Attendance allowance	—	—	—	6	25	38	66	102	136	175	193
Mobility allowance	—	—	—	—	—	—	—	—	8	21	49
Invalidity pension	—	—	—	—	—	—	—	12	37	48	72
Lump sums to pensioners	—	—	—	—	81	3	3	—	—	98	126
Administration	143	167	186	230	246	292	376	538	608	675	747
Total Government expenditure	3,410	3,659	3,927	4,578	5,178	5,723	7,171	9,751	11,575	13,874	16,490

* Including lump-sum payments to pensioners amounting to £79 million in 1973/4 and £90 million in 1974/5
Source: Central Statistical Office

Health and Social Security. At the next level all services were integrated within the fourteen Regional Health Authorities. As part of an intended move towards efficiency and greater professionalization, the chairmen of these Authorities were paid; and advice was provided by the Regional Advisory Committees, representing the Health Services' staff, and given statutory recognition. Thirdly came the ninety Area Health Authorities, which took over all the functions of the old Hospital Management Committees and Local Executive Councils, as well as most of those of the local authorities. Chairmen were appointed by the Secretary of State, the rest of the members being appointed by local authorities, universities, and the Regional Health Authorities, and had to include at least one doctor and one nurse. Unfortunately there was a serious and disruptive mismatch between these Area Health Authorities and the new local government units.

The miracle of the National Health Service, if newspapers and television were anything to go by, was not that it did so much but that it managed to survive at all: the rumbling malaise of the sixties, apparently, had become feverish crisis. The facts and figures are less conclusive. All had never been completely well with the National Health Service – has it ever been with health provision anywhere in the world? The tale of the seventies is a mixed one: advances in some areas, retreats in others, but certainly not one of unrelieved gloom. Crude international comparisons show Britain spending a lower proportion of the National Income on health than other industrialized countries. Yet anyone who has encountered the sheer terror with which the prospect of hospitalization is faced in many walks of life in North America, or anyone, even, who has encountered the system of retrospective reimbursement of medical expenses to be found on the European Continent, would be hard put to it to maintain that Britain then had inferior services. It was true that qualified medical staff were poorly paid in Britain compared with their counterparts overseas; it was also true that the British service was rather heavily dependent at various levels upon immigrant personnel: the passing of the Medical Act 1978 implicitly recognized that some Asian doctors were not as well qualified in all aspects as they ought to have been.

In general, the National Health Service in the later seventies was distinguished by greater participation at local level than ever before, though most informed commentators doubted whether more efficient management had been achieved. The general practitioner service improved throughout the decade: in 1973 there were 2,386 patients per doctor; in 1978 2,312 (2,148 in Wales and 1,875 in Scotland). On the other hand, the number of fully staffed hospital beds was in decline: 437,000 in 1973 to 395,000 in England and Wales in 1978. The average length of time that people spent in hospital fell, and the average number of patients in hospital each day fell from 436,000 in 1971 to 380,000 in 1978. Taking a longer time-span the number of people treated as in-patients rose from about 5 million in 1961 to over 6.6 million in 1977. In general, waiting-lists steadily lengthened, though there were fluctuations: the total queue in 1976 was 722,000, which actually fell to 715,000 in 1977, before rising to 801,000 in 1978. Total public expenditure on the Health Services rose by 10 per cent at constant prices between 1973–4 and 1978–9, but an alarming and accelerating proportion of expenditure was going on drugs and other medicines. The share of the pharmaceutical services rose by 17.4 per cent between 1951 and 1978. In the same period the shares taken by the general medical, the dental, and the ophthalmic services fell by 5.8, 7.3, and 4.3 per cent respectively. From the middle seventies contraceptives became free through the National Health Service, though the problem remained that too few people availed themselves of this facility. In the opinion of most experts the reformed abortion law of the sixties was now working humanely and under effective supervision, and was much in the interests of the health and well-being of women in general. Equally, a major aim of the National Health Service was that all women having their first babies should have them in hospital. In 1960, 66 per cent of all births had been in hospital; by 1977, 98 per cent of all births were in hospital, and practically all women having their first babies had the confinement there.

Attempts at developing private medical services had not been strikingly successful in the 1960s. Now, in a time of constant rumours of crisis, long waiting-lists, official encouragement to employers to provide welfare schemes, and the new conception of unions, particularly among professional workers, as corporations representing all the interests of their members, there was up to 1975, and again after 1977, a great increase in private medical care through group schemes (though, at the same time, there was actually a slight decline in the number of individual subscribers). Group health schemes contained about 672,000 subscribers in 1978, with most or all of the contributions being paid by employers. Many of these schemes covered dependants, so that, in all, company health insurance schemes were covering about 2.4 million people. Private hospitals and nursing homes contained about 34,500 beds (many of these for the use of wealthy overseas, rather than British, patients).

In 1945 the fundamental housing problem had been that too many people did not have a home of their own, that too many people were crammed into decaying, inadequate properties: in short, that there were too few houses and too many of these were below the standard proper to a civilized community. By 1980 there were, in global terms, more dwellings than there were households and the vast majority of the population did have the basic facilities of inside toilet, bathroom, and so on. The characteristic slums of this era were the heartless public housing estates built in the fifties and sixties and now stuck on a descending spiral into Hades as, a natural target for frustration and vandalism, they increasingly became dumping grounds for problem families. Authority recognized the problem, as authority for a hundred years had recognized the problem of the traditional slums. On paper, new policies of conservation and renovation, and, indeed, of evacuation and even destruction of housing stock less than a quarter of a century old, were now in force, but, alas, the massive sums necessary to remedy the sins of yesterday were not available. The main concern in the post-war years had been with providing housing for the working class as a class: by the late seventies, as was the case in so many other aspects of welfare policy, the problem was no longer seen as a class one, but as one relating to distinctive deprived groups, in this case, black and Asian immigrants, the homeless, and gypsies.

Throughout the United Kingdom in 1978 there were about 19,901,000 households while at the same time the actual number of separate dwellings totalled 21,101,000. In every region there existed more dwellings than families to fill them, though in London the margin was very narrow indeed. Yet many people seeking homes were unable to find them. The trouble was that, as a survey carried out in 1977 indicated, there were about 729,000 dwellings standing empty for various reasons: around 127,000 were being converted or modernized and were therefore uninhabitable; a sizeable number of the remainder belonged to those prosperous enough to own second homes.

House building danced in erratic time with the economy. In 1968 413,700 houses had been built. In 1971 the figure was 350,600, in 1972 319,300, in 1973 294,100, in 1974 269,500, in 1975 313,000, in 1976 315,200, in 1977 302,700, and in 1978 279,200. Within these figures there was a significant shift away from public construction to private construction. In 1978 152,000 houses were built within the private sector and only 136,000 in the public sector. Owner-occupation was on the advance, as the figures for the different types of tenure in Table 5 show.

Table 5: Stock of dwellings: change and tenure

Stock of dwellings – at end of period (millions):	1951–60	1961–70	1971–4	1975	1976	1977	1978
Owner-occupied	6.97	9.57	10.57	10.76	10.96	11.16	11.39
Rented from local authorities or new town corporations	4.40	5.85	6.09	6.40	6.56	6.70	6.79
Rented from private owners	4.31 ⎫						
Tied accommodation	0.93 ⎭	3.77	3.42	3.19	3.09	3.01	2.93
Total	16.60	19.18	20.10	20.35	20.61	20.86	21.11

Source: *Social Trends* (1980)

Again we must remember the variousness of British social geography. Whereas in the country as a whole 54 per cent of dwellings were owner-occupied, with 32 per cent rented from local authorities, and 14 per cent from private owners, the figure for owner-occupation was as high as 62 per cent in south-eastern areas outside of Greater London (where it was only 48 per cent) and 63 per cent in the South-West; in Scotland, the only part of the United Kingdom where local authority housing at 54 per cent accounted for more than half of all dwellings, it was only 35 per cent. There was, of course, a correlation between housing type and social class. But more and more the line of demarcation was occurring within the working class itself. Skilled workers were joining with the professionals in buying houses; more and more it was unskilled workers who formed council tenants.

There are simple measurements of housing standards. A dwelling is judged to be overcrowded if it falls below the 'bedroom standard'. This standard allows one bedroom for each married couple, one each for other men and women aged twenty-one or over, one each for two people of the same sex aged ten–twenty, one for any person aged ten–twenty together with a child under ten of the same sex, and one for any person aged ten–twenty not covered by the above, with one for each two of any remaining children and one for any child remaining. Other major indicators of below-standard housing are the lack of the sole use of a bath or shower and the lack of the sole use of a WC inside the building. A new indicator, and very much a sign of the times, was that of whether or not the house had central heating. As Table 6 shows, there has been considerable all-round improvement since 1971.

Overcrowding and lack of amenities were most heavily concentrated in immigrant households. Overcrowding was more prevalent in Scotland than elsewhere in Britain; but on the whole, largely because of the high proportion of recent public authority housing, Scotland was well off for basic amenities.

A number of pressures combined to push immigrants into the worst decaying areas, often ones scheduled for eventual demolition. Public concern over the special problem of the homeless, officially defined as those housed in local authority temporary accommodation, came to a head in 1974. A number of voluntary organizations, such as Shelter, had already come into being in the 1960s. In 1974, following a recommendation made in the Seebohm Report on the homeless, practical responsibility for providing accommodation for the homeless was vested in the housing authorities rather than the Social Services. The 1974 Government circular 'Homelessness' urged local authorities to work closely with the voluntary housing movement and be ready to make loans or grants to help them. Finally, increasing attention was given in the seventies to the plight of gypsies. Although the Caravan Sites Act of 1968 appeared to require local authorities to provide sites for gypsies, in fact most local authorities took advantage of the exemptions in the Act. All indications suggested that the number of travellers and gypsies was on the increase.

For much of the population, however, the crucial problem was the gigantic inflation in house prices through the 1970s. Although modest Government and local authority support was given to some first-time house-buyers, at no time did the number of mortgages available match the demand. If all forms of public expenditure on housing, including loans and grants in the private sector as well as subsidies to public-sector housing, are taken together, such expenditure was in 1978–9 15 per cent up on 1973–4, 8 per cent down on 1976–7, and 3 per cent up on 1977–8.

Of all the major issues of social policy in the seventies, education engendered most controversy. The Labour Government after 1974 pushed forward vigorously with its policy of directly absorbing public-sector grammar schools into comprehensive schools and indirectly pressuring 'independent' schools to do the same by withdrawing their 'direct grants'. With various degrees of intensity Conservatives opposed this universalist policy, as indeed did some Labour supporters when faced, as parents, with the problem that overall social good might conflict with the educational

Table 6: Housing standards: by tenure, 1971 and 1978

Percentages

| | below bedroom standard | | lacking sole use of | | | | with central heating | | Total sample size (= 100%) | |
| | | | bath/shower | | wc inside building | | | | | |
	1971	1978	1971	1978	1971	1978	1971	1978	1971	1978
Owned outright	3	2	12	5	13	6	39	52	2,654	2,634
Owned with mortgage or loan	4	3	4	2	5	2	57	73	3,206	3,478
All owner-occupiers	4	3	7	3	9	3	49	64	5,860	6,109
Rented from local authority/New Town	10	6	3	5	5	2	24	43	3,691	3,999
Rented privately unfurnished	8	4	33	19	37	18	15	28	2,043	1,309
Rented privately furnished	19	14	58	52	57	51	17	27	320	283
All tenures	7	4	12	6	13	6	34	52	11,914	11,700

Source: *Social Trends* (1980)

prospects of their child. In fact, the debate over whether or not the absorption of grammar schools into comprehensive schools meant a lowering of standards or not was a confused one. Alas, both sides seemed more concerned to make a case than to get at objective facts. But whether well-founded or not, fears were spreading among parents and educationists alike that standards in British schools were not as high as they might be. Independent schools now had to charge far higher fees but, along with the public schools, they tended to prosper as it became clear that many parents would prefer to buy their way out of a state system which they increasingly distrusted. The Labour Party at last brought positive proposals for ending the privileged position of the public schools into its programme; though once more, between 1974 and 1979, nothing was actually done. Labour, at the very least, could be accused of inconsistency, and indeed of a hostility towards the middle class, thrown into relief by its tenderness towards the upper class, when in pushing through its policies of making the entire state secondary system comprehensive, it left open increasingly expensive independent and public schools for the privileged to escape to.

The arguments for a universal comprehensive system, as with the arguments for a universalist national health service, are very strong indeed. But they become seriously weakened when loopholes are left. Beyond that, it became apparent that, as in the United States, comprehensive schools in certain better-off areas had higher standards than comprehensive schools in impoverished areas. Thus, the comprehensive principle in itself was very far from abolishing inequalities. Altogether the total number of school pupils declined slightly after 1977, which would probably stand out as the peak year of the century, to 11,221,000. Of these 614,000 were in assisted or independent schools.

At another level, probably the most serious educational problem towards the end of the decade was the high level of teacher unemployment and of unemployment among the academically qualified in general. Even before the return of the Thatcher Government in 1979 public-spending cuts were affecting all aspects of higher and further education, as well as schooling in general. If public expenditure at constant prices on education is taken as 100 for 1977–8, it had stood at 102 in 1973–4, 104 in 1976–7, and was slightly up again to 102 in 1978–9, before the more drastic cuts struck.

In introducing the concept of the Welfare State as it emerged in the post-war years, I suggested that apart from the four major areas of social concern, a welfare state could also be taken to embrace a miscellaneous range of other pieces of social legislation. Such other legislation, indeed, indicates changes in the areas of social concern. In the 1970s, apart from questions of race and sex discrimination which I deal with elsewhere, the major special concerns were with the environment and consumer protection. Under the latter head, one might note the Control of Pollution Act 1974, the Community Land Act 1975, and the Inner Urban Areas Act 1978, designed to assist the regeneration of inner-city areas; and under the second head, such legislation as the Consumer Safety Act of 1978.

If we take together the economic and geographical aspects discussed in Chapter 12 together with the social policy issues just discussed, we arrive at the actual living conditions of British people in this period. Broadly, British people in the late seventies were healthier and had higher life expectancy than ever before, but one or two killers of the contemporary age were strengthening their grip, particularly cancer and heart disease.

On the vexed matter of real income the long-term perspective is well worth bearing in mind. Using 1975 prices, average earnings for a man in manual work rose from the equivalent of £31 a week to £54 a week between 1951 and 1975. The proportionate increase for women was rather greater. Put another way, a manual worker with average earnings would have had to work thirty-four minutes to buy a pint of beer in 1950, but only eighteen minutes in 1977.

For all of their intrusive quality, and the agony they caused, high-rise flats housed only a minority of British people. In fact four out of five households were accommodated in houses not flats. The traditional terraced housing of the early part of the twentieth century still provided dwellings for one quarter of all households. Families or individuals with private households of their own totalled 97 per cent. The official hand-book, *Britain 1979*, expressed the essence of British aspiration, even if a slightly embellished view of reality: 'Many British families now live in houses grouped in small terraces, or semi-detached or detached, usually of two storeys with gardens, and providing two main ground-floor living rooms, a kitchen, from two to four bedrooms, a bathroom, and one or two lavatories.' Over one half of all families owned their own homes, though half of these were still paying off mortgages. One third of all families moved house every five years.

Spending patterns did not alter drastically in the seventies from those established in the first era of affluence. In many respects it was more of the same: in the late seventies about 50 per cent of households had a telephone, about 52 per cent use of at least one car, and 11 per cent use of at least two cars, 88 per cent a fridge, 71 per cent a washing machine, but only 3 per cent a dishwasher. The big development in central heating has already been noted; by 1978 natural gas was being piped to fourteen million homes, and nearly six million used it for central heating. The most significant new modern convenience was the deep-freezer. In 1970 only about 4 per cent of households owned one, by 1972 this had risen to about 8 per cent, and by 1978 to 41 per cent. Correspondingly there was a sharp rise in the 1970s in the purchase of frozen foods. Five other areas, which tell us something about the fashions and fads of the time, are also of significance. Traditionally the British had been addicted to unhealthy white bread, tasting of tissue paper. Yet 12 per cent of all bread eaten in 1977 was of the wholemeal type and there was a general increase in the consumption of 'health' foods. Secondly, an enormous boom was apparent in do-it-yourself. In 1978 over one billion pounds was spent on do-it-yourself products: householders (often women) pasted nearly one million kilometres of wallpaper and used about one hundred million litres of paint. Over roughly the same period, to move to another significant area, it was reckoned that forty-four million pairs of jeans were bought, and that about four in every ten people bought at least one pair of jeans over a twelve-month period. Fourthly, in 1974 a small, but steady, expansion in the use of pedal bicycles began. Finally, while tobacco sales declined, sales of alcohol, and most particularly sales of wine, increased.

This chapter began with a reference to the essay 'Changes in Living Standards Since the 1950s' published in *Social Trends* No. 10, the 1980 edition. There a summary was attempted:

Perhaps there are three changes which stand out amongst the others. Firstly, the range of opportunities open to young people widened enormously. For example, as the three decades moved on, increasing proportions of young people made use of the opportunity to continue education after the statutory minimum school-leaving age. The same group of people could afford to buy their own radios, hi-fis, and cars; and, later on, they could afford to move into homes of their own at increasingly earlier ages.

Secondly, women – particularly mothers – were more likely to have some sort of paid job in the 1970s than in earlier years. This meant that the proportion of families with more than one earner increased.

Thirdly, people at work were entitled to longer holidays as the years went on, and enjoyed a small decrease in the number of hours that they worked each week. Thus working people had more time for other pursuits such as DIY and leisure activities.

The first of these points brings out a difficult issue in regard to the pace of social change. Over three decades no doubt what is said about young people was true; yet, in 1980, what struck observers most was the bleak outlook which faced young school-leavers and, indeed, at a more prosperous level, the problems now facing first-time home-buyers.

It would be absurd to deny that, whatever the deeper economic realities, the British were still enjoying unprecedented levels of material prosperity at the end of the 1970s. But this was to make the problem of being a have-not in a have society particularly serious; and it meant too that unemployment was a drastic threat to those with heavy hire-purchase commitments on the appliances of affluence.

However, the final words of the essay in *Social Trends* read as follows:

It is not possible to produce a figure, or set of figures, which shows that we are *x* per cent better off than we were in 1951. It is clear that there was a substantial improvement in real disposable incomes and in material conditions between the 1950s and the 1970s, but many of the changes described in this Commentary are simply *differences* in the ways people live – whether they are for the better or worse is left for the reader to judge.

It is in the next chapter, in considering questions of customs and behaviour, the family, and social deviance and law and order, that I move towards the difficult area of the quality of life.

15

'Gimme a Man After Midnight'

The title is that of a hit song of 1978 by the pop group Abba. Many were the signs of a world turned upside down as far as relations between the sexes were concerned. Earlier in the decade a woman agony columnist in a London evening newspaper, replying to a nervous young man who said that when entertaining young women in his bedsitter he was embarrassed by the prominent position of his bed, advised that since the bed was the most important item of furniture on such occasions he should use every device to make it the focal point of the room. Another woman journalist, speculating on the possibility of a male contraceptive pill, pointed out that the important thing about the old-fashioned male sheath was that at least one could see that it was on. A standard truism to Malcolm Muggeridge and other pundits of his generation had been that women are incapable of being humorous about sex. In fact, the most hilariously bawdy novel of the time was Molly Parkin's *Switchback* (1978). Less than a generation before, women were not supposed to think the thoughts expressed in this and many other books, let alone set them down in print. The opening lines of *Switchback* could have been designed to bring apoplexy to the traditionalists:

Blossom Tree opened her eyes. It wasn't light yet, but she had been rudely awakened (an apt description, she thought) by her husband's heavy erection twitching between her warm buttocks. Nosing its way in like a determined torpedo.

'Bugger me!' she exclaimed crossly. 'I don't know about that!' and sliding over to face him she took his tool in her hand. The firm touch seemed to satisfy the taut, questing flesh; by the time Blossom had drifted to sleep once again, her handful had subsided to nothing.

Meanwhile, some 290 miles away in London, Blossom's twin, June Day, was awakening too. But in quite different circumstances. The man sleeping beside her was a stranger as far as she could tell. She felt cautiously. Circumcised. Nothing much to write home about, neither dressing to left nor to right, but centrally and in the perpendicular – Christ – suddenly there was *heaps* to write home about!

For a time, the woman's magazine *Cosmopolitan* (founded in 1972) had published pin-up pictures of nude males, but these soon disappeared; apparently women actually preferred looking at pictures of nude females, so that those now regularly appearing in the *Sun* and other popular news-papers could scarcely be represented as the exclusive products of male chauvinism. However, male strippers were increasingly in demand at women's clubs and women's outings. 'Role reversal' was a modish, though probably not very exact phrase (rendered for commercial purposes as 'unisex'). Catherine Storr published a very funny novel, *Unnatural Fathers* (1976), which postulated the idea of males actually giving birth. More rel-evant, perhaps, to the reality of changing social attitudes in this sphere was an advertisement for a convenience food broadcast on commercial radio: after repeated complaints from her ill-mannered husband, the housewife discovers the magic of this particular convenience food; but the punch-line is that she then divorces her husband 'and marries a much nicer man'.

The key feminist tract of the 1970s, as already mentioned, was Germaine Greer's *The Female Eunuch*, reissued as a paperback in 1971. Referring to the suffragette era as 'the first feminist wave', Dr Greer declared her book to be 'part of the second feminist wave': 'The new emphasis is different. Then genteel middle-class ladies clamoured for reform, now ungenteel middle-class women are calling for revolution.' In a work of high literary quality and deep scholarship, she made some disturbing points:

Women have very little idea of how much men hate them . . . The universal sway of the feminine stereotype is the single most important factor in male and female woman-hatred. Until a woman as she is can drive this plastic sphere out of her own and her man's imagination she will continue to apologize and disguise herself, while accepting her male's pot-belly, wattles, bad breath, farting, stubble, baldness and other ugliness without complaint . . . Is it too much to ask that women be spared the daily struggle for superhuman beauty in order to offer it to the caresses of a subhumanly ugly mate?

But let us leave questions of the relationships between the sexes (to which I return in discussing the family) and turn to other aspects of customs and behaviour. Commercial radio makes a good starting point. Commercial broadcasting of more or less continuous pop music from 'pirate' ships had begun in 1964, but had been squeezed out by effective Government counter-action. Under the Heath Conservative Government licensed local radio stations were set up. They clearly met a felt need, and the advertisements, broadcast as separate inserts, not, as in America, by the disc jockey himself, were not noticeably more irritating than the kind of condescending self-indulgent chat which still too often formed the official notion of informality as presented on BBC local radio. Local radio, of both kinds, at any rate, did represent and enhance a spirit of local participation and involvement, a mode of the sixties which developed impressively in the seventies.

Participation, involvement, consumer protest and action, these were all present in the sixties, but they were dominant motifs in the seventies. The Campaign for Real Ale was founded in 1971, and really burst into significant effectiveness around the middle of the decade. In the 1960s the 'big six' brewery combines had gone hell for leather in fulfilment of the theory that what the nation wanted was a handful of bland beers each supported by a brand name, heavily advertised. Small breweries were bought up and either converted into making big-name beer or, more often, closed down; as the motorway boom reached its peak it was believed that a few massive breweries producing pasteurized beer could deliver it to every corner of the kingdom. That cost accountants make lousy beer is to be expected; with a major petrol crisis on the way, even their economic forecasts were shaky.

Real beer is not pasteurized, and should not be served under carbon dioxide pressure. Unlike continental and North American lager-style beers, it is intended to continue 'conditioning' in the barrel. It therefore has a relatively short life, and needs to be handled and served with skill and care. By the late seventies the big breweries were in retreat. Watney's, who had been the leaders in the movement towards massification and gasification, employing the idiot television slogan 'Watney's Red Revolution' and painting all of their pubs red, now brought back two traditional bitters, and began to scrape off some of the red paint. Even more of a classic case is that of Whitbread's. This historic family firm had been taken over, its beautiful old brewery in Chiswell Street on the borders of the City of London closed down, and a modern beer factory built at Luton beside the M1 motorway thirty miles north of London. Whitbread's then bought up many local breweries and, final mad tribute to the idea of the brand name, marketed a whole range of different-tasting beers as 'Whitbread Trophy'. By the late seventies the Trophy labels were being ripped off and good local beers were being given their proper names back and also being served properly, without benefit of carbon dioxide.

However, repentant sinners should not gain their rewards too easily. A nice parable of the new balance between the local brewer of traditional ales and the conglomerate-owned national brewer could be seen in the relationship between the two breweries Shepherd Neame and Whitbread Fremlins which stand opposite each other in the small Kent town of Faversham. In April 1980, the Chairman of the former, Robert Neame, also Chairman of the Kent County Council Finance Committee and of the South-East England Tourist Board, was able to declare: 'It has really paid off remaining independent. Fremlins previously had the reputation of being Kent's premier brewers. That accolade has now passed to us.' Although Whitbread Trophy was now once again being called Fremlins Bitter, 'It's difficult,' Mr Neame commented, 'for them to regain their reputation. Even if they restore the old name, people realize who controls them.' None the less, the revival of real ale remained a relatively minor phenomenon compared with the expansion of the market for lager – most of it brewed in Britain (despite foreign names) and of poor quality.

In the gloom of the seventies, not all of the battles went to the big battalions, nor were the righteous always vanquished. It is sometimes said that social behaviour and fashion go in cycles, or that innovation is inevitably followed by reaction. Thus the sixties, a time of radical change (which it certainly was), is said to have been followed by the conservative seventies. In fact, in much of what is most important in manners and life-styles, change is cumulative. Perhaps violence, race tension, and terrorism are the most important social phenomena of the seventies; yet the decade was also increasingly characterized by a greater tolerance, by a progressive breaking-down of rigid stereotypes in social relationships. No doubt when old rules and old customs lose their force there is uneasiness and even aggression. Yet most often the confrontation and challenge had taken place in the sixties; in the seventies there was much more genuine acceptance for, in the cliché, 'doing your own thing'. If stereotypes were collapsing as to the respective roles of 'them' and 'us', governors and governed, media magnates and viewers, producers and consumers, men and women, so too were they collapsing with regard to the respective roles of age and youth. Still in the sixties, style in appearance and dress was very much a function of age. For generations, nay centuries, it was accepted that as a person moved through the progression so decisively defined in Shakespeare's 'All the world's a stage' so the appropriate style and the appropriate manner must be adopted. Lines, as far as fashion was concerned, were perhaps more vertical than horizontal in the later seventies: many different styles coexisted in the same age group, and the same styles could be observed over different age groups. Here, in itself, was another aspect of the loosening-up of society. Fashion – that is to say something determined by 'them' on behalf of 'us' – no longer asserted its old tyranny: more and more (within, of course, the limits always imposed by the human desire to conform with one's peer group, however that is defined) individuals chose to dress and present themselves as individuals.

Among the young, certainly, there were exaggerated fashions pertaining to different cliques and sects. The new stylized groupings of the seventies had been the Skinheads, who expressed an exaggerated reaction to the long hairstyles of the sixties, and the Punks, who, with dyed hair and clownish make-up (for both sexes), brought a genuine verve and colour to teenage style. In the later seventies there were revivals from earlier decades: Teds (who, without sideburns, emerged as Rockabilly Rebels), Mods (sometimes smartened-up Punks), and Rockers. 'Skins' took to pork-pie hats and thereby became Rudies. But these are all segmentations within one basic age group: they did not represent one consolidated youth style ranged against the whole of the rest of society.

The single biggest leisure activity of the majority of all British people was watching television. The number of viewing-hours had risen fairly sharply at the end of the sixties, but held steady, with perhaps a very slight increase, in the seventies. In the 1977–9 period, average hours viewed per week were sixteen in the summer and twenty in the winter. Children and the elderly tended to watch the most television, while women watched more than men; but the differences between the different categories were not very marked. The largest audiences would be recorded for royal occasions, major sporting events, light entertainment, and certain specially popular films, and varied from twenty million for light entertainment and fifteen–twenty million for sporting events or films to seven–eight million for documentaries and five–six million for current affairs. The average number of hours of radio listened to per week in 1978–9 was about nine hours, of which about seven and a half hours was provided by BBC radio, with the remainder provided by commercial and independent local radio.

An official Household Survey carried out in 1977 attempted, by asking questions about activities participated in over a four-week period, to identify and quantify major leisure activities apart from watching television. Top of this list came 'going out for a meal or a drink': 71 per cent of men had done so in the four-week period, 57 per cent of women (but what a daft bureaucratic category: what almost all of the men and most of the women had actually done was visit the pub). Next came listening to records or tapes: 64 per cent of men and 60 per cent of women. Then came reading books (57 per cent of women and 52 per cent of men – figures almost certainly about as high as would have been found in any other country in the world). After that, for men, came house repairs and do-it-yourself (51 per cent, 22 per cent of women) and gardening (49 per cent, 35 per cent of women) and for women needlework and knitting (51 per cent, as against a not altogether surprising 2 per cent for men). Other activities in which women appear to participate more than men were attending leisure classes (3 per cent women to 1 per cent men), dancing (16 per cent women against 14 per cent men), social and voluntary work (9 per cent women as against 8 per cent men), and going on outings to the seaside, the country and parks (7 per cent, 5 per cent, and 4 per cent as against 6 per cent, 5 per cent, and 3 per cent respectively) and on visits to historic buildings, and theatre, opera, and ballet (9 per cent and 6 per cent, as against 8 per cent and 4 per cent respectively). The last two groups of figures may have represented women's continuing responsibility in regard to entertaining children. However, when it came to visiting museums and art galleries the men had it by 4 per cent to 3 per cent.

Other important activities included walks, climbing, etc. (lumped together as 'countryside activities'), involving 31 per cent of men and 27 per cent of women; going to the cinema, involving 11 per cent of men and 10 per cent of women; amateur music and drama, involving 4 per cent of men and 3 per cent of women; home-based games of skill, 21 per cent of men and 16 per cent of women; and hobbies, 12 per cent of men and 3 per cent of women. After a steady decline since the fifties, cinema attendances actually staged a rally in 1978: the characteristic new phenomenon, which enjoyed an enormous expansion in the middle 1970s, was the multi-screen complex, in which three small cinemas performing simultaneously were housed in the gigantic antediluvian shell of a 1930s cinema. Watching football was still a major pastime, though it no longer held the modish appeal it had attained in the 1960s. In face of the counter-attraction of colour television and the deterrent of football hooliganism attendances were holding up reasonably well. Of outdoor sports in which people actually participated, football was also the most popular. The 1977 Household Survey showed 6 per cent of men interviewed as having played football within the last four weeks. The most popular sport of all was darts, involving 15 per cent of the men and 4 per cent of the women interviewed. Betting on horses, dogs, or through football pools was a fairly consistent activity among men in different social groups: it was an activity of 29 per cent in the Household Survey, and, also consistently across social classes, of 11 per cent of women. Bingo, however, was very much an activity of women in the semi-skilled and unskilled groups: 17 per cent of women in this group as against only 6 per cent in the professional and managerial group. On average, 5 per cent of men indulged in bingo.

Throughout the sixties an English historian, a long-time exile in the University of Glasgow, had been wont to speak of 'the Misery (Scotland) Act', his all-embracing explanation of the killjoy tedium of Scottish social life. Suddenly, in the late seventies, Scotland shot ahead of her southern neighbour in one traditionally fraught area. As a result of Section 64, Subsection 3, of the Licensing (Scotland) Act of 1976 (there was no English counterpart) certain pubs were enabled to stay open all day, from eleven in the morning till eleven at night. The crucial clause read:

After considering the application and any objections made thereto, a licensing board may grant an application for the regular extension of permitted hours if, having regard to the social circumstances of the locality in which the premises in respect of which the application is made are situated or to activities taking place in that locality, the board considers it is desirable to do so . . .

Officially, a holiday is a period of four or more nights away from home considered by the respondent to be a holiday. On this basis, the total number of holidays taken by British people rose from twenty-seven million in 1951 to thirty-four million in 1961, to forty-one million in 1971, and up to a peak of forty-nine million in 1973: the figures in 1976 and 1977 were forty-five million and forty-four million respectively, then there was a revival in 1978 with the figure going up to forty-eight million. In 1978, also, the figure for holidays abroad was at its highest yet: nine million, as against eight million in 1977 and 1973, seven million in 1971, four million in 1961, and two million in 1951. By far the most popular foreign destination was Spain, taking a good 30 per cent of all foreign holidays.

New overseas influences on British customs and leisure activities were strongly marked by the middle seventies. British society was showing the effects of continental travel, of closer commercial links with Europe brought about by membership of the EEC, and of having growing Asian and West Indian communities located within its midst. Often now the traditional fish-and-chip shop might be run by Indians, Pakistanis, or Greeks, offering curry or kebabs in addition to the old standard fare. For almost every sector of the market there were Italian restaurants, Chinese restaurants, of varying levels of sophistication. Shops and markets offered avocados, mangoes, peppers, artichokes, and aubergines. When consideration is given to the racial views described in Chapter 13, and to the growing evidence from opinion polls of hostility to the Common Market, it has to be said that Britain in the later seventies had acquired a new cosmopolitanism without shedding its old xenophobia.

For the country as a whole there was no change in the secular decline in religious observance, though there was in the seventies a definite growth in fringe religion – Moonies, gurus, and so on – and also a quite striking expansion of interest in astrology. Openness to outside influences, both American and oriental, was one factor here; as to the other bases of religious or quasi-religious need at a time of decline in institutional religion, it is only possible to speculate.

My opening remarks were concerned with sexual attitudes; on sexual behaviour, none of the evidence suggests that there was anything in the way of a puritan reaction in the seventies. The most thorough and up-to-date survey of sexual behaviour among teenagers and women in their early twenties was that published in April 1980 in 19 magazine, based on questionnaires filled in by 10,000 readers. The majority (77 per cent) of those responding fell within the age range sixteen–twenty-four, though there were also younger girls and older women. Some of the results, therefore, were manifestly less representative than others. Of the relatively small number of those aged sixteen or less, fully 46 per cent said that they were not virgins. In each cohort the number claiming virginity declined: at seventeen, 43 per cent; at eighteen, 22 per cent; at nineteen, 17 per cent; at twenty–twenty-one, 12 per cent; at twenty-two and over, 8 per cent. Taking all girls under twenty-one, and this is probably the most reliable and representative statistic, 26 per cent claimed to have had their first sexual experience before the age of sixteen. Of all sexually experienced girls (again a slightly less representative statistic) 39 per cent claimed to have had sexual experience at under sixteen years of age. Of sexually experienced single girls 72 per cent had had two or more partners. Over one half of those who started sex early had had four or more partners, and a quarter claimed to have had ten partners or more.

What, then, were the implications for that enduring institution, marriage? Evidently, as the organizers of the survey commented, 'the virgin bride has become a rarity in our society'. However, 77 per cent of all those participating in the survey disagreed that marriage was becoming old-fashioned and obsolete. Only one in ten said that they would prefer unmarried living together to marriage; but eight out of ten said they would be willing to live with their man with or without reservations or marriage prospects. From subjective evidence it is clear that the condition whereby couples live together in a relatively stable relationship without actually being married had become an accepted social institution, though the incidence was not in fact widespread enough to show up significantly in official statistics. The number of first marriages was certainly in steady decline in the 1970s: first marriages for both parties numbered 377,000 in 1971, 273,000 in 1976, and 266,000 in 1977. Here, certainly, was a reflection of the change in attitudes of younger people towards marriage. But the overall popularity of marriage as an institution was sustained by the increasing number of second marriages. The divorce rate rose slowly, and stood at 10.4 per thousand of the married population in 1977; on the other hand, the average age of the re-marriage of divorced people was falling. The figures, then, suggest, not a destruction of marriage, but a greater and more flexible range of options: stable unmarried relationships, later marriages, more frequent divorce, more frequent re-marriage. The convenience food commercial was not so wide of the mark.

Some traditional customs, still detectable in the early fifties, such as 'churching', appeared to have died out altogether. Attitudes towards children had continued to soften, yet Britain in many respects remained one of the most backward countries in the world in this area. While corporal punishment of children was against the law in Saudi Arabia (much featured in the press as a brutal, atavistic Muslim state) it remained in existence in many British, and, above all, in Scottish schools. Unlike Scandinavian countries, Britain had no special legislation protecting children's rights against, for instance, their parents.

From within families, the problem given most attention was that of how to handle teenage children. Self-evidently, the statistics of teenage sexual behaviour cited above contained within them their own problems for parents. Then there was violence, drink, drugs, and even just sheer waywardness. The drug scene of the late seventies was rather smudgier than that of the sixties: facts were even less certain; voices of both takers and opponents were, in keeping with the more tolerant pluralistic trends already mentioned, much less strident; there was even a strong do-it-yourself element. If there was any general problem of addiction and abuse among children and young people it was rather in relation to alcohol; and here their elders scarcely set a good example. The major new development of the mid-seventies was that of sniffing glue, and this became quite a widespread open-air habit among young males, particularly on housing estates. Surveys, however, suggested that glue was simply a cheap alternative to alcohol which would be resorted to as soon as the funds were available.

The avowed use of cannabis may have reached a peak early in the seventies, when perhaps about a third of all students in higher education were indulging, with about half that figure among young people of the same age group outside higher education, and perhaps 10 per cent of school pupils. But it may well be that the total number of cannabis users remained at least the same throughout the seventies. Some authorities believed the habit was spreading among working-class youth, including skinheads. What was certain was that use of cannabis was becoming much more private. Whereas it was difficult at the beginning of the seventies to be in a university and not be aware, at least, of its use in the later seventies those who were not involved tended to have no contact with those who were. At the same time, the attitudes of the law became rather more sensible and humane: first-time offenders caught in possession of cannabis had risked a prison sentence in the early seventies; thereafter, at most, they risked a fine.

Far other was the case with the hard drug heroin. By 1980 there was far more heroin around in the country than there had ever been before, and an organized black market on a scale unknown in 1970. Even the official seizure figures give some indication: in 1973 a little over 3 kg were seized; by 1978 the figure had risen to 60 kg. The situation had not yet reached the seriousness of, for instance, New York, where much crime was directly related to drug addiction, but some experts predicted that, while abuse of cannabis was scarcely a problem, the growth of heroin addiction, apart from the personal damage done to addicts, could become a further cause of violent crime in Britain.

Overall there was actually a decline in the number of serious criminal offences recorded by the police in 1978 and 1979, and a decline in the number of persons prosecuted. However, crimes of violence against the person, and crimes by young people, particularly personal violence and vandalism, increased. Although rape had, very properly, become a matter for serious concern and protest among feminist groups, the number of such offences actually slightly declined also.

What perhaps helped most of all to colour attitudes about the direction British society was taking and to spread disenchantment among the articulate was the number of cases involving corruption and conspiracy. It is hard to be sure whether those in authority, in the civil service, in local government, in the police, in financial institutions, were really becoming more corrupt, or whether the police were becoming more zealous and public morality, if one can use such a phrase, becoming less tolerant of high jinks on the part of those who in a former era might well have contrived concealment behind the majesty of office.

To cope with a great diversity of problems there were the police forces (still under the control of local authorities, not of the central Government) totalling 120,000, including 8,890 policewomen: one policeman to every 450 members of the population, in fact. As noted in Part Two, increasing the numbers might not necessarily affect the detection, or even the prevention, of crime. But, without doubt, when it came to riot and civil disturbance, the forces were often dangerously stretched. They were now, however, grouped together more rationally than had been the case in the forties and fifties. For the whole of Great Britain there were now just sixty-seven regular police forces, ranging in size from about 130 in the remoter parts of Scotland, to about 21,200 in the Metropolitan Police. The particular problem within the realm of law and order which gained most publicity at the end of the decade was that of gross overcrowding in Britain's prisons: prison strikes and demonstrations, of which there were many, would, experts predicted, soon culminate in some great explosion.

In general, as indicated in Part Two, the police tended to have the respect and support of the British people. How far they had had the support of submerged minorities in the past is dubious. But the clear message of the seventies was that they were very definitely faced with the active hostility of disinherited youth, white as well as black. In witness to this the 1980s began with the quite spectacular violence in St Paul's, Bristol, at Brighton and Scarborough a few days later on the Easter Bank Holiday of 1980, and then on the evening of the Easter Monday at Finsbury Park in North London. The omens were not good; but taken all in all it would be absurd to say that they were all bad. The two contrary elements suggesting hope on the one hand, and despair on the other, form the title of my next chapter.

16

Tolerance and Confrontation

Previous chapters in Part Three have indicated why, as mentioned in the Introduction, by the end of the 1970s books and articles were being published on different variations of the 'Is Britain Dying?' theme. Apart from the problems of the economy, race, and civil violence, some writers also pointed to Britain's poor performance, after the excitements of the sixties, in the realms of intellect, arts, and entertainment.

It certainly appeared that while such artists as Elisabeth Frink, David Hockney, and Bridget Riley continued to produce excellent work, they had no true successors. London theatre was probably still the best in the world, but economies were showing, and again there seemed nothing quite to match the innovations of the sixties. British art merged anonymously into the major international trends; and these trends, blurring the distinctions between 'high art' and popular art, stressing literalness and 'super realism', pushing political messages, and emphasizing feminism and homosexuality, were not themselves of a sort to assist the revelation of distinctively national or personal genius.

The best dramatists, Pinter, or Tom Stoppard (*Rosencrantz and Guildenstern are Dead, 1967; Jumpers*, 1972), say, had made their names long since. This would hold true too for poets and for musicians. Innovation tended to be at the unspectacular, and perhaps necessarily transient level, taking the form of multimedia events and of happenings involving audience participation. However, it was in the mid-1970s that the National Theatre at last entered into its magnificent new architectural complex and thereafter continued to present a range of plays which could by no stretch of the words be deemed conservative or unimaginative.

The most significant development in the indigenous novel was, as hinted at at the beginning of the previous chapter, the emergence of the liberated woman novelist. However, such writers as Angela Carter and Fay Weldon seemed, in their very different ways, to run against the problem that in the real contemporary world there was no prospect of full women's liberation as feminists envisaged it; woman's own nature seemed to be against it. Thus some feminist writers took off into various forms of fantasy, surreal or futuristic worlds where alone, they seemed to be suggesting, women could be completely free. Angela Carter's *The Passion of New Eve* (1977), set in a horrifically violent America of the near future, has a handsome predatory man captured by a women's group and subjected to an operation which turns him into a highly desirable, and vulnerable, young woman. The vulnerability, as much as the unconquerability, of women appeared to be major themes in *Sweet William* (1975) by Beryl Bainbridge, and *Praxis* (1978) by Fay Weldon. If, where it is possible to identify social and political trends in creative writing, one such trend stressed the woman's viewpoint, another tended to take a rather right-wing view of society. The tone of Tory sourness had been well struck in Kingsley Amis's poem of the sixties, 'A Tribute to the Founder', republished in the *Collected Poems* of 1979.

> By bluster, graft, and doing people down,
> Sam Baines got rich, but, mellowing at last,
> Felt that by giving something to the town
> He might repair the evils of his past.
>
> His hope was to prevent the local youth
> From making the mistakes that he had made:
> Choosing expediency instead of truth,
> And quitting what was honest for what was paid.
>
> A university seemed just the thing,
> And that old stately home the very place.
> Sam wept with pleasure at its opening.
> He died too soon to weep at its disgrace.
>
> Graft is refined among the tea and scones,
> Bluster (new style) invokes the public good,
> And doing-down gets done in pious tones
> Sam often tried to learn, but never could.

That tone had become a dominant key by the mid-seventies, giving a special power to Amis's own masterpiece, *The Alteration* (1976), in which he created a Britain as it might well be had the Reformation never taken place. While back in the fifties the 'popular' espionage-and-thuggery novels of Ian Fleming eventually abandoned their cold war complexion, the 'quality' spy novels of John Le Carré were increasingly informed by a sense of the barbaric obscurantism of the Soviet régime. Malcolm Bradbury's *The History Man* (1975) was portrayed as a nasty, lefty, trendy, university sociologist. However, the *Daniel Martin* of John Fowles's big novel of 1977, a highly successful British Hollywood screen writer, managed to preserve liberal and even social-democratic attitudes in musing on the structural weaknesses which had made Britain a feeble, sluggish country compared with the USA. A conversation between Piers Paul Read's *A Married Man* (1979) and his sister and brother-in-law

made him most pessimistic about his ideals; for his sister and her husband seemed to exemplify a new bourgeoisie which had expropriated and exploited the Welfare State. Instead of scrambling to save money to send their children to private schools they schemed to get them into some chosen comprehensive which, because word had gone around among like-minded members of the state-employed élite, was then packed with the progeny of up-and-coming couples while the children of the working classes were relegated as before to the second-class schools.

All the paradoxes of Britain's record in science and technology sharpened in the seventies. Much had been done in the sixties to develop science teaching in all types of secondary schools, yet in the seventies there was a swing back in student choices from science to arts subjects. There was still a strong élitist atmosphere about university science, yet, despite economic stringency, British scientists retained their enviable eminence in the international community. Developments were particularly arresting in 'the life sciences', in microbiology, molecular biology, and immunology: the 'physicists' war' had become the 'biologists' peace'. Basically it was the achievements in immunology which made possible the transplant surgery which attracted so much attention in the press. Most attention of all was focused on the arrival, early in 1979, of the world's first 'test-tube' baby, resulting from the partnership of Robert Edwards, physiologist at Cambridge University, and Patrick Steptoe, gynaecologist at the distinctly unfashionable Oldham General Hospital. Peter Medawar, himself one of the most illustrious figures in the realm of immunology, emerged (in partnership with his wife) as *the* science philosopher to rival Sir James Jeans of an earlier age: the elegant and profound *The Life Science*, by P. B. and J. S. Medawar was published in

1977. In the world of technology much attention was focused on the silicon chip developed in the United States which made possible very complex computerization within a small space. In the 1960s, research into robot technology at Hawker-Siddeley and Guest Keen and Nettlefold was as far ahead as any in the world, and significant advances were achieved at the University of Nottingham in the early 1970s. Yet there was remarkably little practical sign of the micro-electronic revolution in the Britain of the seventies. Its most obvious manifestations appeared to be in pocket calculators, new cash registers in shops, and sophisticated children's toys. While from the very beginning of the seventies the Japanese, and in lesser degree other West European countries, exploited the possibilities of automated 'robot' factories, in Britain really significant developments only came at the very end of the decade. The automated Mini Metro factory at Longbridge, Birmingham, was shown off to the press in September 1980. None of the robots were of British manufacture. It was right at the time when unemployment was soaring alarmingly that a number of other firms announced lay-offs due to automation based on micro-electronic robot technology. Never was the failure to integrate technological and social planning shown up more sharply.

However little understanding there was of the relationship between science and technology and society and government, there was probably till the early seventies general acceptance of the view that science and technology offered great boons to society. Only in the seventies, with the development of the environmental movement, the growth of fears about the uses to which 'data banks' might be put, and the questioning of the effect on the human mind of constant exposure to television, did this fundamental liberal-optimist assumption begin to be questioned. Again, as with so many of the issues raised by science and technology, this was a worldwide, not a purely British matter. In fact – to extend further the whole paradoxical nature of the matter – Britain could be singled out as making particularly effective use of the potential of television: many drama series, both contemporary and classical, and such general service programmes as *The World at War* (on ITV) or *The Voyages of Charles Darwin* (on BBC) were the admiration of the world. As the Medawars rightly said, 'Most of the problems that beset mankind call for political, moral and administrative rather than scientific solutions.'

There were serious problems at humbler levels. Some of the less healthy features of the book industry have already been noted. But only in the middle seventies did the proud position still held by British publishing in face of all rivals begin to disintegrate. Book prices shot up; hitherto impregnable firms turned in large trading losses; retrenchment and redundancy struck suddenly and often arbitrarily; North Americans found it no longer sensible to order British books, nor indeed to seek to have their own works published by British publishers. Among popular bestsellers, the rage was for works of terror, and, above all, occultism and exorcism: almost all the market leaders were American-originated.

The story of the press is not much happier. Thus a further Royal Commission on the Press (the second since the war) was set up in May 1974. In its *Final Report* (July 1977) the Commission noted that sales of national dailies had fallen from 15.8 million per day in 1961 to 14.0 million in 1976; while the provincial press generally prospered the national press was in a condition of recurrent financial crisis. The Commission divided the press into a number of categories: first the 'qualities' – *Daily Telegraph, Sunday Telegraph, Financial Times, Guardian, The Times, Sunday Times,* and *Observer* – and the 'populars' – *Daily Mirror, Sunday Mirror, Daily Express, Sunday Express, Sunday People, Daily Mail, Sun,* and *News of the World* (later there arrived the appalling *Daily Star*); 'the *Morning Star*' (the Communist Party newspaper), said the Commission, 'does not fit easily into either classification'. Next came the weekly 'Journals of Opinion': *The Economist, Spectator, New Statesman, Tribune,* and *New Society.* Then the 'Alternative Press', creation of the sixties, well nourished in the seventies: *Gay News* (which, launched in 1962, had a bigger circulation than the *Spectator* or *Tribune*), *Private Eye* (which had at one time achieved a circulation of 100,000), and *Time Out* (steady sale of about 48,000). The Commission's next groupings were the 'Provincial Mornings', of which there were now only twelve in England and Wales, compared with eighteen in 1948 (Scotland still had four), and the 'Evenings', of which nine had closed since 1961, leaving no single provincial city with more than one evening paper (London had two, though they were to be amalgamated in November 1980). Finally the Commission came to a series of categories, either launched, or greatly expanded, in the seventies: 'freesheets', product of participation and consumerism, providing information on entertainments and tourist attractions, financed by advertisements; immigrant newspapers; 'general periodicals', including the old war-horses like *Reveille* and *Titbits,* the newer specialist magazines orientated towards pop music, say, or Do-It-Yourself, and the increasingly explicit sex magazines; and the 'women's press' made up of the more traditional weeklies and monthlies such as *Woman* and *Good Housekeeping,* the newer 'emancipated' monthlies such as *Cosmopolitan* (founded in 1972), the firmly feminist organs such as *Spare Rib* (also founded in 1972), and the mass of girls' magazines which form such an important source for the student of changing moral attitudes.

This varied progeny of Gutenberg's epochal invention was in fact (with minor exceptions) owned by ten large companies, four of which were, in the last analysis, controlled from outside Britain: the Thomson Organization, Atlantic Richfield, News International (the Australian owners of the *Sun*) and Beaverbrook Newspapers (ultimately owned by the French finance company, Générale Occidentale). The six others were: Reed International (formed by a merger with IPC in 1970), S. Pearson and Son, Associated Newspaper Group, Guardian and Manchester Evening News Ltd, Daily Telegraph Ltd, and Morning Star Co-operative Society.

In addition to the menace of mergers, the Commission also identified four other major problems: the invasion of privacy by 'investigative' reporters; the weakness of the Press Council in maintaining the highest journalistic standards; the growing control of the major alternative source of information, television, by the newspaper companies; and poor industrial relations:

One debilitating legacy to national newspapers from the post-war days of easy profits and weak management has been the exceptionally high earnings of print workers and a disposition among publishers to yield easily to threats of unofficial action. Industrial relations in Fleet Street have been notoriously bad for a generation and their improvement has been the regularly falsified hope of everyone who has attempted to set the industry on the path of modernisation.

Throughout 1979, indeed, Times Newspapers were paralysed as managers and men failed to agree over the introduction of computerized techniques. When their representatives appeared on television to express their differences and, ultimately, to explain their agreement, their accents, naturally, were those of, on the one hand, the public-school-educated upper class (represented in this case by Marmaduke Hussey) and, on the other, the intrepid London artisanry.

How far, then, were social and political values changing? What of that secular Anglicanism of which I have spoken once or twice? In the previous chapter one of my main arguments was that, contrary to what was being said about the disintegration of traditional values, it was the continuing vigour of the Anglican tradition which permitted a peaceful accommodation to consumerism, participation, youth culture, and feminism. Tolerance had not fled the country. But there could be no gainsaying the facts of violence simmering on the surface, and, as a new decade opened, more frequently bursting devastatingly into the open.

It is particularly difficult when dealing with a past so immediate that it merges into the present, to distinguish between what actually was happening and what political and social commentators hotly in pursuit of fundamental causes and universal remedies declared was happening. Here, I choose four major areas of the political and industrial history of the seventies, none of which clearly demonstrates a disintegration of values, a continuation of values, or a replacement of one set of values by another. As always, the areas overlap and inter-relate. They are: first, trade unions, industrial relations and strikes; second, developments (a better word, here, than changes) in the way in which national economic and social decisions were arrived at, sometimes described, though in my view quite inadequately, as representing a move towards 'corporatism'; third, the position of the Labour Party, appearing at one moment as the country's national governing party, at another as a body ready at any moment to splinter between right, centre, and left elements, while at the same time apparently choking in apathy and lack of funds; and, fourthly, the radical Conservative attitudes of Thatcherite conservatism which, it can be argued, helped to hold Labour, the trade unions, and the left together in the middle years of the decade, and then, after 1979, began to effect a reorientation of political and social values.

As noted in Part Two there was a great and rising upsurge of strike activity between 1968 and 1972. As we also saw, there are different ways of measuring the intensity of strike activity. Taking the number of days lost, these reached their peak figure of 23,909,000 in 1972. There was then a sharp reduction to a figure little above that for 1969, 7,197,000. As the Heath confrontation intensified and Labour Governments took over in confused circumstances, the figure more than doubled again in 1974 to 14,750,000. The prime years of the social contract, 1975 and 1976, had figures back around late sixties' levels of, respectively, 6,012,000 and 3,284,000. There was a slight up in 1977, and then a slight down again in 1978, the figures, respectively, being 10,142,000 and 9,405,000. In 1979, as the social contract collapsed, the figures rose up beyond the proportions of the 1926 General Strike. Within these figures the central phenomenon was that, in keeping with the trend beginning at the end of the sixties, strikes were now not so often small-scale, unofficial efforts, but frequently involved large unions and many workers, and had official backing. It appeared as though strikes were becoming more 'political' than 'industrial' in purpose (though, as I have already suggested, there is some unreality about this distinction). The weight of trade-union leadership was thrown against the Heath Government's Industrial Relations Act and in favour, till the very end at least, of Labour's social contract and policy of wage limitation. In formulating the stages of the wage policy and the concomitant bargains struck in the social contract, the Labour Government was operating in close co-operation with the trade-union leadership; and there may well be truth, too, in the story that Heath had hoped to work in much closer collaboration with the trade-union leadership than his policies of confrontation would suggest. Certainly, in July 1976, he gave his support in this respect to the Labour Government: 'The agreement between the Government and trade unions' was in the national interest especially since 'those countries which had had greater success in dealing with the industrial situation were those which had the closest form of consultation with both sides of industry'.

The phenomena of flying pickets and 'secondary picketing' had been introduced in the early seventies. Then in 1974 the miners' leaders deliberately acted to restrain violence. But the issues remained live ones even during the period of relative quietude in industrial relations in the middle seventies, coming to the fore again in the Grunwick strike, and then much more forcefully, in the steel strike of 1980. Truly the energies of activists in earlier generations of the trade-union and Labour movement had been directed much more towards the traditional activities of propaganda and organization than towards picketing and intimidation. Yet the new type of picketing was little more than an updating and intensification of the activism of the hunger marchers in the thirties. Certainly it could be held to be undesirable in that it became a focal point for militants on both left and right who had little to do with the trade-union movement, that it was liable to create violence, and that it interfered with the livelihood of employers and employees not in any way directly involved with the particular strike in question. To that extent there was a case both for legislation and for a return to the kind of self-discipline which the British trade-union movement had so long exercised.

Despite the revived interest in workers' control and industrial democracy in the 1960s little had been done. The whole saga of industrial democracy in the later seventies tells us much about the contemporary trade-union movement and its attitudes, and very much suggests, not that radical, disruptive, ideas were taking over, but that the traditional stance had shifted little. However, with a Labour Government back in office after 1974, and a General Council of the TUC, together with the most influential trade-union leader of the time, Jack Jones of the Transport and General Workers strongly committed to their own version of industrial democracy, the matter was very much back on the agenda. Furthermore, the Government began to surmise that the extent of worker participation in management in European countries, particularly West Germany, might have something to do with their greater economic success. In his first address as Prime Minister to the Labour Party Conference in 1976, James Callaghan spoke of successive governments having 'failed to ignite the fires of industrial growth in the ways that Germany, France, and Japan, with their different political and economic philosophies, have done'. Worker participation schemes, on Government directions, were introduced into the British Steel Corporation, British Leyland, and Chrysler.

Yet there was still great resistance to the whole concept from within the trade-union movement itself: opposition was particularly strong from the Electricians, the Engineers, and the General and Municipal workers. Among the public at large, it appeared that something over half of all adult employees did favour worker participation in management, but that most people were against industrial democracy being imposed by law. There was public opposition, too, among trade-unionists as well as non-trade-unionists, to the TUC scheme, whereby worker directors would be nominated through trade unions; there was also opposition to any idea of worker directors being in a majority on boards. As governments so often did in such circumstances, the Callaghan Government in December 1975 appointed a Committee of Inquiry under the Chairmanship of Lord Bullock. The Bullock Committee had an enormously difficult task in front of it and in the end produced a majority report, a minority report, and a note of dissent. Basically the Bullock Report proposed that its scheme for industrial democracy would only come into practice in a company where at least one third of the employees expressed a wish for such an arrangement. But where the scheme did come into effect workers' representation on the board would be controlled entirely by the trade unions. It was on this point that the minority – desiring that representation should be directly from the workforce as a whole, not through the unions – split from the majority. An elaborate scheme for the composition of boards would ensure that though in appearance there would be 'parity' between employers and employees, the addition of a co-opted 'third group' meant that workers' (or, in effect, union) representatives could never be in a majority, and thus could always escape responsibility for serious, or unpopular decisions. At the same time the Report went out of its way to stress that unions would still retain their traditional independence.

As was to be expected, the proposals were not well received. Employers drew back now from the prospect that industrial democracy might become a reality; liberals (in all parties) joined with the minority in opposing the vesting of control of workers' representation exclusively in the hands of the unions; and such union leaders as John Lyons, General Secretary of the Electrical Power Engineers' Association, expressed the old reservations: 'Employee representatives on boards à la Bullock will tie the unions into the management process.' Thus when the Labour Government came to frame its own proposals on the subject they departed quite far from Bullock. The Government proposed a two-tier scheme, with worker representation only on a 'Policy Board', not involved in the day-to-day running of the company, which would be reserved to a more traditional 'Management Board' exclusively composed of the usual 'professional' managers; even on the Policy Board, workers' representatives would have no more than one third of the seats. Elections for these seats would be carried out by the workforce as a whole, not through trade unions. Once more, little had been done to implement the proposals by the time the Labour Government fell from office.

Several of these issues bring us towards the heart of the discussion as to whether Britain was or was not becoming a corporatist society. One of the few political leaders who boasted of running a corporatist state was Mussolini, the Italian dictator, so the term has a pejorative quality to it. It implies that instead of the country being ruled by a democratically elected parliament, major decisions are made through bodies representative of various vested interests (in particular trade unions and employers' associations) interacting directly with the government. That ordinary Members of Parliament have been losing influence since the late nineteenth century is a historical truism. That MPs carry less respect than they once did among their peer groups in the upper and middle classes is also true; how much they actually meant to the masses in the nineteenth century is a moot question. But direct influence upon Parliament and Government by vested interests and pressure groups is nothing new whatsoever. As modern society has become more complex, so the balance of forces behind political decision-making must become more complex. Political commentators have focused attention on such pressure groups as: the Child Poverty Action Group whose campaigning and lobbying did much to bring about the introduction of Child Benefits; the Abortion Law Reform Association and the Society for the Protection of the Unborn Child which between them provided much of the ammunition for the parliamentary debates on abortion; and the National Association for Mental Health which did much to reorientate the National Health Service towards this traditionally neglected and suspect area. In an ideal world it would be better if MPs themselves had control of the research facilities offered by such organizations; but on the whole these pressure groups cannot unreasonably be seen as representing that element of participation and commitment which was one of the more encouraging legacies of the sixties, husbanded and developed in the seventies.

In the general election of February 1974, 78.8 per cent of the electorate voted, a figure which, marking a reversal of the trend of declining electoral participation since the fifties, suggested that political apathy was not going to be a cardinal sin of the seventies. Labour polled half a million less votes than they had in the election they lost in 1970, but the Conservatives lost still more seriously at the hands of Nationalists and Liberals. With 37.9 per cent of votes cast the Conservatives returned 297 MPs; Labour with 37.1 per cent of votes cast actually returned 301 MPs; the Liberals with 19.3 per cent had 14 MPs, the Scottish Nationalists with 2 per cent and the Welsh Nationalists with 0.6 per cent had 7 MPs and 2 MPs respectively. Nevertheless, events which followed suggested that Labour really was establishing itself as the natural governing party. With the old flair and skill Wilson ran a minority Government till October when he chose his moment for a further general election. This time Labour polled 39.2 per cent of all votes cast to 35.9 per cent for the Conservatives. By traditional standards Labour's majority was still tiny, yet Wilson, and then Callaghan, seemed to govern with confidence. There was a desperate sterling crisis in the late summer of 1976, but thereafter, despite continuing recession and very high unemployment, there was something of a recovery, and it appeared that inflation was being brought under control. Fear of an alternative Conservative Government under Mrs Thatcher helped to keep the unions and the left in line.

However, for a younger generation of militants there was no joy at all in seeing a Labour Government presiding over wage controls, high unemployment, and spending cuts. Within many sections of the party the grouping known as the Militant Tendency gained in strength. Outside of the party much unfavourable comment was evoked by the behaviour of leftist students in generally making it impossible for right-wing opinions to be heard in student unions or at student meetings. This sort of totalitarian intolerance did suggest that serious flaws were developing in the Anglican tradition of fair play and free speech. As the Labour Government went into the dismal winter of 1979 and on to electoral defeat, the problems within the party came out into the open. Was the survival of Labour as a broad-based, non-ideological institution, designed primarily for the purpose of getting workers' representatives into Parliament, now menaced? Many of the objectives on which Labour had set its sights in the thirties and forties had indeed been accomplished. The social contract had committed the Labour Government to bringing 'about a fundamental and irreversible shift in the balance of power and wealth in favour of working people and their families'. But how high a priority was to be given to that aim, compared with just somehow trying to keep the economy afloat? Traditionally the broad-based non-ideological Labour Party had been a factor for stability in British society; in 1980 it was still too early to say that it was now ceasing to be so.

It would be a mistake to see the Conservative election victory of 1979 as marking anything like a revolution in British social and political values. Self-evidently, most of those who believed in consensus politics or some form of collectivist socialism continued to do so. On the other hand, already in the seventies politicians in the Labour Party as well as in the Conservative Party were claiming that trade-union powers must be curbed and that encouragement must be given to thrift and enterprise. As long as inflation was running at a few per cent per year it was generally taken by politicians, privately if not publicly, as being no bad thing; but as inflation rose sharply in the seventies greater credence was given to arguments that above all it was the duty of governments to provide for a stable economic environment in which each individual could plan his future on a rational basis.

However, whatever a few self-conscious political theorists might think, whatever the developments in the Labour Party, whatever the truth or falsity of the fears that Britain was becoming a corporatist society, and whatever the activities of the trade unions, great interest still attaches to the fundamental views, or lack of them, of the ordinary mass of the British people. A much cited worldwide Gallup opinion survey conducted in 1977 suggested that, on their own valuation, the British people were among the happiest in the world. Of course, this evidence could be interpreted in two opposite ways. Some commentators, such as the American author of *Britain: The Future That Works*, argued that it was better to be happy and relatively poor, than relatively prosperous and subject to stress and unhappiness. Other commentators, particularly those of a Thatcherite cast, saw the poll as indicating the very thing that was wrong with Britain, a determination to put personal tranquillity and happiness far ahead of hard work and serious endeavour. That this – whether one saw it as a good thing or a bad thing – was true of a large section of the British people seemed to be confirmed by a *New Society* survey carried out on 28 April 1977. In a sample of 1,081 adults nearly twice as many considered it better to work only for as long as was necessary to live a pleasant life than considered it more important to work as hard as they could for as much money as they could get. Most of those interviewed appeared to be fairly content with their incomes and over half considered that a rise of £10 a week or less was all that they needed to live without financial worries. These results were consistent across all social classes.

Had the British always had such attitudes? If not, how far back did they go? The nation, or at least certain members of it, had surely shown great energy and initiative in the period of the building-up of the British overseas Empire from Elizabethan times onwards, and still more so during the period in which Britain became 'the workshop of the world'. It was in the inter-war years, J. M. Keynes thought, that the British upper class, many of whose fathers had built up industrial empires in the nineteenth century, began to become complacent and unadventurous. Perhaps, with the diffusion of affluence throughout society after the Second World War, this complacency percolated down through all classes of society.

Most commentators writing at the end of the decade were concerned with 'crisis': crisis in the economy, crisis in law and order, crisis in racial and industrial relations. From the point of view of the survival of the nation as a whole as a stable and relatively prosperous (as, of course, in comparison with the rest of the world Britain undoubtedly was) society these commentators may very well have been right. But from the point of view of the vast majority of the British people, as little interested as ever in major national concerns, the most significant changes in values were probably those related to sexual mores and social relationships: the tight little society of the late forties had expanded much, and the movement begun in the sixties, towards more humane, more civilized, and more libertarian attitudes and towards a more comprehensive notion of what should be included in the term social welfare, continued on its upward trajectory right to the end of the 1970s.

Then again, perhaps these changes loomed so large only because of the essential conservatism and insularity of the British people. The ultimate irony of 1980 was that the task of blasting the British out of their conservative ways was in the hands of a government labelled 'Conservative'.

17

The Winter of Discontent and the Summer of the Fire Bombs

The winter is the winter of 1979; the summer is the summer of 1981. In their different ways these mark a kind of culmination of the time of troubles, an intensification of the 'crisis' of which commentators were speaking at the end of the seventies. As ever, the talk was exaggerated; none the less, certain of the events of 1979 to 1982 do deserve special attention. Laurence Olivier's virtuoso performance in the fifties film *Richard III*, and particularly the distilled venom in the rendering of the opening words, 'Now is the winter of our discontent...', meant that the phrase probably had an unusually high recognition factor among the British public; it seems to have been used first by Peter Jenkins in the *Guardian* and it stuck. The phrase signified the excessively high number of days lost to industrial action (higher in 1979 than in the year of the General Strike, 1926), the irritations caused to the public, and above all the inconvenience inflicted by strikes on the part of formerly rather docile public employees (whereby, for example, piles of rotting rubbish were left uncleared in streets, schools, and hospitals), and the discontent of higher-paid workers who resented Government attempts to hold down pay settlements to the official norm of 5 per cent. The industrial action was actually of two rather distinct types. On the one hand, at a time when inflation was not being effectively controlled, many of the big unions, rank-and-file as well as leaders, were losing patience with the policies of statutory limits on wage increases and of the 'Social Contract', which promised welfare benefits (most useful to the least well-off workers) in place of cash increases, and wanted a return to the 'free collective bargaining' that had always benefited the big battalions. But also there was a revolt among the least-considered members of the workforce, increasingly organized in the National Union of Public Employees (NUPE), whose membership over the previous ten years had risen from 265,000 to 712,000.

It was in July 1978 that a Government White Paper indicated the intention to limit pay settlements to 5 per cent. This was rejected by the Labour Party Conference in September, which supported NUPE in its campaigns for a national minimum wage of £60 per week. In the same month Ford workers embarked on a nine-week strike, which ended in their winning a 17 per cent pay rise. Shortly the Transport and General Workers Union (TGWU) was claiming a 22 per cent rise on behalf of the road haulage drivers, turning down an offer of 13 per cent. Early in January 1979 the drivers came out on strike, marking what is usually taken as the beginning of the Winter of Discontent. There followed a day of action on 22 January when 1.5 million public service workers came out on strike, as a prelude to the series of selective strikes, which had the much publicized results of denying children school meals, or even the right to bring packed lunches, of rubbish piling up in festering mounds, and, in Lancashire, of the dead not being buried; all this amid the snows of a particularly cold winter. There was genuine desperation; there was pride among the low-paid (very many of them women) that at last they were taking positive action; but there was also, as a TGWU official in South Wales put it, 'not bloodymindedness' but 'bloodymindlessness'. The situation was not nearly as bad as that of 1974, but in the inventive stories of the right-wing press it sounded bad, on television it looked bad, and for millions of discomfited citizens it felt bad.

The Conservative victory in the general election of May 1979 was certainly no landslide, though Mrs Thatcher called it 'a watershed'; at least the Government, unlike its Labour predecessors, did have a secure parliamentary majority (forty-three overall). But for the time being the signs of crisis intensified. The first reason for this was that the international trade recession sharply worsened. In this context the Government's determination to adhere strictly to the principles of monetarism and to ruthlessly curtail public spending had very serious repercussions. Unemployment in 1979 had eased to 5.7 per cent. In 1980–81 it took off astronomically and by the end of 1982 had more than doubled, with a rate of 13.4 per cent, and a highest-ever number of people out of work 3,190,621. De-industrialization was striking with a vengeance. After only a dozen years the magnificent new aluminium smelter at Invergordon, in Scotland, was shut down. A bitter and violent strike in the steel industry in 1980 failed to stop closures and job losses (the Government, however, for the time being avoided any confrontation with the miners). The West Midlands joined with Scotland, the North and Wales as areas in which manufacturing industry was drastically shrinking, the queues for unemployment benefit lengthening. Yet the rate of inflation, down to 9.3 per cent in 1978–9, almost doubled in 1979–80 to 18.4 per cent, and was running at 13.0 per cent in 1980–81, though down to 8.6 per cent in 1981–2. Government spending controls meant that there was a significant erosion in the spending power of welfare benefits. Over the period 1979–83 manufacturing production declined by more than 15 per cent.

The Labour Party, I have said, could still in the 1970s be regarded as a force for stability. But as radicalism triumphed in the Conservative Party, so militant left-wing elements became stronger and stronger in the Labour Party, particularly on some major local authorities, such as the Greater London Council and the Merseyside Metropolitan Council. Thus was the scene set for as sharp a set of confrontations as had ever been seen between local and central government. But, in a time of rapidly rising unemployment, major confrontations between the Government and the unions did not materialize. Two Employment Acts (Trade Union Acts in all but name) were passed: the first in 1980 outlawed secondary picketing and removed immunity for most secondary actions, such as sympathetic strikes, declaring certain firms 'blacked', etc.; the second one of 1982 made union funds liable to actions for damages in the event of strikes being undertaken outside the strict letter of the law. The level of support that the TUC managed to get for its 1982 day of action against this legislation was most unimpressive. Union leaders were no longer being consulted by Government: if ever there had been a corporatist phase, it was now clearly over. Needless to say, the whole idea of industrial democracy was totally dropped. The number of days lost due to strikes declined so that by 1983 the figure was the lowest since the war. For the moment the real trouble-spots were elsewhere.

It was actually in April 1981 that a new horrific level of urban rioting appeared, pointing the way to the summer of the fire bombs. The location was Brixton in South London, over the long weekend 9–13 April. Seventy-six shops and homes were seriously damaged, as, in addition, were many police and private motor-vehicles: 143 policemen were taken to hospital, one seriously ill with a fractured skull; at least thirty civilians were treated in hospital; 199 people were arrested. At once it was announced that a public enquiry would be undertaken by Lord Scarman. A week later, on 20 April, there was another riot in London, this time at Finsbury Park in the north-east: thirty-two members of the public were injured, sixty police, and there were ninety-one arrests. The Scarman inquiry was still sitting when, on Saturday 4 July, there was a violent confrontation between skinheads and Asians in Southall, West London, fought with bricks and then petrol bombs. That same day in Toxteth, Central Liverpool, there were clashes between police and young blacks, who complained of police harassment, and also involving white youths suffering all the frustrations of unemployment. On 6 July, *The Times* reported:

> For the second successive night the Toxteth district of Liverpool became a battlefield last night as mobs of young rioters fought police.
>
> Buildings blazed as the rioters, some little more than children, attacked police lines with barrages of missiles, driving hijacked milk-floats and a concrete-mixer into their midst.

Rioting continued over several weeks. The police took heavy punishment, but were themselves accused of brutality, particularly in the use of vehicles to charge rioters. One twenty-two-year-old white man, crippled since childhood, was run down and killed by a police vehicle. A week after the beginning of the Southall and Toxteth rioting, there was a further outbreak in Brixton, and also in Moss Side, Manchester, as well as in Bristol, Leicester, and Wood Green in North London. In the press and on television, the images of burned-out streets and of police, dressed in riot gear, aggressively wielding their truncheons, were stark ones. Published in December, the Scarman Report indicated the extent to which insensitivity and, indeed, provocation on the part of the police had contributed to riots, which, however, were largely born out of frustration in an economic recession that weighed most heavily on black youth. In the spread of the riots there was a copy-cat element; there was also an element of premeditation – both reacting with a volatile mix of unemployment, frustration, and over-intensive policing.

In the urban riots of 1981 only one person was killed – a fact which must in large measure be attributed to the continuing tradition whereby the British police are not armed. There had actually been some talk of calling in the Army, and it should be noted that such suggestions were totally dismissed by the Government. One part of the United Kingdom where the police were armed, and where the Army was being deployed, was Northern Ireland. The central objective of IRA terrorism (helped since around 1970 by the availability of plastic explosive, one of the most potent technological developments of our time) was to pressure the

British authorities into withdrawing the troops from Northern Ireland. On 20 July 1982 two IRA bombs packed with nails, one hidden in the bandstand in Regent's Park in Central London, and the other detonated from a car as the Household Cavalry marched past, killed a total of eleven soldiers and viciously wounded many others. The next day crowds turned out to cheer the Household Cavalry on parade. Whatever the divisions within, attacks from without only served to show the continuing cohesion of British society. This was a cohesion which, much as it might puzzle the rational, and infuriate the revolutionary, seemed to find a focal point in the Royal Family, whose popularity after a relatively low ebb in the austerity years had been steadily growing. This was encapsulated on 29 July 1981 in one great piece of pageantry, the wedding of Charles, Prince of Wales, to Lady Diana Spencer. No doubt there was a touch of kitsch in the *Times* account; yet the light-hearted reference to other events of that July was not entirely unjustified:

> Riotous behaviour gripped the heart of London yesterday. More than a million jubilant demonstrators took to the streets, confronting nearly 4,000 police, reinforced by thousands of servicemen, and keeping hundreds of ambulance men at full stretch. All along the procession route the Royal Wedding proved a riot of colour, good humour, and fun.

Early in 1981 four leading Labour politicians (the 'Gang of Four' – Roy Jenkins, David Owen, William Rodgers and Shirley Williams) had established the Social Democratic Party (SDP) as a party that rejected both the incipient corporatism of such leaders as Wilson and Callaghan, and, more strongly, the extreme socialism of the militant Left, and that hoped to make an appeal to the middle ground in British politics. The Labour Party, now led by Michael Foot, did not look a particularly bright electoral prospect. But when in the autumn of 1981 Shirley Williams won the Crosby by-election with 49.1 per cent of the vote, the opinion polls were putting the Alliance formed between the SDP and the Liberals well ahead of the other two parties, with the Conservatives scrambling to avoid third place. In March 1982 Roy Jenkins, leader of the SDP, won the formerly safe Labour seat of Hillhead, in Glasgow. It was, at the same time, no secret that many influential Conservatives felt the policies of the Thatcher Government not only to be electorally disastrous, but to be utterly wrong in both practical and moral terms. Limits on the powers of the unions, a proper respect for small business enterprise, seemed to be here to stay; but there was every reason to believe that there was a solid political basis upon which older policies of managing the economy so as to maintain employment, of acknowledging full State responsibility for looking after those unable to look after themselves, and of fostering the unity of the nation, would be re-established, perhaps in a Conservative Government without Thatcher, perhaps, after a general election, in a Government in which the new Alliance would play a crucial role. For an analysis of the nature and timing of change we must move on to Part Four.

Part Four

Privatization, Polarization and IT 1982–9

18

The Processes of Change

The life and leisure of the British people by the early seventies was rather different from what it had been in the late forties. Most historians would agree that the most profound causes of the change were the great expansion in world trade from the fifties into the sixties, which despite the chronic weaknesses in the British economy brought increased production and general affluence, and technological advances in the consumer sphere. Within that international setting there were, I argued, a number of particular processes that came together in the cultural transformations of the sixties. Favourable trading conditions helped to conceal the problems of low investment in manufacturing industry (British banks had a very poor record compared to their German or French counterparts), lack of long-term consistency in Government economic policy, a mixed economy that put too much emphasis on large units, whether public or private, and gave no encouragement to small business enterprises, inflexible practices and vested interests in marketing, in the professions, in the unions, and among the workers. By the later seventies these weaknesses were clearly in evidence: inflation no longer seemed a harmless adjunct to rising living standards; monetary restraints were being applied by Labour's Chancellor of the Exchequer, Denis Healey. Of course, there was no going back on the emancipated and exuberant life-styles developed in the sixties; but there was no denying the general sense of pessimism and gloom.

By the late 1980s, it was widely being claimed, the pessimism and gloom had been dispelled, there was a new purpose in British life, an 'enterprise culture' was coming into full flowering; life-styles and leisure activities, though this was less commented on, were probably continuing along the directions they had, for the majority, begun to take in the sixties. Britain in the mid-seventies, when both inflation and unemployment rose menacingly, and in the early eighties, when they rose catastrophically, was directly affected by the deepening world trade recession. After 1982 trade revival, and in particular the renewed growth of the American economy, was certainly a critical factor in the growing sense of well-being of the later eighties. Does this then mean that the endeavours of politicians, businessmen, labour leaders, and social theorists are of no significance? Certainly the tenor of this book has been to discount the importance of changes of Government with respect to the conditions and activities of the mass of the people. Still, I would not argue that the notion of 'Mrs Thatcher's Revolution' is an utterly inaccurate one, simply that, as is inevitable with such an encapsulation, it is not accurate enough. That following the re-election of the Thatcher Government in June 1983, legislation aimed at reversing the direction of social policy, as described so far in this book, was enacted at accelerating pace and with increasing certainty, is beyond dispute; as it is that every aspect of Government policy reflected the will of Mrs Thatcher, quite the most commanding figure seen in British domestic politics for nearly a century. Thus, in explaining the changes of the eighties, more weight than a social historian such as myself would generally allow must be allocated to the accidents and contingencies of politics, and to the vagaries of personality.

Thatcher's dedication, resilience, and dominating personality were the more effective because of the absence of strikingly qualified senior politicians either in her own party, or more critically, in Opposition (highlighted, for example, in the failure to exploit the Westland Affair of January 1986, in which Downing Street looked extremely vulnerable to the charge of dirty tricks in its discrediting of Cabinet minister Michael Heseltine and his case for a European, rather than an American, purchaser for the British helicopter company Westland). With its new-found genius for self-inflicted wounds, the Labour Party contrived to withhold the succession to James Callaghan from its most experienced and formidable figure, Denis Healey. Another formidable figure, David Owen, was in various ways rendered politically impotent. While the consequences were scarcely fully predictable in the period 1981–3 when Labour under Michael Foot was at its most ineffectual for generations, the establishment of three-party politics served mainly to assist Mrs Thatcher. However, behind the reforms of the Thatcher Government was a longer-term series of policy adjustments and critiques going back to the seventies or earlier.

The Radical Right had not been alone in thinking that, were it only possible, some limitations on the rights of unions would be beneficial to the economy as a whole. The two trade union Acts of the first Thatcher Government were probably both the most important legislative steps towards later changes, and the most widely (if sometimes covertly) supported. (A third Act, this time with the official title of Trade Union Act, followed in 1984, making secret ballots compulsory in trade union elections and prior to any industrial action.) Criticism of the way in which the economy was actually operated had been endemic since the early sixties, with growing appreciation that financial management was lax, economic decision-making unpredictable, and the power given to the big battalions inimical to genuine individual initiative. The principle of universality in the Welfare State had long been abandoned, both to try to contain costs, and to target aid where it was most needed. Most important of all in looking at the background to the Thatcherite innovations of the later eighties were the responses that planners and local officials in the seventies were making to the redevelopment blunders of the sixties. Two representative and informative documents, both published in 1980, are the *Birmingham Central Area District Plan*, and the *Manchester City Centre Local Plan Report and Survey*. The latter neatly contrasts the ideologies of 1968 and 1980:

Implicit in the City Centre Map (1968) was a belief that in the face of ever-growing pressures upon the City Centre there was a need to be restrictive and to 'channel', or in some cases 'deflect' activity. To this extent our objective would now be fundamentally different, with the whole emphasis being on the 'promotion' of the regional centre and the 'encouragement' and 'nurturing' of activity. Apart from the much changed world in which the City Centre Map now finds itself, the great weakness of many of its proposals – which found expression in numerous advisory schemes – was that they did not relate well to the existing fabric of the City. Moreover, they depended upon wholesale and large-scale change and needed to be implemented as a whole in order to be coherent.

The *Birmingham Plan* noted that: 'A good environment, full of variety and interest and well maintained, can be a major factor in attracting private investment of all kinds.' J. C. Holiday, to whom I am indebted for these two quotations (R. L. Davies and A. G. Champion (eds.), 'City Centre Plans in the 1980s' in *The Future for the City Centre*, 1983) sums up the new city centre plans of the early eighties as follows:

The plans are paperback statutory working documents, in contrast to some of the hardback glossies of the 1960s and 1970s. But at the same time exhibitions and leaflets show the improvement in public relations and a recognition of the need not only to sell but to share issues with the public.

To which he adds:

Employment is now a major issue in all plans, perhaps most strikingly seen in the encouragement given to industry, which received little attention in most earlier plans.

Did the drastic monetarist policies of 1980–81 contribute to the sense of well-being that people were beginning to express in opinion polls in 1982 and 1983? Had the world trade situation not improved, would voters have been less pleased, would the Government itself have plunged into crisis? Economists have little calculations that they can do in response to such questions, but since they still tend to disagree both over the calculations and the conclusions to be drawn from them, I shall not myself presume to attempt answers. I will simply restate that the accidents of politics and personality, and the longer-term ideological trends, have always to be set in the context of the international economic situation. And what of developments in technology? We move, as my general heading indicates, into the age of IT (Information Technology). IT-based instant communication enhances the control and cohesion of multinational corporations, but IT is also highly supportive of individualistic, 'desk-top' enterprises. If its effect on employment patterns and social geography was often a highly distorting one, it was certainly a most important growth area with respect to employment and profit-making opportunities, and it permeated many aspects of work and leisure. These topics will be developed further in the chapters that follow. For the moment I am simply re-establishing the truism that many of the most important characteristics of the period we are now studying had little to do with political choices or events.

However, there is one rather large event which I wish to bring under scrutiny: the Falklands War of the spring and summer of 1982. Now it is certainly true that the 'Falklands factor' has been over-worked as a self-sufficient explanation of the re-election of a revitalized Thatcher Government supremely determined to carry through its 'Revolution'. Yet from the evidence of the opinion polls and of intelligent speculation by political experts, it is very clear that of the various possible outcomes of a future general election a victory by the Conservatives under Margaret Thatcher seemed, in early 1982, the least likely. There were many predictions of revolt within the Conservative ranks, with the restoration to power of a leader with a more traditional concern for social reform and class unity. Despite the defects of Michael Foot as a national leader, Labour looked secure in its traditional strongholds and appeared to be regaining some of the ground lost at the general election. The Social Democrats were in full cry; some even predicted that they might form a Government, or certainly participate in one. The news of the Argentine occupation of the Falklands (2 April), if anything, further lowered the standing of the Government. Through its own defence cuts the Government had gravely weakened its ability to defend such remote outposts, and indeed had seemed to imply that it had no will to defend them, or at least it clearly failed to give a contrary signal to Argentina whose ambitions in the area, of course, were long-standing. (The Foreign Secretary, Lord Carrington, most honourably, resigned, incidentally removing another respected Tory traditionalist from the Cabinet – Gilmour and Soames had been ousted in September 1981.) But Mrs Thatcher, at her best in a crisis of this sort, acted with great decisiveness in mustering and dispatching a task-force. While there were very proper doubts about the Government's own responsibility for this situation, and about the appropriateness in the late twentieth century of resort to military solutions, it was virtually impossible for the Opposition to mount an effective critique, particularly once the lives of British servicemen were at stake; Argentina had violated international law, was denying basic rights to the Falkland Islanders, and was ruled by a particularly vicious military dictatorship.

National pride, loyalty to the community, and its symbols and surrogates (songs, flags, football teams, etc.), remain a potent force (too often mistaken for, and therefore written off as, something slightly different – imperialism). On 14 June, after feats of great heroism and military skill, the British forces secured the surrender of the occupying Argentine force. In the intervening months the Government had commanded the political stage. In May the Government jumped into the lead in the opinion polls with a figure of 50 per cent. In the succeeding weeks all major ships, including the main troop carrier, *Canberra*, returned to home base, to scenes of great patriotic jubilation and pride. Thereafter, the Government continued to have a commanding lead in the opinion polls. So aware were Conservative advisers of the 'Falklands factor' that many wished Mrs Thatcher to cash in with an immediate general election. It is one of

Mrs Thatcher's most admirable points of honour that she scorns such short-term political manoeuvring. But the breakthrough had been made: not the Conservative Party, but the Thatcher Conservative Government was in the ascendant; many, probably a majority in the electorate, remained opposed to much of her social philosophy, but she not only offered, but was now palpably perceived to be offering, a toughness and leadership that could not be matched anywhere else in the political spectrum. There were other factors, but the 'Falklands factor' was the critical one in bringing them fully into play and in neutralizing whatever effective resistance there might have been to the political triumph of Thatcherism. In the election held in June 1983, voter turn-out was down again to 72.7 per cent. The Conservatives won nearly 700,000 less votes than in 1979, their share of the poll dropping by 1.5 per cent to 42.4 per cent. At 27.6 per cent, Labour just managed to stay ahead of the Alliance (at 25.4 per cent). British elections, we should remind ourselves again, are won at the margins and do not accurately reflect popular voting preferences: the figures in the House of Commons were 397 Conservatives, 209 Labour, 23 Alliance. Mrs Thatcher, quite manifestly, did not have majority support in the country at large, but, what is crucial to this chapter, insofar as a politician ever is in a position to change social trends, she was in that position.

Much, I shall be continuing to argue, is unamenable, or irrelevant, to political action. It could not be said that the first Thatcher Government had had much success in resolving Britain's fundamental economic problems. Manufacturing industry, in fact, had suffered its heaviest blows yet. For many years it had been a commonplace in academic circles that the era of manufacturing industry was over and that the world was moving into the 'post-industrial age': economic activity would now be based on IT, services, and leisure. Yet there were still purchasers for motor cars, oil tankers, advanced passenger trains, oil rigs, sophisticated industrial machinery of many sorts, air frames and aero engines, and an immense range of consumer goods; human beings were still continuing to wear manufactured clothing and footwear and to consume manufactured food and drink. 'Post-industrial' or not, Japan, West Germany, the United States and many other countries were continuing to cater to these needs. Politicians and economists like to talk about 'restructuring': the need to abandon old industries and develop new ones. Without doubt it was *easier* to supply services than to make the right kind of decisions in manufacturing industry. There was indeed to be, as we shall see in

Chapter 20, some important and admirable growth in certain sectors of manufacturing industry, but Britain by the end of the eighties had not dispelled the impression of being a country that bobbed around helplessly upon international currents, rather than one that, in the manner of Japan, set out to control and exploit them. The shrinking of Britain's industrial base was apparent in the late seventies; in the main, it continued throughout the eighties.

The 'roads to freedom', which I identified as opening up in the 1960s and saw as extending through the 1970s, were not suddenly blocked off, despite the overt hostility of Thatcherites to sixties-style permissiveness, and much talk of a 'new piety'. Pop culture and youth culture went through many surface changes and reversions, but essentially retained and extended the vigour it had discovered at the end of the fifties; British television (for the time being!) continued to adhere to the standard of commitment and disrespect for authority established in the sixties; the numbers of those cohabiting without benefit of the traditional institution of marriage loomed larger and larger in the population and census statistics. The appearance of herpes and then (far more horrific and devastating) AIDS reintroduced a sanction upon sexual promiscuity as old as human society; certainly it had nothing to do with Thatcherism. In this book I have sought to divide the course of social history since 1945 into sub-periods that do genuinely exhibit characteristics particular and distinctive to themselves: that the later eighties was a period of certain distinctive and potentially very far-reaching changes is not to be denied – but nor is the persistence of behaviour patterns established in earlier periods.

What, then, of my fourth main topic of 'secular Anglicanism': the deeper stability and unity of British society, the tendency towards consensus that I postulated? 'Polarization', as suggested in my general heading for Part Four, was certainly a marked characteristic of this period, seen most obviously in the contrast between a prospering South and declining North, between well-off suburbs and market towns, and decaying and conflict-ridden urban centres, and, this was the cruel new twist, between the urban habitations of the poor, and the redeveloped leisure centres and bijoux residences of yuppiedom ('yuppie', significantly an American coinage, meaning the 'young, upwardly mobile', usually employed in finance or the service trades, was perhaps the word of the age to match 'permissive', a purely British coinage, as the word of the sixties). The very fact of a strong Government with intense ideological commitment and a determination to force through change, set within a society in which it did not in fact command majority support, was a likely recipe for friction and confrontation. Confrontation and violence there undoubtedly were, on a scale unprecedented in the entire period under review. But large sections of the British population also showed, in the traditional way, a facility for adjusting peacefully to change, where such change could be seen to have its positive aspects, as with the greater openness to the forces of the market, while at the same time preserving a strong commitment to the spirit of community welfare established in the 1940s. Part Four, then, considers a new phase in the social history of Britain, within the context of the developments since 1945 that we have already examined, of powerful reactions against some of these developments, and of the deliberate actions of a Government committed to the ideology of the Radical Right. The catastrophic rise in unemployment was already seriously undermining the power of the unions: this was driven home by Mrs Thatcher's refusal on ideological grounds to consult with union leaders in the way that all previous Governments had done. The international trade cycle played its part in the revival and triumph of Thatcherism: recession, as much as Government policy, crippled the unions; reviving world trade helped win back the voters.

19

The Geography of 'Post-Industrialization': Mainland Britain and Northern Ireland

Much of the world is subject to violent climatic conditions and natural disaster, as the floods in Bangladesh and, above all, the 1988 earthquake in Soviet Armenia poignantly reminded the inhabitants of more fortunate countries. Whatever the political storms, Britain remained a country distinguished by a very temperate climate. The hurricane that built up across the English Channel around midnight on Thursday 15 October 1987, and that between 2.00 a.m. and 6.00 a.m. on Friday 16 October created a broad band of devastation from Dorset to the Humber Estuary, was all the more of a shock. Had the hurricane struck during crowded day-time hours, the death toll would have been enormously greater than the seventeen fatalities recorded. Buildings were destroyed, thousands of trees, many very rare, were uprooted, hundreds of thousands of people went for many days without electricity and other essential services: the total damage ran into millions of pounds. The elegant south-coast city of Brighton took the full brunt. A report in the *Independent* captures the scene the morning after:

Driving to Brighton from the south exit of the M25 was like entering a valley where a major war had taken place. Mile after mile of naked and uprooted trees, some of them split like firewood, showed the northward path of the hurricane as it swept over southern England at more than 100 m.p.h. The further south you travelled the greater the devastation.

Entire forests seemed to be leaning like drunken men, with smaller woods flattened. Thirty-ton lorries lay toppled haphazardly and houses seemed to have lost their heads.

But nothing could prepare you for Brighton. It looked as if an airliner had made a forced landing on the seafront and ploughed up Palace Parade, running straight through the town, scattering debris by the ton. At one point the screaming wind was sucking up shingle from the beach and firing it like bullets up the side streets. Windows 300 yards away were peppered and smashed as if by gunfire. Roofs from beach huts and large wooden signs torn from their hinges sliced through the air and embedded themselves into walls. Three trees well over 90 feet high came down like guillotines and split the roof and walls of a three-storey block of flats in Queens Court.

Inside the Royal Pavilion, its blue polymer sheeting ripped to pieces, part of a minaret weighing over three tons was ripped off and fell into the famous Music Room, where it shattered on to a priceless carpet.

A forecaster in the Netherlands actually issued warnings as early as the Wednesday morning; French forecasters were issuing warnings by the Thursday afternoon. But a BBC forecaster in his Thursday evening bulletin specifically denied that there was any chance of a hurricane. What was all too easy to predict was that the responsibility for this gross error was blamed on the computer (just not up to the job, poor thing). The hurricane largely spared the north and west, the areas not only socially deprived in comparison with the south and east, but also the areas that generally suffered markedly cooler and wetter weather than the sheltered and relatively sunny south-east corner of England.

To turn from elemental forces to the more enduring features of social geography, the pattern that unfolds is certainly one, not just of industrial decline, but of whole industrial complexes removed from the face of the land, of the sharpening contrast already touched on between North and South, but also of some signs of bustle and activity in areas that really had appeared hopeless at the end of the seventies. The traveller through Britain's cities in 1988 would certainly note that much was different from what was to be seen in 1979 or 1980. Whether such changes meant a new optimism and a new prosperity, or whether they were simply cosmetics concealing the poverty and squalor afflicting many urban dwellers, was a matter for considerable debate.

The population of Scotland continued to decline, to 5,112,000 in 1987, while unemployment continued to rise, to 13.7 per cent in 1986, easing marginally to 13.3 per cent in 1987. Glasgow, which once proudly called itself the second city of Britain, provides an excellent focal point for the debates going on about what was really happening around Britain. Population was still in decline but at a much reduced rate compared with that of the sixties and of the seventies. As with Britain's other historic ports, the inner docks were completely closed; there was a container terminal downstream at Greenock, but no large-scale new development had taken place, partly because of the hilly terrain, largely because Glasgow faced towards the wider world, not towards Europe. Both the steel industry and the shipbuilding industry were practically finished (though at Motherwell, east of Glasgow, the bulk steel-making plant at Ravenscraig, constantly under threat, continued to operate); there was only partial compensation in the way the growth of the oil industry had brought some business in steel-pipe making and the construction of oil rigs. Yet Glasgow, under its perennial Labour council, had initiated the Glasgow Eastern Area Renewal in 1976, and in the eighties, under the slogan 'Glasgow's Miles Better', had launched a determined effort to alter its image as a centre of deprivation and violence. The appearance, most certainly, was striking: for the first time since before the Industrial Revolution, Glasgow looked clean. Pedestrian precincts had been an innovation of the 1960s but were a badge of the 1980s; Glasgow's famous Sauchiehall Street, of course, became one; Glasgow had its Garden Festival (another badge of the times) in 1988; in 1990 it was to be European Cultural City of the Year. In fact, Glasgow had always been a city of high culture, home of the Scottish (subsequently Scottish National) Orchestra, of the Glasgow Orpheus (later Phoenix) Choir and of Scottish Opera. It had long held one of the finest privately assembled art collections in Britain, the Burrell Collection; now, amid great publicity, this was rehoused in a specially built gallery on the southern outskirts. The optimists' case was that Glasgow, run by a Labour council but operating in a Thatcherite context, had demonstrated its refusal to die, its determination to attract business and to milk tourists for all they were worth. The city centre was jammed with buses of many colours, a consequence of deregulation: it was said that local citizens were now totally baffled as to which bus would take them where. Without doubt, Glasgow was a much better place to visit, particularly when comparison was made with its condition a quarter of a century before, when the then Labour council was determinedly tearing down beautiful Victorian housing in order to construct an urban motor-way; for its poorer citizens, particularly those living in the massive housing estates on the periphery, it was still as awful as ever.

Let us move the forty miles east to Glasgow's great rival, Edinburgh, a city that, in its long-established traditional occupational structure, was well suited to benefit from the processes of de-industrialization. Edinburgh had never been a centre of heavy industry, but it had always been a town of bankers and accountants, as well as lawyers. The development of the offshore oil industry (Edinburgh faced in the right direction) and the arrival of many foreign companies, particularly in connection with the computer industry, enabled Edinburgh to develop quite notably as a major provider of financial services. Always a relatively cosmopolitan city, Edinburgh attracted a growing number of non-Scottish yuppies. The accoutrements of the international commercial style were everywhere in evidence: the old Waverley Market, for instance, became an arcade of little shops selling the sort of things little shops were selling round the world. Historically, Edinburgh had been a Conservative city. When Labour took over in the 1980s, the new council, following a policy that seemed to contrast with the one currently being pursued in Glasgow, set out to make the famous Edinburgh International Festival less appealing to the moneyed élites, and more to the humbler general public. Edinburgh seemed a city divided within itself in several ways. Most notoriously, Edinburgh's outlying housing estates, a far cry indeed from the carefully restored late-medieval Old Town and the immaculately preserved Georgian New Town, had become the worst centres of drug abuse in Europe, and, inevitably, the most prolific breeding ground for AIDS.

The major development discussed in Part Three was that of North Sea oil. Aberdeen had been a true boom city in the late seventies, had gone into slight recession in the early eighties, but was again in the second half of the decade presenting the outward face of prosperity, together with all the little shops and all the little eating-places of the service culture. The bar whose drinks list I printed in Chapter 12 was now less brashly Americanized, more genteel, offering a wider range of services (including solidly decent food) in more comfortable surroundings. The latest drinks list I shall reserve for a later chapter. The period of feverish development of the oil industry was over, but there were still direct benefits for several different parts of Scotland. Further up the east coast oil-rig construction yards were being developed in the Cromarty and Moray firths, and a new oil terminal was opened at Nigg Bay in the same area. Directly or indirectly North Sea oil was still responsible for 100,000 jobs. The indirect effects were seen in the engineering and petrochemicals industries: a major new ethylène plant at Mosmorran in Fife began production in 1985, reinforcing the prominent position Scotland was assuming in chemicals.

Engineering, in all of its aspects, accounted for over a quarter of the manufacturing workforce. The major area of expansion, which now attracted the attention once focused on North Sea oil, was that of electronics. By mid-1986 Scotland's 'Silicon Glen' (comprising roughly what was more conventionally known as the Lowlands) had one of the biggest concentrations of electronics manufacture in western Europe. Over 250 plants employing around 43,000 workers produced over 50 per cent of Britain's output of integrated circuits, 15 per cent of total European output. Most of the firms were foreign-owned; much, though not all, was routine assembly, often performed by women. An important reason for the establishment of 'Silicon Glen' had been (and this parallels the situation in the original, Californian 'Silicon Valley') the pool of expertise available in the Scottish universities; most notably in the sphere of artificial intelligence, associated with its brilliant pioneer, Donald Michie. Much of the most important higher level work took the form of adapting American products to the nuances of the European market. Other factors were Government grants and, relative to most of Europe, cheap labour.

Four new factors affecting developments in the Highlands were: the availability from 1982 of funds from the European Economic Community channelled through the Integrated Development Programme for the Western Isles; the new emphasis on small business; the production of luxury primary food products based on fish farming and red-deer estates; and the advent of a more systematized approach to tourism, with centres for skiing, angling, climbing, and hill-walking, as well as craft shops. Most of the new business ventures were in weaving, knitwear, sheepskins, food products or crafts. A telegraph-pole factory at Fearn, Easter Ross, with forty-seven employees, was shipping out 300,000 poles a year to the Mediterranean and Middle East. With fish farming mainly concentrating on the higher-priced species – salmon, turbot, eels and shellfish – Scotland had become the most important inshore-fishing area in Britain. With only 4 per cent of Scotland's population, the Highlands had 25 per cent of the tourist accommodation. The traditional whisky industry had suffered in the recession, but was now again reviving under the stimulus for higher consumer demand. Tree-planting was being subsidized by the Government through tax concessions, much to the anger of environmentalists, who claimed that natural wild beauty was being ruined by afforestation.

The North, to take now the standard region that includes both Cumbria in the west and Northumberland and Durham in the east, continued to suffer the highest rates of unemployment on mainland Britain, though it did share with the West Midlands the distinction of a slight decline in 1986 (unemployment eased in the West Midlands in both 1985 and 1986).

In the North unemployment figures were: 1982, 13.6 per cent; 1983, 14.9 per cent; 1984, 15.6 per cent; 1985, 15.7 per cent; 1986, 15.4 per cent; 1987, 14.3 per cent. The problem of the North, in a nutshell, was that having lost the bulk of its heavy industry, shipbuilding and coal mining (any coal that was mined was kept within the region for electricity production), it failed to attract light manufacturing industries such as electronics, computers, and consumer goods. Yet again there could be seen, in the region's largest city, Newcastle, the Janus-face of 'post-industrial' Britain. Operating as a service centre for the whole area, Newcastle had attracted commercial enterprises and much new office building. In the city centre was a modern leisure complex and the fashionable Eldon Square Shopping Centre. The Labour council had installed a highly subsidized, and very efficient, trendy-looking rapid-transit Metro rail system. Teesside remained one of the world's largest chemical centres, but unfortunately from the point of view of employment prospects this industry was becoming increasingly capital-intensive. Cleveland still had its bulk steel-making plant at Redcar/Lackenby. In Cumbria there remained the now no longer glamorous nuclear power station, together with reprocessing facilities. In the rural areas sheep farming and forestry predominated; fishing was undergoing a slight revival. Population was in steady decline till 1986, when it stood at 4,899,000; there was a tiny shift to 4,900,000 in 1987.

The standard region of the North-West came second only to the North for high unemployment levels, just displacing Wales in this dismal league table in 1983. The percentages were: 1982, 12.4; 1983, 13.7; 1984, 13.9; 1985, 14.1; 1986, 14.2; with an easing to 13.0 in 1987. Population decline showed no sign of abatement, with the figure standing at 6,370,000 in 1987. Large numbers of the textile mills that had become engineering factories now stood empty or had been demolished. There were still a few modern deep mines between Wigan and St Helens, much of the output of two million tonnes per year being exported through the new port at Garston. The older chemical industry had declined along with textiles, but as in other parts of the UK there was significant growth in petrochemicals – unfortunately, as already noted, not an industry offering large-scale employment. The reduced motor-vehicle industry was showing some signs of recovery in the Ford plant at Halewood and the Vauxhall one at Ellesmere Port. At St Helens, Pilkington was maintaining its position as the world's largest flat-glass maker. The decline and near disappearance of the old shipbuilding and dock activities has been noted as a part of an earlier phase of de-industrialization: there were still vestiges of shipbuilding at Birkenhead, and some quite prosperous port industries such as flour milling, oil-seed crushing and cattle-feeds production, and paper making and paints. The main port now was the Royal Seaforth container terminal. Oil refining was taking place at Eastham and Stanlow, with large tankers off-loading at the Tranmere Oil Terminal. Most buoyancy was to be found in the food-processing and food-manufacturing industries: the Unilever complex at Port Sunlight was still a large-scale employer, and the Kellogg cereal factory in Manchester seemed to be going from strength to strength. In general, the other confectionery, biscuits, and bread manufacturers were not large-scale employers. Manchester had become an important centre for computer manufacture, which seemed to be on the upturn in the second half of the decade. 'Post-industrial' development on the American model was most obviously to be seen in the establishment of the Wirral Science Park, and the Birchwood Science Park near Warrington, factory estates designed to attract electronics and other high-tech enterprises.

The metropolitan counties of Merseyside and Greater Manchester, having been established in the seventies in recognition of modern patterns of commuting inward from far-flung suburbs, and with the intention of ensuring that prosperous suburbs should contribute to the cost of city-centre amenities, were abolished in 1985. District councils were encouraged to participate in deregulated local transport, so Manchester and Liverpool, too, now had their varied arrays of buses. Liverpool most obviously shared with Glasgow the image of a city revived, while, as in Glasgow, those with local knowledge continued to insist that the worst problems of urban deprivation had not been solved. In the aftermath of the Toxteth riots much attention was focused on Liverpool, a civil service task force was established, and highly publicized efforts were made to attract private capital into urban renewal developments. The prototype for this new age of private involvement in civic enterprise was the reclamation of 350 hectares of derelict land for the 1984 Garden Festival. The most famous of the new initiatives, a classic instance of what came to be termed the 'heritage industry' (see Chapter 23), was the conversion of the Albert Dock, the largest group of Grade One Listed Buildings in the United Kingdom, into a complex of shops, offices, pubs, restaurants, private residences, a maritime museum and the Granada TV News Centre. The dock had closed in 1972; conversion work began in 1982. With the opening of a Liverpool Tate Gallery, occupying the largest warehouse in the dock, the project was complete. The gallery had been designed by one of Britain's most internationally renowned architects, James Stirling (see Chapter 23), and it displays exhibits on loan from the Tate Gallery in London. Stirling had been brought up in Liverpool and had studied architecture at Liverpool University; the Tate family had made their fortune out of the Liverpool sugar trade. But these fashionable developments did little for the inhabitants of Liverpool 8, Toxteth. According to a report in *New Statesman and Society* (9 December 1988), 'the net result of "recovery" in Liverpool 8 is one street into a boulevard, a smattering of housing, one leisure centre, a handful of projects – and a great deal more misery'. In the early eighties Liverpool had been ruled by a militant Labour council that had energetically built council houses, but on borrowed money due for repayment to Japanese banks in 1989; for lack of maintenance, some of this housing rapidly turned into slums.

Manchester, while it did have a more satisfactory manufacturing base than Liverpool, developed along similar lines. Inner Manchester had been declared a partnership area in the seventies, and everywhere there were signs of reclamation and renovation. In keeping with the Government philosophy that prioritized road transport over rail, much of the hope for economic regeneration was placed on increasing still further Manchester's already considerable urban motorway network. But Manchester also offered colourful evidence of a completely different geographical development: accelerating Chinese immigration from Hong Kong. Manchester now had a clearly designated Chinatown; indeed, the attention of the media fixed on the sinister activities of the Chinese Triads there (Glasgow had already had one alleged Triad murder).

Up till 1981 the unemployment rate in Wales had been higher than in the North-West: in 1982 the principality shared with the North-West the figure of 12.4 per cent; after figures of 13.2 in 1983, 13.5 in 1984, 14.1 in 1985, Wales was back on the level of the North-West with a figure of 14.2 in 1986; the figure dropped to 12.8 in 1987. Contraction of coal, iron and steel, and the movement of industry from the valleys of South Wales to industrial estates on the coast, continued. The workforce in the great steel plants of Port Talbot and Llanwern halved between 1980 and 1986, though Wales continued to contribute one third of Britain's total steel production. Agricultural and rural pursuits (sheep and cattle rearing in the hill areas, dairy farming in the lowlands, and forestry) continued to do reasonably well. Small-scale light-industrial developments were taking place on the North Wales coalfield around Wrexham, and also in the small towns in the rural areas of mid- and North Wales. The most striking development was in electronics: an influx of over 200 overseas-owned, or overseas-associated, firms brought employment to around 45,000 people in South Wales. Compared with Scotland, the industry in Wales had a relatively low number of technically skilled and managerial employees, and an overwhelming number of routine assembly workers. There was some moderately high-level work in adapting foreign products for European markets, for example providing television sets with teletext facilities, but in the main the South Wales plants served their foreign owners as export platforms for the European and British markets. The population of Wales had gone on rising till 1980, when it stood at 2,816,000; the decline that followed was arrested in 1985, and by 1987 the population was higher than ever before, at 2,836,000.

Areas of undoubted expansion lay in the financial business services. The fabric of Cardiff underwent some of the changes characteristic of the other cities we have looked at: in April 1987 a development corporation was set up for the Cardiff Bay area. Milford Haven, surrounded by a prospering refinery complex, remained one of Britain's major oil ports. Systematized tourism advanced in such coastal resorts as Tenby, Saundersfoot, Rhyl, Llandudno, Colwyn Bay, Porthcawl and Barry, and in the National Parks of Snowdonia, the Brecon Beacons and the Pembrokeshire coast. Perceptions varied. The distinguished author Gavin Young gave South Wales a great write-up in the *Observer* (8 January 1989): 'Clean, smallish modern factories, leisure centres, golf courses and now – of all things – tourism are replacing the familiar dull and dirty sprawl of slag heaps.' And he quoted a distinguished citizen of Merthyr: 'It's a cheerful place now. There's work. And tourist attractions.'

In part the attractiveness of South Wales to foreign electronics firms lay in its position at the subsidized end of the famous 'M4 corridor', the M4 being the motorway linking London with South Wales. Part of this corridor, the most sophisticated and prosperous area of electronics production in Britain, lay in the standard region of the South-West, and part in the South-East. The three main towns of what has been called 'England's new industrial axis' were, going east, Swindon, Newbury, and Reading. Swindon housed the European headquarters of Intel, the American electronics giant, and was characterized by the recent development of large office complexes. Apart from electronics, there was also growth in the pharmaceuticals industry. Newbury, formerly little more than a market town, was now dominated by light engineering, particularly computers and microprocessors. Reading in the later eighties was noteworthy for growth in electrical engineering, electronics, computers, plastics and office employment. In general, this was an area of Government military and research establishments, classically a stimulus to electronics technology. While the towns just mentioned were expanding in population, Bristol to the west was declining, though, by the later eighties, showing many signs of prosperity. The aerospace plant at Filton, north of Bristol, very much formed a part of the electronics complex of the M4 corridor. Going to the south, Plymouth, despite the decline of the Devonport dockyard, was expanding in population, and sponsoring a new range of light industry; television sets, chewing-gum, baby foods, small boats, scientific instruments and hydraulic equipment. The traditional farming activities of the counties to the far south-west – Somerset, Devon, and Cornwall – continued to do reasonably well. Small business ventures in early vegetables, flowers, cider apples, and fish processing were expanding. In the fisheries area, shellfish, most of it exported, had become the biggest earner. Tourist shops, holiday accommodation, leisure facilities and restaurants were everywhere in evidence; about 20 per cent of all people holidaying in Britain went to the South-West. Eastwards along the south coast, a major new growth area had appeared in the interstices between the older towns of Portsmouth, Southampton, Bournemouth and Poole, particularly at Fareham, the New Forest and Christchurch.

The population of the South-West rose steadily throughout the eighties, to 4,588,000 in 1987, as did that of the South-East, which had reached 17,318,000 in the same year. Unemployment in the South-East reached levels that once would have been considered shocking, rising from 7.0 per cent in 1982 to 8.4 per cent in 1986, easing to 7.2 per cent in 1987. The figures were rather higher in the South-West: 8.1 per cent in 1982, 9.8 per cent in 1986, and 8.4 per cent in 1987. The population of Greater London, still an all too recognizable blob on the map, though no longer governed by one authority (the Greater London Council having been abolished in 1985), continued to decline, though there was considerable growth in what could be termed the Outer Metropolitan Area, extending from the Cambridgeshire border in the north almost to the Sussex coast in the south, and from Reading in the west to the coast of Essex in the east. Aspects of the old London – Fleet Street as the centre of the newspaper industry, and the Docks as a fully functioning port – had gone for good; in other respects London and the whole of the South-East, traditionally a centre for services of every kind, was well suited to profit from the characteristic developments of the post-industrial age. By the later eighties the range of activities included the production of food and drink, instrument engineering, electrical and electronic engineering, clothing, furniture, electronic printing (in various areas inside and outside of London), financial and business services, advertising, market research, wholesale distribution, and, along the Thames, oil refining. Of all employees in London and the South-East, 75 per cent were in the service sector. Tourism, too, was important, London being number one on the lists of all visitors. In 1980 part of London's derelict docklands was designated an enterprise zone and a year later handed over to the London Docklands Development Corporation, which was funded by the Government on the analogue of new-town development corporations. London, east of Tower Bridge, became the single biggest expression of what enterprise and renewal meant in the currency of the later 1980s. A ride along the new Docklands Light Railway made a splendid trip for tourists; there was an undoubted brightness and vivacity about the new developments; but older inhabitants were heard to complain of being forced out of their homes by redevelopment and astronomical prices. Much of Central London itself was assuming the aspect and noise of a permanent building site, so long known to denizens of North American cities.

As in the previous decade, East Anglia was the fastest-growing region in Britain, with respect both to population and employment, though unemployment rates were not negligible, rising from 7.7 per cent in 1982 to 8.4 per cent in 1986 (7.0 per cent in 1987). Agriculture was still the mainstay, though the structure of agriculture itself was changing: on the one hand were the moves to large farms, to large fields (the disappearance of traditional English hedgerows was much lamented) producing one single crop, and to contract farming (in which a food company contracts for the entire crop); on the other hand there was intensive development in market gardening. In common with farmers in most other agricultural areas, East Anglian farmers welcomed the subsidies provided by the European Community for the growth of oil-seed rape. Many were the complaints about the miles of monotonous yellow; more serious complaints were raised when it became apparent that these rape fields were fertile breeding grounds for the pollen beetles that were beginning to attack English gardens. On the industrial side the most important developments were the spread throughout the region of high-tech industry, continuing advances in food processing, further growth in the container ports, particularly Felixstowe, and the expansion in financial and business services, particularly in Peterborough, but also in Cambridge, Ipswich and Norwich. Peterborough was perhaps most obviously representative of the new urban face that I have described several times. East Anglia recorded the highest car ownership throughout Britain: 66 per cent of all homes had a car. The plight of those in remote areas without access to cars was as bad as ever.

Apart from a marginal decline registered in 1982, the East Midlands had continued to show a small but steady increase in population, the rise being from 3,853,000 in 1981 to 3,920,000 in 1987. Unemployment figures fell on the better side of the middle of the range, being 8.8 per cent in 1982, 9.8 per cent in 1983, 10.1 per cent in both 1984 and 1985, 10.3 per cent in 1986, and 9.2 per cent in 1987. Concentrated in the East Midlands were two thirds of Britain's footwear, hosiery and knitted goods industries, which began to do reasonably well out of consumer affluence. There was also the smaller southern end of Britain's most productive coal field (65 per cent of Britain's deep-mined coal), the rest of which is situated in Yorkshire. There was other heavy industry in the form of iron-castings and steel tubes. At best it could be said that the East Midlands was adapting more successfully to 'de-industrialization' than the West Midlands, which had long been one of Britain's main concentrations of manufacturing industry and which still in 1982 accounted for 38.3 per cent of total employment in the region, compared with the national average of 27.81 per cent. The break-down in Table 7 shows the diversity, but also reveals the importance of motor-vehicle manufacture, whose very British decline was a West Midlands catastrophe.

Table 7: Percentage employed in manufacturing industries in the West Midlands

1982	Percentage of total employment
Food, drink, tobacco	2.3
Chemicals, coal, oil products	1.0
Metal manufacture	4.2
Engineering, vehicles	22.1
Textiles, clothing	1.9
Bricks, timber, others	6.8
Total	38.3

Source: Neil Punnett and Peter Webber, *The British Isles* (1984)

Population in the West Midlands fluctuated slightly: from being 5,186,000 in 1981 it dropped to 5,180,000 in 1982, then was up to 5,183,000 in 1985, down slightly to 5,181,000 in 1986, and up to 5,198,000 in 1987. Unemployment had hit really hard at the beginning of the eighties, going up to 12.2 per cent in 1982; it went as high as 13.1 per cent in 1983, and 13.0 in both 1984 and 1985, then was down slightly to 12.8 per cent in 1986, and 11.2 in 1987. Birmingham City Centre underwent some of the same developments we have detected elsewhere, and at the end of the decade was striving here to undo the devastation wrought by earlier city-centre planning. It was in 1979 that the Birmingham partnership area was established, involving the Government, Birmingham City Council, the West Midlands Metropolitan County (abolished in 1985) and the Birmingham Area Health Authority. Away from the urban centre the characteristic sign of new enterprise was the industrial park: Monks Path Industrial Park at Solihull was built by private enterprise. Depression in the North, depression in Wales could be attributed to over-dependence on the early industries of the Industrial Revolution: depression in the West Midlands brought home the national failure to invest intelligently in the motor industry.

Yorkshire, as noted, contained the main part of Britain's most productive coalfield; through the coking plant at Orgreave, outside Sheffield, there was an organic link to the bulk steel mill at Rotherham. The woollen industry enjoyed a slight recovery in the latter part of the period, but was still a shadow of its former self; the same could be said of the Sheffield steel industry. However the York confectionery industry was buoyant. Population was in decline from 1981: standing at 4,910,000 in 1982, it had fallen to 4,899,000 in 1986 (up again slightly to 4,900,000 in 1987). Unemployment rose steadily: 10.7 per cent in 1982; 11.7 per cent in 1983; 12.0 per cent in 1984; 12.3 per cent in 1985; and 12.7 per cent in 1986, moving down to 11.6 in 1987. Some expansion did take place in light engineering, but the most obvious signs of a growth of a sort were the new office developments in Leeds, and the proposed combined conference, leisure and shopping centre in Sheffield.

As, having completed another anticlockwise tour of Great Britain, we cross the Irish Sea to the United Kingdom's most depressed region, and the storm-centre for one of the most intractable problems facing British Government and British society, we shall have to inject a little history into the geography. Before the First World War British Liberals had wanted to concede to the Irish a 'Home Rule' Parliament in Dublin, with

Ireland, however, remaining part of the United Kingdom. Unfortunately, the province of Ulster in the north was dominated by the descendants of Scottish and English settlers of the seventeenth century (about two thirds of the population there) who were vehemently opposed to even limited home rule, and determined to maintain their integral relationship with Britain. In the violence that followed the First World War an independent Irish Republic was established excluding, however, Protestant-dominated Northern Ireland, upon which was thrust, in Belfast, exactly the kind of local parliament that the Liberals had intended for Dublin. Protestant pride in being British was intensified by a deeply atavistic hatred of Catholicism; thus Catholics in the North were treated as second-class citizens, and often denied basic civil rights. The contemporary phase of the Northern Ireland problem began in 1968 with civil rights demonstrations. The Royal Ulster Constabulary (RUC), the only British police force to carry arms, resorted to its usual repressive methods. The Irish Republican Army (born in the original struggles against British rule) had been quiescent for quite some time, but now its extremist offshoot, the Provisional IRA, sprang into action. On the other side were the RUC, the Ulster Defence Volunteers, and other Protestant paramilitary formations. There is evidence to suggest that quite a number of Catholic citizens welcomed the arrival of British troops in 1969, charged with the desperately difficult task of keeping the warring factions apart. The British Government took over direct rule of Northern Ireland in 1972, and subsequently endeavoured to establish an executive in which Protestants would share power with Catholics, but this initiative was defeated by the general strike organized by the Protestant working class in 1974. Further attempts at producing devolved administrative structures were unsuccessful. Meantime, violent and murderous outrages became a regular part of the Northern Ireland scene (though there were areas that remained quite unscathed) while, as we saw, there were a number of terrorist incidents on mainland Britain. From 1973 the Emergency Powers Act gave special powers of arrest with respect to crimes associated with the various paramilitary organizations, and these crimes were tried before non-jury courts. British troops were the main (though not the only) targets of the Provisional IRA. On 30 January 1972, 'Bloody Sunday', troops of the Parachute Regiment shot dead thirteen unarmed civilians in Londonderry. For years there was a desperate and bloody military stalemate, with no significant political initiative till the Anglo-Irish Agreement of November 1985 was, against the bitter hostility of Protestant leaders in the North, concluded between the British Government and the Government of the Irish Republic. The Agreement recognized a united Ireland as an ultimate possibility but ruled that no change in the status of Northern Ireland could come about without the consent of a majority of its people, and provided for co-operation on security matters. For the suffering people of Northern Ireland the Agreement brought no abatement in violence (see Chapter 21).

Even without the sectarian divisions and the Provisional IRA, Northern Ireland had its problems. Topographically it is far from unattractive, bounded on two sides by the indented coastline of the North Atlantic and the Irish Sea, with the largest freshwater lake in the British Isles, Lough Neagh (381 square kilometres, 147 square miles) at its centre, and the mountains of Mourne rising sharply to the south-east. It is bounded on the south and west by its 480-kilometre (303-mile) border with the Irish Republic. Its most persistent climatic feature is rain, so land is more suitable for pasture than for arable farming. The population is small (just over 1.5 million), so there is no substantial domestic market on which industry and commerce might be built. Commerce southwards is limited, too, because of the Irish Republic's desire to protect its own industries. Nor have prospects been favourable in other directions: Northern Ireland sits very much on the periphery of Britain and Europe: importing and exporting over the sea crossing is expensive. Added to that, Northern Ireland is lacking in natural mineral and power resources. In the nineteenth century two major industries had been established, linen manufacture and ship-building, but, they, alas, are the very epitome of the sort of trades that do not thrive in 'post-industrial' society.

Farms in Northern Ireland were generally rather smaller than those in the agricultural areas of Britain, with most farming activity being concentrated in the areas of livestock and dairy products: there was intensive pig and poultry farming, with over 20 per cent of United Kingdom bacon coming from Northern Ireland. Amalgamation and mechanization were resulting in a reduction in the farm labour force, and in general there were the obvious symptoms of rural decline – ageing population, low levels of income, and diminishing services. There were in the 1980s about 1,000 fishermen in Northern Ireland and some developments took place recently in the realm of fish processing.

In the sixties and seventies Government incentives tempted ICI, Courtaulds and DuPont to establish production in man-made fibres to replace the traditional linen industry. But there was a series of closures at the beginning of the eighties, ICI switching its polyester production from Carrick Fergus to Pontypool in Wales, with the loss of 5,000 jobs. In fact, the relatively newly established man-made fibres industry went from 10,000 employees down to 2,500 within the space of a few years. Northern Ireland's greatest industrial employer had been Harland and Wolff, the famous Belfast shipyard. Despite having gone through an extensive modernization programme, it had no secure future: employment had been at 25,000 in 1970, but was down to 6,000 in 1983. Another great name was that of Short Brothers, still in the later eighties employing 6,000 in the manufacture of aircraft, missiles and components. Short specialized in small commuter airliners like the Short 360, while the US-owned company Lecaria was building Learfan executive aircraft at Aldergrove, just north of Belfast.

Even without the sectarian violence, which was certainly a deterrent to many major firms, Northern Ireland had serious basic economic difficulties. As in the rest of the United Kingdom there was some development in small manufacturing firms, crafts and services. The newest developments were in synthetic rubber, vehicle components, oil-well equipment, electronics, telecommunications equipment, carpets, food processing and packaging. The discovery of lignite around Lough Neagh offered possibilities; experiments were actually taking place in the growing again of flax. It could be said that the British Government had not done much to help Northern Ireland when it might have counted; industry continued to depend on expensively produced energy from oil-fired power stations. Yet Britain was pouring in considerable financial support, with building grants, machinery grants, start-up grants, free factory rentals for five years, loans, help for transferred workers, training grants, tax allowances and research and development grants. Enterprise zones were established in Belfast and Londonderry; Aldergrove Airport was declared a 'free port'. In 1986–7 the United Kingdom Government pumped nearly £1,700 million into Northern Ireland.

In many respects the province had some remarkable achievements. The annual Belfast Festival at Queen's University is the second largest international festival in Britain. Pianist Barry Douglas won the International Tchaikovsky Competition in Moscow in 1986; the flautist James Galway and soprano Heather Harper were already famous. In popular sport, the boxer Barry McGuigan and the snooker player Denis Taylor were true local heroes. The province had a vigorous local press. Bombings were not conducive to city-centre life, but there had been, in Belfast and

Londonderry, the same sort of city-centre changes noted on mainland Britain: heritage refurbishment, pedestrian precincts. Yet there remained the basic problems of housing worse than anywhere else in Europe – in housing estates segregated by religion – and of unemployment as high in some areas as 43 per cent. In the eighties people were leaving Northern Ireland at the rate of 8,000 a year. But the birth rate there was high: 18.5 per thousand, compared with the UK average of 13.5 per thousand. Thus the Northern Ireland population, 1,528,000 in 1979, 1,538,000 in 1982, had reached 1,575,000 in 1987. Overall unemployment, of course, was by far the highest in the United Kingdom, standing in the same years at 8.2, 14.7 and 17.9. Northern Ireland had some very special problems of its own (which, in turn, helped to create some very special problems for mainland Britain). It was also an extreme case of the problems of de-industrialization. At the same time, it showed some indications of the urban change detectable elsewhere – signs of enterprise and revival according to some; merely superficial gimmickry according to others.

The Americanization of Britain had been alleged for many years. In particular, J. B. Priestley, whose *English Journey* I referred to in the first chapter of this book, had felt American influences to be the most potent ones on the 'new' England he perceived in the 1930s. Priestley, like many others, grossly exaggerated the American influence, and underestimated the resilience of native British culture. But it did seem in the later eighties that the arrival of the heritage trade, shopping arcades, leisure cities, theme parks, were making parts of Britain seem more homogenized, and more Americanized, than they ever had been before. A tour round the country certainly sustained the widely publicized view of a North/South divide, a North in which manufacturing industry was not being adequately replaced, a South enjoying prosperity based very largely on the service sector. Smeared over everything, however, was this veneer of international commercial culture, while, at the same time, inner-city squalor and desperately run-down housing estates existed in London and southern towns as well as northern ones.

Table 8: Indices of production (1980 = 100)

	1976	1978	1979	1980	1981	1982	1983	1984	1985	1986
Coal export and solid fuels manufacture	100.9	97.0	97.0	100.0	97.5	93.4	89.6	32.9	66.5	79.0
Oil and gas extracts	16.2	68.9	98.7	100.0	110.3	125.6	137.6	147.1	150.3	153.0
Iron and steel	151.0	155.0	165.4	100.0	120.5	114.9	119.2	104.3	126.0	136.3
Basic chemicals	106.5	107.7	111.3	100.0	98.4	95.2	106.1	115.8	118.8	114.8
Pharmaceuticals	97.2	104.7	103.9	100.0	102.5	107.8	114.5	118.5	127.3	136.6
Machine tools and engineers' tools	112.6	112.4	106.4	100.0	72.8	68.5	64.6	72.4	81.2	79.0
Computers and office machines	58.6	77.8	93.4	100.0	86.3	95.8	144.7	207.2	270.6	247.8
Telecommunications equipment, etc.	79.1	85.7	93.8	100.0	100.9	105.6	110.5	121.0	123.8	123.8
Motor vehicles and their engines	126.1	124.1	114.6	100.0	80.2	77.2	81.1	74.8	85.4	79.0
Shipbuilding and repairs	124.2	113.8	106.5	100.0	104.2	111.3	100.4	92.3	86.2	76.0
Bread, biscuits and flour	101.4	99.2	101.5	100.0	101.1	99.9	98.2	97.5	96.9	100.0
Ice-cream and chocolate/sugar confectionery	104.3	109.3	106.4	100.0	97.8	105.1	107.4	113.9	114.1	113.4
Animal food stuffs	94.2	95.4	99.1	100.0	98.6	106.2	107.1	103.0	99.8	104.5
Miscellaneous foods	97.1	96.5	96.2	100.0	98.3	103.8	106.4	111.6	112.6	112.5
Spirits	86.7	100.1	100.8	100.0	91.5	88.2	85.3	87.1	90.4	91.9
Brewing and malting	100.9	102.9	104.1	100.0	95.6	92.5	93.3	92.8	92.2	92.0
Soft drinks	84.5	89.1	97.6	100.0	102.3	109.3	114.4	120.8	122.8	143.3
Tobacco	92.2	98.1	97.3	100.0	97.2	90.7	90.4	90.1	82.7	74.1
Woollens and worsteds	123.9	124.3	115.6	100.0	90.4	86.0	87.1	89.4	95.1	99.0
Printing and publishing	93.6	105.5	105.4	100.0	95.4	92.7	92.4	97.5	101.0	106.1
Processing of plastics	95.2	106.5	110.6	100.0	94.7	99.0	110.2	121.3	125.1	138.5

20

The 'Enterprise Economy'

Table 8 is an abbreviated version of Table 8.2 from the *Annual Abstract of Statistics for 1988* (regrettably no analogous table was published in 1989). For each industry the index of production in 1980 is taken as 100.0, and the table shows indices of production for preceding and succeeding years. Not all statistical tables are as packed with useful information as this one, but here we really do have a splendid bird's-eye view of important aspects of the economy. I'd like at this stage to try to actually involve readers in my discussion, so I am going to pose a number of key questions that can be answered from the table. I will supply answers immediately afterwards from an analysis of the table.

1. Where do we see the evidence of the basic decline in major manufacturing industries?
2. Where is there evidence of some revival in such industries?
3. Where is there evidence of striking growth in the 'post-industrial' industries?
4. Are there any other odd or striking figures on which it might be worth commenting?

Here are the conclusions I would draw from the table:

1. The coal industry, which seemed to have staged a modest rally in 1980, is steadily shrinking thereafter (with the national coal strike reflected in the particularly bad figures for 1984 and, to a lesser degree, 1985). Iron and steel, in the early eighties, is considerably below the figures for the late seventies. The figures for machine tools and engineers' tools are among the most depressingly significant, perhaps paralleled only by those for motor vehicles and shipbuilding (the decline of the last is occurring

slightly more slowly, but to similar dimensions). Further down the table, two among the oldest of all British industries evidently in decline are brewing and malting and woollens and worsteds.

2. There is a clear upturn in iron and steel in the last two years under review; the recovery and advance in basic industrial chemicals is also worthy of note. Recovery and development in plastics, by now quite a long-established industry, might also be included here. Limited recovery may possibly be detected in woollens and worsteds.

3. The obvious areas are computers and office machines, which after a two-year pause took off again in 1983, and telecommunications equipment, which shows a steady expansion throughout. The figures bring out the continuing and developing importance of North Sea oil and gas.

4. The sharp downturn reflecting the miners' strike has already been mentioned. The rise in soft drinks can be related to a number of factors: growing consumer affluence, change in consumer tastes, the American image, the growth of small outlets for such products, the decline in brewing. The decline in tobacco production relates to the swing in social mores against smoking.

From the end of the Second World War till the late 1970s the economic orthodoxy shared by most politicians, most civil servants and most political commentators was Keynesianism. According to this doctrine, it was a prime duty of Governments to manage total national expenditure in such a way that levels of demand would be sufficient to maintain full or near-full employment; Labour Governments tended to stress the importance, in addition, of direct Government intervention in the economy, particularly through the nationalized industries; both Conservatives and Labour recognized the need to maintain the Welfare Services, and the taxation policies that that entailed. The fruits, the Radical Right argued, had been low growth, gathering inflation, the stifling of enterprise and initiative, too much dependency upon the State. Openly and avowedly, the different Thatcher Governments aimed to create a culture in which enterprise would thrive, in which the value of the pound would be held steady, and individual initiative and freedom would replace dependency. There are various technical terms to describe the type of economic policies these Governments aimed to pursue. Attention was turned from demand management to the 'supply side' of the economy: better to ensure cheap and efficient production of goods that people actually wanted to buy, than simply to inflate purchasing power. There should be strict control of the amount of money in circulation (too much money chasing too few goods is the classic recipe for inflation), particularly by limiting Government borrowing and Government spending: this is the philosophy of 'monetarism'. The standard monetarist remedy for an excess of money (which entails inflation) is high interest rates, which make credit much more expensive to obtain and also suck up the resources of many existing borrowers (for example, house purchasers). The Thatcher Governments also aimed at reductions in direct taxation on the economic principle that hard work and enterprise would thus be encouraged, and the moral one that choices about the disposal of income should rest as much as possible with individuals rather than the State. The fundamental philosophy was that the most efficient economic decisions, the ones that would most benefit the country as a whole, were the ones that took place in a free market-place undistorted by Government intervention. One important aspect of deregulating the market-place took the form of curbing trade-union power. Another showed itself in regional policy now operating (apart from Northern Ireland, covered by separate legislation) on a two-level system of Development Areas (still quite fully resourced) and Intermediate Areas (with resources much reduced compared with the 1970s), with money mainly being channelled to small business.

Arguments raged over how far such policies actually produced the consequences intended, and indeed over whether the Government was actually carrying them out. It is no part of the function of this book to go into arguments of that sort, or at least no further than is required for a brief identification of the main features of economic and technological change. Some commentators claimed that having been tried between 1979 and 1982, and having failed disastrously, monetarism was buried thereafter. It was certainly true that the Government generally failed to keep within its own stated borrowing limits, and that its own expenditure continued to rise, particularly since so much was being paid out in unemployment benefits. But the very definite restrictions on expenditure in certain areas, the whole concept of 'level funding', that is to say funding that did not automatically make adjustments for inflation or pay settlements (as had been the general principle in the 'consensus' period), and the ready resort to high interest rates, continued to give Government policy a distinct monetarist flavour. Critics of the Government argued that market mechanisms alone did not ensure that the required investment was put into manufacturing industry, that high direct taxation was a better and fairer way of reducing consumer spending and inflation than high interest rates, and that high interest rates anyway both reduced investment and resulted in an overvalued pound (high interest rates attract foreign money into London), which in turn made British goods seem overpriced in foreign markets, and was thus a further handicap to British industry.

There had been an enterprise culture of a sort in the 1960s, with pop groups, experimental theatre companies, underground publications of various sorts, and boutiques, though none of these were very relevant to the basic problems of British industry. It was around 1972 that a growth in small businesses of a more orthodox character began to become apparent. D. J. Storey ('The Economics of Small Businesses' in A. Amin and J. Goddard (eds.), *Technological Change, Industrial Restructuring and Regional Development*, 1986) has identified the swing of certain circumstances against large enterprises and in favour of smaller ones, including the rise in oil prices, which disproportionately put up the costs of both energy and transport; the manner in which foreign protectionist measures were particularly aimed at the large exporting firms; the targeting of Japanese and Third World competition at the big-firm areas; and the general consumer orientation towards specialized services and one-off goods. As a lust after bigness had been a commonplace of the post-war years through to the sixties, so in the seventies it was becoming part of the common wisdom that large enterprises were beset by many inefficiencies and that small was indeed beautiful. Much of Italy's famed economic miracle had been based, it was coming to be realized, on small artisan enterprises, organizationally, if not technologically, of a rather traditional sort. Now the initial wave of electronics and microprocessors opened up new opportunities for small firms. But there was no direct and effective encouragement of small businesses, with grants and loans, till the advent of the Thatcher Governments. In this sphere, certainly, the much vaunted title of 'enterprise culture' was fully justified. True, the impact of the Government's Business Expansion Scheme, allowing for tax relief on investments up to £40,000 in unquoted companies, was not great. But there was a considerable expansion in privately sponsored venture capitalism (companies investing in small businesses for a high stake in the potential profits). In 1986 venture capitalists invested £436 million in 766 companies, 34 per cent more than in 1985 and more than double the 1983 figure. Yet while there was quite significant growth in small businesses, dogged application of the principles of the market-place allowed greater scope than ever before for foreign take-overs of British businesses, and for increasing purchase on the economy by multi-national corporations. When it came to the allocation of defence contracts, the Government most righteously showed no favouritism towards British industry. In December 1986, to take one famous example, the Government cancelled the £960 million GEC Nimrod programme for early-warning aircraft, with the loss of more than 2,000 jobs, and opted instead for the Boeing AWACS. The promise was that subcontracting to British firms would create high-technology business and 4,500 new jobs: by the spring of 1988 it was being complained that these jobs were not materializing. Twenty of Britain's top thirty employers in the later eighties were multinationals. The Government argued that multi-nationals on balance created employment, and that they brought with them the latest technology. Critics pointed out that some of the most devastating decisions with respect to the creation of unemployment were taken by multi-national companies, which could readily close down a factory in Britain and set another one up in some other country. The Government responded to attacks on it for failing to prevent foreign take-overs of British companies by pointing out that in the eighties there had been significant growth in British take-overs of foreign companies, which may or may not have been a consolation to British workers objecting to their new owners. It did rather seem that the free market included the freedom to reduce the freedom of the market.

Overseas companies, particularly Japanese, were providers of employment in areas that much needed it, for example Central Scotland, the North-East of England, South Wales. A new style of industrial relations was established: on the one side, no-strike agreements, greatly reduced powers on the shop-floor for shop stewards, and the exaction of a high level of company loyalty from employees; on the other, greater worker participation in decision-making, a less distant and snooty management. The EETPU (Electrical, Electronic, Telecommunication and Plumbing Union – expelled from the TUC in 1988) was a pioneer in agreeing to the new style.

Was British information technology, then, entirely foreign-dominated? What was the impact of IT on the British economy and British society? What exactly is IT? The relationship of American, and increasingly Japanese, companies to the British information technology industry is rather reminiscent of that of Hollywood to the British film industry. In the early eighties it did seem that Britain had a particularly innovative and robust home-computer industry, led by Sinclair Research and Acorn.

But like the British film industry, British computers, unsupported by effective Government policies, ran against the problems of chronic under-capitalization and lack of access to, and penetration of, sufficiently wide markets. And the innovative expertise, never properly funded and supported in Britain, remained almost exclusively in America and Japan. Thus British companies, for example Rodime, have felt obliged to expand into America or Japan in order to keep in touch with latest developments. The home-computer industry underwent an expansion of nearly 50 per cent between 1982 and 1983, and the figures we looked at earlier showed the enormous upsurge in the whole area of computers and office machines from 1983 onwards. Here certainly were clear signals of an enterprise economy, though the element of foreign tutelage cannot be wished away. IT (which, to quickly dispose of my third question, includes computers and electronic office machinery, telecommunications, and electronic video and satellite equipment) is, in the jargon, 'a heartland technology', having an often decisive influence on other technologies. However, a motor industry, dependent upon robotics, remains a motor industry; an iron and steel industry, whose processes are set by computer, remains an iron and steel industry.

IT is important because it has brought redundancies, because it has created new job opportunities and new sources of prosperity, because it has polarized working skills – between those who understand something of the principles involved, and between those who simply assemble components. IT is important for all the service trades based on it, particularly financial services. IT is important for the political and administrative developments that would not be possible without it, for example the complex privatization of local authority services, the introduction of the community charge ('poll tax') in place of rates. IT is important for the way in which it has affected banking (for example in the automated payments between banks through the Bankers' Automated Clearing Service and, of course, the widespread use of electronic cash cards), policing, newspapers, telephonic communication, television, video and other entertainments. In telecommunications the most important developments have been the conversion to fully electronic exchanges, and the conspicuous growth in private exchanges of associated IT products resulting from the way in which telecommunications, computing and office equipment interacted; developments have also been taking place in optical fibre systems, which transmit signals on modulated beams of light. IT is important in that it has brought into being, often almost randomly, banks of information, sometimes quite inaccurate, on private citizens. Legislation giving every individual rights of access to such information, which came into effect in 1988, was certainly a necessary, if perhaps inadequate, safeguard. But IT was not, as the enthusiastic and the fearful declared, the sole key to what was happening in Britain in the later eighties. In the newspaper industry the breakthrough point came in December 1985 when Rupert Murdoch, proprietor of the multi-national conglomerate News International, dismissed his print workers for refusing to co-operate with the new computerized technology, and moved his four newspapers to the custom-built plant at Wapping in the London Docklands. The new technology did make possible the launching in October 1986 of a new quality newspaper, the *Independent*; but it could not be argued that the general character of British newspapers changed a great deal, though some of them reflected their lower costs of production by growing much fatter.

One policy that the Government followed with determination and consistency was that of selling off to private buyers nationalized industries and other Government-owned assets. Between 1983 and 1987 the main sales were of: Jaguar cars, British Telecom (in preparation for privatization, this had been split off from the remaining postal services of the GPO), British Aerospace, Britoil, Cable and Wireless, the Trustee Savings Bank, British Gas, British Airways, and Rolls-Royce. 'Selling off the family silver' was the phrase used by critics, especially when at times the prices seemed over generous to potential purchasers: 2.3 million applicants came forward for British Telecom shares, 2.1 million for Rolls-Royce, 1.1 million for British Airways. The percentage of the British people owning shares rose from 7 per cent to 19 per cent. The private enterprise effect extended to sport and culture, where sponsorship was now a commonplace. Private sponsorship in 1986 amounted to £600 million.

Commercial sponsorship of sport (and, in lesser degree, cultural activities) goes back at least to the nineteenth century. In what might perhaps be thought of as the twentieth-century pre-history of sponsorship, the main protagonists were the press, creating events which then could be extensively reported, and the oil companies whose particular interest was motor racing. As with so many other developments in contemporary Britain, the critical changes began to take place in the sixties. The Sports Council set up a working party to study the subject in February 1970: in its report of June 1971 it estimated the amount spent at £2.5 million, almost certainly an underestimate. The first major investigation outside the world of sport was *Sponsorship*, published in 1973 by the commercial research body System Three. This reported that throughout western Europe and North America there had in the last ten years been a 'massive increase in the industrial support given to the sports and, less dramatically, to the performing arts'; it remarked that a huge 'fillip' had been given in Britain by the ban on television advertising of cigarettes. The key to the developments of the sixties was an 'uneasy' turning (the adjective is exact for this initial phase in the sixties) from sponsorship's 'origins in patronage of cultural excellence and towards being an additional marketing medium for influencing a wider public'. Top of the list was motor racing, attracting sponsorship around £3 million; then came horse racing (around £700,000); golf (around £500,000); association football (around £300,000); cricket (£270,000); then, in sixth place, came the arts (around £250,000), followed by tennis (£230,000). A survey of 1976 put the total sponsorship figure at £16 million, remarking that over a quarter of the firms consulted had been sponsoring since before 1968. In 1978 the figure was reported as being £20 million; by 1981 it was at least £40 million, according to the Compton Report. (All of these later figures refer only to sports sponsorship.) The most significant feature of the eighties, when the total sum devoted to sports sponsorship rose to over £60 million, was the way in which sponsorship, rather low-key and isolated in the 1960s, had become part of the basic fabric of the nation's spectator sport, association football. According to the 1983 Howell Report for the Central Council of Physical Recreation, football was attracting £12 million in sponsorship, second only to motor sports with £19 million.

A whiff of the commercial spirit had many beneficial results with respect to the preservation and display of the nation's older buildings, cathedrals, and artistic treasures, though the main art galleries, with the exception of the Victoria and Albert Museum in London, continued to resist pressure to charge for admission. Privatization, and the involvement of commercial interests in the national heritage, assumed the dimensions of notoriety following the proposal of the Dean and Chapter of Hereford Cathedral to sell its unique medieval treasure, the Mappa Mundi, through the famous London sale-room of Sotheby's, having been informed by a firm of accountants that the Cathedral needed a sum of £7 million to cover both major repairs and immediate running costs. (After much protest the decision was eventually rescinded.)

The claim being made at the time of the 1987 general election was that the British economy was now firmly set on a new course, with industry booming, and productivity rising. In 1987 the growth rate of 4 per cent was achieved, though this fell back again in 1988. How one assessed Government claims depended on whether one took the baseline as 1979, when the Conservatives first came into office, or 1982, when the economy was just beginning to recover from the intervening recession. It also depended upon what weight was put on manufacturing output, as distinct from services, and North Sea oil production. It was in April 1983 that Britain for the first time in its industrial history became a net importer of manufactured goods. At the end of 1988 the balance of payments deficits were building up on a scale which would once have been a matter for very serious concern. The Government had succeeded in going a long way towards its intended reductions in tax rates, the basic level having gone down from 33 per cent to 26 per cent, and the highest tax rate from 80 per cent to 60 per cent. Interest rates, however, were back up to 14 per cent. The traditional restrictionism of the London stock-market had been opened out by the 'Big Bang' of October 1986. The City seemed to come through this triumphantly, and also to weather effectively the New York stock-market crash of a year later. But for all the talk of a Thatcherite Revolution it did rather seem as if one traditional failing was being perpetuated: too much emphasis on the world of finance, too little on that of productive industry.

'Post-industrial' is a word I have used several times, usually in quotation marks since it seems to me a term that is both inexact and loaded. Other jargon terms that tended to come up in discussions of economic trends were 'de-skilling' and 'post-Fordism'. De-skilling is the process whereby an increasing proportion of the workforce simply does routine work, assemblage of printed circuits for instance, the old attributes and crafts-manship of the skilled working class being lost. As with most jargon terms of this sort, the description was an inadequate one, as indeed Sayer and Morgan point out when, on page 162 of the collection edited by Amin and Goddard (*Technological Change, Industrial Restructuring and Regional Development*) they refer to 'crude notions of de-skilling'. While the sheer absence of manufacturing employment is not to be gainsaid, a central problem remains the one identified earlier in this book: a lack of the skills necessary in an IT-oriented society. 'Fordism' refers to the large-scale assembly-line production usually associated with the pioneer American manufacturer Henry Ford; 'post-Fordism' refers to the trend towards small businesses and greater entrepreneurship even among members of the working class. These developments were summarized by one authority

(David Clutterbuck, in *New Patterns of Work*, 1985) as: intrapreneurship (employees returning as entrepreneurs within the company); decruitment (employers or managers planning to step down in the future); employees being shed, and then returning as independent contractors; job-sharing; sabbaticals (presumably unpaid); and increased skills and knowledge among secretarial workers.

However, it would be quite wrong to assume that arduous work in unpleasant conditions (the distinguishing characteristic, I said earlier, of being working class) did not continue. In retail outlets, new and old, the trend was towards longer opening hours: a boon to shoppers, but also a source of exploitation of the workforce, increasingly being hired on short contracts of less than sixteen hours, which was an effective way of evading most of the legislation governing the conditions of shop workers. In many places of employment it was an open secret that union agreements about the amount of time that could be spent continuously working at a visual display unit were being ignored. A new anxiety (or rather the revival of an old anxiety, a very Victorian one) about the work-place and elsewhere, which began to surface more and more in newspaper reports, was that an enterprise economy put too great an emphasis on economy and profit-making, at the expense of safety. Such work-places as construction sites and scrap-metal yards were particularly dangerous. Small firms in general tended to evade safety regulations. The Health and Safety Executive reported at the beginning of December 1988 that 'many of the 19,000 new work-places visited were found to be working in ignorance of legal requirements and basic standards for occupational health, safety, and welfare'. Around the same time, the chairman of the Government's Health and Safety Commission commented: 'I cannot conclude that 1987/88 was a satisfactory year for industrial health and safety.' Prosecutions for breaches of safety law increased by 300 in 1988, the year in which British Petroleum was fined £750,000 over the deaths of three men, killed in two separate explosions in nine days at its Grangemouth Refinery in Scotland. This issue was glaringly highlighted by an unprecedented series of tragic disasters running through 1987, 1988 and into 1989. On 6 March 1987 the Townsend Thoresen cross-Channel ferry *Herald of Free Enterprise* capsized while leaving Zeebrugge Harbour in Belgium, killing 193 passengers and crew; on 18 November 1987, in the early evening, just as the rush-hour was coming to an end, fire swept through a section of King's Cross Underground Station in London, killing thirty-one people; on 6 July 1988 the Piper Alpha North Sea platform exploded, killing 167; on the morning of 12 December 1988 three trains were involved in a crash near Clapham Junction in London, killing thirty-five; on 20 December 1988 a Pan-Am jumbo jet blew up over the borders of Scotland and crashed down on the town of Lockerbie (a bomb was the cause; the questions raised were about safety precautions – the announcement early in January 1989 that additional checks were to be imposed on air passengers together with the screening of cargo effectively confirmed that previous safety procedures had been inadequate); on 8 January 1989 a British Midland Boeing 737 crashed on the M1 motorway, causing nearly fifty deaths (none on the ground); early in March there were rail accidents at Purley, South London (five killed), and Glasgow (two killed). Appalling luck played a part each time; yet each case (save perhaps the Lockerbie disaster) did reveal clear signs of economy and profits being higher concerns than safety. The immediate cause of the Townsend Thoresen disaster was that the seaman responsible for closing the bow doors had fallen asleep, so the ship was destabilized by the water pouring into its car deck. Four earlier occasions had been recorded of ferries departing in this desperately dangerous fashion, yet the directors of the company resolutely refused to introduce any safety measures, such as warning lights on the captain's bridge. The *Independent's* report on the *Herald of Free Enterprise* inquiry, 12 June 1987, records:

> They rejected out of hand repeated complaints from captains of grossly over-loaded ships, carrying hundreds more passengers than the management had recorded on their manifests . . .
>
> They pressured already overstretched and tired crews into turning round their vessels in shorter and shorter times.

In preparation for its abolition of the Greater London Council, the Government in 1984 had separated London Transport from that body, renaming it London Regional Transport. From that moment deliberate cost-cutting policies had a manifest effect on safety. The report of the official investigation into the King's Cross Underground fire by Desmond Fennell Q C was less forthright in its criticisms than were many observers, but in one short paragraph of measured prose the link between the ethos of enterprise and economy and a disastrous deterioration of safety standards is clearly revealed (*Report*, Cm499, November 1988, page 149):

> There was a feeling among London Underground managers that the financial climate would rule out proposals to increase spending in certain areas. The lift

and escalator manager, Mr Styles, for example, said that between 1985 and 1987 he did not press for investment to relocate the water fog controls or replace the wooden parts of escalators with metal ones. He did not do so despite their recommendation by internal enquiries into escalator fires and his support for such investment because he felt that they would have stood on only a thin chance of being authorized. There was also evidence that when the budget for escalator cleaning was reduced, the effects were not fully considered at an appropriate level.

The Piper Alpha disaster was above all a tragedy for one community, Aberdeen. Stories were legion in the oil business of men fearing to report breaches in safety regulations for fear of losing their jobs. In Piper Alpha two factors were involved. First of all the entire structure was inherently unsafe in that, unlike Norwegian platforms, there was no effective segregation between production areas and living-quarters. Secondly, on the more immediate level, prior signs of leakage were ignored. Piper Alpha was, of course, American-owned. But, as I have already suggested, in blatantly seeking the best of American enterprise culture, the Government seemed also to be lumbering the country with the worst. (It may be noted here that another kind of tragedy had taken place on 19 August 1987 in the quiet town of Hungerford in the M4 corridor when, in just under an hour, twenty-seven-year-old Michael Ryan shot dead sixteen people, wounded fourteen others, and terrorized many families, before barricading himself into a school and then finally shooting himself at 6.45 p.m. It would be unscholarly to draw any direct correlations with political or economic policy; but again a frightening commonplace of American life had entered once tranquil British terrain.)

The immediate cause of the Clapham Junction disaster was a trailing wire that interrupted the signalling system. In conditions of heavy pressure on qualified staff, supervisory procedures were found to be inadequate. British Rail itself had failed to act upon an earlier warning of the fault. The commuter train where most of the deaths occurred was grossly overcrowded. One must be cautious here in forcing too many links with the general economic environment, as also in the case of the Lockerbie air disaster. Nevertheless, a Transport Select Committee of the House of Commons had two years previously made a number of recommendations designed to prevent bombs being taken on board aircraft with the cost of the additional precautions being met by the re-establishment of the aviation security fund, levied on the industry, which had been abolished in 1983. John Newman, Deputy General Secretary of the transport union

NUMAST (National Union of Marine, Aviation and Shipping Transport Officers) commented on the inadvisability of devolving key security tasks to organizations with a direct commercial stake in air transport, characterizing this as typical of a philosophy that put profit and deregulation before safety. At time of writing the verdict on the M1 air disaster had not been pronounced; what had come out was that, under commercial pressures, quality control at Boeing had deteriorated. During the early hours of Sunday 20 August 1989 the cruise boat *Marchioness*, carrying over a hundred party revellers, was in collision on the River Thames with the dredger *Bowbelle*; twenty-six young people lost their lives.

Moving from this gloomy and ghoulish subject, it must be added that in some areas efforts towards cost-effectiveness and meeting the needs of the market were improving a transport system that had never in the past lived up to the claims of previous Labour Governments that they were developing an integrated national transport policy. Only at the beginning of 1988, for example, was effective integration between London's different modes of transport instituted; such developments had come a little earlier (often under Labour local authorities) in certain provincial centres. Determined attacks were made on the problem of traffic-flow blockage in urban areas due to carelessly parked cars. However, since the responsibility for wheel-clamping or towing away was handed over to private companies the suspicion arose that private profit-making again was outweighing contributions to the public good.

The sorry story of British car manufacture went far back, as we have seen, before the 1980s. The restructuring initiated by Michael Edwardes resulted in the early eighties in the rationalization of volume car production under the title of Austin Rover. In July 1986 the new chairman, Graham Day, an enthusiastic supporter of Government ideology, symbolically abolished British Leyland and re-christened the much reduced enterprise the Rover Group. Within a frame of overall drastic decline, there were signs of recovery in 1986 and 1987. The long tale of woe is most easily expressed in the percentage of British-made cars sold in the home market:

1972	1976	1978	1979	1980	1981
76.5	62.1	50.7	43.7	43.3	44.3

1982	1983	1984	1985	1986	1987
42.3	43.1	42.5	41.9	44.0	48.0

For those engaged in car manufacture, or living in the areas where once this had been the basic industry, the outlook was still not much less than bleak. But for those engaged in the selling of cars (foreign as well as British, of course) an air of jubilation had returned. The 1988 edition of *The UK Passenger Car Market* declared roundly: 'To the extent that such a thing can exist, this is a golden age for the UK car market.' For the British economy as a whole the verdict might well be: buying and selling, yes, manufacturing, maybe. And in the world of food production and marketing a sad little drama was played out in the early months of 1989 that neatly expressed the perilous relationship between enterprise, safety and Government authoritarianism and secrecy: a confused public learned of the unquantified dangers of eggs, chicken, soft cheeses and apparently many other foodstuffs as well, without the help of clear pronouncements or reassuring action from a Government for whom protection of consumers was apparently a very low priority.

21

Workers, Yuppies and Hooligans

What had made the British class structure distinctive (though not, I have always maintained, critically different from that of other industrialized countries) was, on the one hand, a long-established working class thoroughly steeped in its own attitudes and traditions, and, on the other, a continuing upper class, adept at socializing new recruits into attitudes and traditions just as long-established. It is the middle class – so often cited by commentators as if it were a kind of homogeneous universal explanatory factor for everything – that was most variegated (as we saw, for instance, with respect to educational qualifications). The critical developments in the years of privatization were an acceleration in the breaking up of the rigid frontiers of the working class (a process long talked about, but less readily perceivable as an actual reality), and more abrupt openings to positions of power and influence for people who had not taken the trouble to absorb the traditional upper-class life-style. The much talked-of 'yuppie', though over-publicized, did have corporeal existence. This era of buying and selling (in information services, shares, land for development – in one notorious case the Westminster Council sold off, for practically nothing, cemeteries in its care – and goods of all kinds) there were large incomes and commissions to be earned in finance, accountancy, law, in agencies and consultancies of all kinds, as well as in commerce. That, combined with vigorous propaganda on behalf of the notion that success was far more important than social origins (the results of which were far from totally successful, given the weight of tradition that lies on all societies), was the basis for the yuppie phenomenon. Exact statistics are lacking, but impressionistic evidence indicates that working-class and lower-middle-class forms of speech, and provincial accents, were being heard as never before in the world of finance and the commercially oriented professions. (I have already attributed the accent breakthrough to the sixties, but in the areas I am now speaking of, upper-class accents, whether natural or assumed, would have been expected throughout the seventies.) Change was most obvious in the Conservative Party itself, as each successive Conservative victory brought into Parliament more successful entrepreneurs, consultants, etc., who had not been beneficiaries of the traditional upper-class tradition, while upholders of traditional upper-class culture were (up to a point) in retreat.

Earlier, in order to demonstrate continuing upper-class dominance, I analysed Mrs Thatcher's first Cabinet of 1979. Some measure of change, and the limits upon it, can be derived from a similar analysis of the Cabinet she established immediately after her election victory in June 1987. Wykehamist, farmer and landowner Viscount Whitelaw was still there (though before long forced to retire through ill health, to be succeeded as Leader of the Lords by Lord Belstead – educated at Eton and Christ Church). Lord Hailsham had gone, though replaced by Sir Michael Havers (soon Lord Havers), son of Sir Cecil Havers, Q C, and educated at Westminster and Corpus Christi, Cambridge; so had Lord Carrington, Francis Pym, James Prior, Sir Ian Gilmour, Michael Heseltine, Nicholas Edwards, Humphrey Atkins, John Nott, David Howell and Angus Maude. So we come to the Foreign Secretary, Sir Geoffrey Howe, who, as I suggested previously, was fully socialized into, if recently arrived in, the upper class. Commentators have made much of the fact that Nigel Lawson, Chancellor of the Exchequer, came from an immigrant family. Yet he was educated at Westminster and at Christ Church, Oxford (where he was both a Scholar and took a First in PPE); such rapid ascent into the upper class (by my admittedly contentious definition) was not specially unusual (the Mond family had done it in the nineteenth century), and Lawson certainly had the accent (plummy), manners (abrasive) and figure (ample). The Home Secretary, Douglas Hurd, grandson of a knight, and son of a baron, and himself educated at Eton and Trinity College, Cambridge, unambiguously stands in the upper class. Likewise George Younger (Secretary of State for Defence), whom we have already encountered; Nicholas Ridley (Secretary of State for the Environment), younger son of the third Viscount Ridley, and educated at Eton and Balliol; John Wakeham (Leader of the House), an old-style landed Tory, son of a major, educated at Charterhouse, but not at university; Paul Channon (Secretary of State for Transport), son of Sir Henry Channon, part of the mighty Guinness connection and educated at Eton and Christ Church, Oxford, and a former second lieutenant in the Royal Horse Guards. Probably Tom King (Secretary of State for Northern Ireland) – man of business and man of the shires (MP for Bridgwater, commissioned in the Somerset Light Infantry), educated at Rugby and Emmanuel College, Cambridge – should be included as well. Less easy to be dogmatic about are Norman Fowler, probably to be ruled out, as a grammar school boy and subsequently graduate of Trinity Hall, Cambridge; Kenneth Baker, son of a middle-rank civil servant and grandson of a docker, educated at St Paul's and Magdalen College, Oxford; John MacGregor, son of a Scottish doctor, educated at one of Scotland's upper-middle class schools, and at St Andrews and King's College, London; and Malcolm Rifkind (Secretary of State for Scotland), solidly Scottish upper-middle class with an education at George Watson's and Edinburgh University. Quite definitely not upper class in background, though now no doubt establishing themselves in it, were, apart from the Prime Minister herself: Peter Walker (whose background has been detailed earlier); Lord Young of Graffham, seen by many as the perfect Thatcherite – solicitor (leaving school at sixteen, he had studied law in the evenings), businessman (Great Universal Stores), and property developer; Kenneth Clarke, son of a Nottingham miner who left the pits to open a jeweller's shop after the war; John Major (middle-class father, fallen on hard times), a young banker (he was forty-four in 1987), without a university education; John Moore, working class in origins, but with a degree from the London School of Economics; and Cecil Parkinson, also working class in origins (son of a railway worker), but with a degree from Emmanuel College, Cambridge. (On 15 October 1983 the tabloid paper the *Sun* had declared Parkinson 'so weak he destroyed himself' – a reference to his resignation over his much publicized affair with party worker Sara Keays – while nobly recording that 'the overwhelming mass of the nation are right behind Fighting Maggie'. Now 'Fighting Maggie' had brought back one of her special favourites.) Out of a Cabinet of twenty-one, then, my reckoning is that fully eight were in the traditional upper-class mould, while only seven distinctively were not. Change, certainly, but change within strong traditional limitations.

Evidently the number of manual workers employed in manufacturing industry was shrinking drastically, while the numbers of those performing the tasks of the skilled manual worker, but as self-employed entrepreneurs, were increasing. However, a reduction in the size of the working class did not necessarily mean that the boundary between working class and lower-middle class was any less solid, or that a sense of working-class awareness had diminished. Fortunately we have the carefully presented results of a well-conceived survey carried through in the period 1 March to 3 July 1984 (published in 1988 as *Social Class in Britain Today*, by Gordon Marshall, Howard Newby, David Rose and Carolyn Vogler). Of a final sample of 1,770, over 90 per cent were readily able to place themselves in a specific class category. Adjusting the responses to exclude refusals and don't-knows, the authors come up with the figures of 58 per cent working class and 42 per cent middle class (the authors, wrongly in my view, make no allowance for an upper class: since the upper class tend to be concentrated in particular areas, and since there is a polite convention that one does not call oneself upper class, surveys tend anyway to under-estimate this element). The actual raw responses are shown in Table 9.

Table 9: Survey of social class in Britain, 1984

Class	Per cent
Upper	0.2
Upper-middle	3.0
Middle	23.7
Lower-middle	11.8
Upper-working	11.1
Working	37.6
Lower-working	4.2
(Refused)	2.8
(Don't know)	5.6

Source: *Social Class in Britain Today*, p. 144

What these figures tell us is of a very clear sense that classes still exist. The exact allocation to class is of course personal and subjective, but the broad figures do coincide remarkably well with the hard statistical information we have on different types of occupation, manual and non-manual. Usually there is a slight tendency for a few of those, who by other economic and social criteria definitely are working class, to allocate themselves to the middle class. Thus, we probably would not be far wrong if we took the 58 per cent figure as an accurate one for the size of the working class in the mid-1980s and if we compared this with the 69.8 per cent figure produced by Richard Scase in 1972, we would have a good measure of social change in the intervening period. Perhaps 39 per cent would be a roughly appropriate figure for the middle class (to be compared with 19.3 per cent in 1972), leaving about 3 per cent as the figure for the upper class. Some of the general conclusions drawn by Marshall, Newby, Rose and Vogler are very persuasive (*ibid.*, pages 137–8):

> Such upward mobility as has existed is the result of changes in the *shape* (rather than the *openness*) of the class structure. The growth of the service class and contraction of the working class reflects the transformation in the occupational division of labour in Britain since the war – the decline of manufacturing and manual labouring together with the expansion of the services sector and of professional, administrative, and managerial jobs – it does not signify a reduction in the inequalities of class life-chances. More 'room at the top' has not been accompanied by greater equality in the opportunities offered to get there.

The authors demonstrate conclusively that, as I have myself insisted, there is a very high sense of class awareness in this reduced working class, though little class consciousness in the Marxist sense. Class, they show, has not ceased to be an important factor in political choices. There has always been a substantial section of Conservative voters within the working class, but the class as a whole has certainly not turned away from Labour to the Conservatives; there is, however, wide-spread disillusionment with all political parties. And, of course, the secure base for Labour is much smaller than it used to be. The authors make a particular point of drawing attention to the inequalities with regard to mobility, earnings, etc., suffered by women. And, of course, they recognize the salience of race, the disadvantages and the political significance (a strong likelihood of voting Labour) of being nonwhite. The continuing relevance of class was shown up very starkly in such development areas as the London Docklands. The very high investment of public funds, a representative of the London Docklands Consultative Committee reported to the Institute of British Geographers in January 1989, was benefiting the new middle-class and upper-class residents, while long-established working-class families were being squeezed out. Was there, therefore, open conflict between the classes? The middle 1980s were marked by one unprecedentedly violent and prolonged industrial dispute, by horrendous urban riots, by terrorism, and by much sporadic strife, which continued into the later eighties, when a kind of quiescence seemed to settle over the arena in which capital meets labour. Overall, despite the very real evidence of confrontation in many different areas, Britain was not obviously any more riven by class conflict than she had ever been.

From the Second World War to the end of the seventies Governments had been careful to pay heed to the views of trade union leaders. Trade unions, still less their leaders, cannot, of course, be simply equated with the working class, though the leaders did, despite their relatively high salaries, tend to keep up a working-class image. The many consultations between union leaders and Government during the 1970s were notorious for being accompanied by beer and sandwiches. Co-operation between Government and unions (and industry) has been termed 'corporatism', though the term is not one I personally greatly favour: the original basis was a genuine sense of respect for different points of view within a sense of common purpose – secular Anglicanism in practice, in fact. It was perhaps in the 'winter of discontent' of 1979 that the basis was more clearly seen to be flawed; when the unions were perceived as grasping and inconsiderate of the well-being of the community. With the advent of the Thatcher Government and the economic recession, the balance of both power and sentiment swung quite strongly against the unions. Some union leaders were moved to caution; some, apparently, to despairing frenzy; some completely misread the realities of the situation. The occasional violence of the seventies, repeated in stronger form during the 1980 steelworkers' strike, manifested itself in a more concentrated form than ever before: first in a relatively small strike in 1983, then in the epic miners' strike of 1984–5.

Consider this account of events on 29 November 1983 at the Stockport plant of provincial newspaper proprietor and enthusiastic proponent of the new information technology, Eddie Shah, and note both the invocation of Northern Ireland and the reference to one of the special police groups – in this case the Tactical Aid Group, Manchester's equivalent of London's Special Patrol Squad – whose very un-Anglican appearance and deportment became a classic feature of the eighties (D. Goodhart and P. Wintour, *Eddie Shah and the Newspaper Revolution* (1986), page 12):

> The Tactical Aid Group were finally sent in, and cut through the crowd with their batons flailing. Soon the road round the back of the plant looked like an Ulster riot – with burning barricades, felled telegraph poles and groups of riot police with clubs chasing after pickets. There were excesses on both sides. Some members of the Tactical Aid Group in full riot gear clearly enjoyed the night out. But individual acts of police thuggery were in part provoked by the impersonal

violence of the missiles which hailed down from the Kop [the nickname given by the pickets to a mound on which they took up position – the reference, revealingly, is to the terracing occupied by home fans at the Liverpool football ground].

The National Graphical Association (NGA) was battling to maintain its closed shop in the Shah Group. It had steadily increased its picketing throughout the autumn, and members of other unions, including in particular Scottish miners, had become involved. But (*ibid.*, pages 12–13):

most of the pickets were stunned by the efficiency and ruthlessness of the police-clearing operation and started to hurry away. John Ibbotson, later the NGA's deputy general secretary, said the next day: 'A large number of our members, middle-aged blokes who've never been in that kind of scene, were horrified. They're the sort of people who have always been supportive of law and order but they changed their views about the police last night.'

An ominous wind was blowing: the police had also called in Police Support Units (thirty men, three sergeants, and an inspector); more, they had blocked off exits on the M62 motorway to prevent pickets reaching the plant.

'You never seem to be able to get the numbers right in this industry,' lamented Sir Norman Siddall, who bravely filled the gap between the Coal Board chairmanship of Sir Derek Ezra, supreme servant and subtle bureaucrat of consensus, and that of Sir Ian MacGregor, *vieux terrible* of confrontation: 'there is either too much or too little.' The general story, of course, was of 'too much', of declining demand for coal, of competition from oil, nuclear energy, and more cheaply mined coal from abroad. The broad implications had not been contested by Joe Gormley, president of the National Union of Mineworkers till 1982, who had accepted a carefully paced contraction, with good redundancy terms and high wages for remaining miners. The incoming Conservative Government of 1979 sought a drastic reduction of production and accelerated closures, with a view to making the coal industry self-supporting by 1983–4. Gormley threatened to ballot all mineworkers in the certainty of securing support for an all-out strike; the Government, in February 1981, backed down. Gormely had to retire the following year, and was succeeded by Arthur Scargill, a left-wing socialist who believed it was the destiny of the working class (led by the appropriate leaders) to overthrow capitalism, and the mission of the miners to act as the working-class vanguard. Scargill had been the hero of the flying pickets of the early seventies, and was a powerful and charismatic orator. Gormley, and other informed observers, did not believe that Scargill alone could alter the moderate policies long favoured by the miners' union. As others had underestimated Margaret Thatcher, so they underestimated Scargill's ability to impose his will on his followers.

With regard to the year-long miners' strike, three questions arise immediately. Why did it break out in the first place? Why was it so prolonged? Why was it so violent? Really, there is no mystery with respect to any of these questions. Most miners expected the strike to last only a few weeks at the outside (which, of course, is a factor in explaining the actual outbreak of the strike: going on strike – for a while – is quite good fun, particularly if the alternative is working down a mine). But that was a singularly badly informed calculation, and, of course, as the strike went on, yielding no results but poverty and broken homes, frustration, and therefore violence, mounted. The major question of relevance to this chapter is the significance of the strike in illuminating social relationships, particularly relationships within the working class, and relationship between striking miners and the various agencies of authority. The basic problems of the industry were obvious: over-production, declining demand, pits that were uneconomic to work. The Thatcher Government had not retreated from its determination to make the industry face the naked laws of the market, to become self-supporting. No miners' leader could have accepted the Government's plans without resistance. The two circumstances that made a strike, and a prolonged strike, inevitable were that the Government was not prepared for any compromise over its basic objectives, and that Scargill actually welcomed the prospect of a strike as one battle in the class war that would both remove the Thatcher Government and open the way to a better society.

Opinion will differ as to what sorts of compromise were possible or practicable. One could argue that, given all the uncertainties attending both oil production and the production of nuclear energy, the coal industry was a national asset worth preserving, that if power stations could be built to use imported coal, they could be built to use home-produced coal, and that if coal could be imported, it could also be exported. One could argue that whatever closures and whatever changes in working practices were necessary, the closing down of whole communities was simply unacceptable. Other European countries took a balanced view of their coal industries, the French paying a subsidy of £19.19 a tonne, the West Germans £12.06, while the British figure was only £4.11.

Government policies, though narrowly conceived and inhumane in their implications, were at least rational. Scargill's belief in the revolutionary potential of the miners simply defied all experience (though it was apparently subscribed to by many academics). On the other hand, the right of a union to defend the employment prospects and living standards of its members is a basic one, while the maintenance of social unity might well be seen as an equally basic duty of Government. Scargill, however, was exceptional among union leaders in that he himself could be plausibly represented as a threat to social unity and due democratic processes, and therefore a justification for Government intransigence. The appointment of Ian MacGregor to the chairmanship of the Coal Board in September 1983 was an earnest that cost-effectiveness and the right to manage were to be the cornerstones of Government and Coal Board attitudes; if from the miners' side there was a capitalist enemy, MacGregor perfectly embodied it. The preparations of Scargill and his closest associates (though no one was very close) aimed at instigating a strike. The preparations of the Government were more open-ended but much more effective: the buying-in of extra coal stocks for the power stations was actually seen by Scargill as a concession to the miners' power – thus do the purveyors of crazy theory and wild rhetoric delude themselves – when, of course, it was designed to ensure that even if there were a strike there would be no power cuts. That the strike would be long, and that it would be bitter and violent, was made certain by the Government's determination to make a very public show of not intervening in any way, leaving the Coal Board, and of course the police, to fight it out with the miners.

Since becoming miners' president, Scargill had already called for industrial action on the issues of wages and pit closures, but in October 1982 he was defeated in a national ballot. Throughout 1983, however, there were a number of industrial disputes in different coal-mining areas. In November 1983 a special conference was called to impose an overtime ban. The most fateful development, however, had come in March 1983 when Scargill indicated that (since he was unlikely to get a majority under union rule 43, which required first a national ballot and then a majority of 55 per cent in favour of a strike) he might make use of rule 41, under which the different mining areas could call out their own men on strike, with or without a ballot, as their own area rules dictated. Such a proposal was put to the union executive on 4 March, but the moderates insisted that there should be a ballot of the membership, and this resulted in

Scargill's second defeat, 61 per cent of the membership voting against strike action. On 1 March 1984 the director of the South Yorkshire area, on instructions from the Coal Board head office, announced that Corton Wood colliery was to be closed, despite the fact that not long before miners had been assured that it would be kept open for another five years. The Coal Board and its local director had made an unutterable blunder, which Energy Secretary Peter Walker, despite his best efforts, was unable to recoup. Not surprisingly, the Yorkshire area went on strike from 9 March. Meantime, Scargill, very properly, had insisted on a meeting with the Board, held on 6 March, to discuss exactly what was intended in the way of closures – Scargill spoke dramatically, but not altogether unjustifiably, of MacGregor's 'hit list'. It appeared from the meeting that the Board were planning the closure of twenty pits. Scotland immediately joined Yorkshire in deciding to go on strike. The national executive now crushed any attempt at having a national ballot, and gave advance approval to any other areas that decided on strike action. When a further call was made for a national ballot at the executive meeting on 12 April, Scargill ruled it out of order on the grounds that a decision had already been made on 8 March. The 'rolling' national strike was already well under way, that is to say a strike in which areas came in without necessarily balloting their own members, and without, of course, any national ballot.

Trade union legislation in the nineteenth century had declared peaceful picketing legal. One intention of the first Thatcher trade union legislation had been to ensure that picketing really was peaceful, and to outlaw secondary picketing, that is to say picketing of premises not directly involved in a dispute. Immediately the strike started in Yorkshire, pickets streamed down into the Nottinghamshire coalfield, where, as a ballot subsequently showed, majority opinion was against the strike. During this first phase, picketing was also directed towards ensuring that there was solidarity within the Yorkshire coalfield, as also within Scotland (where the men at Bilston Glen did not wish to come out), South Wales and, shortly, Durham. The police went quickly into action in a manner quite alien to the traditions of British policing, the establishment of a National Reporting Centre at Scotland Yard being a large step towards the establishment of a nationally co-ordinated police force. Unprecedented methods were adopted to prevent pickets travelling to Nottinghamshire, where, at such pits as Harworth, Ollerton, Thoresby and Welbeck, the first stone throwing, barricade building, and damaging of cars was taking place. On 14 March a twenty-four-year-old Yorkshire picket, David Jones, was crushed to death in a mêlée between local people and the pickets. The first phase came to a kind of culminating point when, on 2 May, a record total of 8,000 pickets turned out at Harworth.

Phase two was dominated by the mass picketing at the Orgreave coking plant on the outskirts of Sheffield, a supplier of coke to the big steel plant at Scunthorpe. Scargill's attitude towards other unions was a mixture of contempt for the official leadership of the TUC and of several other unions, an assumption that other unions ought unquestioningly to support the miners, and a supreme faith in the potency of the miners' own picketing. There was supposed to be a triple alliance involving the steelworkers (whom the miners had supported in 1980) and the railwaymen. Action on the part of the steelworkers was constrained by the slimming-down process in their own industry, the fear that the Ravenscraig complex had received only a temporary reprieve in 1982, and the insurmountable fact that blast furnaces not kept in commission could be permanently damaged. More support was forthcoming from the railwaymen, but British Rail craftily avoided any victimization of railmen who refused to move coal or steel, and thus kept their own system in almost full operation. Tension was very high at Ravenscraig early in May where convoys of lorries were bringing in the coal necessary to ensure the safety and survival of the works. The words of local union spokesman Tom Brennan (*The Times*, 3 May 1984) speak worlds for both the class solidarity that did genuinely exist, and the intolerable strains that were being put upon it:

> Today we have failed to impress upon the miners our need for the extra coal. It is a very sad and daunting position that faces us now because we do not want to go outside the fraternity of the trade union movement.

However, it was Orgreave that established the images, relayed on television, indelibly associated with the coal strike. Controversially, police were for the first time deployed in riot gear; even more open to criticism was the way in which mounted police were deployed. At times, however, the police were under enormous provocation. The worst abuse on the police side was the repeated indiscriminate use of truncheoning, a particularly horrific example being caught by ITN cameraman Frank Harding; Harding, however, was clear that when the four mounted police were sent in to charge the crowd, police had undergone a long spell of stone throwing protected only by one long line of riot shields. The first convoys at Orgreave began on 23 May, with the real violence starting on 29 May,

just when secret talks were due to take place between the mine-workers'
leaders and the National Coal Board. Police claimed that the new level of
violence was connected with the arrival of Scargill himself. As *The Times*
reported on 30 May:

Trouble began yesterday morning when 35 lorries, heavily protected by wire
mesh, arrived at the coke works to load up. Pickets surged forward under a hail
of missiles and firecrackers, and police, using riot gear for the first time since the
dispute began, went in to make arrests. One officer broke a leg falling from his
horse. The convoy got through.

Violence broke out again when the lorries returned, and pickets scattered across
a field as a posse of mounted police pursued them, followed by officers carrying
riot shields. Fighting continued as the second convoy left for Scunthorpe.

Police struggling with pickets outside the plant entrance applauded their
mounted colleagues, but Mr Scargill said: 'Anyone who has been here today has
seen police tactics of the most brutal nature. We have seen riot shields and riot
gear in action. We have seen truncheons and staves in action. We have seen
mounted police charging into our ranks.

'I was appealing to the police to show restraint. There were baton charges. I saw
truncheons wielded and I saw our people hit. I saw people punched to the ground.
Quite honestly, there were scenes of brutality which were almost unbelievable.

'What you now have in South Yorkshire is an actual police state tantamount to
something you are used to seeing in Chile or Bolivia.' He urged miners and the
whole trade union movement to 'come here in your thousands to make everybody
aware that we are not prepared to see this kind of brutality inflicted against
working men and women'.

The aim of the picket was to persuade lorry drivers not to go in to the plant; it
might take some days, but he was convinced they would succeed.

Mr Tony Clement, Assistant Chief Constable, who was in charge of the 1,700
officers from 13 forces at Orgreave, said: 'The pickets began throwing stones, half
house-bricks, wood torn from fences, and our officers were being injured.

'That was the time for me to order officers to go in with shields to prevent that
sort of thing happening.' He agreed that was 'a deployment of the last resort' . . .

Supt Pratt said the police were not prepared to remain under bombardment.
He said spikes, ball-bearings and potatoes with nails stuck through them had been
used as missiles against the police.

The report noted that the 200 full-time coke workers at the Orgreave
plant had tried unsuccessfully to persuade the lorry drivers and contract
loaders not to move the coke. Sixty-four people were injured and eighty-

four people arrested. Next day Scargill was arrested, together with thirty-five others; sixteen were injured, most of them policemen. When the miners dispersed, police said they left behind 'barricades, a telegraph-pole "battering-ram", barbed wire, a burning Portakabin and a wire stretched across the road intended to bring down police horses'. Among missiles the police said had been found were a '2 lb hammer, an 18-inch cast iron pipe, a steel coach-bolt and steel nuts with nails'. Some police officers regretted the police violence, many protested that the police were being left to do the Government's and the Coal Board's work. Some miners showed obvious disgust at the violence on their own side. The Government never condemned police violence, as Scargill never condemned the pickets' violence; when asked to do so, he repeatedly produced the irrationally glib response (which alienated much potential support), 'I have always condemned police violence.' The final mass picket, 10,000 strong, came on 18 June. The coke had run out, but Scunthorpe was being supplied from elsewhere in any case; the miners had achieved nothing.

The third phase began quietly in the coalfields, then the violence of Orgreave transferred itself there in the autumn, as more and more men tried to go back to work. Briefly in July, when the dockworkers had a dispute of their own over the Dock Labour Scheme, but were also sympathetic to the miners, it looked as though a kind of working-class solidarity was putting real pressure on the Government: for a time workers at Dover, not affected by the Dock Labour Scheme, joined in. Newspapers spoke of the country's economic and industrial crisis: interest rates were put up by 2 per cent. 'Britain counts the cost to pits, ports and City of Mrs Thatcher's worst week,' ran the main headline of the *Observer* of 15 July; the same issue quoted a jubilant Scargill:

'There has to be no fudge, no compromise. We have to win this dispute if we believe in what we have been fighting for,' he declared. He said the NUM was not even prepared to talk about the closure of pits on economic grounds, and suggested that the miners had the opportunity to pave the way for a Labour victory at the next general election.

But the crisis passed; vigorous action by lorry drivers (again!) broke through the bottleneck at Dover.

Attention shifted back to Yorkshire, where some of the most notorious incidents took place around Arnthorpe, after three working miners had been bussed through into Markham Main colliery; things got worse as local people stoned a convoy of police support units. It was at this period that the police introduced the intimidatory tactics (very quickly dropped again) of beating rhythmically on their riot shields; it was also at this time that, in pursuit of pickets, they smashed their way into private houses. This was the most horrific period of the strike: greater intimidation of and violence against miners returning to work, and their families; pitched battles with the police, dangerous missiles thrown, oil spread on roads, cars set on fire. In South Wales, all through the first phase of the strike, there had been sporadic attempts to stop coal convoys moving along the M4 motorway. Then a concrete block was dropped on a taxi bringing a working miner to the Merthyr Vale colliery: taxi driver David Wilkie was killed. Martin Adeney and John Lloyd in their excellent *The Miners' Strike, 1984–5: Loss Without Limit* (1986), page 126, pinned down the characteristics of the third phase in this way:

> The concentration of action in the last months of the strike in and around the pickets' home pits brought police into prolonged daily contact not just with pickets, but the communities from which they came. It was this interaction which brought about some of the bitterest and most emotional reactions of the strike, and perhaps sometimes of the longest-lived. It is the behaviour of the police in the villages, not so much in the heat of the picket-line confrontation, that many miners are most bitter about. Those who are critical blame the out-of-town police, often the London Metropolitan Police, for their behaviour.

From December, matters quietened down as it was widely realized that the strike had been utterly futile and that there was no prospect of substantial concessions for the miners. Behind the scenes negotiations intensified, involving particularly Norman Willis, General Secretary of the TUC; but the miners' executive were not open to any agreement acceptable to the Coal Board. On 3 March 1985 a miners' special delegate conference agreed to a return to work, but without any agreement at all having been made.

The striking miners received no strike pay from the union, though a pittance was usually paid to those on picket duty. After the first few fiesta-weeks, the strikers and their families endured great hardships. The traditional working-class characteristics of loyalty to workmates, unions and community had been very much in evidence. At the same time the miners who insisted on working showed great determination and courage, often giving as the reason for their stance that disrespect had been shown to the proper procedure of a full national ballot. Workers in other industries did show considerable fellow-feeling for the miners, but they also had their own concerns and their own loyalties. Thus the strike was no great testament to the unified class consciousness (as distinct from class awareness) of the British working class. Nor were 'bourgeois' interests universally ranged against the miners, to whom in fact local building society officers extended mortgages, and local banks offered credit, acting out of a mixture of self-interest – backed by the miners' proven record of financial integrity – and support for the local community, tinged no doubt with some fear of reprisals. Much of the mining management had sympathy for and a sense of common purpose with the miners. MacGregor, indeed, had been brought in specially to enforce 'the rights of management'. A few managers did single themselves out through their enthusiastic prosecution of this approach, notably Albert Wheeler, Scottish director of the Coal Board, whose management, according to the verdict of an independent inquiry conducted by a QC, was responsible for the flooding of the Polkemmet pit.

Many police forces clearly cherished their tradition of neutrality: of maintaining the peace, but of never taking sides. Government strategy pushed the police more blatantly than any time since 1945 into being the upholders of Government and of management. Although the Government had itself brought in legislation against secondary picketing it ensured that this legislation was not used. Given its objective, Government strategy was brilliant, though not actually consistent in its 'hands off' philosophy: leaked documents published in the *Daily Mirror* on 6 June revealed that the Government had intervened to secure a pay settlement for the railwaymen, in order not to have to cope with a combined rail and coal strike. Mrs Thatcher and her ministers made it conclusively clear that they felt no responsibility for the promotion of social harmony and that, in the pursuit of longer-term aims, they found confrontation and violence entirely acceptable. The Government was tough, consistent (on the whole), and victorious. For the Labour Party, the strike was a massive embarrassment; Labour leaders continuously disowned picket-line violence. The strike, which in Scargill's fantasies was to demonstrate the power of Labour, demonstrated only the weaknesses of Labour, and enhanced the position of Mrs Thatcher. But it did also reveal the capabilities and resilience of the miners' wives, who not only bore the brunt of material deprivation, but unprecedently played a very active and political part in sustaining strikers and pickets.

As the men returned to work there was sullen fatalism in the coalfields.

Closures, flexible working, the six-day week followed. Those miners who had strongly opposed the strike centred on Nottingham, forming a separate Union of Democratic Mineworkers. Though now a much sub-dued figure, Scargill still commanded sufficient loyalty to secure re-election to the presidency of the NUM by a two-thirds majority over a moderate opponent. Militancy was on retreat throughout the trade union world, but it seemed that the new bitterness and violence, the openly confrontational tactics of the police, had come to stay. Economic and technological imperatives affected other industries than coal, notably newspaper publishing and cross-Channel ferries. The move of News International to Wapping, together with the refusal of staff to accommo-date to the new technology, resulted, early in 1986, in picketing at Wapping of the type now indelibly associated with Orgreave. Picketing and clashes continued well into 1986. Then on 24 January 1987, 7,000 pickets and demonstrators gathered in forceful commemoration of the anniversary of the move to Wapping. They were confronted by 1,000 police officers; clashes were violent, and about 300 people were injured, including 162 police officers. Many allegations of police brutality were made, and after an independent investigation of more than 440 allegations by a senior member of the Northamptonshire police force, twenty-six summonses were issued, with fourteen Metropolitian police officers being suspended from duty. The seamen's strike of 1987 did little more than demonstrate the helplessness of a small union facing adverse economic circumstances, ruthless employers and a determined Government.

Catastrophic violence, none the less, had struck again well before the end of 1985; the root cause this time was again urban deprivation and racial tension; once more confrontational police methods were sharply exposed. The first area to be put to the torch was Handsworth in Birming-ham, an area of high unemployment, bad housing and drug peddling, where 60 per cent of the population consisted of a mix of Afro-Caribbeans and a variety of Asians, several of whom were relatively prosperous shop-owners. Police attempts to crack down on drug dealing over the previous months had created resentment, particularly among young blacks who depended on it for their only source of income. Monday 9 September was the night of rampaging mobs, terror, and arson; two Asians died in the burnt-out wreck of their shop. Within three weeks similarly horrific events were taking place in Brixton. Here there was a background of armed police raids on targeted suspects. Early on the morning of 28 September such a raid went particularly badly wrong when armed police shot and seriously wounded Mrs Cherry Groce in a search for her son. As the *Observer* reported next morning:

Tension rose until the early evening when youths broke into the back of Brixton police station and set its upper stories ablaze with petrol bombs. Scores of riot police poured out of the station, dispersing the crowd but spreading the violence.

Brixton Road, the central spine of the area, rapidly became 'no go' for police. Youths broke into a petrol station and used the fuel to make dozens of petrol bombs. Police retreated south without sealing off the area and more rioters were able to pour into the streets. Ordinary motorists strayed into the riot and some were attacked.

In almost every side street running off Brixton Road cars were overturned and set on fire. On the west of Brixton Road an entire terrace of shops were smashed, looted and then set ablaze. There were reports of stabbings. Occasionally police vans raced into the area before retreating under a hail of bricks and petrol bombs.

People were feared trapped in the biggest blaze covering a block of three buildings, flats and shops in Gresham Road.

During the morning of Tuesday 1 October rioting broke out in Toxteth; some observers declared that the situation was worsened by the provocative tactics of the special police unit, the Operational Support Division. The dreadful roll-call reached its appalling climax at the Broadwater Farm housing estate in Tottenham, North-East London. Again the trigger issue was a badly bungled police raid in which a sick black woman (Mrs Cynthia Jarrett) died, having been knocked to the floor and refused any medical assistance. The next day at noon police and community leaders met at Tottenham police station. But a riotous mob was already assembling, clearly determined to inflict as much damage on the police as possible. Three policemen and two journalists received shotgun wounds, and in a total of 200 police casualties, several others were very seriously wounded. Most horrific of all, P C Keith Blakelock was savagely done to death with knives and a machete. For their part, in their own major co-ordinated counter-offensive the policy returned to the intimidatory tactic of the rhythmic beating on their shields first tried out in the miners' strike. They succeeded in pinning down the rioters in the centre of the estate, but did not retake this area till 4.35 a.m. the next morning.

The first evidence of a new level of destructive violence in British society had appeared in the early seventies. Just as one ingredient then had been I R A terrorism, so it was an important factor in the violence of the middle eighties. On 12 October 1984, while the miners' strike was at its height, the IRA made its most direct and daring attack on British authority, when it attempted to wipe out the British Government by placing a bomb under the sixth floor of the Grand Hotel, Brighton, where Mrs Thatcher and other senior delegates to the Conservative Party Annual Conference were staying. The hotel was wrecked, four people were killed (a fifth died a month later), and there were many extremely serious injuries. Norman Tebbit, then Industry Secretary, was dug out of the rubble after being entombed for four hours; his wife was permanently paralysed. Mrs Thatcher's bathroom was destroyed, though she herself was unhurt. As always, atrocity in Northern Ireland itself aroused less concern; however, two incidents produced reactions that suggested that the Irish issue was lodged more firmly in the British consciousness then at any time since the Second World War. First, on Remembrance Sunday 1987, when the ordinary people of Enniskillen had gathered to commemorate the dead of both World Wars, an IRA bomb placed near by exploded, killing eleven people. 'IRA terrorism plumbed the darkest depths,' commented a British Sunday newspaper. 'We can't take any more,' wrote the local newspaper. Only a few months later, on 19 March 1988, two British soldiers who blundered into a Republican funeral were beaten up and then murdered (the whole episode being all the more nightmarish because parts of it were even relayed on television). Terror returned to England when in August 1988 an explosion at Inglis Barracks in North London killed one soldier and injured nine; miraculously there were no casualties in the bombing of Clive Barracks, Shropshire, in February 1989.

To look for a common cause for all of these different types of confrontation and violence would be absurd. Britain was still a society with a very strong sense of class, with an intermixed problem of race and urban deprivation that was certainly not getting better, and a society that could not pretend immunity from the historically determined communal conflicts in Northern Ireland. International forces making for de-industrialization – forces unmodified by the kind of interventionism that had been an accepted norm from the end of the war to the end of the seventies – did not help. In a society in which many of the differences between the haves and the have-nots were sharpening, in which there were broad trends towards polarization and confrontation, the deeper sources of potential strife were bound to come into play. Class, race, the national and religious tensions of Northern Ireland, are important phenomena. So also are the historic nationalities of mainland Britain. For substantial majorities in Wales and, above all, in Scotland, there was the special indignity of being subject to radical Conservative policy promulgated in London when they themselves had voted Labour – the Conservative Party was a dwindling force in Scotland. Scottish national-ism had been stimulated in the seventies by the developments of North Sea oil. In the 1980s de-industrialization heavily affected both Wales and Scotland. Parts of Wales felt the pressures of rich outsiders moving in from England; in Scotland, particularly in Edinburgh and Glasgow, development of financial and other professional services also brought an English influx. In Wales protest most noticeably took the form of arson against English-owned property, and other violent acts, some directed against reservoirs mainly created for English use. In Scotland there was more of a political movement. Within the Labour Party, several prominent members threatened direct action against the community charge (or poll tax); the Scottish National Party appeared to be cresting to the top of another wave when late in 1988 Jim Sillars, formerly a popular Labour Party figure, overturned an apparently impregnable Labour majority at Govan in Glasgow. Back in 1979, when the Scots failed to turn out in sufficient numbers to carry devolution, the *Glasgow Herald* cartoonist Turnbull had drawn the Scottish lion as lying down and moaning, with regard to the responsibilities of self-government, 'I'm feart.' Sillars (in *Scotland – The Case for Optimism* (1986), page 180) projected a re-found confidence:

Unemployment can be conquered. There is no need for Scots to listen any longer to the depressing defeated wails of Neil Kinnock or wince under the grocer-shop nonsense that pours out of Mrs Thatcher. We have a choice. To remain as we are and go on as we are, downward. Or to take control and tackle the issue in our own way, on our own terms and in accordance with our own priorities. That is the only road to full employment.

Orgreave, Enniskillen, Handsworth, Tottenham; these mark the geo-graphy of the extremes of violence that scarred the eighties as no previous decade in Britain's recent history had been scarred. But there was another name, still further afield than Enniskillen, which sent round the world the message that Britain was no longer *the* country of stability, tolerance, and non-violence. That name was Heysel, the name of an antiquated football stadium in Brussels, venue for the European Cup Final between the English club Liverpool and the Italian club Juventus held on 29 May 1985. In the riot that day thirty-seven Juventus fans, and a thirty-seven-year-old Northern Ireland archivist working in Brussels, were killed. Only two weeks before fifty-three people had died in a grandstand fire at Bradford (the blame here rested with lax safety precautions, not with violent fans), and one fifteen-year-old boy had been crushed beneath a collapsing wall at Birmingham (this time rioting fans were to blame). Vicious rampages, and violent confrontations between groups of rival fans, had become a regular characteristic of English football matches. In Scotland, where the drunken loutishness of, in particular, the fans of Celtic and Rangers (both Glasgow clubs) had been notorious, the problem had very largely been solved by banning drink and drunks from grounds and from transport to and from them. In England, Liverpool were generally perceived as having a quite well-behaved and good-natured (indeed witty) following. *The Times* (31 May 1985) recorded the build-up and horrific climax at Heysel:

It was on Monday [i.e. 27 May] evening that police in Ostend reported the first trouble with Liverpool fans as they began drinking their way towards Brussels. It was the start of a two-day orgy that was to end in the horror of the Heysel Stadium.

In Brussels itself, with its large Italian population, the excitement had been building up. Thousands were pouring in by coach and air. By Wednesday afternoon, the first skirmishes between drunken Liverpool supporters had begun.

There were a number of stabbing instances and police were increasingly busy, miles from the stadium, keeping fans apart. Hours before the start of the game, they made the long trek to the ground, arriving in warm sunshine with time to kill and drink to get rid of.

The red and black banners began to go up at the Liverpool end – some abusive of Manchester United not Juventus. Scuffles with knives began here and there. Fireworks began to fly.

An hour before kick-off, the Liverpool end behind the goal was packed. The neutral stand from which they were divided by a thin-wire fence and a few policemen, looked invitingly empty. Moreover, it contained a few hundred Juventus fans, flying *their* banners. Alcohol, boredom and a desire to increase territory all played their part.

19.22 (by the Belgian police watches): the first wave of violence crashed against the thin green fence. It was repulsed, but the Liverpool fans' blood was up. They began ripping at the wire, pulling out the metal stanchions which held it up.

19.24: With their new weapons they attacked again. This time the Belgian police melted away to call up reinforcements. According to the Ministry of Interior there had been 40 policemen, but there seemed far fewer as the second Liverpool wave went forward.

The Juventus fans panicked and started running to the back, to the pitch, to the wall ... anywhere to escape the red Liverpool hordes, with their metal bars, bottles, scarves and terrifying reputation.

The wall at the end was more than 50 years old, its cement cladding crumbling away from the rotting brickwork. It was supposedly there to hold back the hundreds of desperately clawing, fighting, pushing fans.

19.27: Part of the old wall collapsed. It was scarcely four feet high and perhaps 20 feet long. But as it burst open the pent-up pressure of aggression and terror burst outwards and downwards. Bodies tumbled among the rubble, the injured lay trampled in their blood, as others crunched over them in panic-stricken flight.

19.32: The Belgian riot police swarmed in. They had taken eight minutes from the first alarm call and had difficulty forcing themselves past the crowds. There was what seemed to be a riot going on around a small piece of broken wall.

Their colleagues had been driven back with some savagery – some 13 policeman were eventually taken to hospital – and they were in no mood to look for people in need of help.

Batons flailing behind their shields they charged forward, smashing at anyone in sight. As the area at the foot of the terraces was cleared, the enormity of what had happened came through to them and relief workers were called.

The Red Cross were there within minutes, tending as best they could with their pitiful first aid equipment, to people in need of the maximum aid. Calls went out to the hospitals and ambulances fought through the crowds. The first stretcher arrived, after 40 minutes.

A good deal of blame rested with the Belgian authorities and the Belgian police – whose behaviour reminds one, by contrast, of the high standards traditionally observed by the British police (complacency on that score, however, was severely jolted when, on 15 April 1989, just after the start of the Liverpool–Nottingham Forest semi-final at the Hillsborough ground, Sheffield, crowd control and crowd safety systems collapsed disastrously, resulting in the crushing to death of over ninety Liverpool supporters). But there was no escaping the existence and prevalence of what foreigners called 'the British disease' – football hooliganism. Investigations showed that most major clubs had associated with them (through no design of the clubs, of course) carefully organized gangs (often including young men in quite respectable middle-class occupations) whose sole purpose was to engage in physical combat with the gangs attached to rival clubs and to establish their existence by terrorizing any ordinary citizens who happened to be around. Among the most vicious gangs were: the Inter City Firm (associated with West Ham United), the Headhunters (linked to Chelsea), the Zulu Warriors (Birmingham City), the Bushwhackers (Millwall), the Leeds Service Crew (Leeds United), and the Baby Squad (Leicester City). There was evidence, too, of the presence of members of the extreme right-wing National Front, particularly at Heysel and on other international occasions. Added to all this was the influence of drink, particularly on young unemployed fans for whom licentious and riotous behaviour at the weekend provided a high point in an otherwise rather gloomy and frustrating week.

Over the next few years following the Heysel disaster, extreme violence at home games did begin to diminish as the police developed more sophisticated supervisory techniques. But then in June 1988, during the European Championship finals held in Germany, rampaging English football hooligans abroad were once again grabbing the headlines. Actually, as German police agreed, much of the aggression in fact came from German youths: whether or not the English had set the example, football hooliganism was clearly an international phenomenon. But it was English clubs that were banned from European competitions, and it was English grounds, whatever the improvements, that still aroused fears about the safety of the ordinary good-natured, family-minded fan who wished to attend. Early in 1989 the Government began to develop its measures for a scheme that would make it impossible to attend a football game without an identity card; guilty fans would have their cards confiscated. As was its way, the Government had identified an enemy, even though earlier it had refused to countenance any action, such as the confiscation of passports (which would have prevented potential hooligans from travelling abroad), on the grounds that the matter was not a national issue, but a matter for the football clubs and the football authorities themselves to sort out. Now, indiscriminate action was being aimed at everyone interested in football, detached followers of the *game* as well as fanatical followers of the *club*; the national sport itself, where the less fashionable clubs were already menaced by adverse economic circumstances and increased commercialization, was being put at risk, but then it was at its core a working-class game.

Hooliganism – indiscriminate, but often highly organized violence on the part of young people (and, sometimes, not so young) – was apparent all over the country, even in areas with no association whatsoever with football. Another term of the middle eighties, to go with 'enterprise culture', 'heritage industry' and 'yuppies', was 'lager louts'. Ritualized

Easter-holiday violence had been prevalent from the 1960s onwards. But now violence was appearing everywhere and often apparently quite randomly. Addressing a conference in Surrey on alcohol-related crime in January 1989, the local Chief Constable declared that 'stronger family and church ties, and teachers able to mete out physical punishment, were needed to quell the "rising violence"'. Left-wing commentators, of course, put the blame on high unemployment; despair and aimlessness among the country's youth; the fostering of aggressive economic selfishness; and the policies of polarization and confrontation pursued by the Thatcher Government. But the traditionalist police view was not altogether wrong. What was happening was that the old reference points by which individuals and groups measured their behaviour, by which their behaviour was constrained, had drastically changed. Society had been more unified under policies that deliberately sought to avoid unemployment and to sustain social benefits, policies which recognized the place of trade unions in society, and policies that upheld tolerance and civilized behaviour as important values. Football hooligans at home saw themselves as fighting for their own particular community; football hooligans abroad, ironically, saw themselves as demonstrating British might. All this was, however distortedly, in keeping with the values of the aggressive market-place and the Falklands War. There were no longer national communal values to which all but the most desperate and alienated subscribed. Loyalty was now to the individual peer group. And for many gangs of young people the highest value attached to demonstrations of contempt for citizens and families bent on enjoying the modest rewards of a quiet and industrious life. Acquisitiveness was now being publicly sanctioned; why not brutally attack those blessed with goods one does not have oneself? Structural trends were breaking up old national loyalties and communal networks: those in authority were hastening the trends, and putting nothing appropriate in the place of the loyalties and networks. In November 1988 a demonstration held at Westminster by 16,000 students, against Government proposals to introduce student loans, was marred by the Trotskyite element who hurled missiles at police, to which the police responded by mounting terrifying charges on otherwise peaceful students. Despite apparent quiescence, and some signs of economic upturn, Britain towards the end of the eighties was still, as she had never been since 1945, a country of confrontation.

22

Social Policy and Social Life

In Chapter 3 I defined the basic concerns of the Welfare State as social security, medical services, housing, and education. In Chapter 14 I listed six trends affecting the development of social-welfare provision in the seventies. In the eighties, as then, professional opinion continued to be important as well as political principle. Demographic changes, particularly the increase in the numbers of dependent elderly people, were more insistent than ever. New types of need continued to be uncovered. However, without doubt, the great imperative was the political will to curtail public expenditure, and to wean the British people away from what the Government saw as the 'dependency culture' created by an over-lavish welfare system. Job protection and income protection no longer had the priority they had at last just managed to secure in the seventies. Housing and education were no longer unambiguously 'welfare-state' issues (the term itself was rather out of fashion) and were bound up with other aspects of Government policy. Greater emphasis than ever was placed on the personal social services, administered by the local authorities and by voluntary bodies, and dealing, in particular, with the elderly, the disabled, and with children.

The new spirit that was to inform social security provision was made clear in the 1985 White Paper *Reform of Social Security: Programme for Action*, which spoke of giving 'greater responsibility and greater independence to the individual'. The new spirit, and a new structure, were embodied in the Social Security Act of 1986, whose main provisions came into effect in April 1988. Administratively Social Security was again separated from Health, as it had been in the original Welfare State, each now occupying a separate department with a separate Secretary of State. One purpose of the new legislation was to simplify and systematize the quite extensive, and arguably confusing, list of benefits and allowances – for clothing, housing, furniture, etc. – that had grown up since the 1960s. Critics claimed that the upshot was an overall reduction in what those in need could claim, and this seemed to be supported by specific instances quoted in the press. Means tests were made more rigorous; applicants for unemployment benefit had to demonstrate that they were genuinely available for work. Supplementary benefit was replaced by income support, which, in the interests of targeting benefits where they were felt to be most needed, was divided into two components: a personal allowance, and then additional premiums for families, single parents, pensioners, and long-term sick and disabled people. The new housing benefit scheme operated on a similar basis to that of income support: both schemes denied benefits to persons with more than the most modest amount of capital, thus dealing harshly, as it was again pointed out, with pensioners possessing a house, whose saleability, in reality, might be pretty well nil. On the other hand, the new family credit scheme did appear to be benefiting many more families than the old family income supplement; maternity and widows' benefits were also improved. Sickness and disablement benefits remained much as before. One remnant of the old universalist policies of the 1940s continued: child benefit, costing the State £5 billion a year. In place of the former single payments to cover various eventualities there was now a social fund, which offered loans not grants: the irony was that the poorest and neediest, being in no position to pay back loans, were denied the resource they needed (to visit a sick child in hospital, to buy a pram, etc.). Family credit, paid to those on low incomes, because of the 'poverty trap' (as income rose, benefits decreased) almost seemed designed to cage people in the worst-paid jobs. Apologists said that the poverty trap was simply a temporary inconvenience till people moved into a new level of occupation where benefits would be unnecessary. Many preferred to steer well clear of family credit (there was only about a 40 per cent take-up at the end of 1988). The philosophy of encouraging independence appeared more like a philosophy of perpetuating deprivation. The forms to be filled in for family credit were long and complex, and a formidable deterrent in themselves. It was the right-wing Adam Smith Institute that remarked in its paper *Needs Reform*, published in January 1989, that the

chosen course of all governments would appear to be one of rationing by squalor – that social security should be sufficiently difficult, sufficiently degrading and sufficiently inconvenient to limit the numbers that will have access to it.

The other major aspect of the Act, very much in keeping with Government philosophy, was the encouragement of personal pension schemes through banks, building societies and trusts, with provisions for contracting out not just of the State Earnings-Related Pension Scheme but also employers' schemes. Benefits from the State scheme payable in the next century looked to be somewhat less favourable.

Many of the forces already discussed operated on the medical services, which were also affected by developments in medical science. Some commentators suspected the Government of not being truly committed to the principle of the National Health Service and of hankering after a fully Americanized system. As it was, the main actual developments took the form of introducing outside managerial skills into the various levels of the service; the privatization of many ancillary services; the encouragement of the private sector; and the advocacy of contracting out of services on a competitive basis, even within the National Health Service. In Chapter 14 I spoke of the 'miracle' of the National Health Service, the miracle that, despite all the talk of crisis, it managed to keep going. By the later eighties it was absolutely clear that the National Health Service was failing. The Government had made a concerted effort to reduce waiting-lists, and had deliberately diverted resources from London to the less well-served regions. But from all quarters came well-authenticated stories of units closing, of beds standing empty, of postponements and delays in vital operations. Protests rained in from distinguished doctors and surgeons. In November and December 1987 there was a crescendo of protests from patients, heart surgeons, health districts, and from the Presidents of the medical Royal Colleges. On Monday 14 December the *Daily Telegraph* carried a poll showing the highest-ever level of public concern about the Health Service. The Government claimed, perfectly correctly, that it was spending more than ever in history on the National Health Service: £21,000 million in 1987, compared with about £8,000 million when they took office (see Table 10). However, the Government's case had a number of serious weaknesses (to which it almost seemed to admit, when, as a result of the December protests, it allocated additional funds to the Health Service). First of all, after an initial burst for which the Government was fully entitled to claim credit, the proportion of the Gross National Product being spent on the National Health Service was steadily in decline: standing at 5.98 per cent in 1980, it had reached an all-time high of 6.29 per cent in 1983, then fallen to 6.02 per cent in 1985, and down to 5.2 per cent at the end of 1987. Worse, the costs of medical

Table 10: Summary of Government expenditure on social services and housing (years ended 31 March, figures in £million)

	1977/78	1978/79	1979/80	1980/81	1981/82	1982/83	1983/84	1984/85	1985/86	1986/87	1987/88
Education[1]	8,305	9,169	10,617	13,049	14,088	15,158	16,084	16,681	17,439	19,042	—
National Health Service	6,896	7,835	9,195	11,944	13,267	14,385	15,383	16,312	17,344	18,651	20,598
Personal social services	1,249	1,423	1,785	2,230	2,420	2,552	2,789	2,940	3,467	3,413	3,844
Welfare foods	23	27	29	35	52	70	86	98	113	120	129
Social security benefits	14,410	17,080	20,142	24,426	29,968	33,946	37,190	40,211	43,246	46,867	48,923
Housing	4,583	4,946	6,101	6,304	4,764	4,353	4,744	4,643	4,348	3,868	3,543
Total Government expenditure	35,466	40,480	47,869	57,988	64,559	70,464	76,276	80,885	85,957	91,961	—
Current expenditure	31,447	36,357	43,027	53,039	60,629	66,500	71,567	76,163	81,439	87,778	—
Capital expenditure	4,019	4,123	4,842	4,949	3,930	3,964	4,709	4,722	4,518	4,183	—
Total Government expenditure	35,466	40,480	47,869	57,988	64,559	70,464	76,276	80,885	85,957	91,961	—
Central Government expenditure	24,841	28,851	34,000	41,716	47,932	52,884	57,222	61,282	65,440	70,423	—
Local authorities	10,625	11,629	13,869	16,272	16,627	17,580	19,054	19,603	20,517	21,538	—
Total Government expenditure	35,466	40,480	47,869	57,988	64,559	70,464	76,276	80,885	85,957	91,961	—

[1] Includes school meals and milk
Source: Central Statistical Office

care had shot up astronomically compared with prices as a whole. First, new medical technology (the advances in neo-natal intensive care, for example) was extremely expensive; the cost of basic drugs was rising at about five times the rate of general inflation. And the Government quite simply failed to take account of wage and salary rises, expecting them to be met out of savings, which it was impossible to make. Then the increased numbers of elderly people needing treatment imposed a special burden. There might have been some sympathy for the plight of the Government (though there was sympathy also for Neil Kinnock's claim that Mrs Thatcher was simply 'making a fool of herself' when she endlessly repeated the statistics of National Health Service financing), if it were not for the fact that its most cherished policy was making conditions considerably worse. In sponsoring the private sector, the Government was simply encouraging the creaming off of trained personnel and resources from the National Health Service. There was a considerable weight of expert opinion that services financed privately or through insurance were con- siderably less cost-effective than a taxation-financed National Health Service. Already the result of Government policies was the development of two very different systems: a hard-pressed public service with long waiting-lists; a luxurious private system catering to a small minority, yet parasitical upon the public service. At the end of 1987 the Government announced charges for eye tests, and the abolition of free medical check- ups. The sale of spectacles was extended to those without ophthalmic qualifications. There remained validity in the universalist argument that if the rich opted out into private medicine, there would be no influential customers to complain about second-rate service in public medicine.

Back in 1945, when housing had been the single issue on which most members of the electorate felt most strongly, the problem had been an absolute shortage of housing. Since that no longer was *the* problem, it was reasonable that policies on housing should have shifted. One unresolved problem was that of the massive, bleak housing estates of recent origin, now dilapidated slums (some of the worst areas of deprivation were where shoddy Labour housing policies – and many Labour councils, for example Camden in North London, had abysmal records in the management of their property – intersected with stingy Conservative welfare policies). The new elements of the eighties were the encouragement of private ownership, the encouragement of private building, and the wish to make the renting of accommodation a purely market-place transaction. The governing legislation was contained in the main Housing Act of 1980 and the consolidating one of 1985. In many respects these Acts gave new rights to council tenants (to exchange homes or take in lodgers, for instance), in response to the numerous complaints about the petty despotisms exercised by many local authorities over their housing estates; moves were in hand to enable public-sector tenants to change their landlord if dissatisfied with the local authority. Most important was the provision that council tenants of at least two years' standing could buy their house or flat at a discount. By the end of 1987, 1.1 million council, housing association and new town homes had been purchased in this way. At this same date 64 per cent of all dwellings in the country were owner-occupied. Officially, the number of households identified as homeless was 128,345. However, the housing pressure group Shelter, in its *Christmas Report on Homelessness 1988*, declared that the real figure was probably far higher, counting by individuals – into the millions. One fundamental part of the problem was that households were splitting up much earlier than formerly, with large numbers of single young people looking for accommodation. More immediate causes were the virtual cessation of local-authority house-building and the sharp rise in prices in the now predominating private market. Private landlords were unwilling to rent to unemployed young people, themselves adversely affected by the social-security changes I have just discussed. As the Shelter report put it: 'Without somewhere to live they can't get on to a Youth Training Scheme. Without YTS they get no income support. Many young people are literally being forced on to the streets.' But by the last year of the decade it was clear that disaster was also striking those rather higher up the social scale. In 1987 one in a hundred house buyers were losing their homes through failing to keep up their mortgage payments, and the figure was rising. House prices had gone up by 14.6 per cent in 1986–7, though were levelling off by 1989. However, by this time the much more serious problem of continually rising interest rates, which meant a frequent adjustment upwards of mortgage payments, was striking hard. Redundancy, too, could affect business and professional families. One other cause of people losing their homes was rather peculiar to the times. Many young unmarried couples, employing the device that allowed them both to claim tax relief on the same mortgage, were buying houses together: some dispossessions were a direct result of the relationship breaking up. Tax relief on mortgages was allowed up to the sum of £30,000, the original justification having been that this was compensation for not making demands on subsidized public housing for which, of course, house buyers were paying through taxes and rates. Some argued that given the inflation in house prices the limit ought to be raised, others that this tax relief amounted to no more than a free hand-out to those who were prosperous enough already. The arrangement whereby two people could claim tax relief on the same mortgage was ended in the 1988 budget.

Utopians, fascists, even grim Victorian industrialists had always believed that the quality and nature of education would shape a country's future. Education in the United Kingdom continued to be ruled by the genuine, though flawed 'secondary education for all' principles of the 1944 Butler Education Act (there were always separate Acts to meet the particular structures of Scotland and Northern Ireland, respectively), as applied and interpreted by the different local authorities. The Education Reform Act of July 1988 was widely held to have a significance equal to the Acts of 1944, 1918, 1902, and 1870, not least by the publicity-conscious Education Secretary, Kenneth Baker. The respected education journalist Peter Wilby concurred (*Independent*, 29 December 1988):

> 1988 has been an educational watershed as perhaps no other year has been this century. The Education Reform Act has irrevocably changed the balance of power. It provides that local authorities will lose control of the polytechnics and larger colleges next year. Gradually, too, councils will lose control of schools. Governors will have the power to hire and fire heads and teachers as well as to control budgets. The curriculum will be determined by statutory orders made by the Secretary of State for Education. Some schools will apply to opt out of local authority control and take direct funding from Whitehall; the threat of opting out will be enough to persuade most councils to avoid conflict with heads or governors. New parents' rights to claim places in any school where there is space will make council catchment areas largely irrelevant.

> Thus, heads in future will take their cues from parents and central government rather than from town and county halls. Since their funds will be tied by law to how many pupils they can attract, they will be operating rather as if they were running small (or, in some comprehensives, quite large) businesses. The cultural change for headteachers – many of whom are temperamentally opposed to the very idea of marketing – will be enormous.

Some of the administrative changes, actually, were embodied in the Education Act (No. 2) of 1986, which also introduced performance appraisal for teachers. Behind the Education Reform Act lay twenty years of agonizing over whether educational standards were slipping, and whether poor economic performance was linked to low standards. Thus, there was much to be said for the introduction of a national curriculum (in England and Wales – guidance along similar lines was to be issued by the Scottish Education Department) containing the 'core subjects' of mathematics, English and science, as well as the 'foundation subjects' of history, geography, technology, music, art, physical education and (for secondary pupils) a modern foreign language. To combat over-specialization in the higher levels of English secondary education, the traditional A-level was to be supplemented by Advanced Supplementary (AS) levels, which would, for example, enable students specializing in the arts to continue mathematics and technological subjects to the new level. More dubious were the rigid assessment procedures to be applied at the ages of 7, 11, 14 and 16. Through the special training of teachers and the supply of microcomputers, it was intended to integrate information technology throughout the school curriculum. As with the National Health Service, the sums put into education continued to rise: but, as with the National Health Service, that did not prevent well-founded stories being publicized of publicly funded schools (which still catered for 93 per cent of the country's children) being starved of essential books and other educational materials. Historians have tended to neglect one massive step taken in 1986 towards making Britain a normal civilized European country. Under pressure from the European Union, the Thatcher Government abolished corporal punishment in all schools, save for a few private cranky ones.

It would not be an exaggeration to say that the nation's universities felt themselves to be in a condition of war with the Government. Throughout the eighties Government policies of 'level funding', of refusing to accept the real implication of inflation in educational costs, of salary increases, etc., meant that all universities were suffering from cuts in posts and facilities, and some were in desperately dire straits. The Education Reform Act replaced the University Grants Committee, once the symbol of expansionism in higher education and of freedom and independence for universities, by the Universities Funding Council, which was clearly intended to take a more business-oriented line. Security of tenure for academics was to be phased out as new appointments, or promotions, were made. Open Government encouragement of technology and business studies (sensible enough in itself) seemed to menace the standing, not just of the arts and humanities, but of pure science. Maintenance grants for students were already being severely squeezed, with the aim of putting the onus back on parents. Subsequently it was revealed that the Government intended to move to the American system of loans, rather than grants; at the beginning of 1989 the American model of mixed funding was being openly extolled.

Social policy, of course, affects social life. But there are many other factors, totally, or to a great extent, outside Government control. With regard to relationships between the sexes, changing population statistics were becoming increasingly important. Actually, the sixties had been the first decade in which the population balance began to tip in favour of women: in the 1971 census, for the first time since records began, men outnumbered women in both the 15–29 and 30–44 age groups (consistently more male than female children are born, but only now were more males surviving into adult life). By 1988 there were 212,000 more males than females in the 16–35 age group, and 59,000 more in the peak marriage years of 20–24. Surveys among teenage girls, however, suggested that what researchers perceived as 'masculinist' attitudes still prevailed. But the force which, with chill primeval power, set aside the plans and calculations of modern society was that of the disease AIDS (Acquired Immune Deficiency Syndrome). In the early eighties the sexually transmitted disease causing worry to active heterosexuals was herpes, whose symptoms were unpleasant and painful, but not fatal. AIDS, for those who had heard of it, was thought to be exclusively confined to gays and drug addicts. It was not until 1985–6 that it became clear that heterosexuals were also seriously at risk. The first Government public education campaign, costing £20 million, was launched in late 1986. An official report published in 1988 calculated that at the end of the previous year between 20,000 and 50,000 people were infected in England and Wales. Of these, between 2,000 and 5,500 had been infected by heterosexual contact. However, once drug users and those infected by contaminated blood transfusions were added, the number of heterosexual adults infected was probably between 6,000 and 17,000. The average expectation of life once AIDS had been diagnosed was nine months.

The *British Social Attitudes 5th Report* of 1988 claimed to have detected a swing back to stricter moral standards compared with 1985. Actually the figures do not seem overwhelmingly conclusive:

Percentage saying 'always'/'mostly' wrong

	1983	1984	1985	1987
Pre-marital relations	28	27	23	25
Extra-marital relations	83	85	82	88
Homosexual relations	62	67	69	74

The key question, it would seem to me, concerns what is still slightly quaintly described as 'pre-marital relations' (the activity most likely to concern most young people directly): here one can see that the 'level of permissiveness' is still higher than it had been in both 1983 and 1984. Slightly different considerations come into play with regard to the two other headings: certainly such tolerance as there was for homosexual relations was lessening, and evidently fears about the potentially disastrous consequences of extra-marital adventures were having their impact (but one can see that such relations were in any case considered on an utterly different plane from the activities of the unmarried – 79 per cent of those aged 18–24 regarded pre-marital sex as 'rarely wrong' or 'not wrong at all'). The impact of AIDS was actually curiously double-headed: in a most ironic way the Government educational campaigns (a more forceful one was initiated early in 1988) brought to British television screens an anatomical explicitness, and an open acceptance of the sexual urges of young females as well as males, that would not have been contemplated in the sixties. Fear of AIDS was undoubtedly a stimulus towards fidelity, towards maintaining one partnership, rather than embarking on several. But there was no real evidence of a return to pre-sixties morality, and some evidence to the contrary (for example Margaret Bones's 1986 survey, *Trends in Pre-marital Sexual Behaviour in Scotland*, or the Birth Control Trust's *Teenage Pregnancy in Britain*). Clever talk of 'the new piety' seemed, as such talk often does, to miss the realities of actual behaviour; some feminists had, for more than ten years, been arguing that, rather than a romantic ideal, sexual involvement with a man was a dangerous drug to be avoided; young women were certainly more self-aware and less gullible than they had been in the sixties; gay relationships for women as well as for men were much more openly acknowledged. But the most striking figure yielded up by the official statistics is that of people of opposite sexes living together without bothering about the ritual of marriage. This may well be seen as a sign of emancipation among women; at any rate, the figures are given in the form of 'percentages of women cohabiting': in the age group 18–49 the figure more than doubled from 2.7 per cent in 1979 to 6.4 per cent in 1987; for those in the age group 18–24 the respective figures were 4.5 per cent and 11.5 per cent.

However one estimated responsibility for the origin and spread of AIDS, there could be no doubt that drug trafficking and drug addiction were man-created afflictions. Towards the end of Chapter 15 I noted the alarming rise in heroin abuse and its potential for social violence and disruption. In fact, cocaine was the drug of the eighties, the highly purified form, crack, being the staple of one facet of yuppie life-style (used in a highly controlled way, its supporters claimed), while less pure forms (together, of course, with other hard drugs) were widely diffused. In a 1986 report, *Danger: Drugs at Work*, the Confederation of British Industry warned that drug abuse was a threat from shop-floor to board-room: unless companies took action in monitoring their staff, profits would shrink and inefficiency would grow. A Scotland Yard Assistant Commissioner (Specialist Operations) reckoned that UK drug trafficking amounted to £400 million in 1984, and £500 million in 1985. In the late summer of 1986 David Mellor, then Minister of State at the Home Office, visited the South American countries producing cocaine. 'There is no way,' he reported in September, 'in which any Government, however dedicated to eradicating the drug problem, can guarantee to seize but a limited proportion of what comes here.' In 1987 the Customs and Excise did have an unprecedented success when they made a single haul of 208 kilos of cocaine. But, discounting that exceptional seizure, the figure for cocaine seizures increased by, to use the word of the Chief Investigation Officer, a 'sinister' figure of 80 per cent. He identified cocaine as 'the greatest concern for the future'. Yet heroin, after an apparent falling off in 1986, was again also pouring into the country. Cannabis was clearly back in fashion and, more worryingly, LSD. Apart from drugs coming in from South America and the Indian subcontinent, often via the United States or European countries, there was manufacture within Britain itself of the second most widely used drug, amphetamine sulphate. The first-ever co-ordinated Government strategy against drugs was initiated in 1984, with a major publicity campaign in 1985; in 1987 this merged into the campaign over AIDS. Drug trading (on a small scale, and often involving cannabis rather than hard drugs) was built into the fabric of many deprived urban communities: police action could be a flash-point for trouble.

Right down the age scale there was a cheap, do-it-yourself, but scarcely less pernicious, version of the drug habit – solvent-sniffing among young children (one of whom died in 1988). The growth in the problem can be charted by Government reactions: voluntary guidelines were drawn up in 1983 for retailers to curb the sale of solvents (glue, lighter-fuel, etc.), while legislation passed in Scotland added solvent misuse to the list of grounds on which a child might be considered to need compulsory care; in 1985 there was English legislation making it an offence to supply such substances to children (such sales had been prosecuted successfully under common law in Scotland); a further campaign aimed at retailers was launched in 1987.

Given these developments, and the ones identified in previous chapters, Britain was clearly a disturbed place in which to live. Much, of course, depended upon where you lived, what class and race you belonged to, how old you were, whether you were male or female. According to the 1989 *Social Trends*, the number of notifiable offences recorded by the police in England and Wales rose by 5.5 per cent per year between 1981 and 1987; in a single year 1986–7 crimes against the person increased by 12 per cent. Recorded cases of violent and sexual crimes rose again in 1988 (partly because allegations of rape were now recorded, although the total number of convictions actually declined), some of the credit being given to neighbourhood watch schemes. Old people in run-down housing estates felt at risk (statistics scarcely reassuring them to the contrary): in January 1989 an elderly couple were burned to death because they had installed a safety door which made it impossible for fireman to reach them in time, and very shortly afterwards there was an almost identical repetition of this tragedy. Many old people spoke of their total fear of going out. Women's 'Right to the Night' campaigns had begun in the seventies. Many of the danger spots were located in the abysmal redevelopment projects of the 1960s, but the Government of the eighties showed great reluctance to follow up simple remedies, such as the provision of better street lighting. A survey carried out by the Middlesex Polytechnic Department of Criminology, reporting in May 1988, drew attention both to bad street lighting and to the remedies women were adopting for self-protection. As the *Independent* (20 May 1988) reported:

Bad street lighting and fear of crime are forcing women to go armed with scissors, knives, umbrellas and 'street savvy' at night, according to the first controlled survey of the effect of lighting on crime.

Many women wear flat shoes for a quick escape, keep their door keys in their hands for a quick entry, and some always take their dog.

A draft report of the survey in the Borough of Enfield in North London gives statistical proof to a widely held assumption that the number of assaults on women and their fear of crime could be drastically reduced by simply ensuring that the lights work and are properly positioned.

In the mid-eighties society became aware of another group at risk, partly because of highly publicized developments in Cleveland, where large numbers of alleged child abuse victims were identified. No doubt child abuse there had a long, subterranean history; no doubt also the number of cases in Cleveland was exaggerated by the over-zealous paediatrician Dr Marietta Higgs and her colleague, Dr Geoffrey Wyatt, both criticized by the official Butler-Sloss report 'for the certainty and over-confidence with which they pursued the detection of sexual abuse in children referred to them' and for failing to consider whether their practice 'was in the best interests of the children, their patients'; but such expert bodies as the National Society for the Prevention of Cruelty to Children were clear that the actual number of cases was on the increase. Though the roots of child abuse may often lie in personal histories, the organizations most concerned identified as 'trigger-factors' many of the other general social problems I have already discussed. In 1985 the National Children's Home launched the campaign called 'Children in Danger' to counter what it saw as the effects of

rising poverty, increased drug misuse, deteriorating housing, escalating family break-down, a continuing high level of physical and sexual abuse, and cuts in services for children.

For the majority, prosperity did increase throughout the 1980s, real household disposable income per head rising on average by 3 per cent per year between 1981 and 1987 (women in full-time employment, despite reductions in the differential, still earned on average only two-thirds of what a man in full-time employment earned). For the rich, Britain was a better place to be than at any time since 1939. Everybody in full-time employment did fairly well, those in traditional manufacturing industries doing least well. Those outside the circle of general prosperity fell into a number of categories. There were the older unemployed men in the former industrial areas, their womenfolk often in highly pressurized part-time employments. There were the old, the single-parent families;

there were the rootless young, who formed a significant proportion of those sleeping rough in London. There was plenty of evidence that conditions for many of the people in these groups were extremely harsh.

It is, finally, when we look at leisure activities and patterns of consumer spending that we see the way in which long-term social trends continue irrespective of who wins general elections. The most significant changes (as recorded in *Social Trends*, No. 20, 1989) were the advent of the video recorder (the number of households possessing these more than doubled between 1983 and 1986, and had reached 47 per cent by 1987), home computers (17 per cent of households in 1986), and microwave ovens (23 per cent of households in 1986), and the great expansion in the use of the telephone (83 per cent of households in 1986). The deep-freezer continued its march towards indispensibility: it was to be found (usually combined with a refrigerator) in 72 per cent of households in 1986. Households with access to at least one car had gone up to around 62 per cent, those with two or more cars to 20 per cent. The amount of time spent on watching television had risen quite significantly, to 25.5 hours per week on average. Of other leisure activities (calculated as before on the basis of responses to questions about activities participated in over a four-week period), playing records or tapes had displaced going out for a meal or a drink (now listed as separate activities; perhaps the researchers had read my comments in the first edition of this book!) as top of the list: that people's activities would become more and more home-based was, of course, a cliché of the IT revolution. Going out for a drink remained for all men and for younger women the most popular extramural activity. Going out for a meal actually came fairly close, and well ahead of all other activities, so clearly the freezer had yet to establish total hegemony. For all women, reading books (nothing electronic about that) had apparently gone up slightly in popularity (now 64 per cent), and beat going out for a drink. The reading figure for men had not changed in ten years, remaining at 52 per cent, but reading a book had a higher appeal than going out for a meal. The other leisure activities showed no significant variations from 1977.

Nor did the amount of alcohol consumed change significantly between 1978 and 1987: for women it was slightly up, for men slightly down. But, alas, there was a problem with the statistics, as *Social Trends* (1989) recognized: 'Consumption of alcohol is difficult to measure from social surveys, which consistently record less consumption than would be expected from Customs and Excise statistics of alcohol released for home consumption.' (It is a well-known phenomenon that people overestimate the amount of sex they are getting, underestimate the amount of alcohol they are consuming.) What is indisputable is that alcohol abuse was now being recognized as a very genuine health and social problem, and that the problem of drinking and driving was being faced up to with great seriousness throughout society.

The real-ale movement continued to hold its position, and its activities combined with the entrepreneurial spirit of the times to ensure that in addition to the traditional ales now universally offered by all the big breweries, a large number of local, in effect 'home-brewed', varieties were available. To the British-brewed lagers with foreign names there were added heavily advertised Australian brands – a reflection both of growing Australian economic power, and of an agreeable fashion for all things Australian. An existing trend towards the drinking of wine (in pubs and wine bars) was overtaken by another one for drinking exclusive foreign beers, genuinely imported in bottle. But the great innovation of 1988 was the appearance of beers with practically nil alcoholic content. At the beginning of Part Three, I printed the list of drinks on offer in a large Aberdeen bar that had formerly been the city's finest restaurant. By the autumn of 1988 the bar had seemingly moved slightly up market, presenting a more genteel appearance, with tables nicely set out for lunch, and less of an American feel. The list of drinks may be compared with the one I printed on page 155.

Spirits		*Bottled Beer*	
Whisky	80p	LAGER	70p
Vodka	80p		
Gordon's Gin	80p	EXPORT	70p
Rum	80p	Stout	70p
Bacardi	90p	PILS	£1.00
Brandy	95p	BECKS	£1.00
		Carlsberg Special	£1.00
Canadian Club	95p	Newcastle Brown	£1.10
Southern Comfort	95p	Whitbread	£1.10
Glenyfydch	95p	GROLSCHT	£1.30
Malt Whisky	95p	Furszenburg	£1.30
		BLACK & TAN	£1.30
De Luxe	95p	CIDER BABY	£1.25
Sherry	75p	*Soft Drinks*	
Port	75p	Split	60p

Spirits		*Soft Drinks*	
Martini	85p	Soda and Lime	70p
		Perrier WATER	65p
Liquors		APPLETIZER	65p
Pernod	95p	DASHES	15p
Contreau	95p	Britvic 55	60p
Advocatt	95p		
		Babysham	60p
Draught Beer		Snowball	60p
Lager	£1.00		
Export	£1.00	*Wines*	
Cider	£1.00	by the glass	90p
½ PINT	55p		
80	£1.10		
Guinness	£1.20		
½	60p		

I have tried to reproduce faithfully the idiosyncrasies of spelling and local custom: '80' is an abbreviation for '80-shilling ale', a conscious revival of an archaic term – a response to the real-ale fashion – for what to the customer was 'heavy'; '½' signifies a half-pint of Guinness'; 'De Luxe' refers to those superior whiskies that contain a higher proportion of malt than the ordinary blends.

Also clearly on sale – on draught, though not on the price list – were Greenmantle (a privately brewed Scottish real ale) and low-alcohol beer. The classy foreign beers, of course, are the 'Grolscht' and 'Furszenburg', outshining even Pils and Becks. Scottish pubs like this one were now open all day. From August 1988 a similar privilege was granted to the English drinking classes, though in fact many pubs continued to stay closed in the afternoons, and all adapted the new permissible hours to suit their own particular circumstances.

Just as drinking and driving was coming to be positively frowned upon, so also smoking was becoming increasingly socially unacceptable, many public buildings and many sectors of public transport being declared no-smoking areas. In 1972, 52 per cent of all males, and 42 per cent of all females had declared themselves to be smokers. By 1980 the figures were down to 42 per cent and 37 per cent respectively, and by 1986 to 35 per cent and 31 per cent. The annual cost to the National Health Service of smoking-related diseases was estimated to be around £5,000 million. In 1987–8 over £0.2 million was spent on grants to voluntary organizations for anti-smoking campaigns and on publishing tar and nicotine levels. The Health Education Authority spent a further £1.1 million in anti-smoking advice. One sign of the new campaigning zeal was the national 'No

Smoking Day' held annually in March. In 1987 it was estimated that 800,000 people gave up on that day, and that 50,000 may have done so permanently.

For all its vicissitudes association football seemed to be maintaining its appeal for a large number of the British people. As a participatory activity, football (essentially confined to young or youngish males) was actually slightly less popular than keep-fit/yoga (a growth area, almost exclusively confined to females), and stood on a par with such sports as squash, cycling, and tennis. But it was still by far the most popular spectator sport: attendances, having dropped sharply between 1971 and 1982, were stable in England and Wales by mid-decade, and were rising in Scotland. More important, league football was an absolute essential to television scheduling.

In their leisure pursuits the British were sharing in trends common to all the advanced countries (though football was the classic case of the British-invented sport that far outweighed any American games in world-wide popularity). However, social attitude surveys continued to reveal uniquely British characteristics, few of them conforming to Thatcherite ideas. A Gallup Poll carried out for London Weekend Television in August 1986 revealed that the British people were nothing like as interested in getting rich as the Japanese or the Americans. Only 9 per cent of Britons said that their main goal in life was to get rich, whereas 38 per cent gave this answer in Japan and 15 per cent in the United States. The great majority of British respondents said that their main aim in life was 'to live as I like' (77 per cent). *Social Trends* No. 15 (1984) had commented on the widespread pessimism expressed in 1983 about prospects both for inflation and unemployment. *Social Trends* No. 19 (1988) reported 'a clear overall increase in public optimism about the economy', but, it added, 'the picture is still somewhat patchy' (and it was certainly far from Thatcherite):

Inflation and unemployment are seen as ever-present threats, and a sizeable minority of the population, largely concentrated in the lowest income groups, seem to be sceptical that any general improvements in the economy will actually benefit them. Concern about unemployment in particular, despite the lessening gloom about its likely growth, remains very high. By a margin of over three to one (73 per cent to 23 per cent), respondents feel that the government should give higher priority to bringing down unemployment than to reducing inflation. Indeed, this view has slightly hardened in the last 5 years, possibly because inflation during the period has been consistently rather low. Something approaching a consensus among the various population subgroups exist on this issue, although pensioners and (more noticeably) the self-employed are more likely than average to give priority to tackling inflation.

All in all there was no sharp disjuncture between the social trends of the eighties and those we have been following through since 1945. Despite a Government openly admiring of American ways of doing things, and the spread in Britain, as never before, of a universalized American style and gimmickry, the Britishness of British life was still abundantly in evidence.

23

The Hallmark of a Civilization: 'An Ace Caff with Quite a Nice Museum Attached'

In 1985 the Arts Council published a slim but glossy prospectus ('designed by the Jenkins Group') entitled *A Great British Success Story*. It introduced itself thus:

This prospectus sets out the case for an increase in public investment in the arts. It argues that a thriving arts and entertainment industry of high quality is essential for deepening the experience and enjoyment of the people of Great Britain, for richly enhancing the nation's prestige overseas, and most significantly for the good of the British economy. A small increase in public funding will bring quick and sizeable returns.

Why invest in the arts?

The arts are the hallmark of a civilization; the lifeblood of a nation. They fulfil the individual, releasing creative talents – in music, dance, drama, mime, opera, the visual arts, crafts, photography, literature, film, video, they reach out to the spectator and the audience, lifting the imagination and widening experience; and they bring communities together in shared achievements – in orchestras and drama groups, arts centres, dance classes, steel and brass bands. The arts inspire a sense of identity.

But the arts are more than a personal preoccupation. Nations have always been judged and valued by their creativity – from classical Greece through Renaissance Florence to our times. A nation needs economic success to take care of the basic requirements of its inhabitants, but 'where there is no vision the people perish'. The arts provide that vision.

This is not just a question of national pride. Our achievements in the arts demonstrate to the world that we are creative, imaginative, innovative and resourceful; they represent an important strand in our export drive, both producing real profits and preparing the way for further enterprises. The arts matter.

Few nations can match the artistic achievements of Britain since the 1940s. The arts have been one of our greatest success stories – perhaps the greatest. We are asking the nation to invest in this well-proved 'product'; to provide the cash to ensure that past glories do not become insubstantial memories, and that present achievements can be built upon for even greater returns in the future.

The 'vital' or 'central' core of the arts, the document further explained, is funded by the Government, but it 'badly needs more cash now to fulfil its potential'; 'it offers an excellent product now' and 'sows seeds for the future'; 'rarely in the arts,' furthermore, 'do these research and development costs have to be written off as a wasted investment'. Indeed, while ten years ago 'public investment' meant Government investment, it becomes clear that the phrase has a new Thatcherite meaning: investment by members of 'the public' (rich ones usually). Not surprisingly, the document speaks openly of the 'arts industry', which it defines as embracing both high and low culture and all structures and activities relating thereto:

It is the Edinburgh International Festival with its ever expanding Fringe, and the sights and sounds of Carnival filling the streets of Notting Hill . . .

It is Space-Time System's box office computer system (BOCS) developed in British theatres, and the world-wide consultancy service of Theatre Projects promoting British technical achievements in sound, lighting and state engineering.

Then on to the 'dividends'. The nation benefits from investing in the arts, it is explained, because: most of the money is quickly recouped in taxes; the arts increase employment at low cost (thus incidentally producing savings in welfare payments); the arts help the regeneration of depressed inner cities; the arts vitalize the wider entertainment industry; the arts raise the nation's prestige; the arts are a substantial tourist attraction and foreign currency earner; and (last, but conceivably not least) the arts give great pleasure to millions of people. Throughout, the document stresses the interrelationship between the growth of the arts and the growth of leisure in contemporary society. It concludes with a word on 'productivity and efficiency': 'our product offers excellent value. On average our companies earn around 45 per cent of turnover, a much higher figure than our rivals in Germany and France . . .'

From the setting up of the Arts Council at the end of the war, the place of the arts in British society had scarcely been in doubt; but the case had never quite been put in this way before. Lord Clark, Huw Weldon, Melvyn

Bragg, Sir Roy Shaw (great communicators and protagonists of the arts) would all have argued for the arts as 'the hallmark of a civilization'. But the blatant commercial associations were something different, and inspired deep mistrust. Similarly those who had shared the ideas crystallized in the Robbins Report of the 1960s were highly mistrustful of Government attitudes towards higher education. Such people were upholders of liberal humanism, political pluralism, traditional freedoms, all perceived within a framework of broad consensus and the tolerance of secular Anglicanism. To them the Government appeared vulgar in its attitude to the arts and matters of the intellect, and authoritarian in its attitudes towards freedom of thought and expression.

To these issues I shall return later in the chapter, after turning to other 'hallmarks of civilization', in particular questions of the maintenance of law and order, of freedom of expression, and of political and social values. The tradition (outside of Northern Ireland) of an unarmed and (on the whole) non-violent police force was a proud one, which probably more than any other single factor explained why for all the fire-bombing and urban rioting loss of life in Britain was, by international standards, very low. However, the tradition was beginning to seem a little threadbare in the aftermath of the blunders in Brixton and Tottenham, and of police actions in the miners' strike and subsequently. Very properly there was considerable sympathy and support for the police in a world which generally did not adhere to British standards of decent behaviour: on 17 April 1984, for instance, WPC Yvonne Fletcher, on duty outside the Libyan People's Bureau in St James's Square, London, was shot dead from inside that building. But earlier grave doubts about police responses and police training were aroused when a totally innocent man, Steven Waldorf, was shot and seriously wounded in mistake for a convicted criminal, David Martin. Further along the law and order chain the utterly disgusting conditions in many of Britain's ancient and grossly overcrowded prisons, together with growing disaffection among prison officers, were generating a situation of extreme crisis. At the same time the Government itself appeared to be operating in an increasingly high-handed and authoritarian way. Issues of policing, national security, freedom of expression, and, of course, Northern Ireland, tended to interact with each other.

Towards the end of 1988 an issue relating to the Government's perceptions of national security, which had been rumbling along for quite a considerable time, was brought to a nice conclusion: the issue concerned the rights of certain newspapers to publish material from an autobiographical account of British Secret Service activities, the book *Spycatcher* (whose contents were now very widely known, largely thanks to the Government's attempts to suppress the book, particularly in Australia). The Government had adopted the tactic of fighting the newspapers through the civil courts. Giving judgement for the newspapers, Mr Justice Scott declared:

> The Press has a legitimate role in disclosing scandals in government. An open democratic society requires that that be so . . . The ability of the Press freely to report allegations of scandals in government is one of the bulwarks of our democratic society.

How well equipped was the British press (and British television) to preserve the values of democracy? There was evidence that the tabloids were plumbing lower depths for irrelevance, misrepresentation and invention than ever before. In 1988 juries awarded unprecedentedly high and punitive levels of damages for individuals whose private conduct had been libelled in these papers, while at the same time an MP was trying to bring in a bill that would compel papers to print corrections from individuals who had had misstatements made about them. The country's most popular tabloid, the *Sun*, together with two of its most respected quality papers, *The Times* and the *Sunday Times*, were all owned by the Australian multi-national media magnate Rupert Murdoch, who made no secret of his devotion to Margaret Thatcher and her policies. On the other hand, thanks mainly to the breaking of the power of the print unions and the installation of new technology, the quality papers, which had seemed in terminal crisis in 1981, were now more securely established than they had been at any time since the nineteenth century. In October 1986 the *Independent* was launched: it so quickly justified its title that it was given the ultimate accolade of honest reliability by being declared 'a newspaper of record' by the British Library. The broadcasting authorities, the BBC and the ITA, together with the companies it supervised, manifested the highest standards of professional integrity, on a par with the best of the quality press. However (and this is where the Irish element begins to intrude), this was not the view of the Government. In the summer of 1985 the BBC programme *At the Edge of the Union* was banned by the Home Secretary Leon Brittan: the objection was to any publicity for the IRA, though in fact the programme demonstrated that organization's merciless disregard for human life, while also demonstrating the bigotry of a Protestant extremist. Two years later the Government sought to persuade the ITA to ban a Thames Television programme, *Death on the Rock*, which was an attempt to investigate what actually had happened when members of the special military force (the SAS) shot three IRA terrorists as they were trying to leave Gibraltar. Lord Thomson, chairman of the ITA, refused to give way to Government pressure, and the programme was duly broadcast. Government ministers, and the Government-supporting press, made many wild accusations against the programme, and against individuals who appeared on it (one secured libel damages). But the Government let it be known at once that it didn't accept the verdict. The programme was finally vindicated through an independent inquiry, reporting early in 1989, that was conducted by Lord Windlesham, a widely respected hereditary peer and former Conservative Home Office and Northern Ireland Minister, and Richard Rampton, QC. To expect politicians (or whatever party) to admit to their own errors would probably be to expect too much. Nevertheless, a less ignoble regime might have taken the opportunity to rejoice in the vindication once again of the independence and integrity of British television.

Of the many examples of the Government's authoritarian tendencies, one of the most celebrated was the prosecution of Clive Ponting, an official in the Ministry of Defence, who had communicated information about the sinking of the Argentinian cruiser the *General Belgrano* during the Falklands War (a subject on which the Government had always been less than candid). Mr Justice Cantley took the Government line, equating the national interest with what is good for the Government of the day, but in one of these incidents which demonstrated that there were characteristics of British society that would not be suborned by Government, the jury acquitted Ponting (the satirical journal *Private Eye* brilliantly caught the essence of the affair in having Mr Justice Cantley ask of the jury foreman 'And is that the verdict of you all?' as the foreman raises two fingers to him). The Government hastened ahead with its Official Secrets Bill, which would make impossible the defence that the leaking of a secret was in the public interest, and its Security Services Bill, which would deny any parliamentary control over the activities of the security services. Also in 1988 it published its White Paper on the future of broadcasting. The Government was clearly unhappy with what was internationally recognized as the best television service in the world (though perfectly happy with a press which, in its lower levels, was among the worst in the world). In 1988 a ban was imposed on all interviews with members of Sinn Fein (the political wing of the IRA). In the same year a group of academics and intellectuals launched Charter '88, whose primary claim was for a Bill of Rights that would establish the rights and liberties of the individual (against, for instance, the Government, the security services, the holding of secret files, etc.); it also represented a cross-party rallying point against the Government, given the continuing weaknesses of the parliamentary opposition.

But what was the nature of the opposition to the Government? That there was a majority in the country against Thatcherite policies was beyond dispute. But equally beyond dispute was the existence of a majority against the socialism that the Labour Party claimed to espouse. Whether there was anything like a majority for the kinds of issues that the disaffected intellectuals focused on was highly dubious. Perhaps the most interesting political critique was *The Unprincipled Society* (1988) by David Marquand. Marquand argued that there had been nothing, in principle, wrong with Keynesianism, but that Keynesianism, and consensus politics in general, depended upon a genuine spirit of national community, something which had perhaps existed in the forties, but which had very clearly broken up in the seventies when unions were as guilty as anyone else of self-seeking and adversarial attitudes. The real alternative to Thatcherism, with its encouragement of private acquisitiveness, he said, was a 'principled society' in which individuals and groups accepted their responsibilities to each other. Just how this was to be achieved was less clear: presumably by a Government combining the moral principles of the Attlee Government with a recognition that unions and those on the Left could be just as selfish as those on the Right. The problems of securing an alternative Government still seemed enormous. Labour could still build up large majorities in traditional working-class areas (though some of its seats in Scotland were now looking vulnerable), but there was little evidence that it could regain enough ground elsewhere to secure a majority. The Liberals and the Social Democrats had now (since the late summer of 1987) merged into one party yet, a trifle ludicrously, could not get all of their members to accept one name – the party appeared both as the Democrats and as the Social and Liberal Democrats (SLD). The subsequently elected leader, Paddy Ashdown, was both a 'caring' politician and possessed of great personal dynamism. But without a new electoral system that would enable a party's strength in the country to be accurately reflected in the House of Commons (something the Conservatives would be most unlikely to concede), there seemed little hope of gaining more than a handful of seats. In any case opinion polls were putting the new party's rating at below 15 per cent. David Owen had refused to accept the merger, so that, to add to the general confusion and the ineffectiveness of the attempt to establish a third force in British politics, there remained a party calling itself the SDP under his leadership. Neil Kinnock was making a determined effort to broaden the appeal of the Labour Party, but his own greatest strength was probably that having spent practically all of his working life within the Labour Party he was (the discomfited hard Left apart) greatly liked and respected within the party: that he had never led any kind of successful life outside of politics was thought by some commentators to be a considerable handicap in making an appeal beyond traditional Labour voters. As a historian, my own general belief is that economic and technological forces, social trends, and international crises have greater significance than individual personalities: the fissiparous state of the opposition parties, the continuing unpopularity among large sections of the electorate of unilateral nuclear disarmament (in fact dropped at the 1989 Labour Party conference), of the prospect of high taxation, and of many aspects of trade unionism, were factors limiting the possibility of securing a majority behind the case against Thatcherism; but there was also, to say the least, the problem of matching someone who looked like a credible Prime Minister to deliverable votes in the country. The most impressive witness to the cause of nuclear disarmament was borne by the women who camped out year after year at Greenham Common: but undoubtedly as the superpowers moved towards multilateral disarmament the old appeal was becoming muted. The new cause which was palpably making its way in the later eighties (and earning lip-service at least from the old parties) was that of the environment – once again an issue whose major beginnings lay in the 1960s.

Serious criticisms could be made of Government policy towards the universities and towards the arts; but these were not issues of great appeal to the majority of voters – indeed heritage industry refurbishment, leisure centres, and theme parks both brightened up the built environment and had genuine family appeal. My long quotation at the beginning of this chapter very much conveys the essence of the new policies, represented also in the appointment in 1983 of Luke Rittner, a former Conservative counsellor in Bath and organizer of the Association for Business Sponsorship of the Arts as Secretary General of the Arts Council; in the launching in 1984 of the Business Sponsorship Incentive Scheme with matching grants from Government of up to £25,000; and in the National Heritage Act of 1983. This Act removed responsibility for historical buildings and monuments from the Department of Environment, vesting in it a new Historical Building and Monuments Committee for England, generally known as English Heritage (in Wales responsibility for historic monuments rests with Cadw – Welsh Historic Monuments – and in Scotland with the Historic Buildings and Monuments Directorate of the Scottish Development Department), and removed limitations on the sale of artistic treasures. Clause 35 of the Act empowered the Commission to set up companies with the following objectives:

(a) the production and publication in England of books, films or other informative material relating to ancient monuments or historic buildings;

(b) the production in England of souvenirs relating to ancient monuments or historic buildings;

(c) the sale in England of souvenirs or of informative material relating to ancient monuments or historic buildings; and

(d) the provision in England of catering or car parking or other services or facilities for members of the public visiting ancient monuments or historic buildings.

One can admire or deplore the tone set by English Heritage advertising: 'Visit an English Heritage property and enjoy a range of spectacular entertainment!'; love or loathe the advertisement for the Victoria and Albert Museum (alluded to in my title): 'Ace Caff with Quite a Nice Museum Attached'. Robert Hewison, in his powerful and influential work *The Heritage Industry: Britain in a Climate of Decline* (1987), stated the case against Government policies:

A change in cultural perception has taken place which narrows the imagination and cramps the spirit. In the nineteenth century museums were seen as sources of education and improvement, and were therefore free. Now they are treated as financial institutions that must pay their way, and therefore charge entrance fees. The arts are no longer appreciated as a source of inspiration, of ideas, images or values, they are part of the 'leisure business'. We are no longer lovers of art, but customers for a product. And as the marketing managers of the heritage industry get into full swing, the goods that we are being offered become more and more spurious, and the quality of life becomes more and more debased.

Was the condition of the arts ('the hallmark of a civilization') so utterly irredeemable? In 1986 private sponsorship of the arts was running between £250,000 and £300,000 (excluding the £500,000 gifted by John Paul Getty to the National Gallery, and Sainsbury's £250,000 for building the National Gallery extension). A grand debate continued over the state of British architecture, much enlivened by the interventions of the Prince of Wales who, for example, successfully aborted the proposed modernist extension to the National Gallery by terming it a 'monstrous carbuncle'. The highly salutary reversal of sixties trends (a reversal which, of course, had originated in the seventies) towards an emphasis on traditional forms (usually neo-Georgian) and renovation, and an attempt to bring real distinction and relevance to modernist design continued. If not particularly original, Richard Siefert's National Westminster Bank Tower in the City of London (1981) – at 183 metres it was Britain's highest tower block – was rather more elegant than his Centrepoint (1971). More important, three younger architects (by this time not terribly young) burst into a new prominence. The senior figure was James Stirling, born in 1926, the son of a Scots marine engineer. The other two were Richard Rogers, born in Florence in 1933 of Anglo-Italian parents, and Norman Foster, born in 1935 into a very non-intellectual Manchester milieu. Given the theme that I have developed throughout Part Four, it is significant that all three spent time in America: as Deyan Sudjic has put it in his *Norman Foster, Richard Rogers, James Stirling: New Directions in British Architecture* (1989), 'America alone seemed able to pursue technologically advanced modernism.' All were respecters of tradition, but insistent that each age should have an advanced architecture suited to its particular needs. Back in 1958, Stirling had written: 'One has only to compare the Crystal Palace to the Festival of Britain, or the Victorian railway stations to recent airports, to appreciate the desperate situation of our technical inventiveness today, compared to the supreme position which we held in the last century.' It would be facile, but not totally irrelevant, to recall here that Margaret Thatcher herself put great faith in the restoration of Victorian values.

The Engineering building for the University of Leicester, built between 1959 and 1964 by the Stirling and Gowan partnership, had achieved world-wide fame, as had the Cambridge History Faculty building, completed in 1968 by Stirling and Michael Wilford, but in general Stirling had been starved of work throughout the sixties. That Stirling was indeed a figure of international renown was driven home in 1984 when, in partnership with Wilford, he completed the much praised and much commented-on extension to the Staatsgallerei in Stuttgart. At home, Stirling and Wilford were responsible for the new Clore Gallery at the Tate Gallery. Richard Rogers had already entered the world limelight when the

Beaubourg Centre in Paris was completed in 1977. It was in the same year that Norman Foster completed the Sainsbury Centre for Visual Arts at the University of East Anglia; his Headquarters of the Hong Kong and Shanghai Corporation, a much discussed and unmissable feature of the Hong Kong waterfront, was completed in 1986. *The* architectural event was the completion in 1986 of the new Lloyds of London, close by the National Westminster Tower, to the design of Richard Rogers. The analogy of the Meccano set has been applied to both this building and the Beaubourg. Rogers likes to speak of 'served' and 'servant' spaces: he has said of the Lloyds building, 'Whereas the frame of the building has a long life expectancy, the servant areas, filled with mechanical equipment, have an extremely short life, especially in this energy-critical period.' Deyan Sudjic explains that the building is:

an arrangement that will allow for any foreseeable growth to be accommodated without compromising the single-space underwriting room. The centre of the building is a twelve-storey-high barrel-vaulted atrium that rises up through the middle of a series of regular rectangular office floors . . . The underwriting room is on the principal floor, just above street level, and future growth will take place by spilling over into the lower levels of office space around the atrium, which is criss-crossed by escalators. Surrounding the atrium are six towers, containing lifts, stairs, washrooms and service ducts. The towers are expressed as the dominant elements in the overall composition . . .

If, with respect to international recognition and, it should be said, distinctiveness of style, Hockney had been *the* artist of the sixties and beyond, then the partnership of Gilbert and George constituted *the* artist of the seventies and beyond. Dubbing them 'God's Eastenders', a *Guardian* article of 15 July 1987 began:

Gilbert and George are frequently described as two men working as one artist. In practice they are four men working as one artist, two pairs of G and G. The first pair makes the pictures. The second promotes them.

The first pair is secretive, sad, obsessed with low life and sex, yet by one of those curiously British artist artistic paradoxes, they align themselves alongside Mrs Thatcher – whom they recently described as the most 'moral' Prime Minister of their times – as upholders of a set of strict, Victorian moral values. They have never really been out of fashion but they have never been more in fashion than now.

A Gilbert and George exhibition 'Pictures 1982–6' (sponsored, it may be noted by Beck's Bier), had toured Brussels, Basel, Madrid and Munich, before coming to the Hayward Gallery, London, in July 1987. Gilbert and George pictures, usually very large, are best described as photo-pieces: they incorporate photographic images of themselves together with various young men. In keeping with the conceptualist tradition that had developed in the seventies, the titles of the pictures – 'Finding God', 'Drunk with God', 'Death after Life', etc. – are incorporated in the pictures, often referred to as allegories of our time. According to the guide to the Hayward Gallery exhibition the most recent 'allegories of our time' by Gilbert and George 'have taken the image of the youth of their world – working class, unemployed, or facing unemployment – and elevated it to the status of ideal male protagonist, of hero'. An older painter, Lucian Freud (born in 1922), hitherto best known for his nudes, entered a new phase in the 1980s, signalled by such works as 'Large Interior W11 (after Watteau)', and achieved great international acclaim.

It would be a harsh critic indeed who, touring the provinces, as well as visiting the galleries of London, would deny that there was life and variety in contemporary British painting. One of the most commented-on exhibitions was that held in the autumn of 1988 in the Serpentine Gallery, London, featuring more than twenty years of paintings by the Portuguese-born Paula Rego, a painter, said Germaine Greer, whose power is 'undeniably, obviously, triumphantly female'. The quotation is from an article in *Modern Painters*, an important new quarterly journal of the fine arts launched in 1988 by the distinguished art critic Peter Fuller. Fuller had abandoned an earlier Marxism, and was critical of much in contemporary British modernist art: but to see in the art world any universal swing towards either naked commercialism, or conformity with Thatcherite conservatism, would be to miss the variety I have just mentioned.

For those who like to set up a target of bloated establishment art, opera earns a special contempt. Certainly connections could be made between the commercial sponsorship of opera, and the commandeering of excessively expensive seats for purposes of business entertainment. Yet, at the same time – apart from the marvellously inventive productions of Opera Factory – Scottish Opera, Welsh Opera, the English National Opera, and, indeed, the Royal Opera House were all putting on innovative productions of most of the great classical and romantic operas. That opera was not an archaic art form was demonstrated by the productions of Harrison Birtwhistle's *The Mask of Orpheus* (English National Opera, 1986) and Nigel Osborne's *The Electrification of the Soviet Union* (Royal Opera House, 1987).

It would be difficult indeed to maintain that British theatre betrayed a conformist trend. Leading left-wing writers such as Howard Brenton, David Hare and David Edgar did not suddenly go into retirement. Indeed, Brenton and Hare collaborated on the runaway success at the National Theatre *Pravda*, a satire whose target was quite manifestly Thatcherite newspaper magnate Rupert Murdoch. The target of Caryl Churchill's *Serious Money* was the stock-market of eighties' yuppiedom. A staple attraction for tourists continued to be classical plays imaginatively staged. The sensation of 1984 was Antony Sher's portrayal of Richard III at Stratford-upon-Avon as a 'bottled spider', an embittered cripple on crutches. In November 1983 Sher was musing on how 'a tradition has evolved of playing it [*Richard III*] as black comedy'. He states in *Year of the King: An Actor's Diary* (1985):

It seems to me that Richard's personality has been deeply and dangerously affected by his deformity, and that one has to show this connection.

But the problem in playing him extremely deformed is to devise a position that would be 100 per cent safe to sustain over three hours, and for a run that could run for two years. Play him on crutches perhaps? They would take a lot of strain off the danger areas; lower back, pelvis and legs. And my arms are quite strong after months in the gym. Also I was on crutches for months after the operation so they have a personal association for me of being disabled . . .

The crutches idea is attractive, too attractive at this early stage. Must keep an open mind on the subject.

Opening night was Wednesday 20 June 1984. In his diary Sher commented that Michael Caine should have the last word on the (rapturous) reviews:

'What about these reviews, then?' he said.
'I don't read them.'
'Don't read them? *You wrote* them, didn't you?'

Gilbert Phelps (in volume 9 of *The Cambridge Guide to the Arts in Britain*) has written of the 'genuine poetic imagination' of J. G. Ballard, and of 'the extraordinary amalgam of Dickensian richness, of the quirky circumlocutions of Laurence Sterne, of grim realism, extravagant farce, fantasy, magic, and symbolism' in the work of Salman Rushdie, who in 1989 gained a peculiar and unwanted fame when, after his *Satanic Verses* had been burned – terrible sign of the times! – by incensed Muslims in Bradford, a death sentence was pronounced on him by the Ayatollah Khomeini. But in the main, British novels continued to be accounts –

often highly inventive – of the manners and morals of the age. Fay Weldon remained an exuberant guide to post-feminist sensibilities: *Leader of the Band* (1988) portrays the sex-pot musician out of lust for whom the narrator, Starlady Sandra, has given up her work as a brilliant astronomer. David Lodge, whilst still offering a nice commentary on contemporary intellectual fashion, entered the world of industry in post-industrial Birmingham; *Nice Work* (1988) could well be *the* novel of life in Thatcherite Britain. 1986 is Industry Year: universities are encouraged to appoint one 'Industry Year Shadow', who, by following a local industrialist around, will learn about the vital importance of making money. Robyn Penrose is the 'Shadow', Vic Wilcox the industrialist. Here is part of their first conversation:

'My field is the nineteenth-century novel,' said Robyn. 'And women's studies.'

'Women's studies?' Wilcox echoed with a frown. 'What are they?'

'Oh, women's writing. The representation of women in literature. Feminist critical theory.'

Wilcox sniffed. 'You give degrees for that?'

'It's one part of the course,' said Robyn stiffly. 'It's an option.'

'A soft one, if you ask me,' said Wilcox. 'Still, I suppose it's all right for girls.'

'Boys take it too,' said Robyn. 'And the reading load is very heavy, as a matter of fact.'

'Boys?' Wilcox curled a lip. 'Nancy boys?'

'Perfectly normal, decent, intelligent young men,' said Robyn, struggling to control her temper.

'Why aren't they studying something useful, then?'

'Like mechanical engineering?'

'You said it.'

Robyn sighed. 'Do I really have to tell you?'

'Not if you don't want to.'

'Because they're more interested in ideas, in feelings, than in the way machines work.'

'Won't pay the rent, though will they – ideas, feelings?'

'Is money the only criterion?'

'I don't know a better one.'

'What about happiness?'

'Happiness?' Wilcox looked startled, caught off balance for the first time.

'Yes, I don't earn much money, but I'm happy in my job. Or I would be, if I were sure of keeping it.'

'Why aren't you?'

When Robyn explained her situation, Wilcox seemed more struck by her colleagues' security than by her own vulnerability. 'You mean, they've got jobs for life?' he said.

'Well, yes. But the Government wants to abolish tenure in the future.'

'I should think so.'

'But it's essential!' Robyn exclaimed. 'It's the only guarantee of academic freedom. It is one of the things we were demonstrating for last week.'

'Hang about,' said Wilcox. '*You* were demonstrating in support of other lecutrers' right to a job for life?'

'Partly,' said Robyn.

'But if they can't be shifted, there'll never be room for you, no matter how much better than them you may be at the job.'

This thought had crossed Robyn's mind before, but she had suppressed it as ignoble. 'It's the principle of the thing,' she said. 'Besides, if it wasn't for the cuts, I'd have had a permanent job by now. We should be taking more students, not fewer.'

'You think the universities should expand indefinitely?'

'Not indefinitely, but —'

'Enough to accommodate all those who want to do women's studies?'

'If you like to put it that way, yes,' said Robyn defiantly.

'Who pays?'

'You keep bringing everything back to money.'

'That's what you learn from business. There's no such thing as a free lunch. Who said that?'

In late 1989 London buses were carrying massive advertisements for *London Fields*, the latest novel by Martin Amis (son of Kingsley), who had burst on the literary scene in the seventies with *The Rachel Papers* (1973), a sort of last fling of sixties' youth, and *Dead Babies* (1975), a vicious drug-laden binge set in a future whose super-rich, arrogant characters marvellously anticipate the nastiest acolytes of Thatcherism. *Money* (1984) is narrated by a yuppie pornographic film-maker, John Self. Feminists declared Amis a sexist, but may have been falling into the elementary error of confusing author with character. 'Post-feminist' journalist Julie Burchill produced a first novel, *Ambition* (1989), in which the uninhibited female chauvinism of central character Susan Street is almost a mirror image of the male chauvinism of John Self.

The up-and-down story of the British film industry, so often undercapitalized and confused as to its objectives, was generally on an 'up' in the later eighties. Richard Attenborough secured international commercial success with his *Gandhi* (directed by David Lean); *The Last Emperor* was another successful blockbuster. But consistent success was to be found among the low-budget films sponsored by television's Channel Four. Particularly interesting were *My Beautiful Laundrette* (involving British Asians and non-hetero-sexual relationships), *Mona Lisa* (in which the dominant figure is a beautiful black woman), and *Wish You Were Here* (featuring a liberated young woman, Lynda, in 1940s Britain).

Here is an extract from David Leland's script for *Wish You Were Here*. Lynda, who has left home (her mother is dead) is working in a tea-room; her father (Hubert) turns up as a customer:

MANAGER: You're fired, you are dismissed, get out.

[*Everybody is now watching, the café is at a standstill.*]

LYNDA [*To everybody, about the* MANAGER]: This one goes around with his brown nose, up in the air, down on the carpet, lardy-dah this, lardy-dah that. [*Announces*] The cook spits in the buns and we all piss in the teapots.

[*A customer holds her mouth, another chokes on her tea.*]

MANAGER: Out! Ladies and gentlemen –

HUBERT: She's a bad lot, that's the truth, nothing but trouble. That's the way it's always been.

LYNDA: This is my father.

HUBERT [*Gives testimony*]: Ever since she could speak she's uttered nothing but filth. From the day she uttered her first word. Her tongue has caused nothing but trouble.

LYNDA: This is my father speaking.

HUBERT: Sometimes I doubt it.

LYNDA: An insult to my dead mother.

MANAGER [*Who has gone very pale*]: I'm sorry, but this cannot go on.

LYNDA: I'm up the duff! That's what's up his nose. I'm pregnant. In the club!

[*Shock horror.*]

MANAGER: Right! That's it! That's enough.

LYNDA: A man's willy has entered my person and left a little visitor behind.

[*More shock horror. The* MANAGER *marches purposefully in one direction, then the other, like a chicken with no head.* LYNDA *is by now standing on a chair.*]

Whatever people might say about Thatcherite 'morality' and the 'new piety', that the roads to freedom laid down in the sixties could not suddenly be blocked was apparent, to choose but one example, in continuing developments in British film censorship. Early in 1989 the Board proposed that in between the 15 category (suitable for showing to those over fifteen) and the PG category (parental guidance required) there should be a new 12 category. As reported in the *Independent* on 27 January 1989, James Firman, director of the British Board of Film Classification, stated:

Crocodile Dundee is the best example of all. We had to give that a 15 on the single word 'fucking'. It's lunatic that 12, 13 and 14-year-olds should be stopped seeing such an otherwise suitable film because of one word that they probably hear every day.

The report continued:

The Board has recently stopped giving films a PG certificate which include 'shitting' and 'arse-hole', but which are unobjectionable in other ways. However, it feels that putting such movies into the 15 class is unduly restrictive.

There was, of course, no way of reinventing the pop revolution of the sixties. But in March 1984 the *Observer* was reporting that 'Britain has returned to its customary position as the world leader in pop music'. The groups singled out at that time (the occasion was the annual American Grammy Awards) were Culture Club, The Police, and Duran Duran. Later in the eighties the popular music scene was noteworthy for the strong Irish influence: unkind comments were made about the musical talents of Bob Geldof, but he certainly, and very deservedly, held centre stage for his notion of Band Aid, using popular performers to raise money for the starving in Ethiopia; in March 1985 *Rolling Stone* nominated the Dublin group U2 as 'band of the eighties'. In April 1987 the group appeared on the cover of *Time* (only The Beatles and The Who had managed this previously). U2's album *The Joshua Tree*, released in March 1987 quickly went to the top of the album charts in both the UK and the USA. The point to bring out at the end of this inevitably hasty catalogue is that U2 songs were distinguished by a strong element of social criticism and political protest.

Early in this book I made much of British achievements in science. In the eighties the worry was that scientific funding was now seriously inadequate, a point almost inadvertently touched on in passing in the most famous work of scientific popularization of the decade, *A Brief History of Time: From the Big Bang to Black Holes* (1988) by the Lucasian Professor of Mathematics at Cambridge University, Stephen W. Hawking.

Hawking explained and summarized latest developments in our under-standing of the universe, many the product of his own work. The universe, it seems, *is* expanding, though at a decreasing rate (see above, page 67). Hawking's aspiration was the unification of quantum mechanics and general relativity, offering the new possibility

that space and time together might form a finite, four-dimensional space without similarities or boundaries, like the surface of the earth but with more dimensions. It seems that this idea could explain many of the observed features of the universe, such as its large-scale uniformity and also the smaller-scale departures from homogeneity, like galaxies, stars, and even human beings. It would even account for the arrow of time that we observe. But if the universe is completely self-contained, with no singularities or boundaries, and completely described by a unified theory, that has profound implications for the rôle of God as Creator.

The rather odd *mélange* of values contained in the long quotation with which I began this chapter are very open to criticism, and their perpetuation could well lead to the long-term impoverishment of British culture. But as things stood in 1989 it would not be accurate to see the hallmark of that culture, or of British political values generally, as either conformity or stagnation. However, there were two major problems. First, the forces of pluralism and dissidence still lacked any effective political mechanism. Second, the threat to British life from a homogenized 'Ameri-canization' (a travesty, in fact, of so much that is delightful about American life), something over which so many had so often cried 'wolf' in the past, was now a very pressing danger. It was a danger brought not by American soldiers defending democracy, nor even by free cultural exchange, but over a 'welcome' mat laid out by Her Majesty's Government.

Part Five

A Society at Odds with Itself
1989–97

24

Divisive Bequests: Cultural and Political

It is impossible to understand British society today without keeping firmly in mind two distinctive bequests from earlier decades. On the one side we have the irreversible cultural transformations of the 1960s (fully examined in Part Two), which, above all, dispelled the lingering miasma of Victorianism, yet at the same time reinforced both the historic tradition of independence and tolerance embodied in what I have called 'secular Anglicanism', and the more recent surge of community spirit engendered by the Second World War. On the other side we have the political legacy of the seventies and eighties: that polarization between 'loonie left' and Thatcherite radical right, which was quite alien to the Anglican instinct for consensus and respect for the other person's point of view. When leading Cabinet colleagues squeezed a weeping Mrs Thatcher out of office in November 1990 because they realized that she was now an electoral liability, behind the almost audible sigh of relief which ran through the country there was a sense that a new era of conciliation and caring politics was about to begin. The new Prime Minister, John Major, expressed his wish to preside over a society 'at ease with itself'. Seldom were decent hopes more callously dashed. The mumbo-jumbo of market economics became an unquestioned mantra, the ethics of Scrooge a central principle of government. Bare-faced authoritarianism and unabashed contempt for the rules of accountability reached heights unparalleled since the early nineteenth century. The disturbing trends I identified in Part Four – disregard for public safety; ordinary people, talked into buying their homes or taking out private pensions, being unable to keep up payments on the former, and finding the latter falling far short of what had been promised; beggars in the streets; the homeless in cardboard boxes – far from being reversed, became endogenous characteristics of a society manifestly 'at odds with itself'.

The sixties are out of fashion, save for the fashion for phoney nostalgia. Yet the policies that led to the steady weakening of the British economy – absurd overseas commitments, under-investment in the manufacturing economy and its infrastructure, a 'mixed economy' with too much emphasis on large units, whether public or private, too little on small business enterprises – were not initiated in the sixties. To get to the real heart of that vital decade we should ignore the tiny posturing minority and instead compare the lot of all sorts of ordinary people in the middle fifties with what it had become for analogous individuals and groups by the early seventies, and has remained ever since. Consider the teenage girl, not just the one who is already pregnant, but all the others who are terrified of becoming pregnant; consider the young person (male or female) with talent for design, drawing, acting, music-making, football; consider the disabled of all ages and either sex; consider the homosexual; consider the young people (male or female) tied to home till they can establish a marriage of their own; consider the couple trapped in an unworkable marriage; consider the young women in the dancehalls forever shuffling expressionlessly backwards; consider the sniggering furtiveness, the guilt over sex; consider the dominance over all walks of life, from government to entertainment, of those with the correct education and the correct accents; consider the earnings, the material circumstances and the leisure activities of the working class and lower-middle class; consider the ubiquitousness of the tinny songs of Guy Mitchell and Doris Day, and the feebleness of British movies after the collapse of Ealing; consider the slavish adherence to fashion and proper decorum; consider the contortions of female sunbathers endeavouring to combine maximum exposure to the sun with minimum outrage to public pudicity. If the cultural revolution of the sixties had its male chauvinist aspects, it also contributed to the launching, partly in very response to the manifestations of decontrolled male sexuality, of activist feminism. These developments of the sixties have continued, and, despite Thatcherite pieties and John Major's empty and hypocritical cry of 'back to basics', have steadily accelerated: as we shall see, they lie at the heart of British social behaviour today.

Since early Victorian times Britain was admired abroad for, and prided herself on, her political institutions and stability, her high levels of civic loyalty and the standards of public service maintained by that special élite within the class structure, known, in a slightly mocking fashion that is rather characteristically British, as 'the great and the good'. She gained little admiration – till the Second World War at least – for her high culture, and still less for her popular culture. The British were reckoned drab, inhibited, and Philistine. Young people in the fifties looked to America for popular culture, and to Italy for fashion. But, for the very reason that Britain had very little in the way of authentic, up-to-date, popular music, there was an empty vessel waiting to be filled, and that vessel was in fact filled to overflowing by the young groups playing mainly in working-class areas, still household names and exemplars for all that followed. With pop music came pop fashion, and also a period of vigorous innovation in British film and British television. And, as we have seen, British high culture flourished, just barely being menaced in the eighties by the introduction of 'productivity and efficiency' criteria.

Fundamentalist tendencies in both left and right began to manifest themselves around the same time, the early to mid-seventies. Among trade unionists the basic influence was that of orthodox (or 'vulgar') Marxism, and the outcome was seen in the struggles culminating in the winter of discontent, in Scargill's disastrous leadership, and in the high profile assumed by Militant Tendency. Among intellectuals (most significantly in educational institutions), the influence was that of neo-Marxist post-structuralism (subsequently subsumed under the blanket term 'postmodernism'). Inflation and high-handed trade union activism under the Wilson and Callaghan governments (in themselves far from being extremist) left a general legacy of mistrust for Labour policies among certain sections of the electorate. Labour's marked movement to the left after 1979, under fundamentalist pressure, simply increased this mistrust, further augmented by the corruption, kowtowing to public service unions, and questionable use of funds (in support of gay and lesbian activities, for example) among certain left-wing Labour local authorities. Fashionable postmodernist ideas (representing correct speech and grammar, for instance, as instruments of 'bourgeois power') began to appear incompatible with the maintenance of basic educational standards. Thus, while rampant Thatcherism produced an increasingly divided and polarized society, the forces of pluralism and dissidence, and, one might add, the supporters of a genuinely civilized and caring society, lacked, as I put it at the end of the last chapter, any effective political mechanism. The fundamental principles of the radical right, upheld by John Major, and, a few setbacks apart, triumphant throughout the State, were utterly at odds with the liberating spirit of the sixties, predominant (though, of course, not uncontested) throughout society.

Margaret Thatcher's general standing was seriously undermined by the unpopularity of the poll tax. Her position within the charmed circle of Cabinet politics suffered a blow when her Chancellor of the Exchequer, Nigel Lawson (who, in having the pound 'shadow' the German mark, was following a 'European' policy while Thatcher persisted in giving her ear to her 'anti-European' personal adviser, Professor Alan Walters; in effect, Lawson was overvaluing sterling, while at the same time stimulating a dangerously unsustainable boom) had the sense to resign while his spurious reputation as a financial wizard was still intact. She was all but terminally damaged when her increasingly strident anti-European statements (together with her graceless treatment of him) provoked not just the resignation of Sir Geoffrey Howe, but a resignation speech of such merciless acuity and wit that it was as devastating as it was unexpected from that sheep-like source. Challenged to a leadership election by Michael Heseltine, Thatcher actually secured a majority just short of what was required for outright victory in the first round, but was persuaded (notably by Kenneth Clarke) that to go to a second round would be to court humiliating defeat. The beneficiary was Major, Thatcher's own preferred choice, but, despite what was said at the time, it seems unlikely that any other available Conservative would have broken decisively with Thatcherism. The world had now moved into recession, and Britain, thanks to Lawson's excesses, was in deeper than most. Even formerly moderate Conservatives ('wets') had sold their souls to the god of naked market economics, while undistinguished right-wingers were in the ascendant on the back benches. Major's policy, in face of the dreadful condition of the national finances, was one of unrelenting retrenchment; but no leading Conservative, least of all Heseltine, spoke out seriously against it.

The poll tax was rapidly abolished (though thousands of non-payers continued to be pursued), and replaced by a modified form of the old rating system, the Council Tax; the revenue shortfall was to be met by increasing VAT. Major's great personal initiative was the Citizen's Charter, setting targets for public services, and empowering citizens to claim financial compensation where targets were not met – a cheap and ineffectual alternative to improving the services in the first place. Labour had stood high in the opinion polls at the height of Mrs Thatcher's unpopularity over the poll tax, but had fallen behind again with the accession of

John Major. Neil Kinnock, having secured the dropping of the commitment to unilateral nuclear disarmament in 1989, was, all informed critics agreed, doing an excellent job in 'modernizing' the Labour Party and extending its appeal. As the general election approached – Major had decided to go for April 1992 – the polls began to put Labour in the lead. Private Labour surveys suggested that the public rated Labour's front bench more highly than the Government, but Major consistently came out with higher ratings than Kinnock. The polls, in fact, had built-in flaws (since corrected) and the odds, in reality, remained slightly against Labour. An independent columnist of the Conservative *Sunday Times* put things perceptively a couple of months before the election in an article entitled 'Ruthless grip on the levers of power gives the Tories the edge':

> Ministers have displayed a ruthlessness in manipulating the levers of power that would have won the admiration of many a fallen Communist party boss . . .
>
> Ministers have all the resources of the state . . . at their disposal: advantages that would, by themselves, be enough to make it an unequal struggle. But these are only a fraction of the weapons in the Conservatives' arsenal.
>
> They have, for a start, much more money. In addition to government advertising, the Tories are likely to outspend Labour three-to-one in newspaper and poster advertising. They also have the press . . . seven national dailies, with a combined circulation of almost 10 million copies, support the government, compared with only two (the *Daily Mirror* and *The Guardian*), with a circulation of 3.5 million, that back Labour. Actually, the imbalance is more pronounced than that, for the figures fail to measure the seething, partisan mendacity of such papers as the *Mail* and the *Express*, which, on their day, can make the equally partisan *Mirror* look like the *Christian Science Monitor*.

All that apart, canvassers continued to find distrust of Labour and doubt about its tax plans, and, most notably, hostility towards Kinnock. It is just possible that in a situation tilting away from Labour a truly charismatic leader, without previous associations with the left, might have managed to attain the hung parliament that preoccupied so many commentators. But, in the event, the Conservative victory, 7.6 per cent over Labour in votes cast, 64 seats over Labour, and 21 over all, was not really very surprising. Kinnock resigned from the Labour leadership, to be succeeded by the earnest, honest, moderate, and wickedly witty shadow Chancellor John Smith; sadly, it took Smith's untimely death in May 1994 – after he had succeeded in democratizing Labour's internal voting procedures – to reveal the enormous respect in which he was held in all sections of the community. With an instinct for success it had not always shown, Labour chose as successor the young, personable and ultra-moderate Tony Blair.

Leadership elections and general elections notwithstanding, certain clusters of issues across the years from 1989 to 1995 consistently reveal Britain as a more divided nation than at any time since the aftermath of the First World War. It would be naïve to point the finger solely at politicians, even the worst ideologues of right and left. There is a wider framework of economic, technological and global factors, forming in the eighties but only fully in place in the nineties, which introduced new insecurities into the lives of people of all social classes and made establishing the proper balance between constructive government action and untrammelled private enterprise more problematic than either the Keynesians of the sixties or the Thatcherites of the eighties had ever envisaged. But that does not, of course, exonerate politicians from an obligation to act responsibly and rationally.

Nineteen eighty-nine was the second year of the ill-judged Lawson–Thatcher boom during which, as had tended to be the case throughout the eighties, too much investment went into unproductive sectors of the economy such as services and property. 1990 and 1991 were years of deepest recession, in which GDP declined and official unemployment figures went up over 3 million. At the beginning of 1992, the oft-threatened death sentence on the Scottish Ravenscraig steelworks was finally pronounced. But redundancies were now striking too at middle-class jobs in the hitherto prosperous South of England. The event which gave rise to most intensive political controversy was the so-called Black Wednesday (16 September 1992 – in its jovial way, the *Sun* newspaper subsequently always insisted on referring to 'White Wednesday'). Lawson had resigned over Thatcher's hostility to his informal attempt to link sterling to the mark, yet by October 1990 informed opinion (Labour as well as Conservative) was that formally joining the European Exchange Rate Mechanism (ERM) would be the ideal means of ensuring monetary stability and low inflation – the pound would be tied to a band running at 6 per cent on either side of DM 2.95. John Major, Lawson's successor as Chancellor, was responsible for implementing the decision; in August 1992 he was telling journalists that he could envisage sterling replacing the mark as the anchor currency of the ERM – a classic pronouncement from a Government long on assertion and dismally short on performance.

Within weeks massive international currency movements were putting pressure on Europe's four weakest currencies, the escudo, the peseta, the lira and the pound. The Government announced its commitment to keeping the pound within the ERM band. On 13 September the lira was devalued; Chancellor Norman Lamont rejected the very notion of any devaluation of the pound. On the morning of 16 September the Bank of England was desperately buying sterling; at 11 a.m. the interest rate was put up from 10 to 12 per cent; at 2.15 p.m. to 15 per cent; at 7.30 p.m. down to 12 per cent again, as Lamont at the same time announced Britain's withdrawal from the ERM; and next day back to 10 per cent. The Prime Minister waited for a convenient moment before sacking a bitterly protesting Lamont (who was succeeded by Kenneth Clarke). Government pretensions had been ripped apart, though as the pound slipped down (by about 15 per cent) to a realistic value, exports benefited. At the same time the world economy, and therefore the British economy, were moving out of recession. By the beginning of 1995 some of the figures were looking quite impressive: 3.5 per cent growth over 1994; unemployment (on the Government's own not universally trusted figures) down well below 3 million; inflation at a 27-year low of 2 per cent. Yet, as opinion polls amply demonstrated, there was no sense of well-being throughout the country; Government plans to increase VAT on domestic heating drew attention to the fact that overall people were being more highly taxed under the Conservatives than they had been at the end of the last Labour Government. That a backbench revolt inflicted a humiliating defeat on this issue scarcely served to raise the credibility of the Government.

Much of what happened in Britain was governed by international trends, including trends in science and technology (most obviously the continuing and accelerating IT revolution). Of major scientific and technological discoveries, a smaller proportion than at any time for two centuries was emanating from Britain. The reduction in scientific investment initiated by Thatcher continued under Major. What *A Great British Success Story* had been for the arts, the White Paper, *Realising Our Potential: a strategy for science, engineering and technology* (May 1993), was for the sciences. Introducing it, William Waldegrave, the responsible minister, declared that it

puts science and engineering back where it belongs – on top of the agenda for solving our current problems and raising our future prosperity – and closer to the heart of government . . . (*Independent*, 27 May 1993)

There was to be no advance on the £6 billion currently allocated to research; in the authentic Thatcherite style the research councils were to be reconstituted under the control of chief executives, scientists themselves being sidelined; the number of science PhDs was to be cut. Short-term accountancy and concern for immediate returns are no more helpful to the sciences than they are to the arts. Denied essential resources, leading scientists were already leaving the country, two or three a year. This brain drain was accelerated by changes in the National Health Service, starving it of research funding. When two leading medical scientists left in July 1994, the editor of *Gene Therapy*, in sentences which could be applied across the board to the Government's 'reforms' of research, scholarship and higher education, commented:

These people are the leaders of British science. Why should they waste their time on committees carrying out hours of paperwork when they should be allowed to get on with the research that is so desperately needed? (*Independent*, 22 July 1994)

Arguments may legitimately rage over economic policy; one cannot assume that an alternative government would have done better; Conservatives were entitled to claim that pain in 1990–91 would yield steady growth in the future. But on the matter of the collapse of standards in public life there can be no debate. On 17 January 1994 the Committee of Public Accounts of the House of Commons (an all-party committee whose membership reflected the overall Conservative majority in the House, but which was chaired by a widely respected Labour MP) published what will come to be regarded as one of the key public documents of the time, a report entitled *The Proper Conduct of Public Business*. It began in the thunderous yet measured tones of such documents down the years:

1. In recent years we have seen and reported on a number of serious failures in administrative and financial systems and controls within departments and other public bodies, which have led to money being wasted or otherwise improperly spent. These failings represent a departure from the standards of public conduct which have mainly been established during the past 140 years. This was the period following the publication of the Northcote and Trevelyan Report which condemned the nepotism, the incompetence and other defects of the Civil Service and brought about fundamental change. It is from that period that we acquired the principles and the standards which have come to be copied by some

countries and admired by many more. It is our task to retain these standards.

2. There have recently been fundamental changes in the way in which government departments and public bodies such as those in the NHS carry out their work. These changes, which include the introduction of executive agencies and the growth in numbers of non-departmental public bodies, are intended to improve the provision of public services through greater delegation of responsibilities, streamlining and a more entrepreneurial approach to the work. The attention of staff at all levels is rightly focused on making a success of these changes.

3. But at a time of change it is important to ensure that proper standards are maintained in the conduct of public business. Annex 1 to this report sets out a number of failings on which we have reported in key areas of financial control, compliance with rules, the stewardship of public money and assets, and generally getting value for the taxpayer's money . . .

The 'fundamental changes' mentioned, and to some extent identified, in paragraph 2 originated in the third Thatcher Government (Next Steps Initiative of 1988, aimed at reducing the number of civil servants and contracting out government work, National Health Service and Community Care Act of 1990), and were enthusiastically extended by the Major Governments (notably in the 'Efficiency Measures' of 1991). Basically they involved transferring power from civil service departments, from elected local authorities, and from bodies of professional experts (scientists, doctors, academics, etc.) to agencies staffed by government nominees (right-wing businessmen and Thatcherite politicians) – the notorious 'quangos' (quasi-autonomous non-governmental organizations), which had existed under Labour Governments, but which then numbered over 1,500 and exercised power in a hitherto unheard-of fashion. The 'internal market' was introduced into the NHS (see next chapter), market testing and performance-related pay were principles applied throughout, and vast salaries were available to executives and managers, balanced by redundancies among those who did the real work, doctors, nurses, lecturers, teachers. The 'failings' mentioned in paragraph 3 ranged from incompetence on an astronomical scale to downright corruption, costing the public finances at least £2.5 billion in 1992–3. Among the most notorious cases were the Overseas Development Administration's illegal spend of £234 million on the Malaysian Pergau dam project, and several examples of the purchase under dubious circumstances, and at enormous cost, of computer systems which subsequently did not work (£48 million spent by the Department of Employment, £20 million by the Wessex Health Authority – yet the mad rush after inadequately thought-out and inadequately tested computer systems spread throughout the country and used up cash which could have been spent on the nurses, teachers, etc. mentioned above). The report revealed clearly the gap yawning between what, traditionally, public service in Britain was believed to entail with respect to moral standards, and the laxity and bungling the 'fundamental changes' actually entailed. The very language of the report, and, indeed, the meritorious fact of its actually having been written, demonstrated that the traditional image of British public service remained very strong; its content demonstrated a tragic disjunction between how the British public (or at least those who thought about such matters) believed public business ought to be conducted, and how it actually was being conducted.

Among traditional local authorities it was generally Labour councils which stood accused of misuse of public funds, with Lambeth council continuing to be a notorious example. But in January 1994 it became public knowledge that throughout the eighties the Conservative council in Westminster had been following policies described by the District Auditor as 'disgraceful and improper'. In brief, the council had been using housing funds and housing stock to bring into marginal wards owner-occupiers who would be likely to vote Conservative, while deliberately denying rented accommodation to homeless families who would be likely to vote Labour. In 1995 the multiple scandal that attracted most attention was concerned with the manner in which the privatization policy initiated by Margaret Thatcher (for privatization by year see Table 11) had been carried out; the perquisites which had fallen to politicians themselves closely involved in specific privatizations; the general conduct of the privatized utilities and the share options and vast salary increases the directors of these utilities were awarding themselves. As earlier chapters in this book have indicated there is no question of either public ownership, or private ownership, being in themselves 'a good thing'. Everything depends on the precise circumstances: much of the early Thatcher programme can be credited with the laudatory aims of securing much-needed investment and of widening the circle of share ownership. What was thought scandalous in the mid nineties was that almost as a matter of routine Government Ministers who had been involved in privatizing a particular industry soon appeared among the directors of the newly privatized firms; in almost every case, shares in the new companies had

Table 11: List of privatizations by year

British Petroleum	1979–87
British Aerospace	1981–85
Cable and Wireless	1981–85
Britoil	1982–85
British Telecom	1984–93
British Gas	1986–90
British Airports Authority	1987
British Airways	1987
Rolls-Royce	1987
British Steel	1988
Water companies (England and Wales)	1989
Regional electricity companies (England and Wales)	1990
Electricity generating companies (England and Wales)	1991
Scottish electricity companies	1991
Northern Ireland electricity	1992–93

been sold at bargain prices; the new privatized utilities both followed pricing and service policies which were unfriendly, or even punitive, towards their poorest customers, and instituted large-scale redundancies among their workpeople; at the same time their directors granted themselves 'rolling' payments and share options which offered total insurance against ever being dismissed, and took grotesque pay rises – the *cause célèbre* was that of Cedric Brown, head of British Gas, who in late 1994 received an increase of 75 per cent which took his salary to £475,000 (but, as Table 12 shows, this, in 1993–94, was no exceptional figure).

Bonuses and share options could add a good deal more – in the case of David Morris, for example, shares worth £400,000.

The Conservative-supporting *Sunday Times* is a good guide to when issues become a serious threat to popular forbearance. 'Time to halt the gravy train' was the title of a thunderous leader in August 1994 (dealing largely, but not exclusively, with newly privatized companies):

Against a background of tight pay restraint, life in many boardrooms seems increasingly other-worldly to ordinary folk.

Reports of telephone number salaries, two- and three-year rolling employment contracts, share options worth millions and enhanced pension rights had become too frequent to ignore.

*

Table 12: Salaries of Chief Executives in Privatized Utilities

		£
Sir Iain Vallance	British Telecom	650,000
Cedric Brown	British Gas	475,000
John Baker	National Power	375,000
Ed Wallis	PowerGen	351,000
Sir Desmond Pitcher	North West Water	338,000
David Jefferies	National Grid Co.	330,000
David Morris	Northern Electric	300,000
James Smith	Eastern Group	269,000
Henry Casley	Southern Electric	258,000
Ian Preston	Scottish Power	255,000
Bryan Townsend	Midlands Electricity	250,000
Michael Hoffman	Thames Water	250,000

The *Sun* (which had claimed credit for the Conservative election victory, but which had taken to referring to John Major as 'the grey dwarf', and which had been scathing about VAT increases) was characteristically to the point in a leading article (7 February 1995) entitled 'Stop this Greed':

> We've become used to the sickening greed of the privatised company bosses.
>
> They can't pass a trough without plunging their snouts in.
>
> Gas, water, BT. You name it, they'll milk it.
>
> But Powergen's Ed Wallis, who scooped £1.2 million in share options without risking a penny of his own money, is in a class of his own . . .
>
> He says his millionaire status is a reward for Powergen 'doing so well' after shedding thousands of jobs . . .

Alongside was a cartoon showing a self-satisfied middle-aged man walking out of a jeweller's carrying a tray piled high with valuables, including a crown and a sceptre. The place is surrounded by armed police, but the officer in charge shouts: 'Hold your fire . . . it's just an electricity boss!'

The major issues of quangos, corruption, privatization and greed apart, the years 1993 to 1995 were marked by a series of remarkable and often hilarious episodes in which Conservative ministers and MPs were caught with their pants down or their hands in the till. The sexual transgressions would scarcely have been of any account had not the Prime Minister, with that addiction to the feeble slogan which characterizes him, not declared a (quickly buried) campaign of 'back to basics' (family values and such), but incidents culminating in a *Sunday Times* revelation that two ministers had been prepared to accept bribes to ask parliamentary questions, and allegations against a third of improperly accepting hospitality, brought into general currency one word to describe the state of politics, 'sleaze'. On 25 October 1994 the Prime Minister announced the establishment of a permanent (this was unprecedented) standing committee, under Lord Nolan (immediately dubbed 'Sleaze-finder General' by the *Independent*):

to examine current concerns about the standards of conduct of all holders of public office, including arrangements relating to financial and commercial activities, and make recommendations as to any change in present arrangements which might be required to ensure the highest standards in public life.

Manifestly, 'efficiency measures', market testing, and privatization were signally failing to do so.

Suddenly, in February 1995, the Government, under pressure from the Nolan Committee, began to show that it had some inkling of the error of its ways. The thoroughly Conservative *Daily Mail*, in its main leader (7 February 1995), reacted vigorously:

At last, the Government is to come clean (well almost) about the cohorts it appoints to more than 1,300 public bodies.

Yesterday the Uriah Heep of this Tory Cabinet, David Hunt, conceded that in future there would have to be more openness about the way people are chosen to fill such jobs.

Not before time.

There is now an abiding distrust of a system through which a party so long in national office can create a countrywide network of influence and obligation by picking politically sympathetic men and women to run these ever-proliferating quangos.

To be blunt, most objective observers are agreed that ministerial patronage under the Tories has increased, is increasing and ought to be diminished.

Now the placatory Mr Hunt assures us that more of the posts will have to be advertised . . .

Although these modest reforms are to be welcomed, how suggestive that they are announced on the very eve of the Government's own submission to the Nolan committee's inquiry into standards in public life.

Just once in a while, wouldn't it be lovely to hear ministers proclaim their good deed for the day without so obvious a prompt?

Standards in Public Life was published in May 1995. In restrained, gentlemanly language, the Nolan Committee called for full disclosure of MPs' outside interests and remuneration, restrictions upon ministers taking up positions in companies with which they had had official dealings, and regulation of appointments to quangos. Conservative MPs protested bitterly; opinion polls showed that the public did not feel that the recommendations went far enough. Meantime the full report of the Scott Enquiry into whether ministers in the last Thatcher Government had tried to mislead Parliament (and the courts) over changes in the professed policy of a ban on arms sales to Iraq was awaited.

One area in which harmony between society and its rulers might have been expected was that of crime, policing and punishment. Surveys showed that crime was a priority concern throughout the country. In England and Wales recorded crime doubled between 1979 and 1992; there was then a slight easing off, with a fall of two per cent in 1993; none the less, the annual rate was still equivalent to one crime for every ten people. Michael Howard, the Home Secretary, put himself forward as the protagonist of tough treatment for criminals, trouble-makers, and even mere suspects (embodied in his massive and trouble-prone Criminal Justice Act), and in this, though strongly opposed by expert and informed liberal opinion, he was to a great extent representing the sentiments (see Chapter 26) of a majority of the British people. The problem was the gap between Howard's pronouncements and his actual performance. Applause is cheaply won at Conservative Party conferences, but seldom more cheaply than when the Home Secretary declared to the 1993 Conference, 'prison works'. Under his tutelage, prison most assuredly did not 'work', both in the general sense that overcrowded and understaffed jails were quite obviously serving as forcing grounds for criminal and other antisocial activities, and in the simple sense of failing to keep prisoners safely confined. Attention was constantly being drawn to the counter-productive (as well as frequently insecure) character of British prisons in the official reports of Judge Stephen Tumim, who in February 1995 pointed out that young women going into Styal prison in Cheshire were coming out drug addicts.

Early in September 1994 five IRA terrorists and a highly dangerous armed robber shot their way out of the special secure unit in the custom-built maximum security Whitemoor prison in Cambridgeshire; three weeks later Semtex explosive was discovered inside a sealed property store at the same prison. On the last day of the year the imprisoned serial murderer Frederick West escaped, not only from justice, but from any possible exploration of his mental condition, by hanging himself in his prison cell. The new year opened with prisoners at Everthorpe jail, near Hull, going on the rampage on two separate nights, then on 3 January, while these riots were continuing, two very violent murderers and an arsonist got clean away from the Parkhurst maximum security jail on the Isle of Wight. While the three were still at large (they were eventually recaptured still on the island), three more prisoners escaped from Littlehey prison near Huntingdon. It quickly became known that with respect to both of the major break-outs, the Home Secretary, and the highly paid former executive, Derek Lewis, who, though innocent of all prison experience, had, in keeping with Government Next Step and privatization policies, been created Director-General of the recently-formed Prison Service, had been warned well in advance of serious security risks at both prisons, but had taken no action. Specifically, Parkhurst governor John Marriott had called for a touch-sensitive alarm on the perimeter fence – not installed because of the expense. Ignoring persistent and well-substantiated calls for his resignation, Howard instead sacked Marriott (as, subsequently, he refused to renew Tumim's appointment). Howard had promised the Conservative Conference tougher policies all round (while at the same time seeking economies wherever he could find them, not least in the police forces); but, the prison fiascos apart, he encountered another series of humiliations when his ill-considered and high-handed actions were rejected in the House of Lords and in the courts. Noting that Howard was at least succeeding in bringing the prison population up again to close on 50,000, the level-headed Home Affairs correspondent of the *Observer* commented (25 September 1994): 'The direction is towards America – a society at war with itself, with an ever-higher proportion of the population in jail,' continuing:

Under Michael Howard, everything that was imaginative and constructive in criminal justice has been rubbished: rehabilitation itself has become a dirty word. Mauled by the Lords his Criminal Justice Bill may have been – but it will be back with its dismal plans to lock up children, condemning them to abuse and socialization as criminals, and its erosion of the presumption of innocence in the abolition of the right to silence.

In the early nineties grave doubts about the English judicial system were created by some spectacular cases (notably, the 'Guildford Four' and the 'Birmingham Six', all wrongly accused of being IRA terrorists) in which, on appeal, prisoners serving long sentences were released after it had been conclusively demonstrated that the original police evidence leading to their convictions had been fabricated. Opinion polls suggested that the police still retained the confidence of the public, but only just. Certainly reductions in police forces resulting from the cash limits of early 1995 were not calculated to allay public disquiet over crime. As the *Independent* Home Affairs Correspondent reported (25 January 1995):

Chief Constables warned yesterday that a reduction in service and a less visible police force could drive the public into the arms of second-rate private security firms or vigilante patrols.

There was cause for concern at the level of the humble magistrates' court, where there were quite harrowing instances of comfortably-off magistrates practising class war against low-income people in arrears with the (now abolished) poll tax. In August 1994 magistrates in Durham sentenced a 74-year-old former miner, unable to look after himself, and taken into care suffering from malnutrition, to thirty-one days. In October Bolton magistrates sentenced a 46-year-old mother of four, with a physically and mentally disabled 21-year-old son, to twenty-eight days. In January 1995 Lincoln magistrates sentenced a young mother on income support to nine days for poll tax arrears of £22 (all cases reported in the *Independent*, 25 January 1995). All of these sentences, and about 3,500 like them, were contrary to law, and in every case High Court judges ordered release within days – but the sense of the existence within one sector of society itself of intense, punitive animosity towards the underprivileged is one that lingers nastily. In fact these cases, in which the defendants had been denied legal aid, fell foul of the European Commission of Human Rights, which declared the British Government liable for millions of pounds of compensation to those falsely imprisoned (*Independent*, 28 January 1995). On the very same day the British Government was severely criticized by another international body, the United Nations Committee on the Rights of the Child: the Committee was concerned about child poverty, children sleeping and begging in the streets, and Michael Howard's plans for secure centres for child offenders – likely, in fact, to be in breach of United Nations laws.

The British public may not have been too troubled by international criticisms, but no one could be untroubled by the displays of incompetence and disregard for ordinary human rights at all levels of authority. And complaints were widespread too over falling standards of service in every aspect of everyday life. In November 1994 it became known that while British Telecom was making huge profits for its shareholders it was failing to provide proper safeguards for the data it held on its customers. Delays in the underfunded, and sometimes mismanaged, ambulance services could prove lethal. Privatized gas and electricity showrooms stopped servicing gas and electrical appliances and concentrated on selling them. Train and bus services got more expensive, more infrequent and more chaotic. Not surprisingly planned privatizations of the Post Office and of the railways were widely unpopular. Opposition to the former from Conservative backbenchers led to its abandonment. Opposition politicians argued that the Post Office, while remaining in public owner-ship, should be opened to private investment. Suspicions were aroused that the Cabinet's refusal to allow the Post Office to expand its services in this way was due to ideological hostility to anything short of complete privatization. Meantime there was a 'rising storm of complaints' (*The Times*, 29 November 1991) over one group of institutions which never had been nationalized, and so never privatized, but which were joining in the general stampede towards putting shareholders first and customers last, the banks. Small businessmen complained of exorbitant loan charges, while the Consumers' Association reported on 'huge charges, imposed without warning, by banks which bungled time and time again – and then relied on customers to point out what they had bungled'; *Times* cartoonist Calman had a marvellous little drawing in which a bank manager is saying to a protesting customer: 'We're a Caring Bank – we care about making lots of money.' Particularly irritating, and highly characteristic of this society at odds with itself, were the oleaginous television commercials with the bogus slogans, 'the listening bank', 'we're here to make life easier', etc., when, as the Consumers' Association reported in December 1991, one in eight customers was charged incor-rectly, one in six had problems with a direct debit or standing order, and almost one in five was dissatisfied with the way mistakes were handled. Six years later there had been no improvement.

Public disaffection, the desperate divides between government and governed, between consumers and profit-takers, between the mean-mindedness and phoney moralizing of those in power and the tolerant and community-minded spirit of many sections of society were amply displayed in opinion surveys and polls; all of this was very apparent before the year of sleaze and Tony Blair's accession to the Labour Party leadership. Asked, in December 1993 (in an ICM poll published in the *Observer*) with respect to a list of key qualities, 'which party do you trust?', responses (in percentages) were:

	Conservative	Labour	Lib Dem	None	Don't know
Trustworthy	14	23	19	43	11
Caring	13	34	27	29	13
Sincere	12	23	23	40	15
Hard working	32	44	37	24	15
Competent	21	27	21	32	20
Effective	24	19	14	34	21
Clever	44	34	30	23	16
In touch with ordinary people	9	40	28	31	10
Fair with people	12	35	27	31	14

Most striking of all was the clear sense of a Government utterly out of touch with ordinary people. With respect specifically to that Government, responses were:

	Agree	Disagree	Don't know
Tells the truth	14	77	9
Trusted to run the economy well	20	70	10
Remain party of low taxation	25	64	11
Have made Britain more prosperous	21	68	11
Have made start on creating classless society	19	70	12

A further question revealed which professions were most trusted, and which least (in percentages):

	Most	*Least*
Doctors	81	4
Nurses	79	2
Teachers	49	6
Police officers	41	17
Judges	27	21
Civil Servants	20	15
Estate Agents	6	45
Politicians	5	59
Journalists	3	57
Car Salespeople	3	62

It is noteworthy that opinion was most evenly divided, with a marked absence of positive enthusiasm, over judges and civil servants; and there was slightly more positive hostility to policemen than to civil servants. Three general questions revealed profound disillusionment with the then Parliament, yet a persistence in a basic patriotism and faith in British democracy:

	Agree	*Disagree*	*Don't know*
Parliament can be trusted to tackle the country's problems	29	59	11
Voting in elections is a waste of time	16	79	5
Politicians in other countries seem to be better than our own	21	57	22
I would like to emigrate	25	69	5

In January 1994 only 13 per cent of those polled by MORI, as reported in *The Times*, were satisfied with the way the Government was running the country, with 80 per cent dissatisfied. John Major emerged marginally better, with 21 per cent satisfied with the way he was performing as Prime Minister and 71 per cent dissatisfied. Absence of strong positive enthusiasm for Labour was seen in the ratings for John Smith's performance as Leader of the Opposition: 37 per cent satisfied, with an equal number dissatisfied. Paddy Ashdown's leadership of the Liberal

Democrats rated 42 per cent satisfied, 31 per cent dissatisfied. An NOP poll, printed in the *Independent* (23 April 1994), reflected what I have already said about perceptions of Government handling of crime, taxation, and the economy, while also revealing continuing doubts about Labour's policies on the latter two issues. Figures are of the percentages trusting the two main parties to make the right decisions on the three topics:

	Crime	Taxation	The economy
Conservatives?			
Yes	28	18	22
No	64	76	69
Don't know	8	6	9
Labour?			
Yes	44	34	37
No	39	51	47
Don't know	17	15	16

In September 1989 NOP had tested people's views of what would happen if Labour did manage to win the next election, specifically on (a) taxation, and (b) the economy. A new poll, published in the *Independent* on 27 September 1994, indicated that Tony Blair was having some success in projecting the image of 'New Labour', but that on the economy, and still more taxation, strong doubts persisted, as shown in the table below:

(a) Percentages thinking taxation would be higher, or lower:

	Sept. 1989	Sept. 1994
Higher	40	38
Lower	21	20
About the same	32	37

(b) Percentages thinking economy would be stronger or weaker:

	Sept. 1989	Sept. 1994
Stronger	18	25
Weaker	42	29
About the same	34	38

On 'New Labour' the proposition was put that 'Labour has made big changes for the better in recent years', and the results in percentages were:

Agree	58
Disagree	27
Neither/Don't know	15

Pollsters now knew how not to overestimate Labour's strength; yet an ICM poll conducted on that basis, and published in the *Observer* on 11 December 1994, gave Labour an astonishing 54 per cent, with the Conservatives down to 26 per cent, and the Liberal Democrats at 17 per cent. In the new year Conservative support was to drop below 20 per cent. In three successive by-elections the Conservative Government had lost seats to the Lib Dems. At Dudley West on 15 December there was a swing to Labour of 29 per cent. The turnout of 46.95 per cent (compared with 82.1 per cent in the General Election) was said to be normal for a raw December day, but the fact that the total vote for the triumphant Labour candidate actually dropped by over a thousand again suggested an absence of whole-hearted support for Labour, whatever national opinion polls might indicate with respect to the unpopularity of the Government. This impression strengthened as sections of the party expressed open opposition to Blair's successful replacement of Clause IV of the Party constitution (identifying public ownership as a fundamental objective) with a new clause stressing social justice as the fundamental value. The 1995 local elections, first in Scotland, then in England, brought unprecedented humiliation for the Conservatives, but, as the *Independent* (6 May) remarked, 'the low turnout could be a warning to Blair'. The Perth and Kinross by-election later in the same month was another humiliation for the Government but an unalloyed triumph for the winners, the Scottish Nationalists. In July John Major challenged his critics within the Conservative Party by resigning his leadership and offering himself for re-election. His gamble paid off and he gave his Cabinet a slight shuffle away from the right, promoting Michael Heseltine to deputy Prime Minister. But it quickly became clear that policy would be as uncompromisingly Thatcherite as ever.

Clearly there was no question of the nation being united behind Labour; apart from long-enduring mistrust, it was obvious that many people did believe in privatization and market economics. Similarly, though there is undoubtedly strong evidence that the community spirit and libertarian attitudes of the sixties were continuing to grow stronger, in face of the opposition to them of those in authority, it is also clear that, on questions of family values, traditional attitudes were far from vanquished, and that attitudes to improved social welfare were not always coherent: it seemed that, while in principle people might support an improved welfare system, they might also object to any consequent increase in their own personal taxation. Here for the moment are some broad trends (to be examined more fully in Chapter 26), as indicated in NOP figures (in per cent) from December 1993, giving responses to certain propositions relating to community or libertarian issues, in comparison with responses to the same propositions in 1987 (in brackets):

'The Government should spend more on welfare benefits for the very poor, even if it leads to higher taxes.'

Agree	76	(55)
Disagree	13	(22)

'A single mother can bring up her child as well as a married couple.'

Agree	48	(30)
Disagree	41	(51)

'People who want children ought to get married.'

Agree	52	(70)
Disagree	35	(17)

All qualifications made, one can, at the very least, conclude that much of society was at odds with the values promulgated by the Government. Still more potent were the increasingly complex divisions opening up between the very well-off and almost everybody else. Just how utterly torn apart British society had become was graphically revealed with the publication in February 1995 of the Joseph Rowntree Foundation report on Income and Wealth, another great document future historians will clasp to their bosoms. Inequality in Britain was worse than it had been for fifty years, and the rate of growth in inequality was worse than in any other developed country save New Zealand. Between 1979 and 1992 the bottom 10 per cent grew steadily worse off, while the next 10 to 20 per cent derived no benefits from economic growth. The number of people with incomes less than half of the national average trebled. Average incomes rose by 36 per cent, but only the top 30 per cent enjoyed rises as large as, or larger than, that. The incomes of the top 10 per cent rose by 62 per cent. The poor were getting poorer and there were more of them. The convenient myth that as the very rich got richer there would be 'a trickle-down effect' to the poor was exposed for the empty propaganda that it was. At the beginning of the nineties the majority were still doing quite well. With the recession of 1990–91, entailing further job losses, and new curtailments in welfare provision (discussed in the next chapter), the poor got still poorer; but the hitherto prospering now too were afflicted by redundancies, market testing, performance appraisal, insecurity and short-term contracts, as well as, in some cases, mortgage repayment problems. Those who were doing very well appeared more and more as a tiny privileged, and not too scrupulous, minority. Many Conservatives were aware of what, despite the confident assertions of the Government, was really happening. 'While we trumpet recovery, the voters do not think the recession has ended ... what we are saying is completely at odds with their experience,' Conservative Party deputy-chairman John Maples reported to the Prime Minister in a secret report, leaked to, and published in, the *Financial Times* (21 November 1994). The Conservatives, he said, had appeared to promise a classless society, but 'the reality is now', he continued (in a phrase worthy of bringing this chapter to a close) 'that the rich are getting richer on the backs of the rest, who are getting poorer.'

25

Social Reform with a Sting

Throughout this book I have defined the Welfare State as 'the totality of schemes and services through which the central government together with the local authorities assumed a major responsibility for dealing with all the different types of social problems which beset individual citizens'. The powerful thrust of Conservative policy since 1979 had been towards greatly reducing that responsibility, while both encouraging growth in private sector insurance and medicine, and introducing the mantra of the market into state services. Extreme right-wing Conservatives, of whom there were several in the Cabinet, enthusiastically envisaged the complete disappearance of the Welfare State and its replacement by the 'Night-watchman State', solely concerned with minimal support for those unfortunates who had no hope of making provision for themselves. Thatcherite ideology was a driving force, as also was the all-encompassing Government determination not to spend money if it could possibly be avoided. Expert professional opinion, as distinct from political interest, had always had an important influence on the development of social policy, and this continued to be true, though to a decreasing extent as the manager came to be rated more highly than the specialist. Prevention of unemployment had long since disappeared as a fundamental background assumption of the Welfare State (Labour promised economic policies deliberately targeted at the reduction of unemployment), while (despite the emergence of homelessness as an insistent issue) housing practically ceased to be matter of state concern. Whether or not education was still considered part of the Welfare State (as distinct from simply being a matter related on the one hand to national efficiency and, on the other, to family choice), the Education Reform Act of 1988 had left a troubled legacy, ensuring that education remained a central political and social issue. In Social Security and in Health and Social Services (to recognize the formal division into two of what now basically remained of the Welfare State), 'reforms' of a Thatcherite character were energetically pursued: on the one hand, all sorts of schemes and devices in Social Security – most notoriously, the Child Support Agency (CSA) – as well as many restrictions on, and reductions in, entitlements; and, on the other, the implementation of the massive changes in the National Health Service entailed in the National Health Service and Community Care Act of 1990.

Looking back over nearly sixty years of the NHS, one key feature, and one key contrast, command attention. The key feature is the enthusiastic participation and support the NHS had secured from the overwhelming majority of the country's doctors and surgeons. The key contrast is that between what happened in Britain and what happened in the United States. In America even a well-off professional person could be bankrupted should a family member fall prey to any serious medical condition; accounts of individuals being denied treatment through lack of funds or relevant insurance coverage were legion. High-earning doctors were in a position of monopolistic strength and, in alliance with other vested interests, were well able to frustrate such attempts as President Clinton's to bring in a comprehensive medical scheme. There seemed, therefore, to be good grounds for the British to strive to maintain the integral relationship between the doctors and the NHS, and to avoid pushing the doctors into an independent position from which they might hold the nation up to ransom, American-style. Partly in compensation for their involvement in the state scheme, senior doctors, and, above all, surgeons, had privileged positions within the NHS, and could operate lucrative private practices in conjunction with their obligations to the NHS (while, at the same time, junior hospital doctors had tended to be grossly, and dangerously, overworked); there were few effective sanctions against doctors offering their patients expensive treatment when possibly something more modest might have sufficed. We saw in Chapter 22 that whatever additional expenditure Governments might make, it never appeared anything like enough. Radical Conservative instincts in that direction apart, a case could be made that drastic changes in the running of the NHS were required if inefficiencies were to be eradicated and money spent in the most effective way. At the same time informed opinion had become very critical of the way care for elderly and physically or mentally disabled people was available only in hospitals or special institutions. Thus the NHS and Community Care Act, drafted and enacted during the last stages of Mrs Thatcher's Government, implemented during the first years of John Major's, aimed both at reorganizing management of the NHS and transferring the provision for those with special needs from institutional care to 'Care in the Community'.

Management reorganization took the form of introducing internal markets within the NHS, appointing a new cadre of managers (with business, but not medical, experience), and thrusting managerial and accounting responsibilities onto doctors themselves. Whether such an approach was suitable for a service in which, it was widely held, an overriding priority ought to be dispassionate assessment of patient need, was a matter of intense controversy. But there could be no disagreeing with the principle of Care in the Community, which, in theory, would end the isolation and ostracizing of those with special needs. It was the way in which Care in the Community was actually implemented which aroused storms of criticism.

The reorganization envisaged in the Act fell into four parts. First, instead of the local health authorities simply being responsible for organizing in their own areas the health services required by law, they were allocated funds to use in purchasing such services for their own residents in whatever seemed the best market, mainly through establishing contracts with hospitals and other health service units (such as ambulance services and community health services), whether or not these were within their own area, whether publicly or privately owned. Second, hospitals, apart from the income received through such contracts, were to be directly funded purely on the basis of the number of patients treated, with the aim, in part, of encouraging GPs to refer patients to the most efficient hospitals even if (again) outside their own area. Third, hospitals and other health service units could apply to become self-governing NHS trusts, independent of local authority control, most of their income coming through the contracts mentioned above, though they could also take in private, fee-paying patients. Each NHS Trust was run by a board of directors, and required to publish its business plan and annual accounts. Many trusts continued to provide medical education and to carry out research. Trusts were rapidly formed in England, and by April 1994 there were 419 of them, handling all but 5 per cent of the NHS hospital and community health services. Fourth, practices with 7,000 patients or more (6,000 in Scotland and Northern Ireland) could apply to become GP fundholders, using the funds directly allocated to them to purchase various kinds of services for their patients, hospital treatment, nursing and health visiting, psychiatric treatment, and so on. In the nature of things, GP fundholding did not quite carry all before it in the manner of the NHS trusts (many practices were simply not big enough), but by April 1994 36 per cent of the population of Britain were registered with one of the 8,800 GPs in over 2,000 fundholding practices. Throughout the health service, market-testing and contracting out of ancillary services had been in operation since 1983, and was now being applied to clinical support services. From 1990 GPs (and dentists) were on performance-related pay schemes. Quality of service was to be guaranteed – or so the Prime Minister appeared to believe – by one general Patient's Charter, and several specific ones related to individual aspects of the NHS. Patients now had three new rights: to be given detailed information on local health services, including quality standards and maximum waiting times; to be guaranteed admission for treatment no later than two years from the date of being placed on a waiting list; and to have any complaint about NHS services investigated, and receive a full reply as soon as possible.

One of the long-standing charges against the NHS had been that it was entirely preoccupied with curing sickness rather than promoting health. The 1992 White Paper, *The Health of the Nation*, was a genuine attempt to meet that criticism and work out a strategy for the nation's health, setting targets for improvements with regard to certain specified harbingers of death and serious illness (coronary heart disease and stroke; cancers; accidents; mental illness; HIV/AIDS and sexual health) and for reducing risk behaviour, such as smoking. The other main health service initiative aroused much opposition, the plan launched in February 1993 to reduce the number of hospitals in London: together with a general policy of redistributing resources from inner cities to the regions.

Evaluation of the health service reforms is not easy. Certain experts, most notably Professor Chris Ham of Birmingham University, argued that they were eliminating inefficiency, waste and sloppy performance, and stimulating innovation. The Government claimed success in reducing waiting times: that, for instance, in England in March 1994 fewer than 65,000 patients were waiting over a year for hospital treatment, compared with more than 200,000 in 1987; and that since March 1988 the average waiting time had fallen from over nine months to less than five. Unfortunately the actual experiences of many patients suggested a different story, and there were many accounts of figures being massaged (with, for example, major cases having to wait still longer, so that less difficult ones could be pushed through more quickly). The evidence of improvement is not wholly persuasive, whereas a mass of material from varied sources suggests that these reforms did indeed have a sting in them. And whatever might be being achieved in theory, a cut in hospital spending in 1993 of £1.6 billion and a programme of closing down 40 per cent of hospital beds over eight years created crisis situations in many trust hospitals. Hospitals short of cash could only survive by refusing to take any patients other than those contracted for by fundholders. From all directions there were indictments of the consequences of Government policy: shortages of hospital places and specialist facilities, different standards of care for different patients, diversion of resources to management and bureaucracy, and unqualified managers taking clinical decisions. A leading surgeon and retiring chairman of the Joint Consultants' Committee of the British Medical Association and medical Royal Colleges warned of a 'sinister' elevation of managerial judgements over medical ones which he suspected of being

a deliberate policy on the part of Government because the managers . . . will accept balancing the books as their number one priority, whereas the doctor will always treat the individual patient. (*Independent*, 28 January 1994)

Articles in the *British Medical Journal* in December 1994 spoke of medical staff critical of the NHS reforms being intimidated into silence. One article maintained:

Most NHS employees feel that restrictions on freedom of speech have become more severe since the health service has become more commercial. Speaking up on deficiencies within a hospital was once a public duty; now it is viewed as a betrayal of the competitive interest of the NHS trust. Gagging clauses have been written into contracts of NHS consultants and other employees and there have been high-profile cases of whistle-blowers being persecuted.

The most telling criticism of the NHS reforms came early in 1995 from a recent chairman of the British Medical Association, who, as a Conservative, had tried to cooperate with the Major Government's policies; now, as he explained in the *British Medical Association News Review*, he was taking early retirement from his post as a consultant haematologist

because I am fed up with what is going on. They are driven by dogma more in tune with the eastern bloc . . . For three years I negotiated with the Government. It was just like slipping down a cliff.

The Care in the Community programme was long on good intentions but short on the funding necessary to make them effective and safe.

Intended in part to humanize the harsher terms of the Mental Health Act of 1983, whose basic premise was that treatment of mental disorders must be in a hospital or institution, Care in the Community, in the lax and penny-pinching way in which it was practised, simply exposed the fundamental flaws in the Act. It also resulted in a couple of truly tragic cases in which mental patients loose in the community carried out murders. An Inquiry by Sir Louis Blom-Cooper, reporting in January 1995, demanded fundamental changes in the system. These, said an *Independent* leader on 17 January, firmly identifying the failure to back Care in the Community with the necessary cash,

would end the chaos of community care: the authorities would have to give a precise description of where patients should live and the treatment they must receive, compulsorily if necessary.

Civil rights would have to be protected. But vulnerable people would at last be sure of a decent life in the community. Psychiatric services would no longer be able to shirk their responsibilities. The Government would have to pay the bill.

If these proposals are ignored, we can only assume that ministers prefer the cheaper, dangerous status quo. If so, they must accept responsibility for the future scandals that will surely follow.

The cry of 'children in danger' had been raised in the mid eighties, leading indeed to the Children Act of 1989: the general thrust in implementing the Act was the laudable, though in practice not necessarily successful, one that children with special needs should wherever possible remain at home with their families. No doubt it would have taken genius well beyond the talents available in the British political establishment to have found answers to all the complications of the horrifying issue of child abuse. There were guidelines and training initiatives. It was made possible for children under fourteen to testify in court through video-recorded interviews. Unfortunately this well-intentioned move did not prove particularly successful in obtaining convictions, and did not help in mitigating the trauma suffered by the children. Leaving the realm of Health and Social Services, and moving to that of Social Security, children (allegedly, at least) were at the centre of the biggest (and most controversial) initiative in that realm. It is important to stress that, in principle, the setting up of the CSA in April 1993 had overwhelming professional and political support. Single mothers endeavouring to bring up children were amongst the most deprived groups in society, with serious consequences for the health and well-being of both themselves and the children.

Their only formal means of securing maintenance payments from absent fathers was through the courts, which was reasonably effective with respect to agreed divorce settlements between the relatively prosperous but almost totally irrelevant to women who had been deserted or who had never had stable relationships. It was intended that the CSA would assume responsibility for assessing, collecting and enforcing child maintenance payments and for tracking down absent fathers. As operated the CSA was a microcosm of everything that was wrong with the Government's attitude to social policy.

A prize example of a 'Next Steps' autonomous agency, the CSA was headed by a chief executive, Ros Hepplewhite, who (in marked contrast with the formal neutrality traditionally expected of old-style civil servants) declared herself a hearty supporter of Government policies; she was on a target-related bonus, the target having nothing to do with the number of children rescued from poverty, but everything to do with the amount of cash the agency succeeded in collecting from fathers. The morality of the CSA was thus that of the ordinary strong-arm debt-collector. Single mothers were harassed into naming fathers when often they had the most pressing reasons, to do with their personal safety and that of their children, for wishing to avoid all contact with their former sexual partners. Fathers who were already making provision for their children (often through court-approved settlements) were much easier and cheaper to trace than the true fly-by-night defaulters, so such fathers, now usually with second families to support, were stung (it is with great deliberation that I again recall the colloquial term of my chapter title) for quite unreasonably high payments, driving some to suicide, and others, by mutual agreement, to part from their second wives. The first year of operations, the official handbook, *Britain 1995*, baldly reported, had 'produced benefit savings of over £418 million' (p. 403). No pretence that they had actually brought any benefit to the mothers and their children. No mention of the misery that had been brought to the children of second families – just this innocent, but all-revealing sentence: 'Changes to the child support arrangements were introduced in February 1994 to take account of concerns raised by members of the public and MPs.' The changes were trivial; the protests and the demonstrations continued; Ms Hepplewhite resigned; towards the end of the year about 350,000 cases that actually required some serious effort were unceremoniously abandoned (along with, of course, the mothers on whose behalf they were allegedly being pursued); in January 1995, the Parliamentary Commissioner or 'Ombudsman' (a sixties creation, incidentally – 1967 to be exact) published a damning indictment of 'failures and mistakes' causing 'undue worry and distress to parents'. This was quickly followed by the White Paper, *Improving Child Support*, which set limits upon the claims that could be made against absent fathers and gave some recognition to court settlements and to the needs of second families. The abandoned cases would remain abandoned; and the cases of single mothers earning a living but not on benefits, which the CSA was intended to take on after 1996, would also be dropped. To encourage single mothers on benefit to take jobs (which would incidentally lose them fringe benefits such as free school milk and dental treatment), a 'maintenance benefit' of up to £1,000, made up of money claimed from the absent father, would be available in a lump sum on their taking up employment. Small minds had laboured hard to bring forth a mouse, and to appease the richer and more vociferous critics; there was, said the Child Poverty Action Group, 'practically nothing to combat the poverty of lone parents and their children'.

The Ombudsman had also criticized maladministration in the other main Next Steps 'executive agency', the Benefits Agency, responsible for paying the benefits defined in the 1986 Act (discussed at the beginning of Chapter 22): its main target for 1994–95 was to save £654 million through its anti-fraud work. With the specific aim of reducing the numbers claiming either sickness or invalidity benefit, the Social Security (Incapacity for Work) Act of 1994 replaced them, from April 1995, with a single Incapacity Benefit, which was subject to stringent medical tests. From April 1996 unemployment benefit and income support for unemployed people were to be replaced by a Jobseekers' Allowance, which would require all unemployed people to enter into a 'jobseekers' agreement', committing them to a plan of action to seek work, and which would be means-tested. Meantime, on the testimony of the City's own financial watchdog, the Securities and Investments Board, it emerged that up to one-and-a-half million people who had followed Government advice in switching since 1988 to personal pensions had lost heavily thereby; compensation for the 350,000 most urgent cases could (if the financial advisers and insurers involved were ever forced to pay up) amount to over £2 billion. In 1993 wages councils, which set minimum wages for 2 million workers, most of them women, were abolished, giving immediate impetus to a trade union and Labour Party campaign in favour of a statutory minimum hourly wage rate.

The debates over social security are fairly straightforward. Almost all commentators were agreed that benefits and services must be targeted towards need in a way they had not been in the original concept of the Welfare State, and that attention had to be given to the elimination of inefficiency and waste. But, said opponents of the Government, these laudable aims must not become swamped in a more general policy of saving money at all costs, which, in turn, it was said, was creating a two-tier system, and denying benefits to those who actually were in need (the fullest statement of the alternative to Government policies is to be found in *Social Justice: Strategies for National Renewal, the Report of the Commission on Social Justice* of October 1994, commissioned by the Labour Party, though not formally Labour policy).

The debates over education are much more complicated. Parts of the British education system worked very effectively, but across education as a whole the record was patchy. Organization for Economic Cooperation and Development figures placed Britain fifth bottom in a list of twenty-four industrial nations for the percentage of the population receiving higher (or 'tertiary') education. For the percentage of three-year-olds attending nursery school, the relative figures were rather better, Britain coming sixth in a list of fifteen; but in absolute terms, there were less than half as many children in British nursery schools as in French or Belgian ones. For standards of literacy, numeracy and geographical knowledge, ordinary British school-children rated poorly compared with those in the other main European countries. The Government aimed to give parents choice in where they sent their children, to test pupils and assess teachers, to publish 'league tables' of school results and to encourage schools to opt out of local authority control and become 'grant maintained' (funded directly by the government; free to parents), all within the overall framework of a rigid control of expenditure. Local authorities (i.e. Labour ones) were associated with lax, 'progressive', teaching. Critics of the Government argued that if better-off parents (who could afford travel costs, etc.) could select their schools, there would be no pressures towards raising standards in the poorer schools. In response, Conservatives spoke of 'the politics of envy' – why should individual children be prevented from taking advantage of the best education available? The most urgent priority, one might think, was a universal levelling up of standards – testing and assessment, while certainly not unreasonable in themselves, manifestly increased burdens on teachers, and certainly did not increase the amount of quality teaching available. But how precisely was such an increase to be achieved? How financed? Meantime the irrelevant shibboleths of both right and left continued to bedevil debate.

Implementation of the many ramifications of the 1988 Education Act proceeded first in an atmosphere of resistance and confrontation, then, with the advent of Gillian Shephard as Education Secretary, within an atmosphere of negotiation and compromise. The National Curriculum was made more flexible; teachers moved towards acquiescence in modified national testing, and even in 'league tables', if these included appropriate information on a school's social circumstances and problems. However, it remained the explicit aim of the Funding Agency for Schools, established under the 1993 Education Act, to replace the local authorities as the main provider of school places. Overriding all other controversies was the crisis of funding. The 'starvation of essential books and other educational materials' (to which I referred in Chapter 22) had become steadily more severe, and, in 1995, despite Government talk of 'recovery', spending cuts looked set to cause further sackings of teachers. There were strong suspicions that reforms in teacher training (a Teacher Training Agency was established in 1994) were designed to get both teaching and training on the cheap, through having teaching done by students and calling it training. In March 1996 Major announced the objectives of greater selection and choice for parents, without reflecting on whether the two were actually compatible, and the ultimate Majorism, 'a grammar school in every town'.

An attempt at addressing the chronic problem of low vocational and technical qualifications, one of the many handicaps carried by the British economy, was made through the introduction of National Vocational Qualifications (NVQs). The difficulty of the narrow base and élitism of British universities was challenged by offering the polytechnics and some other higher-education institutions the right to assume university status, so that the total number of universities leapt to over ninety. It would scarcely be true to say that peace had broken out in the 'condition of war' between universities and government I referred to in chapter 22. But, without doubt, it was the universities which were yielding: research and teaching assessments imposed further burdens on academics; management consultants were everywhere in the ascendant; glossy brochures and mission statements proliferated. Going to university was becoming less of a privilege or a right, more a commercial transaction: there was a strong suspicion that standards were dropping.

Once the responsibility of the Ministry of Health, housing (in England and Wales) was now the responsibility of the Ministry of the Environment. This is probably how it should be in a healthy society where everyone has sufficient income to buy or rent housing of their choice. Alas, Britain was not that healthy society. True, inadequate housing was no longer a primary social problem affecting large sections of the population; rather, it was just another inescapable curse of belonging to the growing underclass. In addition, housing policy (or lack of it) articulated with two headline issues, that of racial conflict, and that (obviously) of homeless beggars in city streets. In working-class areas where low-cost housing to rent was in short supply, and where local authorities, rightly, had an equal obligation to house Asian and Afro-Caribbean families as well as white ones, resentment was easily kindled among whites who felt themselves to be inadequately housed. If we add the further problems of families constrained to live in grossly deteriorated housing estates (many dating from the fifties and sixties), vandalized, lacking amenities, with individual flats often suffering from faulty fittings or damp, and of squatters occupying empty properties, we can see that the sheer need for more decent housing at affordable rents was not yet an outdated concept in social policy.

Within its vision of a society of owner-occupiers, the Government made a number of pragmatic reforms. In the worst conditions of recession houses were standing empty and unsold, while, of course, many people were homeless or living in squalor. In November 1992 a 'housing market package' of £750 million was announced, to facilitate the purchase of such houses (a boon to the property owners) and make them available to meet social needs. In England £580 million was used to enable housing associations to buy 18,000 new, empty or refurbished properties for letting to homeless families. A further £50 million was used to provide cash incentives to housing association and local authority tenants to, in the words of the official handbook, *Britain 1994* (p. 329), 'enable them to buy homes on the open market and release their existing accommodation for housing homeless families'. The passage which follows provides a neat summary:

The promotion of home ownership and more choice in the rented sector are central to Government housing policy. New house construction is undertaken by both public and private sectors, but most dwellings are now built by the private sector for sale to owner-occupiers. Housing associations are becoming the main providers of new housing in the subsidized rented sector. Local authorities are being encouraged to see their housing role as more of an enabling one, working with housing associations and the private sector to increase the supply of low-cost housing for rent without necessarily providing it themselves. This allows them to concentrate their resources on improving the management of their own stock.

In 1950 more than half of all housing had been in the form of dwellings rented from a private landlord. Subsidized local authority housing had steadily grown in importance, while legislation relating to rent control and security of tenure had made offering property for rent a decreasingly attractive proposition for private landlords. By 1989 privately rented dwellings accounted for only 7 per cent of all housing. It was in that year that the Thatcher Government, in the hope of creating a restored private market in rented housing, abolished rent control on all new private lettings (while preserving guarantees of security for tenants). A 'Rent a Room' scheme was developed, a worthy initiative, even if rather reminiscent of such other home-spun wheezes as patients' charters and the 'cones hotline' (motorists disgruntled at finding perfectly good repaired roadway still coned off had a phone number over which to voice their fury – if anyone ever answered): home owners were encouraged to rent rooms to lodgers by being excused tax on rents up to about £62 a week (in 1994). Overwhelmingly, rented accommodation continued to be supplied from already existing local authority housing, supported by a Government subsidy (about £4,000 million in 1993–94). Practically all new rented accommodation was in the hands of the housing associations, supervised by one of the three statutory bodies, the Housing Corporation (England), Scottish Homes, or Housing in Wales. Together these bodies received Government grants totalling about £1,800 million (in 1993–94), a substantial proportion of which they then allocated to the housing associations, which were also encouraged to seek private finance. Over the years various governments had attempted to deal with the fundamentally English problem that it was often impossible to buy older houses outright (freehold), but only on leasehold, the property eventually reverting to the landowner owning the freehold. The Leasehold Reform, Housing and Urban Development Act of 1993 gave residential leaseholders in blocks of flats in England and Wales the right to acquire the freedhold of their block collectively at market price. At the same time the Act introduced a nationwide 'Rents-to-Mortgages' scheme, whereby, after an initial deposit, continuing rent payments would in effect count as mortgage payments, with the balance owing only needing to be paid off if and when the house was sold.

While the house-building role of local authorities had been almost abolished, it was upon them that the statutory duty (as imposed by the Housing Act of 1985) rested of providing permanent accommodation for 'households which they accept as unintentionally homeless and in priority need' (*Britain 1995*, p. 334), including pregnant women, people with dependent children and those rendered vulnerable by old age, mental or physical handicap, or other special reasons. The homeless came from various directions: family break-down or change in circumstances of a relative or friend formerly providing accommodation, abuse in family or institutional home. The number of would-be home owners being dispossessed because of inability to keep up mortgage payments had shot up in the 1980s and shot up again in the early nineties, peaking in 1991, but remaining excessively high in 1992, 1993, and 1994 (see Table 13).

Table 13: Number of mortgages, arrears and repossessions (UK) in thousands

| | | Loans in arrears | | |
	Mortgages	By 6–12 months	By over 12 months	Properties taken into possession
1971	4,506	17.6		2.8
1976	5,322	16.0		5.0
1981	6,336	21.5		4.9
1986	8,138	52.1	13.0	24.1
1988	8,564	42.8	10.3	18.5
1989	9,125	66.8	13.8	15.8
1990	9,415	123.1	36.1	43.9
1991	9,815	183.6	91.7	75.5
1992	9,922	205.0	147.7	68.5
1993	10,137	164.0	151.8	58.5
1994	10,375	153.3	142.2	49.2

Source: *Social Trends 1995*, p. 181, updated for 1994 with latest Council of Mortgage Lenders figures.

The Government had take emergency measures in December 1991 to stem the mounting flood of repossessions: benefits relating to mortgage interest were paid direct to the lenders, who, in turn, were encouraged to develop their own schemes to help borrowers in difficulty. The improved figures in 1994 were partly due to these measures, more to reduced interest rates and falling unemployment. But they were still high, and represented a substantial regular addition to the homeless; with the Government announcing new restrictions on the payment of mortgage interest benefits, the situation looked set to get worse.

It was not always easy for local authorities, especially in London, to find the required permanent accommodation. Table 14 shows the numbers of homeless families in fact being placed in temporary accommodation, of which 'Bed and Breakfast' (i.e. seedy boarding houses) was the most notorious. It was to the credit of the Government that by 1993 it had got this figure down below the 1986 level, though the extent of the continuing misery for many families allowed no cause for complacency.

Table 14: Homeless households living in temporary accommodation (England, Scotland and Wales), in thousands

	Bed and Breakfast	Hostels	Property leased by local authority on short-term basis	Total
1982	2.0	3.7	4.8	10.5
1984	4.2	4.2	5.3	13.7
1986	9.4	5.0	8.3	22.7
1988	11.2	6.8	14.2	32.2
1989	12.0	8.6	19.9	40.5
1990	11.7	10.4	27.0	49.1
1991	12.9	11.7	39.7	64.3
1992	8.4	12.6	46.6	67.6
1993	5.5	12.0	41.0	58.5

Source: *Social Trends 1995*, p. 185.

For visitors to London and its locals one of the most evident consequences of the Thatcher revolution was the sight of street beggars and rough sleepers, in doorways, in the 'cardboard cities' set up in squares and open spaces, and in covered areas such as that under the roundabout at Waterloo. Nobody could miss them, and in 1990 the Government introduced its 'Rough Sleepers Initiative' – a three-year programme, costing £96 million, which provided about 950 new places in short-term hostels, and about 2,200 permanent and 700 leased places in accommodation for hostel dwellers to move on into. After protests that the problem certainly hadn't gone away (though the Government claimed that the number of rough sleepers in Central London had dropped from over 1,000 to less than 270), £86 million was made available in 1994 to continue the initiative until 1996. The Prime Minister and other Ministers denounced 'the culture of begging' and instructed citizens to resist entreaties to 'spare any change', and instead call the police. The straightforward evidence was that denunciations and emergency initiatives were not enough. Certainly there was (as the Government claimed) an issue of acculturation and attitude: but that, in essence, was a direct product of a divided, and increasingly atomized, society – a society, in short, at odds with itself. There was also an issue of rejection, neglect and deprivation: and that, in essence, was a direct product of the running down of the social services and the introduction of 'reforms' aimed more at making future tax cuts possible than at the real needs of those least able to help themselves – abused youth, alcoholics and addicts, the mentally sick and the senile.

In Chapter 20 I identified a series of horrific accidents that took place in the last years of the eighties, raising issues of whether the Government was giving enough attention to questions of public safety, and whether indeed it was encouraging a cut-throat milieu in which safety was being sacrificed to sales – a phrase used in connection with the tragic loss of children's lives in a disgracefully disorganized and ill-prepared South Coast canoeing expedition in the summer of 1994. On the railways there was little sign, even in the aftermath of the Clapham disaster, that safety issues were being taken any more seriously, and much evidence that warnings and recommendations were being ignored. In 1991 and in 1994 there were appalling head-on crashes, the first near Glasgow, the second at Cowden in Kent, on tracks which, for reasons of economy, had been converted to single-line working; in the latter crash a signalman was unable to avert the tragedy because of the absence of two-way radio communication. Questions about the absence of modern means of communication were again raised when, on the remote Carlisle to Settle line on 31 January 1995, one train ploughed into another which had come off the rails ten minutes earlier. During the signalmen's strike of the summer of 1994 there was evidence of disregard for safety on the part of Railtrack (the government-owned company set up by the Railways Act of 1993 to operate track, signalling etc., in preparation for privatization of the twenty-five train-operating units into which British Rail was now divided): the *Observer* (31 July 1994) published a tape recording in which a Railtrack manager answered the concerns of a supervisor over working a signal box with the remark, 'If a mistake is made, then so be it.' In the early morning of 25 August 1994 the ferry *Sally Star*, on overnight freight duty, suffered a major engine room blaze eight miles off Ramsgate, just over a month after the helicopter rescue service at RAF Manston, Kent, had been closed, despite urgent pleas following the *Herald of Free Enterprise* catastrophe that it must be kept open. The hundred people on board were rescued; during a daytime passenger crossing there would have been 1,400. *The Times* headline next day read: 'Anger as near-disaster off Ramsgate raises spectre of Zeebrugge.' On 10 November a coach crashed near Faversham, Kent, killing nine American tourists and the driver. The anti-lock brakes and speed-limiter were faulty; there were no passenger seat belts. The dreadful crash of a school minibus on the M6 in 1994 again raised the question of seat belts and seating arrangements, and drew attention to how poverty-sticken schools had to use the most beaten-up old transport. In January 1995 an *Observer* investigation demonstrated that the recently opened Channel Tunnel was very far from observing standards of safety analogous to those of airlines, as had been promised in Parliament. It did seem that the general spirit, endorsed by the Government, was that, if costs could thereby be saved, corners could be cut. In May 1994 the Government announced the removal of nearly one hundred regulations relating to Health and Safety at Work, many no doubt outdated and overly bureaucratic; but again there was the suspicion that business interests were being put before the interests of safety.

The last, massive blow to strike John Major's government was an almost pure product of the Thatcherism which he had never repudiated and, indeed, had done so much to extend and accelerate – the authoritarian Thatcherism which privileged deregulation and untrammelled profit-making and suppressed all questioning, all dissent. It is true that two elements in the great BSE (Bovine Spongiform Encephalopathy) crisis pre-dated Thatcherism: the encouragement of intensive farming, includ-ing the feeding of meat-and-bone meal ('supplementary feedstuffs') to cows, and the flaw in government structure whereby in the combined Ministry of Agriculture, Food, and Fisheries consumer interests were completely swamped by those of producers. But it was deregulation under Thatcher which permitted the switch in 1981–2 to cost-cutting processing of 'supplementary feedstuffs' at lower temperatures with reduced use of solvents; this permitted contaminated protein, almost certainly the source of BSE, or 'mad cow disease', to be fed to cows. The first 'mad cow' was noted in Kent in April 1985, the first official confirmation issued in November 1986; already there were over 200,000 infected cattle, but BSE was not made a notifiable disease till 21 June 1988. It was at the same time decided that the feeding to ruminants of feedstuffs derived from animal remnants should be banned, but the ban was delayed for one month, so that existing (contaminated) stocks could be used up, thus infecting thousands more animals. In June the Government was also advised that all BSE-infected animals should be destroyed, but took no action till August. Meantime, since there was a possibility of BSE being communicated to humans, the Government set up the Southwood Committee, which eventually became the Encephalopathy Advisory Committee (SEAC). The Government kept up an unjustifiably confident façade, with, in 1990, John Gummer, Agriculture Secretary, blustering in public, and attempting to force-feed a hamburger to his daughter. On the recommendation of Southwood, in November 1989 the sale of specified bovine offal for human consumption was banned, but, again in the spirit of deregulation and cost-cutting, inspection procedures were sloppy and inadequate. Research was discouraged and evidence suppressed. The Americans wisely banned imports of British beef, but even that was not enough to upset Government complacency. The maximum extraction – and maximum profit – policies of the food industry meant that cheap pies and hamburgers were particularly suspect. Deaths began to occur among young people, and could often be linked to the consumption of cheap beef products.

If the issue was dormant, it certainly should not have been, and it blew up in March 1996. The fact that SEAC was about to make a statement of new evidence of the putative link between the spread of BSE in cattle and ten new cases of New Variant Creutzfeldt-Jakob brain disease (CJD) in young people in the previous two years was recorded in a memo written by the Ministers of Agriculture and of Health, Douglas Hogg and Stephen Dorrell, on 18 March 1996. The Government decided on a parliamentary statement to be made on the afternoon of 20 March; but the news was leaked in that morning's *Daily Mirror*. Dorrell's statement intimated that CJD cases might be linked to the eating of beef before the introduction of the specified bovine offal ban in 1989. It was not so clear that the precautions taken in 1989 were sufficient, nor indeed that they were being rigorously enforced. On 25 March the veterinary committee of the European Commission imposed a world-wide ban on the import of British beef and beef by-products.

The European Commission acted very rationally, promising the UK financial help for the destruction of older cattle, and expressing the hope that the ban could be lifted once measures acceptable to the European Union had been agreed. But Major chose to behave in a petulant and obstructive manner, announcing on 21 May that Britain would pursue a policy of 'non-cooperation' with Europe. The agreement reached with the EU in mid-June that subject to European scrutiny of the cattle-slaughtering programme there would be a progressive lifting of the ban, was readily represented as a climb-down on the part of Major. Officially the Government embarked on a programme of slaughtering 60,000 cattle over three years old, every week. But facilities for burning carcasses were inadequate; stories continued to surface of dangerous conditions in slaughter houses where younger cattle were being butchered for the market, and of infected carcasses simply being buried in shallow graves. If ever regulation was needed, it was now; but resources were thin, the ethos of responsibility threadbare.

Modern governments clearly have a responsibility to ensure for their people the delivery of the basic utilities, clean water, gas, electricity, the availability of essential transport systems and the provision of the basic postal and telephonic means of communication. Privatization and (limited) competition in telecommunications undoubtedly resulted in an extension of services that would have been unlikely under old Post Office control (less certainly, though, if the Post Office itself had been permitted to seek private investment). The same sort of claim was plausibly made with respect to privatized British Airways (the problems of still-nationalized Air France being something of a warning) – though little pride could be derived from the dirty tricks campaign waged by British Airways against commercial rivals Virgin Atlantic. With respect to electricity and gas, arguments could be made on both sides, though it has to be said that, at the middle of the decade, neither set of privatized companies stood very high in public opinion. As for the water companies, very serious criticisms were being made of them, well encapsulated in two pieces of quality reporting from the *Observer*. The first dates from the height of the hot summer of 1994:

As England sizzled last week, Lisa and Andy Young had bad news for their four young children: don't get the paddling pool out – we can't afford the water. The children were also reminded not to get themselves or their clothes dirty, because the Youngs have been forced to cut back drastically on baths and washing.

The Youngs, both unemployed, live in Sidmouth, Devon. Water bills have risen faster in the South-West than anywhere else in the country since the water industry was privatized in 1989. A bath in Sidmouth costs twice as much as a bath in London.

This year the Youngs will be required to pay more than £400 for their water – a 25 per cent increase on the previous year. They are £500 in arrears. And now they have a water meter, so they pay for every drop they use.

'We're cutting back on everything,' said Lisa. 'We even change the bed linen less often and try to flush the toilet less. It causes a lot of tension. I find myself shouting at the children if they get dirty. We are being penalized for having a family.'

About 15 miles away in Exeter is the office of Keith Court, chairman of South West Water. Mr Court, 59, has no such problem meeting his bills, since his salary has risen from £41,000 to £136,000 since 1989. His company's pre-tax profit last year was £127 million.

The contrast has been repeated all over the country. The astronomical rise in consumers' water bills since privatization has been matched by spectacular increases in water companies' profits, salaries and dividends. (24 July 1994).

Two months later (25 September 1994) a further article concerned the revolt of the town of Alton in Hampshire against the compulsory installation of water meters:

The residents say metering will leave up to 40 per cent of the town's population worse off. Many will face serious financial problems unless they use less water. Local doctors fear this will put people's health at risk.

The town is seething about being given no choice by Mid Southern Water. There was no trial, no proper consultation. 'Their attitude is totalitarian,' said Allan Chick of the Alton Against Residential Metering (Alarm) action group. 'This is being done purely for profit.'

Eileen Thompson and her husband Peter, 42, are among those who will be hit hard by metering. They have eight children; six of them, aged eight to eighteen, live at home in the family's council house. Mr Thompson's factory job brings in about £200 a week after tax.

It might not be enough after metering. The Thompson's bill will rise from its current £160 a year to more than £500, according to Mid Southern's own estimates. 'We are already very tight,' said Mrs Thompson. 'I don't know what we will do.'

She has made some plans. When the meter is installed, Mrs Thompson will take the children 13 miles for a bath, to unmetered Liphook, where her mother lives. They will go in the family's 21-year-old mini-van, 'when we can afford the petrol'.

The Thompsons never go out. Haven't had a holiday for six years. Use every spare penny to buy the children clothes and shoes and store them up for the Days When the Meters are Here.

The meter will cause friction at home. The girls won't be able to wash their hair as often as they would like. The toilet will be flushed less frequently. The garden and potted plants, Eileen's 'oasis of sanity', will be neglected. Peter will complain about the bills. The TV will go first, then insurance payments. There will be arguments about who's wasting water.

Mrs Thompson said: 'I can't put the kettle on without thinking how much it's going to cost.'

The Thompsons would not be able to expect help from OFWAT (Office of Water Services), the body (in England and Wales) responsible for 'regulating prices and representing customers' interests', since, after all, it was 'the Government's view', as *Britain 1995* makes unambiguously clear (p. 266), that 'water metering is potentially the fairest way of paying for water.' The other water regulatory body in England and Wales is the NRA (National Rivers Authority), responsible basically for water resources and pollution control. A report at the end of 1994 on the dangerously polluted nature of many of England's most popular beaches reflected little credit on privatized water or on the Government's tame regulatory bodies. The regulatory, or as many saw them, non-regulatory bodies for electricity and gas (covering the whole of Britain) were, respectively, OFFER (Office of Electricity Regulation), and OFGAS (Office of Gas Supply). Earliest reports of the 'passenger service requirements' which would be imposed as the railways were privatized gave clear warnings of probable 20 per cent cuts in existing services.

In Chapter 23 I picked out the Environment as a cause, very much part of sixties' attitudes, which came to great political prominence in the late eighties. By the middle of the nineties it was clear that the Government was speaking with two voices. In March 1994 the Department of the Environment issued a Planning Policy Guidance note which in many respects was a courageous counterblast to the prevailing *laissez-faire* ethic and worship of the motor car. The aim of the Guidance note was:

to reduce the need to travel and to maximize the development potential of existing centres. The careful selection by local planning authorities of locations for new development, close to existing facilities and readily served by public transport, will reduce journey lengths and maximize the choice of means of transport other than car. (*Britain 1995*, p. 343)

Such sentiments ran counter to the Government's massive road-building programme, encouragement of motor transport and general hostility to the railways. A study by the consulting firm of Steer Davies Gleave, published in August 1994, demonstrated that Britain's expenditure on rail infrastructure was by far the lowest in Europe, one tenth of that in Italy, one sixth of that in France, and one fifth of that in Germany. As experts had been pointing out for years, road users were not actually paying an economic price for their journeys. Furthermore, contrary to the practice of every other European country, Britain's flat-rate excise duty took no account of engine size.

For environmentalists, the bugle-call came in the form of the *18th Report of the Royal Commission on Environmental Pollution, Transport and the Environment*, issued at the end of October 1994. Hailing the Report as 'a true watershed in transport policy', the Executive Director of the Metropolitan Transport Research Unit, Keith Buchan, noted that behind the Report lay 'a 10-year history of accumulating awareness that the prevailing thrust of policy was literally unsustainable'; the Report's achievement was 'to begin to set out a sustainable transport policy in its place'.

Today, everyone at least talks sustainable: the desire to use cars must be 'managed' and 'restrained', the object of planning is to 'reduce the need to travel'. This is the opposite of predicting seemingly endless traffic growth and then building the roads to keep up. The change is from what is often described as 'predict and provide' to 'predict and prevent'.

Why is this reversal happening so quickly and why is it accepted by such a broad spectrum of decision makers? There are two reasons: first it is abundantly clear that there is no room for the Department of Transport's predicted increases in traffic to take place; even a road-building programme many times bigger than the current £20 billion would offer no guaranteed relief of existing congestion, while promising vast increases in pollution and damage to our social environment. We cannot build our way out of congestion, and I know of no sane professional who believes we can. This was not so universally accepted ten years ago.

The second reason is that there is no technical fix which can make a transport system based on car and lorry use acceptable in environmental terms. People may want to use their cars, but they also want their children to be able to breathe freely, to play and undertake social activity without the constant fear of traffic. 'Calming' the local street is not enough; despite the growth of pedestrian malls, shopping, education and leisure are still most usually concentrated in traditional high streets which are also main roads.

Thus, both in traffic and environmental terms, there is no coherent vision of the future which follows through the logic of a continued growth of car and lorry traffic.

The adversarial nature of British politics, allied to the long relapse of the Labour party, had ensured that ideology and political will had played an unusually strong role in shaping social policy; now perhaps the 'sane professionals', responding to stirrings of consciousness among 'people' and the sheer imperatives of technological development, could begin again to exercise restraint over the mad marketeers.

Care for the environment was something all governments – and all business enterprises – had to make a show of, as also was belief in Equal Opportunities. The two major statutory commissions, the Equal Opportunities Commission and the Commission for Racial Equality, date, respectively, from 1975 and 1976. With regard to sex equality, the Major Governments must be credited with a number of initiatives, even if they do tend to carry that aura of the homespun wheeze to which I have already referred. 'Opportunity 2000' was a private employers' initiative, supported by the Government, aiming at getting more women into the workforce. 'Fair Play for Women', launched by the Department of Employment and the Equal Opportunities Commission, was a regional programme aiming 'to encourage women to realize their full potential in the community'. The 'enterprise culture' was often cruel to women at the lower end of the scale: yet it is right to record that by 1994 more than 740,000 women were running their own businesses, nearly double the number in 1980. On first becoming Prime Minister in December 1990, John Major appointed a woman, Sarah Hogg, as Head of his Policy Unit. The new Head of MI5 was a woman, Stella Rimmington (who was also the first Head of that intelligence organization to be acknowledged to exist). However, at the beginning of 1994, 90 per cent of all top civil servants were men. The Department of Employment, though officially charged with giving the lead in increasing opportunities for women, conformed to the regular pattern. While just two of its thirty top civil servants were women, only three of its 719 typists were men. The European Union average for women in ministerial office was 12.6 per cent; Britain was bottom country with a figure of 7 per cent. Women still averaged only 75 per cent of male earnings. A confidential letter from the Government to the Equal Opportunities Commission, leaked to the *Independent*, 11 October 1993, revealed that the Government wanted women to be dissuaded from bringing equal pay cases because of 'the need to avoid undue burdens on employers which could threaten job opportunities'.

Gay Rights is not a topic which gets any space in the British *Official Handbooks*. A much-publicized visit in September 1991 by the actor Sir Ian McKellen to Downing Street to discuss with the Prime Minister the law as it affected, and failed to protect, homosexuals brought into prominence such issues as the homosexual age of consent (twenty-one, as against sixteen for heterosexual intercourse), the need to outlaw discrimination on grounds of sexual orientation, and the continuance of the situation whereby in the armed forces homosexuality was still illegal. As in so many other areas of social policy, Britain, so much admired in the late forties for what foreign commentators referred to as a 'peaceful social revolution', was now far behind what was standard practice in European Union countries. There were a number of sources of hostility to gays, some perhaps peculiarly British, and possibly even related to class attitudes and notions of an effete upper class. Some prejudices concerning 'the Gay Plague' were dampened by the widely circulated news that new cases of AIDS among gays were tailing off, while those among heterosexuals were still increasing. At the same time, the offensive activities of some gays in public places did give rise to legitimate complaints. Here are two readers' letters about open homosexual activity on Hampstead Heath, published in the *Hampstead and Highgate Express* (30 August 1991), the first from a man, the second from a woman:

> When I reproved a pair in the act of buggery, I was told to 'f*** off!' I replied that the Heath was a public area governed by law. What consenting homosexuals do in private is their business, but when these acts take place on the Heath the law must act . . .
>
> Perhaps gays don't realize what a shock it can be (however broad-minded you are) to come upon two men doing it 'doggy fashion' in the middle of a public path, as I did the other day.
>
> All I ask of people (gay or otherwise) is that they have whatever intimacy they want at home/in private, and protect me from their bare bums, tubes of lubrication, and used condoms. It's my Heath too.

When the question of lowering the homosexual age of consent did come before Parliament, for once the old, and this case rather soggy, instinct for compromise proved irresistible, and the age was lowered only to eighteen.

The question of race really needs to be taken in the context of an overall survey of the British people, their attitudes and their identity (the subject-matter of my next chapter). Government policy towards race relations issues revealed neither vigour nor enthusiasm. Both social policy and economic trends were generally adverse in their effects on the underprivileged, among whom racial minorities formed a disporportionate number. Immigration policies continued to be enforced in the harshest possible ways, harassment of blacks and Asians being notorious. It was in this area that there was a rather grubby little instance of the performance-related-pay fetish. The report by the *Independent* Labour Editor (13 December 1994) makes a sadly appropriate coda to this chapter about social reform, which was usually cheap where it was not actually nasty:

Immigration officers have been given a quota system for refusing foreign nationals entry to Britain, according to internal papers obtained by the *Independent.*

If officials fail to meet the target, their earnings could suffer under a new appraisal system.

Civil servants staffing immigration desks have been told that the number of incomers they refer for interrogation should reflect the average for the entry point concerned . . .

The Home Office has received complaints about the new arrangement from immigration officers arguing that it puts pressure on officials to raise objections to a person's entry simply to ensure that their salaries do not suffer.

26

Class, Race, Identity

In the August 1992 number of the learned sociology journal, *Sociology*, Professors Goldthorpe and Marshall argued that class was still a very important phenomenon in Britain, though class should not be conceived as conforming to the laws laid down by Marxism. This is exactly the position I took in my *Class: Image and Reality in Britain, France and the USA since 1930* (1980, revised edition 1990) and have repeated throughout the various editions of this book.

In the mid nineties the situation in regard to class was, naturally enough, not greatly changed from the situation in the late eighties as I described it in Chapter 21: inequalities in income and living conditions between well-off and badly off were intensifying still further, while, at the same time, the arrival in positions of power of people of nondescript background and varied accents, challenging more and more forcefully the air of easy superiority once so readily assumed by those of upper-class upbringing, together with, lower down the scale, the rejection of the old working-class poverty of desire and principles of solidarity, proceeded unabated. Yet the basic class framework remained, and articles on class continued to appear every two or three years in the quality newspapers. A telling, if slightly over-dramatized one appeared in *Observer Life* (the colour magazine attached to the *Observer* newspaper) on 12 December 1993, accompanied by interviews with individuals said to be representative of 'the working class' (a 44-year-old production line worker at the Ford plant in Dagenham, East London), 'the middle class' (a young mother of two children who worked as a gardener and in her husband's computer consultancy), 'the upper-middle class' (a director of an exclusive merchant bank), and 'the upper class' (the eleventh Duke of Devonshire). For reasons explained throughout this book, I would regard the merchant banker as being in the upper class – that, I am sure, is how the car worker and the middle-class woman would regard him. In Britain today it is still considered in bad taste to describe yourself as 'upper class', even when everybody else can see that that is what you are; hence the polite fiction of 'upper-middle class'. Dukes, actually, are not really very important – there are extremely few of them, and along with figures from the lesser aristocracy and gentry, they simply set the kind of historical tone to which the other members of the upper class aspire. Single interviews with such 'representatives' must, of course, be taken with great caution; yet these particular ones do highlight important points based on much wider evidence, and offer certain insights that merit further comment. There may have been journalistic intervention – but, on the whole, the now ubiquitous deployment of the tape-recorder does offer a guarantee of authenticity.

The car-worker is manifestly something of a traditionalist; his comments about young workers, only interested in such television soap operas as *Coronation Street* and *Neighbours*, indicate a continuing fragmentation of the traditional working class. For all that, there is an unambiguous sense of that classic notion of being working class being equivalent to serving a life-sentence from which there is little hope of escape.

In our plant there really is a class society, you've got the management canteen and car park, workers' canteen and car park, and we all know our place.

The union is strong in the plant, but you can't get the allegiance out of the younger workers. A lot of them don't have any allegiance to the Tory party, the Labour party, the trade union – nothing. If they're all right, it's bugger anyone else. I don't know why they're different because my dad was a trade unionist and so was his dad. The younger lot don't seem to know anything apart from sport and what's happening in *Coronation Street* and *Neighbours*.

Do I come into contact with other classes? Not much, all my friends are working class . . .

Now I can't afford to re-educate myself and try something entirely different, and haven't got the time.

We earn £6.50 an hour, in fact you get paid by the minute. If you're five minutes late you miss five minutes' pay. It's a 39-hour week, so we earn about £14,000 a year.

It's enough for a mortgage, we live in a nice little house in a cul-de-sac, I'm happy where I live, but as far as I am concerned the Halifax Building Society owns my house, it's the curse on my household.

Now for the middle-class woman, resident of a small village in Norfolk. What she says coincides with a point I made earlier in the book about the middle class (or classes) coming from the most variegated origins and not being defined by any one particular type of education. In part at least, her class position derives from that of her husband. Bur from the start it is absolutely clear that she perceives an upper class above her (to be mocked) and a working class below her (to be pitied and criticized for their inertia).

Class is something I talk about a lot with my close friends. We take the mickey out of upper-class people and their style of life, having people doing things for them. But we are probably more condemning of people below us than of upper-class twits. We can almost accept upper-class twits can't do anything about themseves – and why should they change things? But people at the bottom are always going on about how things don't suit them, and they'd like to change things, but then they choose not to do so . . .

Most middle class people, particularly the young, think people should be allowed to do what they want. I think the upper class like to control other people and I think the majority of the working class like to be controlled. I might sound snotty, but . . . we have three dogs, they like to know where the boundaries are, where they can tread. They are not actually able to think for themselves that much and when they do things tend to go terribly wrong.

Most working-class people are pretty decent people but they like to know where the boundaries are. They want to be told this is acceptable and this isn't and work between the two lines.

Don't you think you are in control of your own life and you can do whatever you want to do? I didn't go to private school, I was brought up on a council estate, I know people who've been sent to private schools and have ended up a complete low-life. If I could afford to send my children to a private school I would but it's more important that the whole family has a balanced existence.

I think the middle class is energetic but not in a particularly daring way, they are generally nice, and almost sum up Britishness, non-controversial, let's-not-stir-anything-up type attitude. I joined the Tory party when Mrs Thatcher was kicked out. I don't believe at the end of the day that socialism works, never have done. People should be allowed to do what they want to do, I want my own spending power.

Both my parents are Irish and working class. I think other people define me as middle class but I think deep down I like to consider myself working class, part of it is wanting more street cred, and you don't want to be associated with the toff types. I do sound middle class and I spoke better than the other children on the estate, but I was at a good Roman Catholic girls' comprehensive, where my accent was influenced I suppose. My God, I have just worked out where my accent came from!

Fabulous testimony, isn't it? – about accent, Britishness, Irishness, working-class origins, middle-class aspirations. It seems clear that the woman herself was born and brought up in England (on a working-class housing estate); whether her parents were Catholics from Northern Ireland or immigrants from the Republic is uncertain, but whatever the origins of her parents, she clearly sees herself as 'British' (very noteworthy that she says 'Britishness', not 'Englishness'). It is not unusual for a state-funded Catholic school to put more emphasis on such matters as accent than an ordinary comprehensive school (secular, but with a broadly Protestant morning service) would do. And nothing here of the dreary certitudes of Marxist or Weberian analysis. Escaping from the working class, as the previous document suggested, is not as easy as she implies, but none the less her image of the middle class as, in part, being formed of those who take hold of their own destiny has more truth than conventional sociology would allow. At times she thinks of herself, and *likes* to think of herself, as working class, though in fact, partly through education and personal initiative, but basically through marriage, she has achieved a middle-class life-style, and is perceived by others (a very important indicator of class) as middle class. Her parents had exercised choice in sending her to a Catholic school (with high traditional standards), and most certainly she would like to have choice in where she sends her own children – though, a most important point, she cannot afford a private school (that privilege, increasingly, being an indicator of upper-class status). It was this question of choice that lay at the heart of the education debate (notoriously, the Labour leader, Tony Blair, had picked a particular direct-grant Catholic school for one of his own children). There is a brief sense of shock in her reference to Margaret Thatcher, but that enables us to see all the more clearly the mountain made up of the attitudes of moderate, far from unperceptive, middle England, that the Labour Party still had to climb.

Our merchant banker (aged 37) owns an old rectory in Cornwall, where he joins his wife at weekends, living during the week in a flat in London, a life-style beyond the means of most truly middle-class families; his father was an army officer, and his mother came from a well-established naval family (both fairly reliable indicators of upper-class status). He was educated at a private school and took a degree at Exeter University. Usually, for choice, the offspring of the upper class study at Oxford or Cambridge (where certain colleges are ranked as more prestigious than the rest – e.g. Christ Church, or Balliol, Oxford; King's, Cambridge – and within these colleges there are exclusive élite societies). The other universities with upper-class associations are Durham, St Andrew's (in Scotland) and Exeter. A fashionable term for gilded upper-class youth (perhaps a little dated by the nineties) was 'Sloanes' or 'Sloane Rangers', from the expensive area behind Sloane Square bordering on Chelsea and Kensington, to the west of Central London. In responding to his interviewer, the banker had this to say:

Until you called I hadn't really thought about the class issue for a few years. When all the Sloane Ranger books came out ten years ago it was quite amusing, but I've always tried to fight against being thought a Sloane, I've never wanted to be categorized by class. I would say I am upper middle class. Class is a combination of values, your approach to life, employment, as well as how you have been brought up. But above all else, education conditions attitudes that last a long time. But there is such an enormous middle class where people are bound to have much in common. I suspect the definition of middle class today is people that have been educated.

If you go back thirty or forty years in the City, management would have been much more narrowly drawn, there is more of a mixture these days. But although we have more of an egalitarian society I do feel class divisions are still very pronounced, as if the mixing has made people more aware of it, more self-conscious.

It soon becomes clear that, for all his protestations, he does feel himself to be in a class above most middle-class people, and he does recognize that the way he speaks, his accent, is different – in fact, though he doesn't like to say it (in itself an indicator of upper-class good taste), he is upper class (a class above his wife, who, it would appear, was actually well up in the middle class).

A lot of my friends are media or creative and I married a woman who was not of my class but through her own efforts made sure she was very well educated. Now she stays in Cornwall and is trying to write, after working as a technical publishing director.

I feel lucky I have had more incentive to open my eyes than many other people.

The upper middle classes in particular are guilty of being narrow mixers socially. Their life-style reinforces division so they perhaps ought to make a bigger effort to break away.

My job is lending money to medium sized companies and the people running these are not upper middle class. I deal with a broad cross-section and after fifteen years or so of working the view you form of people is far more meritocratic than based on class – are they people you respect, trust, find interesting? But I do feel embarrassed at times. If I'm in a room full of industrialists the way I speak could be a disadvantage. It could be taken by some as projecting a form of arrogance . . .

Again a neat indicator of upper-class status: having an accent and manner which projects 'a form of arrogance'. Again an immensely rich and rewarding document. By contrast the interview with a genuine landed aristocrat (aged 73, it must be noted) is of little more than curiosity value: the hint that an interest in football is one of Britain's great class levellers is well worth taking seriously (only a silly female interviewer from *The Times* would assume such an interest to be lower-class . . . or an affectation); the confusion between middle class and working class (shared by Winston Churchill, for instance) is not uncommon among the ancient upper class (Mrs Thatcher's father was a middle-class shopkeeper, and very prominent citizen in Grantham).

A lot of people do try to pigeonhole people by class. I take a passionate interest in association football, but there was nothing I could say in an interview when I completely failed to convince a woman from *The Times* that this wasn't an affectation on my part.

Class is like beauty, it's all in the mind's eye, isn't it? I think the system is breaking down. Mrs Thatcher came from what used to be called the working class, and for better or worse the aristocracy has ceased to be any force in the country . . .

Let me, just one more time, play my revealing little game of analysing the class composition of the Cabinet, this time that reshaped by John Major in July 1994. With reference to the Thatcher Cabinet of June 1987, I reported that out of twenty-one members, 'fully eight were in the traditional upper-class mould, while only seven distinctively were not.' Of this seven, low-born lads Parkinson, Moore and Young, as well as the low-born lady herself, had all gone: Major and Clarke (now Chancellor of the Exchequer) remained: no one else quite so humble joined Major's Cabinet of twenty-three. Of Thatcher's aristocrats only Hurd (now Foreign Secretary) remained, but he had been joined by two even grander figures, William Waldegrave (Minister of Agriculture), younger son of the twelfth Earl of Waldegrave, and Viscount Cranborne, from the majestic Cecil, or Salisbury, family (Lord Privy Seal), and five others of perhaps just slightly lesser rank. These were: Jonathan Aitken, son of Sir William Aitken, and scion of the powerful Beaverbrook connection, educated at Eton and Christ Church, Oxford (Financial Secretary to the Treasury); Ian Lang, from a prestigious family of Scottish insurance brokers, educated at a Scottish prep school, Rugby, and Sidney Sussex, Cambridge (Scottish Secretary); Sir Patrick Mayhew, son of an oil executive, himself a barrister and farmer and ex-Dragoon Guardsman, educated at Tonbridge and Balliol, Oxford (Irish Secretary); Virginia Bottomley (Health Secretary) was from a family of public servants (some with left-wing leanings) – her grandfather was secretary of the League of Nations, her father, Dr Maxwell Garnett CBE, who was educated at Rugby and Trinity, Cambridge, ran the Industrial Society, her uncle and aunt were the Labour patricians Douglas and Peggy Jay, and her husband, a Conservative MP, is the second son of Sir James Bottomley, former Ambassador to the United States; and Stephen Dorrell, from a traditional family firm of overall manufacturers, educated at prep school, Uppingham and Brasenose, Oxford (National Heritage Secretary). Dorrell had been an old-fashioned supporter of industry against the flash, lower-class manipulators of money who were coming to dominate the Conservative Party. And Michael Heseltine had returned (President of the Board of Trade). That gives nine indisputably upper-class figures. Jeremy Hanley (Minister without Portfolio, Chairman of the Conservative Party), an accountant with the prestigious firm of Peat, Marwick, Mitchell, was the son of a well-known actor and a famous actress, and had married the ex-wife of Viscount Villiers. The rest of the Cabinet were much more solidly upper middle class than Thatcher's last Cabinet had been. Michael Howard (Home Secretary), John Gummer (Environment), Peter Lilley (Social Security) and Michael Portillo (Employment) were all Cambridge graduates; Tony Newton (Leader of the House), Gillian Shephard (Education) and John Redwood (Wales) were Oxford ones. Lord Mackay (Lord Chancellor) came from a fraction lower in the solid Scottish middle class than Malcolm Rifkind (Defence Secretary). Brian Mawhinney (Transport) was from the equally solid Northern Ireland middle class. David Hunt (Chancellor of the Duchy of Lancaster, responsible for the Citizens' Charter, and Science) was a graduate of Montpellier University in France, and Bristol University. Britain was no classless society; and this was a classless Cabinet only in the sense that all of its members came from the upper, or the upper-middle, class.

In the eighties there had been appalling episodes of violence in which members of racial minorities had both been leading protagonists and suffered as victims, and in which police ineptitude, or worse, had often been a primary element. It was common ground among social commentators, and perhaps, above all, among American observers, black and white, of the British scene (Thomas Cottle, obviously, but also many others) that Britain had been slow and feeble in facing up to problems of racial prejudice and tension. However liberating the trends of the sixties, they had not done much to liberate Britain's Blacks and Asians. Now, in closing Part Five, it is important, first, to be absolutely clear about the population statistics (only in the 1991 census were there, for the first time, questions about ethnic origins), and about the distribution of jobs, as well as of unemployment; and, second, to set discrimination and tension in Britain within an international context (to include America as well as other European countries). My conclusion will be that, given that racism is manifest in every advanced country, the levels of integration achieved by Britain in the mid nineties were better than might well have been predicted ten years earlier; at the bottom of the scale black youths were still suffering disproportionately, but this (as in America) was becoming more and more a class, rather than a purely racial, issue – in the 'enterprise culture' all of the poorest were getting poorer (while some small businessmen, particularly Asian – and Chinese – were doing quite well). The figures first (Table 15, overleaf).

As can be seen, ethnic minorities are not spread evenly throughout the country. In the London borough of Brent they make up nearly 45 per cent of the population, the highest proportion in the country, and they are more than a third of the population of the boroughs of Newham, Tower Hamlets and Hackney. Brixton (in the borough of Lambeth) and Notting Hill (in the run-down part of Kensington) had for years had the reputation almost of black ghettos. Slough, west of London, and Luton, north of London, also have heavy concentrations, while in the provinces the main concentrations are in Bradford, the West Midlands and the Pennine conurbation, with a number of smaller areas, such as Toxteth in Liverpool, also being well known from the newspaper headlines. The ethnic minority population, 47 per cent of whom had been born in Britain, was young and growing: a large proportion of them (33 per cent) were under sixteen (only 19 per cent of the white population were under

Table 15: Population by ethnic group and region in thousands and percentages

	Black	Indian, Pakistani or Bangladeshi	Other ethnic groups	All ethnic groups	White	Ethnic groups as a percentage of total
Britain	891	1,480	645	3,015	51,874	5.5
North	5	21	13	39	2,988	1.3
Yorkshire & Humberside	37	144	33	214	4,623	4.4
E. Midlands	39	120	29	188	3,765	4.8
E. Anglia	14	14	15	43	1,984	2.1
South-East	610	691	395	1,695	15,513	9.9
Greater London	535	521	290	1,346	5,334	20.2
Rest of S. East	74	170	104	349	10,179	3.3
South-West	22	17	24	63	4,547	1.4
W. Midlands	102	277	45	424	4,726	8.2
North West	47	147	50	245	5,999	3.9
England	875	1,431	605	2,911	44,144	6.2
Wales	9	16	16	42	2,794	1.5
Scotland	6	32	24	63	4,936	1.3

Source: *Social Trends 1994*, p. 25.

sixteen). Employment patterns are well worth studying. Blacks and Bangladeshis in the professions were so few that they didn't show up in the percentages (see Table 16), but Indians, both male and female, are highly represented here. Unskilled jobs were largely done by Blacks and Whites (though the percentage of Blacks is double that of the Whites).

From these figures we can see that there was integration of ethnic minorities into the major sectors of the labour market; but if we consider unemployment rates among the different ethnic groups (*Social Trends 1995*, p. 78), then we see that there was also serious disadvantage. By a fraction, the highest percentage of overall unemployment was to be found among the Pakistanis and Bangladeshis, at 27.9 per cent, with Blacks only a shade less badly off. But Blacks were worst off with regard to long-term (over a year) unemployment, at 15.8 per cent; the percentage of Pakistanis and Bangladeshis was only a fraction lower. Among Whites, by contrast, overall unemployment was at 9.1 per cent and long-term at 4.0 per cent. The Indian long-term unemployment rate was about twice that of the White, with the overall rate at about 14 per cent. (Again figures are for spring 1994.)

Table 16: People in employment by ethnic group, occupation, and sex, spring '94

	Black	Indian	Pakistani or Bangladeshi	Other ethnic minority groups	All ethnic minority groups	White	All
Males							
Professional	—	13.7	—	19.5	11.7	8.2	8.4
Intermediate	25.2	30.5	18.3	28.2	26.3	31.1	0.9
Skilled non-manual	13.7	13.5	15.7	16.8	14.7	11.6	11.8
Skilled manual	28.6	22.3	33.5	19.2	25.3	31.6	31.3
Partly skilled	17.2	17.0	22.9	11.1	16.9	13.4	13.5
Unskilled	9.4	—	—	—	5.1	4.1	4.1
	94.1	97.0	90.4	94.8	100.0	100.0	100.0
Females							
Professional	—	7.0	—	—	4.8	2.6	2.6
Intermediate	35.1	23.2	28.7	30.9	29.4	30.3	30.3
Skilled non-manual	28.8	34.2	40.7	35.9	33.5	37.0	36.8
Partly skilled	14.2	26.7	—	13.0	18.7	15.5	15.7
Unskilled	9.7	—	—	—	5.5	6.6	6.5
	87.8	91.1	69.4	79.8	91.9	92.0	91.9

Source: *Social Trends 1995*, p. 20.

On the positive side, incidents of police provocation had declined greatly, and, indeed, almost seemed to have been replaced by the close consultation between police and ethnic communities required by law. Slowly, Black and Asian numbers were increasing in the police forces, as also in local government and many other walks of life. Some of the most-worshipped international football and athletics stars were Black. The kind of rioting which had been new to modern British life in the 1980s continued, as we shall see: but it was usually White-inspired, often multi-racial, and only occasionally motivated purely by the grievances of a racial minority. Special resources for providing English language teaching were a particularly valuable integrative tool; unfortunately they began to disappear in the economies of early 1995. Apart from the tragedy of high youth unemployment, the most serious developments were the increase in violent racist attacks (on, in particular, Asians), the high tensions, exploited by the racist British National Party (BNP), in areas of inadequate housing, and, on the other side, the increasing fundamental-ism of certain Muslim groups. In the five years 1988–93, reported racist attacks doubled; in that latter year, a BNP member briefly won a local seat in the run-down former London Docks area of the Isle of Dogs. Some politicians from all parties called for stronger anti-racist legislation. That probably was needed; however – and this of course is no excuse – all the same sorts of problems were highly visible in all the Western countries, where events made it clear that it simply was inaccurate to single out Britain as a country peculiarly beset by race problems.

That Britain now indisputably was a multi-racial society comes out in the statistics of membership of the different churches (Table 17), though what these figures demonstrate most forcibly is that majority Britain, White Britain, was overwhelmingly a secular society.

The figure of 6.44 million members of the traditional churches amounts to no more than 15 per cent of the UK adult population, the lowest church membership figure in Western Europe. A deeply secular society indeed, where Christian Democracy of the continental type would simply be impossible. The British Conservative Party was now somewhat to the right of European Conservatives and frequently expressed irritation when the British churches gave voice to their social conscience. It is worth noting that the highest level of church membership in the European Union is in the Republic of Ireland, and that church membership is also high in Northern Ireland: here is a very critical difference between mainland Britishness and Irishness of either variety. On the mainland, 11.7 per cent of adults attend church once a week or more. If we turn away from actual church membership, and regular church attendance, we find that slightly over 70 per cent of adults in the UK claimed to have some religious affiliation – interestingly this is about the same proportion as in 1970; that is to say, though not practising church-goers, a substantial majority of British people retained a sentimental attachment to religion (and use the churches for life's major ceremonies, particularly marriage and burial). The constancy of the number of practising Jews is noteworthy; there are, of course, far more Jews in the population as a whole, but they are very much integrated into secular society. The figures reflect the growth of Asian communities, and also the growth of the Greek popu-lation. There has also been a growth in fundamentalist and American-inspired inspirational religions (Mormons, etc.).

I have already discussed (in Chapter 24) the intimidating growth of crime, and want to come now to the prevalence of rioting and general

Table 17: UK church membership (aged 16 and over) (in millions)

	1970	1980	1992
Traditional British Christian			
Anglican	2.55	2.18	1.81
Presbyterian	1.64	1.51	1.24
Methodist	0.69	0.54	0.46
Baptist	0.30	0.24	0.23
Other Free Churches	0.53	0.52	0.66
Roman Catholic	2.71	2.34	2.04
Total	8.42	7.33	6.44
Greek Orthodox	0.19	0.20	0.28
Non-traditional			
Mormons	0.09	0.11	0.15
Jehovah's Witnesses	0.06	0.08	0.13
Spiritualists	0.05	0.05	0.04
Others	0.08	0.11	0.14
Total	0.28	0.35	0.46
Non-Christian			
Muslims	0.25	0.31	0.52
Sikhs	0.08	0.15	0.27
Hindus	0.05	0.12	0.14
Jews	0.11	0.11	0.11
Others	0.05	0.05	0.08

Source: (Adapted from) *Social Trends 1995*, p. 222.

violence. Obviously the decline in the churches is part of the widespread decline of agencies of social control and propagation of ideas of right and wrong and correct social behaviour. But if religion no longer dominates and controls, it has left its indelible mark on British society. Secular Anglicanism and the Anglican legacy of tolerance have been referred to many times in this book. Methodists, Baptists, and other Free Churches are historically known as 'Nonconformists' – they refused to conform to the practices of the Anglican Church. They have contributed to the general heritage of nonconformity and independent-mindedness which, of course, came so spectacularly alive in the 1960s. These churches, too, along with the established Presbyterian Church in Scotland, have left a legacy of social commitment, and with respect to the Presbyterian Church in particular, a deep sense of democracy.

Britain in the eighties, I remarked at the end of Chapter 21, was a country of confrontation, of demonstrations and riots; and so it continued in the nineties. Throughout the country there were decaying urban areas, and modern, but utterly dilapidated, suburban estates, where the threat of rioting accompanied by destruction of property and violence against the person was endemic, particularly in the summer months. Such riots could be touched off by police attempts to interfere with anything from drug dealing to local youths (known as 'hotters') turning streets into race tracks (using stolen vehicles), by incidents of racial discrimination, by police acting in an inappropriately violent manner, or by almost any act, malicious or unintentional. More spectacular were the demonstrations in the centres of major cities against the many unpopular aspects of Government policy, quickly turned into violent rioting by some miscalculation or provocative action by the police, or by the 'rent-a-mob' minority of professional agitators. On I April 1990 the *Observer* front page carried a photograph of a shirtless demonstrator in front of a blazing building, with the headline: 'Scores hurt, buildings blaze in poll tax riot'. Inside were stunning photographs of mounted riot police charging fleeing demonstrators, a demonstrator lying unconscious on the street, and riot police making an arrest (pictures, of course, duplicated in all the papers). Two reports give a fair impression of the appropriate distribution of blame between police and certain demonstrators. From the front page:

Buildings were set on fire, police vehicles overturned, cars set ablaze, shops looted and scores of people injured, including at least fifty-one policemen, some of them seriously, when violence erupted at a massive poll-tax demonstration near Downing Street yesterday.

The full-scale riot began when an initially peaceful demonstration – attended by an estimated 200,000 people – erupted into one of the most violent in London for a generation. Two men in their twenties received serious head injuries and one was in a critical condition in St Thomas's hospital last night . . .

The poll-tax battle began in Whitehall as police in riot gear drew truncheons and charged at crowds that had streamed down from Trafalgar Square, where demonstrators had gathered after taking part in anti-poll tax marches across London. Mounted police were called in and charged the crowds.

Protesters responded by showering police with placards, milk crates and traffic bollards. Several Portakabins, attached to a large building, were then set on fire.

In Cranbourn Street a car showroom was smashed with rocks, torn up paving slabs and iron rods, and all the cars had their windows broken. Terrified theatre-goers huddled in doorways . . .

Flames . . . were seen coming from the ground floor of South Africa House. But a fleet of four fire engines that had been sent to tackle the blaze were pelted with missiles and prevented from getting through until police, in vans and on foot, managed to force a way. Fire crews finally put out a blaze in a seven-storey office block in Trafalgar Square at 7.30 pm . . .

Several police vehicles were overturned in the riot during which more than 300 people were arrested and many people were taken away with blood streaming from head wounds. A Scotland Yard spokesman said one officer knocked unconscious outside the Cabinet Office had suffered serious head injuries. More than 100 police officers were treated in mobile hospital wagons behind Whitehall at the height of the riot . . .

Passers-by took refuge in the Lumière cinema while demonstrators smashed windows and looted shops. Others set fire to cars . . .

The report inside quoted a photographer:

'People were upset, crying, and frustrated because of the crush and the fact they could not escape. The police had cut off both ends of the roads and kept trying to push people through to the main body of Trafalgar Square,' he said . . .

'People had got very frightened; some were even hysterical. Others were upset because they were split from their friends in the crush. It was a crazy situation; in just three quarters of an hour it had turned from a fun family atmosphere into an angry, tense occasion. There was a mob on the streets . . .'

An almost identical pattern emerges in the accounts, four-and-a-half years later, of the demonstration on 9 October 1994 against certain clauses of the Criminal Justice Bill. The main report in *The Times* began with this summary:

Riot police were involved in running battles with protesters last night after violence broke out at the end of a demonstration against the Criminal Justice Bill in London. Officers with batons and riot shields charged repeatedly into crowds in Hyde Park and surrounding streets after being pelted with missiles that included bottles and CS gas canisters.

A policewoman in hospital with serious chest injuries after being hit with a concrete slab was among nineteen officers injured. Eight officers and two members of the crowd were treated for the effects of gas. At least thirty-nine arrests were made and nineteen demonstrators were treated in hospital . . .

The detailed report inside stressed that the protest march 'started in a warm carnival mood . . . before descending into a series of violent clashes', and referred to 'a colourful collection of demonstrators' converging on London 'to show their opposition to proposals to strengthen the law against squatters, rave parties, festivals and other gatherings of New Age travellers'. Chief Superintendent Cullen blamed 'a hard core of six or seven hundred' who came fully prepared with bricks and CS gas. One witness, writing to the *Independent* (12 October 1994), claimed to have seen 'anarchists' retrieving previously hidden crowbars and half-bricks. The *Independent*'s careful analysis on 11 October quoted civil liberties observer Mary-Ann Stephenson as describing the policing as 'a shambles', and as saying 'she had seen several unprovoked attacks on demonstrators by the police'. According to Labour MP Jeremy Corbyn, what started the trouble was the police decision to seal off the exits to Hyde Park, so that demonstrators wishing to leave peacefully felt trapped.

Mr Corbyn said police deliberately charged demonstrators when everyone was leaving, and a number of people, including children, were seriously hurt. 'Police tactics were monumentally ill-conceived,' he said.

In some ways the most interesting comment was that published two days later in the *Independent*, from a young Black police constable:

. . . it was obvious to me that an intolerable amount of vicious and intense violence was used against police officers by a hard core of what can only be described as rent-a-thugs. These nasty, bitter and twisted yobs hijacked a legitimate and harmless demonstration by a wide cross-section of society, whose sole aim, I am sure, was to exercise their democratic right to protest against a Bill before Parliament. The yobs were out to further their own perverse, anarchistic aims, i.e., to force a violent confrontation with police and undermine the value of the excellent bridge-building dialogue that continues between London's police service and the many and diverse communities of the capital . . .

I have policed two previous anti-Criminal Justice Bill demonstrations and on both occasions I was spat on, punched, kicked, and verbally taunted with phrases such as coconut (meaning 'black on the outside, white on the inside'), black traitor and white man's nigger – all this from white adults who complain about the police race relations record and a lack of black police officers. Not once did I retaliate. Not one arrest did I make.

The most eloquent testimony to there indeed being effective 'bridge-building dialogue' in London is that while violent rioting, particularly in the summers of 1991 and 1992, took place in various provincial centres, there was no rioting at all in any of the former London trouble-spots. The one general factor behind the riots in Leeds, Oxford, Birmingham, Cardiff, Tyneside, Coventry, Manchester and Bristol was that, with economic recession, young people, White as well as Black, are the first to lose their jobs. They are thus more than usually frustrated, short of cash, and have extra time on their hands. Hot weather, probably only a marginal influence in itself (certainly, riots do not take place in drenching rain or snow storms), has its effect largely through intensified consumption of beer. Because of tighter policing, violence had almost disappeared from football grounds, though it did sometimes reappear in the streets, and never more pervasively than when, on Wednesday 4 July 1990, Germany knocked England out of the World Cup in Italy. Window-smashing rampages took place the length and breadth of England. A 33-year-old man was killed as he tried to restrain a mob near Southampton; a 67-year-old Brighton pub landlady died of a heart attack after rioters smashed her windows; in West London, a 30-year-old man was killed when hit by a police car. In Leominster youths draped in Union Jacks attacked police. In Woking a Scot wearing a German football shirt was beaten up. On Sunday 28 July 1991, when temperatures topped 80°F, a family carnival on a patch of open ground to the south of the seedy Chapeltown area of Leeds degenerated into a night of stone-throwing, careering around in stolen cars, and attacks on a Latvian club and an Asian video centre. The police response was admitted by West Yorkshire's assistant chief constable to have been 'less than appropriate', while local officers claimed that to have rushed in reinforcements could have sparked more serious violence.

The London *Evening Standard* (3 September 1991) wrote of 'Madness in the heat of the night', Home Office Minister John Patten spoke of 'mindless hooliganism and yobbery for which there can be absolutely no excuse': over three to four days there had been rioting on the Blackbird Leys estate, Oxford, the Ely estate in Cardiff, and in the Handsworth area of Birmingham. A week later there were nights of intense violence on the Meadow Well estate on Tyneside. The 1992 rioting season began in the Wood End estate, Coventry, in May, and spread, most notably to the Ordsall estate in Manchester, and the Hartcliffe estate, Bristol, in July. Blackford Leys was regularly the venue for youths (hotters) to show off their driving skills in stolen high-performance cars, drawing many admirers but also greatly disturbing most of the local residents; the riots were a response to police attempts to put a stop to the fun. In Cardiff the trouble began when an Asian shopkeeper, notorious for his hard line with shop-lifters, took out an injunction against a neighbouring Welsh newsagent who had taken to selling basic foods at lower prices. The Handsworth riots came when a power failure and blackout provided the opportunity for massive looting. Meadow Well had become a centre for stolen cars, used for ram raids on shops: the riots began when two car thieves were killed in a police chase. Wood End's problem was young motorbikers, rather as at Blackbird Leys, using the estate as a race track and demonstration area; the trouble flared when police attempted to arrest one of the bikers. The Ordsall estate was a battleground for drug gangs using stolen vehicles; it was attempted police intervention which provoked the riots. At Hartcliffe the rioting began when two men riding a stolen police motorcycle died in a collision with an unmarked police vehicle. The twee pastoral names of many of the estates speak of earlier aspirations after decent housing standards for all. At Ordsall attempts were actually being made to renovate the run-down property; at Wood End and Blackbird Leys there were hard-working citizens who welcomed the interventions of the police. Certainly it would be simplistic to blame the police; they were, after all, faced with manifest wrongdoing, whose basic common denominator was alienated youth without constructive outlets for energy and talent. However, heavy-handed police action (it was claimed that two officers had assaulted a mother while in pursuit of her brother) was cited as the immediate cause of rioting which broke out in the mainly Asian district of Manningham in Bradford, spreading over the nights of Friday and Saturday 9 and 10 June 1995. On 5 July riots broke out on the Marsh Farm estate in Luton, followed on 10 July by rioting in the Hyde Park area of Leeds. That throughout all types of rioting and demonstrations there was little loss of life must above all be attributed to the British police not being armed.

One success claimed for the Majorite continuation of Thatcherite policies was that in 1994 the statistics for strikes were the lowest ever since records began in 1891; it really did appear that the days of great industrial struggles were over. This was not quite true. There was a six months' ambulancemen's strike in 1989–90 and over two months of sporadic action by signalmen in the summer of 1994, in each case strikes by skilled and responsible members of the community. Both revealed the separation of Government from society in that both had widespread public support; but neither made much in the way of real gains for the strikers. In 1995 both teachers and parents were incensed by the Government's refusal to fund teachers' pay awards, while nurses and midwives prepared for action by abandoning their historic no-strike policies. Disaffection from Government showed itself particularly impressively in two other ways, noteworthy for their involvement of substantial middle-class elements. Campaigns of civil disobedience against the Government's road-building programme, in the form of the physical occupation of sites either of great natural beauty or where local home-owners would be gravely affected, and obstruction of the actual work, had a long history. Protesters against the M11 link road in Leytonstone, east London, developed staggeringly ingenious methods – concealed tunnels, 'rat-runs' at first-floor level, masses of netting across trees and houses – to hold up demolition of housing. Protesters camped out in Pollock Castle Woods, a prized local amenity on the south side of Glasgow and site of construction works for a projected M77 extension, achieved a spectacular, and agreeably comic, success in February 1995: apparently Conservative M P and junior Minister in the Scottish Office Allan Stewart had come out, with his son and half-a-dozen others, to confront the protesters and tear down their banners; Mr Stewart's injudicious action in picking up a fiercesome-looking pickaxe led directly to his becoming the fourteenth Minister to resign from John Major's accident-prone administration. However, it was the persistent series of obstructions at seaports and airports against the export of live calves destined for continental veal crates that drew such headlines as: 'The middle class goes militant' (*Observer*, 22 January 1995); 'Ideology is dead . . . long live animals!' (*Independent* leader, 21 January); 'Grief and fury over veal "martyr"' (*Independent*, 3 February 1995). Jill Phipps had been crushed to death by a livestock lorry two days previously outside Coventry airport. Active, though almost entirely non-violent, civil disobedience at Shoreham in West Sussex had tied up 1,000 riot police and succeeded in having the port closed to the live-animal trade until a much-criticized judicial decision in favour of the live-animal traders. The *Independent* leader just referred to concluded:

> We should celebrate this week's victory by the animal rights campaigners. It shows that politics has not died in the post-Communist West. Environmentalism demonstrates that people have global concerns. They have not become introverted in their politics. Even modern technology and the police cannot frighten them. People can still bind together in a common, worthy cause and win.

So what values were closest to the hearts of a majority of the British people in the 1990s? The most complete picture is provided by the annual

British Social Attitudes reports, published for Social and Community Planning Research by Dartmouth Publishing Company Limited. What emerges, remembering what I have already said about the complexities and contradictions of human responses, suggests the persistence of secular Anglicanism, the continuing growth of tolerance and the community spirit, but also a strong element of traditional hard-headedness and even harshness or philistinism (with regard, say, to education, scrounging on state benefits, authority, censorship, crime, and culture and the arts). Tables 18–23 (all from *British Social Attitudes 1995*) relate to major issues discussed throughout this book.

There is no extremism, no fundamentalism in these figures, and considerable evidence of differences of outlook. The balance is well in favour of the Welfare State, but strongly conservative views come through too.

Table 18: Higher welfare spending versus lower taxes (per cent)

	1983	1986	1990	1993
If the Government had to choose it should . . .				
reduce taxes and spend less on health, education and social benefits	9	5	3	4
keep taxes and spending at the same levels as now	54	44	37	29
increase taxes and spend more on health, education and social benefits	32	46	54	63

Table 19: Attitudes to Government spending on specific items (per cent)

	More	Same as now	Less
Health	87	9	1
Education	79	16	1
Old-age pensions	78	17	1
The police and law enforcement	68	25	3
The environment	54	36	3
Unemployment benefits	48	39	8
The military and defence	21	40	33
Culture and the arts	10	38	44

Table 20: Attitudes to welfare (per cent)

	Agree	Neither agree nor disagree	Disagree
The welfare state makes people nowadays less willing to look after themselves	41	24	34
The welfare state encourages people to stop helping each other	32	29	36
Most people on the dole are fiddling one way or another	31	30	38
Around here, most unemployed people could find a job if they really wanted one	27	20	52
Most people who get social security don't really deserve any help	24	25	50
If welfare benefits weren't so generous, people would learn to stand on their own two feet	25	22	52

There is wide agreement on severe punishments for crime. Thus (recalling also the civil disobedience campaigns I have just been discussing) the statistic indicating relative tolerance for the breaking of laws which are 'wrong' is particularly interesting. Overall one can see why the famous utterance associated with Tony Blair while still Shadow Home Secretary should have had such resonance, 'tough on crime, tough on the causes of crime'. Finally, Tables 22 and 23 illustrate, on the one hand, the growth of environmentalist and community-based attitudes with regard to road-building and public transport, and, on the other, a resurgence of the traditional belief in the value of school examinations.

News reports and viewing figures at Christmas 1994 indicated that the Queen's annual Christmas broadcast was no longer considered an event absolutely central to the family Christmas; news reports for several years had been revealing all the details of the marital misfortunes and extra-marital activities of the younger royals, the Prince and Princess of Wales and the Duke and Duchess of York. Enthusiasm for the monarchy, as polls revealed, was on the wane. There was still acceptance of the monarchy as an integral part of the constitution, but about three-quarters of all voters felt that it should no longer be a charge on the taxpayer. While cost

Table 21: Respect for authority, tradition, law

	Per cent who agree
Schools should teach children to obey authority	88
Young people today don't have enough respect for traditional British values	74
Censorship of films and magazines is necessary to uphold moral standards	65
The law should be obeyed, even if a particular law is wrong	43
People who break the law should be given stiffer sentences	85
For some crimes, the death penalty is the most appropriate sentence	74
In favour of the death penalty	65

Table 22: Roads versus public transport (preferences in per cent)

	In towns or cities		In country areas	
	1991	1993	1991	1993
If the government had to choose it should				
improve roads	44	39	38	34
improve public transport	55	59	61	64

Table 23: Value of exams (in secondary schools)

Per cent agreeing that:	1987	1990	1993
Formal exams are the best way of judging the ability of pupils	44	47	53
A pupil's everyday classroom work counts for too little	70	62	60

was undoubtedly the main issue, the position of the monarchy is also bound up with questions of national identity and the nature of the United Kingdom, which I shall take up at the very end of this chapter.

Before that I want to conduct another overview of life-styles and leisure

Table 24: Percentage of households possessing main consumer products

	1986	1988	1990	1992
Car	62.4	66.0	66.8	67.6
One	44.3	45.0	43.9	45.1
Two	14.9	17.5	19.1	18.7
Three	3.2	3.6	3.8	3.8
Central heating	70.1	76.5	79.3	81.8
Washing machine	82.9	84.6	86.3	87.9
Refrigerator	96.9	98.0	98.1	99.2
Freezer	69.2	75.2	80.1	83.5
Television	97.1	98.0	98.1	98.3
Telephone	80.9	84.7	87.4	88.4
Home computer	15.1	16.9	16.8	19.1
Video recorder	36.3	50.2	61.2	69.3

Source: *Annual Abstract of Statistics 1994*, p. 259

activities, arts and entertainments, and sexual attitudes and behaviour. With regard to life-styles and leisure activities there is little to add to the summary I gave in Chapter 22, save that, in one major initiative that really was in tune with the deeper movements in British society generated in the sixties, the Government was freeing pubs, shops, and race-courses from the last of the Victorian shibboleths and restrictions: citizens (and tourists) could take their children into pubs, and throughout Sunday could buy anything at all, including alcohol, or bet on a horse and watch it run. Basically the steady acquisition of the main consumer products characteristic of the modern Western way of life continued.

The major trend is towards increasingly home-based leisure activities; more than other Europeans the British were video addicts, borrowing from the vast number of video shops that had appeared in the last few years. Television viewing figures changed little; but at the end of 1993 satellite TV had about three million subscribers, 12.1 per cent of all TV households. However, at least in the short-term, the general insecurity of which I have spoken once or twice was reflected in a greater caution in consumer purchases. The neat twist was that sales of the old-fashioned printed book rose (by 5.2 per cent in 1993). On average, the British were spending £43.73 per head per adult on books, compared with £39.98 in France, £30.80 in the Netherlands, £49.98 in Germany and £53.43 in the United States. Against these latter figures it has to be added that the

British make far greater use of public libraries than anyone else – loans run at eleven per person per year, compared with under two in France and Germany, and less in the USA.

Alas, that moral and cheering note is lost in cacophony as we are forced to register that various incidents suggested that British sport, and particularly professional football, which had seemed to be undergoing a renaissance at the end of the eighties, was being contaminated by the swell of corruption so characteristic of the early nineties, and that the appalling prevalence of drug-dealing and drug-consumption described in Chapter 22 was escalating still further. Drug seizures, by value, in 1993 were as follows: cannabis, £176 million; cocaine, £110 million; heroin, £98 million; synthetics (ecstasy, amphetamines, LSD), £133 million – up 215 per cent. Drug dealing was now inextricably bound up with professional criminal gangs linked to violence of all types, including killings. Still more horrific was the development of large-scale drug-taking on the part of children. The prediction for 1995 was that one eleven-year-old in five would have taken drugs, compared with fewer than one in ten in 1989; and that almost half of all sixteen-year-olds would have done so.

Drugs, sleaze, insecurity: were the times propitious for the arts? This is a sphere, above all others, in which simple correlations must not be attempted. As in the eighties there were individual successes in all branches of the arts, but it is difficult to escape from an overall impression of decline, of the energy and innovation that sprang out of the sixties not being sustained, of market testing and performance appraisal being applied in a domain where they were at their most utterly inappropriate. The British, we have noted, were not at all enthusiastic about Government patronage of the arts; the Government was not very enthusiastic either – and just as there was in the Civil Service, the NHS, and in Social Security, so there was reorganization in the administration of the arts, from 1992 placed in the hands of the newly created office of Secretary of State for the National Heritage. On 1 April 1994 the Arts Council of Great Britain, already a much scoffed-at shadow of the noble enterprise which had emerged from the Second World War, was replaced by separate Councils for England, Scotland and Wales. Due credit should be given to initiatives developed to provide facilities for the disabled, and to encourage the arts in minority communities.

In public building, the ubiquitous, tricky, eclectic, 'postmodernist' style was beginning to become downright boring, but Britain undoubtedly still had international giants in Richard Rogers (who emerged as a thunderous critic of the Government's *laissez-faire* attitudes to urban planning) and Norman Foster. They were joined by Nicholas Grimshaw, who in 1994 won the Royal Institute of British Architects' Building of the Year award for the London terminal for Channel Tunnel trains, Waterloo International, and Terry Farrell, architect of Embankment Place (on top of Charing Cross station). Four years earlier a new tallest building in Britain had joined the London skyline: the 800-foot Canary Wharf (exempted from planning restrictions, because situated in the Government-designated Docklands Enterprise Zone), designed by American-Italian architect, Cesar Pelli. 'The impact on the skyline', said a leading British architect, Francis Tibbalds, 'is quite dreadful. It's just not in the same league as classic sky-scrapers like the Chrysler building in New York.' Several major issues are united in the case of the National Opera House for Wales at Cardiff Bay. The competition for the commission to build the Opera House was won, towards the end of 1994, by an architect who was both an Iraqi and female, Zaha Hadid. The design was excitingly original and modernist in the most uncompromising sense, with not a smidgen of fashionable postmodernist tat about it. The local newspaper and the Welsh National Opera Trust (which tried to institute what was in effect a re-run of the competition) were against it. This was sheer common or garden philistinism, quite certainly, rather than racism or male chauvinism; fortunately the original decision was confirmed early in 1995. In the visual arts, it continued to be true, as I put it in Chapter 23, 'that there was life and variety in contemporary British painting'. But the fashion was for a kind of neo-Surrealist radical avant-gardism produced by extremely young artists (many from hitherto down-market Goldsmith's College) – of whom the most written-about in the tabloid press, and the most commercially successful, was Damien Hirst. As *Independent* critic Andrew Graham-Dixon put it in an article (16 February 1993) entitled 'Radical chic and the schlock of the new': 'In a culture dedicated to novelty, precedence begins to count for everything: it is not the depth of the idea that matters, but the fact that no one else had it before.' Whatever their status as art, the products of this approach are important as the very embodiment of the weird combination of brash commercialism and pedantic political correctness everywhere to be found infecting the artistic, intellectual, and academic worlds. Perhaps Marc Quinn's *Self* of 1991, a cast of the painter's own head made by pouring nine pints of his own blood into a mould and then freezing it, can be taken as a paradigmatic example. Graham-Dixon commented:

it looks less horrific than it sounds; you need to be told that it is made out of blood for its unpleasantness to work. It seems probable that this is the first time such a gesture has been performed by an artist, so Quinn can at least claim to have risen above the crisis of originality. But outlandishness can't make up for witlessness . . . Profound claims have been advanced for it as a sculpture for the AIDS era but, if anything, that makes the work even less engaging. So it isn't even enigmatic: its oddity is hedged round with worthy social concern.

Although there were still just about enough experimental theatres and classical presentations to keep falling audiences happy, retrenchment was the most obvious characteristic in the world of drama: 'the nation's repertoire has become progressively conservative,' the Theatrical Management Association reported in October 1994. Retrenchment or hype: heavy advertising and the appearance of popular television performer John Thaw contributed to the commercial success at the Royal National Theatre of veteran David Hare's play about an unelectable Labour leader losing an election, *The Absence of War*. Hype and commercialism now seemed also to surround the country's most talked-of avant-garde novelist, Martin Amis. Critic D. J. Taylor attacked (*Sunday Times*, 15 January 1995) the way, as he saw it, most leading novelists were sacrificing character-drawing to (politically correct) cultural determinism, and spoke up for the traditionalist Antonia (A.S.) Byatt, now, indeed, emerging as a kind of *grande dame* of English letters:

> More so than any other English novelist now writing, she has a sense of the emotional limits within which the average person works – no bad thing in an age where the average novel is simply a riot of personal neuroses and an author's advance is somehow more newsworthy than what he writes.

Once again, David Lodge produced an observant novel, *Therapy* (1995). In hospital, the wealthy narrator (writer of a popular television comedy series) encounters a National Health Service patient admitted three days previously: 'nobody had come near him since'; 'he seemed to have dropped into some kind of black hole in the system'. Some words also on 'recession – depression': 'People get depressed because they can't get a job, or their businesses collapse, or their houses are repossessed.'

The British film industry had seemed to be on an 'up' in the late eighties, but it was clear in the nineties that, although there were some sparkling individual successes, there was to be no real recovery, and that the vacuum where government support for film might have been was greater than ever. Figures in the *Film and Television Handbook 1994* indicated that in the Netherlands 13.7 per cent of films shown in 1992 were made in the Netherlands; in Italy, 24 per cent; in France, 35 per cent; in Britain the figure was 3.7 per cent. But the successes really are worth noting: *The Crying Game*, directed by Irishman Neil Jordan, in part set in troubled Northern Ireland, but as one critic (Tom Shone) has put it, a 'florid, thematic thicket of religion, politics and sex'; *Much Ado About Nothing* (Kenneth Branagh), immaculate Shakespeare; *Four Weddings and a Funeral* (Mike Newell), a craftily romantic anti-romantic comedy, neatly catching the manners and morals of the early 1990s, phenomenally successful in the United States; and *Shallow Grave* (Danny Boyle), a black comedy set among young Edinburgh professionals, very Scottish and very, very funny.

The Broadcasting Act of 1990 led to the replacement of the Independent Broadcasting Authority (which, as the ITA, had, in the golden days of British Television, shared the honours with the BBC in maintaining the very high standards obtained across the board in British television; it had also, within living Conservative memory, supported the Thames Television programme *Death on the Rock*) by the Independent Television Commission (ITC), the Radio Authority, and National Transcommunications Ltd, which was immediately sold off to Mercury Asset Management. One of the first jobs of the ITC was to conduct an auction for the allocation of new commercial television franchises, an auction described by Richard Brooks (*Observer*, 20 October 1991) as bettering 'the wildest plots of any soap opera writer'. The decision to disenfranchise one of independent television's most distinguished companies, Thames, and grant the franchise to Carlton, which simply continued the most successful Thames programmes without itself creating anything of any distinction, was widely criticized. For the first time national commercial radio services were introduced, the first being Classic FM, which began operations in September 1992; it was markedly American in character, broadcasting little gobbets of classical music, and obsessed with compiling hit parades of classical recordings. Promotion by Classic FM was an important factor in the remarkable popular success of the Symphony of Sorrowful Songs by Polish composer Henryk Gorecki. In the world of music generally, retrenchment, once more, was the key-note; yet the array of talent with respect to composers and performers was still quite dazzling, an adjective which perhaps above all applies to solo percussionist Evelyn Glennie. In my *Culture in Britain since 1945* (1991) I noted that standard studies of music always omit Andrew Lloyd Webber, but that his phenomenal success with such musicals as *Cats, Phantom of the Opera,* and *Sunset Boulevard* really did cry out for attention, as did his recent theatre building ventures in Germany and Switzerland. A highly successful crossover initiative (February 1993) was the *Juliet Letters,* sung by pop singer Elvis Costello, with the classical Brodsky Quartet. But the days of British hegemony in rock/pop seemed to be truly over. The *Guardian* (15 December 1993) lamented 'the erosion of British rock', while the *Independent* (23 February 1994) pointed out that 'in 1965 fifteen of the thirty best-selling US singles were British. In 1993 . . . two.' Such groups as Take That, Suede, Blur and Oasis were lionized by teenage girls at home, but scarcely had the international status of Britain's former world-conquerors. Shortly, however, emblematic of what was referred to as 'girl power', there came the Spice Girls, the all-female multi-ethnic Beatles of the nineties.

The notion of teenage girls cavorting with randy rock players had lain at the heart of one aspect of the sixties 'sexual revolution'. Now AIDS was the (almost) ever-present *doppelgänger* in any engagement with sex, though, as I have already remarked, Government campaigns had created an atmosphere of even greater frankness and explicitness than ever. Concern about AIDS was a major motivation behind the idea of a National Survey of Sexual Attitudes and Life-styles, which originated in late 1986 with a group of epidemiologists and statisticians at three of London's most famous medical schools. General approval from the Department of Health was established over the period June to October 1987, and a pilot sample of 977 was interviewed in the autumn of 1988. Long delays then followed over the release of government funds; in September 1989, it became known that Mrs Thatcher had vetoed the project, though no official statement giving reasons was ever made. In the event, the privately funded Wellcome Trust took over the financing with a grant of £900,000. Between May 1990 and November 1991, interviews, confined to mainland Britain, were completed with 18,876 men and women aged 16–59 (out of an original sample of 26,393). The survey was eventually published as Kaye Wellings *et al., Sexual Behaviour in Britain* (Penguin Books, 1994).

The first issue addressed was that of the age at which first sexual intercourse takes place. Three recent trends were identified: 'a progressive reduction . . . in the age at which first intercourse occurs, an increase in the proportion of young women who have had sexual intercourse before the age of sexual consent [sixteen] and a convergence in the behaviour of men and women'. While the survey did suggest that press reports of teenage sexual activity were slightly exaggerated in that their interviews were usually focused on those who manifestly were already sexually active, rather than on a sample of the population as a whole, it was in no doubt that a 'sizeable minority of young people are now sexually active before the age of sixteen': in the 16–19 age group, 18.7 per cent of females had had sexual intercourse before the age of sixteen, and 27.6 per cent of males; both change and convergence are demonstrated by the statistics that of women in the age group 55–59 only 1 per cent had had sex before sixteen, while the figure for men was 5.8 per cent. The median age for young people (male and female) was seventeen. In general the researchers found no difference between ' "permissive" south and "puritanical" north' (though females in Scotland and in East Anglia tended to lose their virginity about a year later than in other parts of the country): sex is indeed a great unifying and democratic force! With regard to the spread of AIDS, it was found that 'non-use of contraception at first intercourse has declined steadily over recent decades, and was reported by fewer than a quarter of women and fewer than a third of men aged 16–24.'

There had been a sharp increase in the use of condoms among the young; use of the pill, hailed in the sixties as the great herald of freedom, was highest among women aged 25–34. That even very young women were taking more control over their lives was shown by the way in which first intercourse had increasingly become a matter of deliberate choice:

First intercourse seems to have been characterized by more planning and less spontaneity in recent years. Younger women in the sample were less likely than older women to report first intercourse having been mainly associated with being 'carried away by their feelings'.

The ideal of monogamy was in decline. Well into adult life the number of people continuing to experience sex with more than one partner, usually serially, but sometimes concurrently, was increasing: 'Only 43.1 per cent of cohabiting men and 59.9 per cent of cohabiting women reported monogamy over the last five years, with 24.3 per cent of men and 12.7 per cent of women reporting concurrent partnerships.' Loss of sexual inhibitions was shown in the growth of variation in sexual practices:

for both men and women experience of oral and non-penetrative sex appears to have increased through the decades of the 1950s and 1960s, reaching a steady level of more than 80 per cent of those who experienced their first sexual intercourse in the 1970s onwards.

The survey also cast light on one other particularly obscure area. The propaganda of gay activists had tended to give the impression that gays were a substantial minority group. The survey suggested that all previous estimates of the number of gays were greatly exaggerated, summarizing its own findings in the following cautious way:

Several estimates of the prevalence of homosexual behaviour are provided. These range from 6.1 per cent of men and 3.4 per cent of women reporting any homosexual experience in their lifetime to 1.1 per cent of men and 0.4 per cent of women reporting having had a homosexual partner in the past year. For many, it seems, homosexual experience is transitory and unlikely to lead to a permanent behaviour pattern. It is more likely to be reported by men than by women.

The data show clearly that there is no 'typical' homosexual profile. Homosexual behaviour is reported across a broad range of social and demographic back-grounds. The main exception to this is the higher prevalence in London, which seems likely to be attributable to the more hospitable climate and the greater range of amenities existing there.

From accelerating permissiveness, two important facts, set out clearly in *Social Trends 1994*, follow. Large numbers of people were now cohabit-ing in stable relationships without actually bothering to get married, and there was a substantial number (the largest in Europe) of 'single-parent families' (in fact almost exclusively 'single-woman families'). In 1992 those cohabiting without actually being married amounted to eighteen per cent of the total number of unmarried adults (it was now formally correct to refer to the person you are living with as your 'partner'). *Social Trends 1994* summarized the second phenomenon as follows:

There were about 1.3 million one-parent families in Great Britain in 1991, containing about 2.2 million dependent children. Between 1971 and 1991, one-parent families with dependent children as a proportion of all families with dependent children more than doubled. The rate of increase has quickened in pace recently, mainly due to the increase in lone mothers. In the four years up to 1991 the number of single lone parents grew, increasing by 24 per cent, while the number of dependent children in one-parent families increased by half a million, from 1.7 million in 1987. In 1991 just over 17 per cent of families with dependent children were headed by a lone mother compared with just over 1 per cent headed by a lone father. The figures reflect the rise in both divorce and births outside marriage.

In fact, divorces more than doubled between 1971 and 1991 (in which year there was one divorce for every two marriages).

Contrary to foreign myths about the British, what the national sex survey demonstrated was that the British did not in general suffer from hang-ups about sex. In the words of the survey, 'most people, more than two-thirds of women and more than three-quarters of men, judged their first intercourse to have been well timed'. More broadly:

The view which emerges predominantly from these data is one of the British as a nation strongly committed to the idea of the heterosexual monogamous union, but of considerable relaxation in attitudes towards teenage sexuality and, in particular, sex before marriage. Although there is no widespread support for a lowering of the age of sexual consent, views on the age before which sexual intercourse is thought to be inadvisable accord remarkably well with the current patterns in behaviour. Nor is there apparent widespread opposition to the idea of sexual intercourse occurring before marriage. Acceptance of pre-marital sex is now nearly universal, as indeed is its practice.

British attitudes towards sex, then, are characterized, on the whole, by pragmatism, commonsense, tolerance, and a certain respect for traditional monogamous ideals.

But the dread spectre of AIDS was always there, now clearly an issue for the overwhelming heterosexual majority. In the year to the end of March 1994 the number of cases reported was 1,704, a rise of 9 per cent on the previous year's total. Taking these two years together the number of cases reported in women increased by 44 per cent (from 149 to 214). Total numbers of heterosexuals infected increased by 33 per cent (226 to 300). Those infected through drug injection increased by 61 per cent (from 83 to 134). At the end of March 1994 there had been notification of a grand total of 21,718 HIV infections. Homosexual activity accounted for 60 per cent of this total; this remained by far the largest group, but was decreasing – down to 57 per cent of cases in the previous year. Sixteen per cent of all HIV cases had resulted from heterosexual intercourse; but in the most recent twelve months, up to March 1994, the proportion had gone up to 28 per cent.

Turning from that grim subject, let us conclude this chapter by turning to questions of nationality and identity, which, because of Labour Party proposals for devolution for Scotland and Wales and regional assemblies for parts of England, and because of the dramatic turn for the better in Northern Ireland, were very much issues of public concern. An ICM/ Rowntree Trust poll in 1994 attempted to elicit from sample groups of Scots, Welsh and English their sense of national identity. Each sample group was asked: 'Which of these five alternatives best reflects how you regard yourself?'. Replies, in per cent of each national sample, were:

	Scots	Welsh	English
Scots, Welsh, English (as appropriate), not British	37	28	16
More Scots, etc., than British	27	20	12
Equally Scots, etc. as British	25	30	43
More British than Scots, etc.	4	7	10
British not Scots, etc.	6	14	15

Clearly the strongest sense of a separate national identity is to be found among the Scots, while it is among the English that there is the strongest sense of British identity. But even among the Scots a substantial majority (62 per cent) admit to at least some sense of British identity. And within Scotland (as within England, and as, indeed, throughout the world) there is a complex of more local affiliations – rivalry, and even hostility, between the two major cities, Glasgow and Edinburgh is strong. Many English people are conscious of being first of all, say, Yorkshiremen (or women), 'Geordies' (from North East England), 'Cockneys' (long-established, London-bred, Londoners, i.e. not incomers from elsewhere in Britain, and not, of course, suburbanites), 'Scousers' from Liverpool, and so on. There is also a way in which those born anywhere in the North of England feel themselves to be different from Southerners, more rugged, more honest, less effete (this is traditional and cultural, not simply related to current economic circumstances). Who was more to blame, the English hooligans who beat him up, or the Scot (living, note, in England) who provocatively put on a German football shirt? The Scots take their separate identity in sport much more seriously than the English, who would be surprised to know that most Scots are delighted to see teams from England (historically 'the Auld Enemy') defeated. But for all these qualifications there is a common Britishness (seen in the sex survey I have just quoted from and in the social attitudes I was discussing earlier). Inevitably

Britishness is dominated by Englishness, yet it is also inflected by elements from the Celtic fringes. At the heart of Britishness in its ideal mode (but whenever does one find anything in ideal mode?) lies an obligation to certain civic virtues, and perhaps (less admirably) an acceptance of certain traditional hierarchies, combined with a thorough disrespect for the centralized state.

In Northern Ireland the Protestants, the majority, cannot but see themselves as in some sense Irish; but also, more fundamentally, they feel themselves to be British, more British than the Welsh, the Scots, or even the English, for they are the 'Unionists', the 'Loyalists'. But to the Welsh, the Scots, and the English, they are un-British in the fervour of their commitment, in their confidence in their own righteousness, in their religious bigotry and in their conspicuous lack of essential ingredients of the British self-image as held in Britain itself, tolerance, restraint, and fairness towards the minority. British governments placed British troops in Northern Ireland because, in a British sort of way, they recognized that, as a consequence of British sins in the past, Britain had a responsibility for preventing militants from both communities from totally drenching the province in bloodshed and violence. So ensued the apparently unbreak-able deadlock and the IRA terror campaign, which continued, on both sides of the Irish Sea, right up to 31 August 1994, when the IRA declared its ceasefire. By the end of the year talks between British Government, Irish Government, and Sinn Fein, the political wing of the IRA, were well under way. The most abrasive, and most detached, element was the Northern Ireland Unionist leadership: what was uncertain was whether these uncompromising politicians represented the views of their constitu-ents, or whether the people of Northern Ireland, at last living something like a normal life, would themselves become a force demanding that the talks be kept going until a genuinely permanent peace could be estab-lished. High tension returned with the release at the beginning of July 1995 of Private Lee Clegg, after he had served two years of the life sentence imposed on him upon his conviction for the murder of a joy-rider; while meantime the peace process stalled.

Wittingly or not, the British Government projected a sense of wanting the IRA to admit the error of their ways; indeed to, as the IRA perceived it, surrender. The British Government could not quite see that the urgent prior problem was that of conflict resolution, not of rights and wrongs, while Sinn Fein could not avoid seeing how dependent Major was on the Ulster Unionists for his parliamentary majority. One very immediate danger was of the Protestant paramilitaries reacting to the possibility of any kind of agreement with increased violence. Sensibly, the British Government issued reassurances that it was certainly not committed to a united Ireland, and that there could be no question of the people of Northern Ireland being forced into such a union. The Protestant paramilitaries, assured that there had been no secret deal with the Provisionals, declared a ceasefire of their own on 13 October 1995. But very soon it was apparent that one disruptive annual fixture that would not go away was that at Drumcree. Trying to show sensitivity to Nationalist sentiment, the RUC prohibited Orangemen from marching from the church at Drumcree back along the nationalist Garvaghy Road in Portadown, the route they considered to be hallowed by tradition. David Trimble, law lecturer at Belfast University and MP for Upper Bann, emerged as an uncompromising spokesman for the Orangemen. Despairing of the stalled peace process, the Ulster Unionist party leader, James Molyneux, resigned, to be succeeded by Trimble. For the moment this suggested still greater intransigence amongst the Unionists. Clearly what was needed was some *deus ex machina*. And so indeed President Bill Clinton of the United States arrived in November 1995 for visits both to Northern Ireland and to the Republic, anxious to contribute positively to the peace process. A major initiative was the establishing of an international body, chaired by the former US senator George Mitchell, to deal with the decommissioning of weapons and the initiation of all-party talks.

The Mitchell Report, accepted by the British Government, was delivered on 24 January 1996. It recognized that the paramilitary organizations would not undertake decommissioning in advance of all-party talks. It therefore suggested that decommissioning should take place *during* all-party negotiations, not *before* as the British had been insisting, or *after*, which was the Sinn Fein position. The British Government appeared confident that progress was being made, but if it was now prepared to believe in the permanence of the ceasefire, it was too late. On 4 February 1996 a massive bomb at Canary Wharf in London, which killed two, and injured over a hundred, with more than £85 million of damage, announced the end of the IRA ceasefire. There was a further enormous blast, though no deaths, in Manchester on 15 June.

What, finally, of Europe? All the main structural trends – population movements, patterns of trade – together with leisure activities – holidays, European football competitions – were pulling Britain closer to the Continent, and away from former ties of language and family with the

English-speaking areas of the wider world. Two events of 1994 were, respectively, of great geographical and great symbolic importance: the opening of the Channel Tunnel provided a totally new physical link, and the inauguration of the National Lottery meant that Britain now had a national pastime which had been standard in continental countries back into the mists of time. Radio and television weather forecasts now routinely included continental European countries. Mistrust of European bureaucracy and its mania for an unreflecting uniformity, very properly, remained high. The time of regarding oneself as, say, Scouse, English, British *and* European, or Glaswegian, Scottish, British *and* European, was not yet at hand, though the concept was not intrinsically absurd. European sentiment had to have some genuine roots to survive the constant anti-European onslaughts of the right-wing tabloids. The *Sun* celebrated the fiftieth anniversary of D-Day with a leader (6 June 1994) entitled 'We're Still Fighting in Europe':

> Our role in Europe in 1994 may not be as it was in 1944.
>
> But we are still fighting dictators – the Eurocrats who want us to bow to their laws and life-styles.
>
> Your vote in Thurdsay's Euro elections is a blow in the battle to keep our country British
>
> Not a suburb of Brussels.

Investigating constituency reactions in the Lincolnshire seat of Gainsborough and Horncastle to Conservative leadership splits over Europe, the *Independent* (29 November 1994) found that three young mothers out shopping 'put succinctly views echoed across the constituency' (with clarity, if not necessarily with enthusiasm): 'Britain was in Europe to stay.'

People can make their attitudes and aspirations count. But they can also be helpless in face of the actions and inactions of governments. For governments, choices are not always crystal clear: efficiency and fairness, economic growth and social justice, can be in conflict. But, in respect of the very widest social and cultural issues, Britain's rulers, by 1997, were facing a stark, though multi-faceted, set of choices, involving both internal and external policies. Was Britain to become more and more like America, privileging private interest over public good, callous towards the poor, treating the arts as price-tagged consumables? Or was Britain to rediscover its own generous traditions, melding them with continental concepts of citizenship and social (or Christian) democracy, and sharing a European perception of the arts as essential to a civilized society?

The issues, of course, were not put like that in the general election which took place on 1 May 1997. What was obvious was that the Major Government was dying on its feet (indeed its parliamentary majority totally evaporated when on 3 November 1996 the Conservative MP for Wirral South died). All the polls predicted a substantial Labour victory, though, as I noted on page 355, there was always the fear of a low turnout (a fear partially justified in 1997, and more than fully justified in 2001). In the conventional language of British politics, Tony Blair's 'New Labour' won a 'landslide' victory, in fact the product of the British first-past-the-post electoral system and extreme disenchantment with the Conservatives; certainly, as we can see if we scrutinize the figures, Blair was some distance from having won an overwhelming popular mandate.

General Election, 1 May 1997
Electorate 43.85 million   Turnout 71.2 per cent

	Labour	Conservative	Lib Dem	Nationalist	Others
Total votes	13,518,167	9,600,943	5,242,947	782,580	2,141,647
Percentage	43.2	30.7	16.8	2.5	6.8
Seats	418	165	46	4 Welsh	20
				6 Scottish	

Others are mainly the various Ulster Unionists

Compared with the total number voting for Major in 1992, Blair was actually down by nearly half a million; he had won just 1.3 per cent more of the total vote, 43.2 per cent not really being terribly impressive, though, to be fair, it was slightly better than Thatcher's habitual percentage. The turnout was nearly 6.5 per cent down. Subsequent to the election, Labour's score in public opinion polls did reach some astonishing heights, and some polls indicated that people were claiming to have voted for Blair and Labour when manifestly they could not have done so! But the point I want to drive home, as we come to the end of Part Five, is that, at the time of the election, Labour's massive majority in parliamentary seats was not an accurate reflection of voters' reactions in the country at large, though the low poll for the Conservatives, 4 per cent below that of Kinnock in 1992, certainly is noteworthy.

Part Six

A Faltering Return Towards Consensus? 1997–2002

27

The Odd Shape of the Nation

Apart from a few cliffs toppling into the sea, some modifications to the climate as a consequence of global warming, and certain areas becoming subject to repeated flooding, physical geography, naturally, did not change. But in social geography (conceived broadly in this book to take in political and institutional developments) there were new relationships and new dispositions concerning central government, Scotland and Wales, the English regions, the European continent and, inevitably, Northern Ireland. Veteran class warriors, trendy postmodernists and exuberant celtic nationalists declared that the very notion of there being a unified nation state called 'Britain' was now disintegrating. Exaggeration though this was, Her Majesty's Stationery Office did own to a minor change of perception for 2002: its annual publication, *Britain: an official handbook* (inside which it was always explained that 'Britain' was shorthand for 'The United Kingdom of Great Britain and Ireland'), was now given the brand new title, *UK 2002: The Official Yearbook of Great Britain and Northern Ireland*. Elected to office in May 1997, the Blair Government was committed both to maintaining the unity of the nation state, under the sovereignty of the monarchy, and to reforming aspects of its government.

Devolution for Scotland and Wales, and the abolition of the House of Lords, had been under discussion since the late nineteenth century. Always the devil had been in the detail, and the devil had always been strong enough to prevent any proposals going ahead. A particular problem with devolution, as manifested in the referendums of 1979, had been the lack of unbounded enthusiasm for it among the majority of Scots, and the lack of enthusiasm of any sort among any but a very small minority of the Welsh. But the really big problem for modernizers is that the United Kingdom divides up in a very odd way (compared, say, with America with its fifty states, Germany with its roughly equal *länder* created at the end of the war, or Italy with its even more recently created regions). In population and wealth it is overwhelmingly dominated by England, which has nearly ten times as many inhabitants as Scotland, over sixteen times as many as Wales, and about twenty-five times as many as Northern Ireland. In territory Wales and Northern Ireland are tiny; Scotland is three-fifths the size of England, but much of its territory, as we have seen, is mountainous and sparsely populated. If Scotland had a separate parliament, shouldn't England have one too? But that would add absurdity to oddity, an absurdity only to be overcome by dividing England into separate regions each with at least a local assembly. If Scotland had a separate parliament, but nothing was done about England, how could it be right for Scottish MPs still to come to Westminster and discuss matters purely relating to England? This last point was known as the 'West Lothian question' since it had been posed by the upper-class, Catholic, MP for West Lothian in Scotland, Tam Dalyell, who was as opposed to Scottish self-government as he was to foreign adventures by the British Government.

The question which had always bedevilled House of Lords reform was that of what was to be put in the place of the hereditary house. Because Britain was not shaped to a federal design, the kind of second chamber which existed in the United States, or Germany, could not readily be established, and certainly not in advance of the creation of regional assemblies. In any case, devotees of the British constitution, including Blair and his colleagues, maintained that the establishment of another elected house would derogate from the prestige and powers of the House of Commons. Predictably, progress was slow, with Conservatives claiming that Blair intended a house of 'Tony's cronies'. In November 1999 a compromise was reached whereby 91 hereditary peers would retain their right to sit and vote in a 'transitional' House of Lords. After being re-elected in July 2001, the Government proposed a 600-member chamber, with only 20 per cent elected, while 20 per cent would be nominated by an independent commission, and 60 per cent by the political parties. With backbench Labour MPs demanding a wholly elected chamber, the Conservatives (now led by Ian Duncan Smith) embarked on a mighty policy reversal, proposing a 300-member chamber, only 60 of whom were to be appointed by the independent commission, with the rest being elected, though for deliberately protracted terms of up to fifteen years; the elections would be held in regional constituencies by the traditional first-past-the-post system. For their part many back-bench Conservatives were utterly opposed to this scheme.

By comparison devolution went like greased lightning. As early as September 1997, referendums were held in Scotland and Wales. This time the Scottish vote could scarcely have been more decisive, the Welsh scarcely less. The Scots voted by 1,775,045 votes (74.3 per cent) to 614,400 (25.7 per cent) for a Scottish Parliament, and by 63.5 per cent to 36.5 per cent in favour of that parliament having the power to vary income tax by up to three pence in the pound. In Wales the vote for a National Assembly was 559,419 (50.3) per cent, against 552,698 (49.7 per cent). Wales, nonetheless, would have an Assembly of 60 members (40 elected in the traditional way from single-member constituencies, 'topped up' with 20 elected from party lists by proportional representation), just as Scotland would have a Parliament of 129 MSPs (73 from traditional constituencies, 56 by proportional representation). Elections were held on 9 May 1999. From the start the Scottish Executive took the form of a coalition between Labour and Liberal Democrats; and from October 2000 the Welsh Assembly was run by a similar coalition.

The effect of proportional representation had been to deny Labour the total control in the two countries which the exaggerated effects of complete first-past-the-post voting would have guaranteed. On the whole the Liberal Democrat presence was beneficial in helping to emancipate both administrations from subservience to the Labour Government in London. In Scotland, Liberal Democrat pressure secured the abolition of tuition fees in the Scottish universities; and, while teachers in England and Wales continued to be grossly overworked, Scottish teachers were guaranteed a maximum working week of 35 hours. In contrast with much criticized practices in England and Wales, free personal care for older people in Scotland was to be introduced in April 2002. Against that it was widely claimed that the devolved Scotland, especially after the death of the original First Minister, Donald Dewar, was all too prone to the cronyism and minor corruption that for decades had been endemic in the Scottish Labour Party; it was specially noted that Scotland's most able political figures (Gordon Brown, Robin Cook, etc.) preferred serving in the UK government to serving in the Scottish one. There were also some lamentable incidents of English residents deciding to leave in face of anti-English racism, heartily condemned by the official Scottish Nationalist Party which, in fact, welcomed people of all national and ethnic backgrounds. The most important single point to make is that while life in Scotland was already showing an exciting new vibrancy (the reincarnation of Glasgow as a postindustrial city, historic central Edinburgh's world famous Hogmanay street celebrations, etc.) well before the enactment of devolution, political change did provide a significant further stimulus.

Scotland, Wales – so far, so good. But one of the greatest curiosities bequeathed by Margaret Thatcher was that there was no self-government, no unified administration, for the nation's capital. Thatcher, we saw, had reacted against poor standards of government in the Labour-controlled conurbations. The new Labour Government envisaged salvation through the introduction of directly elected mayors. Ironically, Thatcher's adversary, 'Red Ken' Livingstone, expelled from the Labour Party for standing against the official Labour mayoral candidate, was, in May 2002, elected first mayor of the newly created Greater London Authority, and head of its elected Assembly of 25 members. Actually, the mayor had even less power than the Welsh first minister: nonetheless Livingstone went ahead vigorously in pursuit of solutions to London's appalling transport problems, thereby bringing himself into direct conflict with the Labour government. Other elections followed, with the next major city due to get a mayor being Birmingham, against considerable resistance from traditional Labour municipal politicians. In the meantime, London became on official region, to be counted separately from the South-East.

Among the eight 'genuine' English regions (i.e. not including London) the strongest case for devolution was made by politicians and businessmen in the North-East, who now felt themselves seriously disadvantaged in comparison with their neighbours in Scotland. In fact, Government policy went little beyond the setting up of Regional Development Agencies in each of England's officially designated regions, each allocated a government grant, but charged also with attracting private money. The commonplace with regard to the English regions was that of a 'North/South divide'. The 2001 edition of the Stationery Office publication *Regional Trends* refers specifically to the 'often-quoted difference' that 'income is higher in the south-east and lower in the north:'

Over the period 1997–2000, average gross weekly income for households in London was more than one-and-a-half times that of households in the North East. London and the South East also have the highest proportion of people with a personal taxable income of £50,000 or more. However, this does not give a full picture as weekly household expenditure and housing costs for those living in the south are higher than the national average and house prices continue to rise at a faster rate. The increase in house prices in the South East between 1999 and 2000 was almost 19 per cent compared with increases of 3 and 4 per cent in the North East and North West respectively.

One's heart may not immediately start to bleed over the high costs of living in the South-East, but in fact this bland civil service prose conceals the regrettable realities behind the extreme imbalance in the geographical distribution of wealth: streets of derelict houses in the North; desperate shortages of essential workers like nurses, fire-fighters, bus drivers and police officers, all hard-pressed to obtain the basic amenity of decent housing in the South East.

Regional Trends then goes on to make the vital qualification to conventional wisdom; that while regional averages give a 'broad picture', they also 'mask considerable variability within regions'. With average weekly earnings over the UK standing at £409, ten per cent of London men were earning less than £259 – the average for the North-East was £366. But then the employment rate there was only 67.4 per cent compared with 74.3 per cent for the UK, 80.6 per cent for the South-East, 71.9 per cent for Scotland, 69.4 per cent for Wales and an appalling 64.9 per cent for Northern Ireland. Population statistics, of course, are an absolute fundamental, determined in part by birth and death rates but, by this stage, overwhelmingly by movements out of depressed and dangerous areas and into prospering ones. Over the last two decades of the twentieth century the population declined slightly in both the North-East (by 2.2 per cent) and the North-West (by 0.7 per cent), against an average of 6.8 per cent growth for England. The smallest growth was in Yorkshire and Humber (under 3 per cent), the highest in the South-West (13.6), the East (12.5) and the South-East (only in third place at 12 per cent) – London's growth was 8.4 per cent. The former industrial areas of Wales, for example Merthyr Tydfil, suffered population loss as high as 7.8 per cent, while some of the rural areas had increases as high as 13 or even 18 per cent (Ceredigion); the capital city, Cardiff, reflecting both the boom in service trades and the effects of devolution, increased by 14.2 per cent. Overall Welsh population growth was 4.7 per cent. But Scotland's population had gone down by 1.3 per cent, though it was stabilizing itself at the beginning of the new millennium. Dundee had declined by nearly 16 per cent, Glasgow by 14.5 per cent, and the Shetlands and Western Isles (now re-baptized in Gaelic as Eilean Siar) by nearly 14, and nearly 15 per cent, respectively. However, the Highland local government region had increased by 7 per cent, and the Borders (or Southern Uplands) by 5.6 per cent; slightly surprisingly, the capital, Edinburgh, had only gone up by 1.7 per cent, in part a reflection of the increased popularity of commuting from, say, the Borders. For the entire United Kingdom the rise in birth rate was 11.8 per thousand, with few parts departing very far from this. Interestingly, the South-West, with the biggest population increase, actually had the lowest birth rate (10.6), followed by the North-East (10.7), Scotland (10.8), and Wales (10.9). Northern Ireland, where 42 per cent of the population was Catholic, had the spectacular birthrate of 13.6 per thousand, but even this was eclipsed by London, home to the highest proportion of ethnic minorities, with 14.5. Overall population growth in Northern Ireland was 10 per cent, but that concealed a 10.7 per cent decline in Belfast, heart of the national and religious conflicts.

In the 1997 election Sinn Fein took 17 per cent of the Northern Ireland vote, winning two seats (though it still refused to send its two members to Westminster). It could now claim that it did have a legitimate electoral base. The SDLP had remained stuck on three seats for 24 per cent of the vote. With a second IRA ceasefire being declared in July 1997, a new phase of all-party discussions began. In September an International Commission on Decommissioning (of weapons), chaired by the Canadian General John de Chastelain, was set up by the British and Irish governments. Up to the last, the multi-party talks in Belfast always seemed at risk of breaking down but, helped perhaps by the direct intervention of Tony Blair, the 'Good Friday Agreement' was concluded on 10 April 1998. The Agreement was first to be submitted to referendums in Northern Ireland and the Republic. A new Northern Ireland Assembly of 108 members was to be elected on 25 June 1998. By 10 March 1999 that Assembly was to have appointed a multi-party Executive (proportional to party strengths in the Assembly) to which responsibility for governing the province would be transferred (restoring the devolution which had been taken away by the introduction of direct rule in 1972). There was to be a North/South Ministerial Council, together with 'implementation bodies', a British–Irish Council, which would bring in representatives of the devolved governments of Scotland and Wales, and a British–Irish Intergovernmental Conference. Both governments recognized that Northern Ireland would remain a part of the United Kingdom as long as a majority of its people so wished, the Irish Government undertaking to remove the claim to Northern Ireland from the Irish Constitution; and should the Northern Ireland people ever decide in favour of a United Ireland, the British Government would immediately facilitate this.

All parties to the Agreement committed themselves to use their best efforts to achieve decommissioning of all paramilitary weapons within two years of the referendum (i.e. by 22 May 2000) and to work with the Independent International Commission. An independent commission (chaired by Conservative, and Catholic, Chris Patten) would make recommendations on the future of the RUC – greatly mistrusted by Catholics. The major Patten recommendations were incorporated in the Police (Northern Ireland) Act 2000 and were to be implemented in 2002: to enhance accountability of the police service, a Policing Board of ten Assembly members and nine independent ones was to be established; there was to be a positive policy of recruiting Catholics; the official name of the service was to be changed to the 'Police Service of Northern Ireland (incorporating the Royal Ulster Constabulary)' – the parenthesis was designed to appease Unionist sentiment, but in fact the operational title was simply to be 'Police Service of Northern Ireland'. Arrangements were put in train for an accelerated release of paramilitary prisoners. On 22 May, 80.9 per cent of the Northern Ireland electorate took part in the referendum; there was a 55.5 per cent turnout in the Irish Republic. The votes in favour of the Good Friday Agreement were, in Northern Ireland and the Republic respectively, 71.1 per cent for to 28.8 per cent against, and 94.3 per cent for to 5.6 per cent against. After the elections the distribution of seats in the new Assembly was: Ulster Unionist 28; SDLP 24; Democratic Unionist (Ian Paisley's extreme Protestant party) 20; Sinn Fein 18; others 18. David Trimble was to be First Minister, with Seamus Mallon of the SDLP as Deputy First Minister.

Extremists were not reconciled to the Agreement, the splinter group Continuity IRA carrying out an atrocious attack, in which 29 people were killed, at Omagh in August 1998. Orangemen continued to insist on their right to march along the traditional routes through Catholic areas – each summer Drumcree was a storm-centre as, under heavy siege from Orangemen, the RUC strove to hold out against any march down the Catholic Garvaghy Road. As the deadline for handover of power approached, many obstacles lay in the way of completing the setting up of the Executive. Trimble maintained that the Unionists could not permit representatives of Sinn Fein to take up places on the Executive until decommissioning of IRA weapons had begun: 'no guns, no government', was the slogan. When, at Easter 1999, the cross-party Executive was still not in place the British and Irish prime ministers issued the Hillsborough Declaration, calling upon the IRA to put a token quantity of weapons 'beyond use'. Sinn Fein rejected this. In August the Northern Ireland Secretary, Mo Mowlam, thought by the Unionists to be too sympathetic to the Nationalists, was forced by certain violent episodes to contemplate the possibility that the IRA ceasefire was breaking down, but decided against making such a judgement. That matters had got even this far owed much to the good offices of President Clinton of the United States, and to the detailed negotiating work of ex-Senator George Mitchell. The latter was now persuaded to chair further talks between the parties. These were hopelessly acrimonious until Mitchell had the idea of moving them to the American ambassador's residence in London, Winfield House. Here there was a perceptible thaw. Trimble softened from demanding decommissioned guns immediately to accepting a renewed commitment to the peace process leading to eventual decommissioning. Meantime Mowlam had been replaced by Peter Mandelson, whom the Unionists found more congenial. Suddenly, on Tuesday 16 and Wednesday 17 November there emerged statements of a remarkably conciliatory nature, first from both the Ulster Unionists and Sinn Fein, then by the IRA. The IRA undertook to appoint a go-between to discuss decommissioning with General de Chastelain, and Trimble decided it was now possible for the Unionists to participate in the power-sharing Executive. Meeting on 27 November, a divided Ulster Unionist Council supported Trimble's decision by 480 to 349. At midnight on 1 December 1999 devolution returned to Northern Ireland. However, Trimble signed a post-dated letter of resignation which would take effect if decommissioning had not begun by February 2000.

The crunch point came on 11 February: there had been no decommissioning. Without that Trimble's party would not continue to support power-sharing. The only way of preventing the visible, and all too terminal, collapse of the Executive was – though both Sinn Fein and the Irish Government refused to acknowledge this – for Mandelson to suspend its operations and return for the time being to direct rule. Once more Trimble demonstrated some flexibility in attempting to get things moving again, and once more the American connection proved invaluable. It was in Washington in March that the idea was conveyed to Adams that Trimble would accept some gesture well short of immediate decommissioning. The specific proposal taken up at a Belfast summit meeting early in May was of IRA arms dumps being open to inspection and then sealed, so that they were 'completely and verifiably put beyond use'. At midnight on 29 May the power-sharing Executive came back into existence. In June, and again in October, several IRA arms dumps were inspected by a specially appointed commission of Cyril Ramaphosa, former Secretary-General of the South African National Congress, and former Finnish President Martii Ahtisaari. But it went no further than that; so once again the pattern of accelerating Unionist disgruntlement asserted itself. Trimble's first move was an attempt to get Sinn Fein members excluded from the North/South Ministerial Council; then, in May 2001, he wrote another letter of resignation to take effect on 1 July if no significant progress on decommissioning had taken place.

Thick gloom descended with the results of the June elections, which greatly strengthened the position of the extremists and weakened that of Trimble's Unionists, from whom the Democratic Unionists took three seats and Sinn Fein two. In July Trimble carried out his threat to resign and, in August, rejected a new IRA proposal on a means of disposing of weapons, well short, as usual, of actually disposing of them. Once again the Irish Secretary, now John Reid, averted complete collapse of the Executive by suspending it. Belief in the eventual restoration of the peace process was at its lowest point. Then came the apalling atrocity and tragedy of the 11 September terrorist attack on the twin towers of the World Trade Center in New York. Before attributing the next development in Northern Ireland entirely to the repercussions of that terrible event, it is important to reflect that Republicans had made, and were continuing to make, considerable gains from the peace process which, itself, was very much supported by ordinary voters across Northern Ireland: reform of the RUC was under way; the British Government was prepared, particularly if it could be assured that there were no weapons dumps readily accessible to IRA dissidents, to dismantle army surveillance posts in South Armagh, something very much desired by the local inhabitants. And, indeed, the IRA was already moving (slowly!) in the direction of some form of decommissioning. But all that said, 11 September and the general 'war on terrorism' which followed undoubtedly provided a powerful incentive for a quick and open disavowal of any association with the modes of international terrorism for, in short, making serious start to actual decommissioning. Which is exactly what happened in October.

Joy unconfined for Trimble, one might have thought. Not a bit of it. While, at the beginning of November, the Nationalist parties were happy to ensure that he would have an overall majority in the Assembly for his resumption of the First Ministership, he was foiled by the cunningly crafted rules which specified that he must have a majority of both Nationalists and Unionists. In fact, with opinion polls showing that Protestant and Unionist voters did not regard the recent IRA act of decommissioning as sufficiently significant, Trimble was being faced with the crucial defection of one – a woman – from his own loyal band within the Ulster Unionists. There followed an exquisite piece of Northern Ireland jiggery-pokery (in a good cause) in which the Assembly and Executive were (once again) put into suspension, just giving enough time for some members of the non-aligned minority parties to declare that they were in fact Protestants (and so, Unionists), while, for the necessary short period, the Assembly and Executive were put into suspension. The Trimble-led Executive was saved, but his Unionist opponents were so infuriated that they brought some of the violence of the streets into Stormont itself, in what became known as 'the brawl in the hall'.

For violence in the streets there certainly was, despite the fact that the devolved system (when not in suspension) was working with notable efficiency and sensitivity (former IRA hard man and continuing member of its Army Council, Martin McGuinness as Education Minister was even-handed in allocating funds to Protestant schools and won applause from teachers by abolishing school league tables – something not attempted in Scotland). At the beginning of the year attention had focused on Larne, in County Antrim. 'The cease-fire's a joke,' declared a 38-year-old Catholic man, who lived in Larne with his Protestant partner and his 14-year-old son. 'It doesn't matter what the politicians say, it's a different ball game in Larne' (*Guardian*, 15 January 2001):

It's not one-off incidents, it's a continuous flow. The fear is always there for Catholics. It's taken over their lives. Couples take turns at sleeping, they're on tranquillisers, they're ringing their children on mobile phones if they're five minutes late home from school.

Maybe it wasn't really such a different ball game in the notorious Ardoyne area of North Belfast, where there was particularly vicious street fighting in both June and July. Orangemen returning from their 12 July marches provided the occasion for the latter, but the RUC believed that the violence was organized by the IRA. However, by the end of the year a clear pattern had emerged whereby nearly three-quarters of all killings were being committed by 'loyalists', many the result of internecine feuding between UDA, UVF, and LVF. The good news at the beginning of 2002 was of a continuing long-term decline in deaths by paramilitary action and of a fairly full and normal life being lived in most parts of the province: over the previous three years there had been an annual average of 14 killings, against an average of 34 over the three years previous to that, and 56 and 92 for the two three-year periods before that (*Independent*, 31 December 2001, 4 January 2002). The bad news was that in certain areas, and particularly North Belfast, historically determined sectarian divides were, if anything, intensifying. A survey of people aged 18 to 25 found that 68 per cent of those interviewed 'have never had a meaningful conversation with anyone from the other community'. The main approach to Holy Cross Catholic Primary School is through a Protestant area, where Protestants claimed they were under threat from Nationalist paramilitaries. But nothing could excuse the appalling scenes occurring for twelve weeks in the autumn when Protestant gangs violently intimidated terrified children being escorted to the school by their mothers. At the turn of the year there was a collossal recrudescence of sectarian hatred, particularly vicious on 9 and 10 January when Catholics and Protestants, hurling bombs and stones, setting cars on fire, attacked each other; and, bravely caught in the middle, police and soldiers; masked paramilitaries entered Our Lady of Mercy Secondary School, smashing cars and panicking the pupils while, not far away, frightened Protestant schoolchildren had to be ferried home in armoured police Land Rovers. To this spectacle of mass barbarism, involving paramilitaries, but incorporating the 'recreational rioting' (as the phrase was) of jobless young people reared in bigotry amidst substandard housing and non-existent community facilities, was added, a few days later, the gruesome horror of a young Catholic postman, Daniel McColgan, being shot down as he turned up for work. Would the almost universal shudder of revulsion now give politics a chance, permit the Executive and Assembly to pick up on the decent beginning they had been embarked on a year previously, or were sectarian bitterness and the myths of the past too deeply ingrained?

No such bitterness, no such myths on mainland Britain, of course. Or had core values been changing significantly? Was what I referred to as 'traditional hard-headedness, harshness and philistinism' growing in strength? Were secular Anglicanism, social unity and community spirit disintegrating? The comparison we have noted between high church attendance in Northern Ireland and very low in England, Scotland and Wales persisted, but so did the growth of devoted religious attendance among Muslims, Sikhs, and Hindus – could that be a potential cause of a new sectarian bitterness, particularly after 11 September and the launching of the war in Afghanistan against fundamentalist Muslims? I'll address that question in Chapter 28 when we encounter the bigotry and barbarism breaking out in northern English cities in the summer of 2001 – 'And we thought only the Irish rioted like this', was the headline to the *Sunday Times* report (15 July 2001) on the previous week's rioting in Bradford. Since, with regard to the wider issues, I shall be returning to the legacies of Thatcherite thinking at the beginning of the next chapter, it is very important to record here the vigorous conclusions on 'the robustness of British civil society', arrived at by the *18th British Social Attitudes* report (2001):

The well-documented decline of social capital in the United States, and the associated decline in social trust are not mirrored in Britain. Civil society here remains as strong and active as it was. There is evidence in Britain, as elsewhere, of a gradual decline in electoral turnout, political trust and democratic engagement, but for the moment this does not seem to be explained by changing levels of social trust. To a significant – and sustained – extent, British people tend to trust one another, help each other out, and spend proportions of their discretionary time in the service of community goals – a situation that many other societies would envy (p. 194).

Given what I said in Part Five about a collapse in public standards, and over whether the British were looking more towards an American privileging of private interests over public good, or towards integrating with European concepts of social service, this quotation is worth pondering carefully; I shall refer to it again.

The Conservative Government had been suffocating in sleaze; it was condemned, too, for the excessive salaries and share options awarded to 'fat cats' (see Table 12 on p. 346). It should be said at once that corruption in high places had continued to be much less prevalent, and on a much less spectacular scale in Britain than in countries such as America, France, Italy and, even, Germany. Then one must immediately add that 'New Labour' (despite election promises on the matter) did not arrest the fall in standards, did not stop fat cats from becoming fatter, and brought to new prominence a special sin of its own, 'spin' – presenting polices and achievements in glowing terms which were always specious and sometimes dishonest. Among dubious associations was that between Blair and the media monopolist Rupert Murdoch. Though continuing to be hysterically anti-European, the *Sun* had supported Blair in the general election. It was perhaps understandable, though scarcely commendable, that Blair wished to retain the support of the Murdoch press, especially since a central calculation behind many of his actions was that if Labour was to carry through its modernization of Britain, it must do what no previous Labour Government had ever achieved, win a second full term of office. No excuses were to hand when the new government, instead of fully implementing its promise to abolish tobacco sponsorship of all sporting events, exempted motor racing, whose leading figure Bernie Ecclestone had donated one million pounds to Labour Party funds. Three Cabinet ministers were forced to depart from office – Peter Mandelson (twice), Geoffrey Robinson, and Keith Vaz (not reappointed in June 2001) – for alleged improprieties. All of these ministers, and certain other powerful parliamentarians, had been subject to investigation by the Parliamentary Commissioner for Standards, Elizabeth Filkin. For doing her job too conscientiously, she found it, towards the end of 2001, being downgraded, while she was told that she would have to reapply for the now enfeebled post. She refused. The Labour chairman of the Commons Public Administration Committee put the matter in an (unanswered) question to the Prime Minister:

Do you know of any public institution apart from this one where the people who are regulated have the ability to choose and dismiss the person who regulates them?

On fat cats the greatest scandals were when two egregious failures, Gerald Corbett and Lord Simpson, the chief executives respectively of Railtrack and Marconi, were given massive pay-offs. The excuse for 'spin' was that Labour Governments in the past, faced anyway with a largely hostile press, and prone to splits and internal discord, had generally been inept in their public relations. But bland, dissembling statements and the re-announcing of old allocations of money as if they were new ones, far from winning over voters, simply created greater disillusionment. A culminating point came when, at the time of the 11 September outrage, a 'spin doctor' in the Department of Transport, Jo Moore, sent an e-mail calling on press officers to take the opportunity to 'bury' bad news. If restoration of consensus and trust in government was an aim, it was not being very effectively pursued. An NOP poll in October 2000 found that 49 per cent regarded 'financial sleaze in government' as a 'major problem', with 39 per cent calling it a 'minor problem'. Results on other indicators were: 'ministers appointing friends to important public posts' – 50 per cent, major problem (36 per cent, minor problem); 'the government using spin doctors to manipulate the media' – 57 per cent, major problem (30 per cent, minor problem); 'the granting of peerages and honours to large donors' – 52 per cent, major problem (32 per cent, minor problem); 'government ministers putting interests of business before people' – 58 per cent, major problem (29 per cent, minor problem); 'government ministers not being truthful' – 66 per cent, major problem (26 per cent, minor problem).

Blair had also promised to end political 'tribalism', to reform the adversarial name-calling character of politics. For progressives there was a particular appeal in the idea of an accommodation between Labour and Liberal Democrats, with the introduction of some form of proportional representation ensuring that the latter had seats in the House of Commons commensurate with their strength in the country, since this would end the situation where the Conservatives held power while actually getting only a minority of votes. There was also the argument that the de facto two-party system – based on first-past-the-post elections – led to short-termism in policy-making, an inability of governments to think beyond the next election and the need to appease voters, and an absence of long-term planning and investment such as was to be found in continental countries. For a time there was a new Cabinet Council, which involved the active participation of the Liberal Democrat leader, Paddy Ashdown. Modified proportional representation, we saw, was introduced for Scotland, Wales and Northern Ireland, and a similar system for the entire United Kingdom was proposed by a commission under Lord Jenkins (founding member of the SDP and now a Liberal Democrat peer); full proportional representation was used in the European elections of 10 June 1999. Ashdown retired from politics having, in reality, secured few concession from the government; his successor, Charles Kennedy, set the Liberal Democrats back on a route of resolute independence from Labour.

William Hague had fought the election on the issue of 'saving the pound', of refusing to join the European common currency. From the election results it was clear that the British electors did not share Hagues's obsession, though, from other evidence it was apparent that a substantial majority continued to be highly suspicious of the euro – see Table 25.
For pro-Europeans there was comfort in the second question, though in fact the trend after the 2001 election proved to be one of a hardening against the euro, till the successful conversion in January 2002 to use of the euro across the continent provoked further thought.

Table 25: British views on the single currency, October 1999

If there were a referendum, would you vote to join a European single currency or not?

	All, per cent	Labour, per cent	Conservative, per cent
Vote to join	34	38	20
Vote not to join	54	48	70
Don't know/would not vote	16	14	10

Do you agree or disagree with the statement: 'if the European single currency turns out to be a success, Britain can't afford to stay out of it'?

	Per cent	Per cent	Per cent
Agree	58	64	42
Disagree	30	23	50
Neither/don't know	12	13	8

The formal position of the Blair government was that if, and when, five economic tests were satisfied, demonstrating the clear economic advantages of joining, it would so recommend, holding a referendum, in order that the people have the final say. On the same Sunday (6 January 2002), shortly after Euro coins had started to circulate on the continent, two leading papers, the *Telegraph* and the *Sunday Times*, reported the very different results of a couple of opinion polls. Under the heading, 'We still don't want euro, say Britons,' the former reported on an ICM poll for (perhaps significantly) the anti-European 'No Campaign', giving a figure of 73 per cent against the Euro. In the *Sunday Times*, however, the headline was, 'Majority of Britons warm to euro entry'. The questions in a YouGov poll had been cunningly set to elicit responses of genuine political significance: an overall majority of people (52 per cent) would either join the euro immediately (18 per cent) or when economic conditions were right (34 per cent) – hardline opponents, saying Britain should never join, amounted to 25 per cent. An NOP/Barclays Capital poll, given the rather over-enthusiastic heading, 'Britons would back euro' by the *Independent* (24 January), actually indicated that, if the government came out strongly in favour, then 40 per cent would vote for the euro, 39 per cent against – hardline opponents amounted to 27 per cent.

So, summing up the essential geography, we have a less centralized United Kingdom, where 'English' could never again be used as a synonym for 'British', where complex, but rational arrangements with that 'other Island', Ireland (in both its constituents) had at last been established, and where awareness of indeed being part of Europe was manifesting itself in all kinds of ways. Was it an illusion that the nation was also playing a more important and more honourable part in world affairs? In December 1998, Britain was the only country to join with the Americans in air attacks on Iraq, provoked by Saddam Hussein's interference with UN weapons inspections. Attacks continued sporadically, usually in connection with policing the 'no-fly zones' imposed on Saddam – notably in February and September 2001. There was much principled opposition within Britain, mixed with many signs of a robotic anti-Americanism. With regard to that eternal trouble spot, the Balkans, none of the European powers had behaved with wisdom or courage when first faced with the aggressive, 'ethnic cleansing' policies of the Serbian President of what remained of Yugoslavia, Slobodan Milosevic, and with the resultant atrocities against the Muslim inhabitants of Bosnia. When Milosevic turned his brutal activities against the Albanian majority in Kosovo, Britain was the strongest supporter of American-sponsored NATO action against him. The bombing campaign, which began on 24 March 1999, resulted both in the intensification of the eviction and killings of Kosovar Albanians and in many direct civilian casualties. Nonetheless, on the evening of 9 June 1999, Serbia's top generals signed a military agreement with the NATO commander, British General Sir Michael Jackson, on their withdrawal from Kosovo; eventually, Milosevic was ousted by his own people. There were the usual entrenched criticisms from the left, but also criticisms from the right, based on an equally entrenched none-of-our-business certainty that foreigners should be left to get on with slaughtering each other. The right had no qualms about the 'war against terrorism', waged by America in Afghanistan from October 2001, with the enthusiastic participation of Britain and the support of an international coalition. There were a number of left-organized anti-war demonstrations (once more with hints of ritualistic anti-Americanism); on 1 November in the House of Commons 17 MPs opposed the bombing in Afghanistan (11 Labour, 4 Plaid Cymru, and 2 Scottish Nationalist); on Sunday 18 November 15,000 protesters marched from Hyde Park to Trafalgar Square. Tony Blair took upon himself the punishing mission of touring foreign capitals with the aim of maintaining and strengthening the international coalition against terrorism. Did this demonstrate a revived 'special relationship' with America or merely Blair acting as US President George W. Bush's poodle?

The British Prime Minister, in fact, was operating within a realistic appraisal of the only relationship possible between the world's sole super-power and a country which, at best, could be accounted one of Europe's top four powers (he was far more perceptive than, say, Harold Macmillan had been in the late fifties), making intelligent use of the historically determined fact that Britain was uniquely placed to operate as a conduit between America and Europe. Other more awkward facts were that both the Falklands and Gibraltar were British territories and wanted to remain British. In early 2002 Argentina was in a mess, and Spain was asserting its claims to Gibraltar. In dealing with both countries, British foreign policy (now in the hands of Jack Straw, Robin Cook having become Leader of the House of Commons after the election) was sensitive and sensible. If we add that British contributions, both governmental and private, to overseas aid, and to the international disaster funds which succeeded each other with such tragic frequency, in generosity compared very favourably with those of other developed countries, we may well give the United Kingdom (whatever the recent blemishes) some credit for striving to be a decent member of the world community. I make this positive point now because my next chapter is stuffed with intensifications of the negative comments on British policies and attitudes made through-out Parts Four and Five of this book.

28

Service with a Scowl

By the criteria of conventional economics, Britain was doing rather well in the last years of the twentieth century and at the beginning of the twenty-first. Both official statistics (always concerned now to print comparisons with other European Union countries) and figures compiled by the private consultancy, Oxford Economic Forecasting, demonstrated that inflation was lower than in any of the other countries, the annual rate of growth higher (2.7 per cent, compared with, say, 1.8 per cent in Germany). In 2001 Gross Domestic Product (GDP) per head, long limping along well behind that of Britain's neighbours, shot into the lead, 5 per cent ahead of Germany, 7 per cent ahead of France, and 16 per cent ahead of the EU average. In 1995, taking overall EU GDP per head as 100, Germany's was 110, France's 104, and the UK's well back at 96. The spurt was just beginning to show in 1998, when the analogous figures were: 108, 99, and 102. 'Britain,' exulted the *Sunday Times* (23 December 2001), in reporting the latest statistics, 'is the rich man of Europe', while the *Independent*'s conservative economics columnist, Hamish McRae, posed the self-gratifying question: 'Does Britain's new-found prosperity offer lessons for other countries?' Though the world economy had for some time been moving into recession, a process accelerated by reactions to the events of 11 September 2001, Britain was enjoying a consumer boom with, over the Christmas period, shops reporting unprecedentedly high levels of spending. Of what they earned, Britons were spending a higher proportion than was the case in the other countries; and of their household expenditure a higher proportion than in the rest of Europe went on recreational and leisure activities and goods – in the words of the *Sunday Times*, 'we spend the most on having fun'. Here are the comparative statistics:

Percentage of household spending which goes on leisure and recreational activities and goods

UK	21.3
Ireland	19.7
Sweden	18.4
Luxembourg	18.3
Austria	17.7
Netherlands	17.4
Germany	16.8
Belgium	16.4
Spain	15.4
Denmark	15.3
Finland	14.8
France	14.5
Greece	13.3
Portugul	12.9
Italy	10.9

Fascinating figures, aren't they? Look at that astonishing contrast between Italy and Sweden: but, of course, each statistic embraces many circumstances, from drinks and restaurant prices to richness of cost-free community and family life.

Anyway, back to booming Britain. It is not the principal task of a social history to allocate credit and blame to politicians, so let me seek the assistance of the chapter 'Industry' by Sir Geoffrey Owen, Senior Fellow at the London School of Economics, in Anthony Seldon's indispensable collection, *The Blair Effect: The Blair Government 1997–2001* (the recession referred to is that of the early 1990s):

The government was fortunate in taking office at a time when recovery from the recession was well under way. But the fact that the upswing continued, at a steady and sustainable pace, was due in part to New Labour's policies, including, most importantly, the delegation of monetary policy to the Bank of England and the strict control of public expenditure. By 2001 the British economy was in its ninth year of growth – the longest period of uninterrupted expansion since the war – and this had been achieved with low inflation and steadily falling unemployment.

This was a refreshing contrast with the crisis management that had characterised the Labour governments of the 1960s and 1970s. Hardly less remarkable was the new focus on competition. The government declared its intention to let markets work, and to intervene only where there was clear evidence of market failure. (If ministers needed further evidence that politicians and civil servants should not try to run commercial enterprises, it was provided by the embarrassing failure of the Millennium Dome) (p. 215).

Another quotation richly worthy of sustained contemplation! Clearly some credit for an expanding economy goes back beyond the advent of the Labour Government, perhaps back as far as Margaret Thatcher (note the remarks about pre-Thatcher Labour governments). Since my main topic in this chapter is: (following upon everything I said in Part Five about the decline in standards and in safety) what, if anything, was happening under New Labour to public (and private) services? I shall need in a moment to make a final attempt to get to grips with the big issue of the Thatcher legacy.

First, more on economic and technological developments. 'Strict control of public expenditure' – not exactly a recipe for expansion in the public services, though it can of course be argued that without a sound economy there will be no money for public services anyway – was certainly a feature of New Labour's first years in office; more positively, the 'prudent' Chancellor of the Exchequer, Gordon Brown, assisted by higher-than-expected revenues from an increasingly buoyant economy, reduced government borrowing and indeed directed resources towards paying off some of the enormous national debt built up by the Conservatives, annual interest payments on which amounted to as much as was spent on social security. As Philip Stephens, editor of the *Financial Times*, puts it in the Seldon collection already cited:

In 1996–7 public sector net borrowing had amounted to 3.6 per cent of national income. Three years later the public finances had moved into sizeable surplus, with a net repayment of 2 per cent of GDP recorded in 1999–2000. In the same year the surplus on the current budget reached £20bn. The stock of public sector net debt meanwhile fell from fractionally over 44 per cent of national income in 1996–97 to below 35 per cent in 2000–01 (p. 192).

But there was no improvement in Britain's chronic balance of payments deficit and, indeed, in 2000 the deficit on trade in goods was, at £28.8 billion, the largest on record (it had been £18.7 bn in 1990, £11.7 bn in 1995, £20.6 bn in 1998, and £26.2 bn in 1999). These potentially alarming figures (save that no one was alarmed – a big trade deficit, certainly, being one function of consumer prosperity – America being the classic example) were far from redeemed by modest surpluses on trade in services: down at £4 bn in 1990, then up to £8.9 bn in 1995, and £12.6 bn in 1998, and down slightly in 1999 to £11.3 bn and, again, in 2000 to £11.0 bn. From the time of Thatcher British macro-policy had, in comparison with continental countries, been one of relatively low taxes and distinctly high interest rates (while that policy continued there could be no genuine economic 'convergence' such as to make joining the euro a real option). Operating to the Government target of a 2.5 per cent per annum inflation rate, the now independent (in this respect) Bank of England set interest rates at 6.25 per cent, going steadily up to 7.5 per cent in June 1998, then falling back to 6 per cent at the beginning of 2000 and then, miracle of miracles, to 4 per cent for the whole of the last part of 2001. The higher rates imposed a heavy burden on British exporters, particularly while the euro was falling in value. On taxes, the Government kept to a pre-election pledge not to raise income tax. However, there were what the Conservatives condemned as 'stealth taxes' – notably, the phasing out of mortgage interest relief and the married couple's income tax allowance, increased escalation of fuel duties, and abolition of dividend tax credits and advance corporation tax.

The massive swing in the economy away from manufacturing and into service trades continued: between 1978 and 2000 jobs in the service industries rose by 36 per cent, while jobs in manufacturing fell by 39 per cent. To a considerable degree, obviously, this was due to the exploitation of advances in technology: employment in information technology increased by 45 per cent in the five years up to the spring of 2000, when the total workforce in this area amounted to 855,000. Overall unemployment figures looked good, standing in the spring of 2001 at 1.5 million, that is 4.9 per cent of the labour force, considerably lower than in the other EU countries. However, such figures were, in part, the product of increasing employment among women, mainly in low-paid jobs, and masked the series of devastating closures in major manufacturing centres which entailed massive male redundancies. In March 2000 the German owners, BMW, decided to pull out of Rover car manufacture at Longbridge near Birmingham; by the year's end Ford had announced the cessation of car manufacture at Dagenham in East London and General Motors took the same action with the historic Vauxhall plant at Luton; in February Corus, product of a 1999 merger between British Steel and the Dutch Hoogevens, announced the end to steel-making in Ebbw Vale. The last *Sunday Times* of 2001 (30 December), noting that unemployment was now very slowly creeping up, announced that job prospects, particularly in leisure, retail and telecommunications, as well as in manufacturing, were, according to Manpower, the recruitment agency, at a thirty-year low.

So, nothing is straightforward. And nothing, it was becoming ever more clear, was less straightforward than the legacy of Thatcherism, particularly with regard to the provision of both public and private services. Self-evidently a prosperous economy is an essential basis for decent public services; a third world economy yields third world health care, social security, etc. However, the reverse is not automatically true: the wealthiest nation on earth, America, has a health-care system so awful that it terrifies even solid middle-class professionals and, for the poor, a social security system of monstrous inadequacy. But let us start with the question of whether Thatcherism, with whatever side-effects, was essential to the (qualified) prosperity enjoyed by the UK in the later 1990s – was the gain based on unavoidable pain? I believe that vital clues lie in the policies being put forward by the still-moderate, still-consensual supporters of Thatcher when she was just a recently elected Leader of the Opposition. One of the great 'lost political programmes' (as distinct from 'lost leaders', of whom we tend to hear rather more) of recent British history is *The Right Approach to the Economy: Outline of an Economic Strategy for the Next Conservative Government* (October 1977) by Geoffrey Howe, James Prior, Keith Joseph, David Howell, and edited by Angus Maude. This called, naturally, for a 'more stable economic climate', 'strict control by the Government of the rate of growth of the money supply', 'firm management of government expenditure', 'lower taxation', and 'the removal of unnecessary restrictions on business expansion' (p. 6). The 'overriding objective', the document declared with a touch of poetic drama, 'is to unwind the inflationary coils which have gripped our economy' (p. 8). 'State ownership' must be reduced (p. 47), but the authors have first made it clear that they are firm supporters of manufacturing industry (pp. 39–42) – which, as we saw, was, in fact, to be savaged by Thatcher in her first years in office. The tone throughout is consensual and opposed to political tribalism. It is recognized that the then Labour government was 'now belatedly trying to pursue' correct policies (p. 8) and that, 'urged on by the Conservative Party, has taken the first steps' in the right direction; 'the need for control of the money supply and of government expenditure has been accepted on both sides of the House of Commons'. The authors explicitly disavow any belief that 'one has only to follow the right money supply path and everything in the economy will become right'. Britain should learn lessons from Germany and our other competitors (pp. 9, 17). There should be both a 'more independent role for the Bank of England', and joint discussions between the Bank, both sides of industry and then Parliament, through the National Economic Development Council (which, in office, Thatcher first ignored, then dismantled in 1987, final abolition being carried out by Norman Lamont in July 1992). Monetary discipline would be extended gradually (p. 8), not as 'a prescription for poorer social provision', 'but as a recipe for better housekeeping in all public services'; there would be no 'savage and indiscriminate cuts in public programmes' (p. 10). The term 'inclusiveness' had not yet been coined, but this was indeed a programme for inclusiveness and against confrontation:

We see the trade unions as a very important economic interest group whose cooperation and understanding we must work constantly to win and keep, as we have done in the past. We do not seek confrontation and see no need for it!

Calling for 'fuller participation at work' (p. 50), the authors continued:

We are looking at ways in which people at work can be given the right to information about the big decisions affecting them. And we shall encourage the development in a variety of ways and means for employees to influence these decisions. (p. 51)

Finally, the document taunted those in the Labour Party still evincing 'blatant hostility' to the EEC (pp. 52–3).

Readers will need no prodding from me to see the similarities between these Conservative policies of 1977 and those of New Labour twenty years later. Is it not the case that if these policies had been implemented in the 1980s, British society would have enjoyed the benefits of necessary economic reforms without the adverse effects of Thatcherism? Thatcher, of course, hated *The Right Approach to the Economy* and, unhappily, when in office, none of its authors was prepared to stand up for it. With respect to British public services at the beginning of the twenty-first century there are three points to be made about the Thatcher legacy. First, we have to recognize that without the reforms affecting productivity, enterprise and restrictive practices, there would not have been the required economic stability upon which to base social and other services – though with the codicil that the reforms could have been carried out in a more moderate, consensual way, and with a good deal less collateral damage. Second, however healthy the economy, it was not possible to make up in one fell swoop (even if the Labour Government had attempted that) for the arid period in the eighties and nineties of inadequate investment in transport and the social services, deliberately initiated by Thatcher and continued by Major. Third, the purveying and sanctioning of attitudes and values which privileged the individual over the community, prized deregulation over concern about the well-attested dangers of unrestrained private enterprise, and legitimated greed, selfishness, and any sharp practice which produced a profit. Such attitudes, very much contrary to the values on which the British had formerly prided themselves, spread and became entrenched because they were now endorsed by politicians and the media, and discouraged only by a discredited Labour Party. Matters, as I have said, are not straightforward. Thatcher, as I pointed out in Part Five, was, much as she hated the sixties, not successful in reversing the freedoms and disdain for convention and authority developed during that decade; but then these were enjoyable, contributed to self-gratification and, in any case, were in many respects compatible with the radical individualism of Thatcherism. Further complication: what I have just been saying about selfishness and greed seems to contradict the findings on the robustness of British civil society published in the *British Social Attitudes* report already quoted. The explanation, known to all historians, is that in any society, at any time, some people think and behave in one way, others in another, and some people think and behave in one way in certain circumstances, and another in other circumstances. Most notoriously people can be in favour of higher welfare benefits for the poor and against paying the higher taxes needed to finance such benefits; it also seems to be true that from the mid-eighties to the late nineties there was a feeling that to be in favour of low taxes was to be a virtuous supporter of economic growth, whereas, at the end of the nineties, as the furore intensified over the dismal state of the public services, virtue began again to be perceived as entailing support for higher taxes in order to improve public services. The *Social Attitudes* findings were well substantiated, and offered grounds for believing that there was still a lot that was admirable about British society. In general, those who were primarily users of services of all types, public and private, behaved in a community-spirited way. It was those responsible for organizing services, and above all, for squeezing out profits from them, who tended to put personal gain above concern for the community and for customers. The preoccupation was with, as the phrase had it, shareholder value, not with satisfying the consumer or, in public services, with meeting the paper targets and arbitrary economies imposed (often at government behest) by account-ancy-minded executives, rather than doing what the qualified experts knew to be necessary; the masters of slick management-speak were put in control of those who could actually do the job that needed doing. The central problem was that Tony Blair liked the company of the rich, liked being popular with them and, in utter defiance of overwhelming evidence, had a childlike faith in the talents of private entrepreneurs. He could scarcely fail to see that the French and German railway systems were utterly superior to the British; somehow he failed to register that both were owned and run by the state. He somehow also failed to note that what the wealthiest British entrepreneurs were best at was not creating new enterprises but buying up other people's. Behind the fawning on the private sector lay the deep fear of investing public money, which would necessitate increasing taxation: better to bring in private investment no matter what the longer term costs to the nation would be.

The watchwords in all spheres continued to be 'cost-cutting' and 'downsizing', the paramount action the cutting back of staff to the bare minimum, imposing overtime when necessary, contracting out wherever possible. Short-term profits were the be-all and end-all. Hardly was the BSE crisis (though not necessarily the long-term effects) over than there was a foot-and-mouth crisis (see next chapter), created and prolonged by lax practice all round and, in particular, a Government-created shortage of veterinary experts. During 2001 and into 2002 it became apparent that leading supermarkets, quite unwittingly, were (thanks to a nefarious trade in condemned meat acquired free, then reintroduced into the food chain) selling dangerously contaminated meat products (*Sunday Times* 20 January 2002). The privatized utilities sold gas, or water, or electricity but did not offer service, repairs or spare parts. The big department stores sold electrical appliances but would not install them, and furniture, but would not deliver it, nor remove the old furniture being replaced. The poor standard of customer service provided by most banks, noted in Part Five, did not significantly improve.

Everything that was occurring elsewhere was writ large in the railways, whose crazy mode of privatization, determined solely by the Major Government's desire for a quick sell-off at knock-down prices, was, as also noted in Part Five, a sure recipe for disaster. Disaster duly followed. From the inception of the privatized system complaints mounted about late-running and cancelled trains, the difficulties of obtaining advance information about train services, dirty and overcrowded trains, unjustified fare rises, and withdrawal of economy fares. There were frequent reports of inadequacies in track maintenance and failure to maintain safety systems on trains. Then came successive crashes outside the London mainline station, Paddington, at Southall (19 September 1997) when seven people were killed and thirteen seriously injured, and Ladbroke Grove (5 October 1999) when 31 died. Incredibly (or, rather, all too credibly) nothing of significance was done with respect to the appalling mismanagement of Railtrack (good only at paying high dividends and excessive rewards to its executives, while pulling in an enormous government subsidy). On 17 October 2000, a Leeds-bound express was derailed at Hatfield, north of London: four people were killed. The cause was a cracked rail which had actually been spotted as far back as November 1999 but, as rail expert Christian Wolmar comments, 'due to a series of blunders by Railtrack and its maintenance contractors, Balfour Beatty, the rail had not been replaced'. Three absolutely fundamental errors had resulted from the hasty and ill-thought-out privatization. First, fragmentation between Railtrack and operating companies had entailed a dissipation of the indispensable accumulation of vital railway skills built up over the years, not least in engineering – hence the deeply unsatisfactory resort to the use of outside contractors, such as Balfour Beatty. Second, while state-run British Rail had been a world leader in railway research, that expertise was lost when, on privatization, BR Research was effectively disbanded. Railtrack did not set up a research department of its own so that such research and development as was undertaken had (in the now fashionable manner) to be subcontracted, putting Railtrack at the mercy of outside consultants. A third 'remarkable result of the upheaval of privatisation', as Wolmar puts it, was that:

Railtrack, a company whose principal function was supposed to be organizing the maintenance of one of the nation's primary engineering resources, was largely run by people with no relevant technical background. There were just two engineers on the board, and the most senior, Richard Middleton, the commercial director, was responsible for dealing with the train operating companies and therefore not in a position to exercise influence over engineering decisions. (Christian Wolmar, *Broken Rails: How Privatisation Wrecked Britain's Railways*, p. 3)

Thus, although Railtrack was aware, before Hatfield, about the specific phenomenon which had caused the crash, known as gauge corner cracking, they had no understanding of the extent of the phenomenon or of the speed at which it could spread. They panicked: having failed, despite plenty of warning, to impose even a speed limit at Hatfield, they now, unable to distinguish genuine dangers from non-existent ones, imposed thousands of speed restrictions across the network, causing chaos for millions of travellers.

Government policy was embodied in the ten-year transport spending plan of July 2000 and the Transport Act 2000. By the former, £60 billion was to be spent on the railways, half, however, to come from private investors. A further £120 billion (again dependent on private investment) was to be spent on local transport, roads, etc. The Act set up a Strategic Rail Authority, with grand objectives, but rather ill-defined powers, and (against strong resistance within the Labour Party), a Public–Private Partnership (PPP) to take over National Air Traffic Services Ltd (NATS), the body responsible for air traffic control. Transport for London, working with the newly established Mayor and Assembly, was to devise plans to deal with the congested mess which was transport in London – the Government, however, wanted direct private investment here too, despite the opposition of the mayor and most of those who had tried to do the sums. In October 2001, Transport Secretary, Stephen Byers, placed Railtrack in administration, i.e. declared it bankrupt: the fat cats had already creamed off their winnings, while ordinary railworkers found the shares they had been persuaded to buy worthless. In a manner eerily reminiscent of Arthur Scargill constantly repeating that he had 'always opposed police violence', Byers took to constantly repeating that he had 'taken a difficult decision'. Actually, he had made no decision at all: pending something turning up – Byers intended a not-for-profit successor to Railtrack to which private investors were expected to flock. It was difficult to see who now was running the railway infrastructure. It was not at all difficult to see that conditions for the travelling public were deteriorating still further, from awful to abysmal. During a hostile interview in the ultra-right magazine, the *Spectator* (12 January, 2002), Minister for Europe, Peter Hain, volunteered the truth: 'We have the worst railways in Europe. We started transport investment far too late. It's an intractable problem. We should have been more radical earlier.' A friendly German commented that the trouble was that the British are too easy-going, putting up with a railway service that Germans simply would not tolerate. He was kind but wrong. The difference lay with governments: the German, French, and all other intelligent governments understood the utter essentiality, on both social and economic grounds, of an efficient railway network. British governments were too busy counting the pennies.

If there was any condition lower than abysmal, it was encountered in January 2002 as two-day strike actions by the RMT union (representing guards and station staff) in the London area were set to spread across the country. At the outset of privatization the new train operating companies had behaved as every good downsizer should and got rid of substantial numbers of experienced engine drivers. Very soon they had to:

(a) recruit young, untrained would-be drivers (possibly a contributory factor in the Ladbroke Grove crash); and

(b) offer substantial wage rises in order to tempt experienced drivers away from other companies.

Again the folly of fragmentation was demonstrated. Seeing drivers (who had their own union, Aslef) pulling in higher wages, RMT demanded rises for their own railworkers. Simple really, but hell for the travelling public. During the strike at South West Trains, Byers kept tediously repeating that it was not for the Government to intervene in a private dispute. What *was* the Government for? passengers began to wonder. One of them, a former railway employee, writing a letter to the *Independent* (29 January 2002), set matters out in bold colours:

The bulk of today's problems are caused directly by under-manning on the part of Railtrack and the train operating companies – a consequence of the desire to cut costs and boost profits. Until all stations are manned during operating hours, backup trains and repair crews kept on standby and regular track and signal maintenance carried out by dedicated teams rather than outside contractors, the system will stay locked into a vicious spiral of increasing fare-dodging, dilapidation, vandalism, accidents, delays and cancellations. Where the money to pay the increased wage bill will come from, I do not know; renationalization would be a start. But I do know that unless it is found, and the railway system returned to the hands of those who wish to run it as a railway, not as a business, all we long-suffering passengers face a dismal future.

During this mayhem, up, at least, till the disruptions following Hatfield, there was an astonishing expansion in the numbers of rail travellers, a function mainly of economic growth, and of further migration to ever more far-flung commuter regions. Continuing my mission to convert the world to the excitements of perusing statistical tables, here is another revealing government one (the rail link between Paddington and Heathrow airport, a growth area in itself for those who could afford it, is not included):

Passenger Traffic on Rail, Underground and Selected Light Rail Services (in million passenger/km.)

	1990—91	1995—96	1998—99	1999—2000	2000—01
National railways	33,200	30,000	36,300	38,400	39,200
London Underground	6,164	6,337	6,716	7,171	7,456
Glasgow Underground	40	41	47	49	46
Docklands Light Railway	33	70	144	172	200
Greater Manchester Metro	–	81	117	126	152
Tyne and Weir Metro	290	261	238	230	229
Croydon Tramlink	–	–	–	–	96
Centro West Midlands Metro	–	–	–	50	56
Stagecoach Supertram	–	20	35	37	38

It's consonant with the official ethos that (where relevant) we get the names of the private operators, though not necessarily the community being served; Stagecoach Supertram operated in South Yorkshire.

In the press headlines at the beginning of 2002 there was a kind of Punch and Judy competition over which was the more appalling, the condition of the railways, or the condition of the National Health Service. With regard to the latter there were still intolerably long waiting-lists, occasional horror stories of patients being left unattended on trolleys, and a general sense of crises and shortages. Early in 2002 a handful of patients were being financed by the NHS to go for treatment in a French private hospital. France was spending 9.6 per cent of GDP on health care, Germany 10.7 per cent, the UK only 6.8 per cent. Was it all a matter of money, or was the British NHS fundamentally flawed? Rather than a fundamental flaw, there was a 'serious potential weakness', one which affected the entirety of British welfare provision. People were entitled to health care, pensions, etc. because Parliament (i.e. the Government) had so decided, hoping to meet the cost almost entirely out of general taxation, not because, as on the continent, they contributed, along with their employers, to state-run insurance schemes. Under the British system of parliamentary sovereignty, what Parliament had given, Parliament could take away. Thus, as, first the economy performed badly, then tax revenues were cut, and all the time, the costs of state-of-the-art treatment mounted, people began to be denied the first-class treatment they had once thought they were guaranteed in perpetuity. From the start of the NHS the Government had felt bound to permit hospital consultants to carry on private practice alongside their NHS work: consultants gave priority to private work and that contributed to NHS waiting times. In the more recent period encouragement was given to the building of private hospitals. With respect to size, facilities and the complexity of treatment undertaken, these were greatly inferior to NHS hospitals. They did routine work for substantial remuneration; they also creamed off staff who had been trained, at public expense, in NHS hospitals. The fallacy of regarding private as inherently superior to public was tragically exposed when, nine days after giving birth to twins in one of the most expensive maternity hospitals in the country, a woman died due to staff negligence, the coroner criticizing 'medical and nursing standards, training and discipline at the hospital' (*Independent* 19 January 2002). A consultant obstetrician at Nottingham City Hospital declared that

... the woman would have received better care at the worst example of a failing NHS trust. At a time when the Secretary of State is recommending the private sector take over management of some NHS trusts it behoves us to ask serious questions about how it manages itself. Patients intending to use the private sector should choose carefully.

Conservative reform, we have seen, was aimed at introducing an internal market, with the purchaser/provider split and budgets devolved to GP fundholders. Professor Howard Glennerster, in the Seldon collection, reckons that the reforms had some success in the aim of providing a better service for consumers and praises the Labour Government for maintaining much of them, while abolishing fundholding (pp. 399–400). Labour introduced Primary Care Trusts (2000), Primary Care Groups (1999), and the National Institute for Clinical Excellence (1999). Worthy moves all, though the NHS, as Glennerster neatly put it, 'was weary with change'. A series of targets, and more money, were announced in the NHS Plan of July 2000. Something, but not enough, was done about making nursing more remunerative; moves to get in more doctors would take longer. The shortage of beds was largely a function of the shortage of trained staff. The most encouraging sign was both Blair and Health Secretary Alan Milburn declaring that they were ready to be judged harshly at the next election if they had not, by then, significantly improved health care. As for the perceptions of ordinary people, they were already deeply unfavourable by 1999.

Great Britain: Percentages satisfied with Local Hospital and Community Health Services

	1991	1999
Hospital services		
Quality of medical treatment	65	66
Time spent waiting for an ambulance after a 999 call	n.a.	60
General condition of hospital buildings	40	53
Time spent waiting in outpatient departments	17	28
Time spent in accident and emergency departments before being seen by a doctor	24	20
Waiting lists for non-emergency operations (including such disabling conditions as hip replacements, etc.)	13	20
Waiting time before getting appointments with hospital Consultants	14	17
GP services		
Quality of medical treatment by GPs	73	76
Being able to choose which GP to see	72	71
Amount of time GP gives to each patient	65	69
GP appointment systems	54	54

On the whole, Britons were strong supporters of the basic principles of the NHS, notably that of treatment being free at point of delivery: in 1998, asked in a Gallup poll whether the NHS had been a success or a failure, 89 per cent said 'success'; in December 2001 the figure was down to 76 per cent (*Daily Telegraph*, 14 January 2002). In France treatment must first be paid for, the cost then being claimed back from the state health fund; the system is expensive to run; nurses are overworked and deeply discontented. Still, among the French public overall satisfaction with the running of the health services is, at 65 per cent, higher than in Britain (57 per cent) or Germany (57.5 per cent). Here are the crucial statistics behind the satisfaction ratings (*New Statesman*, 4 February 2002):

	Germany	France	UK
Doctors per 1,000 people	4.2	3.03	1.6
Nurses per 1,000 people	9.6	4.97	5.0
Hospitals beds per 1,000 people	7.1	4.3	2.0
Percentage occupancy of beds	76.6	75.7	1 million on waiting list

British expenditure on what was now officially called 'social protection' (pensions, welfare benefits, etc.), was slightly lower than the EU average, with Britain ranking ninth, above Italy, Finland, Ireland, Spain, Greece and Portugal. Government policy had four distinct strands. The first two had a harsh American feel to them, being concerned, respectively, with getting people off benefits and into work, and with controlling costs. The third strand was concerned with cutting cumbersome duplication and could result, as with the concept of the 'single gateway' to the multiplicity of benefits, in positive gains to recipients; and the fourth with delivering increased benefits to those who manifestly needed them. The major aims were to be realized through the Welfare Reform and Pensions Act, which came into force in November 1999; the major intentions were apparent in the title of the new Department for Work and Pensions, established in June 2001. To try to get them into work, snakes and ladders were constructed for, in particular, the disabled and single mothers – people not always best fitted to climbing the ladders – to approach the 'single gateway': all claimants of working age had to attend personal interviews about job possibilities. In the attempt to get young people into jobs, the nationwide 'New Deal' was launched in April 1998, with the subsidized jobs being financed through a one-off windfall levy on the privatized utilities. In comparison with other EU countries employment levels for young people were high in Britain, and the scheme was subsequently opened to the older unemployed. The Conservative concept of a Jobseekers' Allowance (rather than Unemployment Benefit) was retained; to encourage 'jobseekers' to take on part-time work a Back to Work Bonus was introduced. The demographic fact of an increasing proportion of retired people would set the alarm bells ringing for any government. Labour was determined not to restore the link between old-age pensions and the standard of living: hence the derisory inflation allowance of 75p, which in the spring of 2000 severely jolted the Government's standing. There was a steady stream, though without anything spectacular, of specific gains for poorer families, principally through Income Support, Child Benefits, and the new Working Families' Tax Credit. Such families also benefited from raising the earnings point at which income tax became payable, and from halving the bottom rate to ten per cent. In 1999, for the first time in the country's history, a statutory minimum wage was introduced. Do we have enough here to indicate a return to a consensual social policy? Probably not; but there was one of these encouraging omens which we can detect from time to time in the setting up from the outset in 1997 of the

Social Exclusion Unit within the Cabinet Office: great aims, great ideology, though as so often with this Government, fewer concrete achievements.

Labour's highest priority in 1997 was, as Tony Blair put it, 'education, education, education'. In fact, in almost all aspects Labour's educational policies were a product of Blairism at its worst: frenetic, ill-directed activity, much meddling, no strategy, sound and sound-bites galore, loads of spin (Stephen Byers had a spell as Minister of State at the Department for Education and Employment), only limited results. Failures in the NHS, chaos on the railways, these were obvious; the inadequacies and inequalities in the educational systems of England and Wales (I leave out Scotland's less problematic non-selective system) were more deep-rooted and more complex. Civilized countries saw it as a primary obligation to ensure that every locality had its own free, state-run, high-quality schools. England and Wales never attained that level of civilization: educational opportunities were greatly extended after the Second World War, but then the unstable compound of old Labour and radical Conservative policies left a patchwork of, according to geographical location, top-notch state schools and ones which could only be termed 'sink schools', together with selective grammar and special schools, and private fee-paying ones. The Labour government ostensibly set out to address 'standards', not 'structures'. It was also, as we know, committed in its first two years to keeping that other 's', spending, to the limits set by the Conservatives. Over the period of the first Blair government education spending rose less than it did between 1991 and 1995. Then large sums did start coming through – though not nearly enough. The shortage of teachers was even more critical than that of medical staff or railway workers, but much shouted-about recruitment policies were touched by the usual twinges of meanness. As Professor Alan Smithers puts it in his contribution on Education Policy to the Seldon collection:

By the time of the 2001 pay settlement the government had belatedly accepted that there was a serious problem, if not a crisis. But instead of making sufficient money available to restore the earlier status of teachers, it only allowed the School Teachers' Review Body to make adjustments with the limit of the rise in average earnings.

Instead of raising standards across the profession the Government introduced the dubious ploy of merit pay (how did you assess merit?) and proposed the deployment of low-cost 'teaching assistants'.

Credit must, however, be given to the Government for successes in its policy of concentrating on 'standards'. In essence it followed the paths pioneered by the Conservatives, in fact rather overdoing the testing, inflicting on pupils and teachers an embarrassment of tests for every possible age group; however, unlike its predecessors, the Government did support its attempts to raise standards with real resources, and its initiatives in literacy and numeracy were well judged. It also exerted tighter control over curricula and methods than any British government had ever done before – not necessarily a bad thing when one looks at other countries, particularly France. From being pretty well bottom in European educational leagues tables, the UK actually was beginning to climb into world prominence. But when it came to what Smithers rightly calls England's 'monstrously untidy and unfair secondary education system' (i.e. 'structure'), Labour, apart from some moves towards 'inclusiveness' (grant maintained schools reabsorbed into local authorities as 'foundation schools', for example), fiddled while parents fumed. There was much talk of 'diversity' (a favoured mantra) and 'parent choice', while in fact parents often found there was no decent school in their vicinity, or no school that they could get their children into, or that they had to send their children on journeys of three hours each way, or set up their own schools, or teach their children at home.

Taken all in all the standards at British universities were still very high and the most prestigious ones were among the best in the world. Neither Government nor tax-payers were enthusiastic about providing the funding needed to maintain this position. The Teaching and Higher Education Act of July 1998 laid it down that higher education students must pay up to £1,025 a year of their tuition costs, while at the same time it reconstructed the loan system for both fees and maintenance, loans being repayable when the successful graduate's income reached a certain level. The full tuition levy was paid by families with incomes over £26,000 – not a princely sum when compared with fat cat salaries; those with family incomes below £16,000 paid no fees; however, maintenance costs remained an obstacle. As it became clear that potential students were being deterred from taking up university places, one had to conclude that England was still some distance away from civilized educational services and that education remained a divisive factor.

29

The Pleasures and Pains of Life

Back in February 1993, in Liverpool a two-year-old toddler, James Bulger, was abducted by two ten-year-old boys, Jon Venables and Robert Thompson, taken to a railway line and beaten to death; in April of the same year, a gifted black student, Stephen Lawrence, was murdered at a bus-stop in South-East London by a racist gang, the incompetence and racial prejudice of the police being fully exposed in the exhaustive public enquiry conducted in 1999 by Sir William Macpherson. Right into the new century there were other crimes which forced more than routine agonizing over the type of society Britain had become: on 1 June 2000 eight-year-old Sarah Payne was assaulted and murdered by a known paedophile; another eight-year-old, black Anna Climbie, practically under the eyes of the social workers, died an unimaginably horrible death from the neglect and abuse of her great aunt and great aunt's boyfriend; in November 2000 a ten-year-old, hard-studying Nigerian schoolboy, Damilola Taylor, was stabbed in the deprived, drug-ridden North Peckham estate in south London and left to bleed to death. Treated in England as criminally responsible at the age of ten (they would not have been in other West European countries), Venables and Thompson were placed in secure custody. However, in June 2001, by the decision of the Parole Board and the Home Secretary, they were released, the High Court earlier having ruled that they should have the right to live anonymously for the rest of their lives. Both decisions were subject to hysterical attack in sections of the press; there was also a campaign in support of lists of known paedophiles being made available to the public, an obvious incitement to vigilante action. Again (with specific reference to the Bulger case) one may seek the more measured voices among the British public (Letters, *Independent*, 25, 26 June 2001):

An adult that goes off the rails in the way Venables and Thompson did is probably beyond rehabilitation, but 10-year-olds should not be. If our young offenders' system can set two normal individuals free it would be a better tribute to James Bulger than a further damaging incarceration, and also prove that the society that helped create two child killers is also strong enough to reform them.

More surely than the killing of James Bulger itself, the reaction to the possible release of the boys who killed him has shown what a sick and nasty country England has become. I am disgusted by how the cheap media in this country . . . has fanned the flames of hatred by giving air and space to every low-life willing to give them a suitably inflammatory quote.

. . . My experience is that most people believe that it is wrong to keep these boys incarcerated in an adult prison for a crime committed as immature children. But that view is hardly reflected at all by the British media, who are much happier quoting those who would prefer to see them meet a violent end.

Polls did consistently show that the greatest concern of the British people was crime. Two major issues were levels of policing and levels of punishment. For all the exposures of police frailty, the public continued to tell pollsters that what they most wanted was more policemen on the beat. Labour's first Home Secretary, Jack Straw, while by no means in the same mould as his Conservative predecessor, definitely projected a tough image, at the end of 1998 implementing Michael Howard's policy (and one imitative of America) of setting a minimum prison sentence for those committing a third burglary, though with the introduction of some discretion for the courts. Britain had the largest prison population in Europe: the Government's response that this showed that Britain was catching most criminals suggested a lamentable failure to give the crime problem the serious, professional attention it needed. David Blunkett, formerly Education Secretary, was more flexible than Straw, though, unfortunately he was immediately greeted by the unsavoury problem of an apparent need for many more prison places for female offenders. Worse still was the steady increase in serious crime among young people, which doubled in the seven years up to 2000; meantime, in the decade since the Criminal Justice Act of 1991 had promised to abolish jail for fifteen- and sixteen-year-olds, the number of them in prison had actually doubled. Blunkett's White Paper, *Policing a New Century* (December 2001) called for the setting up of civilian patrols – better than nothing, but essentially a cut-price way of trying to deal with street crime.

Two areas of criminal activity attracted special attention. The European Commission's 1998 *Annual Report* on the state of the drugs problem reported that in Britain, among both teenagers and adults, consumption of drugs was higher than anywhere else in Europe. Huge drug seizures were announced from time to time, but the problem seemed to get only worse, increased drug-taking being reported first among pre-teen boys, and then among teenage girls – drug-taking correlated closely with the crime figures. At first Government policy was as hard as could be, however 'soft' the drug. At the end of May 1999, however, a better, if still modest, strategy was announced, aimed at rehabilitation rather than punishment. Most encouraging development of all, perhaps, towards the end of 2001 the vulgar press, to whose nasty punitive attitudes I recently alluded, was beginning to suggest that the drugs scourge required more imaginative policies. Here is a boldish leader from the *Daily Mirror* (12 November 2001):

The hardline war on drugs has simply not worked.

The illegal drug industry in this country is worth £6 billion a year. It leads to half the property crime, costing the nation another £3 billion.

The policies of successive Governments have done nothing to slow the rise in drug-taking ... We should understand ... that a different approach to drugs is needed ...

The signs were that police forces and, perhaps even the Government, were just, very tentatively beginning to finger 'a different approach'. Britain was 'the drugs capital of Europe'. It was probably not the 'paedophilia capital of Europe', that dishonour perhaps belonging to Belgium, maybe run close by Ireland. But from the mid-nineties onwards there was a spate of well-documented cases of institutionalized child abuse: the stories children, and adults, told were now (rightly) being listened to, when previously they were being dismissed. At Ashworth secure mental hospital it was actually a patient, in October 1996, whose complaints of paedophilia, and other goings on, prompted the setting up of an enquiry in February 1997 which produced a disturbing report at the end of 1998.

Despite the several dank pockets of gloom and despair, overall developments in the world of law and order offered glints of hope, with respect both to a decline in crime figures and to the growth of more responsible attitudes among the police. Police statistics of 'recorded crime' are known to be very imperfect and so are taken in conjunction with the *British* (and *Scottish*) *Crime Surveys*. In broad terms crime in England and Wales fell by a third from its peak in 1995, and by 12 per cent between 1999 and 2000. *Social Trends 2002* (pp. 150–53) explains that international crime comparisons are invariably given in percentage changes rather than absolute rates. Thus when comparing 1995 with 1999, crime recorded in England and Wales fell by 10 per cent compared with 1 per cent in EU countries. The figure for Scotland was 8 per cent. By the end of the century there was justifiable concern about an almost American level of gun-ownership and use ('The British become trigger happy', reported the *New Statesman*, 5 November 2001). However, for the three-year period 1997 to 1999 the average homicide rate in EU countries was 1.7 per 100,000, with the highest rates in Northern Ireland (3.1), Finland (2.6), Spain (2.6) and Scotland (2.1), while England and Wales had the dulcet rate of 1.5; the true haven of tranquillity was Austria, with only 0.8 murders a year per 100,000 of the population. There were both reforms, and a sharp drop, in the use of stop and search powers by the police, particularly disliked by ethnic minorities; and in September 2000 the police in London came out with their guide to sensitive policing of minority communities, *Policing Diversity: the Metropolitan Police Service handbook on London's religions, cultures and communities.*

Alas, police and race were subjects which still seemed to inevitably go together. And, to pick up again one of my eleven central topics, social cohesion, there were in the spring and summer of 2001 many tangible signs of an absence of it, mainland Britain in places, as I already noted, looking ominously like Northern Ireland. Indeed Northern Ireland once more spilled over into England with number of attacks by the dissident Real IRA, including a bomb explosion at the BBC television centre, west London, on 4 March and at a post office in Hendon, north London, on 14 April. However, no Irish assistance was needed as rioting flared through Oldham and Burnley in Lancashire and Bradford in Yorkshire, all areas in which whites and Asians lived in segregated contiguity, with the police frequently excoriated and attacked by both sides. This may well sound like a reprise of episodes discussed earlier in this book, and in many ways it was; yet, in my search for indications that Britain, after the internecine struggles of the Thatcher and Major years, was, however deeply flawed Blair and his cronies, beginning to rediscover some of its better instincts, I do believe that the riots of 2001 had a special importance in that they stimulated a new quest for 'community cohesion' (the very phrase seems almost to have been borrowed from me). And, incidentally, some reprise!: the 2001 riots were the worst since the years of Thatcher's supremacy. For the misbegotten thugs of the National Front a banned march is the next best thing to an unbanned march. The series of violent events which zig-zagged back and forth between the former mill-towns on either side of the Pennines was touched off on Saturday 5 May by the arrival in Oldham, Greater Manchester, of would-be marchers, planning to inflame the existing tensions between white and Asian gangs, and being obligingly met by anti-Nazi protesters.

Three petrol bombs were thrown into roads by Asian youths, and gangs of white males smashed windows and damaged houses while shouting racist abuse at residents. A couple claimed they had their car attacked and the back windscreen smashed as they rescued a 17-year-old white youth who was being beaten up by an Asian gang. They said they were surrounded by young men wielding baseball bats . . .

As tension mounted in Oldham, the violence spread to Bradford, West Yorkshire, when two white men were attacked and beaten, leaving one unconscious, by a gang of Asian youths. The two men, brothers aged 26 and 28, were set upon by up to 12 Asian men as they walked through the Westgate area of the city. One of the men suffered a fractured skull and was taken to Bradford Royal Infirmary. (*Independent*, 7 May 2001)

With the general election approaching, the British National Party kept up an active presence in Oldham, where it was contesting both parliamentary constituencies. On Saturday 26 May an argument outside a chip shop in the deprived Asian area of Glodwick between an Asian and a white teenager (each aged thirteen or fourteen) turned into the worst riot in Oldham's history. Asian shops and houses were attacked with stones and petrol bombs; then a gang of Asian youths mounted similar attacks on the Live and Let Live pub. *Sunday Times* journalist Melanie Philips summed up (3 June 2001);

The situation in Oldham is complex. Asian community leaders admit there have been attacks on whites, and there are tensions between Bangladeshis and Pakistanis. They say parental authority in Asian families has broken down and their young men who have higher rates of unemployment than whites are no longer prepared to control their frustration.

As for the police, they seem to have been trapped by their desire to protect lawful freedom of movement into appearing to allow racial thuggery. Their apparent insistence on treating white racist yobbery and Asian defences as equivalent has provoked the Asians into violence, over which the BNP and National

Front are rubbing their hands. This incendiary mix of grinding deprivation, disaffected white people and volatile Asian youths, with white extremists poised to supply the lighted match is present not just in Oldham but in many of our cities.

Too true! Less than a month later (22 June) the explosion was located in Burnley, where the trigger was a row over a noisy party. Two of the main gangs involved, white and Asian, were both embroiled in drug dealing, but the violence was quickly generalized, Asians attacking a pub, whites an Asian business; then young Asians fought the police and fire-bombed a pub. Doomsday in Bradford was Saturday 7 July, and the two following days. New weapons, called 'air bombs' – fireworks reinforced with lumps of metal – replaced petrol bombs; Manningham Ward Labour Club was set on fire with members trapped inside; but there was also evidence of racial mingling across the battle lines. The important outcomes were, first, a report on Bradford by Lord Ouseley, former head of the Commission for Racial Equality, and, still more important, the reports of the community cohesion review team set up by the Government. Ouseley described Bradford as a city in a grip of fear:

There is a fear of people talking openly and honestly because of possible repercussions, recriminations and victimization. There is the fear of challenging wrongdoing because of being labelled racist. There is the fear of confronting the gangs culture, the illegal drugs trade and the growing racial intolerance, harassment and abuse that exists.

That was honest *diagnosis*. The community cohesion team's *prescription* was dynamite. Back on p. 133, I remarked on the failure of Government to enunciate policies designed to ensure that a multicultural society was also a cohesive one. The dynamic Home Office documents, *Building Cohesive Communities*, and *Community Cohesion*, produced by the team chaired by Ted Cantle, after noting that faith-based schools (another of Blair's absurd fancies), separate places of worship, segregated employment, housing and schooling, entailed communities operating 'on the basis of a series of parallel lives,' trumpeted:

the importance of open and constructive debate about citizenship, civic identity, shared values, rights and responsibilities. It is only through having such a debate that we will have the basis for bringing together people of different races, cultures, and religions in a cohesive society and within cohesive communities . . .

It will be important for Government to be clear about some key, but contentious issues in this debate. In an open liberal democracy, citizenship is founded on fundamental human rights and duties. The laws, rules and practices that govern our democracy uphold our commitment to the equal worth and dignity of all our citizens. We must tackle head on racism and Islamophobia. It will sometimes be necessary to confront cultural practices that conflict with these basic values, such as those which deny women the right to participate as equal citizens. Similarly, it means ensuring that every individual has the wherewithal, such as the ability to speak English, to enable them to engage as active citizens in economic, social and political life (*Building Cohesive Communities*, p. 20).

Inevitably the 'constructive debate' began with the legions of the politically correct denouncing the very ideas of 'confronting cultural practices' and expecting an 'ability to speak English'. In fact, the very next words of the document were: 'Common citizenship does not mean cultural uniformity . . . There is no single culture into which all must be assimilated'. Lofty aims? Just words? For the first time ever Britain was beginning to formulate a policy for the integration of cultural diversity and national cohesion. The foundations were perhaps a little more solid than the precedent rioting had indicated. It's no great shakes, perhaps, but it's certainly something: race relations in Britain were definitely more tranquil, less marred by atrocities than those in Germany or France.

How about class? According to Blair, speaking in December 1998: 'slowly but surely, the old establishment is being replaced by a new, larger, more meritocratic middle class'. In that same month the old official classification of people into Classes I–V, which dated from 1911, was replaced by a more complex system, broadly suggesting that almost everyone was now middle class. Had the working class disappeared, the fortunates moving into the middle class, the unfortunates into an underclass? With manufacturing now contributing only 20 per cent of GDP, the traditional working class had certainly shrunk but, particularly given that there are many other working-class occupations, from transport workers to labourers, from butchers and bakers to electricians and plumbers, it had not disappeared, nor had age-old working-class attitudes. Although trade union membership had dropped greatly (though now actually firming up), the view that it was no part of a worker's responsibility to participate in any way in management – a sentiment echoed by many managers, and one still at the heart of many of the country's economic difficulties – persisted. The persistence of class attitudes was suddenly illuminated in the House of Commons when criticisms of the Speaker, Michael Martin (who had been one of those to undermine

Elizabeth Firkin), were interpreted by him and his supporters as being criticisms of his working-class manner and coagulated Glasgow accent (he was being referred to as Gorbals Mick). It would be quite wrong to believe that working-class and 'peasant' accents do not exist in other countries, but somehow those whose accents remain unmodified do not make it to prominent parliamentary positions. Perhaps that was actually beginning to become the norm in Britain too; Martin's predecessor, Betty Boothroyd, had been equally working class, but her accent approximated to a middle-class regional norm. Both she and Martin were true to traditional working-class prudishness in refusing to sanction breastfeeding in parliament.

Quite obviously Blair's 'meritocratic middle class', as he envisaged it, extended to the proliferating fat cats who, in fact, could readily join, and reinforce, the ever-enduring upper class. Class content, certainly from the time of Thatcher, was in flux; class attitudes much less so. The terrible situation with regard to public and private services on which I animadverted had some odd consequences: competent plumbers and electricians were so hard to find that the intelligent skilled worker could build for himself an above-average middle-class income (say £60,000 a year – *The Times*, 12 February 2002). What most securely underpinned the class system was the educational mess already described; what most palpably demonstrated it was inexcusable economic inequality, actually growing under the Blair governments, though it had been at its highest between 1985 and 1992. The figures, taken from *Social Trends 1992* and *1991* concern those on 'low income', which, by E U agreement, means those on less than sixty per cent of median national income. The figure was fairly steady in the 1960s, 1970s, and early 1980s, fluctuating between 10 and 15 per cent, then it rose steeply from 1985 (the 'Thatcher effect', as they say!) to a peak of 21 per cent in 1992. From the mid-nineties onwards, it stuck at around 18 per cent, whereas it was at 16 per cent in France and Germany; only two E U countries had a higher proportion on low income than Britain, Portugul and Greece.

Was there a town–country divide to add to the various other ones? Rather suddenly, during 2000, a soi-disant Countryside Movement came to prominence with a somewhat mixed, not to say contradictory, agenda. Some complained about the devastating effect on rural life of the decline in rural transport. Others, however, owning cars as big as small houses, were more concerned about the possibility of legislation banning hunting. Such legislation had been a Labour-supported objective, but had apparently succumbed to Blair's determination never to stir up powerful enemies (devolved Scotland went ahead). City intellectuals (mainly) raised protests about intensive farming and genetically modified crops; the Countryside and Rights of Way Act of 2002 began the process of opening up, against the resistance of many farmers, the countryside to 'the right to roam', unlikely to be consummated till 2005. Compared with, say, Germany, the Green Movement was pretty weak in the UK. Finding affordable rural housing was a problem, mainly through rich people from the cities buying up second homes; which brings out that the real divide was not town *versus* country, but the wealthy *versus* the rest. This was confirmed by the epidemic of foot-and-mouth disease which broke out in February 2001 and lasted for the rest of the year, probably caused by a combination of the import of infected meat and the slovenly habits of certain pig farmers. For small- and medium-sized farmers the epidemic, during which nearly four million animals were slaughtered, was a desperate disaster, many being forced on to income supplements and even charity; owners of small hotels and other businesses dependent on tourism also suffered disastrously. But the big farmers did very well out of government compensation payments, many fiddling things to their own advantage; some collected private insurance payments as well as ones from the government (Judith Cook, *The Year of the Pyres: The 2001 Foot-and-Mouth Epidemic*, 2001, pp. 180–1). The biggest culprit was the Government, ill-prepared and complacent, possessed of no lessons from the last epidemic in 1967. The Ministry of Agriculture, Fisheries and Food, as we saw from the BSE crisis, had far too cosy a relationship with the farmers; only partly closing the door long after the horse had bolted, the Government, following the June election, replaced it with the Department for Environment, Food and Rural Affairs (a Food Standards Agency had been set up in April 2000). Short of qualified staff, thanks to all the cuts in the name of deregulation, it was dilatory and sometimes careless, insisted on massive slaughter (perhaps not always necessary) and refused to countenance vaccination (this would temporarily have halted the British meat trade). The hope was that there would now be a reappraisal of the country's entire farming strategy, a turning away from the industrialized production of cheap (and oftimes nasty) food, to a concern for the environment and the production of quality food. Trying to dig out such earnests of better things to come from contemporary disasters is one of the two main purposes of this chapter; the other is to pose the question: were the British, nevertheless, getting pleasure out of life?

The circumstances of private life were continuing to change rapidly, the most striking structural phenomenon being the rise and rise of the singleton, followed by the rise and rise of the lone parent, the two, obviously, entailing the decline of the traditional two-parent plus dependent children family.

Types of Households: Great Britain percentages

	1961	1971	1981	1991	2001
One-family households					
Living alone	4	6	8	11	12
Couple					
No children	18	19	20	23	24
Dependent children	52	52	47	41	39
Lone parent	3	4	6	10	10
Other households	12	9	9	4	5

We must note that in this sphere the eighties was a more significant period of change than the nineties, though there was a striking increase in cohabitation at the expense of marriage in the latter decade. An official statistical exercise carried out in 1996 estimated that there were just over a million and a half cohabiting couples in England and Wales, about one in six of the adult non-married population. Phrased another way, more than 15 per cent of British couples were now cohabiting (compared with 5 per cent in 1986). So, where's the pleasure? Let's sample people's opinions, then get down to the sex. In summarizing what the *18th British Social Attitudes* survey reported on opinions about marriage and cohabitation, the *Independent* used the headline 'Marriage is just a lifestyle choice for many Britons', declaring that 'the report suggests views on marriage have shifted dramatically over the past two decades as increasing numbers of couples choose to cohabit'. Always mistrust that dead horse of an adverb, 'dramatically', is my advice. Actually the *Social Attitudes* interviews confirm, what we saw in the previous table, that there was no sharp change in the late nineties; and, indeed, that when taken with earlier reports and, say, the figures I quote on p. 356, the changes, as I have insisted throughout this book, began during the cultural revolution of the long sixties, then accelerated throughout the succeeding decades – with, in some respects, a levelling off in the late nineties (change is not eternal and monodirectional): in 2000 *fewer* in the age group 25–44 agreed that 'it is all right for a couple to live together without intending to get married' than, among the analogous age group, had done so in 1994 (p. 35). What this *18th Social Attitudes* report does bring out brilliantly is that change towards more permissive attitudes is increasingly to be found among the older age groups (those getting past it) and the highly religious (those who felt guilty about it), who previously had stood out against the permissive trend (gathering force, to repeat, since the sixties). Altogether only 9 per cent dismissed marriage as 'just a piece of paper', with nearly 60 per cent regarding it as 'still the best kind of relationship', while at the same time, being 'no longer seen as having any advantage over cohabitation in everyday life'. Is that clear? People, I have said, are not always totally consistent. But the drift *is* clear, and meant that a quarter of all children were now being born to cohabitants ('partners', in ordinary speech). Marriage in 2000 was at its lowest level since 1917 (a year disrupted by war), while the divorce rate (though in decline since 1992) was still the highest in the EU. There was general support for giving partners (gay as well as straight) the same kind of legal rights as married couples; by the end of 2001 noises from the Government indicated that this might just happen sometime in the future. The report, in fact, paints a rather cheerful, pragmatic, British mix of cohabitations, separations, marriages and divorces, and certainly not a breakdown in family life, if that term is interpreted in a positive, non-guilt-ridden way.

Now to the wondrous 'National Survey of Sexual Attitudes and Life-styles, 1999–2001 (Natsal 2000)', published in the medical journal, *Lancet*, of 1 December 2001, and which can be compared with 'Natsal 1990', the study edited by Kaye Wellings, which I discussed on pp. 406–9. Interviews, confined to those in the 16–44 age group, were conducted with 4,762 men and 6,399 women, women always being more forthcoming in talking to strangers about their sex lives – men boast to each other. With respect to numbers of heterosexual partners there was 'substantial heterogeneity' between the sexes: 81.9 per cent of men and 76.4 per cent of women reported more than one lifetime partner, whereas 34.6 per cent of men and 19.4 per cent of women reported at least ten lifetime partners. This somewhat skewed definition of 'heterogeneity' is rather obscurely explained: crudely put, men continue at it longer. In the previous year, 31.2 per cent of men and 21.4 per cent of women had formed new heterosexual or homosexual partnerships. The mean number of new partnerships varied from 20.4 among single men aged 25–34 years to 0.05 among married women aged 32–44 years.

Of the total number of new partnerships in the past year formed by all male respondents, 81.0% were reported by single or previously married men who together constitute only 43.7% of all male respondents. The equivalent figures were 77.8% and 37.6% for female respondents. 56.5% of men and 42.8% of women with new partners in the past year reported having sex with their most recent partner within 1 month of meeting . . .

Using the dates of first and last intercourse for the three most recent sexual partnerships in the past 5 years, we estimated that 14.6% of men and 9.0% of women had concurrent partnerships – i.e., sexual partnerships which were ongoing simultaneously at some time in the past year.

Greater London was consolidating its reputation as sin city, many activities apparently being more frequent there than in the rest of the country: mean number of heterosexual partners; paying for sex among men in the past five years; male and female homosexual partnerships in the past five years; and concurrent partnerships among women in the past year. However, the general picture was that of sexual activity in the rest of Britain catching up with, or surpassing that in London, permissiveness, once again, touching those previously struggling to remain immune.

Men and women were generally similar in the proportion reporting specific sexual practices – e.g. heterosexual anal intercourse. However, we continue to observe higher mean numbers of reported partners in men than women . . . Of particular relevance to the current survey is that, as expected, there was a higher proportion of single men than single women in Natsal 2000, reflecting the earlier age at first marriage and cohabitation among women, and their tendency to choose older male partners.

Of course, we all have our limits. There are considerable variations in the frequency of sex, but in 2000 the average man and woman was having sex no more often than ten years previously, once a week. The fact that twice as many men were now paying for sex may have had less to do with increased sex drive and more to do with improved service (for once!) from such seductive facilities as table-dancing clubs and the like.

As with Natsal 1990, preoccupation with the sexual behaviour of young people was strongly motivated by concern for their sexual health. In the 1960s and 1970s, Natsal 2000 recorded, the impetus to research was provided by unease surrounding rates of conception among young unmarried people, whereas in the 1980s and 1990s the focus shifted to the risk of HIV transmission. By the end of the twentieth century the UK had the highest rate of teenage births in western Europe, and an upward trend in the rates of sexually transmitted infections. Age of first intercourse is a relevant factor:

Following the steep decrease in age of first intercourse among women up to and including the 1970s, in many countries there is evidence of subsequent stabilization. In several European countries this stabilization occurred in the early 1980s. In the USA it occurred in the late 1980s. In Britain and New Zealand, however, heterosexual intercourse continued to occur at earlier ages throughout the 1980s.

A number of factors affected both the earliness of the age of first intercourse and whether it was safe or not. One tribute to governments was that school-based lessons were now the main source of information about sexual matters for young people; but class was a crucial factor. Early, unprotected intercourse was prevalent among those who left school at 16 and those whose parents were manual workers. But 'early intercourse was also more commonly reported by women who were less that 13 years old at menarche'. Early intercourse tended to lead to expressions of regret at not having waited longer, particularly among women. Among females, 26 per cent had sex before the legal age of 16, an increase since 1990. However, the signs were that the age was stabilizing; on the matter of safe sex the conclusions were also cautiously optimistic. Summarizing the 1990 survey I suggested that British attitudes towards sex were characterized by 'pragmatism, common sense, tolerance, and a certain respect for traditional monogomous ideals'. That judgement can stand for 2002, save that the ideals were steadily yielding to still more pragmatism.

There was much there about differences between men and women. Social, economic and political discrimination continued. However, through deliberate positive discrimination (subsequently ruled illegal), Labour had ensured that in May 1997 there were 101 women (rather ambivalently termed 'Blair's babes') among its ranks in Parliament. The number fell in 2001, but seven women did reach the Cabinet. Women constituted 45 per cent of the workforce, but only five per cent of company directors, seven per cent of university professors, and ten per cent of judges. Some role reversals were not entirely happy ones. Because of the shrinkage in traditional male manufacturing jobs, in many households the principal earner was a woman, often herself on low wages. But at school, and increasingly at university, girls, showing great powers of application, as well as confidence that there were jobs to be obtained in telecommunications, design, teaching, information technology, office administration and the liberal professions, were outperforming boys.

Back in 1977, we saw (p. 225), the British, while not the most hard-working, were among the happiest, people in the world. By the end of the twentieth century much had changed, the British now being notorious for over-working: in November 2001, half the workforce were breaking the legal limit on working hours. Was money now more important than leisure? Or is money essential for quality leisure? We saw in the previous chapter that the British spend more of their income on 'fun' than any other Europeans. And there was a fascinating study of living standards and job satisfaction among teachers in the *Times Education Supplement* of 1 February 2002. This reported that: 'today a typical teacher lives in a detached house, owns a new-ish car, holidays abroad, and likes the job'. Yet only three in five teachers expected to be still teaching in five years: the problem was excessive hours, and, what contributed to the same thing, too much bureaucracy. The headline was: 'Happy teachers' only gripe is long hours'. The opening sentence: 'Too much work, rather than too little pay, is the major worry for teachers, who are generally satisfied with their jobs and standard of living.' It is difficult to generalize but, on the whole, the British do again come over as a relaxed, pleasure-loving people. After all, the liberating, self-expressive, anti-authoritarian developments of the sixties had continued. Thatcher was gone; the Conservatives had, as one paper put it, 'returned to planet earth', i.e. were again paying attention to the concerns of ordinary people. If public life was flawed, private life was there to be enjoyed. But perhaps the British were just too relaxed: little exercise, low participation in sport, growing obesity. In several respects the national sport, association football, was symptomatic of many of the things wrong with the country. Young players were not coming forward in the way they used to. Clubs preferred buying in talent from abroad to investing in nurturing it at home. Searching for a competent national coach, England had to sign up the Swede, Sven Goran Eriksson; Scotland followed with the German, Berti Vogts. To state that football, a spectator sport which at the highest levels could pull in massive television revenue, was mega business was to state the most banal of platitudes; rugby union, once the priggish guardian of amateurism, was now big business too. But let us recognize that the English Rugby Union team was up there among the top two in the world, and that the Ireland team, uniting North and Republic (welcome breath of sanity, this), and the Irish provincial teams were doing hearteningly well. More, British premier football, played at terrific speed, was the most exciting in the world. While handing out the plaudits, let me just mention the eleven golds, ten silvers, and seven bronzes won by Britain at the 2000 Sydney Olympics.

If the bulk of the British did not care too much for exercise, they were undoubtedly more bewitched than ever by the latest miracles of IT. In 2000–01, 40 per cent of all households in the UK owned a personal computer, while 47 per cent owned a mobile telephone, practically a threefold increase since 1996–97, and almost 4.5 million households were subscribing to satellite and 3.3 million to cable television. The steady increase in the ownership of video players was accompanied by the increase in video cassettes purchased, from around six million in 1986 to 114 million in 2000. Nine per cent of VCR owners rented at least one video a week, with fewer than half never renting one. Digital Versatile Disc (DVD) was launched in the UK in April 1998. Over 800,000 DVD players and 17 million disks were sold in 2000, compared with under 250,000 players and four million disks the previous year. The institution of the National Lottery, run in very high tech (and very lucrative) fashion by Camelot, had been the perfect memorial to John Major; in 1999, 72 per cent of the adult population in mainland Britain took part in some form of gambling, mostly on the National Lottery.

Virginia Bottomley, at the Department of National Heritage, had, in the last year of the Conservative administration, attempted to popularize the phrase coined by the American *Newsweek* magazine, 'Cool Britannia', to symbolize the alleged creativity in British business and the arts (much the same thing, it was beginning to seem), from Britart to Britpop. The new Labour Government took up the idea, while applying a mercy killing to National Heritage, replacing it with a Department of Culture, Media and Sport. In November 2001, the latest Minister, Tessa Jowell, pronounced official obsequies over the unlamented notion of Cool Britannia. But signs of genuinely *bella* Britannia were: the setting up of the immensely popular Tate Modern gallery of international art in a former London power station; the dropping of admission charges in all museums (with a resulting jump in attendances); the institution of government subsidies for film-makers; and new genres of intelligent, and sometimes side-splittingly funny, crime stories (Minette Walters, Ian Rankin, R. D. Wing-field), thirty-something singleton novels – also known as 'chicklit' – (Helen Fielding, Jenny Colgan, Jane Green), and children's literature, with an adult bite (J. K. Rowling, Philip Pullman). Britart was not well served by the clique which controlled the Turner prize, recent winners being notable for their ineffable boringness, but only a jaded Tory or a tedious cultural theorist would fail to be exhilarated by some of the work, at least, of Chris Ofili, Jake and Dinos Chapman, Sarah Lucas and Tracey Emin. Britpop wasn't really that special, but it did keep up an international presence. Films continued to be too dependent on American investment but, as we have seen happening throughout this book, notched up some notable successes, including the two great thirty-something movies, *This Year's Love* (David Kane, 1999) and *Bridget Jones's Diary* (2001).

The Labour governments showed a slightly higher appreciation of the need for investment in science than its predecessors had, much scientific effort now being integrated with the EU. The UK was responsible for about 4.5 per cent of global expenditure on science, produced about 8 per cent of scientific publications and received 9 per cent of citations. The Sanger Centre at Hinxton in Cambridgeshire (funded mainly by the Wellcome Trust) contributed a third of the sequence data to the international Genome Project, while, on the same site, the Medical Research Council (MRC) Human Genome Mapping Project Resource Centre also played an important part in work on the human genome. The near complete set of human genes, product of scientists working in six countries, was announced in February 2001. At the University of Edinburgh, the Centre for Genome Research has established a position of world eminence in stem cell biology.

For all the many failings of the Blair governments, the prospect in February 2002 was much brighter than it had been in early 1997, the forces of consensus just perceptibly beginning to win out against those of fragmentation. Nasty riots there had been, including the anti-globalization protests of May 2000 and, especially, of May 2001 – yet commentators were not altogether wrong to detect warning signs of a regeneration of the caring international spirit of the sixties. Deplorable that in 2002 it seemed still true that the poor are always with us, but at least the concept of challenging social exclusion was on the agenda. In human history, migrations, would-be immigrants, and asylum seekers, have also been something of an eternal problem. In 2002 Britain was far from finding an effective and humane answer to that one. Yet really what the British people, still showing some inventiveness and some of the traditional virtues, most needed were politicians with guts and civil servants with brains, both sharing the normal European's understanding that investment is a necessity and state regulation of public services a blessing.

Note on Sources and Guide to Further Reading

When I was commissioned to write the first edition of this book, back in the 1970s, the idea was the conventional one that I should cover the whole of the twentieth century, from, say, 1914, up, to, say, the 1960s. I insisted that the time had come for a pioneering shot at a history confined to the contemporary period, that is to say, *beginning* in 1945. There was at that time a scarcity of 'secondary sources', as we professionals call the scholarly accounts written by other historians, amounting to an almost total shortage for the period after about 1955. Thus I was forced to rely very heavily on 'primary sources', the vast profusion of materials originated within the period being studied by individuals and groups going about their daily lives, pursuing their own particular purposes, rather than consciously striving to produce scholarly history. I ended the book with a very elaborate *Note on Sources and Guide to Further Reading* (I do not like the term 'Bibliography': historians work from many other artefacts apart from books) which, after summarizing the different categories of primary source, set out the main sources (primary and secondary) that a conscientious reader might find useful in following up each of the 'eleven main clusters of interrelated social facts and developments' upon which the book is structured. With each edition this section just grew and grew. Now, when the reader can be confidently directed towards a selection of excellent secondary sources written since my original venture was published, is the time to take the secateurs. What follows is drastically pruned guidance, very much aimed at utility. After a few comments on primary sources, I proceed to a simple list of some of the best secondary sources available today.

Primary Sources

Fundamental for a social history are the Government publications providing statistics and trends, principally *The Annual Abstract of Statistics, Social Trends*, and *Regional Trends. UK 2002* and its predecessors (e.g. *Britain 2001*) contain valuable data, though also much spin – however, to spin-doctors, historians, being experts in analysing every kind of documentation, are deadly enemies. Almost as important are Government surveys and reports, a few specially luscious ones being: *Report of the Ministry of National Insurance for the Period 17 November 1944 to 4 July 1949* (1950), *The Report of the Committee on Broadcasting (Pilkington Report)* (1961), *The Proper Conduct of Public Business* (1994), *Investigation into the King's Cross Underground Fire* (1988), *Building Cohesive Communities* (2002).

I do have to stress that a serious work of history is based on evidence drawn from a myriad sources, not just a few plum documents. Government reports need to be supplemented by private surveys and reports, for example those of the Joseph Rowntree Foundation, the *British Social Attitudes* reports, or sociological surveys like *Tradition and Change: A Study of Banbury*, by Margaret Stacey and her associates (1960). As sex becomes more sophisticated, so do the surveys: just compare Geoffrey Gorer, *Sex and Marriage in England Today* (1971) with Natsal 1990, published as Kaye Wellings *et al*, *Sexual Behaviour in Britain* (1994), and Natsal 2000, published in the *Lancet*, 1 December 2001. Also very useful are contemporary studies of geography, social psychology, the arts, etiquette, etc. Sometimes party political documents are actually worth reading: I have made much of *The Right Approach to the Economy: Outline of an Economic Strategy for the Next Conservative Government* (1977). For my own specialist work on the social consequences of World War II and the Cultural Revolution of the Long Sixties, I have done much work in ARCHIVAL SOURCES (Modern Records Centre, Warwick, Imperial War Museum, etc.), but this book has made great use of PUBLISHED MEMOIRS AND DIARIES, for example the J. L. Hodson diary, *The Way Things Are* (1947), or the J. D. Watson memoir, *Double Helix* (1968). Some historians are snooty about NEWSPAPERS. True, it is absurd to quote the self-serving pontifications of proprietors or editors and declare these to be 'public opinion'; on the other hand eye-witness reports, or personal investigations, by trained journalists can be of great value, as can the scientific public opinion polls published from time to time. In my specialist researches I make great use of letters written by members of the public to their MPs; in writing this book, I have found letters to the press most illuminating. I have a profound interest in THE ARTS (POPULAR AND ELITE) and believe that no study of society is complete without a study of that society's films, novels, paintings, music, etc. Another little homily: all sources require caution and deep specialist knowledge, but this has to be particularly borne in mind with artistic products and practices, which too often induce in historians a self-congratulatory and, therefore, uncritical rush of blood to the head.

Select Guide to Further Reading

In their books relating to contemporary society, many journalists (for example, Andrew Rawnsley, Peter Riddell, or Hugo Young) and professional biographers (for example, John Campbell) uphold the same scholarly standards that historians should aspire to – Young and Campbell, for instance, have both written excellent biographies of Margaret Thatcher. In this list I include some books by authors who are not professional historians, but have omitted books which are basically concerned with politics rather than society.

A. Aldgate, *Censorship and the Permissive Society: British Cinema and Theatre 1955–1965* (1995)

C. Barnett, *The Verdict of Peace: Britain Between Her Yesterday and the Future* (2001)

L. Baston, *Sleaze: The State of Britain* (2000)

A. Briggs, *History of Broadcasting in the United Kingdom*, vols. IV and V (1980–87)

J. Childs, *Britain since 1939: Progress and Decline* (2002)

D. Gowland and A. Turner, *Reluctant Europeans: Britain and European Integration 1945–1998* (1999)

P. Hennessy, *Never Again: Britain 1945–51* (1992)

D. Hero, *Black British, White British: A History of Race Relations in Britain* (1991)

R. Hewison, *Culture and Consensus: England, Art and Politics since 1940* (1997)

J. Lewis, *Women in Britain since 1945* (1992)

R. Lowe, *The Welfare State in Britain since 1945* (1993)

E. Mallie and D. McKittrick, *Endgame in Ireland* (2001)

A. Marwick, *Class: Image and Reality in Britain France and the USA since 1930* (1990)

A. Marwick, *Culture in Britain since 1945* (1991)

A. Marwick, *The Sixties: Cultural Revolution in Britain, France, Italy and the United States, c. 1958–c. 1974* (1998).

A. Marwick, *A History of the Modern British Isles 1914–1999: Circumstances, Events and Outcomes* (2000)

A. Marwick, *The Arts in the West Since 1945* (2002)

K. O. Morgan, *Britain since 1945: The People's Peace* (2001)

T. Morris, *Crime and Criminal Justice in Britain since 1945* (1989)

G. Parsons, *The Growth of Religious Diversity: Britain since 1945*, 2 vols. (1993, 1994)

A. Seldon, (ed.), *The Blair Effect: The Blair Government, 1997–2001* (2001)

N. Timmins, *The Five Giants: A Biography of the Welfare State* (1995)

C. Wolmar, *Broken Rails: How Privatisation Wrecked Britain's Railways* (2001)

Index